Charles Seale-Hayne Library
University of Plymouth
(01752) 588 588
LibraryandITenquiries@plymouth.ac.uk

The Cognitive Neuroscience of Working Memory

The Cognitive Neuroscience of Working Memory

Edited by

Naoyuki Osaka,
Department of Psychology,
Graduate School of Letters, Kyoto University,
Kyoto, Japan

Robert H. Logie
Human Cognitive Neuroscience,
PPLS-Psychology, University of Edinburgh,
Edinburgh, Scotland

Mark D'Esposito
Helen Wills Neuroscience Institute and
Department of Psychology, University of California
Berkeley, CA, USA

OXFORD
UNIVERSITY PRESS

OXFORD

UNIVERSITY PRESS

Great Clarendon Street, Oxford OX2 6DP

Oxford University Press is a department of the University of Oxford.
It furthers the University's objective of excellence in research, scholarship,
and education by publishing worldwide in

Oxford New York

Auckland Cape Town Dar es Salaam Hong Kong Karachi
Kuala Lumpur Madrid Melbourne Mexico City Nairobi
New Delhi Shanghai Taipei Toronto

With offices in

Argentina Austria Brazil Chile Czech Republic France Greece
Guatemala Hungary Italy Japan Poland Portugal Singapore
South Korea Switzerland Thailand Turkey Ukraine Vietnam

Oxford is a registered trade mark of Oxford University Press
in the UK and in certain other countries

Published in the United States
by Oxford University Press Inc., New York

British Library Cataloguing in Publication Data

Data available

Library of Congress Cataloging in Publication Data

Data available

Typeset by Cepha Imaging Pvt. Ltd., Bangalore, India
Printed in Great Britain
on acid-free paper by
Biddles Ltd., King's Lynn, Norfolk

ISBN 978-0-19-857039-4

10 9 8 7 6 5 4 3 2 1

Whilst every effort has been made to ensure that the contents of this book are as complete,
accurate and up-to-date as possible at the date of writing, Oxford University Press is not
able to give any guarantee or assurance that such is the case. Readers are urged to take
appropriately qualified medical advice in all cases. The information in this book is
intended to be useful to the general reader, but should not be used as a means of
self-diagnosis or for the prescription of medication.

Contents

Contributors

Glenda Andrews
School of Psychology
Griffiths University
Logan
Australia

Alan Baddeley
Department of Psychology
University of York
York
England

John D. Bain
School of Psychology
University of Queensland, Griffiths University
Queensland
Australia

Rosemary Baker
School of Psychology
University of Queensland
Queensland
Australia

Pierre Barrouillet
Department of Psychology
Université de Genève
Genève
Switzerland

Chandramallika Basak
Beckman Institute
University of Illinois
Urbana
USA

Damian Birney
School of Psychology
University of Sydney
Queensland
Australia

Gordon D. A. Brown
Department of Psychology
University of Warwick
Warwick, UK;

And School of Psychology
University of Western Australia
Crawley, Australia

Michael Bunting
Assistant Research Scientist
University of Maryland Center for Advanced
Study of Language
College Park
USA

Valérie Camos
LEAD CNRS
Université de Bourgogne and
Institut Universitaire de France
Dijon
France

John Cerella
Center for Health and Behavior and
Psychology Department
Syracuse University
NY
USA

Zhijian Chen
Department of Psychological Sciences
University of Missouri
Columbia, MO
USA

Susan M. Courtney
Department of Psychological and Brain Sciences
John Hopkins University
Baltimore, MD
USA

Nelson Cowan
Department of Psychological Sciences
University of Missouri
Columbia, MO
USA

Meredyth Daneman
Department of Psychology
University of Toronto
Mississauga, Ontario
Canada

Anne Depoorter
Department of Experimental Psychology
Ghent University
Ghent
Belgium

Maude Deschuyteneer
Department of Experimental Psychology
Ghent University
Ghent
Belgium

Simon C. Duff
Department of Clinical Psychology
University of Liverpool
Liverpool
England

Mark D'Esposito
Helen Wills Neuroscience Institute and
Department of Psychology
University of California
Berkeley, CA
USA

Shintaro Funahashi
Department of Cognitive and
Behavioural Sciences
Graduate School of Human and
Environmental Studies, Kyoto University
Kyoto
Japan

Adam Gazzaley
Department of Neurology and Physiology
University of California
San Francisco, CA
USA

Graeme S. Halford
School of Psychology
University of Queensland, Griffiths University
Queensland
Australia

A. Cris Hamilton
Center for Cognitive Neuroscience
University of Pennsylvania
Philadelphia, PA
USA

Brenda Hannon
Department of Psychology
University of Texas at San Antonio
Texas
USA

Graham Hitch
Department of Psychology
University of York
York
England

William J. Hoyer
Center for Health and Behavior and
Psychology Department
Syracuse University
NY
USA

Kara Kopp
Psychology Department
Wofford College
Spartanburg
SC, USA

Stephan Lewandowsky
School of Psychology
University of Western Australia
Crawley
Australia

Robert H. Logie
Human Cognitive Neuroscience,
PPLS-Psychology
University of Edinburgh
Edinburgh
Scotland

Petter Marklund
Department of Psychology
Stockholm University and Stockholm Brain
Institute
Stockholm
Sweden

Randi C. Martin
Psychology Department
Rice University
Houston, TX
USA

Julie McCredden
School of Psychology
University of Queensland
Queensland
Australia

Kaye Mills
Department of Psychology
University of Southern Queensland
Toowomba
Australia

Candice C. Morey
Department of Psychological Science
University of Missouri
Columbia, MO
USA

Ian Neath
Department of Psychology
Memorial University of Newfoundland
St. John's, NL
Canada

Lars Nyberg
Department of Integrative Medical Biology,
Physiology Section
Umeå University
Umeå
Sweden

Klaus Oberauer
Department of Experimental Psychology
University of Bristol
Bristol
UK

Mariko Osaka
Department of Psychology
Osaka University of Foreign Studies
Osaka
Japan

Naoyuki Osaka
Department of Psychology
Graduate School of Letters, Kyoto University
Kyoto
Japan

David G. Pearson
School of Psychology
University of Aberdeen
Aberdeen
Scotland

Steven Phillips
Cognitive and Behavioral Science Group
National Institute of Industrial Science
and Technology
Tsukuba
Japan

Bradley R. Postle
Department of Psychology
University of Wisconsin-Madison
Madison, WI
USA

Jennifer K. Roth
Magnetic Resonance Research Center,
Department of Diagnostic Radiology
Yale School of Medicine
New Haven, CT
USA

Bart Rypma
School of Behavioural and Brain Science
University of Texas at Dallas
Dallas, TX
USA

Joseph B. Sala
Department of Psychology
Stanford University
Stanford, CA
USA

Aimée M. Suprenant
Department of Psychology
Memorial University of Newfoundland
St. John's, NL
Canada

Arnaud Szmalec
Department of Experimental Psychology
Ghent University
Ghent
Belgium

Gerald Tehan
Department of Psychology
University of Southern Queensland
Toowomba
Australia

André Vandierendonck
Department of Experimental Psychology
Ghent University
Ghent
Belgium

Paul Verhaeghen
Center for Health and Behavior and
Psychology Department
Syracuse University
NY
USA

William H. Wilson
School of Computer Science
and Engineering
University of New South Wales
Kensington
Australia

Tarryn Wright
School of Psychology
University of Western Australia
Crawley
Australia

Yanmin Zhang
Center for Health and Behavior and
Psychology Department
Syracuse University
NY
USA

Acknowledgments

The international conference on working memory that inspired this book was convened by the Japan Society for Working Memory (JSWM), directed by the president Naoyuki Osaka. The conference was held in August 2004 at the beautiful Kyoto International Conference Hall which sits at the foot of Mount Hiei, surrounded by Lake Takaragaike.

We would like to express our thanks to The International Scientific Committee for the conference comprising Naoyuki Osaka (Chair, Kyoto University), Mark D'Esposito (University of California), Shintaro Funahashi (Kyoto University), Michael Kane (University of North Carolina), Robert Logie (University of Edinburgh), Akira Miyake (University of Colorado), Mariko Osaka (Osaka University of Foreign Studies), and Satoru Saito (Kyoto University). The members of the local organizing committee were Naoyuki Osaka (Chair), Shintaro Funahashi, Masanao Morishita, Mariko Osaka and Satoru Saito. We are grateful to our colleagues on these committees for making the conference so successful. We also express thanks to the conference staff including Nobuyuki Hirose, Takashi Ikeda, Mizuki Kaneda, Ken Kihara, Daisuke Matsuyoshi, Rie Nishimura, Yuki Otsuka and Hiroyuki Tsubomi from Kyoto University.

We are deeply indebted to Martin Baum, our senior commissioning editor at Oxford University Press for his enduring support and to his assistant Carol Maxwell for her help with assembling the manuscript.

Finally, many thanks go JSWM, Japan Society for the Promotion of Sciences (JSPS), Inoue Foundation, Kayamori Foundation, Kyoto University Foundation, and Kyoto University 21st Century Centre of Excellence (COE) Program (D-2, Kyoto University) for their financial support.

Working memory capacity, control, components and theory
An editorial overview

Robert H. Logie, Naoyuki Osaka and Mark D'Esposito

John Locke (1690), the British philosopher, referred to 'contemplation'. Joseph Jacobs (1887), reputed to have invented the digit span technique, referred to it as 'prehension'. William James (1890), the American philosopher and psychologist, referred to 'the specious present', and during the middle decades of the twentieth century, experimental psychologists on both sides of the Atlantic referred to 'short-term memory'. The term working memory was originally used by Miller, Galanter and Pribram in 1960 but was described very briefly and in very general terms as a system for temporary retention of plans and goals. The concept of working memory was very substantially developed and empirically tested by Baddeley and Hitch (1974). Their view was of a cognitive system that was broader than the prevailing focus at the time on verbal short-term memory, and included some form of visual and spatial temporary memory (the visuospatial scratch pad), together with a range of control processes (a central executive) to allow for selection and implementation of strategies, in addition to serial ordered verbal memory (the phonological loop). The Baddeley and Hitch model has been highly influential since its first publication, although there are now several different instantiations of the working memory concept, and in its various guises this concept is now the subject of substantial research effort worldwide (see for example Miyake and Shah 1999).

The motivation for this book came from the Second International Conference on Working Memory that took place from 17–20 August in the International Conference Hall in Kyoto, Japan in 2004, organized by the editors and some of the authors in this book, and led by Naoyuki Osaka. The date of the conference coincided with the thirtieth anniversary of the seminal Baddeley and Hitch (1974) article. However, the conference also was a showcase for leading edge research on all contemporary concepts of working memory using techniques from experimental psychology, single cell recording, neuropsychology, cognitive neuroimaging and computational modelling. Conference presenters were invited to write chapters covering the work of their own laboratories and from their own theoretical perspectives with a focus on behavioural and neural correlates of working memory. The result was this text, which has chapters from most of the leading international figures in working memory research and these chapters complement a separate set of papers arising from the conference that appear elsewhere (Logie and D'Esposito 2007).

In their opening chapter, Baddeley and Hitch provide an account of the history of the working memory concept and of their own substantial contributions, in addition to summaries of their ongoing research programmes. The broad scope of their chapter offers contexts for many, if not all of the chapters that follow. For example, their historical discussion argues that heralding the demise of short-term memory was premature in the 1970s and 1980s, and this can be contrasted with the chapters by Marklund and Nyberg, and by Postle. Hitch's own current research on computational modelling of serial order links neatly with the chapters by Lewandowsky et al., Tehan and Mills, and Neath and Surprenant, as does Baddeley's recent work on the irrelevant speech effect. The research by Hitch and colleagues on a time-based account of working memory span sets the scene for the chapters by Daneman and Hannon, Barrouillet and Camos, Osaka and Osaka and Logie and Duff. Their recent joint work on binding in working memory and the episodic buffer complements the chapters by Martin and Hamilton, by Funahashi and by Gazzaley and D'Esposito.

Following the chapter by Baddeley and Hitch, four chapters discuss the concept of working memory capacity. Daneman and Hannon focus on the very substantial evidence base for working memory capacity reflecting a core cognitive ability that differs between individuals, that offers a set of measures with high internal reliability and that accounts for substantial amounts of individual variance in a wide range of other cognitive abilities, most notably language comprehension. They conclude that the key aspects of language comprehension predicted by working memory measures involve remembering new text, retrieval from long-term memory, making inferences and integrating knowledge. The concept of 'working memory capacity' was also the title of a recent book by Cowan (2005) and represents a major source of debate as well as an important interface between working memory, attention, and general mental ability. In the current chapter, Cowan, Morey, Chen, and Bunting emphasize that working memory represents more than just general efficiency of information processing and is closely linked to the capacity of single, limited capacity attentional resource. They also demonstrate how working memory capacity differences may be assessed without the need for tasks that have two major components (processing and storage). Barrouillet and Camos develop their interpretation of the working memory span task as reflecting the rapid switching of a single, limited capacity attentional resource between the processing element and rehearsal of the items for recall. They argue that the memory trace is subject to decay over time and demonstrate that when attention is captured by demanding processing tasks that prevent time for rehearsal, the result is poorer memory performance. Their view then is of a system in which capacity is limited by time and by attention. This is broadly consistent with the arguments from Cowan and colleagues, as is the argument presented by Verhaeghen and colleagues who point to evidence from task-switching paradigms that a single flexible attentional resource may place limitations on working memory capacity. This limitation may vary up to a maximum of four chunks of information with sufficient practice on the task. They conclude by suggesting that the task-switching elements of the working memory span task may offer additional insight into the precise characteristics of this limited resource. In their chapter, Osaka and Osaka present functional magnetic resonance imaging (fMRI) data that explore the basis for individual differences in working memory span capacity. They identify three major and separable working memory functions, namely the focusing, shifting and inhibition of attention with neural networks connecting the dorsolateral prefrontal cortex (DLPFC), anterior cingulate cortex (ACC) and superior parietal lobule. This raises the question as to whether there are quite distinct operations for attentional control, even if there is only a single limited capacity attentional resource that is subject to such diverse control. Logie and Duff present data on this issue that are not consistent with the single flexible resource view. They describe empirical work that extends their previous findings to demonstrate that memory maintenance can continue even when participants are occupied by a time-demanding processing task. They also present evidence from a large participant sample suggesting that processing speed and memory capacity are largely unrelated in a working memory span task. This last result is also consistent with evidence reported by Daneman and Hannon. This kind of evidence cannot readily be explained by the concept of a single limited capacity attentional resource that switches between memory and processing. It is much more comfortable with an account that draws on the concept of multiple cognitive resources that can operate in parallel, and a multiple component model of working memory. This argument is echoed in the chapters by Baddeley and Hitch, by Funahashi, by Martin and Hamilton, and by Vandierendonck and colleagues.

Although the broader concept of working memory has replaced the more traditional focus on short-term verbal memory, there remain significant research questions about how humans achieve temporary retention of verbal material, and particularly serial order. Several different models have been produced, some of which are described and addressed here. Lewandowsky, Wright and Brown focus on the role of timing in the presentation of verbal material for immediate ordered serial recall. There is an established finding that items which are temporally isolated from other items in the list are rather better recalled. This finding is one source of support for models that view temporal markers as important for retaining and reproducing serial order. Lewandowsky *et al.* argue that these results can be interpreted as reflecting alternative encoding strategies for items that stand out from the list because of the timing of presentation. Therefore, timing itself might not be crucial, and selective encoding strategies might be more important for recall success. Tehan and Mills address whether there is a common short-term verbal memory system that supports simple (e.g. forward serial recall span) and more complex (e.g. backward serial recall) verbal span tasks. They present data demonstrating that phonological coding appears to be used in both forward and backward recall, suggesting that the same memory store might be involved in simple and complex verbal memory. One contrast is that word length effects are present for forward but not backward recall, and this is offered for further investigation. Neath and Surprenant offer a potential solution by pointing to evidence indicating that word length effects even for forward recall might be unreliable and prone to alternative encoding strategies. They refer to a range of formal models of serial recall and demonstrate how their own feature-based model may account for a range of phenomena associated with verbal serial recall tasks as well as accounting for how these phenomena may differ between younger and older participants. Martin and Hamilton point to a feature of serial recall that is less commonly considered, namely that recall is better for real words than it is for nonwords, letters or digits. Performance is even better if the word list comprises a meaningful sentence. This demonstrates an important role for semantic knowledge in immediate serial recall tasks. Conversely, Martin and Hamilton report evidence from patients with verbal short-term memory deficits who nevertheless have intact language comprehension, showing that the latter skill does not depend on adequate functioning of the phonological loop. Moreover, amnesic patients appear able to retain semantic information over short periods of time, despite their severe difficulty in accessing long-term memory. As mentioned in the Baddeley and Hitch chapter, Baddeley has addressed these shortcomings by proposing the 'episodic buffer' as a temporary store for meaningful material and representations of coincident information from different sensory modalities. Martin and Hamilton discuss dissociations between patients with deficits of phonological short-term memory and those with deficits of semantic short-term memory. This in part serves as the basis for their own model of short-term memory comprising a range of different competencies.

Gazzaley and D'Esposito use the vehicle of visuospatial representations to explore broader issues of the top down modulation of association cortex linked to activity in the prefrontal cortex (PFC). One general emerging view from brain imaging, neuropsychological studies and from single cell recording is that the control and maintenance functions of working memory appear to be linked with PFC activity (see also the chapter by Postle). Gazzaley and D'Esposito offer both fMRI and event-related potential (ERP) data, demonstrating how the PFC might contribute to the inhibition of irrelevant visual information while focusing on and maintaining visual information that is relevant to the task in hand. Some of their recent work using transcranial magnetic stimulation (TMS) to induce temporary lesions offers a promising additional source of evidence for this form of top-down modulation of visual processing. The argument applies to visual information from stored knowledge, such as in mental imagery tasks, as well as the filtering and processing of visual sensory input, but is presented as a model of broader control in working memory function. Funahashi points to evidence from single-cell recording in primates that cells in the DLPFC show sustained activity following removal of a visual stimulus, thereby offering a neural mechanism for maintenance in working memory. Some of these cells also show activity related to an activity that will be required following the delay, akin to maintenance of intended actions (e.g. saccades) or prospective remembering. Consistent with this, DLPFC cells appear to support the link between visuospatial representations and representations of motor activity. The argument is broader, however, in suggesting that DLPFC has a general information processing role and is not just confined to visuospatial and motor representations. It receives signals from a range of different sensory association areas, and sends signals to those areas for top-down modulation of their function. The DLPFC is then equated with a domain general information processing and control system akin to a central executive, while sensory association areas offer domain-specific aspects of working memory that can be controlled through top-down modulation by the executive. This offers a neurological implementation of a multiple component working memory. The chapter by Pearson discusses the body of evidence linking physical movement, eye movement and attentional control with retention of visual and spatial features of stimuli. He describes work suggesting that oculomotor control has a close association with retaining movement sequences, such as in the Corsi blocks task, and that the effects of eye movements can be separated from the effects of shifts of visual attention. He then goes on to describe a theory based on indexing individual objects, with executive or attentional control required to keep track of multiple objects moving in the visual field.

Vandierendonck and colleagues explicitly argue for top down modulation with respect to conflict resolution and response selection, both of which are seen as important functions on a central executive, while concurrent cognitive functions may operate in parallel, modality-specific systems providing demands on two or more tasks do not require response selection. They argue that this fits with a multiple component model of working memory. A consistent view of executive control is described by Halford and colleagues who offer evidence that a major function of an executive is to support relational processing involved in planning, reasoning and comprehension. Rypma examines the changes in executive functions with age, drawing on behavioral and brain imaging data. Like Vandierendonck, he focuses on response selection as an important executive function and concludes that this function deteriorates with age because of increased noise in the neural signals, making it difficult for older adults to decide between alternative responses. He suggests that a major change in older adults is a reduction in neural efficiency, particularly in the DLPFC, which contributes to the deterioration in executive function with age. This is a conclusion that is consistent with behavioral data demonstrating the slowing of cognitive processing in older adults, for example in the chapter by Verhaeghen (see also Salthouse, Babcock and Shaw 1991).

Marklund and Nyberg review positron emission tomography (PET), fMRI and ERP studies of episodic memory retrieval, working memory and of executive control, and conclude that working memory may comprise a range of control functions linked with the operation of the prefrontal cortex that serve to retrieve information from long-term memory in more posterior areas and to maintain the information in an active state. This views the memory components of working memory as comprising the currently activated areas of long-term memory rather than a quite distinct temporary memory system. Postle offers a similar argument, drawing on brain imaging data linked with spatial, visual and verbal representations, thereby expanding on the arguments by Marklund and Nyberg. He also seeks to address some of the counterarguments to this view by introducing the concept of multiple encoding. Oberauer offers a model in which there is no limit to the amount of activation available, with the possibility of multiple distinct activations. However limitations arise if there are too many representations active at one time, leading to competition and interference, and a requirement for an inhibitory process for activations that are not relevant for the task in hand. He suggests that efficiency of inhibitory function might offer a major source of individual differences in working memory capacity. In common with Cowan's model, he suggests that at any one time there is a set of activations that are readily accessible, and there is a subset of these that are in the focus of attention. He is specific about competition between activations for the focus of attention. This last concept is described as a processing bottleneck. Courtney, Roth and Sala discuss a neurological implementation of a model that allows for concurrent activation of multiple representations that are distinct from activated areas of long-term memory, that may be domain-specific and involve activations associated with integrated objects arising from the binding of several different sensory features. Rather than referring to a focus of attention, their argument builds on the Desimone and Duncan (1995; Duncan 2001) biased competition model in which the relative activation of these different representations influences activation elsewhere in the brain and consequently influences action.

The scope of this book is intentionally broad, and this breadth demonstrates clearly the wide appeal of the concept of working memory as an explanatory construct for everyday cognition, for phenomena observed in the laboratory, and as a stimulus for substantial and fruitful empirical research. Several of the debates from the early 1970s have remained salient. The more recent brain imaging techniques have given rise to a new debate about their status with regard to developing cognitive theory (e.g. Coltheart 2006; Henson 2005; Page 2006). That debate aside, working memory as on-line cognition in particular lends itself to investigation using fMRI, magentic encephalographic (MEG) and ERP techniques with humans, and single cell recording techniques with animals, leading to further questions about how it might be implemented in the brain. There are also broader sets of contrasting views expressed in the pages of this book. However, it is clear from the present chapters that we know a great deal more about brain organization and about cognitive organization than did the memory research community in the early 1970s. The growth of interest, the volume and quality of the research more than three decades on appear unabated.

References

Baddeley, AD and Hitch, GJ (1974). Working memory. In G. Bower (ed), *The Psychology of Learning and Motivation, Vol. VIII*, 47–90, New York: Academic Press.

Coltheart, M (2006). What has functional neuroimaging told us about the mind (so far)? *Cortex*, *42*, 323–331.

Cowan, N (2005). *Working Memory Capacity*. New York: Psychology Press.

Desimone, R and Duncan, J (1995). Neural mechanisms of selective visual attention. *Annual Review of Neuroscience*, *18*, 193–222.

Duncan, J (2001). An adaptive coding model of neural function in prefrontal cortex. *Nature Reviews Neuroscience*, *2*, 820–829.

Henson, R (2005). What can functional neuroimaging tell the experimental psychologist? *Quarterly Journal of Experimental Psychology*, *58A*, 193–233.

Jacobs, J (1887). Experiments on 'prehension'. *Mind*, *12*(45), 75–79.

James, W (1890). *Principles of Psychology Vol. 1*. 1902 Edition. London: Macmillan and Co.

Locke, J (1690). *An Essay Concerning Human Understanding*, Book II, Chapter X, paragraphs 1–2. University of Aberdeen, UK. Special Collections.

Logie, RH and D'Esposito, M (eds) (2007). *Working Memory in the Brain: A special issue of Cortex*. Amsterdam: Elsevier.

Miller, GA, Galanter, E and Pribram, KH (1960). *Plans and the Structure of Behavior*. New York: Henry Holt and Company.

Miyake, A and Shah, P (eds) (1999). *Models of Working Memory: Mechanisms of active maintenance and executive control*. Cambridge: Cambridge University Press.

Page, MPA (2006). What can't functional neuroimaging tell the cognitive psychologist? *Cortex*, *42*, 428–443.

Salthouse, TA, Babcock, RL and Shaw, RJ (1991). Effects of adult age on structural and operational capacities in working memory. *Psychology and Aging*, *6*, 118–127.

Working memory

Past, present ... and future?

Alan Baddeley and Graham Hitch

As the longest serving residents of the province of working memory, the two of us have been invited to introduce this volume by saying a little about our particular experiences of how it all began.

One of us (AD Baddeley – ADB) had cut his research teeth on the 1960s controversy concerning the nature of memory, whether unitary as proposed by the previously dominant stimulus–repsonse (S–R) associationist view with learning based on the building up of associations and forgetting due to interference (Keppel and Underwood 1962; Melton 1963; Postman 1975), or whether it was necessary to assume two or more separate memory systems, interpreted in terms of the new information-processing concepts that came to be known as cognitive psychology (Broadbent 1958; Brown 1958; Miller 1956; Peterson and Peterson 1959). The Medical Research Council Applied Psychology Unit (APU) in Cambridge lay at the heart of this latter approach and our respective mentors, namely Conrad (ADB) and Broadbent (GJ Hitch – GJH) played central roles in the early development of the concept of a separate short-memory (STM). During the 1960s the single versus multiple systems controversy became a very hot issue, with a large number of novel paradigms being developed, and what seemed like an equally large number of explanatory models, many of them mathematically based (for 13 such models see Deutsch and Deutsch 1975). However, as Murdock observed, these tended to have a great deal in common, broadly resembling the most influential example, that of Atkinson and Shiffrin (1968), which Murdock dubbed the modal model.

Lacking even moderate mathematical competence, ADB preferred to concentrate on studying phenomena that might help distinguish between the two hypothetical systems, identifying as possible candidates acoustic versus semantic coding (Baddeley 1966a, b), two-component tasks, where one component is durable and attributable to long-term memory (LTM) and the other a more fragile potential STM component (Baddeley 1968a; Glanzier and Cunitz 1966). A third approach resulted from the opportunity to collaborate with Elizabeth Warrington in the study of a group of dense but very pure amnesic patients, who showed preserved performance on tasks associated with STM, despite their grossly impaired LTM (Baddeley and Warrington 1970). As such these provided a double dissociation when contrasted with patients with a lesion in the left temporoparietal lobe who showed impaired STM and preserved LTM (Shallice and Warrington 1970).

GJH in the mean time was completing a PhD on STM, attempting to investigate the mechanism whereby acoustic similarity of items impairs recall. It was well known that acoustic similarity increases order errors (Wickelgren 1965), but unclear how this effect occurs. Experiments comparing different methods of probing STM for recall of a single item suggested that item and order information were stored separately, order being coded positionally rather than through interitem (i.e. chaining) associations (Hitch 1974). However, it was not possible at that stage to link these observations to an account of the acoustic similarity effect. This had to wait a number of years, as will be described later.

In 1971, GJH moved from Cambridge to Sussex to work on a grant to study the relationship between STM and LTM with ADB, who had just returned from a year with George Mandler and Donald Norman in California.

Between our application and starting the grant, however, the scene had changed markedly, and STM was no longer a fashionable topic. It is unclear whether this was because the plethora of new experimental paradigms and the plethora of models did not match up, or whether people were beginning to think like Don Norman (personal communication 1971) that we had already solved the problem of STM. It rapidly became clear, however, that Don's assessment of the situation was a little optimistic.

If we take the Atkinson and Shiffrin (1968) modal model as an example, it was beginning to encounter two major problems. The first of these was the assumption that learning, the transfer of information from the short-term to the long-term store, occurs automatically, with the degree of learning depending on the time in the short-term store (STS). It was becoming increasingly clear that simply maintaining an item in STS does not guarantee learning (Craik and Watkins 1973), consistent with the proposal by Craik and Lockhart (1972) of the Levels of Processing hypothesis, according to which the probability of learning was dependent on depth of processing. Hence with verbal material, requiring the subject to make a judgment about the visual characteristics of the word led to very little learning, judgments of its sound were somewhat better but not nearly as good as processing in terms of its meaning. This issue rapidly eclipsed studies of STM in popularity, and was indeed sometimes claimed to be a refutation of the STM–LTM distinction (Postman 1975), despite the fact that Craik and Lockhart themselves assumed the importance of a short-term component which they termed primary memory.

A second dramatic change in the intellectual scene was prompted by the PhD dissertation of an MIT computer science student that attempted to develop a language comprehension programme. Such a programme needed to store the meaning of the constituent words, and it did so by proposing a hierarchal storage scheme (Quillian 1969). This led to an experimental test, which appeared to support the hypothesis (Collins and Quillian 1969). Although subsequent research identified flaws with this original study (Conrad 1972), the work stimulated intense interest in the important but neglected topic of how meaning is stored. This interest was intensified and crystallized by Tulving's (1972) classic paper proposing a distinction between knowledge-based semantic memory, and episodic memory, the capacity to recollect specific experiences. We ourselves seemed to have chosen yesterday's problem as the focus of our first grant.

Paradoxically, a glimmer of hope was provided by a second problem with the modal model. Atkinson and Shiffrin proposed that their short-term store acted as a working memory, performing the wide range of coding and manipulation activities that are needed for complex cognition. The term working memory appears to have been coined by Miller, Galanter and Pribram (1960), although they said little about its nature. Furthermore, although this was an important feature of the Atkinson and Shiffrin model, it was one they had not explored, concentrating instead on producing a mathematically specified model of the retention of lists of unrelated words. Had they attempted to tackle the broader cognitive capacity of their model, they might well have been perturbed by the fact that the patients with STM deficits studied by Shallice and Warrington (1970) appeared to have few problems in their everyday life: indeed one was a very efficient secretary. If the short-term store acted as a working memory, such patients should have been grossly functionally impaired.

We therefore decided to tackle the question of what function the short-term store might serve, if any. We did not have access to appropriate patients, and instead used dual task methods to turn our student subjects into patient substitutes. We did this by requiring them to perform a range of complex cognitive tasks such as reasoning, learning and comprehension, while simultaneously holding and reciting digit sequences ranging in length from zero to eight items. According to the modal model, this should lead to a cumulative decrement in performance as digit load increased, until performance was virtually obliterated when the digit sequence reached span. In the case of a syntactic reasoning task, for which performance correlates with intelligence (Baddeley 1968b), completion time increased with load, but even with eight digits it was only 50 per cent higher than the control level, while accuracy remained stable at around 5 per cent regardless of concurrent load. We found similar results for learning and reasoning tasks and concluded that the modal model required revision.

We proposed to replace the concept of a single short-term store with a three-component system comprising an attentional controller, the central executive, aided by two subsidiary systems. The first we christened the articulatory loop, since we proposed that rehearsal involved vocal or subvocal articulation. We have subsequently changed the name to phonological loop, transferring emphasis to the storage system, rather than its means of rehearsal. The second system we initially called the visuospatial scratchpad, changing this in turn to sketchpad on the grounds that a scratchpad could be used for making verbal notes as well as visual sketches.

We began by investigating the two peripheral systems, on the grounds that these appeared to offer a more tractable problem than the central executive, especially in the case of the phonological loop for which extensive evidence already existed based on the standard verbal STM literature.

Things were going well, despite disruption from a move from Sussex to Stirling University, at which point we were invited by Gordon Bower to contribute to a prestigious annual review series he was currently editing. We hesitated, since our model was far from complete, but eventually succumbed to the temptation and submitted the chapter that became Baddeley and Hitch (1974).

By the time the paper was published, we had moved again, back to the APU where ADB had succeeded Broadbent as Director. Although we both moved to Cambridge, our research paths diverged at this point.

Baddeley's programme

The sketchpad

Work on the visuospatial component of the system was initially prompted by a paper by Atwood (1971), who claimed to find marked differential effects of simple verbal and spatial tasks on whether material was held visually or verbally. In common with a number of other investigators, ADB repeatedly failed to replicate the Atwood effect, although convinced from personal experience that such a distinction existed. A series of ingenious studies by Brooks (1967, 1968) provided a much more robust paradigm that not only identified a reliable effect, but also was able to demonstrate that it was spatial rather than visual in origin (Baddeley, Grant, Wight *et al.* 1973; Baddeley and Lieberman 1980). He concluded that the system was spatial in nature, a conclusion that failed to convince a sceptical Scottish post doctoral colleague, Robert Logie, who went on to demonstrate that the system could store either spatial or visual characteristics such as shape and colour, depending on the task (Logie 1986), a line of research he has continued to develop successfully in subsequent years (Logie 1995). Subsequent research using neuroimaging has provided additional evidence for a fractionation of the sketchpad into at least two and possibly more components. The issue of precisely how to characterize these remains controversial. One view links the components to the spatial and object-based visual processing streams (Smith and Jonides 1997) while another view argues for a later post-LTM interpretation (Della Sala and Logie 2002).

The phonological loop

As mentioned earlier, a good deal of existing evidence could be used to develop a simple model of the phonological loop, comprising a temporary store, together with an articulatory rehearsal system which can be used either to maintain items through repetition or to register visually presented material within the store by a process of articulatory naming. We were unsure quite what to call the store. Conrad (1964) referred to the system as acoustic, but since visually presented material could be stored, the term acoustic did not seem quite appropriate. The term phonemic was then adopted, but subsequently abandoned when it transpired that this had a rather precise linguistic connotation that did not seem justified either. Phonological was the third attempt; it appears that this also can have a more precise connotation than intended, but there is a limit to the number of times one can change terminology without exhausting the patience of one's colleagues. No doubt one day someone will specify precisely the nature of the code, but given the lack of success of earlier attempts (Hintzman 1967; Wickelgren 1969), this will not be an easy task.

We concentrated instead on attempting to identify robust phenomena that would place clear constraints on any model, arguing that any progress made in this direction would be valuable in providing a foundation for subsequent theories, even if our own rapidly fell by the wayside. The first of these phenomena, the phonological similarity effect had already been discovered by Conrad (Conrad 1964; Conrad and Hull 1964), and further extended by Baddeley (1966a, b) and Wickelgren (1965). It was assumed to reflect the phonological nature of the short-term store. The articulatory rehearsal system on the other hand was assumed to be reflected in the word length effect, the tendency for immediate serial memory span to decline with number of syllables in the words to be remembered (Baddeley, Thomson and Buchanan 1975).

Our initial word length study was almost abandoned on the grounds that any result would have multiple interpretations, but given the robust and strikingly lawful results we obtained, we were able to rule out some at least of the alternative explanations in terms of the semantic, lexical or frequency characteristics of the constituent words. As my colleague Neil Thomson pointed out, the linear relationship between word length, the speed with which the material could be articulated, and span was consistent with the assumption that the memory retrace faded rapidly, becoming inaccessible after about two seconds, unless rehearsed. The subsequent observation by Nicolson (1981) that both memory span and maximal rate of articulation increased systematically with age in young children appeared to offer further support for a simple model involving a fading trace that could be reactivated by subvocal rehearsal, a process that increased in speed and efficiency as the children developed.

Finally, our evidence seemed to support an interpretation in terms of trace decay rather than interference. Our conclusion came from the observation that when our subjects were required to recall sequences of disyllabic words, performance was better for words with short vowels and rapid pronunciation (e.g. *bishop, wicket* vs *harpoon, Friday*). Everything seemed to fit neatly into the simple model of a fading trace and a time-based articulatory rehearsal system. Alas, things were not so simple, and although there is till a strong case for thinking that the initial simple model holds (Baddeley, in press), it has since been under continuous attack.

Some apparent criticisms could reasonably be regarded as clarifications: a good example of this is the demonstration by (Cowan, Day, Saults *et al.* 1992) that much of the forgetting observed in recalling sequences of long words occurs not only during rehearsal, but also because long words take longer to articulate during recall, as indeed would be predicted by the model. In fact both rehearsal and recall effects of word length can be demonstrated (Baddeley, Chincotta, Stafford *et al.* 2002).

A second line of attack has focused on our long and short vowel result, with subsequent studies able to replicate our own results with our material, but showing different results for other sets of apparently equally appropriate material (see Lovatt and Avons 2001 for a review). However, these studies in turn have been criticized for failing to match the relevant groups in terms of phonological similarity (Baddeley and Andrade 1994), a claim denied by Caplan and Walters (1994). The latest development in this saga is provided by an extremely careful series of experiments by Mueller, Seymour, Kieras *et al.* 2003) who observed that they can give a good account of the data from all the studies in terms of phonological similarity and spoken duration, finding little or no support for the opposing interpretation in terms of word complexity. A further blow to the complexity hypothesis comes from the observation that when long and short words are mixed, no difference in overall recall between the long and short words was found (Cowan, Baddeley, Elliot *et al.* 2003; Hulme, Surprenant, Bireta *et al.* 2004). The results do not however conform simply to a total spoken time hypothesis, suggesting the need to assume factors other than simple decay, possibly reflecting discriminability of the items at retrieval. This seems likely to be an area of active continuing controversy.

A second area that remained controversial is that of the influence of irrelevant sound on immediate serial recall. In the early 1980s, a French visitor, Pierre Salamé spent a sabbatical year at the APU, tasked with carrying out a one year programme that was unconstrained, except that it had to involve noise. As this was not an active research area at the APU at that time, it was agreed that noise could include the disruptive effect of irrelevant speech. He and ADB agreed an experiment, but disagreed on their predictions. The experiment involved immediate serial recall of sequences of nine digits under quiet conditions, or when ignoring sequences of meaningful words, or sequences of nonsense syllables. One of us (ADB) predicted no effects, Pierre predicted a disruptive effect of irrelevant meaningful words but not syllables. We were both wrong, as we would have known if we had read an earlier paper by Colle (1980). Irrelevant spoken material disrupts recall, regardless of meaning, whereas white noise of a similar loudness does not. Our experiments (Salamé and Baddeley 1982), and a series of subsequent studies extended Colle's findings and interpreted them within a phonological loop framework, identifying the effect with storage rather than rehearsal. We found an effect of music and of complex meaningless sounds, but not of noise pulsed within the same sound envelope as the irrelevant speech (Salamé and Baddeley 1987, 1989). At this point, Salamé's laboratory switched direction requiring him to work first on sleep, then on alcohol, and subsequently on schizophrenia, and ADB's direct involvement in the area paused until reactivated by a new collaboration (Larsen, Baddeley and Andrade 2000; Larsen and Baddeley 2003).

Research on irrelevant sound was carried on by Dylan Jones and his group, who substantially extended the investigation of the acoustic characteristics needed for an irrelevant sound to disrupt serial verbal recall, leading to the development of the changing state hypothesis (Jones 1993) which proposed that only sounds that changed will disrupt memory. Jones (1993) further proposed that serial recall depends on the representation of a chain of items within a multimodal space. The irrelevant sound disrupts recall by providing a competing chain, the object-oriented episodic record (O-OER) hypothesis (Jones 1993). While there is no doubt that the careful study of the nature of the sounds needed to disrupt performance by Jones and his group has made a major contribution, many features of his memory model are questionable, including his assumption of a common verbal/visuospatial system underlying his results. The O-OER model's assumption of a single chaining mechanism for serial recall is also problematic (see Henson *et al.* 1996), as is its failure to address neuropsychological and neuroimaging evidence (see Baddeley, in press). Neath (2000) provides further discussion.

Articulatory suppression

When subjects are required to repeatedly utter an irrelevant word such as "the", memory span is reduced, and with visual presentation, the phonological similarity effect is removed (Murray 1968). The latter may be attributed to suppression preventing the subvocal naming and recoding of the visually presented material, as when the material is presented auditorily the similarity effect returns (Baddeley, Lewis and Vallar 1984). Regardless of presentation modality, suppression removes the word length effect, presumably because it prevents the articulatory rehearsal that is assumed to be the basis of the effect (Baddeley *et al.* 1975). Jones also interprets this effect in terms of a changing state hypothesis, although it is not clear why hearing a single repeated word does not substantially disrupt recall (allegedly because it does not form a changing state) whereas repeatedly saying a single word has a major effect (for further discussion see Baddeley, in press; Larsen and Baddeley 2003).

Perhaps the major problem with the initial phonological loop model was the absence of a precise specification, and in particular in its absence of a mechanism for storing and retrieving serial order. Fortunately, as GJH describes, others have done an excellent job in filling this gap.

Hence, although the concept of a phonological loop has engendered continued controversy, in our opinion it remains in good health. The question still arises, however, as to whether it is a sufficiently important component to justify the considerable efforts put into its investigation. Is it anything other than a way of keeping cognitive psychologists busy? We argue that it is, and that it has evolved as a mechanism to facilitate the acquisition of language, applying it both to first language and to later language learning, a position discussed extensively by Baddeley, Gathercole and Papagno (1998), who present evidence for impaired vocabulary learning when the phonological loop is limited either neuropsychologically (Baddeley, Papagno and Vallar 1988), developmentally (Gathercole and Baddeley 1989), by the nature of the material (Papagno and Vallar 1992), or by concurrent articulatory suppression (Papagno, Valentine and Baddeley 1991). It is also becoming clear that the loop can play a valuable role in the control of behavior, providing a reliable, attentionally undemanding if limited source of self-instruction (Baddeley, Chincotta and Adlam 2001; Luria 1959a, b; Miyake, Emerson, Padilla *et al.* 2004; Saeki and Saito 2004).

The central executive

Some ten years after the initial Baddeley and Hitch paper, ADB began a monograph that attempted to pull together the work that had been done in that decade (Baddeley 1986). On nearing the end of the book, it became embarrassingly clear that he had made no progress on the all-important central executive, other than to use it as a convenient homunculus that could take care of all the complicated issues that appeared to be beyond the remit of the two subsystems. Like Attneave (1960), we think that homunculi can be useful chaps, but only if kept in their place. They can be valuable markers for problems that are yet to be solved, but this is only helpful if the problems are identified and in due course tackled, gradually reducing the remit of the homunculus, who it is hoped will eventually retire. In an attempt to identify the jobs being performed by the homunculus, a chapter on the central executive was added.

An obvious place to search for inspiration for a possible model was in the literature on attention. Although this was a well-developed field, the vast majority of work concerned the role of selective attention in perception. At the time, only one model appeared to tackle the role of attention in the control of action, that of Norman and Shallice (1986). This approach divided the control of action into two distinct mechanisms, one of which was automatic and dependent on existing habits and schemata, the other was an attentionally demanding system for modifying and controlling action when the habit-based system failed, either through overload, or from encountering a novel problem. The latter system which they labelled the Supervisory Attentional System (SAS) was adopted as a possible model for the central executive component of working memory (Baddeley 1986). It still gives a very good general account of the two principal ways in which action is controlled (Baddeley, 2007).

Analysing the SAS is therefore dependent on analysing attentional control, no mean task. One way into the problem is to attempt to go back to first principles, deciding what characteristics virtually any attentional control system would require, and then searching for evidence of these in working memory. Baddeley (1996) proposed four basic functions – the need to focus attention, to divide attention across different sources, to switch attention between tasks, and to use attention to link working memory with LTM.

Evidence of the focusing of attention is abundant. One example is provided by the task of retaining a chess position, or selecting the optimal next move. Whereas articulatory suppression has no effect on performance, suggesting no verbal contribution, a concurrent attentionally demanding task such as random generation impairs positional memory and has an even greater effect on move selection (Robbins, Anderson, Barker *et al.* 1996; Saariluoma 1995).

Divided attention was studied principally through research on Alzheimer's disease, where patients proved to have disproportionate difficulty in dividing attention between tasks, a deficit not present in normal elderly people (Baddeley, Bressi, Della Sala *et al.* 1991; Logie, Cocchini, Della Sala *et al.* 2004). Evidence for a specific capacity to switch attention between two tasks proved more elusive. One series of studies (Baddeley, Chincotta and Adlam 2001) found that the phonological loop was playing a greater role than the executive in switching in the case of one task, while switching may even enhance performance under certain conditions. For example, the speed of repeatedly writing a single letter (aaaa...) is slower than writing a series of different letters (abcabc...) as found by Nohara (1965) and replicated by Wing, Lewis and Baddeley (1979). It seems likely that switching may be achieved in a number of different ways, only some of which will depend on executive resources (Schumacher, Seymour, Glass *et al.* 2001).

The episodic buffer

The search for the process whereby working memory and LTM interact also proved complex. The situation was further complicated by the attempt to treat the executive as a purely attentional system with no storage capacity (Baddeley and Logie 1999). This resulted in a range of problems, issues that could not be handled readily within the existing three-component model. The issue was brought to a head by the attempt to account for the memory performance of a single patient, a densely amnesic but intellectually well-preserved man who had a capacity to perform normally on the immediate recall of a prose passage comprising some 25 different idea units, greatly exceeding the assumed capacity of any of the components of working memory (Wilson and Baddeley 1988), followed by the discovery of a small number of similar patients who appeared to be able to use a high level of preserved intelligence to temporarily maintain a prose paragraph (Baddeley and Wilson 2002). This highlighted the fact that the three-component system also failed to give a good account of recall of prose in normal subjects, and of the crucial phenomenon of chunking, in which existing knowledge is used to increase span (Miller 1956). In order to cope with these and a range of other problems, a fourth component of working memory was proposed: the episodic buffer (Baddeley 2000).

The episodic buffer was assumed to be a limited capacity attentional storage system based on a multidimensional code. Control is exercised by the central executive and retrieval via conscious awareness. It is episodic in that it stores episodes of information that are chunked into higher-order representations. It is a buffer in that it is a limited-capacity system which by its multidimensional nature is capable of providing a link between the more specialized subsystems of working memory.

In the few years since the concept was proposed, it appears to have evoked a reasonable amount of interest. It certainly has the advantage of providing a bridge between the European approach to working memory which has typically been bottom-up, attempting to begin by studying the simpler subsystems, and the predominant North American approach, which tends towards a more top-down emphasis on executive control. The crucial question remains however, whether the concept can really earn its living by generating fruitful experiments that genuinely enhance our knowledge of working memory, or whether it will simply become a handy method of placating editors who want more theoretical speculation in the discussion section of empirical papers.

Hitch's programme

Going back to the point when we both moved to the APU, GJH's intention was to start a research programme on the role of working memory in arithmetic. There was already a substantial amount of research at the Unit on reading and it seemed a good strategy to complete coverage of reading, writing and arithmetic (at the same time Alan Wing started a programme on writing and spelling). In my case (GJH) this work culminated in a model of mental arithmetic performance in which errors could be predicted from the implications of the calculation strategy being employed for the need to store temporary information (Hitch 1978). Put simply, the longer information had to be left in store while other attention-demanding operations were carried out, the more likely it was to be forgotten when the time came to recall it. This model was developed to explain adult performance, and it seemed important to extend the application of ideas about working memory to children's arithmetic. However, at that time MRC advised that they had a separate unit for research on children, making it difficult to continue this approach in Cambridge with any confidence. I therefore moved to a position at Manchester University, where this apparently bureaucratic constraint would not apply. At the same time I turned towards investigating the broader question of the development of working memory, while at the same time continuing to investigate the role of working memory in children's arithmetic (see e.g. Hitch, Arnold and Phillips 1983; Hitch and McAuley 1991; Furst and Hitch 2000; Adams and Hitch 1997).

Development of working memory in children

Nicolson's (1981) data on the relationship between memory span and reading rate in children stimulated particular interest in whether our model of working memory could be applied to children more generally. Given that the model was based entirely on evidence from adults, the answer was not at all obvious. If the model could be shown to be applicable to children, then this might open up new insights into children's cognitive development and education. A research grant from the UK Economic and Social Research Council held at Manchester University with Sebastian Halliday, a developmental psychologist, provided the opportunity to study this topic.

It turned out that Nicolson's data were robust and easy to replicate (Hitch and Halliday 1983; Hulme, Thomson, Muir et al. 1984). The existence of a linear relationship between memory span for words of different length and speech rate from early childhood onwards suggested that the developmental increase in span reflected more efficient use of the phonological loop. However, a competing interpretation was that a general increase in speed of information processing rather than speech rate underpinned the developmental improvement in recall (Dempster 1981). However, when we compared these two accounts with one another directly, we found that variation in span with age and materials was better explained by speed of articulation, consistent with the phonological loop (Hitch, Halliday and Littler 1989).

Older children and adults show similar sensitivity to word length and phonemic similarity in immediate serial recall regardless of whether the stimuli are spoken words, written words or nameable pictures. However, in the course of our work we noticed that children younger than about 5 or 6 years old showed different patterns of performance depending on whether items were presented auditorily or visually. These younger children showed standard effects of word length and phonemic similarity when items were presented auditorily, but not when presented with a series of pictures and tested on immediate serial recall of the picture names. In the latter condition they were unaffected by word length or phonemic similarity of the picture names (Hitch, Halliday, Dodd *et al.* 1989). Instead, younger children recalled fewer items when the pictures were visually similar and when the sequence was followed by visual rather than verbal interfering stimuli (Hitch, Woodin and Baker 1989; Hitch, Halliday, Schaafstal *et al.* 1988), suggesting they were relying on the visuospatial sketchpad. This pattern of observations implies a marked developmental transition from using the sketchpad to using the phonological loop to remember nameable visual stimuli. It was intriguing to note that such a progression is consistent with the hypothesis that auditory inputs gain direct access to the phonological loop whereas visual inputs require an optional process of verbal recoding (Baddeley, Lewis and Vallar 1984), if one makes the plausible assumption that the more controlled process develops after the more automatic process (Shiffrin and Schneider 1977).

Thus, our evidence suggested that the working memory model is not only applicable to children, but can generate novel insights in describing the pattern of developmental change. However, changes in children's performance in STM tasks are only one aspect of the development of working memory. A broader set of questions concern the relationship between working memory and cognitive development more generally. An influential approach to these issues originated in North America and focused on individual and developmental differences in complex span tasks (Daneman and Carpenter 1980; Case, Kurland and Goldberg 1982). Complex span assesses the ability to hold temporary information at the same time as carrying out mental operations. The classic example is reading span, the number of unrelated words that can be held in mind at the same time as reading for comprehension. Daneman and Carpenter (1980) showed that individual differences in reading span in college students were a much better predictor of their scholastic skills than digit span, the standard measure of STM. They interpreted complex span as measuring the size of a central workspace in which functions of processing and storage compete for common resources, a concept isomorphic with the central executive in our original model (Baddeley and Hitch 1974). There followed a rapid increase in investigations of reading span and other complex span tasks and their links to cognitive abilities, especially in adults (see e.g. Engle, Kane and Tuholski 1999).

Research on working memory in children was stimulated by Case *et al.*'s (1982) work on counting span, a task involving counting the number of targets in a series of visual arrays and then recalling all the totals. Case *et al.* found that counting span increases with age in direct proportion to the speed at which children count, which also gets faster. Using the same view of complex span as Daneman and Carpenter, Case *et al.* inferred that the resources needed to support processing decrease with age while the size of the workspace remains constant, leaving more available for storage. This explanation seemed to be widely accepted. However, to the best of our knowledge it had never been tested.

A collaboration with John Towse led to a series of experiments in which we found that counting span was sensitive to the duration rather than the attentional load of counting operations when these two factors were separated out (Towse and Hitch 1995). This was somewhat surprising, as according to the model of a central workspace one would expect more difficult operations to require more resources, resulting in lower spans. Instead it seemed that time per se was important, suggesting to us that what might limit span was forgetting of stored totals while attention was switched away from storage and on to counting subsequent arrays. We tentatively proposed a 'task switching' account according to which children switch back and forward between processing and storage functions during complex span rather than sharing resources simultaneously. We tested this idea in a series of experiments in which we prolonged the time temporary information had to be held in store while attempting to hold processing load constant. We found the same pattern of effects in a range of different complex span tasks (reading span, listening span and counting span) consistent with task-switching in children and adults (Towse, Hitch and Hutton 1998, 2000). At the same time we confirmed that complex span is highly correlated with children's reading and mathematics attainment. Complex span even predicted children's attainment one year after the initial assessment (Hitch, Towse and Hutton 2001) consistent with the idea that working memory plays an important role in the learning and acquisition of cognitive skills, an idea that has received substantial support in subsequent work (Gathercole, Pickering, Knight *et al.* 2004; St Clair-Thompson and Gathercole 2006). For example, children with low complex spans have difficulty following instructions in the classroom (Gathercole and Alloway, in press).

Subsequently, other investigators have challenged our task-switching account (Saito and Miyake 2004; Barrouillet, Bernardin and Camos 2004). Barrouillet *et al.* present evidence for a particularly interesting model that involves what they call 'resource-limited task-switching', in which the switching back and forth occurs on a much finer timescale than we proposed and is constrained by capacity limitations. We accept the importance of these contributions, noting that they agree with us in emphasizing the importance of forgetting in working memory while differing on the detailed mechanisms (Towse, Hitch and Horton 2007). Our own recent work has concentrated on developing the idea of measuring the temporal duration of working memory directly, i.e. how long temporary information can be maintained in an immediately accessible state. We find that it is possible to measure duration as reliably as complex span, and that duration is an equally good predictor of individual differences in children's cognitive abilities (Towse, Hitch, Hamilton *et al.* (2005). Others have shown that the domains of processing and storage (visuospatial vs verbal) are an important determinant of the resources utilized by complex span (Jarrold and Bayliss, 2007). It seems that unpacking these widely used tasks theoretically is likely to continue to present a challenge for some time to come. The rewards could be great, however, given that working memory appears to be an important resource in cognitive development.

Modeling the phonological loop

The concept of the phonological loop has proved durable, despite the challenges described above. This is partly because it gives a simple, easily graspable account of a robust set of phenomena that can be readily applied to tackle new problems. However, towards the end of the 1980s it became evident that this simplicity came at a price. For example, evidence that the phonological loop plays a key role in the learning of new word forms (Baddeley, Gathercole and Papagno 1998) was making it increasingly awkward that the loop contained no mechanism for long-term learning. In addition, and as already noted, the loop did not address the basic question of how serial order information is maintained. At about the same time as these omissions were coming to the fore, interest in more detailed modeling of memory received a substantial boost, particularly from the advent of connectionism, a methodology that involves constructing artificial neural networks and examining their behavior through computer simulation (Rumelhart and McClelland 1986). Elements or nodes within such networks transmit and receive activation to and from other nodes by means of connections with modifiable strengths. The plasticity of connections allows networks to adapt and provides a mechanism for learning.

The phonological loop seemed ripe for detailed modeling, given the large amount of empirical data available to inform and constrain the form of such models. Moreover, some connectionist modeling carried out by George Houghton drew attention to a potentially important mechanism called 'competitive queuing' for controlling serial output in recalling verbal sequences (Houghton 1990). In competitive queuing (see also Grossberg 1978), the element corresponding to the most active node is selected for output and is strongly suppressed immediately following its output, gradually recovering as the inhibition wears off. Such a mechanism prevents a strongly activated node from capturing the output system and provides a basic model of sequencing. It may be related to the Ranschburg Effect in immediate serial recall where memory for the second occurrence of a repeated item tends to be inhibited (Jahnke 1969).

At about this time I was fortunate to come into contact with Neil Burgess, who was completing a PhD in theoretical physics and had skills in neural network modeling. We developed a deliberately simplistic network model of the phonological loop that assumed separate but interconnected mechanisms for order and for items (Burgess and Hitch 1992). Order was coded via an internal context signal that varies with the timing of item presentation and items were coded via nodes representing words and their phonemes. Encoding a sequence involved strengthening connections between simultaneously active context, item and phoneme nodes while serial recall involved driving the model with successive states of the context signal and selecting the strongest item at each step, inhibiting it rapidly thereafter by means of competitive queuing. Rehearsal was assumed to be analogous to recall, and all connections were subject to decay over the same timescale as in the original model of the phonological loop.

This model successfully generated the key effects associated with the phonological loop, namely word length, phonological similarity, articulatory suppression and their interactions. These effects arose straightforwardly from choosing to include time-based decay of connection weights in the model. However, as required, the new model went further in generating serial order effects such as bow-shaped serial position curves and the characteristic human tendency for errors to be items presented adjacent to the correct item. These effects arose through the operation of the context signal and competitive queuing. An interesting incidental feature of the model was that it succeeded in addressing the problem of relating effects of phonological similarity and order information that had arisen in GJH's PhD thesis. We went on to show that the model was also capable of generating more complex effects of serial order such as those that occur when items are temporally grouped during presentation, resulting in multiply bowed serial position curves and systematic changes in the pattern of order errors (Ryan 1969; Frankish 1985). These effects followed straightforwardly from assuming that grouping recruits a second context signal reflecting the timing of groups, thus increasing the effectiveness of context as a cue during recall.

As well as explaining a wider range of phenomena than the original concept of the phonological loop, our network model had the desirable feature of generating novel predictions. For example, one prediction was that temporal grouping effects should be largely independent of phonological similarity, word length and articulatory suppression. This followed from the assumption of a context signal separate from the speech-based component in the model. A series of experiments confirmed these predictions (Hitch, Burgess, Towse et al. 1996).

The computational approach was obviously attractive and a number of competing models of the phonological loop soon emerged, especially in the UK (Brown, Preece and Hulme 2000; Henson 1998; Page and Norris 1998). Brown et al.'s OSCAR was broadly equivalent to Burgess and Hitch (1992), but with more emphasis on how the timing signal could be implemented in terms of temporal oscillators. Page and Norris's Primacy Model presented an important contrast. As in Burgess and Hitch (1992), serial recall involves selecting items using competitive queuing, with stored information subject to rapid decay, and retrieval of an items' phonological content following after item selection. However, Page and Norris assume items are selected according to their level of activation in a descending primacy gradient that extends over all the items in a list. This type of mechanism stands in contrast to forming associations between items and states of an internal context/timing signal coding position within the list.

Is it necessary to assume a timing signal? The Primacy Model is certainly simpler and more parsimonious than Burgess and Hitch (1992). However, it has not so far addressed temporal grouping, and would have difficulty explaining 'protrusion' errors whereby intrusions from previous lists retain information about their serial position (Henson 1999). Moreover the Primacy Model remains a model of STM and does not (so far) address LTM. In a subsequent development of our own model we included LTM by allowing changes to connections to have both short-term (rapidly decaying) and long-term (slowly decaying) effects (Burgess and Hitch 1999). This allowed us to explain long-term learning when a sequence of items such as digits or letters was repeated, as in the Hebb repetition effect (Hebb 1961). This effect was attributed to cumulative changes in context-item connections with list repetition. As before, the model was capable of generating novel predictions. Thus, learning a repeated sequence was expected to be sensitive to factors affecting the timing signal while being insensitive to phonological variables (connections involving items and their phonemic constituents were assumed to be already saturated due to pre-experimental item learning). We confirmed these predictions experimentally. However, others failed to confirm the model's prediction that learning involves the strengthening of independent position-item associations (Cumming, Page and Norris 2003), while we ourselves came to a similar conclusion from evidence that sequence learning involves building from the start of the list (Hitch, Fastame and Flude 2005). Moreover in another of our own experiments we found that people could learn two sequences simultaneously. This ought to be impossible given a single set of 'hooks' with which to form position-item associations.

These failures posed the familiar dilemma of whether to abandon the model and start again or try to modify it so as to accommodate the new findings. Fortunately, a relatively simple modification had the desired effect of maintaining the strengths of the 1999 model while addressing its shortcomings (Burgess and Hitch, in press). This third version assumes there are several sets of context signals rather than just one, each set having its own pattern of associations to items. When encoding a sequence the model compares the match between the current input and the associations for each context set. It does so cumulatively as the sequence unfolds, reducing the cohort of context sets until the current list is either 'recognized' as one that has been encountered before (and strengthened further) or treated as 'new'. The process is broadly analogous to the cohort model of spoken word recognition (Marslen-Wilson 1989) but operating at a higher level of analysis. With this simple but important modification, the model retains its strengths while at the same time succeeding in learning different sequences at the same time, building them up from the start of the list rather than via independent position-item associations. The revised model continues to have the desirable property of generating new predictions, such as 'capture' effects where a well-learned sequence disrupts the learning of a new sequence that shares a similar beginning (Burgess and Hitch, in press). At the time of writing it is too early to tell whether these predictions will be confirmed. Moreover, quite different competing models are emerging that address both STM and long-term learning (see e.g. Botvinick and Plaut 2006), suggesting that this topic has some way to run and is likely to be an area of fruitful controversy in the years to come.

Exploring the episodic buffer

Some two years ago, the original Baddeley and Hitch team got together again when ADB moved to York. We are now jointly working on the task of putting flesh on the rather skeletal episodic buffer. We decided to begin by tackling the role of the buffer in binding together diverse sources of information into chunks, a process that is assumed to be central to the role of the buffer in conscious awareness, in learning and potentially in many complex tasks.

We began with the simplifying assumption that binding is a unitary function, and is attentionally demanding. It is important to note however that these are heuristic assumptions, adopted as a means of systematically exploring the episodic buffer, and do not constitute basic tenets underlying the concept. It could of course be argued that by refusing to specify assumptions that are crucial to the concept, it becomes untestable. The episodic buffer does not however pretend to be a fully specified model, but rather an addition to the existing working memory framework that will, we hope, allow us to ask questions about the relationship between working memory and LTM, to which the answers will be useful, even if the concept itself is consequently abandoned. The use of a loosely specified but coherent theory as a framework for guiding research has served us well in the past, and we trust it will continue to do so in the future.

Returning to the episodic buffer, how far have we got? We decided to begin with two contrasting examples of binding, one visual and simple and the other verbal and complex. In the visual case we asked whether binding a color and shape together into a unitary colored object that is retained over a brief delay was dependent on general attentional capacity. This topic has already begun to be explored by colleagues from the field of visual attention (Luck and Vogel 1997; Vogel, Woodman and Luck 2001; Wheeler and Triesman 2002). Our aim was to tackle the problem using the type of dual task methodology we had used widely in the past. Our subjects were presented with one or more patches of color, achromatic shapes or colored shapes, after which we tested retention of either the individual features or their binding together into an object comprising the appropriate shape with the appropriate color.

As expected from earlier studies, we found no effect of articulatory suppression, suggesting that verbal coding was not used in this task. A demanding executive task such as counting backward did impair overall performance, but did not differentially disrupt the process of establishing the binding between color and shape (Allen, Baddeley and Hitch 2006). We are finding a similar result when the color and shape are presented simultaneously, but at separate locations, and plan to increase the complexity of the binding operation, expecting at some point that general executive processes will be needed, perhaps when crossmodal binding is required. Although this may seem a disappointingly negative result, we regard it as placing valuable constraints on the role of general attentional resources in binding in short-term visual memory. We do not of course conclude from our study that other forms of more perceptually based attention (see e.g., Posner and Petersen 1990) may not be involved. However, we would not regard these as intrinsic to the episodic buffer.

In the case of verbal binding, we chose to tackle the role of language in the capacity for binding through chunking in the serial recall of sentences. One problem with tackling such a question is that whereas span for unrelated words is around five or six, sentence span ranges up to 15 words or more, depending on the precise sentence and its meaning. In order to avoid this problem we developed a tool which we term constrained sentence span in which sentences are generated from a limited set of subject nouns, verbs, object nouns, adjectives and adverbs. By varying the number of adjectives and adverbs, it is possible to vary the length of the sentence systematically without substantially changing the nature of the rather inane semantic content. Our method succeeded in reducing immediate verbal memory span to a surprising degree. Hence, using sentences culled from a broadsheet daily newspaper (e.g. Car headlights that can help motorists see round corners will finally be introduced sometime in the next year) we observed that people could recall up to about 15 content words in the correct order. However, for constrained sentences (e.g. Lucy the old pilot rapidly borrowed the small red book) this reduced to between seven and eight content words, and for equivalent words in scrambled order (e.g. John car instantly large borrowed white), the number reduced even further to between five and six words.

Again we used our dual task technique, comparing constrained sentences of nine words with sequences of seven scrambled words. In one study, the items were presented auditorily while subjects performed concurrent tasks designed to load the phonological loop and the sketchpad, both with and without a substantial concurrent executive demand. We achieved this by using an N-back task in which N could be either zero-back, effectively shadowing, or two-back, a task that involves considerable combined storage and manipulation of information, hence heavily loading the central executive. Our verbal task involved sequences of digits, and our visual task cells within the sequence of 3 × 3 matrices. We found clear effects of both visual and verbal processing, and in each case the impairment was greater with the executively demanding two-back task. There was in addition substantially more interference from the verbal tasks than the visual, with the visual shadowing having a minimal impact on performance (Allen and Baddeley, in press; Baddeley, Allen and Hitch, in prep).

The crucial question concerns the effect of the concurrent tasks on binding. This splits into two subquestions: does binding occur, and is it differentially disrupted by an attentionally demanding secondary task? Our results showed that with auditory presentation, the advantage from sentential form remained, and although executive processing impaired performance, it did so to approximately the same extent for random sequences and sentences. Under these circumstances therefore it appears, perhaps surprisingly, that chunking does not depend heavily on executive processes. It is important to note however that with auditory presentation, material is likely to gain direct access to the phonological loop, even though the verbal tasks will prevent it being subsequently rehearsed. Could it be that the extra second or so of storage provided by the loop is enough to allow any additional processing needed to take advantage of the linguistic redundancy to take place? We tackled this in a second experiment.

This time we used visual presentation, since it is known that articulatory suppression disrupts the phonological recoding of visual presented material (Baddeley, Lewis and Vallar 1984; Murray 1968). We again used zero-back and two-back using auditorily presented digits. We did not include visual tasks since this would have directly interfered with reading the stimulus material. We again got an effect of zero-back, and a greater effect of the more demanding two-back task. However this time, we obtained an interaction with the sentential material being more disrupted than the random word strings, suggesting that when the phonological loop is blocked, utilization of the redundancy provided by our syntactic and semantic knowledge is dependent on executive processes (Baddeley, Allen and Hitch, in preparation). We plan to explore our preliminary studies further, possibly combining them to look at the role of semantic factors in visual-verbal cross modal binding.

The future

What of the more distant future? One of us (ADB), after completing a new book attempting a rather broad overview of working memory, has become interested in the role of emotion in working memory, and working memory in emotion. This is turn raises the further question of motivation. Working memory is concerned with control, but what is controlled? Why do we do anything? In the longer term, it seems that we shall need to discover a way of reintroducing some form of concept of energy into our understanding of how working memory controls action. Too hard a question to hope to settle over the next couple of years, but at least we can start asking questions.

In the case of GJH, the problems of serial order and learning will continue to be of central interest. Computational models of verbal working memory have proved an inspiration here, helping to sharpen our understanding by making assumptions explicit and, crucially, generating new predictions that can be put to experimental test. Such tests are valuable in producing results that feed back and inform model development. One problem of particular interest is how to model the control of serial order at multiple hierarchical levels, such as phonemes, words and phrases in the verbal domain, and how to model the interaction between STM and LTM in the learning of new word forms.

So how does it feel to be working on the same project after 30 years? A recurring theme in our work is that asking general questions and developing broad theoretical ideas to capture what we know at any point always leads to further questions. Attempting to answer the new questions generates new data and these in turn necessitate further developments to our theoretical ideas. A second theme is that of keeping the theory as simple and as widely applicable as possible, with progress driven by a wide variety of different types of data (e.g. from neuropsychology to – more recently – neuroimaging). This simple but eclectic approach seems to have led to cumulative scientific progress, albeit necessarily on a relatively slow and modest scale in the wider perspective. On a personal level the whole process continues to be immensely enjoyable, with one particular highlight being the opportunity to work with some highly stimulating colleagues on a variety of problems. We don't detect any signs of running out of steam just yet, either in ourselves or in the topic, but that is of course for others to judge.

References

Adams, JW and Hitch, GJ (1997). Working memory and children's mental addition. *Journal of Experimental Child Psychology*, *67*, 21–38.

Allen, RJ, Baddeley, AD and Hitch, GJ (2006). Is the binding of visual features in working memory resource-demanding? *Journal of Experimental Psychology: General*, *135*, 298–313.

Allen, RJ and Baddeley, AD (in press). Working memory and sentence recall. In AT Thorn and M Page (eds), *Interactions Between Short-term and Long-term Memory in the Verbal Domain*. Hove, UK: Psychology Press.

Atkinson, RC and Shiffrin, RM (1968). Human memory: A proposed system and its control processes. In KW Spence (ed.), *The Psychology of Learning and Motivation: Advances in research and theory* (Vol. 2, pp. 89–195). New York: Academic Press.

Attneave, F (1960). In defense of humunculi. In W. Rosenblith (ed), *Sensory Communication*. (pp. 777–782). Cambridge, MA: Holt, MIT Press.

Atwood, GE (1971). An experimental study of visual imagination and memory. *Cognitive Psychology*, *2*, 290–299.

Baddeley, AD (1966a). Short-term memory for word sequences as a function of acoustic, semantic and formal similarity. *Quarterly Journal of Experimental Psychology*, *18*, 362–365.

Baddeley, AD (1966b). The influence of acoustic and semantic similarity on long-term memory for word sequences. *Quarterly Journal of Experimental Psychology*, *18*, 302–309.

Baddeley, AD (1968a). How does acoustic similarity influence short-term memory? *Quarterly Journal of Experimental Psychology*, *20*, 249–264.

Baddeley, AD (1968b). A 3-min reasoning test based on grammatical transformation. *Psychonomic Science*, *10*, 341–342.

Baddeley, AD (1986). *Working Memory*. Oxford: Oxford University Press.

Baddeley, AD (1996). Exploring the central executive. *Quarterly Journal of Experimental Psychology*, *49A*, 5–28.

Baddeley, AD (2000). The episodic buffer: A new component of working memory? *Trends in Cognitive Sciences*, *4*, 417–423.

Baddeley, AD (2007). *Working Memory, Thought and Action*. Oxford: Oxford University Press.

Baddeley, AD, Allen, RJ and Hitch, GJ (in prep). The role of attention in the sentence superiority effect.

Baddeley, AD and Andrade, J (1994). Reversing the word length effect: A comment on Caplan, Rochon, and Waters. *Quarterly Journal of Experimental Psychology*, *47A*, 1047–1054.

Baddeley, AD, Bressi, S, Della Sala, S, Logie, R and Spinnler, H (1991). The decline of working memory in Alzheimer's Disease: A longitudinal study. *Brain*, *114*, 2521–2542.

Baddeley, AD, Chincotta, D and Adlam, A (2001). Working memory and the control of action: Evidence from task switching. *Journal of Experimental Psychology: General*, *130*, 641–657.

Baddeley, AD, Chincotta, D, Stafford, L and Turk, D (2002). Is the word length effect in STM entirely attributable to output delay? Evidence from serial recognition. *Quarterly Journal of Experimental Psychology*, *55A*, 353–369.

Baddeley, AD, Gathercole, SE and Papagno, C (1998). The phonological loop as a language learning device. *Psychological Review, 105*, 158–173.

Baddeley, AD, Grant, S, Wight, E and Thomson, N (1973). Imagery and visual working memory. In PMA Rabbitt and S Dornic (eds), *Attention and Performance V* (pp. 205–217). London: Academic Press.

Baddeley, AD and Hitch, GJ (1974). Working memory. In GA Bower (ed.), *The Psychology of Learning and Motivation: Advances in research and theory* (Vol. 8, pp. 47–89). New York: Academic Press.

Baddeley, AD, Lewis, VJ and Vallar, G (1984). Exploring the articulatory loop. *Quarterly Journal of Experimental Psychology, 36*, 233–252.

Baddeley, AD and Lieberman, K (1980). Spatial working memory. *Attention and Performance VIII*, 521–539.

Baddeley, AD and Logie, RH (1999). Working memory: The multiple component model. In A Miyake and P Shah (eds), *Models of Working Memory: Mechanisms of active maintenance and executive control* (pp. 28–61). Cambridge: Cambridge University Press.

Baddeley, AD, Papagno, C and Vallar, G (1988). When long-term learning depends on short-term storage. *Journal of Memory and Language, 27*, 586–595.

Baddeley, AD, Thomson, N and Buchanan, M (1975). Word length and the structure of short-term memory. *Journal of Verbal Learning and Verbal Behavior, 14*, 575–589.

Baddeley, AD and Warrington, EK (1970). Amnesia and the distinction between long- and short-term memory. *Journal of Verbal Learning and Verbal Behavior, 9*, 176–189.

Baddeley, AD and Wilson, BA (2002). Prose recall and amnesia: Implications for the structure of working memory. *Neuropsychologia, 40*, 1737–1743.

Barrouillet, P, Bernardin, S and Camos, V (2004). Time constraints and resource sharing in adults' working memory spans. *Journal of Experimental Psychology: General, 133*, 83–100.

Botvinick, M and Plaut, DC (2006). Short-term memory for serial order: A recurrent neural network model. *Psychological Review, 113*, 201.

Broadbent, DE (1958). *Perception and Communication*. London: Pergamon Press.

Brooks, LR (1967). The suppression of visualization by reading. *Quarterly Journal of Experimental Psychology, 19*, 289–299.

Brooks, LR (1968). Spatial and verbal components in the act of recall. *Canadian Journal of Psychology, 22*, 349–368.

Brown, GDA, Preece, T and Hulme, C (2000). Oscillator-based memory for serial order. *Psychological Review, 107*, 127–181.

Brown, J (1958). Some tests of the decay theory of immediate memory. *Quarterly Journal of Experimental Psychology, 10*, 12–21.

Burgess, N and Hitch, GJ (1992). Towards a network model of the articulatory loop. *Journal of Memory and Language, 31*, 429–460.

Burgess, N and Hitch, GJ (1999). Memory for serial order: A network model of the phonological loop and its timing. *Psychological Review, 106*, 551–581.

Burgess, N and Hitch, GJ (in press). A revised model of short-term memory and long-term learning of verbal sequences. *Journal of Memory and Language*.

Caplan, D and Waters, GS (1994). Articulatory length and phonological similarity in span tasks: A reply to Baddeley and Andrade. *Quarterly Journal of Experimental Psychology, 47A*, 1055–1062.

Case, RD, Kurland, DM and Goldberg, J (1982). Operational efficiency and the growth of short-term memory span. *Journal of Experimental Child Psychology, 33*, 386–404.

Colle, HA (1980). Auditory encoding in visual short-term recall: Effects of noise intensity and spatial location. *Journal of Verbal Learning and Verbal Behaviour, 19*, 722–735.

Collins, AM and Quillian, MR (1969). Retrieval time from semantic memory. *Journal of Verbal Learning and Verbal Behavior, 8*, 432–438.

Conrad, C (1972). Cognitive economy in semantic memory. *Journal of Experimental Psychology, 92*, 149–154.

Conrad, R (1964). Acoustic confusion in immediate memory. *British Journal of Psychology, 55*, 75–84.

Conrad, R and Hull, AJ (1964). Information, acoustic confusion and memory span. *British Journal of Psychology*, *55*, 429–432.

Cowan, N, Baddeley, AD, Elliott, EM and Norris, J (2003). Items are not lists in short-term memory: Opposing global and local effects of word length. *Psychological Bulletin and Review*, *10*, 74–79.

Cowan, N, Day, L, Saults, JS, Keller, DA, Johnston, T and Flores, L (1992). The role of verbal output time in the effects of word-length on immediate memory. *Journal of Memory and Language*, *31*, 1–17.

Craik, FIM and Lockhart, RS (1972). Levels of processing: A framework for memory research. *Journal of Verbal Learning and Verbal Behavior*, *11*, 671–684.

Craik, FIM and Watkins, MJ (1973). Role of rehearsal in short-term-memory. *Journal of Verbal Learning and Verbal Behavior*, *12*, 599–607.

Cumming, N, Page, MPA and Norris, D (2003). Testing a positional model of the Hebb effect. *Memory*, *11*, 43–63.

Daneman, M and Carpenter, PA (1980). Individual differences in working memory and reading. *Journal of Verbal Learning and Verbal Behavior*, *19*, 450–466.

Della Sala, S and Logie, RH (2002). Neuropsychological impairments of visual and spatial working memory. In AD Baddeley, MD Kopelman and BA Wilson (eds), *The Handbook of Memory Disorders*. Chichester: Wiley.

Dempster, FN (1981). Memory span: Sources of individual and developmental differences. *Psychological Bulletin*, *1*, 63–100.

Deutsch, D and Deutsch, JA (1975). *Short-term Memory*. New York: Academic Press.

Engle, RW, Kane, MJ and Tuholski, SW (1999). Individual differences in working memory capacity and what they tell us about controlled attention, general fluid intelligence, and functions of the prefrontal cortex. In A Miyake and P Shah (eds), *Models of Working Memory: Mechanisms of active maintenance and executive control* (pp. 102–134). Cambridge: Cambridge University Press.

Frankish, C (1985). Modality-specific grouping effects in short-term memory. *Journal of Memory and Language*, *24*, 200–209.

Furst, AJ and Hitch, GJ (2000). Separate roles for executive and phonological components of working memory in mental arithmetic. *Memory and Cognition*, *28*, 774–782.

Gathercole, SE and Alloway, TP (in press). Working memory and classroom learning. In K Thurman and K Fiorello (eds), *Cognitive Development in K-3 Classroom Learning: Research Applications*. Mahwah, NJ: Erlbaum.

Gathercole, SE and Baddeley, AD (1989). Evaluation of the role of phonological STM in the development of vocabulary in children: A longitudinal study. *Journal of Memory and Language*, *28*, 200–213.

Gathercole, SE, Pickering, SJ, Knight, C and Stegman, Z (2004). Working memory skills and educational attainment: Evidence from national curriculum assessments at 7 and 14 years of age. *Applied Cognitive Psychology*, *18*, 1–16.

Glanzer, M and Cunitz, AR (1966). Two storage mechanisms in free recall. *Journal of Verbal Learning and Verbal Behavior*, *5*, 351–360.

Grossberg, S (1978). Behavioral contrast in short-term memory: Serial binary memory models or parallel continuous models? *Journal of Mathematical Psychology*, *3*, 199–219.

Hebb, DO (1961). Distinctive features of learning in the higher animal. In JF Delafresnaye (ed.), *Brain Mechanisms and Learning* (pp. 37–46). Oxford: Oxford University Press.

Henson, RNA (1998). Short-term memory for serial order: The start–end model. *Cognitive Psychology*, *36*, 73–137.

Henson, RNA (1999). Positional information in short-term memory: Relative or absolute? *Memory and Cognition*, *27*, 915–927.

Henson, RNA, Norris, DG, Page, MPA and Baddeley, AD (1996). Unchained memory: Error patterns rule out chaining models of immediate serial recall. *Quarterly Journal of Experimental Psychology*, *49A*, 80–115.

Hintzman, DL (1967). Articulatory coding in short-term memory. *Journal of Verbal Learning and Verbal Behavior*, *6*, 312–316.

Hitch, GJ (1974). Short-term memory for spatial and temporal information. *Quarterly Journal of Experimental Psychology, 26*, 503–513.

Hitch, GJ (1978). Role of short-term working memory in mental arithmetic. *Cognitive Psychology, 10*, 302–323.

Hitch, GJ, Arnold, P and Phillips, LJ (1983). Counting processes in deaf children's arithmetic. *British Journal of Psychology, 74*, 429–437.

Hitch, GJ, Burgess, N, Towse, JN and Culpin, V (1996). Temporal grouping effects in immediate recall: A working memory analysis. *Quarterly Journal of Experimental Psychology, 49A*, 140–158.

Hitch, GJ, Fastame, C and Flude, B (2005). How is the serial order of a verbal sequence coded? Some comparisons between models. *Memory, 3–4*, 247–258.

Hitch, GJ and Halliday, MS (1983). Working memory in children. *Philosophical Transactions of the Royal Society London, Series B, 302*, 325–340.

Hitch, GJ, Halliday, MS and Littler, JE (1989). Item identification time, rehearsal rate and memory span in children. *Quarterly Journal of Experimental Psychology, 41A*, 321–337.

Hitch, GJ, Halliday, MS, Schaafstal, AM and Schraagen, JMC (1988). Visual working memory in young children. *Memory and Cognition, 16*, 120–132.

Hitch, GJ and McAuley, E (1991). Working memory in children with specific arithmetical learning difficulties. *British Journal of Psychology, 82*, 375–386.

Hitch, GJ, Towse, JN and Hutton, U (2001). What limits children's working memory span? Theoretical accounts and applicaions to scholastic development. *Journal of Experimental Psychology: General, 130*, 184–198.

Hitch, GJ, Woodin, M and Baker, SL (1989). Visual and phonological components of working memory in children. *Memory and Cognition, 17*, 175–185.

Houghton, G (1990). The problem of serial order: A neural network model of sequence learning and recall. In R Dale, C Mellish and M Zock (eds), *Current Research in Natural Language Generation* (pp. 287–319). London: Academic Press.

Hulme, C, Surprenant, AM, Bireta, TJ, Stuart, G and Neath, I (2004). Abolishing the word-length effect. *Journal of Experimental Psychology: Learning, Memory, and Cognition, 30*, 98–106.

Hulme, C, Thomson, N, Muir, C and Lawrence, WA (1984). Speech rate and the development of short-term memory span. *Journal of Experimental Child Psychology, 38*, 241–253.

Jahnke, JC (1969). The Ranschburg Effect. *Psychological Review, 76*, 592–605.

Jarrold, C and Bayliss, D (2007). Variation in working memory due to typical and atypical development. In ARA Conway, C Jarrold, A Kane, A Miyake, and JN Towse (eds), *Variation in Working Memory*. pp. 134–61. New York: Oxford University Press.

Jones, DM (1993). Objects, streams and threads of auditory attention. In AD Baddeley and L Weiskrantz (eds), *Attention: Selection, awareness and control* (pp. 87–104). Oxford: Clarendon Press.

Keppel, G and Underwood, BJ (1962). Proactive inhibition in short-term retention of single items. *Journal of Verbal Learning and Verbal Behavior, 1*, 153–161.

Larsen, J and Baddeley, AD (2003). Disruption of verbal STM by irrelevent speech, articulatory suppression and manual tapping: Do they have a common source? *Quarterly Journal of Experimental Psychology, 56A*, 1249–1268.

Larsen, JD, Baddeley, AD and Andrade, J (2000). Phonological similarity and the irrelevant speech effect: Implications for models of short-term verbal memory. *Memory, 8*, 145–157.

Logie, RH (1986). Visuo-spatial processing in working memory. *Quarterly Journal of Experimental Psychology, 38A*, 229–247.

Logie, RH (1995). *Visuo-spatial Working Memory*. Hove, UK: Erlbaum.

Logie, RH, Cocchini, G, Della Sala, S and Baddeley, A (2004). Is there a specific capacity for dual task co-ordination? Evidence from Alzheimer's disease. *Neuropsychology, 18*, 504–513.

Lovatt, PJ and Avons, SE (2001). Re-evaluating the word-length effect. In J. Andrade (ed.), *Working Memory in Perspective* (pp. 199–218). Hove: Psychology Press.

Luck, SJ and Vogel, EK (1997). The capacity of visual working memory for features and conjunctions. *Nature, 390*, 279–281.

Luria, AR (1959a). The directive function of speech in development and dissolution, Part I. *Word*, *15*, 341–352.

Luria, AR (1959b). The directive function of speech in development and dissolution, Part II. *Word*, *15*, 453–464.

Marslen-Wilson, WD (1989). Access and integration: Projecting sound onto meaning. In WD Marslen-Wilson (ed), *Lexical Representation and Process* (pp. 3–24). Cambridge, MA: MIT Press.

Melton, AW (1963). Implications of short-term memory for a general theory of memory. *Journal of Verbal Learning and Verbal Behavior*, *2*, 1–21.

Miller, GA (1956). The magical number seven, plus or minus two: Some limits on our capacity for processing information. *Psychological Review*, *63*, 81–97.

Miller, GA, Galanter, E and Pribram, KH (1960). *Plans and the Structure of Behavior*. New York: Holt, Rinehart and Winston.

Miyake, A, Emerson, MJ, Padilla, F and Ahn, JC (2004). Inner speech as a retrieval aid for task goals: the effects of cue type and articulatory suppression in the random task cuing paradigm. *Acta Psychologica*, *115*, 123–142.

Mueller, ST, Seymour, TL, Kieras, DE and Meyer, DE (2003). Theoretical implications of articulatory duration, phonological similarity, and phonological complexity in verbal working memory. *Journal of Experimental Psychology: Learning, Memory, and Cognition*, *29*, 1353–1380.

Murray, DJ (1968). Articulation and acoustic confusability in short-term memory. *Journal of Experimental Psychology*, *78*, 679–684.

Neath, I (2000). Modeling the effects of irrelevant speech on memory. *Psychonomic Bulletin and Review*, *7*, 403–423.

Nicolson, R (1981). The relationship between memory span and processing speed. In M Friedman, JP Das and N O'Connor (eds), *Intelligence and Learning* (pp. 179–184). New York: Plenum Press.

Nohara, DM (1965). Variety of responses and reactive inhibition. *Psychonomic Science*, *2*, 301–302.

Norman, DA and Shallice, T (1986). Attention to action: Willed and automatic control of behaviour. In RJ Davidson and GE Schwarts and D Shapiro (eds), *Consciousness and self-regulation: Advances in research and theory* (Vol. 4, pp. 1–18). New York: Plenum Press.

Page, MPA and Norris, D (1998). The primacy model: A new model of immediate serial recall. *Psychological Review*, *105*, 761–781.

Papagno, C, Valentine, T and Baddeley, AD (1991). Phonological short-term memory and foreign language vocabulary learning. *Journal of Memory and Language*, *30*, 331–347.

Papagno, C and Vallar, G (1992). Phonological short-term memory and the learning of novel words: The effect of phonological similarity and item length. *Quarterly Journal of Experimental Psychology*, *44A*, 47–67.

Peterson, LR and Peterson, MJ (1959). Short-term retention of individual verbal items. *Journal of Experimental Psychology*, *58*, 193–198.

Posner, MI and Petersen, SE (1990). The attention system of the human brain. *Annual Review of Neuroscience*, *13*, 25–42.

Postman, L (1975). Verbal learning and memory. *Annual Review of Psychology*, *26*, 291–335.

Quillian, MR (1969). The teachable language comprehender: A simulation program and theory of language. *Communications of the ACM*, *12*, 459–476.

Robbins, T, Anderson, E, Barker, D, Bradley, A, Fearneyhough, C, Henson, R, Hudson, S and Baddeley, A (1996). Working memory in chess. *Memory and Cognition*, *24*, 83–93.

Rumelhart, DE and McClelland, JL (1986). *Parallel Distributed Processing: Explorations in the microstructure of cognition. Vol. 1: Foundations*. Cambridge, MA: MIT Press.

Ryan, J (1969). Grouping and short-term memory: Different means and pattern of grouping. *Quarterly Journal of Experimental Psychology*, *21*, 137–147.

Saariluoma, P (1995). *Chess Players' Thinking: A cognitive psychological approach*. London: Routledge.

Saeki, E and Saito, S (2004). The role of the phonological loop in task switching performance: The effect of articulatory suppression in the alternating runs paradigm. *Psychologia*, *47*, 35–43.

St Clair-Thompson, HL and Gathercole, SE (2006). Executive functions and achievements in school: Shifting, updating, inhibition, and working memory. *Quarterly Journal of Experimental Psychology*, *59A*, 745–759.

Saito, S and Miyake, A (2004). On the nature of forgetting and the processing-storage relationship in reading span performance. *Journal of Memory and Language, 50*, 425–443.

Salamé, P and Baddeley, AD (1982). Disruption of short-term memory by unattended speech: Implications for the structure of working memory. *Journal of Verbal Learning and Verbal Behaviour, 21*, 150–164.

Salamé, P and Baddeley, AD (1987). Noise, unattended speech and short-term memory. *Ergonomics, 30*, 1185–1194.

Salamé, P and Baddeley, AD (1989). Effects of background music on phonological short-term memory. *Quarterly Journal of Experimental Psychology, 41A*, 107–122.

Schumacher, EH, Seymour, TL, Glass, JM, Lauber, EJ, Kieras, DE and Meyer, DE (2001). Virtually perfect time-sharing in dual-task performance: Uncorking the central cognitive bottleneck. *Psychological Science, 12*, 101–108.

Shallice, T and Warrington, EK (1970). Independent functioning of verbal memory stores: A neuropsychological study. *Quarterly Journal of Experimental Psychology, 22*, 261–273.

Shiffrin, RM and Schneider, W (1977). Controlled and automatic human information processing: II Perceptual learning, automatic attending and a general theory. *Psychological Review, 84*, 127–190.

Smith, EE and Jonides, J (1997). Working memory: A view from neuroimaging. *Cognitive Psychology, 33*, 5–42.

Towse, JN and Hitch, GJ (1995). Is there a relationship between task demand and storage space in tests of working memory capacity? *Quarterly Journal of Experimental Psychology, 48*, 108–124.

Towse, JN, Hitch, GJ, Hamilton, Z, Peacock, K and Hutton, UMZ (2005). Working memory period: The endurance of mental representations. *Quarterly Journal of Experimental Psychology, 58A*, 547–571.

Towse, JN, Hitch, GJ and Horton, N (2007). Working memory as the interface between processing and retention: A developmental perspective. In R Kail (ed), *Advances in Child Development and Behavior*. New York: Academic Press.

Towse, JN, Hitch, GJ and Hutton, U (1998). A reevaluation of working memory capacity in children. *Journal of Memory and Language, 39*, 195–217.

Towse, JN, Hitch, GJ and Hutton, U (2000). On the interpretation of working memory span in adults. *Memory and Cognition, 28*(3), 341–348.

Tulving, E (1972). Episodic and semantic memory. In E Tulving and W Donaldson (eds), *Organization of Memory* (pp. 381–403). New York: Academic Press.

Vogel, EK, Woodman, GF and Luck, SJ (2001). Storage of features, conjunctions, and objects in visual working memory. *Journal of Experimental Psychology: Human Perception and Performance, 27*, 92–114.

Wheeler, ME and Treisman AM (2002). Binding in short-term visual memory. *Journal of Experimental Psychology: General, 131*, 48–64.

Wickelgren, WA (1965). Short-term memory for phonemically similar lists. *American Journal of Psychology, 78*, 567–574.

Wickelgren, WA (1969). Auditory or articulatory coding in verbal short-term memory. *Psychological Review, 76*, 232–235.

Wilson, B and Baddeley, A. (1988). Semantic, episodic and autobiographical memory in a postmeningitic amnesic patient. *Brain and Cognition, 8*, 31–46.

Wing, AM, Lewis, VJ and Baddeley, AD (1979). The slowing of handwriting by letter repetition. *Journal of Human Movement Studies, 5*, 182–188.

2

What do working memory span tasks like reading span really measure?

Meredyth Daneman and Brenda Hannon

Introduction

What do tasks such as calculating the appropriate amount to tip your cab driver, mentally rearranging the luggage in your car trunk to see if you can cram in that one extra suitcase or reading the latest murder mystery by your favorite crime writer, all have in common? On the surface, they appear to be quite different because the first involves skill at doing mathematical calculations, the second involves skill at spatial manipulations, and the third involves skill at reading comprehension. However, they have at least one important feature in common – they all depend on the temporary storage of information while new information is being processed. If you want to calculate 15 per cent of your $38.50 taxicab fare, you must have access to the results of intermediate stages of processing. Of course, you could always resort to external storage aids such as your fingers or pen and paper. But if you are more adept at math problem-solving, you will likely keep track of the intermediate results mentally. To solve the problem of cramming lots of luggage into your car trunk, you also need to keep track of intermediate results. If you are not very skilled at spatial problem-solving, you may have to lug the baggage in and out as you try out various geometric configurations. You will be at a distinct advantage if you can place and rotate each piece mentally, keeping track of the results of each manipulation in memory. And if you want to understand what the successive words, phrases, and sentences of your murder mystery novel mean, you will also need to have access to the results of earlier processed information. If you couldn't hold the earlier information at least temporarily in mind, you would be continually backtracking to reread parts or even whole sentences and paragraphs: if you can keep at least some of the earlier processed information in mind, you will be at a distinct advantage when it comes to integrating the clues and evidence necessary for understanding the murder mystery and trying to figure out 'who dunnit'.

According to current cognitive theory, a single system is responsible for temporarily maintaining task-relevant information during the performance of these everyday cognitive tasks. This system had been called *working memory* (Baddeley and Hitch 1974; Daneman and Carpenter 1980; see also Baddeley 1986; Miller *et al.* 1960; Miyake and Shah 1999). The system is assumed to have limited resources that must be shared between the work and the memory, between the processing and storage demands of the task to which the working memory system is being applied. Empirical support for working memory's role in complex cognition comes from the finding that working memory capacity is an excellent predictor of performance on a range of complex cognitive tasks, including tasks that tap language comprehension ability (Daneman and Merikle 1996), reasoning ability (Kyllonen and Christal 1990), spatial ability (Miyake *et al.* 2001), and general fluid intelligence (Engle *et al.* 1999). In this chapter, we explore the nature of the well-established correlation between working memory capacity and language comprehension ability.

Background

One of the most widely used measures of working memory capacity is the reading span task, originally developed by Daneman and Carpenter (1980). In a typical version of this task, participants are required to read progressively longer sets of sentences out loud (the processing requirement) while trying to remember the final word of each sentence in the set for later recall (the storage requirement). For example, at the two-sentence level, participants may be asked to read aloud the following sentences: 'He had an odd elongated skull which sat on his shoulders like a pear on a dish; I turned my memories over like pictures in a photograph album.' At the end of the set, they would be required to recall the two sentence-final words, *dish* and *album*. At the three-sentence level, they might read: 'The girl hesitated a moment to taste the onions because her husband hated the smell; The rain and howling wind kept beating against the window pane; He covered his heart with both hands to keep anyone from hearing the noise it made,' and they would have to recall *smell, pane, made*. In a population of university students, the typical finding is that some individuals can recall only two or three sentence-final words, whereas others can recall as many as four or five. Notice that reading span differs from the more traditional short-term memory tasks, such as word span and digit span, because it imposes simultaneous processing and storage demands, whereas the traditional span tasks impose only storage demands by simply requiring individuals to passively repeat back a string of random words (e.g., *cup, shoe, ball*) or digits (e.g., *8, 6, 9*).

The popularity of the reading span task can be attributed, in large part, to the fact that it does a better job at predicting performance on complex cognitive tasks, such as reading comprehension, than do traditional storage-only word span and digit span tasks. In their original study, Daneman and Carpenter (1980) showed that individuals with reading spans of only two or three sentence-final words did more poorly on a global test of comprehension (the Verbal Scholastic Assessment Test or VSAT) and particularly poorly on specific tests of the integration of successive ideas in a text, such as computing the antecedent referent for a pronoun. The correlations ranged between 0.42 and 0.90, and, with an average correlation of 0.66, they were well above the 0.30 barrier that typically plagues research on individual differences (Hunt 1980). In contrast, the correlations between word span and comprehension were in the typical 0.33 to 0.37 range. Daneman and Carpenter's pattern of findings has been replicated many times since the original 1980 study. For example, in a meta-analysis based on data from 6,179 participants in 77 independent studies, Daneman and Merikle (1996) showed that the correlation between reading span (or variants of reading span) and global tests of comprehension was 0.41 (with a 95 per cent confidence interval [CI] of 0.38 to 0.44),[1] and this was significantly higher than the correlation between word span and comprehension (0.28, CI = 0.23–0.33), or the correlation between digit span and comprehension (0.14, CI = 0.10–0.18). These findings suggest that it is the combined processing and temporary storage capacity of working memory, and not simply the storage capacity, that is important for comprehension.

The popularity of reading span notwithstanding, a legitimate concern is that it is too much like reading comprehension itself. Indeed, Daneman and Carpenter (1980; see also Daneman 1982) argued that reading span may be such a successful predictor of comprehension precisely because it captures many of the processing requirements of sentence comprehension, and consequently has an excellent probability of tapping those aspects of working memory that are important to comprehension. By the same token, critics have pointed out that the complexity of reading span

---

[1] The correlation between reading span and specific tests of integration was 0.52 (95 per cent CI = 0.49–0.55); specific tests of integration included the ability to compute the referent for a pronoun, make inferences, monitor and revise inconsistencies, abstract the main theme, and so on.

makes interpretation of the correlation difficult (e.g., Baddeley *et al.* 1985), and they have argued that the language-specific nature of the measure may leave us with the rather trivial conclusion that sentence comprehension (reading span) correlates with paragraph comprehension (the criterion comprehension tests). In the words of one of the leading researchers in the area of language comprehension, reading span may be simply a measure of 'the efficiency with which readers can comprehend sentences and hence store them in long-term memory' (Kintsch 1998, p. 24).

Our goals

The goals of this chapter are twofold. First, we present data to show that reading span is not simply another test of comprehension skill, and then we show just which of the processing and storage requirements of comprehension the reading span measure of working memory capacity does capture.

Is reading span simply another test of reading comprehension skill?

Evidence that reading span is not simply another test of reading comprehension skill comes from a study of ours that used working memory theory to investigate the construct validity of multiple-choice tests of reading comprehension such as the VSAT (Daneman and Hannon 2001). As is typical for most standardized tests of reading comprehension ability, the VSAT requires test-takers to read a series of short prose passages and answer multiple-choice questions about them. For example, one passage might be about nineteenth-century Bohemia, and it would be accompanied by a series of five alternative questions such as the following:

The passage is best described as

1. a refutation of an ancient misconception;

2. a definition of a concept;

3. a discussion of one historical era;

4. a catalog of nineteenth-century biases; or

5. an example of a class struggle.

Test-takers are allowed to consult the passage when attempting to answer the questions. Tests such as the VSAT are supposed to be measuring passage comprehension (Donlan 1984), but do they? In the next few sections, we show how our use of the working memory approach to investigate the construct validity of the VSAT provided evidence that reading span is more than simply another test of reading comprehension skill.

Background concerning construct validity

There has been a long and persistent history of attacks on the validity of multiple-choice tests of reading comprehension such as the VSAT (e.g., Farr *et al.* 1990; Katz *et al.* 1990, 1991). One of the most serious criticisms is that test-takers do not or need not read and comprehend the passages on which the test questions are based. Indeed, Katz *et al.* (1990) demonstrated that test-takers were able to perform at better than chance on as many as 72 per cent of the multiple-choice items of the reading section of the VSAT when they were not given access to the passages. On the basis of findings such as this, critics have argued that multiple-choice reading tests in general, and the reading portion of the VSAT in particular, may largely be measuring factors unrelated to reading comprehension, such as personal opinion, prior knowledge, and general test wiseness. This is a serious allegation, given the widespread practice of using SAT scores in the screening and placement of college applicants in the United States.

Now, it is unlikely that test-takers ignore the passages when they are available. Although students performed better than the 20 per cent chance level in the absence of the passages (Katz, Lautenschlager, Blackburn *et al.* 1990; Powers and Leung 1995), they did not perform substantially better than chance (around 35 per cent), and certainly not at levels that are competitive for college admission. Thus, it is unlikely that students would adopt a strategy of ignoring the available passages when they are taking a test 'that will dramatically affect their futures' (Freedle and Kostin 1994, p. 109). Nevertheless, there is evidence to suggest that when the passages are available, test-takers use a range of strategies that vary in the extent to which they emphasize reading the passages versus reading the questions (Farr *et al.* 1990). At the one extreme, test-takers read the entire passage (and possibly even the entire set of questions) before attempting to respond to the individual questions. At an intermediate level, test-takers read only part of the passage before proceeding to the questions; at the other extreme, test-takers do no global reading of the passage at all, but proceed directly to the first question, read it, and then search the passage for the answer, read the second question, then search the passage for the answer, and so on (see Farr *et al.* 1990 for more details).

Although the strategies identified by Farr *et al.* (1990) all involve consulting or searching local parts of the passage to find information to answer a specific question, there are differences in how much global reading of a passage takes place before the test-taker initiates question-directed search of the passage. To the extent that a reading comprehension test like the VSAT is designed to assess passage comprehension (Donlon 1984), the construct validity of the test could vary as a function of how much passage reading the test-taker actually engages in. In Daneman and Hannon (2001), we directly manipulated the strategy our test-takers used to complete the VSAT test, and we used working memory theory to investigate the extent to which the different strategies tapped reading comprehension processes. In this chapter, we present data from three strategies:

1. advance reading of the entire passage (and the entire set of questions),

2. no advance reading of any of the passage,

3. no passage available.

As will become evident, the results can be used to show that reading span is not simply another test of reading comprehension skill.

The logic behind the working memory approach to investigating construct validity

The working memory approach to assessing the construct validity of the reading portion of the VSAT capitalizes on the fact that measures of working memory capacity are good predictors of performance on a range of reading and verbal reasoning tasks (Daneman and Merikle 1996; Jurden 1995; Kyllonen and Christal 1990), and makes predictions about the relative powers of reading span (as a measure of working memory capacity) and the Nelson–Denny (another multiple-choice test of reading comprehension) at predicting VSAT performance.

Passage-available predictions

When passages are available, reading span should be a good predictor of performance as long as the test-taking strategy sufficiently engages working-memory demanding comprehension processes. Consequently, we might expect a higher correlation for the advance reading strategy than for the question-directed reading strategy if the former draws on reading comprehension more, but similar correlations for the two passage-available strategies if even the question-directed reading strategy engages comprehension processes sufficiently. In either case, the

Nelson–Denny test of reading comprehension (Brown *et al.* 1981) should be better than reading span at predicting VSAT performance because it is structurally very similar to the VSAT (it too involves reading short passages and answering multiple-choice questions about them).

Passage-unavailable predictions

If test-takers achieve better than chance performance as a result of invoking strategies that have no relevance to reading comprehension (e.g., personal opinion, prior knowledge), then reading span should not predict VSAT performance. However, there is reason to believe that test-takers achieve better than chance performance as a result of invoking sophisticated verbal reasoning strategies, such as 'choosing answers on the basis of consistency with other questions and reconstructing the main theme and contents of a missing passage from all the questions and answers in the set' (Powers and Leung 1995, p. 105). These kinds of verbal reasoning strategies are precisely the kinds of strategies that have been shown to draw on the processing and storage resources of working memory (Jurden 1995; Kyllonen and Christal 1990). Consequently, we would expect reading span to predict VSAT performance in the no-passage condition as well. On the other hand, because specific reading processes would be minimally engaged in the no-passage condition (they would be engaged only in the reading of question stems and answer choices), we would expect the Nelson–Denny reading comprehension test to be much more weakly correlated with VSAT performance in this condition than in the passage-available conditions. In other words, we would expect reading span to be better than the Nelson–Denny at predicting VSAT performance when no passages are available, but the reverse to be true for the two passage-available strategies.

The outcome

The correlational results were consistent with the position that test-takers evoke qualitatively different strategies when the passages are available than when they are unavailable (Daneman and Hannon 2001). When passages were available, reading span was a good predictor of VSAT performance, correlating 0.60 with VSAT performance in the advance reading condition and 0.64 with VSAT performance in the no advance reading condition. However, the Nelson–Denny was an even better predictor, correlating 0.74 and 0.76 with performance in the advance reading and no advance reading conditions, respectively. In contrast, when passages were unavailable, reading span was still a good predictor, correlating 0.54 with VSAT performance. However, now the predictive power of the Nelson–Denny was greatly reduced, correlating only 0.38 with VSAT performance. We took these findings to reflect the fact that test-takers invoke a qualitatively different strategy when the passages are available than when they are not available. When the passages are available, test-takers make use of the passages by reading them and answering the multiple-choice questions based on what is stated or implied in them. Working memory capacity plays a role in how well individuals can execute the reading comprehension processes, and so reading span, as a measure of working memory capacity, was a good predictor of performance on the VSAT when passages were involved. However, the Nelson–Denny, a task that has great surface similarity to the VSAT passage-available conditions, was an even better predictor of performance, capturing variance not accounted for by differences in working memory capacity (see Daneman and Hannon 2001). On the other hand, when passages are not available, test-takers do not do much reading at all, and so the Nelson–Denny was no longer a good predictor. However, test-takers do invoke sophisticated verbal reasoning strategies as they attempt to reconstruct the theme and contents of the passage from what the questions and answer choices reveal. Working memory capacity plays a role in how well individuals can engage in complex verbal reasoning, and so reading span, as a measure of working memory capacity, was a good predictor of SAT performance in the no-passage condition.

With respect to the construct validity question, this pattern of results suggests that even if test-takers were to adopt the extreme approach of entirely ignoring the passages when answering some or all of the VSAT questions, the strategy would not compromise the construct validity of the test entirely. The no-passage strategy is qualitatively different from the passage-reading strategies; nevertheless, it implicates sophisticated verbal reasoning skills that are also important for and predictive of academic success. What implications does this pattern of results have for the relationship between reading span and reading comprehension?

Implications for the nature of reading span

We believe that the Daneman and Hannon (2001) findings show that reading span is not simply another measure of reading comprehension skill. If it were, then its predictive power should mirror that of the direct measure of reading comprehension skill that was used in the Daneman and Hannon study, namely, the Nelson–Denny. The reversal of the predictive powers of reading span and the Nelson–Denny argues against Kintsch's (1998) view that you can simply equate reading span with reading comprehension skill. Instead, we think that reading span is a measure of a dynamic system that processes and temporarily stores information in the service of language comprehension (see Miyake 2001, for a review of alternative views).

Which processing and storage components of comprehension does reading span capture?

If reading span is a measure of a dynamic working system that processes and temporarily stores information in the service of language comprehension, which processing and storage components of comprehension is reading span capturing? Or put another way, which aspect of comprehension draws most heavily on working memory resources? To answer this, we need a theory of what the components of comprehension are, and a major problem has been that most tests of reading comprehension ability (e.g., the Nelson–Denny, the VSAT) are largely atheoretical (Daneman 1982). Fortunately, we now have some evidence concerning the components that are tapped by these global tests of reading comprehension; this evidence comes from a study in which we developed and validated a new tool that measures four component processes of comprehension:

1. the ability to remember new text information,
2. the ability to make inferences about the new information,
3. the ability to access knowledge from long-term memory, and
4. the ability to integrate the accessed knowledge with the new information (Hannon and Daneman 2001).

This task is based on a four-component task developed by Potts and Peterson (1985). However, unlike the Potts and Peterson task which has at best low to moderate correlations with reading comprehension ability, all the components of the new component processes task correlate well with performance on standardized tests of reading comprehension such as the Nelson–Denny (Hannon and Daneman 2001) and the VSAT (Hannon and Daneman 2006). First, we provide a brief description of the Potts and Peterson task and our modified version which is a much better predictor of reading comprehension ability. Then we present data to show which components of comprehension are captured by reading span and another commonly used measure of working memory capacity called operation span (Turner and Engle 1989). We believe that these data provide important theoretical insights into the nature of the working memory/comprehension correlation.

The Potts and Peterson (1985) task

In the Potts and Peterson task, participants read a set of short paragraphs and respond to four types of true–false test statements after reading each paragraph. Each paragraph consists of three short sentences that describe the relations among a set of real and artificial terms. One example is:

A JAL is larger than a TOC.

A TOC is larger than a PONY.

A BEAVER is larger than a CAZ.

By using the relations described among the real and artificial terms, participants can construct a five-item linear ordering (JAL > TOC > PONY > BEAVER > CAZ); however, because the fact that a pony is larger than a beaver is not explicitly mentioned, participants need to access their existing world knowledge in order to construct the ordering. Participants study the paragraph at their own pace and then respond to true–false statements of four types. *Text memory* statements (e.g., 'A JAL is larger than a TOC') test information explicitly mentioned in the paragraph; no prior knowledge is required. *Text inferencing* statements (e.g., 'A JAL is larger than a PONY') test for information that can be inferred by integrating information that appears explicitly in the text (i.e., 'A JAL is larger than a TOC; A TOC is larger than a PONY'); again, no prior knowledge is required. *Knowledge access* statements (e.g., 'A PONY is larger than a BEAVER') can be answered by simply accessing prior knowledge; no new information from the text is required. *Knowledge integration* statements (e.g., 'A TOC is larger than a BEAVER') require participants to access their prior knowledge (i.e., that a pony is larger than a beaver) and integrate this knowledge with the text fact (i.e., 'A TOC is larger than a PONY').

Potts and Peterson (1985) found that the pattern of correlations among the four statement types was consistent with the above description. Text memory and text inferencing, the two components that depended on memory for new text information rather than access to prior knowledge, were highly correlated with one another ($r = 0.59$), but neither was correlated with knowledge access, the component that depended only on prior knowledge ($r = -0.04$ for text memory and $r = 0.00$ for text inferencing). On the other hand, knowledge integration, the component that depended on text information as well as prior knowledge, was correlated with the two text-based components ($r = 0.39$ with text memory and $r = 0.44$ with text inferencing), and the pure prior knowledge component, knowledge access ($r = 0.64$). This pattern of correlations suggests that the ability to remember new information and the tendency to use world knowledge are separate skills.

The Potts and Peterson (1985) task was originally developed for purposes other than predicting reading ability. However, on the basis of the findings of previous research examining the relationships between higher-level processes and reading ability (e.g., Hannon and Daneman 1998; Masson and Miller 1983; Oakhill 1982), we were struck by the possibility that all four components of the Potts and Peterson task might tap important sources of individual differences in reading comprehension ability. We administered the Potts and Paterson task in conjunction with the Nelson–Denny test of reading comprehension (see Hannon and Daneman 2001, Experiment 1). Although we replicated Potts and Peterson's basic pattern of correlations among the components, we were disappointed to find that none of the components correlated well with reading comprehension (correlations ranged between 0.16 and 0.38), and together, the components accounted for only 27 per cent of the variance in performance on the Nelson–Denny test.

Upon reflection, it occurred to us that the main problem with the Potts and Peterson (1985) task was that it is just not complex enough to capture the kinds of memory, inferencing, knowledge access and knowledge integration processes that are part and parcel of full-blown reading comprehension. Indeed, more than half of the participants reported performing the task by memorizing a simple mnemonic for the five-term linear ordering (e.g., JTPBC for JAL> TOC> PONY> BEAVER> CAZ) and rehearsing this mnemonic throughout the testing phase. Although developing and rehearsing a mnemonic may be a useful strategy for performing well on the Potts and Peterson task, it is unlikely that such a strategy plays a major role in reading comprehension. So even though part of the original appeal of the Potts and Peterson task was its simplicity, we recognized the need to increase the complexity of the task to increase its predictive power. This was accomplished by increasing the complexity of both the three-sentence paragraphs and the test statements. In the next section, we describe our modified form of the Potts and Peterson four-component task, and we show the extent to which the new components predict individual differences in reading comprehension ability.

Our new component processes task

The first strategy for increasing the complexity of the Potts and Peterson (1985) task was to increase the complexity of the three-sentence paragraphs. The Potts and Peterson paragraphs could be represented as simple five-item linear orderings because they included only one relation among the five terms (e.g., larger than). We increased the complexity of representing and reasoning about the paragraphs by including two to four relations/features. Consider the following three-feature paragraph:

A MIRT resembles an OSTRICH but is larger and has a longer neck.

A COFT resembles a ROBIN but is smaller and has a longer neck.

A FILP resembles a COFT but is smaller, has a longer neck, and nests on land.

As in the Potts and Peterson task, these new paragraphs contain three nonsense terms (e.g., MIRT, COFT, and FILP) and two real terms (e.g., OSTRICH, ROBIN). However, unlike their task, which included only one feature, the new paragraphs include two to four features (e.g., larger than, longer neck and nests on land). The additional features create a complex structure. In this example, the size feature produces the linear ordering MIRT > OSTRICH > ROBIN > COFT > FILP if individuals access their prior knowledge that an ostrich is larger than a robin. The neck feature produces two orderings, MIRT > OSTRICH > ROBIN, and FILP > COFT > ROBIN if individuals access their prior knowledge that an ostrich has a longer neck than a robin. The third feature, nests on land, adds to the complexity of the representation and provides additional ways to test learning. The modified version of the task consists of six experimental paragraphs and one practice paragraph (see Hannon and Daneman 2001).

The second strategy for increasing the complexity of the Potts and Peterson (1985) task was to increase the number and types of test statements. By having more than one semantic feature (e.g., larger than, neck length and nests on land), the number of text memory and text inferencing statements per paragraph could be increased. For example, there are text memory statements testing the larger than relation (e.g., 'A MIRT is larger than an OSTRICH'), the neck length relation (e.g., 'A MIRT has a longer neck than an OSTRICH'), and the nests on land relation (e.g., 'A FILP nests on land'). Similarly, there are text inferencing statements testing all three relations (e.g., 'A FILP is smaller than a ROBIN; A FILP has a longer neck than a ROBIN; A COFT doesn't nest on land'). A second type of knowledge access statement was also included. The *low-knowledge access* statements (e.g., 'An OSTRICH is larger than a ROBIN') are like those used in the Potts and Peterson task in that they use terms (e.g., OSTRICH, ROBIN) and a semantic feature (e.g., larger than) explicitly mentioned in the paragraph. On the other hand, the new *high-knowledge access* statements (e.g., 'A ROBIN lives in Canada, whereas a PENGUIN typically doesn't') require more extensive use of prior knowledge because they use a term explicitly mentioned in the paragraph (e.g., ROBIN), and a term (e.g., PENGUIN) and semantic feature (e.g., lives in Canada) not explicitly mentioned in the paragraph. Finally, two new types of knowledge integration statements were included. The *low-knowledge integration* statements (e.g., 'A MIRT has a longer neck than a ROBIN') are like the knowledge integration statements used by Potts and Peterson in that they test knowledge integration with two terms (e.g., MIRT and ROBIN) and a semantic feature (e.g., longer neck) all explicitly mentioned in the paragraph. The *medium-knowledge integration* statements (e.g., 'A MIRT is larger than a BLUEJAY') test integration of information explicitly mentioned in the paragraph (e.g., MIRT, larger than) with a term not explicitly mentioned in the paragraph (e.g., BLUEJAY). Finally, the *high-knowledge integration* statements (e.g., 'Like PENGUINS, MIRTS can't fly') test integration of a term mentioned in the paragraph (e.g., MIRT) with a semantic feature (e.g., can't fly) and a term (e.g., PENGUIN) not explicitly mentioned in the paragraph. So, in summary, the new task includes more text memory statements, more text inferencing statements, two types of knowledge access statements (low, high), and three types of knowledge integration statements (low, medium, high): see Hannon and Daneman (2001) for more examples of the paragraphs and test statements. In all, the test has 276 test statements.

Our modifications had the desired outcome. The components of the new task showed a similar pattern of intercorrelations as seen in the Potts and Peterson (1985) task,[2] but now the components all correlated well with performance on the Nelson–Denny test of reading comprehension ability. The correlations between the components and reading comprehension ranged from 0.36 to 0.62 (see Hannon and Daneman 2001; Experiment 2). The high-knowledge integration component was the best single predictor of comprehension; it alone accounted for more variance (34.8 per cent) in reading comprehension than all of the components of the Potts and Peterson task combined (27 per cent). The text memory, text inferencing, knowledge access, and knowledge integration components, together with a speed component,[3] accounted for 60 per cent of the variance in performance on the Nelson–Denny which is quite impressive when the reliability of the Nelson–Denny is taken into account; indeed, Form F of the Nelson–Denny accounts for only 59 per cent of the variance in Form E, the form used in our studies (see Hannon and Daneman 2001, Experiment 2). Thus, our new component processes task appears to be as good at predicting reading comprehension ability as is another test of reading comprehension ability. Moreover, there is the added theoretical bonus that our task provides some insights into the nature of the component processes tapped by an atheoretical global reading comprehension test such as the Nelson–Denny (see also Hannon and Daneman 2006, for similar findings with the VSAT). There is also the psychometric bonus that our task provides a practical tool for measuring individual differences in these theoretically important component processes.

Now that we have some theoretical insights into the nature of the major component processes of reading comprehension, and a tool to measure the components, we can examine the nature of the working memory/comprehension correlation more closely. In the next sections, we present data that

---

[2] The two text-based components, text memory and text inferencing, were highly correlated with one another (0.83), and both were at best weakly correlated with the knowledge access components (correlations ranging from 0.18 to 0.30). On the other hand, all three knowledge-integration components were significantly correlated with the two text-based components (correlations ranging from 0.54 to 0.70) and they were also correlated with the knowledge access components, although the correlations were higher for the low-knowledge access component (correlations ranging from 0.34 to 0.49) than for the high-knowledge access component (correlations ranging from 0.22 to 0.31); see Hannon and Daneman (2001; Experiment 2).

[3] This component was based on speed of responding to the test statements (see Hannon and Daneman 2001).

reveal which component processes of comprehension draw more heavily on working memory resources. We have pooled together the data from 206 University of Toronto students, all of whom completed the new component processes task, the Nelson–Denny test of reading comprehension, and two tests of working memory capacity – reading span and operation span. Of these 206 participants, the data for 94 of them are presented in Hannon and Daneman (2001, Experiment 4); the data for the other 112 were collected subsequent to the publication of that article, and have not been published previously.

Tasks and procedures

The 206 participants all completed Hannon and Daneman's (2001) component processes task, the Nelson–Denny (Brown *et al.* 1981) test of reading comprehension, and two widely used measures of working memory capacity, reading span (Daneman and Carpenter 1980), and operation span (Turner and Engle 1989).

Component processes task

The materials consisted of a set of six three-sentence paragraphs (such as the 'MIRT' one described earlier), and their accompanying test statements (276 test statements in all). Each sentence of a paragraph appeared one at a time on a computer screen and in the same standard order. Participants were explicitly instructed to use their world knowledge in performing the task. After a participant had learned all three sentences of a paragraph, the test statements for that paragraph were presented one at a time in a random order. Participants had a maximum of 12 seconds to read and respond to a test statement. If the participant failed to respond within the 12-second deadline, the test statement was removed and replaced by the next test statement. All response failures were classified as errors. Accuracy (i.e., number correct) was the primary dependent measure; however, speed of responding (i.e., average reaction time for correct responses) was also analyzed. A pause screen appeared at the end of the test statements for each paragraph to give participants a break before proceeding to the next paragraph (see Hannon and Daneman 2001, for details).

Nelson–Denny test of reading comprehension

The Nelson–Denny test of reading comprehension (Brown *et al.* 1981) consists of eight prose passages and 36 multiple-choice questions. Participants were given 20 minutes to read the passages and answer the questions.

The reading span test

As one of our measures of working memory span, we used a version of Daneman and Carpenter's (1980) reading span test which was designed to measure the combined processing and storage capacity of working memory during reading. In this version (see also Daneman and Hannon 2001), participants were required to read aloud sets of unrelated sentences (e.g., 'Torrential rains swept over the tiny deserted island,' 'His mouth was twisted into an inhuman smile,' 'The umbrella grabbed its bat and stepped up to the plate.'), and make judgments about the sensibility of each sentence (e.g., respond 'yes' after reading the first sentence, 'yes' after reading the second sentence, and 'no' after reading the third). Then at the end of the set, they were required to recall the final word of each sentence in the set (e.g., *island*; *smile*; *plate*).

The sentences were 8–12 words in length, each ending with a different word. They were presented one at a time on the computer screen. After the participant responded 'yes' or 'no' to indicate whether or not the sentence made sense, the participant pressed a key and the next sentence appeared. The procedure was repeated until a blank screen indicated that the trial was over, and the participant had to recall the last word of each of the sentences in the set. Participants were allowed to recall the words in any order but were encouraged not to recall the last word in the set first. Sentences were arranged in five sets of 2, 3, 4, 5 and 6 sentences each. Participants were presented with increasingly longer sets until all 100 sentences had been presented. Reading span was the total number of sentence-final words out of 100 that the participant could recall.

Operation span test

As our second measure of working memory span, we used Turner and Engle's (1989) operation span test which was designed to measure the combined processing and storage capacity of working memory during the performance of simple mathematical computations. Operation span has been shown to be a good predictor of reading comprehension, but not as good as reading span (see Daneman and Merikle 1996, for a meta-analysis). In this version of the task, participants were given sets of equations and accompanying words (e.g., '$(4 \times 2) - 1 = 7$ girl,' '$(1 \times 6) - 5 = 1$ paper,' '$(9/3) + 3 = 2$ truth).' For each equation-word pair, participants were required to read aloud the math equation and the word, verify whether or not the statement was true (e.g., respond 'true' for the first equation, 'true' for the second, and 'false' for the third). Then at the end of the set, they were required to recall all the words in the set (e.g., girl; paper; truth).

The equation-word pairs were presented one at a time on the computer screen. After the participant responded 'true' or 'false' = to indicate whether or not the stated solution to the equation was correct, the participant pressed a key and the next equation-word pair appeared. The procedure was repeated until a blank screen indicated that the trial was over, and the participant had to recall the words. Equation-word pairs were arranged in five sets of 2, 3, 4, 5 and 6 equation-word pairs each. Participants were presented with increasingly longer sets until all 100 equation-word pairs had been presented. Operation span was the total number of words recalled, the maximum being 100.

The results

Table 2.1 includes the means and standard deviations on the component of the component processes task, the test of reading comprehension, and the two working memory span tasks for our pool of 206 participants. It shows the correlations among the components of the component processes task, and how the components correlated with reading comprehension and with the two working memory span measures.

Component processes task

The internal structure of the component processes task was similar to that found in Hannon and Daneman (2001, Experiment 2). As Table 2.2 shows, the pattern of correlations among the components showed that the two text-based components, text memory and text inferencing, were highly correlated with one another (0.82), showed intermediate correlations with the knowledge integration components (range = 0.57 to 0.75) and much weaker correlations with the pure knowledge access components (range = 0.25 to 0.32).

The power of the components to predict performance on the Nelson–Denny reading comprehension test was also similar to that found in Hannon and Daneman (2001, Experiment 2). As Table 2.2 shows, all the components, including the speed component, correlated significantly with reading comprehension, with the correlations ranging between 0.29 and 0.58. Again, the high-knowledge integration component was the best single predictor, accounting for 33.6 per cent of the variance in reading comprehension performance. In a later section, we present the results of regression analyses which show the proportion of variance in comprehension accounted for by all of the components.

Table 2.1 Means and standard deviations for the components of the component processes task, reading comprehension, reading span and operation span (n = 206)

Test	M	SD	range
Component processes task[a]			
Text memory	78.21	13.84	42.86–100
Text inferencing	70.86	15.32	27.78–97
Low-knowledge integration	86.53	12.35	45.83–100
Medium-knowledge integration	83.68	12.50	47.22–100
High-knowledge integration	73.42	15.79	38.89–100
Low-knowledge access	92.00	6.06	69.44–100
High-knowledge access	88.65	7.83	58.33–100
Speed (in ms)	3778.98	743.09	1967–5764
Tests of reading comprehension and working memory			
Reading comprehension (maximum = 36)	24.02	5.76	11–35[b]
Reading span (maximum = 100)	60.33	11.76	37–95
Operation span (maximum = 100)	76.68	12.08	49–100

[a] Note: Means, standard deviations, and ranges for the components of the component processes task are reported as percentages.

[b] According to the Nelson–Denny norms, this range represents the 2nd to 99th percentiles (Brown *et al.*, 1981).

Working memory span tests

As Table 2.2 shows, the two working memory span measures were highly correlated with one another, r (204) = 0.68, $p < 0.001$, and both were correlated with performance on the Nelson–Denny test of reading comprehension, with reading span being the better predictor of reading comprehension of the two (reading span correlated 0.44 with reading comprehension, whereas operation span correlated 0.33, a difference that was statistically significant, $t[203]$ = 2.19, $p < 0.01$). These findings show that our versions of reading span and operation span replicated the typical pattern of findings in the literature (see Daneman and Merikle 1996, for a meta-analysis). In the next sections, we explore why these processing and storage measures are good predictors of comprehension.

Working memory span and component processes task

Our first step was to examine how reading span and operation span correlated with the different components of the component processes task. As Table 2.2 shows, the pattern of correlations was very similar for reading span and operation span. Reading span and operation span both correlated well with the text-based components, text memory and text inferencing (correlations ranging from 0.42 to 0.50), and with the knowledge integration components (correlations ranging from 0.33 to 0.45). Reading span and operation span showed weaker correlations with the knowledge access components (correlations ranging between 0.19 and 0.25), and even weaker correlations with the speed component (−0.15 and −0.01, respectively). This pattern of correlations suggests that the ability to remember new information, the ability to make inferences about new

Table 2.2 Correlations among components of component processes task, reading comprehension, reading span and operation span (n = 206)

Variable	1	2	3	4	5	6	7	8	9	10	11
1 Text memory	–	0.82**	0.66**	0.73**	0.75**	0.27**	0.30**	0.03	0.50**	0.46**	0.50**
2 Text inferencing		–	0.57**	0.66**	0.70**	0.25**	0.32**	−0.06	0.52**	0.42**	0.43**
3 Low-knowledge integration			–	0.76**	0.64**	0.34**	0.25**	0.03	0.42**	0.33**	0.35**
4 Medium-knowledge integration				–	0.73**	0.37**	0.36**	−0.00	0.50**	0.37**	0.41**
5 High-knowledge integration					–	0.34**	0.35**	−0.07	0.58**	0.43**	0.45**
6 Low-knowledge access						–	0.28**	−0.17*	0.31**	0.25**	0.23**
7 High-knowledge access							–	−0.08	0.29**	0.19**	0.24**
8 Speed								–	−0.36**	−0.15*	−0.01
9 Reading comprehension									–	0.44**	0.33**
10 Reading span										–	0.68**
11 Operation span											–

Note: * $p < 0.05$; ** $p < 0.01$.

information, and the ability to integrate accessed knowledge with new information are comprehension processes that draw most heavily on working memory capacity.

Another way to determine which component processes are tapped by the working memory span measures is through structure equation modeling. In this section, we describe four different structure equation models (SEMs). Our strategy was to first develop a SEM for predicting working memory span that included all of the components of the component processes task, and then to compare the relative strength of this model to other models that included fewer component processes. All of the SEMs that we report were developed by using raw data and LISREL 8, a computer package designed for structural equation modeling (Jöreskog and Sörbom 1993). Based on the recommendations of Hoyle and Panter (1995), we used six different fit statistics to assess the SEMs. These fit statistics were the traditional chi-square test of 'exact' model fit, the chi-square test of 'close' model fit (e.g., Browne and Cudeck 1993), the goodness of fit index (GFI), the adjusted GFI (AGFI) (Jöreskog and Sörbom 1981), the root-mean square error of approximation (RMSEA) (Steiger and Lind 1980), and the comparative fit index (CFI) (Bentler 1989). It is important to note that for the chi-square tests, the hypothesis being tested assumes either an exact model fit for the data or a model fit that is acceptable, and so a good-fitting model is indicated by non-significant results from these tests (i.e., $p > 0.05$); see also Engle *et al.* (1999). For the GFI, AGFI, and CFI indices, we followed the general guideline that good-fitting models are indicated by a value of 0.90 or more. For interpreting the RMSEA statistic, we followed the recommendation that values of 0.05 or less indicate a good-fitting model (Browne and Cudeck 1993).

The first model (the all-components model) included:

1. a *working memory* latent variable that was measured by the observed variables, reading span and operation span;

2. a *text processing* latent variable that was measured by the observed variables, text memory and text inferencing;

3. a *knowledge access* latent variable that was measured by the observed variables, low-knowledge access and high-knowledge access;

4. a *knowledge integration* latent variable that was measured by the observed variables, low-knowledge integration, medium-knowledge integration, and high-knowledge integration; and

5. a *speed* latent variable that was measured by the observed variable of speed.

In order to represent the internal structure of the component processes task, which has been validated by Hannon and Daneman (2001, 2006), we included a path indicating the relationship between the *text processing* latent variable and the *knowledge integration* latent variable as well as a path indicating the relationship between the *knowledge access* latent variable and the *knowledge integration* latent variable. In addition, we included a two-way path between the error terms for low-knowledge integration and medium-knowledge integration. Finally paths indicating the relationships between the *text processing, knowledge access, speed,* and *knowledge integration* latent variables and the *working memory* latent variable were included. Table 2.3 shows the results of the fit statistics for this SEM, and Figure 2.1(a) shows the parameter estimates. In the figure, the ellipses represent the latent variables (e.g., *working memory*) and the rectangles represent the observed measures/variables (e.g., reading span, operation span). Arrows on paths leading from one variable to another variable indicate the direction of influence. Numbers on paths are the standardized path coefficients that indicate the degree of influence.

To reiterate, a well-fitting model is one for which: (a) chi-square tests are not significant, (b) the RMSEA estimate is around or below 0.05, and (b) the GFI, AGFI, and CFI estimates are

Table 2.3 Fit Statistics for Structural Models of Working Memory

	df	χ^2	χ^2 p (exact)	χ^2 p (close)	GFI	AGFI	CFI	RMSEA
All-components Model	26	27.51	.38	.88	.97	.94	1.00	.017
Text+Integration Model	21	13.44	.89	.99	.99	.97	1.00	.000
Text-only Model	22	15.22	.85	.99	.98	.97	1.00	.000
Integration-only Model	22	14.79	.87	.99	.98	.97	1.00	.000

Note: χ^2 p (exact) and χ^2 p (close) reflect the significance levels for the χ^2 p (exact) and χ^2 p (close) tests; GFI = goodness-of-fit index; AGFI = adjusted goodness-of-fit index; CFI = comparative fit index; and RMSEA = root-mean square error of approximation.

above 0.90. As Table 2.3 shows, the results of all six statistical tests suggest that a model that includes all of the components of the component processes task is an acceptable model for predicting working memory.

Of course, it is quite possible that there are more parsimonious models than the all-components model. For example, perhaps a model that includes only the latent variables, *text processing* and *knowledge integration*, is a better and more parsimonious model for predicting working memory. Indeed, the *t*-values for the paths leading from the latent variables, *knowledge access* and *speed*, to *working memory* were not significant in the *all-components* model, both *t*s < 1. To test this possibility, we created three additional SEMs. The first SEM (text + integration) included just the latent variables *text processing* and *knowledge integration* predicting *working memory*; it did not include the latent variables *knowledge access* and *speed*. The second SEM (text-only) included just the latent variable *text processing* predicting *working memory*; it did not include the latent variables *knowledge access, speed,* and *knowledge integration*. Finally, the third SEM (integration-only) included just the latent variable *knowledge integration* predicting *working memory*; it did not include the latent variables *text processing, knowledge access,* and *speed*. The three models are presented in Figures 2.1(b), (c) and (d), respectively, and the fit statistics for these three models are presented in Table 2.3. As the fit statistics indicate, all three of these proposed models (text + integration, text-only, and integration-only) are viable models for describing what is tapped by *working memory*. In order to determine whether these three simpler models fit the data better than the all-components model, we performed three chi-square tests: one comparing the all-components model to the text + integration model, a second comparing the all-components model to the text-only model, and a third comparing the all-components model to the integration-only model. All three of these chi-square tests were significant, χ^2 (5) = 14.07, χ^2 (4) = 12.29, and χ^2 (4) = 12.72, respectively; this finding suggests that all three of these smaller models fit the data better than does the all-inclusive all-components model of working memory. In other words, a model that does not include knowledge access and speed is a better model for discerning what is tapped by *working memory* than a model that does include knowledge access and speed (see also Hannon and Daneman 2001, 2006).

Of course, it is unclear which of these three models (text + integration, text-only, and integration-only) is best for describing what is tapped by *working memory*. In order to answer this question, we conducted three additional chi-square tests: one comparing the text + integration model to

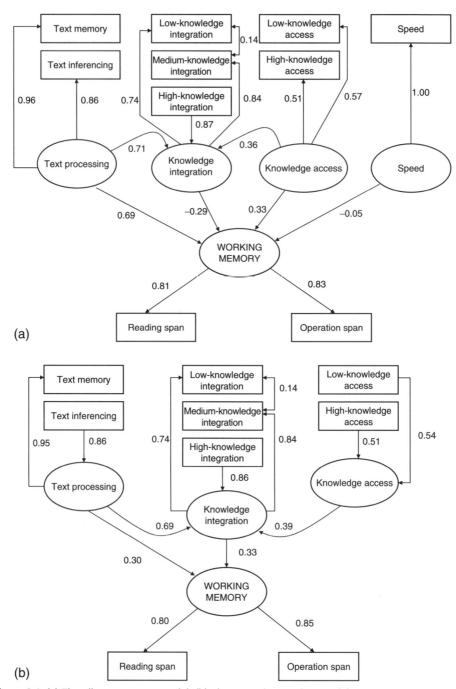

Figure 2.1 (a) The all-components model. (b) The text + integration model.

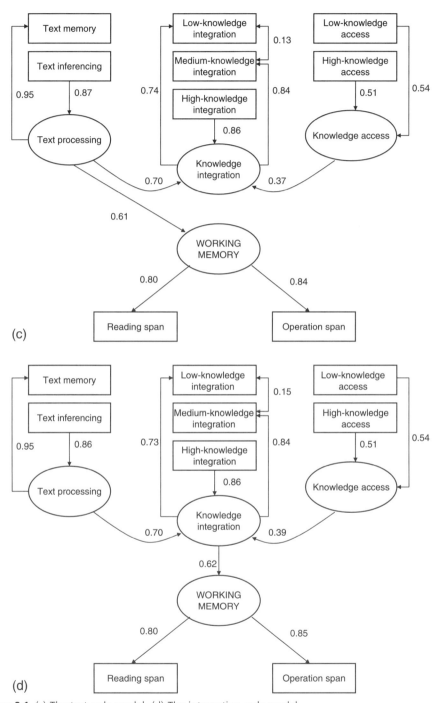

Figure 2.1 (c) The text-only model. (d) The integration-only model.

the text-only model, one comparing the text + integration model to the integration-only model, and one comparing the text-only model to the integration-only model. The results of these tests revealed that none of the three models was significantly different from each other, χ^2 (1) = 1.78, χ^2 (1) = 1.35, and χ^2 (0) = 0.43, respectively. In circumstances such as this one, the general rule is to adopt the most parsimonious model(s). If we adopt such a rule, we can conclude that the text-only and integration-only models are better than the text + integration model for describing what is tapped by *working memory*. All in all, the SEMs supported the zero-order correlations by showing that the two working memory span tests tap the components that draw on the new text information (text memory, text inferencing, knowledge integration) more so than the pure knowledge access components and the speed component.

Working memory span, component processes task and reading comprehension

Our final step was to determine the extent to which the component processes task and the two working memory span tasks, reading span and operation span, made overlapping or independent contributions in their prediction of reading comprehension. To do this, we conducted pairs of stepwise regression analyses: in one analysis, working memory span (either reading span or operation span) was entered as the first predictor into the regression model; in the second analysis, working memory span was entered into the regression model after the variance accounted for by the components of our component processes task was partialed out.[4] Table 2.4 shows the results for the pair of regression analyses using reading span as the measure of working memory capacity. Table 2.5 shows the results for the equivalent pair of regression analyses using operation span as the measure of working memory capacity.

As displayed in Table 2.4(a), when entered first, reading span accounted for 20 per cent of the variance in reading comprehension performance, a finding that is consistent with the reliable correlation between working memory span measures and comprehension (see Daneman and Merikle 1996; Turner and Engle 1989). However, note also that our text inferencing, speed, and high-knowledge integration components accounted for a further 28 per cent of the variance in reading after the effects of reading span were removed. On the other hand, when reading span was entered into the regression equation after the 46 per cent of variance accounted for by the component processes was partialled out, reading span accounted for only an additional 2 per cent of unique variance (Table 2.4b). The picture was very similar when operation span was used as the measure of working memory capacity, although now operation span did not contribute any additional unique variance after the variance accounted for by the component processes was partialed out (see Table 2.5b). Together, these analyses show that the component processes task is accounting for most of the variance in reading comprehension that is tapped by a typical test of the combined processing and storage capacity of working memory. Note that the two working

---

4 Following Dixon *et al.* (1988), our strategy was to test for the unique contribution of a component process by entering it into the regression equation last. If that component process failed to make a unique contribution, it was dropped from the regression equation. After establishing which components made unique contributions to comprehension when added into the regression equation last, we then classified these components as either elementary (low-knowledge access, high-knowledge access, text memory, text inferencing, speed) or complex (low-, medium-, and high-knowledge integration). Elementary components were entered into the equation before complex components on the assumption that more complex component processes (e.g., knowledge integration) are dependent on the presence of more elementary component processes (e.g., text memory, low-knowledge access); see also Hannon and Daneman (2001).

Table 2.4 Regression analyses on reading comprehension scores with reading span and component processes as predictors (n = 206)

Variable	R	R^2	ΔR^2	F
(a) Reading span as first predictor of reading comprehension				
1 Reading span	0.443	0.196	0.196	49.79
2 Text inferencing	0.573	0.328	0.132	39.98
3 Speed	0.647	0.418	0.09	31.16
4 High-knowledge integration	0.694	0.481	0.063	24.25
(b) Reading span as predictor of reading comprehension after variance accounted for by the component processes has been partialed out				
1 Text inferencing	0.517	0.267	0.267	74.19
2 Speed	0.613	0.376	0.109	35.58
3 High-knowledge integration	0.678	0.459	0.083	30.93
4 Reading span	0.694	0.481	0.02	8.48

memory span tasks share most variance in common with the text inferencing component of the component processes task. This is because text inferencing is the component whose predictive power was most reduced by entering working memory span as the first predictor (see also Hannon and Daneman 2001). These findings provide some rationale for adopting the text-only model (Figure 2.1c) over the integration-only model (Figure 2.1d) in accounting for why working memory span tasks such as reading span and operation span are good predictors of comprehension.

Summary and conclusions

There is now considerable evidence that working memory span tasks are excellent predictors of performance on complex cognitive tasks (Daneman and Merikle 1996; Jurden 1995; Miyake

Table 2.5 Regression analyses on reading comprehension scores with operation span and component processes as predictors (n = 206)

Variable	R	R^2	ΔR^2	F
(a) Operation span as first predictor of reading comprehension				
1 Operation span	0.333	0.111	0.111	25.36
2 Text inferencing	0.530	0.281	0.170	48.22
3 Speed	0.627	0.393	0.112	38.01
4 High-knowledge integration	0.681	0.464	0.071	26.39
(b) Operation span as predictor of reading comprehension after variance accounted for by the component processes has been partialed out				
1 Text inferencing	0.517	0.267	0.267	74.19
2 Speed	0.613	0.376	0.109	35.58
3 High-knowledge integration	0.678	0.459	0.083	30.93
4 Operation span	0.678	0.459	0.00	0.00

and Shah 1999). However, the nature of the correlation is not well understood (Miyake 2001), and an increasing number of researchers have been interested in determining what working memory span tasks, such as reading span and operation span, are really measuring (e.g., Kane *et al.* 2001; Towse, *et al.* 2000; see Miyake 2001, for a review). In this chapter, we addressed the well-established correlation between measures of working memory span and reading comprehension ability.

Reading span (Daneman and Carpenter 1980) is a prevalently used measure of working memory in which individuals must read increasingly longer sets of sentences out loud while trying to maintain and then recall the final word of each sentence in the set. Daneman and Carpenter (1980) attributed the high predictive power of reading span to the fact that it assesses the combined processing and storage resources of working memory that can be devoted to language processing, and not simply the storage resources as traditional digit span and word span tasks do. However, a legitimate concern is that reading span is too much like reading comprehension itself, which may leave us with the trivial conclusion that comprehension correlates with comprehension (Kintsch 1998). In the first part of the chapter, we presented data to show that reading span is not simply another test of reading comprehension skill. These data came from a study aimed at investigating the construct validity of multiple-choice reading comprehension tests such as the VSAT (Daneman and Hannon 2001). The study compared the relative powers of reading span and another multiple-choice test of reading comprehension, the Nelson–Denny, at predicting VSAT performance when test-takers could or could not consult the VSAT passages to answer the multiple-choice questions. The study showed a reversal of predictive powers. When test-takers could read and consult the VSAT passages, reading span was a good predictor of VSAT performance, but the Nelson–Denny was an even better predictor of VSAT performance. When test-takers did not have access to the passages, reading span was still a good predictor of VSAT performance, but the predictive power of the Nelson–Denny was greatly reduced. If reading span were simply another test of reading comprehension, then its predictive power should mirror that of the direct test of reading comprehension. We interpreted the reversal of the relative predictive powers as showing that reading span is not simply another measure of reading comprehension skill. Rather it is a measure of a dynamic working memory system that processes and temporarily stores information in the service of complex cognitive tasks such as reading comprehension (passage-available condition) and verbal reasoning (passage-unavailable condition).

In the second part of the chapter, we examined why reading span and operation span, another popular measure of the combined processing and storage resources of working memory, are good at predicting reading comprehension ability. To do this, we introduced a new tool called the component processes task (Hannon and Daneman 2001) that has been shown to measure four important components of comprehension:

1. the ability to remember new information from the text,
2. the ability to make inferences about the new information,
3. the ability to access knowledge from long-term memory; and
4. the ability to integrate the accessed knowledge with the new information.

We then presented data from 206 participants who had completed the two working memory span tasks as well as the component processes task, and we examined the association between working memory span and the component processes of comprehension. The zero-order correlations, structure equation modeling, and stepwise regression analyses all showed that the working memory span measures appear to be tapping the components that act on the new information (text memory, text inferencing, and knowledge integration) more so than the components that access prior knowledge from long-term memory. We think these results provide important theoretical insights into what working memory span measures like reading span and operation span are really measuring, and why they are good at predicting individual differences in reading comprehension ability.

Although the focus of our chapter has been on understanding the nature of the working memory span/comprehension correlation, do our data reveal anything about why working memory span tasks are also good predictors of performance on non-comprehension-related tasks? We think they do. The component processes task was developed and validated with respect to measuring four main components of text comprehension (see Hannon and Daneman 2001, 2006). However, there is reason to believe that the ability to remember different kinds of new information, the ability to make inferences about that new information, the ability to access prior knowledge and the ability to integrate that prior knowledge appropriately with the new information are fundamental processes that underlie skill at a range of complex cognitive tasks. And indeed we already have some preliminary evidence to suggest that the components of our cognitive processes task are good predictors of performance on a battery of cognitive tests that assess general fluid intelligence (e.g., Raven's Matrices) and specific abilities (e.g., verbal and spatial abilities). By extrapolation, then, we could argue that reading span and operation span are good predictors of performance on a range of everyday cognitive tasks because the processing and storage capacity of working memory is important for remembering new information, for making inferences about new information, and for integrating prior knowledge with the new information.

References

Baddeley, AD (1986). *Working Memory*. Oxford: Oxford University Press.

Baddeley, AD and Hitch, G (1974). Working memory. In GH Bower (ed), *The Psychology of Learning and Motivation*, Vol. 8, pp. 47–89. New York: Academic Press.

Baddeley, AD, Logie, RH, Nimmo-Smith, I and Brereton, N (1985). Components of fluent reading. *Journal of Memory and Language*, 24, 119–131.

Bentler, PB (1989). *EQS structural equations program manual*. Los Angeles, CA: BMDP Statistical Software.

Brown, JI, Bennett, JM and Hanna, G (1981). *Nelson–Denny Reading Test*. Chicago, IL: Riverside.

Browne, MW and Cudeck, R (1993). Alternate ways of assessing model fit. In KA Bollen and JS Long (eds), *Testing Structure Equation Models*, pp. 136–142. Newbury Park, CA: Sage.

Daneman, M (1982). The measurement of reading comprehension: How not to trade construct validity for predictive power. *Intelligence*, 6, 331–345.

Daneman, M and Carpenter, PA (1980). Individual differences in working memory and reading. *Journal of Verbal Learning and Verbal Behavior*, 19, 450–466.

Daneman, M and Hannon, B (2001). Using working memory theory to investigate the construct validity of multiple-choice reading comprehension tests such as the SAT. *Journal of Experimental Psychology: General*, 130, 206–223.

Daneman, M and Merikle, PM (1996). Working memory and comprehension: A meta-analysis. *Psychonomic Bulletin and Review*, 3, 422–433.

Donlon, TF (1984). *The College Board technical handbook for the SAT and Achievement Tests*. New York: College Entrance Examination Board.

Dixon, P, LeFevre, J and Twilley, LC (1988). Word knowledge and working memory as predictors of reading skill. *Journal of Educational Psychology*, 80, 465–472.

Engle, RW, Tuholski, SW, Laughlin, JE and Conway, ARA (1999). Working memory, short-term memory, and general fluid intelligence: A latent variable approach. *Journal of Experimental Psychology: General*, 128, 309–331.

Farr, R, Pritchard, R and Smitten, B (1990). A description of what happens when an examinee takes a multiple-choice reading comprehension test. *Journal of Educational Measurement*, 27, 209–226.

Freedle, R and Kostin, I (1994). Can multiple-choice reading tests be construct valid? *Psychological Science*, *5*, 107–110.

Hannon, B and Daneman, M (1998). Facilitating knowledge-based inferences in less-skilled readers. *Contemporary Educational Psychology*, *23*, 149–172.

Hannon, B and Daneman, M (2001). A new tool for measuring and understanding individual differences in the component processes of reading comprehension. *Journal of Educational Psychology*, *93*, 103–128.

Hannon, B and Daneman, M (2006). What do tests of reading comprehension ability such as the VSAT really measure? A componential analysis. In A Mitel (ed), *Focus on Educational Psychology*, pp. 104–146. Nova Publishers.

Hoyle, RH and Panter, AT (1995). Writing about structural equation models. In RH Panter (ed), *Structural Equation Modeling: Concepts, issues, and applications*. Thousand Oaks, California: Sage.

Hunt, E (1980). Intelligence as an information-processing concept. *British Journal of Psychology*, *71*, 449–474.

Jöreskog, K and Sörbom, D (1981). *LISREL V: Analysis of linear structural relationships by the method of maximum likelihood*. Chicago, IL: National Education Resources.

Jöreskog, K and Sörbom, D (1993). *LISREL 8: Structural equation modeling with the SIMPLIS command language*. Hillsdale, NJ: Lawrence Erlbaum Associates.

Jurden, FH (1995). Individual differences in working memory and complex cognition. *Journal of Educational Psychology*, *87*, 93–102.

Kane, MJ, Bleckley, MK, Conway, ARA and Engle, RW (2001). A controlled-attention view of working memory capacity. *Journal of Experimental Psychology: General*, *130*, 169–183.

Katz, S, Blackburn, AB and Lautenschlager, GJ (1991). Answering reading comprehension questions without passages on the SAT when items are quasi-randomized. *Educational and Psychological Measurement*, *51*, 747–754.

Katz, S, Lautenschlager, GJ, Blackburn, AB and Harris, FH (1990). Answering reading comprehension questions without passages on the SAT. *Psychological Science*, *1*, 122–127.

Kintsch, W (1998). *Comprehension: A paradigm for cognition*. Cambridge: Cambridge University Press.

Kyllonen, PC and Christal, RE (1990). Reasoning ability is (little more than) working memory capacity?! *Intelligence*, *14*, 389–433.

Masson, ME and Miller, JA (1983). Working memory and individual differences in comprehension and memory of text. *Journal of Educational Psychology*, *75*, 314–318.

Miller, GA, Galanter, E and Pribram, KH (1960). *Plans and the Structure of Behavior*. New York: Holt.

Miyake, A (2001). Individual differences in working memory: Introduction to the special section. *Journal of Experimental Psychology: General*, *130*, 163–168.

Miyake, A, Friedman, NP, Rettinger, DA, Shah, P, and Hegarty, M (2001). How are visuospatial working memory, executive functioning, and spatial abilities related? A latent variable analysis. *Journal of Experimental Psychology: General*, *130*, 621–640.

Miyake, A and Shah, P (1999). *Models of Working Memory: Mechanisms of active maintenance and executive control*. New York: Cambridge University Press.

Oakhill, J (1982). Constructive processes in skilled and less skilled comprehenders' memory for sentences. *British Journal of Psychology*, *73*, 13–20.

Potts, GR and Peterson, SB (1985). Incorporation versus compartmentalization in memory for discourse. *Journal of Memory and Language*, *24*, 107–118.

Powers, DF and Leung, SW (1995). Answering the new SAT reading comprehension questions without the passages. *Journal of Educational Measurement*, *32*, 105–129.

Steiger, JH and Lind, JC (1980, May). *Statistically based tests for the number of factors*. Paper presented at the annual meeting of the Psychometric Society, Iowa City. IA.

Towse, JN, Hitch, GJ and Hutton, U (2000). On the interpretation of working memory span in adults. *Memory and Cognition*, *28*, 341–348.

Turner, ML and Engle, RW (1989). Is working memory capacity task-dependent? *Journal of Memory and Language*, *28*, 127–154.

3

What do estimates of working memory capacity tell us?

Nelson Cowan, Candice C. Morey,
Zhijian Chen and Michael Bunting

Working memory can be viewed as the collection of mental processes that preserve a limited amount of information in an especially accessible form, long enough for it to be of use in ongoing cognitive tasks. By almost all accounts, working memory is indeed a collection of processes (e.g., for diverse theoretical descriptions of working memory, see the chapters of Miyake and Shah 1999). In our laboratory, we have been investigating 'flavors' of working memory that we believe to be closely related to human conscious awareness, namely the *primary memory* described as the trailing edge of consciousness by James (1890). This chapter serves as a sort of tour of the laboratory's current endeavors, made more or less interactive by the inclusion of a considerable amount of data from recently published studies, presented here in tabular form so it can be explored and questioned.

We examine research that makes four related points in progression:

1. that working memory is an important concept that amounts to more than some notion of general processing efficiency;

2. that the often-discussed relation between working memory and intellectual maturation and aptitude does not depend on using a dual task to examine working memory, but instead depends only on using a task that impedes mnemonic strategies such as covert verbal rehearsal;

3. that working memory performance depends on the notion of capacity, expressed in terms of chunks; and

4. that the core working-memory capacity limit is related to the scope of attention.

Premise 1: working memory is not just general processing efficiency

There is a tradition in the research literature suggesting that developmental differences in working memory and cognitive aptitudes throughout the life span result from a developmental increase, and then decrease, in the speed of processing as neural efficiency improves with maturation in childhood and later declines with aging (e.g., Kail and Salthouse 1994). The theoretical hypothesis is that individuals with a better working memory are able to reactivate information more quickly before it can decay from working memory, and therefore that the speed of processing may be the key factor distinguishing between people with better or poorer working memory. The basis of this claim was a wealth of evidence that processing speed and the accuracy of performance are highly correlated across individuals.

Cowan, Wood, Wood *et al.* (1998) documented a strong correlation between two measures of processing efficiency and performance on a digit span task. The digit span task is one of the oldest measures of the short-term retention processes that form a key component of working memory, and is included in standard tests of intelligence. In this task, a series of digits between 1 and 9, with each digit used no more than once per list, is presented on each trial. The list length starts very short and increases every few trials, with the exact number of trials per list length differing from one procedure to another. If the participant is incorrect on every trial at a given length, the test stops, and therefore the duration of the test is adjusted to the abilities of the participant. Some measure of the length of list that can be repeated is taken as an individual's digit span.

One measure of efficiency examined by Cowan *et al.* (1998) was the rate at which digits were pronounced in lists of a particular length within the span task. The durations of every word in the spoken responses, and the durations of silent pauses between words in these responses, were painstakingly measured using a computer. An oscillographic display of the response was measured with auditory guidance. The notion was that individuals who process information faster would repeat more of this information before it decays. Another measure of efficiency was one devised by Baddeley, Thomson and Buchanan (1975). In this type of measure, a small number of items is to be repeated aloud as quickly as possible, either with a set short enough to be memorized and repeated over and over or with a set that is read rather than remembered. This type of measure was thought to estimate how quickly the participant is capable of covertly rehearsing a longer list of words drawn from the same set, in a span task.

Cowan *et al.* (1998) found that both the speed of retrieval and the speed of rehearsal were significantly related to span. A statistical method (structural equation modeling) was used to characterize the relations between measures. It was found, contrary to the expectations of a single type of efficiency across tasks, that retrieval and rehearsal speed were unrelated to each other. However, they both were related to digit span, to an extent described in Table 3.1. These were both strong, separate relations and together they accounted for 87 per cent of the age-related variance in digit span (and 60 per cent of its total variance).

At the time, this finding provided one of the strongest arguments in favor of some sort of efficiency theory of working memory, although it required that one stipulate the presence of more than one efficiency parameter per individual (because retrieval and rehearsal rates did not correlate with one another). However, it always bears repeating that correlations do not amount to evidence of causation, even with the use of structural equation modeling.

Recently, Cowan *et al.* (2006) showed that at least the retrieval rate factor is not causally related to digit span. Ordinarily, children who are 8 to 9 years old have a smaller digit span than adults and retrieve items (pronounce them in the response) much more slowly. In two different ways within separate experiments, Cowan *et al.* were able to get the children in an experimental group to recall items more quickly. In Experiment 1, this was accomplished by speeding up the stimuli. In Experiment 2, one group of children was simply instructed to speak more quickly in their

Table 3.1 Findings of Cowan *et al.* (1998), Experiment 1

Increase in span resulting from a 1-SD speed-up in retrieval rate (path coefficient)	0.41 SD
Increase in span resulting from a 1-SD speed-up in rehearsal rate (path coefficient)	0.49 SD
The proportion of the total variance accounted for by these two rates	60%
The portion of within-age variance in span accounted for by these two rates	87%

Table 3.2 Findings (retrieval rate; span) of Cowan *et al.* (2006), Experiment 2

Group and experimental phase	Retrieval rate	Span
Training group children, non-speeded Phase 1	1.10 items/sec;	5.37 items
Training group children, speeded Phase 2	2.19 items/sec;	5.37 items
Control group children, non-speeded Phase 1	1.16 items/sec;	5.53 items
Control group children, non-speeded Phase 2	1.41 items/sec;	5.63 items
Adult comparison group, non-speeded	1.63 items/sec;	7.56 items

responses at a certain point (Phase 2 in Table 3.2), and the children were able to do so. In fact, these children sped up their responses to be faster than adults usually speak when recalling lists of an equivalent length. Yet, as illustrated in Table 3.2, speeding up did not affect span at all. The quickly speaking children were still just as far behind the adults in digit span. This study emphasizes that the correlation between efficiency or speed and span does not reflect a forward direction of causation. Perhaps, instead, the most comfortable speed of responding and memory capacity are separate factors that increase during childhood. By analogy, the head and the arms both grow larger during childhood, but one instance of growth does not cause the other; stretching out the arms as far as they can go does not affect the size of the head.

Premise 2: the relation between working memory and intellectual maturation and aptitude does not depend on using a dual task to examine working memory

The traditional view of working memory (Baddeley and Hitch 1974; Baddeley 1986; Baddeley and Logie 1999) and its development (Gathercole and Hitch 1993; Hitch, Towse and Hutton 2001) is one that incorporates storage and processing mechanisms that are assumed to be distinct, both neurologically and behaviorally. From that viewpoint, it stands to reason that, to test the capabilities of working memory, the test should tax or engage both storage and processing. That has been the logical underlying the type of test that has become prevalent in the literature to examine individual and developmental differences in working memory. In the *reading and listening span* tests (Daneman and Carpenter 1980), a sentence is presented and some comprehension is required. The participant is also to remember the last word in the sentence or, in a variation of this procedure, is to remember a separate word. After two or more such sentences, all of the final words are to be repeated. In the *counting span* test (Case, Kurland and Goldberg 1982), the participant is to count arrays of dots while remembering the sums, and then to repeat all of the sums at the end of the trial. In the *operation span* test (Turner and Engle 1989), the participant is to complete multiple arithmetic problems, remembering either the answers to the problems or a separate word presented after each problem. The number of sentences, arrays, or problems that can be processed along with successful serial repetition of the items following the processes (indicating that these items were successfully stored) is taken as the working memory span. In sum, the structure of a trial in these studies is:

Process 1, Store item 1, Process 2, Store item 2 .... Process n, Store item n; Recall of items

The finding has been that this storage and processing type of test generally yields correlations with aptitudes that are considerably stronger and more consistent than the correlations between simple span tasks and aptitudes, and that are general across the processing domains

(Conway, Kane, Bunting *et al.* 2005; Daneman and Merikle 1996; Kane, Hambrick, Tuholski *et al.* 2004). At times, the correlations have been strong enough to suggest that working memory may be the key factor distinguishing between individuals with higher or lower intelligence (Conway, Cowan, Bunting *et al.* 2002; Engle, Tuholski, Laughlin *et al.* 1999; Kyllonen and Christal 1990).

Nevertheless, there are problems with this approach. These correlations are not useful in understanding intelligence unless we can understand what mechanisms are indexed by the tests of working memory. Perhaps the high correlations occur only because the working memory tasks require skills other than the temporary storage of information. For example, consider the original version of the listening and reading span tasks, in which the last word of every sentence is to be remembered (Daneman and Carpenter 1980). It seems theoretically possible that this can be carried out by using long-term memory to retrieve the sentences, using their meaning or grammatical structure as cues. These remembered sentences would serve in turn as strong cues to the last word in each sentence.

This hypothesized retrieval method would lead to the prediction that response times should be much longer for listening or reading spans than for other types of working memory test, in which there are no strong linguistic cues. Indeed, this was found to be the case, by Cowan *et al.* (2003). For example, Table 3.3 shows the mean response durations to two-item lists for three types of span in three age groups. Clearly, in all age groups, responses were longer in listening span than in digit span or counting span, and this difference between tasks was exaggerated in young children. Based on these findings alone, one might consider these original versions of listening and reading span to be potentially invalid measures of working memory, because a long-term retrieval strategy is involved. However, it does not necessarily invalidate the other measures of working memory that incorporate separate processing and storage components.

Another possible drawback of storage and processing tasks is that they require dual-task coordination. For some individuals at least, this poses a difficulty that depends on central executive functioning and can be separate from working memory storage (Logie, Cocchini, Della Sala *et al.* 2004). Fortunately, though, the incorporation of separate storage and processing components may not be necessary after all. Recent studies lead to a reinterpretation of why they correlate so well with aptitudes; that is, why they 'work'.

The original interpretation was that both processing and storage must be involved in a working memory task for it to work well. An alternative interpretation is that the processing episodes merely prevent covert rehearsal, which can become relatively automatic in adults (Guttentag 1984) and can circumvent the need to expend a basic working memory capacity on storage per se. Thus, the difficulty of the processing component of the working memory task is not particularly critical (Duff and Logie 2001). The effectiveness of the working memory task instead seems to depend on how tight the schedule of retrieval and central processing is (Barrouillet, Bernardin and Camos 2004; Conlin, Gathercole and Adams 2005; Friedman and Miyake 2004; Lépine, Barrouillet and Camos 2005), so that it can leave little time for rehearsals to sneak in between processing episodes.

As emphasized by Cowan (2001), there are some sorts of working memory task in which rehearsal is not feasible despite the absence of a dual task. In some of these tasks, an array of items

Table 3.3 Response durations in seconds for two-item lists, after Cowan *et al.* (2003), Experiment 2

Measure	Grade 3	Grade 5	Adult
Digit span	1.57	1.64	1.40
Counting span	2.43	1.94	1.58
Listening span	5.74	3.74	2.48

is presented too quickly for rehearsal to be possible. A classic example is the array memory procedure of Sperling (1960), in which a briefly presented array of characters was followed by a partial-report cue. A more recent example is the visual array comparison task of Luck and Vogel (1997), in which an array of small, differently colored squares is followed by a second array, within about 1 sec of the first, that matches the first array or differs in the color of one square. In one version of the task, to make the decision easier, the second array includes one encircled square and, if any square changed color, it was that one. The task is to indicate whether the square changed color. This task is unaffected by the exact duration of the brief, first array and unaffected by the need to recite digits during the task to suppress, provided that the recited digits do not impose a substantial memory load (Luck and Vogel 1997; Morey and Cowan 2004, 2005). Adults can carry out this task almost perfectly with 3 or 4 squares in each array, but performance drops dramatically as the number of squares increases beyond working memory capacity.

Another example of a working memory task that does not include a separate processing component, but still makes rehearsal infeasible under some circumstances, is running memory span (Pollack, Johnson and Knaff 1959). In this sort of task, a long list of items ends unpredictably, after which the task is to recall as many items as possible (or a certain requested number of items) from the end of the list. If the list is presented very quickly (3 or 4 words per sec, which can be done with spoken words without losing intelligibility), it is impossible to rehearse. In fact, Hockey (1973) found that, with rapid presentation in a running span task, rehearsal instructions led to *worse* performance than instructions to wait passively for the list to end. (With a slow presentation, in contrast, rehearsal instructions help.)

Cowan, Elliott, Saults *et al.* (2005) recently showed that working memory tasks that do not allow much rehearsal, but nevertheless do not include separate storage and processing components, do very well in accounting for variance in aptitude tests. They did not do quite as well as listening span or counting span tests, but the extra variance accounted for by those tests appeared to be mostly task-specific and not general across both types of storage and processing task. Therefore, the tasks such as visual array comparisons and running span could be viewed as purer indicants of working memory capacity. They, like the storage and processing tasks, did much better than simple digit span in accounting for aptitude test results.

An additional expectation could be drawn from our analysis of this single-component type of working memory task. Young children are typically unable to rehearse automatically the way that adults do. Therefore, in young children, even simple digit spans should show a high correlation with aptitudes. This is exactly what Cowan, Elliott, Saults *et al.* (2005) found, as is shown in Table 3.4. In second- and fourth-grade children, digit span had a high value in predicting a general factor of intelligence extracted across verbal and nonverbal tests. In sixth-grade children and adults, in contrast, digit span was of no predictive value.

Table 3.4 Proportion of the within-age-group variance in *g* that is accounted for by three types of tasks in two age ranges, after Cowan, Elliott, Saults *et al.* (2005)

Type of working memory task	Grades 2, 4	Grade 6, College
Traditional storage and processing dual tasks	0.15*	0.15*
No dual task, but rehearsal is not feasible	0.14*	0.11*
Digit span; rehearsal is possible for older participants	0.14*	0.01, n.s.
All working memory measures taken together	0.24*	0.17*

* $p < 0.05$, regression; n.s. = not significant.

Premise 3: Working memory performance depends on the notion of capacity, expressed in terms of chunks

This discussion of what types of test predict aptitudes leads to the question of what core capacity exists and plays a role in aptitude. In a famous paper, Miller (1956) noted that people seem able to recall about seven items in a span test, plus or minus a couple. However, in the same paper he emphasized the importance of the ability to group items together to form higher-level, meaningful units or *chunks*. As a compelling example (not used by Miller), the letter string BBCCIAFBI would be difficult to remember as nine separate letters but it is rather easy to remember if one recognizes three acronyms for well-known agencies, the British Broadcasting Corporation (BBC), the Central Intelligence Agency (CIA), and the Federal Bureau of Investigation (FBI). Then it remains possible that the reason people can remember about seven items is that they rapidly form new, larger chunks of information. The reason why telephone numbers are typically presented in groups of three and four digits is probably to assist in the formation of new chunks. It is also possible that rehearsal of the digits in a repeating loop (Baddeley 1986) is used to form these chunks.

One of the founding fathers of the field of cognitive psychology, Donald Broadbent, recognized that there is probably a core capacity that remains after mnemonic strategies like grouping and rehearsal do not operate (Broadbent 1975). He suggested that this core capacity is three items. (Conceptually, that is three chunks given an absence of grouping.) He gave the example of the list length resulting in perfect performance; usually, across many trials, no more than three items. Another example he gave was that recall from long-term memory requires repeatedly refilling and emptying working memory, as a conduit between the long-term store and voluntary response processes. For example, when one is asked to recall all of the states of the US, the answers come out in bursts of just a few states at a time.

Cowan (2001) looked more systematically for situations in which each item remains a separate chunk because of aspects of the task that prevent grouping and rehearsal. Some of these situations are summarized in Table 3.5. What was remarkable from this survey was that diverse types of situation converged on an estimate of 3 to 5 items recalled in these circumstances.

Table 3.5 Some procedures in which each item remains a separate chunk, after Cowan (2001)

Measuring the number of stimuli that are recalled perfectly, which would not be expected if recall was based on a chunking or rehearsal strategy (Broadbent 1975)
Noting the way in which long-term retrieval depends on repeatedly refilling working memory capacity, so that bursts of items are produced (Broadbent 1975)
Imposing information overload in a spatial array to be remembered (Sperling 1960)
Imposing information overload in a rapid and unpredictable series to be remembered, as in running memory span (Hockey 1973)
Requiring memory of a verbal sequence that was ignored at the time of its presentation (Cowan, Nugent, Elliott *et al.* 1999)
Imposing a rehearsal-prevention task along with a verbal series (Murray 1968)
Using verbal material in which the chunks are too long to rehearse (Glanzer and Razel 1974)
Using materials in which the configuration of items keeps changing, as in multi-object tracking (Pylyshyn and Storm 1988)
Examining how many elements were included in a newly formed chunk (Ryan 1969)

There is something less than completely satisfying about characterizing the number of chunks that can be recalled entirely on the basis of situations in which each item equals a chunk. How do we know that the task analyses are correct, and how do we know whether the same estimate of capacity (3 to 5 chunks) would emerge in situations in which multiple items are grouped together to form a chunk? We have investigated this question intensively in our recent work. There already was some evidence that people can remember 3 to 5 chunks in a situation in which they are to replicate a chessboard, with pauses between groups of pieces defining a chunk (Gobet and Simon 1998). We hoped to extend the evidence to verbal recall, in which there is strong evidence of chunking processes (e.g., Johnson 1978; Marmurek and Johnson 1978).

Tulving and Patkau (1962) already found that presenting material with associations between items resulted in the recall of larger chunks, but not more chunks. Stimulus lists were series of 24 words that varied in the order of approximation to English, ranging from random words at one extreme to perfect English sentences at the other extreme. In between, the orders of approximation made sense for any *n* words in a row, where *n* increased with the order of approximation, but did not make sense for the entire sentence. For example, in a third-order approximation, each sequence of three words is valid, as in *Today I went home with them out or in our house is cold in winter we think*. ... Free recall was required and the results were to be scored according to serial order: Any series of words recalled in the presented order was considered a single chunk. So if the phrase *Think before you speak up again* were recalled as *up again, you speak*, it would be scored as the recall of two chunks. It was found that the average chunk grew larger with increasing levels of approximation to English but that, at all levels of approximation, 4 to 6 chunks were recalled. There are, though, several shortcomings of this method. Each series may not really be a single chunk in the participant's representation, underestimating the number of chunks recalled; and, conversely, an overall representation of some of the ideas might be used, especially in the higher-order approximations to English, reducing the number of words or chunks that had to be separately retained in working memory. Still, the results show at least a rough agreement with estimates of limited capacity that fall between three items (Broadbent 1975) and seven items (Miller 1956).

Cowan, Chen and Rouder (2004) tried to improve upon this sort of method. Monosyllabic words were exposed to participants sometimes as singletons and sometimes in pairs, to manipulate the strength of the learned pairing. For example, the words *brick* and *hat* might be presented sometimes in isolation and other times, for the same participants, as the consistent pair *brick-hat*. After a large number of presentations of this sort, eight-word lists were presented, each of which had been constructed from pairs that had received the same strength of pairing, in a way that maintained the learned pairings. There were five list types, shown in Table 3.6. Recall was scored

Table 3.6 Recall statistics from Cowan *et al.* (2004) Experiment 1

| Type of study | Chunks recalled per list | | |
	Singletons	Intact pairs	Total
Words studied as singletons 0 times, pairs 0 times	1.44	1.40	2.83
Words studied as singletons 4 times, pairs 0 times	1.79	1.54	3.33
Words studied as singletons 1 times, pairs 3 times	1.25	2.13	3.38
Words studied as singletons 2 times, pairs 2 times	1.27	2.21	3.48
Words studied as singletons 0 times, pairs 4 times	0.46	3.04	3.50

in terms of whether a pair of words was retrieved in the order that had been presented in the list (an intact pair). Items recalled not in an intact pair were considered singletons; these comprised words recalled without the paired word, or word pairs recalled with its two items in the reversed order and/or separated by other words.

The number of intact pairs recalled increased as a function of the strength of pair training, as shown in Table 3.6 (middle column of data). Nevertheless, as the table shows in the last column of data, provided that the words had been included in the study phase of the experiment, the total number of chunks recalled (singletons plus intact pairs) remained rather constant across training conditions. The number of chunks recalled was a bit lower when the words had not been studied at all (first row of data in the table). Theoretically, it would be possible for an intact pair actually to be composed of two singletons in the mental representation that by chance happened to be recalled in the presented order, but a mathematical model indicated that this rarely happened.

In a subsequent study, Chen and Cowan (2005) sought an easier way to score the results of such experiments. We also sought to determine how a limit in terms of the number of chunks recalled could be reconciled with the tendency for lists of monosyllabic words to be recalled better than lists of multisyllabic words, the word length effect of Baddeley *et al.* (1975). To examine these issues, pairs of monosyllabic words were taught and tested over and over, in tests in which the first member of the pair cued recall of the second. Other monosyllabic words were presented as singletons intermixed with the pairs. The entire word set was presented repeatedly until both cued recall of each pair and recognition of each singleton as such reached 100 per cent correct. At that point, it was fair to assume that each learned pair was a single chunk and that singletons and learned pairs were equated for familiarity. (Lists of singletons that had not been included formed another control condition, and showed that familiarity training with singletons was actually not very important, probably because they were so familiar to the participants.) Both free and serial recall were used in separate experiments, and list length varied.

Opposing predictions for the proportion of words recalled correctly could be formulated on the basis of a chunk limit or a length limit. According to a chunk limit (Cowan *et al.* 2004), the proportion correct should be similar for a list of n learned pairs and a list of n pre-exposed singletons because both of them contain n chunks. In contrast, according to a length limit (Baddeley *et al.* 1975), the proportion correct should be similar for a list of n learned pairs and a list of $2n$ pre-exposed singletons because both of them include the same number of monosyllabic words and therefore are the same length.

Table 3.7 shows what happened. Under some circumstances, the results conformed to the prediction based on a chunk limit almost perfectly. This happened in free recall when the lists were relatively long (six learned pairs). The results were very similar in serial recall if the data were scored without penalty for order errors, although the table does not include that result. However, under other circumstances, the results conformed to the prediction based on a length limit almost perfectly. This happened when serial recall results were scored as correct only for items recalled in the correct serial positions, provided that the lists were relatively short (four learned pairs). In other circumstances, intermediate results were obtained. Chen and Cowan (2005) suggested a theoretical interpretation in which there is a basic limit in the number of chunks that can be retained in working memory, but in which the core holding mechanism does not do a very good job of retaining the serial order of the chunks. To retain serial order, a phonological rehearsal mechanism (Baddeley 1986) comes into play, and it is limited to about the amount that the participant can rehearse in 2 sec (Baddeley *et al.* 1975). Thus, a length limit applies within the range that the phonological store can manage; that amounts to about eight monosyllables. The serial order-preserving mechanism might have to work in combination with the chunk-preserving mechanism.

Table 3.7 Proportion of words correctly recalled in lists by condition, Chen and Cowan (2005)

Type of recall	Prior exposure to words as	Proportion of words correct	Learned pairs: limiting factor(s)
Free recall	4 Learned pairs	0.84	Both factors?
Free recall	4 Singletons	0.93	
Free recall	8 Singletons	0.60	
Free recall	6 Learned pairs	0.73[a]	Chunk limit
Free recall	6 Singletons	0.75[a]	
Free recall	12 Singletons	0.45	
Serial recall	4 Learned pairs	0.54[b]	Length limit
Serial recall	4 Singletons	0.95	
Serial recall	8 Singletons	0.48[b]	
Serial recall	6 Learned pairs	0.35	Both factors?
Serial recall	6 Singletons	0.54	
Serial recall	12 Singletons	0.18	

Note: Proportions with the same letter superscript do not significantly differ. Serial recall: strict scoring.

Premise 4: the core working-memory capacity limit is related to the scope of attention

What property distinguishes between individuals who do better on tests of working memory, and also do better on aptitude tests, versus those who score lower? According to Randall Engle and his associates (e.g., Kane *et al*. 2001, 2004), a key characteristic is the ability to control attention. For example, Kane *et al*. examined performance in an *antisaccade* task in which the natural tendency to look at a suddenly appearing object is to be resisted; the participant is rewarded for instead looking in the other direction. Similarly, others have argued that what is critical is one particular attention-related executive function, such as the ability to inhibit irrelevant information (Gernsbacher 1993; Lustig, May and Hasher 2001; May, Hasher and Kane 1999) or the ability to update information in working memory (Friedman, Miyake, Corley *et al*. 2006). We (Cowan 2005a; Cowan *et al*. 2005) have explored the possibility that it is not one function of attention specifically, but attention more generally that is important for individual differences in working memory. The focus of attention might zoom out to apprehend the maximum number of items, or zoom in to hold on to a goal in the face of potent interference. Individuals who are better able to apprehend a field of items when the task requires it may also be the ones able to concentrate on a difficult goal when the task requires that.

In a recent study (Cowan, Fristoe, Elliott *et al*. in press), we examined this contention using individual and developmental differences. A task that was assumed to reflect attention zoomed out (i.e., the scope of attention) was the two-array comparison procedure modeled after Luck and Vogel (1997). A task that was used to examine attention zoomed in to maintain a difficult goal (i.e., control of attention) was one in which there was a cue to pay attention either to a list of printed letters or to a concurrent list of spoken digits. After each series, memory for the attended or the ignored list was tested. The measure of the control of attention was the extent to which memory for attended lists surpassed memory for ignored lists. This measure was much higher in adults than in children, who showed little evidence of being able to control their attention in this situation, even in a subsample in which children's accuracy of monitoring the attended channel was matched to the adults. Among adults, there was a significant correlation between the scope of attention and control of attention tasks, $r = 0.34$. A composite measure of intelligence was related to the scope of attention, $r = 0.52$, and also to the control of attention, $r = 0.47$. The two types of attention shared 12 per cent of the variance in intelligence; the scope of attention uniquely contributed another 15 per cent, whereas the control of attention uniquely contributed another 10 per cent. So there appears to be a common attention mechanism that is supplemented by some specialized components for apprehension versus control functions of attention. According to neurological evidence reviewed by Cowan (1995, 2005a, b) these would be primarily parietal versus frontal lobe mechanisms, respectively, working together closely.

In other research we have asked whether the chunk limit in working memory retention is truly a limit in attention, as we have supposed. Morey and Cowan (2004) asked whether the array-comparison procedure could be interrupted by a memory load originating in spoken digits. One would not expect such interference if visual arrays are saved entirely in an automatically held, visually specific buffer like the visuospatial sketch pad of Baddeley (1986). In contrast, one might expect interference if visual arrays are saved at least partly in an attention-demanding manner and attention is needed also for retention of the spoken digits. In their procedure, Morey and Cowan presented acoustic instructions for verbal recitation, followed by two arrays. After indicating whether the arrays were the same or different, the verbal stimuli (if any) were to be recalled. The verbal recitation conditions included:

1. no recitation,
2. recitation of a random two-digit load, which is a very light load,
3. recitation of the participant's own seven-digit telephone number, a light load despite more digits because one's own telephone number can maintained without holding multiple chunks in working memory, and
4. a random seven-digit memory load.

The results are shown in Table 3.8. Neither a two-digit load nor recitation of the known telephone number had much effect on visual array performance. However, a random seven-digit load did have an effect. The effect was particularly severe when the digits were incorrectly remembered, a situation in which attention would have been recruited to the digit-recitation task and away from the visual arrays.

Some remaining issues were addressed by Morey and Cowan (2005). The data are shown in some detail in Table 3.9, separately for different sizes of arrays. The data are shown both in term of the proportion correct and in term of a formula that estimates the number of items retained in

Table 3.8 Proportion of correct comparison of two visual arrays under various digit recital conditions, from Morey and Cowan (2004), collapsed across 4-, 6- and 8-item arrays

Memory load condition	Proportion correct
No memory load	0.91
Two-digit memory load	0.92
Own seven-digit phone number recited	0.90
Seven-digit memory load (all trials)	0.85
Seven-digit memory load incorrectly recalled	0.74

Table 3.9 Proportion correct comparison of two visual arrays (and capacity estimate) under various array and digit load conditions, after Morey and Cowan (2005), Experiment 1

Verbal task condition	Number of items per array		
	4	6	8
No verbal task	0.95 (3.60)	0.87 (4.40)	0.80 (4.80)
Seven-digit load silently held	0.93 (3.44)	0.85 (4.20)	0.75 (4.00)
Seven-digit load recited from before array 1	0.85 (2.80)	0.75 (3.00)	0.65 (2.40)
Seven-digit load recited between arrays only	0.79 (2.32)	0.69 (2.28)	0.62 (1.92)

working memory (Cowan 2001; Cowan *et al.* 2005). The data show that the effect of a memory load was much larger when the load was recited aloud (as was required by Morey and Cowan 2004) than when the load was retained silently (as in other studies, such as Cocchini, Logie, Della Sala *et al.* 2002). Aloud recitation may require more attention, given that silent retention of verbal materials can make use of a rehearsal mechanism that operates without much attention in adults (Guttentag 1984). The data show further that the interference from verbal recitation occurs during the maintenance of the first array; visual array comparison performance was impaired more when verbal recitation began between the arrays than when it began sooner, before the first array. All of this supports the notion that visual arrays are maintained with the assistance of attention.

Although verbal working memory benefits from rehearsal, we are working on obtaining evidence that it, too, relies on attention in certain circumstances. One such circumstance is when the memoranda come from several semantic categories and surpass the ability of rehearsal mechanism, which encourages the use of semantically based chunking mechanisms rather than phonological rehearsal. Bunting and Cowan (2005) presented four words in each of three semantic categories (e.g., body parts, animals and tools), with the words in each semantic category presented in a different color (red, blue, or green). These were followed by a rehearsal cue that was the semantic category (e.g., *animals?*) or a color category (e.g., *blue?*), thus encouraging attention to the color as well as the category during presentation of the list. The main question of the experiment was whether the presentation of the cue in a different color from the targeted words would require extra attention. The color mismatch (second row of data in Table 3.10) had a detrimental effect when the mismatch trials were rare (left-hand column of data), but not when the mismatch trials were common (right-hand column of data). This suggests that when mismatch trials were rare, those rare mismatch trials recruited or required attention and interfered with

Table 3.10 Proportion of targeted words recalled in various retrieval-cue conditions, after Bunting and Cowan (2005)

Type of retrieval cue	Percentage mismatch trials	
	12.5%	50%
Category cue presented in same color as targeted items	0.62	0.55
Category cue presented in a color different from targets	0.54	0.56
Category cue presented in a neutral, black color	0.63	0.56

Note: Color-cue trials (not shown) accounted for half of the different-color (i.e., mismatch) trials in the 50 per cent-mismatch condition, but none in the 12.5 per cent-mismatch condition.

Table 3.11 Response times for different proactive interference conditions and set sizes, after Cowan, Johnson and Saults (2005)

List length	Proactive interference condition (milliseconds)		
	Low	High	Difference
Three items	851	853	2, n.s.
Four items	906	923	17, n.s.
Six items	940	994	54*
Eight items	965	1058	93*

* $p < 0.05$, Tukey Test; n.s. = not significant

recall by drawing attention away from the list items. Converging evidence on the use of attention in verbal recall comes from a task in which running memory span is combined with an attention-demanding, button-press task, presented during the retention interval, that is modeled after the antisaccade task (Bunting and Cowan 2004).

Finally, we have explored other means to draw inferences about the attentional demands of verbal working memory. We have relied upon *proactive interference*, the tendency for retrieval to suffer interference from previous, similar material. The logic is that, if the materials to be remembered are held within the focus of attention, they are less susceptible to proactive interference than if the materials to be remembered are held at least partly in some other portion of memory, where they can be confused with previous materials (cf. Halford, Maybery and Bain 1988). Cowan, Johnson and Saults (2005) presented lists that were followed by a probe item. The task was to indicate as quickly as possible whether the probe item was in the list. On high-proactive-interference trials, the current trial was preceded by several other trials using items from the same semantic category, including some of the same words. Sometimes the lists were presented with all items at once and sometimes they were presented one item at a time, but the results did not differ between those conditions. When the list was short enough to fit within the focus of attention most of the time (three and four items long), there was no effect of proactive interference. However, when the list was longer (six and eight items long), there was an effect of proactive interference, as shown in Table 3.11. The results suggest that three and often four items were held in the focus of attention.

Other theorists have reached different conclusions. Oberauer (2002, 2005) believes that there is a one-chunk focus of attention surrounded by a capacity-limited region or fringe holding up to about four chunks. However, his results also could be explained with the notion that there is a single focus of attention that holds up to about four chunks in the average adult, but with a prioritization of the items in the focus of attention.

Concluding remarks

We have argued on the basis of recent evidence (most of which is summarized in Tables 3.1– 3.11) for four related premises:

1. that working memory is not just general processing efficiency;

2. that the relation between working memory and intellectual maturation and aptitude does not depend on using a dual task to examine working memory;

3. that working memory performance depends on the notion of capacity, expressed in terms of chunks; and

4. that the core working-memory capacity limit is related to the scope of attention.

We believe it to be useful that these premises have been stated separately because evidence against one of them would not necessarily invalidate the others. Together they form a theoretical view (Cowan *et al.* 2005) that has practical, theoretical, and philosophical implications.

Practically, we have shown that considering both the scope of attention and the control of attention can lead to excellent predictions of aptitude in a principled manner (Cowan *et al.* in press). These days when video games are everywhere, measurements of attention may be of higher construct validity than the nonverbal measures within intelligence tests that are used to estimate fluid or native intelligence. Those nonverbal measures were probably intended to examine how individuals deal with novel situations but the situations may be too similar to video games, television shows, or school materials to be sufficiently novel to today's test-takers.

Theoretically, we believe that we are getting closer to an understanding of the basic limits that can be used to predict performance in a range of cognitive tasks. For example, it is helpful to know when chunk limits apply and when length limits apply in verbal recall (Chen and Cowan 2005). It is helpful to understand something about the attention requirements of working memory tasks (Bunting and Cowan 2005; Morey and Cowan 2004, 2005).

Philosophically, the portion of working memory that is based on the focus of attention is closely related to the conscious mind (Baars and Franklin 2003; James 1890). We hope that explorations of this aspect of working memory will lead to a more satisfying understanding of the phenomenological aspect of cognitive psychology, a bridge between behavioral results and our personal understanding of ourselves as human beings.

References

Baars, BJ and Franklin, S (2003). How conscious experience and working memory interact. *Trends in Cognitive Sciences*, 7, 166–172.

Baddeley, AD (1986). *Working Memory*. Oxford: Clarendon Press.

Baddeley, A and Hitch, GJ (1974). Working memory. In G. Bower (ed), *Recent Advances in Learning and Motivation*, Vol. VIII (pp. 47–89). New York: Academic Press.

Baddeley, AD and Logie, RH (1999). Working memory: The multiple-component model. In A Miyake and P Shah (eds), *Models of Working Memory: Mechanisms of active maintenance and executive control* (pp. 28–61). Cambridge: Cambridge University Press.

Baddeley, AD, Thomson, N and Buchanan, M (1975). Word length and the structure of short-term memory. *Journal of Verbal Learning and Verbal Behavior*, 14, 575–589.

Barrouillet, P, Bernardin, S and Camos, V (2004). Time constraints and resource sharing in adults' working memory spans. *Journal of Experimental Psychology: General*, 133, 83–100.

Broadbent, DE (1975). The magic number seven after fifteen years. In A Kennedy and A Wilkes (eds), *Studies in Long-term Memory*, (pp. 3–18). Oxford: Wiley.

Bunting, MF and Cowan, N (2004). *Working-memory retrieval takes attention: Effects of distraction under time pressure*. Poster presented at the annual meeting of the Psychonomic Society, Minneapolis, November.

Bunting, MF and Cowan, N (2005). Working memory and flexibility in awareness and attention. *Psychological Research*, 69, 412–419.

Case, R, Kurland, DM and Goldberg, J (1982). Operational efficiency and the growth of short-term memory span. *Journal of Experimental Child Psychology*, 33, 386–404.

Chen, Z and Cowan, N (2005). Chunk limits and length limits in immediate recall: A reconciliation. *Journal of Experimental Psychology: Learning, Memory, and Cognition*, 31, 1235–1249.

Cocchini, G, Logie, RH, Della Sala, S, MacPherson, SE and Baddeley, AD (2002). Concurrent performance of two memory tasks: Evidence for domain-specific working memory systems. *Memory and Cognition*, 30, 1086–1095.

Conlin, JA, Gathercole, SE and Adams, JW (2005). Children's working memory: Investigating performance limitations in complex span tasks. *Journal of Experimental Child Psychology*, *90*, 303–317.

Conway, ARA, Cowan, N, Bunting, MF, Therriault, DJ and Minkoff, SRB (2002). A latent variable analysis of working memory capacity, short-term memory capacity, processing speed, and general fluid intelligence. *Intelligence*, *30*, 163–183.

Conway, ARA, Kane, MJ, Bunting, MF, Hambrick, DZ, Wilhelm, O and Engle, RW (2005). Working memory span tasks: A methodological review and user's guide. *Psychonomic Bulletin and Review*, *12*, 769–786.

Cowan, N (1995). *Attention and Memory: An integrated framework*. Oxford Psychology Series, No. 26. New York: Oxford University Press. (Paperback edition 1997.)

Cowan, N (2001). The magical number 4 in short-term memory: A reconsideration of mental storage capacity. *Behavioral and Brain Sciences*, *24*, 87–185.

Cowan, N (2005a). Working-memory capacity limits in a theoretical context. In C Izawa and N Ohta (eds), *Human Learning and Memory: Advances in theory and applications. The Fourth Tsukuba international conference on memory* (pp. 155–175). Mahwah, NJ: Erlbaum.

Cowan, N (2005b). *Working Memory Capacity*. New York: Psychology Press.

Cowan, N, Chen, Z and Rouder, JN (2004). Constant capacity in an immediate serial-recall task: A logical sequel to Miller (1956). *Psychological Science*, *15*, 634–640.

Cowan, N, Elliott, EM, Saults, JS, Morey, CC, Mattox, S, Hismjatullina, A and Conway, ARA (2005). On the capacity of attention: Its estimation and its role in working memory and cognitive aptitudes. *Cognitive Psychology*, *51*, 42–100.

Cowan, N, Elliott, EM, Saults, JS, Nugent, LD, Bomb, P and Hismjatullina, A (2006). Rethinking speed theories of cognitive development: Increasing the rate of recall without affecting accuracy. *Psychological Science*, *17*, 63–73.

Cowan, N, Fristoe, NM, Elliott, EM, Brunner, RP and Saults, JS (in press). Scope of attention, control of attention, and intelligence in children and adults. *Memory and Cognition*

Cowan, N, Johnson, TD and Saults, JS (2005). Capacity limits in list item recognition: Evidence from proactive interference. *Memory*, *13*, 293–299.

Cowan, N, Nugent, LD, Elliott, EM, Ponomarev, I and Saults, JS (1999). The role of attention in the development of short-term memory: Age differences in the verbal span of apprehension. *Child Development*, *70*, 1082–1097.

Cowan, N, Towse, JN, Hamilton, Z, Saults, JS, Elliott, EM, Lacey, JF, Moreno, MV and Hitch, GJ (2003). Children's working-memory processes: A response-timing analysis. *Journal of Experimental Psychology: General*, *132*, 113–132.

Cowan, N, Wood, NL, Wood, PK, Keller, TA, Nugent, LD and Keller, CV (1998). Two separate verbal processing rates contributing to short-term memory span. *Journal of Experimental Psychology: General*, *127*, 141–160.

Daneman, M and Carpenter, PA (1980). Individual differences in working memory and reading. *Journal of Verbal Learning and Verbal Behavior*, *19*, 450–466.

Daneman, M and Merikle, PM (1996). Working memory and language comprehension: A meta-analysis. *Psychonomic Bulletin and Review*, *3*, 422–433.

Duff, SC and Logie, RH (2001). Processing and storage in working memory span. *Quarterly Journal of Experimental Psychology*, *54*(A), 31–48.

Engle, RW, Tuholski, SW, Laughlin, JE and Conway, ARA (1999). Working memory, short-term memory, and general fluid intelligence: A latent-variable approach. *Journal of Experimental Psychology: General*, *128*, 309–331.

Friedman, NP and Miyake, A (2004). The reading span test and its predictive power for reading comprehension ability. *Journal of Memory and Language*, *51*, 136–158.

Friedman, NP, Miyake, A, Corley, RP, Young, SE, DeFries, JC and Hewitt, JK (2006). Not all executive functions are related to intelligence. *Psychological Science*, *17*, 172–179.

Gathercole, SE and Hitch, GJ (1993). Developmental changes in short-term memory: A revised working memory perspective. In AF Collins, SE Gathercole, MA Conway and PE Morris (eds), *Theories of Memory* (pp. 189–209). Hove: Lawrence Erlbaum Associates.

Gernsbacher, MA (1993). Less skilled readers have less efficient suppression mechanisms. *Psychological Science*, 4, 294–298.

Glanzer, M and Razel, M (1974). The size of the unit in short-term storage. *Journal of Verbal Learning and Verbal Behavior*, 13, 114–131.

Gobet, F and Simon, HA (1998). Expert chess memory: Revisiting the chunking hypothesis. *Memory*, 6, 225–255.

Guttentag, RE (1984). The mental effort requirement of cumulative rehearsal: A developmental study. *Journal of Experimental Child Psychology*, 37, 92–106.

Halford, GS, Maybery, MT and Bain, JD (1988). Set-size effects in primary memory: An age-related capacity limitation? *Memory and Cognition*, 16, 480–487.

Hitch, GJ, Towse, JN and Hutton, U (2001). What limits children's working memory span? Theoretical accounts and applications for scholastic development. *Journal of Experimental Psychology: General*, 130, 184–198.

Hockey, R (1973). Rate of presentation in running memory and direct manipulation of input-processing strategies. *Quarterly Journal of Experimental Psychology*, 25(A), 104–111.

James, W (1890). *The Principles of Psychology*. New York: Henry Holt.

Johnson, NF (1978). The memorial structure of organized sequences. *Memory and Cognition*, 6, 233–239.

Kail, R and Salthouse, TA (1994). Processing speed as a mental capacity. *Acta Psychologica*, 86, 199–255.

Kane, MJ, Bleckley, MK, Conway, ARA and Engle, RW (2001). A controlled-attention view of working-memory capacity. *Journal of Experimental Psychology: General*, 130, 169–183.

Kane, MJ, Hambrick, DZ, Tuholski, SW, Wilhelm, O, Payne, TW and Engle, RE (2004). The generality of working-memory capacity: A latent-variable approach to verbal and visuo-spatial memory span and reasoning. *Journal of Experimental Psychology: General*, 133, 189–217.

Kyllonen, PC and Christal, RE (1990). Reasoning ability is (little more than) working-memory capacity? *Intelligence*, 14, 389–433.

Lépine, R, Barrouillet, P and Camos, V (2005). What makes working memory spans so predictive of high level cognition? *Psychonomic Bulletin and Review*, 12, 165–170.

Logie, RH, Cocchini, G, Della Sala, S and Baddeley, AD (2004). Is there a specific executive capacity for dual task co-ordination ? Evidence from Alzheimer's disease. *Neuropsychology*, 18, 504–513.

Luck, SJ and Vogel, EK (1997). The capacity of visual working memory for features and conjunctions. *Nature*, 390, 279–281.

Lustig, C, May, CP and Hasher, L (2001). Working memory span and the role of proactive interference. *Journal of Experimental Psychology: General*, 130, 199–207.

May, CP, Hasher, L and Kane, MJ (1999). The role of interference in memory span. *Memory and Cognition*, 27, 759–767.

Miller, GA (1956). The magical number seven, plus or minus two: Some limits on our capacity for processing information. *Psychological Review*, 63, 81–97.

Miyake, A and shah, P (eds) (1999). *Models of Working Memory: Mechanisms of active maintenance and executive control*. Cambridge: Cambridge University Press.

Marmurek, HH and Johnson, NF (1978). Hierarchical organization as a determinant of sequential learning. *Memory and Cognition*, 6, 240–245.

Morey, CC and Cowan, N (2004). When visual and verbal memories compete: Evidence of cross-domain limits in working memory. *Psychonomic Bulletin and Review*, 11, 296–301.

Morey, CC and Cowan, N (2005). When do visual and verbal memories conflict? The importance of working-memory load and retrieval. *Journal of Experimental Psychology: Learning, Memory, and Cognition*, 31, 703–713.

Murray, DJ (1968). Articulation and acoustic confusability in short-term memory. *Journal of Experimental Psychology*, *78*, 679–684.

Pollack, I, Johnson, IB and Knaff, PR (1959). Running memory span. *Journal of Experimental Psychology*, *57*, 137–146.

Oberauer, K (2002). Access to information in working memory: exploring the focus of attention. *Journal of Experimental Psychology: Learning, Memory, and Cognition*, *28*, 411–421.

Oberauer, K (2005). Control of the contents of working memory – a comparison of two paradigms and two age groups. *Journal of Experimental Psychology: Learning, Memory, and Cognition*, *31*, 714–728.

Pylyshyn, ZW and Storm, RW (1988). Tracking multiple independent targets: Evidence for a parallel tracking mechanism. *Spatial Vision*, *3*, 179–197.

Ryan, J (1969). Grouping and short-term memory: Different means and patterns of groups. *Quarterly Journal of Experimental Psychology*, *21*, 137–147.

Sperling, G (1960). The information available in brief visual presentations. *Psychological Monographs*, *74*. (Whole No. 498.)

Tulving, E and Patkau, JE (1962). Concurrent effects of contextual constraint and word frequency on immediate recall and learning of verbal material. *Canadian Journal of Psychology*, *16*, 83–95.

Turner, ML and Engle, RW (1989). Is working memory capacity task dependent? *Journal of Memory and Language*, *28*, 127–154.

4

The time-based resource-sharing model of working memory

Pierre Barrouillet and Valérie Camos

Since Baddeley and Hitch's (1974) seminal proposal to distinguish between short-term and working memory, several influential models and theories have been put forward to account for the structure and functioning of a working memory thought of as the core system of cognition devoted to the maintenance and processing of relevant information. As Engle and Oransky (1999) suggested, ideas about temporary storage in memory during the previous decades have moved from multi-store models and structural approaches championed by Baddeley and Hitch (1974; Baddeley and Logie 1999) to more dynamic or process-oriented models of working memory (Cowan 1995 1999; Engle, Cantor and Carullo 1992; Engle, Kane and Tuholski 1999; Lovett, Reder and Lebiere 1999; Schneider and Detweiller 1987). By conceiving working memory as the activated part of long-term memory rather than as a structure or a set of cognitive structures, these theories have emphasized functional aspects of cognition related to the way activation is produced, maintained or even inhibited, and to the way cognitive processes use the activated items of knowledge. The main question, which seemed to be 'How is working memory organized?' has progressively become 'How does working memory work?'. We do not claim to know how working memory works and admit that the reader will not find the final answer in this chapter. However, we hope to provide some elements to shed light on questions such as 'How is the relevant information maintained active during concurrent processing?', 'What is the nature of the resource to be shared between maintenance and processing?', 'How is this sharing achieved?', and thus 'What are the limiting factors of working memory functioning?'.

Retracing the history of the literature on short-term and working memory, Engle and Oransky (1999) noted that models have become more complex and more flexible. Whereas the first descriptions of working memory functioning mainly concerned the articulatory loop, which is closest in character to the original concept of a short-term store, further models provided thorough descriptions of the relationships between short- and long-term memory, of processes devoted to the activation and maintenance of information, as well as of the role of attention in selecting relevant information and monitoring working memory functioning. Several complex span tasks designed to evaluate working memory capacity proved to be reliable and predictive of high level cognition, and the relations between working memory capacity, controlled attention and general intelligence have been investigated extensively. However, these models might have overlooked an important factor in accounting for cognition, namely time.

Many models of working memory mentioned time as an important factor, but almost exclusively to account for forgetting from short-term memory. For example, Baddeley (1990, 2000) suggested that the traces within the articulatory or phonological loop decay within about 2 s unless they are maintained by a process of subvocal articulatory rehearsal. Cowan (1995) assumed that activation of the information that is outside the focus of attention declines with time. This hypothesis of a time-related decay of memory traces has even been the basis of a recent account of the processes underlying performance on working memory span tasks put forward by Towse and Hitch (1995; Hitch, Towse and Hutton 2001; Towse, Hitch and Hutton 1998, 2000, 2002). Working memory span tasks are complex span tasks in which the participants have to maintain some to-be-remembered items while performing a concurrent activity. For example, in the counting span task (Case, Kurland and Goldberg 1982), the participants are asked to count dots on cards out loud, and then recall the number of dots on each card. The experimenter varies the number of cards to be counted, and consequently the number of values to be recalled after counting. The counting span is the maximum number of cards the participant is able to remember. According to Towse and Hitch's (1995) hypothesis, the difficulty of the working memory span tasks is due to the fact that the memory traces of the items to be recalled suffer from a time-related decay. Because participants have to switch their attention from processing to storage when performing working memory span tasks, their recall performance would depend on the duration of the processing which in turn determines the retention period during which memory traces fade away (see also Halford, Maybery, O'Hare *et al.* 1994). In all of these theories, time affects maintenance because traces are lost over time through decay, but this time parameter does not affect working memory functioning per se. Even in Towse *et al.*'s (1998) proposals, the switches of attention between the processing and maintenance parts of the complex span tasks are assumed to occur in a simple manner that reflects the way working memory span tasks are structured: attention would be entirely absorbed by counting and there would be no active maintenance of stored totals that competes with the execution of counting operations.

In contrast, we assume that the dual function of a working memory devoted to the active maintenance of information while concurrent processing is performed demands a subtle interplay between activities in which time plays the crucial role. The aim of our time-based resource-sharing model (Barrouillet, Bernardin and Camos 2004) is to describe the time course of working memory functioning, the constraints and limits that affect this functioning, how these limits differ from one individual to another and how they evolve with age. We assume that working memory span tasks constitute an appropriate and in fact ideal model to study working memory functioning. Their dual-task structure perfectly mimics the main constraint our cognitive system is faced with: the need to maintain active and ready for treatment transient short-lived memory items while performing sometimes complex and time-consuming activities. Thus, the time-based resource-sharing model has been developed and tested using traditional but also new working memory span tasks in which time parameters are carefully controlled.

The time-based resource-sharing model: the main proposals

Our model is based on four main proposals. First, we assume that both processing and maintenance require attention, which is a limited resource and that, as a consequence, some sharing is needed. Second, following Cowan (1995) and Towse and Hitch (1995), as soon as attention is switched away, the activation of the memory traces suffers from a time-related decay. Refreshing these decaying memory traces requires their retrieval from memory by attentional focusing. Third, as a consequence, any processing that captures attention would disrupt maintenance by preventing the refreshment of these memory traces through attentional focusing. In a first version of the theory (Barrouillet *et al.* 2004), it was assumed that among the activities that capture attention, those that occupy the retrieval process needed to refresh memory traces should have an especially detrimental effect on maintenance because there is a central bottleneck that constrains retrieval activities. This precise point will be addressed here and we shall see that working memory functioning is limited by a central bottleneck that does not only constrain retrievals but probably any central process. Fourth, because the central bottleneck allows only one central process at a time, sharing attention is time-based. It is assumed that within tasks that require attention there are periods of time during which attention is totally captured, preventing memory traces' refreshment. Thus, attention sharing is achieved through a rapid and frequent switching between processing and maintenance that occurs during the completion of the task.

As far as the first point is concerned, the time-based resource-sharing model assumes that processing and maintenance rely on the same limited attention resource. Most of the main working memory span tasks involve complex activities as processing components (e.g., reading sentences, counting dots, arithmetic equation solving, reasoning). These complex activities often require planning multistep strategies, setting goals and subgoals, and maintaining intermediary results. All of these activities are known to require controlled attention, which is a limited resource considered by Engle as isomorphic with fluid intelligence (Engle *et al.* 1999b; Conway, Kane and Engle 2003). The complex activities used in working memory span tasks require attention not only because they involve high level cognition but also in their most elementary processing steps such as retrievals of knowledge from long-term memory. Indeed, within Anderson's Adaptive Character of Thought (ACT-R) framework, activation of declarative knowledge from long-term memory is achieved through attentional focusing on retrieval cues. Interestingly, Anderson (1993) assumes that the total amount of attention considered as source of activation is limited and probably varies from one individual to another (Lovett *et al.* 1999). Thus, the processing component of most of the working memory span tasks require attention. Moreover, several models of working memory assume that maintenance is also attention-demanding. In line with these specific models, we assume that short-term memory is that part of long-term memory attentionally activated above threshold (Anderson 1993; Cantor and Engle 1993; Cowan 1995; Engle and Oransky 1999; Lovett *et al.* 1999). Working memory would thus contain those items on which attention focuses as well as items that are outside of the focus of attention but sufficiently activated to be readily accessible (Conway and Engle 1994; Cowan 1995). As we noted above, activating items from long-term memory requires attention. Thus, both components of working memory span tasks, and more generally the two main functions of working memory that are maintenance of information and processing rely on the same limited attention resource. As a consequence, some sharing of this resource is needed.

As far as the second point is concerned, the items on which attention is focused receive activation, but this activation decays as soon as attention is switched away (Anderson 1993; Cowan 1995, 1999). As a consequence, the memory items to be recalled in working memory span tasks suffer from a time-related decay when attention is switched away from maintenance (Towse and Hitch 1995). The refreshment of these items before their complete disappearance necessitates their reactivation by attentional focusing. In other words, maintaining items in short-term memory in view of their further recall requires the individual to frequently switch attention away from processing to prevent forgetting.

Thus, and this is our third point, memory decay and, consequently, recall performance would be a function of the time during which the concurrent processing captures attention and thus impedes refreshment. As suggested by Barrouillet and Camos (2001), any processing component that captures some part of the available attention capacity should have this detrimental effect. Whether the detrimental effect of the processing component on recall is due to the necessity to share between processing and maintenance a specific central process such as memory retrieval, or just to the fact that the processing component captures attention and thus impedes refreshment remains an open question. Indeed, the effect of processing on maintenance could be accounted for either by the hypothesis of a bottleneck for retrieval or by the hypothesis of a capture of attention. On the one hand, many studies suggest that when two concurrent tasks rely on the same central process, severe interference can be observed. For example, Rohrer, Pashler and

Etchegaray (1998) demonstrated that two memory retrievals cannot be performed simultaneously, suggesting that there is a central bottleneck for retrieval (Pashler 1998). To account for this fact, the authors suggested the metaphor of a spotlight of retrieval that would be directed at only one category at a time in such a way that multiple categories can simultaneously remain activated for a short while, but only one category can be lit. Thus, in the first version of our model, we assumed that the detrimental effect of processing on maintenance would be particularly pronounced when the processing component involves memory retrievals, which is the case in the main verbal working memory span tasks, because the same retrieval process is also needed to refresh the memory traces (Barrouillet *et al.* 2004).

On the other hand, experimental results have shown that attention-demanding processes interfere with each other, suggesting that there is a central attentional bottleneck that allows just one processing step at a time. For example, Garavan (1998) concluded from a study on attention-switching processes that individuals can attend to just one 'object' in working memory at any one time, results that have been replicated and extended by Oberauer (2003). In the same way, Rohrer and Pashler (2003) demonstrated that a secondary task that does not involve verbal material and does not itself rely on retrievals but requires attention (a serial choice-reaction time task) reduces speed and accuracy of recall in a concurrent free recall task. The authors concluded that memory retrieval is subject to severe interference from unrelated central processing. These results are in line with the hypothesis that any processing component that captures attention would impede the refreshment of the decaying memory traces, recall performance depending on the time during which attention is captured. We will see below that our most recent results suggest that the 'capture of attention' hypothesis is probably more plausible than the more restrictive 'bottleneck for retrieval' hypothesis.

Our fourth assumption is that the sharing of attention is achieved through a process of rapid switching of the focus from processing to maintenance and vice versa. However, there is no need to suppose, as Towse *et al.* (1998) did, that this switching only occurs when the participants are presented with a new item to memorize or with a new problem to solve. As demonstrated by Cowan in the field of recall activities (Cowan 1992; Cowan *et al.* 1994), individuals can engage in a covert retrieval process during short pauses to reactivate decaying memory traces. In the same way, it may well be supposed that, while engaged in the counting, operation solving, or reading component of working memory span tasks, participants may keep short pauses free for the brief reactivation of the memory items by means of a simple mental search without engaging in time-consuming activities such as rehearsal (Cowan *et al.* 1994). Thus, we assume that individuals cope with the requirements of the dual task by a fast and incessant process of attention switching. There is really a resource-sharing process in working memory functioning, but it is time-based.

Time and cognitive load

This conception of working memory delineates in turn a conception of cognitive load that departs from more traditional conceptions that conflate cognitive load with complexity. As we noted earlier, the processing components of traditional working memory span tasks involve complex activities such as reading sentences, counting dots among distractors, solving complex equations or reasoning. The rationale of these tasks is to be found within the theoretical framework of resource-sharing and the hypothesized trade-off between processing and storage (Case 1985): because complex activities are especially resource-demanding, they conflict with the concurrent maintenance of the memory items. There is thus a clear difference between simple span measures assessing short-term memory capacity (e.g., the digit span or the word span), and complex span measures involving storage plus processing that assess working-memory capacity (e.g., counting or reading spans). Within this framework, the more complex and demanding the processing component, the better and the more reliable the working memory task.

As far as we know, Towse and Hitch (1995) were among the first to cast doubt on this conception by suggesting that the detrimental effect of processing on maintenance was not due to the cognitive load it would involve but to its duration. However, as we have seen, these authors proposed a simple effect of time by assuming that there would be no active maintenance of stored items while the processing component of the task is performed (Towse, Hitch and Hutton 2002). In this case, memory traces would suffer from an uninterrupted decay during the phases devoted to processing, recall performance depending on their total duration. Short processing phases would thus reduce the delay between storage and recall, resulting in better recall performance and higher spans.

The time-based resource-sharing model departs from both previous conceptions. It assumes that the cognitive load that an activity involves does not depend on its complexity per se, but neither does it depend on the total duration of the activity. Those tasks that frequently capture attention for lengthy periods of time would involve a high cognitive load by preventing the possibility of running another activity or maintaining items active in short-term memory concurrently. By contrast, the activities that require short and infrequent periods of attentional focusing would permit the switching of attention to other activities, involving a low cognitive load. According to the time-based resource-sharing model, cognitive load depends on the proportion of time during which a given activity captures attention in such a way that the refreshment of memory traces or any other activity that requires attention is impeded. As far as processing components involved in working memory span tasks are concerned, the higher this proportion, the fewer and shorter the periods during which pauses can be kept free to divert attention from processing to the retrieval and the refreshing of decaying memory traces of the items to be recalled.

It is worth noting that this conception also accounts for the fact that complex activities proved to be highly disruptive on recall when used within working memory span task. As Kahneman (1973) suggested, complex activities are not demanding because they are complex but because time pressure is inherent to their structure. For example, solving the equations involved in Turner and Engle's (1989) operation span task or reading the sentences in Daneman and Carpenter's (1980) reading span task can not be interrupted for long periods of time without loosing the thread of the activity. However, our model predicts that complexity is not needed. As Barrouillet and Camos (2001) suggested, even a simple task that would require a continuous attentional focusing, for example an uninterrupted series of retrievals from long-term memory, should result in a heavy cognitive load and should have a highly detrimental effect on recall when inserted into a working memory span task.

Many of the predictions issuing from our theory have been tested using such tasks in which participants were asked to maintain letters in memory while performing a secondary task consisting of reading series of digits presented one by one on screen. We named this task the reading digit span task. For this kind of task cognitive load – that is, the proportion of time during which attention is captured – would be a function of the number of retrievals to be performed, their nature, and the total time allowed to perform them. Cognitive load (CL) would thus correspond to the following:

$$CL = \Sigma \; aN/T$$

where N corresponds to the number of retrievals (i.e., the number of digits to be read), a to a parameter that represents the difficulty of these retrievals, that is to say the time during which these retrievals totally capture attention, and T to the total duration of the activity (the duration of the interletter interval). In this case, cognitive load can be assimilated to the number of

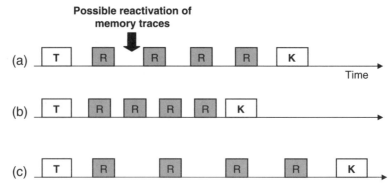

Figure 4.1 Schematic illustration of the time course of the processes involved in a computer-paced working memory span task in which letters must be remembered while the processing component requires successive retrievals (R). The three panels illustrate how variations in the time allowed to perform a fixed number of retrievals constrain the switching process between processing and maintenance. Adapted with permission from Barrouillet, P., Bernardin, S., and Camos, V. (2004). Time constraints and resource sharing in adults' working memory spans. *Journal of Experimental Psychology: General*, 133, 83–100, APA Publisher.

retrievals/time ratio. Reading digits is a very simple activity that cannot be considered as complex. Provided that the digits are presented at a comfortable pace, this activity could allow participants to free up interdigit pauses during which the decaying memory traces of the letters could be retrieved and updated – see panel (a) of Figure 4.1. However, reading the same digits at a faster pace would increase cognitive load by preventing attentional shifting, thus impeding the refreshment of the memory traces and leading to poor recalls. This phenomenon is illustrated in panel (b) of Figure 4.1. By contrast, increasing the time available to read these digits would lead to decrease the cognitive load and would result in better recall performance (panel c).

Two main predictions issue from these proposals. First, working memory spans mainly depend on the rate at which the processing component of the task has to be performed, that is, in our example, on the Number of retrievals/Time ratio. Second, simple activities can have an effect on maintenance which is as detrimental as complex activities provided that they require attention and are also performed at a high rate.

Exploring the cognitive load as the Number of retrievals/Time ratio

The predictions concerning the effect of the Number of Retrievals/Time ratio were tested in a series of experiments using the reading digit span task (Barrouillet *et al.* 2004). The critical aspect of this task lies on the time constraints imposed on the participants, who are not allowed to read the digits at their own pace. In a first experiment (Barrouillet *et al.* 2004, Experiment 4), we manipulated the number of digits to be read while keeping constant the total time allowed to read them. After the presentation of each letter, either 10 or 6 digits were successively displayed on screen at a regular rhythm over a total period of 6 s. In each condition, the length of the series of letters to be remembered was progressively increased from 1 to 7 until the participant failed to recall the letters in the correct order. The time-based resource-sharing model predicts that a larger number of retrievals over a fixed period of time should result in a higher cognitive load and consequently on poorer recall. In line with this hypothesis, the slow-paced condition elicited a higher mean working memory span than the fast-paced condition (4.28 and 2.77 respectively).

In the following experiment, the time allowed to read the digits was manipulated while their number was kept constant (Barrouillet *et al.* 2004, Experiment 5). In the slow-paced condition, participants were given 1s to read each digit, whereas in the fast-paced condition this time was reduced to 600 ms. We predicted that the latter condition would result in a higher cognitive load and thus in poorer recalls. This was exactly what we observed, the slow-paced condition resulting in higher spans than the fast-paced condition (4.76 and 3.01 respectively). This result was of particular interest because it ruled out one of the main predictions issuing from Towse and Hitch's (1995) proposals. Indeed, the fast-paced condition corresponded to a shorter duration of processing. Their theory would predict better recalls because shorter durations of processing involve shorter delays of retention between storage and recall. This was not what we observed, suggesting that, as we surmised, attention must be shared by switching rapidly from processing to maintenance during the intervening activity and that the relative ease of this switching process determines what is called cognitive load.

Finally, we tested the hypothesis that cognitive load is a linear function of the Number of retrievals/Time ratio. Progressively increasing this ratio should result in a smooth and linear decrease in span. For this purpose, nine groups of adult participants were presented with nine different values of the ratio (from 0.4 to 2) resulting from the combination of three different numbers of digits presented (4, 8, or 12) with three total periods (6, 8 or 10 s). As shown in Figure 4.2, recall performance was highly correlated with the ratio, revealing a quasi perfect trade-off between processing

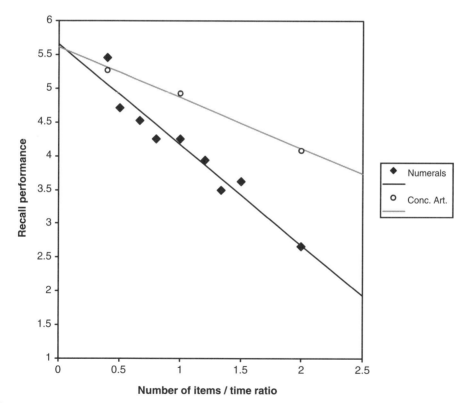

Figure 4.2 Mean working memory spans as a function of the Number of retrievals/Time ratio and the nature of the processing component (reading numerals or saying 'baba') from Barrouillet *et al.* (2004, Experiment 7). Conc. Art. = concurrent articulation. Adapted with permission from Barrouillet, P., Bernardin, S., and Camos, V. (2004). Time constraints and resource sharing in adults' working memory spans. *Journal of Experimental Psychology: General*, 133, 83–100, APA Publisher.

and storage. It could be argued that this relation was merely due to the different levels of articulatory suppression that the nine ratio values involved and not to any cognitive load. Uttering digits would simply block the articulatory loop and impair the rehearsal of the letters. In order to control for this effect, three additional groups of adults were presented with the same task but the digits were replaced by the syllable BA which participants were asked to read aloud each time it appeared on screen. This control involved only three ratio values of 0.4, 1 and 2 (4, 8 and 12 syllables presented respectively over 10, 8 and 6 s). Our theory predicted that spans should decrease as the ratio increases, even when the task consists only in attending to a signal and always pronouncing the same syllable. However, this decrease should be less pronounced in the control condition than when reading numerals because the participants simply have to keep track of a habituated stimulus and always produce the same response. Accordingly, the resulting spans decreased as the number of syllables to be uttered increased but this effect was smaller than that observed with digits (Figure 4.2).

Lépine, Bernardin and Barrouillet (2005) conducted an even more stringent test of the alternative hypothesis of an effect of the Number of retrievals/Time ratio that would only be due to articulatory suppression. In their Experiment 3, they manipulated the time allowed to perform a task that did not involve any articulatory suppression. As in the previous experiments, participants were presented with a task in which letters were to be remembered while digits were successively presented on screen. However, they were not asked to read these digits but to judge their parity by silently pressing identified keys on keyboard for odd and even. The time allowed to judge the parity of each number was 800 ms in the fast-paced condition and 1500 ms in the slow-paced condition. Once more, the former condition resulted in lower recall performance than the latter (mean spans of 3.81 and 5.10).

Overall, these observations lent strong support to the main assumptions of the time-based resource-sharing model. First, time appears to play a major role in determining the impact of the processing component on the concurrent maintenance of information, but in a subtle manner. For example, reducing the total duration of the processing component did not lead to better but to poorer recalls when the amount of stimuli to be processed is kept constant. Keeping this total duration constant led to poorer recalls when the amount of processing was increased. The linear trend reported in Figure 4.2 made clear that as we hypothesized, what matters is the proportion of time during which the processing component captures attention and impedes the retrieval and refreshment of the decaying memory traces. Second, the smooth decrease in span when the difficulty of the processing component increases suggests that there is a quasi perfect trade-off between processing and storage, exactly as the resource-sharing theoretical framework predicts. Taken together, these two points suggest that the resource-sharing that occurs between processing and storage is time-based.

Though these first results were in line with our theory, several counterintuitive claims still needed to be tested. For example, one of the predictions of our theory is that any simple task that captures attention can disrupt concurrent maintenance as efficiently as a complex activity provided that it has to be performed under sufficient time pressure. The studies reported above demonstrated that time pressure has an effect on recall performance, but they did not directly compare the effect of simple processing under time-pressure with the effect of complex activities such as reading or equation solving. Are simple activities as disruptive as complex tasks used in traditional span tasks? The next section addresses this question.

Is cognitive load a matter of complexity?

Intuitively, reading sentences for comprehension or solving complex equations is more demanding than identifying letters or browsing in the numerical chain by adding or subtracting one.

Indeed, we often experience the former activities as laborious, requiring all our attention, and we are well aware of many possible mistakes. By contrast, we rarely experience the latter activities as arduous but instead as undemanding, nearly automatic, the correct answer coming into our mind without any apparent effort. Cognitive psychology echoes these intuitions based on introspective experiences through the widespread notions of controlled and automatic processes, this opposition underpinning most of the theoretical constructs related to working memory. On the one hand, reading sentences and solving equations undoubtedly pertain to those activities that require selection of relevant information among the flow of incoming stimuli and inner knowledge, to select the appropriate and inhibit the irrelevant strategies, and to control their process, that is activities that are known to involve the central executive and to consume cognitive resources (Engle *et al.* 1999a). On the other hand, identifying letters or browsing in the numerical chain probably rely on direct and automatic retrievals from long-term memory that are often considered as leaving the pool of resources intact (Rosen and Engle 1997). However, according to the time-based resource-sharing model, this distinction would only hold when considered in a temporal vacuum. When taking time into account, reading letters or adding 1 to small numbers could become as demanding and consume the same amount of cognitive resource as reading sentences and solving equations! Should we really believe that the former activities can produce the same disruptive effect on concurrent maintenance in short-term memory as tasks that we experience as being so demanding?

This was tested by Lépine, Bernardin and Barrouillet (2005). The authors compared recall performance in either self-paced traditional working memory span tasks involving complex processing components or new computer-paced tasks involving processing components as simple as those we evoked above. They predicted that simple processing components presented at a slow and comfortable pace should have a low impact on concurrent maintenance, thus resulting in higher spans than the complex processing component involved in traditional working memory span tasks. However, according to the time-based resource-sharing model, they predicted that the difference in spans should disappear when simple processing components have to be performed at a fast pace.

In a first experiment, they used a traditional operation span task inspired from Turner and Engle (1989) in which participants were asked to remember series of letters, each letter being followed by an equation to be verified (e.g., '6 + 7 + 2 = 13?'). The equations remained on screen until the participant pressed one of the two keys identified as 'true' or 'false' on keyboard without any limit of time. This task was compared with the continuous operation span task, first introduced by Barrouillet, Camos and Bernardin (2001; see also Barrouillet *et al.* 2004), in which each equation of the former task was replaced by a root (a number from 1 to 9) followed by a series of sign operand pairs (i.e., + 1 or − 1). Such a series can for example take the following form: 5 / + 1 / + 1 / − 1. Participants were asked to read aloud the root, the sign-operand pairs, and to give all the answers aloud (i.e., 'five, plus one six, plus one seven, minus one six'). In the slow-paced condition, participants had 2 s to process each sign-operand pair, but only 1 s in the fast-paced condition. Many studies in cognitive arithmetic have established that adding or subtracting one to small numbers just involves direct retrievals of the answer from memory, retrievals that have been described as automatic (Aschcraft and Battaglia 1978; Barrouillet and Fayol 1998; LeFevre, Bisanz and Mrkonjic 1988). The authors were thus not surprised to observe that the slow-paced condition resulted in higher spans than the traditional operation span task (3.65 and 2.30 respectively). However, and as the time-based resource-sharing model predicted, when the participants were subjected to a fast pace, their continuous operation span dramatically dropped to the same level as the operation span (Table 4.1).

However, the authors acknowledged that this result was not so surprising. As we stated above, the cognitive demand of complex activities such as equation solving lies on the time pressure

Table 4.1 Mean spans (and standard deviations) as a function of the nature of the processing component involved in the working memory span tasks

	Nature of the processing component		
	Simple computer-paced tasks		**Complex self-paced tasks**
	Slow	Fast	
Operation solving	3.65	2.30	2.30
	(0.92)	(0.78)	(0.81)
Reading	4.17	3.11	3.38
	(1.00)	(0.93)	(0.78)

Adapted with permission from Lépine, R, Bernardin, S and Barrouillet, P (2005). Attention switching and working memory spans. *European Journal of Cognitive Psychology, 17*, 329–346.

inherent to their structure. The authors noted that mental arithmetic necessitates keeping track of the problem to be solved, of subgoals and of intermediary results, the memory traces of which suffer from decay and interference. Thus, any interruption or slowing down calculation can lead to irremediable loss of information or failure. Because it could be argued that the processes involved in equation solving are akin to those involved in solving the continuous operations, what this experiment demonstrated was that a time pressure induced by the experimental design has the same effect as the time pressure inherent to the structure of complex activities. Moreover, the processing component of the continuous operation span task involves a memory load because the participant must keep track of the current state of the calculation, a memory load that could have impaired the concurrent maintenance of the letters. Thus, the authors decided to compare the effects on span of two activities that deeply differ in the cognitive process they involve.

In a further experiment, they compared a reading span task inspired from Daneman and Carpenter (1980) in which participants were asked to read aloud and evaluate the plausibility of sentences displayed on screen (e.g., 'A cow lays eggs') with a reading letter span task in which the processing component consisted in reading series of letters displayed successively on screen at a fixed pace. In both tasks, each sentence or series of letters was preceded by a to-be-remembered number presented on screen. Of course, identifying letters is one of the elementary components of reading, but reading series of letters even under time pressure can not be considered as mimicking the activity of reading comprehension. Analyzing the latter activity, Siegel (1994) pointed out that triggering grapheme–phoneme conversion rules, retrieving information about word meaning and processing syntax are cognitive processes involving executive components, all activities that are obviously not needed to read letters. Nonetheless, the authors made the same predictions as in the first experiment because reading letters require attention and a sufficiently fast-paced presentation would prevent attentional switching. In line with this prediction, they observed that the traditional reading span was lower than the reading letter span only when letters were presented at a slow rate (one letter every 1300 ms), but this difference disappeared when letters were presented at a rate of one letter every 675 ms (Table 4.1).

This last result demonstrated that an activity that does not require any memory load or algorithmic process but only the retrieval of overlearned information from memory such as reading letters is sufficient to disrupt concurrent maintenance. As Barrouillet and Camos (2001) surmised, even a fairly simple task that continuously captures attention has the same detrimental effect on span as the complex activities involved in the traditional working memory span tasks. Thus, even if complex activities often involve a high cognitive load, cognitive load is not a matter of complexity. Lépine, Bernardin and Barrouillet (2005) noted that it could be considered as surprising that the simple activities they used in their computer-paced tasks have so great an effect on concurrent maintenance because these activities have been considered as automatic and non-demanding. It has often been suggested that solving simple additions and subtractions used in the continuous operation span task would rely on a process of direct and automatic retrieval of the answer from memory (LeFevre *et al.* 1988; Winkelman and Schmidt 1974; Zbrodoff and Logan 1986). However, they also noted that it had already been pointed out by Kahneman (1973) that a conception of the cognitive demand conflated with complexity was probably wrong. Kahneman reported that when measuring mental effort by arousal and pupillary dilations, easy tasks like the recall of thoroughly overlearned information or retaining five digits for immediate recall induced larger pupillary dilation than apparently more complex activity. More importantly, Kahneman noted that the amount of effort that is required to perform a task could not merely depend on intrinsic characteristics of this task because it is also obviously determined by the rate at which it is performed. The present results confirmed this supposition: even simple tasks can become as, and probably more, demanding than activities considered as complex.

Beyond predicting this counterintuitive result, the time-based resource-sharing model accounts for the fact that we do not usually experience simple activities as demanding. Remember that what matters is time. One of the main properties of the simple tasks we use (identify a letter, finding the answer of 4 + 1) is to extend over very short periods of time. Thus, they can easily be inserted in any activity without interrupting the thread of one's thoughts. These activities capture our attention for such short periods of time that, most of the time, we fail to notice them. They are in fact so fast that we have the impression of performing them in parallel with other more complex activities that obviously solicit our attentional capacities. However, this is an illusion, as their effect on concurrent activities when performed under time pressure made clear.

Although this study demonstrated that our computer-paced tasks can become as difficult as traditional working memory span tasks involving complex activities, an important issue concerning these tasks remained to be addressed. The main interest of the complex span tasks is not that they are more difficult than simple span tasks, or that they allow us to improve our understanding of working memory functioning, but that they provide us with spans that are good predictors of high-level cognition and academic achievement. However, do the spans provided by our new tasks have the same properties as the traditional reading or operation spans? After all, it remains possible that, contrary to the complex activities of reading sentences and solving equations, the simple activities we use disrupt maintenance by affecting peripheral and unimportant processes. In this case, the spans collected through the new tasks would not reflect individual's cognitive capacities and would not provide valid measure of working memory capacity, validity being judged by the correlation between the measure and higher level measures of cognition (Engle, Tuholski, Laughlin *et al.* 1999). In other words, our tasks could lack the predictive power that makes working memory span tasks important for psychology.

Are the new time-constrained tasks as predictive of high level cognition as the traditional working memory span tasks?

This question was addressed by Lépine, Barrouillet and Camos (2005). The authors noted that two alternative hypotheses could be put forward to account for the well-known relationship between working memory spans and performance on high level cognitive activities. According to the first hypothesis, traditional working memory tasks would evaluate some general cognitive capacity that our model describes as an attentional capacity involved in any cognitive process requiring access and maintenance of items of knowledge. This limited attentional capacity would thus underpin and constrain most of the processing steps of the complex activities involved in high-level cognition, such as reasoning or problem-solving. According to this view, complexity is an unnecessary characteristic of the processing component of a valid working memory task because what is required is an activity that solicits and captures attention. Moreover, the temporal constraints of our computer-paced tasks hamper the use of possible strategies for coping with the demands of the dual-task paradigm. It is worth to note that these strategies are allowed by most of the traditional self-paced working memory tasks in which participants are free to interrupt and resume their activity as they wish (Baddeley, Logie, Nimmo-Smith *et al.* 1985; Case, Kurland and Goldberg 1982; Daneman and Carpenter 1980; Turner and Engle 1989). According to the attentional capacity hypothesis, these strategies may produce biased measures of the fundamental capacity by allowing the most skillful participants to overcome their cognitive limits. Thus, this hypothesis predicts that the spans provided by the new tasks will be more predictive of performance in high-level cognition than the traditional tasks.

An alternative hypothesis would be that the ability to plan and use the strategies described above is the basis of the relation between working memory spans and high-level performance. High working memory span individuals would be those who are better able to plan and monitor their activity in complex situations strategically, achieving better performance in working memory dual tasks and in higher-level cognition. In this account, working memory spans are predictive because the traditional tasks mimic high-level cognitive activities, which require the individual to simultaneously maintain goals and intermediary results and to run complex operations. This hypothesis predicts that the traditional spans will have a greater predictive value because the new tasks involve less strategic factors and involve only elementary processes.

The authors tested these two hypotheses by comparing the correlations between academic achievement of 11-year-old children on the one hand, and working memory spans evaluated either by traditional or new span tasks on the other. The tasks were the same as those used by Lépine, Bernardin and Barrouillet (2005) and described above: that is a reading and an operation span task for the traditional tasks and the reading letter and the continuous operation span task for the new tasks. The level of academic achievement was provided by individual scores from the national academic achievement test that each French sixth grader takes at the beginning of the academic year. This test gives compound scores in literacy and mathematics, as well as a global scholastic score in terms of percentage of success. The results were particularly clear and eloquent (Table 4.2).

Table 4.2 Correlations between the traditional and the new working memory span tasks on the one hand and the scholastic scores on the other for 93 French sixth graders

Working memory tasks	Scholastic score		
	Literacy	Mathematics	Global
Traditional			
Reading span	0.30	0.33	0.34
Operation Span	0.32	0.35	0.36
Traditional compound score	*0.34*	*0.38*	*0.39*
Computer-paced			
Reading letter span	0.46	0.48	0.50
Continuous operation span	0.39	0.41	0.42
New compound score	0.50	0.52	0.54

Adapted from Lépine, R, Barrouillet, P and Camos, V (2005). What makes working memory spans so predictive of high-level cognition? *Psychonomic Bulletin and Review, 12*, 165–170, Copyright Psychonomic Society Inc.

Though the traditional reading and operation span were good predictors of academic achieve-ment, both new tasks were better correlated with each of the subcomponents as well as with the global score of the scholastic evaluation. Stepwise regression analyses revealed that the new working memory spans were better predictors of the scholastic scores in mathematics and literacy than the traditional spans, the residual part of variance accounted for by the traditional spans never reaching significance.

The authors concluded that the complexity of the processing component in most of the tradi-tional working memory span tasks is a superfluous characteristic. As we noted above, self-paced working memory span tasks require complex activities to induce the necessary time pressure that is inherent to their structure. However, as soon as the tasks are not self-paced, attentional shifting is strongly constrained and complexity becomes unnecessary. As a consequence, the predictive value of the traditional spans does not stem from their capacity to assess an ability to cope strate-gically with the demands of complex span tasks. Indeed, when the possibility of dealing strategi-cally with the task is reduced by computer-paced presentation, the predictive value is increased. Rather, working memory span tasks measure a fundamental capacity related to the attention required for retrievals from memory during reading of letters or solution of the simple continu-ous operations, but also for reactivation of the decaying memory traces. Thus, those tasks that strongly constrain free attention shifting from processing to maintenance and permit better control of the strategies that undermine the rationale of working memory span tasks provide better estimates of individuals' amount of attention, that is of their working memory capacities.

Discussing the interest of their new working memory tasks, Lépine, Barrouillet and Camos (2005) suggested that another source of the higher predictive power of these tasks could stem from the probable lower interindividual variability in simple processes. Individuals can differ greatly in literacy and mathematics, and these differences in processing efficiency could under-mine a reliable measure of their real cognitive capacities. By contrast, reading letters and brows-ing the numerical chain are universal skills in the literate population, probably with low differences in proficiency. However, does this mean that any simple activity could be used as a processing component within a working memory span task and provide us with a valid measure of working memory capacity? Does any activity that captures attention elicit a cognitive load dis-rupting maintenance in such a way that the recall performance reflects working memory capaci-ties? Answering these questions requires clarifying the mechanisms by which the processing component impairs concurrent maintenance in short-term memory.

Does the nature of the activity matter, or just the capture of attention?

The previous sections established that complexity is not needed to produce cognitive load. Does this mean that the nature of the activity does not matter at all? Is cognitive load simply created by the attentional capture? And what characteristic of this capture is important: its intensity or its duration, or both? Unfortunately, we can not yet answer these questions. What we can do is to suggest some leads.

In order to clearly establish the role of attention in the effect of the processing component, Gavens and Barrouillet (2004) compared two tasks that differed only by a small but crucial detail. They had children to perform a reading digit span task as we described above. In one condition, as in the usual design of this task, the digits to be read between the letters appeared at random, but on the other condition, the same digits were ordered: instead of being presented with series of the form $6 - 3 - 5 - 2 - 4 - 1$, the children were presented with the canonical order $1 - 2 - 3 - 4 - 5 - 6$. Apart from this difference in order of presentation, both conditions presented exactly the same items, required the same activity of reading, and involved the same total duration of processing and the same level of articulatory suppression because the same words were uttered. Nonetheless, the authors predicted that the ordered condition should induce higher recall performance. They reasoned that an ordered presentation would reduce the attentional demand of the task by making it possible to anticipate the nature of the following stimulus and preactivating its phonological representation. By contrast, a random presentation would not only disallow this possibility but would even require to inhibit interferences that could result from spreading activation within the numerical chain. As the authors predicted, the random presentation resulted in lower spans than the ordered presentation in two different groups of children aged 8 and 10 respectively. This experiment clearly demonstrated that the cognitive load of an activity does not depend only on its nature or even on the rate at which it is performed, but that subtle changes on the attentional demand it involves could have substantial effects on a concurrent task. It is interesting to note that all the experiments we ran in our laboratory in order to extend these results to adult participants failed: the difference between the random and ordered conditions disappears with age. This is not perhaps surprising as we can surmise that the access to the phonological representation of digits is highly automatized in adults who no longer take advantage from the ordered presentation.

Although Gavens and Barrouillet's (2004) results indicate that cognitive load depends in some way on attention, they do not provide any evidence that what matters is the duration of this capture. Unfortunately, we did not register the response times during the completion of the task. According to the time-based resource-sharing model, it should be the case that reading times in children are longer for the random than the ordered presentation and that this difference disappears in adults, but we have not yet verified this point. However, Barrouillet, Bernardin, Portrat *et al.* (2007) provided evidence that what matters in the reading digit span is the reading time, and thus probably the duration of the capture of attention. In two experiments, they compared the reading digit span from tasks in which the format of the digits was manipulated. Digits were presented on screen either in their verbal (e.g., 'four', 'six'), Arabic (i.e., 4, 6), or Roman (IV, VI) form. The authors verified in a pretest that the Roman format elicits longer reading times (a mean of 625 ms in adults) than both the verbal and the Arabic forms (446 ms and 442 ms respectively). It can thus be assumed that reading Roman digits captures attention over longer periods of time than reading the same digits written in their Arabic or verbal forms. Thus, they predicted that, when inserted in a reading digit span task, the Roman digits should have a more detrimental effect on span than the verbal and Arabic digits. This is exactly what they observed. The Roman condition in which the digits took longer to be read resulted in lower mean spans (3.87) than the verbal and Arabic conditions, which did not differ in reading times and accordingly resulted in the same level of recall performance (mean spans of 4.50 and 4.54 respectively). In a subsequent experiment, Barrouillet *et al.* (2007) extended this result to a non symbolic representation of digits by using dice-like canonical patterns of 1 to 6 dots. A pretest revealed that identifying quantities of dots (507 ms) took longer than reading the equivalent numbers in their Arabic or verbal form (424 ms and 425 ms respectively). When interleaved into series of letters to be remembered, these different stimuli resulted in recall performance that depended on reading times (75 per cent for dots compared to 82 per cent for both Arabic and verbal forms). Barrouillet *et al.* (2007) observations strongly suggest that in working memory tasks such as the reading digit span task, the detrimental effect on span of the processing component is closely related to the time during which it captures attention. Even small differences can result in significant changes in the amount of information that can be concurrently maintained in short-term memory and recalled. But does the nature of the activity that captures attention matter? Remember that, when presenting the time-based resource-sharing model, Barrouillet *et al.* (2004) suggested that some activities could be more damaging than others for the concurrent maintenance of information in short-term memory.

The effect of the Number of retrievals/Time ratio as well as the results reported in this section suggest that time factors play a major role in the conflict that occurs between the processing and maintenance components of the memory span tasks. According to our theory, this is due to the fact that maintaining items in short-term memory requires their frequent refreshment by a process of retrieval that necessitates attentional focusing (Cowan 1999). However, the locus of the conflict could lie either on the occupation of the process of retrieval or on the capture of attention. According to the first hypothesis, the processing component impedes maintenance as far as it occupies the retrieval process, which is thus unavailable for refreshing the decaying memory traces. As a consequence, the critical factor should be the number and duration of the retrievals that the processing component involves, and secondary tasks necessitating frequent retrievals from memory should have the most detrimental effect on working memory span tasks. According to the second hypothesis, the processing component disrupts maintenance because it blocks the focus of attention. Thus, the critical factor should be here the duration of this capture, whatever the nature of the activity that produces it. As a consequence, activities differing in nature but occupying the focus of attention over equivalent periods of time should have the same effect on concurrent maintenance.

A first investigation of this problem was conducted by Bernardin, Portrat and Barrouillet (2006) who compared the effect on maintenance of two secondary tasks that involved exactly the same stimuli but differed on the processes they involved, depending on whether they needed to retrieve information from memory or not. In both conditions, participants were presented, as in the previous studies, with series of letters to be remembered. After each letter, 7 numbers from 1 to 10 were successively presented on screen over a total period of 9 s. Each of these numbers was displayed either above or below a horizontal line centered on screen. In one condition, which was assumed to involve retrievals, the participants were asked to judge the parity of the numbers by responding either 'odd' or 'even'. In the other condition, they had just to judge their spatial location by responding either 'high' or 'low' when the number was above or below the horizontal line respectively. This latter activity involves a response selection, as in the parity judgment task, but no retrieval from long-term memory. Apart from this difference, both conditions involved exactly the same stimuli presented at the same rate. The results were particularly clear, the spatial task eliciting higher spans than the parity task (mean spans of 4.43 and 3.35 respectively). At a first glance, this difference supports the 'bottleneck for retrieval' hypothesis. A secondary task that calls for retrievals from memory has a more disruptive effect on concurrent maintenance than a task that certainly requires central processes (e.g., response selection), but not retrievals. However, this difference in span is far from being compelling. Indeed, as a posttest using a vocal key made clear, adults are faster in giving their answers to the spatial than the parity task (411 ms vs 560 ms). Thus, the difference in span could also result from differences in the time during which the two tasks captured attention in our participants. The longer this capture, the lower the spans. In order to disentangle the two competing hypothesis, an experiment that would contrast different secondary tasks the duration of which is carefully controlled was needed. We recently ran such an experiment in our lab.

Barrouillet *et al.* (2007) used the same working memory span tasks involving either spatial or parity judgment as in Bernardin *et al.* (2006), except that the participants gave their responses by pressing keys on keyboard. This modification made it possible to easily measure the time that the participants allocated to the secondary task by registering their response times for each stimulus to be processed. Moreover, following the same logic as in many of our previous studies, we varied the rate at which the numbers were presented between the letters. Each letter was followed by series of either 4, 6 or 8 numbers over a fixed total period of 6400 ms. Suppose that the nature of the activity does not matter at all, the time during which attention is captured being the sole and unique factor in accounting for memory loss in working memory span tasks. In this case, as Bernardin *et al.* (2006) observed, the spatial judgment task would result in higher recall performance than the parity judgment task, but when the two tasks would involve the same duration of attentional capture, these differences should disappear. Of course, we can not measure this duration precisely because it is evident, as pointed out by Rohrer and Pashler (2003), that the centrally demanding stages of an activity do not occupy no more than a sizable fraction of the time consumed by this activity. Nonetheless, we assumed that two activities that consume the same time could be considered as capturing attention in approximately the same way. Thus, in each experimental condition, we computed the actual processing time within the interletter intervals by adding the reaction times to the 4, 6, or 8 stimuli that were processed after each letter (this actual processing time is noted $\sum RT$). Obviously, this $\sum RT$ increased with the number of stimuli to be processed and, as we previously observed, the parity judgments elicited longer processing times than the spatial judgments. In line with our previous results, the mean spans decreased as the rate at which the numbers were processed increased, and the spatial task resulted in higher spans than the parity task (Table 4.3). However, our main interest was not in these expected and already known phenomena but on the specific effect of time and tasks on spans. Of course, as we noted, an analysis of variance with the type of task and the number of items presented as independent variables revealed highly significant effects on spans for the two factors without any interaction. However, when the individual mean $\sum RT$ were introduced as covariate in an analysis of covariance, time appeared as a statistically significant covariate whereas the effect of tasks on spans became non significant, the F value dramatically dropping from 19.64 to 0.10. This phenomenon can be illustrated by plotting the observed spans with the $\sum RT$ for each task and by linearly extrapolating what would have been, for example, the recall performance from the spatial judgment task if it had consumed the same time as the parity judgment task (Figure 4.3). As we have seen, the two tasks resulted in quite different overall mean spans (4.48 for the parity and 5.23 for the spatial judgment tasks), but this difference disappeared when imagining that the two tasks would consume the same time.

The main conclusion that can be drawn from these experiments is that the relevant factor in determining the cognitive load induced by a given activity is time, whatever the nature of this activity. Though memory retrievals are needed to refresh the decaying memory traces in short-term

Table 4.3 Mean actual processing times and spans as a function of the nature of the processing component and the number of stimuli to be processed.

Number of stimuli	Nature of the Processing component			
	Spatial judgment		Parity judgment	
	Actual proc. time (ms)	Span	Actual proc. time (ms)	Span
4	1928	5.56	2467	5.16
	(233)	(0.75)	(400)	(0.78)
6	2297	5.52	3251	4.58
	(239)	(0.62)	(316)	(1.23)
8	2827	4.60	3724	3.69
	(266)	(0.82)	(218)	(0.63)

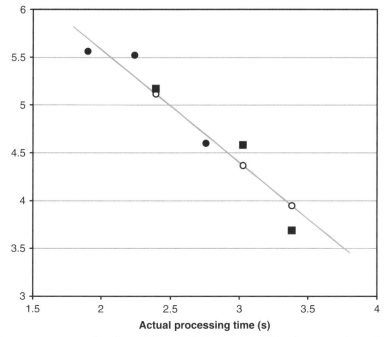

Figure 4.3 Mean spans as a function of the actual time consumed by the processing episodes for a task of spatial judgment (black circles) and of parity judgment (black squares). White circles refer to linearly extrapolated values if spatial judgments had consumed the same time as parity judgments.

memory, secondary tasks that involve frequent retrievals do not disrupt maintenance in a greater extent than other tasks involving other central processes such as response selection. By contrast, the longer the time consumed to perform this task, the lower the resulting span. Of course, these studies only provide us with preliminary results that deserve replication and extension. However, they are sufficient to rule out the restrictive 'bottleneck for retrieval' hypothesis. This is not to say that there is no bottleneck for retrieval, but instead that this bottleneck seems to be a central bottleneck that affects retrievals, but also other central processes. Our results suggest that, in working memory span tasks, recall performance is a function of the actual time during which this central bottleneck is occupied by the processing component, thus lending strong support to one of the main assumptions of the time-based resource-sharing model.

Conclusions and perspectives

The studies reported in this chapter have many implications concerning the way we consider working memory functioning as well as our conceptions about cognitive resources, resource sharing, and cognitive load. Ever since the seminal studies of Moray (1967) and Kahneman (1973) on attention and mental effort, many models have adopted the capacity or resource theory (Navon 1984) and assumed that there is a general limit on the human capacity to perform mental work. Based on a crude physical analogy, this theory posits that mental activities require the allocation of a certain amount of effort and consume energy (Pascual Leone 1970). Difficult tasks would demand more effort, and thus require a greater amount of mental energy. Because the total amount of energy, the total processing space, or the mental power that can be supplied is limited, performance deteriorates when the demands exceed the available capacities or when a part of the limited pool of energy is reallocated from the current task to a concurrent and demanding activity (Case 1985). In line with this seminal conception, most of the current models of working memory assume that there is a limited-capacity central executive involved in all the activities that require controlled attention. This kind of attention would be required in order to select the relevant information from the flow of incoming stimuli and inner knowledge, to select the appropriate and inhibit the irrelevant strategies, and to control their processing (Baddeley 1996; Engle *et al.* 1999a; Norman and Shallice 1986). Other models consider attention to be a kind of mental energy that produces activation and determines which information enters working memory and then becomes available for processing (Cowan 1995; Just and Carpenter 1992; Lovett *et al.* 1999). Despite their discrepancies, all these models share the same basic tenets of resource theories: performance depends both on the amount of resources allocated and on the intrinsic demands of the task, with more difficult and demanding tasks resulting in poorer performance. Thus, the simultaneous completion of two demanding tasks results in a trade-off phenomenon because at any point in time, the cognitive resource is shared between the two competing activities: when resources are reallocated from a task A to a task B, performance on task A deteriorates. Thus, common sense, introspective scrutiny as well as elaborated scientific theories have converged in considering that complex cognitive activities such as reading comprehension, mental calculation, or reasoning on abstract material are among the most resource demanding. Should we abandon these ideas? Certainly not. Our minds are the best witnesses of what is hard for them, and apart from rare and famous prodigies, nobody finds easy to calculate the square of 647 in one's head, apparently for good reasons. Accordingly, when involved in dual-task paradigms, these complex activities proved highly damaging for concurrent processes, suggesting that they annex a substantial part of the available resources, whatever the nature of these resources and the way they are shared.

However, what we demonstrated above is that although complex tasks are the most effective in disturbing concurrent maintenance, complexity is not needed and very simple processes, often described as automatic, can have a highly detrimental effect on spans. Thus, it appeared that the relevant factor is not complexity per se but time! What kind of working memory theory could accommodate this unexpected fact? We claim that the time hypothesis constitutes the simplest way to account for trade-off phenomena, cognitive load, and working memory functioning while retaining the main assumptions of cognitive psychology and even of resource theory.

According to Kahneman (1973), work is done and effort is mobilized in response to the changing demands of the task in which the subject engages. This conception echoes current models of working memory that assume that the role of attention is to update the current content of working memory. This updating would involve encoding relevant stimuli, retrieving items of knowledge from long-term memory, and keeping these items active (Anderson and Lebiere 1998; Cowan 1995). Switching attention from one item to another, selecting among activated responses, and maybe inhibiting irrelevant information are processes that could be added to this list. All these activities, usually considered as executive functions, require the allocation of attention controlled by some central executive (Baddeley and Logie 1999; Cowan 1995, 1999, Engle *et al.* 1999a). In other words, we assume that work is done and effort is mobilized each time the content of working memory is modified by controlled attention, that is each time executive functions are involved.

What are the limits of such a working memory? We assume that there are two main limits, both related to time. The first concerns the activation of those items that are outside the focus of attention because this activation suffers from a time-related decay. Note that this phenomenon would not be a limit per se if it was possible to retrieve these decaying memory traces and thus refresh them through a process of redintegration (Hulme *et al.* 1997) while simultaneously performing other attention demanding operations. However, and this is the second limit, it seems that executive processes are constrained by a central bottleneck and are thus sequential in nature. As a consequence, keeping active the current goals and the information relevant for the activity in hand necessitates frequent interruptions of this activity. When the impairment of maintenance in short-term memory and the further recall performance are taken as a measure of the cognitive load of a given task performed concurrently, this cognitive load is a function of the proportion of time during which this task occupies the central bottleneck and impedes other executive processes to be performed. Thus, as we observed, simple tasks that nonetheless involve executive processes can become highly demanding when performed under time pressure. Moreover, the nature of the executive process that temporarily occupies the central bottleneck does not matter. Whatever this process, it impedes other processes to be concurrently run. As a consequence, what matters is the actual processing time.

Although the time-based resource-sharing model appears to be the opposite of the resource theory exposed above, it is in fact related to this general theory in at least two ways. First, when considering working memory functioning at the atomistic level of the successive elementary processing steps, it is true that our theory contradicts the assumption of a continuous sharing of the resource at any point in time. However, at a macro level of analysis, we can still describe the phenomena we reported in this chapter as resulting from a resource sharing between tasks 'simultaneously' performed. The quasi-perfect trade-off between processing and storage we reported in Figure 4.2 could still be described as a decrease in recall performance while the 'difficulty' of the secondary task increases. Indeed, even if the effect on spans of apparently simple tasks such as reading digits or continuous operations can surprise, those participants who were subjected to fast paces frequently reported the extreme difficulty of these tasks and their firm intention never to take part in working memory experiments! Thus, our estimation of the cognitive load as a time ratio actually reflects conscious experience of mental effort. At this macro level, our results take further and reinforce the physical analogy on which the resource theory is based. Mental activities not only consume energy, but this consumption seems to conform to a general law of physics. We have seen that the recall performance smoothly decreased as the Number of retrievals/Time ratio increased suggesting that the amount of 'resources' consumed by reading digits was a function of this ratio. In other words, the mental power needed to perform a given task corresponds to the rate at which energy is converted, i.e. the amount of work this task demands, here the number of retrievals to be performed, divided by the time taken to perform it. This corresponds to the physical law of power: Power = Work/Time.

Second, at a micro level of analysis, we have assumed that work is done each time executive functions are involved. Let us propose that the energy, the resource that is converted by executive processes is attention. For example, within the ACT-R framework (Anderson 1993; Anderson and Lebière 1998) as well as in Cowan's theory, it is explicitly assumed that attention produces activation and triggers retrievals. Higher amounts of attention result in higher levels of activation. Thus, individual and developmental differences in the amount of attention would account for differences in working memory capacity. Indeed, a higher amount of attentional resources would result in faster executive processes such as retrievals, response selection, updating, and in turn in shorter periods of occupation of the central bottleneck, but also on higher levels of activation and thus on longer periods before the total disappearance of items maintained in short-term memory. Accordingly, Gavens and Barrouillet (2004) demonstrated that even when the difficulty of processing within a continuous operation span task is equated across age, working memory spans still exhibit a developmental increase. The authors suggested that this increase could be underpinned by a greater amount of cognitive resources in older children. Thus, even if the main phenomenon in working memory is probably time sharing, this does not necessarily make the notion of resource useless.

In a fascinating article, Navon (1984) wondered if 'resources' was a theoretical soup stone. The article began with the adaptation of a Russian folktale in which a scamp taught a fool how to prepare a delicious soup that requires nothing but a soup stone. All one has to do is to put the soup stone into boiling water, but adding some vegetables, meat, salt and pepper would not harm the soup and would even achieve a better taste. Navon suggested that if the concept of resource was not sufficient to impose conceptual organization on phenomena in the field, then it might be suspected that that concept is actually a theoretical soup stone that can be taken out, the soup being as good as it was. There are so many issues related to working memory that remain unsolved, and the studies that we reported in this chapter are so limited in scope that we do not know if resources is a theoretical soup stone, but what is clear is that it is difficult and probably premature to take the hot stone out of the soup. Indeed, as we have seen, it remains difficult to account for working memory phenomena without any recourse to the notion of resource. Of course, time plays the major role and central processes seem to use in turn a commodity that can not be shared, but what is this commodity needed by retrievals, response selection and probably other processes? Many models of working memory suggest that it corresponds to controlled attention, the available amount of which could vary from one individual or one age to another, exactly as a resource. Thus, in the present state of our knowledge, the most accurate description of working memory functioning that we can propose corresponds to a time-based resource-sharing.

References

Anderson, JR (1993). *Rules of the Mind*. Hillsdale, NJ: Erlbaum.

Anderson, JR and Lebiere, C (1998). *Atomic Components of Thought*. Hillsdale, NJ: Erlbaum.

Aschcraft, MH and Battaglia, J (1978). Cognitive arithmetics: Evidence for retrieval and decision processes in mental addition. *Journal of Experimental Psychology: Human Learning and Memory*, 4, 527–538.

Baddeley, AD (1990). *Human Memory, Theory and Practice*. Hillsdale, NJ: Erlbaum.

Baddeley, AD (1996). Exploring the central executive. *Quarterly Journal of Experimental Psychology*, 49A, 5–28.

Baddeley, AD (2000). Short-term and working memory. In E Tulving and FIM Craik (eds), *The Oxford Handbook of Memory* (pp. 77–92). Oxford: University Press.

Baddeley, AD and Hitch, G (1974). Working memory. In GA Bower (ed), *Recent Advances in Learning and Motivation*, Vol. 8 (pp. 647–667). New York: Academic Press.

Baddeley, AD and Logie, RH (1999). Working memory: The multiple-component model. In A Miyake and P Shah (eds), *Models of Working Memory: Mechanisms of active maintenance and executive control* (pp. 28–61). Cambridge: Cambridge University Press.

Baddeley, AD, Logie, R, Nimmo-Smith, I and Brereton, N (1985). Components of fluent reading. *Journal of Memory and Language*, 24(1), 119–131.

Barrouillet, P, Bernardin, S and Camos, V (2004). Time constraints and resource sharing in adults' working memory spans. *Journal of Experimental Psychology: General*, 133, 83–100.

Barrouillet, P, Bernardin, S, Portrat, S, Vergauwe, E and Camos, V (2007). Time and cognitive load in working memory. (Manuscript in press.)

Barrouillet, P and Camos, V (2001). Developmental increase in working memory span: Resource sharing or temporal decay? *Journal of Memory and Language*, 45, 1–20.

Barrouillet, P, Camos, V and Bernardin, S (2001). *Temporal decay and resource sharing in working memory span measures: A new paradigm*. Paper presented at the third International Conference on Memory, 16–20 July, Valencia (Spain).

Barrouillet, P and Fayol, M (1998). From algorithmic computing to direct retrieval: Evidence from number- and alphabetic-arithmetic in children and adults. *Memory and Cognition*, 26, 355–368.

Bernardin, S (2004). Mémoire de travail et contraintes cognitives: Le modèle de partage temporel des ressources. Unpublished Doctoral Dissertation. Dijon: Université de Bourgogne.

Bernardin, S, Portrat, S and Barrouillet, P (2006). Impact de la nature et du rythme de realisation de la tâche secondaire dans les tâches d'empan de mémoire de travail. *L'Année Psychologique*, *106*(1), 23–42.

Cantor, J and Engle, RW (1993). Working-memory capacity as long-term memory activation: An individual-differences approach. *Journal of Experimental Psychology: Learning, Memory, and Cognition*, *25*, 1101–1114.

Case, R (1985). *Intellectual Development: Birth to adulthood*. New York: Academic Press.

Case, R, Kurland, M and Goldberg, J (1982). Operational efficiency and the growth of short-term memory. *Journal of Experimental Child Psychology*, *33*, 386–404.

Conway, ARA and Engle, RW (1994). Working memory and retrieval: A resource-dependent inhibition model. *Journal of Experimental Psychology: General*, *4*, 354–373.

Conway, ARA, Kane, MJ and Engle, RW (2003). Working memory capacity and its relation to general intelligence. *Trends in Cognitive Sciences*, *7*(12), 547–552.

Cowan, N (1992). Verbal memory span and the timing of spoken recall. *Journal of Memory and Language*, *31*, 668–684.

Cowan, N (1995). *Attention and Memory: An integrated framework*. New York: Oxford University Press.

Cowan, N (1999). An embedded-process model of working memory. In A Miyake and P Shah (eds), *Models of Working Memory: Mechanisms of active maintenance and executive control* (pp. 62–101). Cambridge: Cambridge University Press.

Cowan, N, Keller, TA, Hulme, C, Roodenrys, S, McDougall, S and Rack, J (1994). Verbal memory span in children: Speech timing clues to the mechanisms underlying age and word length effects. *Journal of Memory and Language*, *33*, 234–250.

Daneman, M and Carpenter, PA (1980). Individual differences in working memory and reading. *Journal of Verbal Learning and Verbal Behavior*, *19*, 450–466.

Engle, RW, Cantor, J and Carullo, JJ (1992). Individual differences in working memory and comprehension: A test of four hypotheses. *Journal of Experimental Psychology: Learning, Memory, and Cognition*, *5*, 972–992.

Engle, RW and Oransky, N (1999). The evolution from short-term memory to working memory: Multi-store to dynamic models of temporary storage. In RJ Sternberg (ed), *The Nature of Cognition* (pp. 515–556). Cambridge, MA: MIT Press.

Engle, RW, Kane, MJ and Tuholski, SW (1999). Individual differences in working memory capacity and what they tell us about controlled attention, general fluid intelligence, and functions of the prefrontal cortex. In A Miyake and P Shah (eds), *Models of Working Memory: Mechanisms of active maintenance and executive control* (pp. 102–134). Cambridge: Cambridge University Press.

Engle, RW, Tuholski, SW, Laughlin, JE and Conway, ARA (1999). Working memory, short-term memory, and general fluid intelligence: A latent-variable approach. *Journal of Experimental Psychology: General*, *128*(3), 309–331.

Garavan, H (1998). Serial attention within working memory. *Memory and Cognition*, *26*(2), 263–276.

Gavens, N and Barrouillet, P (2004). Delays of retention, processing efficiency, and attentional resources in working memory span development. *Journal of Memory and Language*, *51*, 644–657.

Halford, GS, Maybery, MT, O'Hare, AW and Grant, P (1994). The development of memory and processing capacity. *Child Development*, *65*(5), 1338–1356.

Hitch, G, Towse, JN and Hutton, U (2001). What limits children's working memory span? Theoretical accounts and applications for scholastic development. *Journal of Experimental Psychology: General*, *130*(2), 184–198.

Hulme, C, Roodenrys, S, Schweickert, R and Brown, GDA (1997). Word-frequency effects on short-term memory tasks: Evidence for a redintegration process in immediate serial recall. *Journal of Experimental Psychology: Learning, Memory, and Cognition*, *23*(5), 1217–1232.

Just, MA and Carpenter, PA (1992). A capacity theory of comprehension: Individual differences in working memory. *Psychological Review, 99*, 122–149.

Kahneman, D (1973). *Attention and Effort*. Englewood Cliffs, NJ: Prentice-Hall.

LeFevre, J, Bisanz, J and Mrkonjic, L (1988). Cognitive arithmetic: Evidence for obligatory activation of arithmetic facts. *Memory and Cognition, 16*, 45–53.

Lépine, R, Barrouillet, P and Camos, V (2005). What makes working memory spans so predictive of high-level cognition? *Psychonomic Bulletin and Review, 12*, 165–170.

Lépine, R, Bernardin, S and Barrouillet, P (2005). Attention switching and working memory spans. *European Journal of Cognitive Psychology, 17*, 329–346.

Lovett, MC, Reder, LM and Lebière, C (1999). Modeling working memory in a unified architecture: An ACT-R perspective. In A Miyake and P Shah (eds), *Models of Working Memory: Mechanisms of active maintenance and executive control* (pp. 135–182). Cambridge: Cambridge University Press.

Moray, N (1967). Where is capacity limited? A survey and model. *Acta Psychologica, 27*, 84–92.

Navon, D (1984). Resources – a theoretical soup stone? *Psychological Review, 91*(2), 216–234.

Norman, DA and Shallice, T (1986). Attention to action: Willed and automatic control of behavior. In RJ Davidson, GE Schwartz and D Shapiro (eds), *Consciousness and Self-regulation*, Vol. 4 (pp. 1–18). New York: Plenum.

Oberauer, K (2003). Selective attention to elements in working memory. *Experimental Psychology, 50*(4), 257–269.

Pascual-Leone, JA (1970). A mathematical model for the transition rule in Piaget's developmental stage. *Acta Psychologica, 32*, 301–345.

Pashler, H (1998). *The Psychology of Attention*. Cambridge, MA: MIT Press.

Rohrer, D and Pashler, HE (2003). Concurrent task effect on memory retrieval, *Psychonomic Bulletin and Review, 10*(1), 96–103.

Rohrer, D, Pashler, H and Etchegaray, J (1998). When two memories can and cannot be retrieved concurrently. *Memory and Cognition, 26*(4), 731–739.

Rosen, VM and Engle, RW (1997). The role of working memory capacity in retrieval. *Journal of Experimental Psychology: General, 126*(3), 211–227.

Schneider, W and Detweiler, M (1987). A connectionist/control architecture for working memory. In GH Bower (ed), *The Psychology of Learning and Motivation*, Vol. 21 (pp. 54–119). New York: Academic Press.

Siegel, LS (1994). Working memory and reading: A life-span perspective. *International Journal of Behavioral Development, 17*(1), 109–124.

Towse, JN and Hitch, GJ (1995). Is there a relationship between task demand and storage space in tests of working memory capacity? *The Quarterly Journal of Experimental Psychology, 48A*, 108–124.

Towse, JN, Hitch, GJ and Hutton, U (1998). A reevaluation of working memory capacity in children. *Journal of Memory and Language, 39*, 195–217.

Towse, JN, Hitch, GJ and Hutton, U (2000). On the interpretation of working memory spans in adults. *Memory and Cognition, 28*, 341–348.

Towse, JN, Hitch, GJ and Hutton, U (2002). On the nature of the relationship between processing activity and item retention in children. *Journal of Experimental Child Psychology, 82*(2), 156–184.

Turner, ML and Engle, RW (1989). Is working memory task dependent? *Journal of Memory and Language, 28*, 127–154.

Winkelman, JH and Schmidt, J (1974). Associative confusions in mental arithmetic. *Journal of Experimental Psychology, 102*(4), 734–736.

Zbrodoff, NJ and Logan, GD (1986). On the autonomy of mental processes: A case study of arithmetic. *Journal of Experimental Psychology: General, 115*, 18–130.

5

The ins and outs of working memory
Dynamic processes associated with focus switching and search

Paul Verhaeghen, John Cerella, Chandramallika Basak, Kara Bopp, Yanmin Zhang and William J. Hoyer

Recent theories of working memory propose that working memory is not unitary, but is subdivided into concentric regions that differ in the accessibility of the stored information. Cowan's (e.g., 1995, 2001) model has probably been most influential in this regard. This model proposes a hierarchical two-tier structure for working memory, distinguishing a zone of privileged and immediate access, labeled the focus of attention, from a larger activated portion of long-term memory in which items are stored in a readily available but not immediately accessible state. (In accordance with the terminology introduced by McElree [2001], the accessibility of an element in working memory is defined by the time needed to retrieve it; availability is defined by the probability that the element is retrieved correctly.) The focus of attention is capacity-limited, and contains a fixed number of items; the activated portion of long-term memory is not capacity-limited, but items stored in this structure are subject to interference and decay. Note that in this view, working memory is seen not as a separate cognitive system, but rather as an arena consisting of activated elements on which attentional processes operate; the 'central executive' (e.g., Baddeley 1996) is no longer a structural element of the model, but rather is equated with this set of processes.

A logical consequence of this two-tier structure is the existence of a focus-switching process (McElree 2001): as far as we can determine, the term 'focus switch' was coined by Voigt and Hagendorf (2002). When the number of items to be retained in working memory is smaller than or equal to the capacity of the focus of attention, they will be contained in this inner store; there they are immediately retrievable, and access times will be fast. When the number of items to be retained exceeds the capacity of the focus, however, the excess items will be stored outside the focus of attention. Accessing items for processing will necessitate a retrieval operation; this will slow down access time.

Focus switching and the capacity of the focus of attention: the new magical number 2.5 plus or minus 1.5

Cowan's theory provides an operational definition of the capacity of the focus of attention: capacity is measured by the number of items that can be accessed immediately. The measurement can be made for any task that requires retrieval from working memory – when the number of items to be retained is systematically increased, a jump in response times will occur when the limit of the focus of attention is reached.

An aspect of working memory revealed by such measurements is that the capacity of the focus of attention is not fixed but expandable, up to a point. Early studies suggested a capacity of the 'magical number seven plus or minus two' (Miller 1956). This estimate is probably too large. It was derived from forward digit span tasks, and it has been shown that these tasks are contaminated with the effects of rehearsal (Cowan 2001). Following an extensive review of the literature, Cowan ascribed to the focus of attention a size of four (plus or minus one). Evidence for his estimate came from a variety of experiments in a large number of research domains, including cluster size in free recall from episodic memory, the limits of perfect recall from immediate memory, proactive interference effects, the limits of cued partial reports, subitizing spans, multiple-object tracking and the limits of consistently mapped search. The range of the evidence is staggering: Cowan's Table 1 cites 41 key references from 17 different research domains, all pointing to the magical number four. Recent research using evoked potentials to directly assess the capacity of visual working memory as activation in the parietal cortex continues to support a capacity limit of about four items (Vogel, McCollough and Machizawa 2005; Vogel and Machizawa 2004).

Research that relies on the jump in response times to identify focus size, however, has converged on a smaller estimate. At least five such studies have concluded that the focus of attention can accommodate only a single item at any given time (Garavan 1998; McElree 1998, 2001; Oberauer 2002; Verhaeghen and Basak 2005). To illustrate these findings, Figure 5.1 depicts the results from Verhaeghen and Basak (2005, Experiment 1, college-age sample only). Their procedure was adapted from the identity-judgment N-back task used by McElree (2001). A schematic example of a single trial, consisting of 20 to-be-responded-to items, is represented in Figure 5.2. In this procedure the subject sees a series of digits presented one at a time on a computer screen; the task is to indicate whether the item currently presented is identical to the item presented N positions back. In our version stimuli were shown on the screen in N columns defined by their location on the screen and also by unique colors. The subject was instructed to report whether the current item matched the item show previously in the same column. The columnized format relieves the subject of the need to index the item sequence internally.

The critical data are given by the response times (depicted in the bottom left panel of Figure 5.1). The response time by N trace is close to a step function, with a fast time at $N = 1$, and then a jump to slower and statistically equal times for values of $N > 1$. In our view this jump marks the boundary between the focus of attention and the outer store in working memory. When the memory set is two or more, a new item can be accessed only by first switching it from the outer store to the inner store. The duration of the focus-switching operation is defined by the height of the step function, and is quite large – about 250 ms. These data, like similar data obtained by Garavan (1998), McElree (1998, 2001), and Oberauer (2002), imply that only one item is directly accessible at any given time, although the system clearly keeps more items in an available state, testified by high accuracy for at least four items (see the bottom right panel of Figure 5.1).

We are thus faced with conflicting accounts of the capacity of the focus of attention. On one side there is an extensive literature that points to a wide focus of four, and on the other side a set of recent focus-switching studies that claim a narrow focus of one. How can these two accounts be reconciled? One possible resolution arises from the nature of the tasks involved (Garavan 1998). In all the narrow-focus procedures, attention is directed serially to different elements that are either being encoded into working memory or retrieved from it. The serial requirement is likely to necessitate a controlled switch of attention to successive items. What distinguishes narrow-focus outcomes from wide-focus outcomes may be the requirement to shift attention serially between either the stored representations or the to-be-encoded items in the narrow-focus contexts.

Another possible resolution is that the two outcomes derive from different memory structures (Oberauer 2002). Oberauer argues for the existence of not two but three concentric tiers of storage, combining the architecture proposed by Cowan with the architecture proposed by McElree and Garavan. This architecture consists of (a) a focus of attention, containing the item selected as

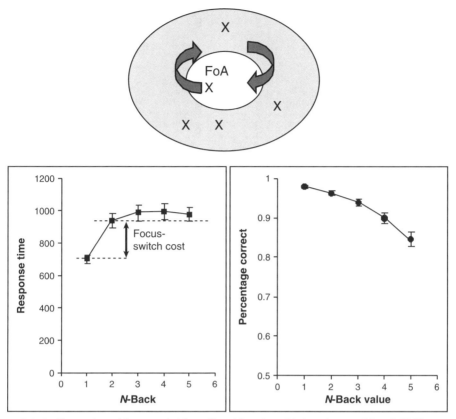

Figure 5.1 An illustration of focus-switching effect (data from Verhaeghen and Basak 2005, Experiment 1). The top of the figure illustrates the two-tier structure of working memory (McElree 2001): within working memory, only the items held in the focus-of-attention (FoA) are immediately accessible. If the number of items present in working memory exceeds the capacity of the focus, item-swapping becomes necessary. The bottom of the figure shows data from our identity-judgment N-Back task, indicating that the focus has a size of one: there is a step function in response times, with the step occurring between $N = 1$ and $N = 2$. The decline in accuracy, which does not measure focus switching, is monotonic over increasing values of N, but not a step function.

the object of the next cognitive operation; (b) a capacity-limited region of direct access corresponding to Cowan's focus of attention, where a limited number of items is stored that are likely to be selected for subsequent processing; and (c) the activated part of long-term memory, that is able to store additional items over brief periods of time. According to this reasoning, narrow-focus results will be obtained when researchers tap into the first store; wide-focus results will be obtained when the second store is being measured.

The limitations imposed on the focus of attention by both the serial-attention explanation and the tripartite-architecture explanation are hard and fast. Both theories treat a focus-of-one as built into the working memory machinery. It seems to us that this view may be excessively rigid. A different perspective comes from theories that view working memory as an attentional system. A basic supposition from this perspective is that attentional capacity can be allocated flexibly across the perceptual/cognitive field, following the needs of the participant, the demands of the task, or both (e.g., Kahneman 1973; Wickens 1984). This points to a third resolution of the

3	5	8	1
3	6	7	1
4	5	7	3
4	5	9	3
3	5	9	8
2	5	9	8

Figure 5.2 An example of what a trial in the 4-back version of the task would look like if all stimuli remained onscreen. In the experiment, stimuli were shown one at a time, in a reading pattern (left to right, then on the next line, etc.); each column was depicted in a different color. The first row was presented at a 2 s/item pace; presentation of subsequent stimuli was participant-paced. The response required was a judgment whether the digit currently projected was identical to the digit previously shown one row higher in the same column.

narrow-focus/wide-focus controversy: perhaps the different values represent the two ends of an underlying continuum of resource allocation (Verhaeghen, Cerella and Basak 2004). Perhaps the focus of attention can vary in size, shrinking to one item when all resources are channeled to the processing of a single item, and expanding up to a size of four when several items can be processed in parallel. On this view, a focus-of-one is not due to a structural limitation of the cognitive system, but rather to the way attention is distributed over the task and stimuli.

One way to test the immutability of the size of the focus of attention is by means of a practice manipulation. Garavan (1998, Experiment 2) enlisted extended practice as a test for a resource-allocation explanation of the focus-of-one outcome in a symbol-counting task. In his study, a substantial focus-switch cost remained after practice: this result has since been replicated by Basak (2005). Both results point to the immutability of the focus size, and by implication, to the existence of a structural limitation.

We took up Garavan's practice manipulation and applied it to our columnized identity-judgment N-Back task (Verhaeghen, Cerella and Basak 2004). This task is simpler than Garavan's or Basak's, especially because the item to be accessed next is always predictable. We hoped that extended practice might lead to automaticity in some of the task components; this in turn should free up resources that could then be applied towards storage inside the focus of attention. The empirical test of this reasoning is straightforward: if the limit on the size of the focus of attention is structural, then we would expect that the N-Back step function (with the step at $N = 2$) will endure over the course of practice (although the height of the step may be diminished). If, however, the location of the step shifts over the course of practice (perhaps settling finally at $N = 5$), this would suggest that a focus-of-one derives from resource limits not structural limits.

In our study, five adults practiced the N-Back task for ten hours each, spread over five consecutive days. Figure 5.3 depicts the evolution over sessions of average response time (RT) and accuracy (Verhaeghen, Cerella and Basak 2004). The critical data are again the response time data (top panel). It can be seen that at the onset of practice, the data conform to the focus-of-one account of working memory: There is a sudden jump from $N = 1$ to $N = 2$, and a flat RT profile thereafter. After ten hours of practice with the task, however, the pattern of response times differed considerably from that of the first session. There is no longer evidence for privileged access in the

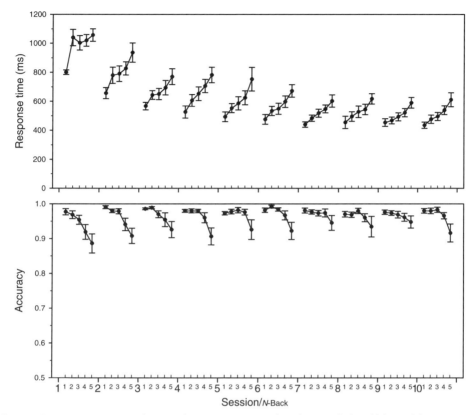

Figure 5.3 Average response times and accuracy over sessions in a study in which participants practiced the identity-judgment *N*-Back task over ten sessions (Verhaeghen, Cerella and Basak 2004). Error bars denote standard errors calculated at the group level. Response times initially showed a step function indicating a focus of size one; at the end of practice, however, the step has disappeared and the focus has expanded to hold four items.

$N = 1$ condition. Rather, the response time increases linearly over the range $N = 1$ to $N = 4$, with a shallow slope of about 30 ms/N. The breakpoint is now situated at $N = 5$: going from $N = 4$ to $N = 5$ the increment in response time is about twice as large as that extrapolated from the linear trend. In other words, it appears that with extended practice participants were able to expand the focus of attention to accommodate four items.

This result suggests that with extended practice the focus of attention can be expanded to hold four items, even in a task requiring serial attention which initially limits processing to a single item. Two additional points are worth noting. First, our data suggest that four may be the ultimate limit of the size of the focus. This may reflect a limit on total activation in the relevant storage structures of the cortex (e.g., Vogel and Machizawa 2004; see Usher, Cohen, Haarmann *et al.* 2001, for a mathematical model of flexible allocation). Second, research has shown that not every task showing an initial focus of one is amenable to a practice-related focus expansion: Garavan's symbol-counting task is not (Garavan 1998; Basak 2005, Experiment 3); neither do all subject groups show this expansion: Basak, Cerella and Verhaeghen (2004 failed to obtain focus expansion in the *N*-Back task in a group of older adults).

To summarize, we believe that the size of the focus of attention is not fixed, but may take any value between one and four. (Put facetiously, the correct magical number may be '2.5 plus-or-minus 1.5'). The size obtained in any particular case appears to be a function of both task characteristics and individual differences, as well as their interaction, the many dimensions of which have yet to be explored.

Focus switching and retrieval dynamics within working memory: a walk down working memory lane

The focus-switching pulse partitions working memory into two zones: a variable-size part characterized by fast access times, and a surrounding part of indefinite size with slower access times. The division raises the question of what type of access process operates within each zone. Interestingly, our studies reveal different retrieval dynamics for the two cases.

Retrieval dynamics within the focus of attention

The extended practice data allow us to examine retrieval processes within the expanded focus of attention. At first blush, one might expect that they are all accessed at the same speed, but this is not necessarily true. In a limited-capacity system, items will compete for activation, and the competition might be greater when the system has to maintain a larger set of items. For instance, in support of a focus size of four, Cowan (1999) cites Trick and Pylyshyn (1994) on the subitizing span, and Fisher (1984) on parallel channels in consistently mapped visual search; both are processes characterized by shallow, positive, load functions. Another memory process showing the same load function is short-term memory scanning (Sternberg 1966). Mathematical models of this process are highly developed, and may converge on the schema of parallel, limited-capacity memory access (Murdock 1971; Ratcliff 1978; Van Zandt and Townsend 1993).

Our data conform to Cowan's expectation: as can be seen over the last sessions in Figure 5.3, there is a significant response time over N slope of about 30 ms/item over the $N = 1$ to $N = 4$ range. The positive slope strongly suggests that the focus of attention is not content-addressable: rather, its contents need to be searched.

Pursuing the hypothesis that the search process within the focus is of a parallel and limited-capacity nature, we conducted an ex-Gaussian decomposition of the response time distributions. The ex-Gaussian model assumes that each response time can be represented as the sum of a Gaussian or normally distributed random variable and an independent exponentially distributed random variable. The ex-Gaussian distribution is described by three parameters: *mu* and *sigma* are the mean and standard deviation of the normal distribution and *tau* is the mean of the exponential distribution. *Mu* and *sigma* determine the location of the leading edge of the distribution; *tau* reflects slow responses at the tail of the distribution (the skew). Hockley (1984, Experiment 1) has shown that the ex-Gaussian signature of the Sternberg search process is a linear increase in *tau* over memory load, while *mu* and *sigma* remain constant. Figure 5.4 (middle panel) presents the results of the ex-Gaussian decomposition for Session 10 of the Verhaeghen, Cerella and Basak study (2004). Clearly, the linear increase in response time over N within the expanded focus of attention is due to an increase in *tau*, as would be expected when a limited-capacity parallel search process is involved.

Thus three operations - our version of N-Back, memory scanning and subitizing - show shallow load functions with about equal slopes, and at least two of these operations - N-Back and memory scanning – have the same ex-Gaussian signature. The processing involved in all three cases may be traceable to the same modus operandi within the focus of attention – an hypothesis that merits more research. The conceptualization of within-focus search as a parallel limited-capacity

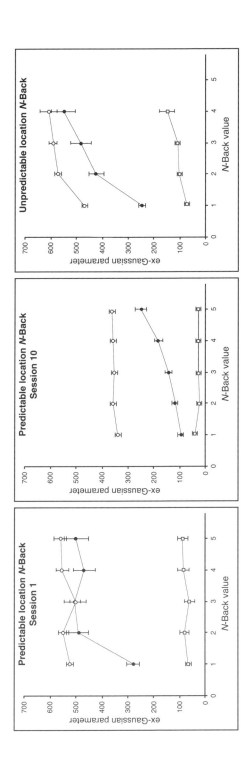

Figure 5.4 Ex-Gaussian decomposition of response times in our identity-judgment N-Back task, under three types of circumstances: predictable switching with a focus size of one (Session 1 data from Verhaeghen et al. 2004), predictable switching with a focus size of four (Session 10 data from Verhaeghen et al. 2004), and unpredictable switching with a focus size of one (data from Basak 2005, Experiment 4). Error bars denote within-individual standard errors for the leftmost and center panel, and group standard errors for the rightmost panel.

process may further explain why the capacity of the focus is not fixed. If access occurs in parallel but capacity-demanding channels, the number of supportable channels is likely to be a function of the total resources available to the working memory system. If a task is very demanding, the residual may allow only a single active channel. As a task becomes automated resources are freed up, allowing the system to open more channels to simultaneous search.

Retrieval dynamics in working memory outside the focus of attention

What about search outside the focus of attention? So far the story seems simple: both Verhaeghen and Basak (2005), and Verhaeghen, Cerella and Basak (2004, Session 1) obtained statistically flat slopes over values of N larger than 1 (see Figures 5.1 and 5.3). Items outside the focus of attention therefore appear to be directly content-addressable, much in the way elements stored in long-term memory are (see also McElree 2001).

However, this conclusion needs to be qualified. First, Verhaeghen and Basak (2005) observed a flat slope only for college-age adults; older adults showed a slope of about 70 ms/item. Second, Basak (2005, Experiment 1) found a slope of about 240 ms/register in focus-switch costs over N in a version of Garavan's counting task. Third, Basak (2005, Experiment 4) found a slope of about 90 ms/N in a modification of the N-Back task in which the item to be accessed could be from any position 1-back to N-Back (making this a hybrid between an N-Back task and a memory scanning task). Taken together, these results suggest that although the region outside the focus of attention can be content-addressable, it will actually be so only under optimal circumstances – predictable switching performed by high-functioning subjects. Under other circumstances, an explicit search process is needed.

This search process is clearly slower, by a factor of at least three, than the limited-capacity parallel search process that seems to govern the focus of attention. Additionally, it has a different ex-Gaussian signature, as can be seen in the right-hand panel of Figure 5.4 (data from Basak 2005, Experiment 4). Whereas the search cost within the focus is due to an increase in the skew parameter alone, the search cost outside the focus seems to involve the mean and standard deviation of the Gaussian parameters as well. Thus, the latter process is probably not a capacity-limited parallel search. Its signature resembles that of a visual search task (Hockley 1984), which is typically considered to be serial and self-terminating. More research is needed to confirm this conclusion, but it is an intriguing hypothesis.

Separating the costs of focus-switching and memory load

A draw-back of our work-horse task, the identity-judgment N-Back procedure, is that the jump from $N = 1$ to $N = 2$ which we attribute to focus switching is confounded with an increase in working memory load. The focus-switch cost is a step function, so that after the initial jump from $N = 1$ to $N = 2$ the cost does not increase with further increases in working memory load. This qualifies, but does not eliminate the confound – there may be something special about increasing the load from its minimum to any other value.

We have conducted two experiments that suggest that the focus-switch cost cannot be due entirely to the increase in memory load. One experiment was based on a new paradigm, a repetition–detection task (Bopp 2003). In that task, participants are presented with a series of stimuli, numbers between 1 and 16, presented one at a time on a computer screen. Within each series, one number is shown twice and the participant's task is to indicate the identity of the repeated stimulus. Progress through the series is self-paced, so that response times and accuracy can be measured. Focus-switching was manipulated by introducing more than one series on the screen, each in a different location and a different color; the subject has to find the repeat within each series. One-column, two-column and three-column conditions were implemented. Working memory load was manipulated by the length of the series. In the increasing-load condition, akin to the load increase in the N-Back task, each series was five numbers long. Thus for the one-column condition the total load is five numbers; for the two-column condition the total load is 10 numbers; and for the three-column condition the total load is 15 numbers. In the constant-load condition, the total number of stimuli was always 15 or 16 items; for the 1-column condition the series was 16 numbers long; for the 2-column condition each series was 8 numbers long; and for the 3-column condition each series was 5 numbers long.

Results are illustrated in Figure 5.5. A focus-switch cost is present in both versions of the task. Importantly, the constant-load condition shows a sizeable focus-switch cost going from one column to two columns of about 200 ms, and then no further increase going from two columns to three columns. This demonstrates that the focus-switch cost is not due solely to an increase in working memory load. The switch-cost is smaller in the constant-load condition than in the increasing-load condition. This demonstrates that increased load probably does play a role in determining the size of the focus-switch effect.

In a second experiment, Basak had participants perform a modified version of Garavan's symbol-counting task (Basak 2005, Experiment 2). In this task, subjects keep a separate running count of different shapes that appeared in a random sequence on a computer screen. Garavan used two shapes and hence two counts: Basak used up to four different shapes and hence four counts. Similar to our other experiments, each shape appeared in a different column and color, making them easier to distinguish. Presentation is self-paced, allowing for the recording of response times. Response times are typically about 500 ms slower when the stimulus shape is changed from the previous trial than when two successive stimuli have the same shape. Such results are understood

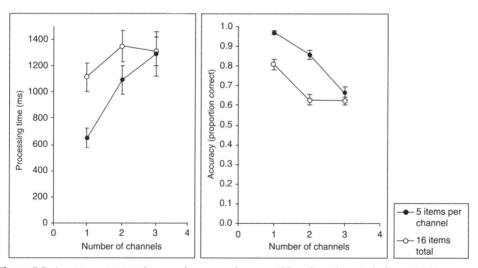

Figure 5.5 Average response times and accuracy in a repetition-detection study (Bopp 2003, Experiment 3). Error bars denote standard errors calculated at the group level. The number of channels and the working memory load were independently varied. Response time results show a focus-switch cost (i.e., an increase in RT from 1 to 2 channels), even in the absence of an increase in load.

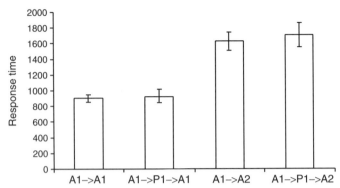

Figure 5.6 Average response times with standard error bars for a symbol-counting task (Basak 2005, Experiment 2). A1 → A1 denotes a non-switch trial; A1 → A2 denotes a switch trial; A1 → P1 → A1 denotes a trial in which a passive count is inserted in a non-switch trial; A1 → P1 → A2 denotes a trial in which a passive count is inserted in a switch trial. The results show that passive intervening items do not influence response times at all, strongly suggesting that the focus switch cost is independent of working memory load.

to show that participants keep separate mental counters active for each stimulus shape; the cost to switch between counters in working memory is the focus-switching cost.

In her version of the task, Basak gave subjects a random start-up count to update from (e.g., the count of circles would start with eight the count of squares with four; the next circle seen would then update the circle count to nine, the next square would update the square count to five). To manipulate load, Basak introduced a condition in which some shapes were designated as 'active', and other shapes as 'passive'. Subjects were given start-up counts for passive shapes but were told to ignore them for the rest of the series (passive shapes would appear, but subjects were not to update their count). At the end of the trial, they were required to give the updated count for each of the active shapes and to recall the start-up count for each of the passive shapes. If working memory load determined the focus-switch cost, the cost should increase with the number of passive items to be retained. It did not. An even stronger result is shown in Figure 5.6: the time to switch the focus of attention from an active shape to another active shape does not increase when a passive shape intervenes; neither does the time to return to the same shape suffer from the occurrence of a passive shape in between. This demonstrates that under certain circumstances, working memory load may have no influence on the focus-switching cost at all – additional items can be completely unreactive (see also Oberauer 2002).

We take up one other alternative explanation of the focus-switch cost here, that it is due to a speed–accuracy trade-off as participants move from the easy $N = 1$ condition to the harder $N > 1$ conditions. Verhaeghen and Hoyer (2007) found a negative correlation between the focus-switch cost in response time and the cost in accuracy, indicating that individuals who slow down most are also more likely to have the largest decrease in accuracy, contrary to what would be expected from a speed-accuracy trade-off mechanism.

The executive suite: focus switching and control processes in working memory

The role of the focus-switching process in working memory may be an important one, but it is far from the only executive control process operating on working memory. It should be informative to investigate the relationship that focus switching has with these other processes. If focus switching is to be elevated to the status of a cognitive primitive, we must be able to differentiate it from other control processes.

Which are these other processes? Empirical attempts to fractionalize central executive processes using the method of confirmatory factor analysis (Miyake, Friedman, Emerson *et al.* 2000; Engle, Tuholski, Laughlin *et al.* 1999; Oberauer, Süß, Schulze *et al.* 2000) have established several categories of processes. The most ambitious of these projects was undertaken by Miyake and colleagues. Miyake *et al.* (2000) investigated the separability of three types of executive processes derived from the neuropsychogical/attention literature – resistance to interference (Miyake *et al.* label this process 'inhibition of prepotent responses'; we prefer the term coined by Dempster; see Dempster and Corkill [1999]), information updating and monitoring and task switching. Miyake's three-factor model indeed provided a good fit to the covariance matrix, indicating factor separability. At the same time, the intercorrelations between the latent factors were quite high, ranging between 0.42 and 0.63, indicating considerable commonality.

In the following sections we examine some of our data pertaining to focus switching and these other control processes, with a goal of showing their independence if possible.

Focus switching and resistance to interference

Resistance to interference is a crucial control process for working memory and is likely to be a major determinant of working memory capacity (e.g., Hasher and Zacks 1988; Kane and Engle 2002). In tasks in which the focus presumably holds only a single item, the focus switch cost occurs at the moment when interfering items are introduced, hence confounding this cost with the need for resistance to interference. The results reported earlier already speak to this issue – a focus switch cost still appears when the total number of items in working memory remains constant.

Another result that suggests that interference is unlikely to be the main source of the focus-switching effect comes from the pattern of auto-correlations between successive response times in the Verhaeghen and Basak (2005) study. These results were not published in the original paper: the development is due to Basak. If a subject is able to resist interference well, then response to the current item should be attuned to and be influenced by only the item in the Nth position back. Hence, in a time-series analysis of response times, the autocorrelation function should show a clear spike in the Nth back position, indicating that performance on the current item is related to performance on the item in the Nth back position, to the exclusion of intervening items. Autocorrelation values should be close to zero for all other positions (with the exception of multiples of N, where lingering activation may still be present). This is just the pattern that was found (see Figure 5.7): Only the correlation between the current item and the item (multiples of) N back was found to be significant. On this measure the working-memory system is supremely efficient in retrieving the one item it needs and in bypassing all others.

Focus switching and updating

A second control process to consider in relation to focus switching is memory updating. In all of our studies, after the basic processing has been completed (e.g., the comparison and identity judgment processes for the N-Back task), the previous item retrieved from the corresponding slot outside the focus of attention needs to be overwritten with the item currently in the focus of attention. If part of the focus-switch cost is due to updating the contents of working memory outside the focus of attention, then the concatenation of the two processes should yield an underadditive interaction.

The identity-judgment N-Back task allows for an examination of the updating process in conjunction with focus switching. In the N-Back task, updating is only necessary when the item presented

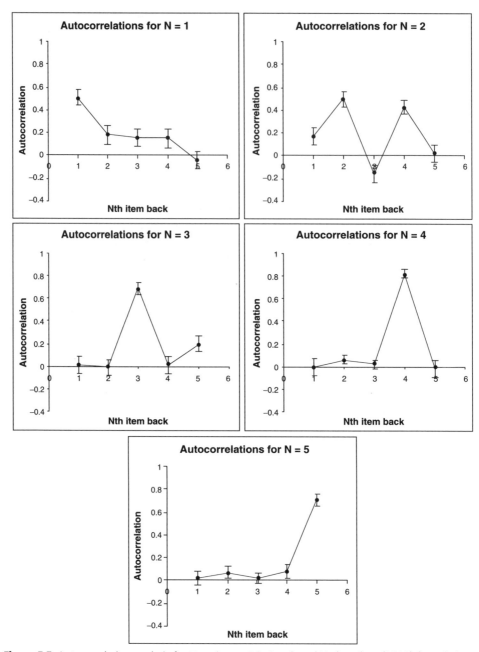

Figure 5.7 Autocorrelation analysis for Experiment 1 in Basak and Verhaeghen (2005) (correlation values with standard error bars). The response time data were treated as a time series. Each panel represents a particular *N*-Back condition; within each panel, the values of the autocorrelation for the item *N*-Back is indicated. For instance, the third panel indicates that in the 3-back condition, only RT for the item 3 back was correlated with performance on the current item. The data indicate that in this task, working memory is only sensitive to the particular item it needs to be sensitive to (or its harmonics), suggesting very efficient resistance to interference.

in the *N*th position back is different from the item currently in focus (a 'no' trial); no updating is required when the two items are identical (a 'yes' trial). Therefore, at least part of any increase in response times from 'yes' to 'no' responses could be attributed to the updating process. In five experiments the update requirement did cause longer response times (Verhaeghen and Basak 2005, Experiments 1 and 2; Verhaeghen, Cerella and Basak 2004; Zhang and Verhaeghen 2005, Experiments 1 and 2). In four of these cases, update status did not interact with focus-switch costs, and in one (Verhaeghen and Basak 2005, Experiment 1) an overadditive interaction was obtained. The findings strongly suggest that updating and focus switching are executed independently and in serial fashion, perhaps with the added cost of unlocking shared resources to support an update following a focus switch.

Focus switching and task switching

A third control process to consider is task switching. Task switching shares a 'switching' logic with focus switching. In focus switching, the task remains the same across trials, but items have to be swapped in and out of the focus of attention. In task switching, the task changes from trial to trial, but ordinarily no storage (and therefore no swapping) of items is necessary. Switching between tasks, like focus switching, typically increases response times (e.g., Jersild 1927; Rogers and Monsell 1995). If the switching logic drives (part of) the focus-switching effect, one would expect an underadditive interaction between task switching and focus switching.

We designed a study (Verhaeghen and Hoyer, in press; see also Verhaeghen and Basak 2005, Experiment 2) to engage both switching processes explicitly. The paradigm was a continuous calculation task modeled after the number-reduction procedure devised by Woltz, Bell, Kyllonen *et al.* (1996). In the continuous calculation task, participants are presented with a string of single-digit numbers, only one of which is visible at any given time. The participants are instructed to perform a calculation on the first pair, type in their answer, combine this answer with the following item to perform the next calculation, and so on. Two types of calculations or rules were used: (a) When the numbers differed by two, the participant reported the average of the two, and used the result to combine with the next number shown on the screen ('midpoint rule'); (b) When the numbers differed by one, the participant reported the next number in the up or down numerical sequence, and used that number to combine with the next number shown on the screen ('up-and-down rule'). To aid participants, items for which the midpoint rule had to be used were presented in yellow, and up-and-down items were presented in blue. Focus switching was manipulated by having the participant work on one continuous series (single condition, no focus switching) versus having the participant work on two series, each one shown in a different column on the screen (dual condition, focus switching). Task switching was manipulated orthogonally by either having the participant work according to a single rule throughout a trial (pure condition) or by mixing the two rules according to a predictable ABAB ... schema (mixed condition). Additionally, a group of older adults was recruited for this experiment, to test for age-related dissociations.

The results are depicted in Figure 5.8. As can be seen, our subjects achieved perfect additivity of focus switching and task switching in response times; the aging manipulation was additive to both these manipulations. Thus, subjects seem to combine task switching and focus switching independently and in a serial fashion. Note that focus switching seems to be the more effortful process – the focus-switch cost in this experiment (around 600 ms) was about three times as large as the task-switching cost. Additionally, the costs in response times for the two processes were correlated only slightly and insignificantly ($r = 0.19$), a further indication that the underlying processes are largely independent.

The accuracy data are of interest because they show an age-related dissociation: the drop in accuracy due to the focus-switch process is (much) larger in older adults than in younger adults,

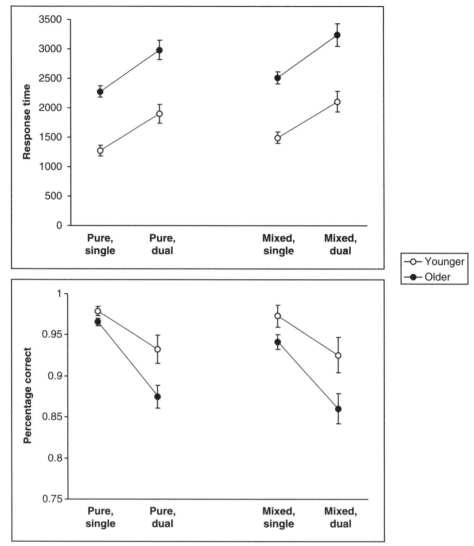

Figure 5.8 Response time and accuracy data, along with standard error bars, for a continuous-calculation task (data from Verhaeghen and Hoyer, 2007). We induced focus switching by using dual processing streams, and task switching by mixing tasks within a trial. Two age groups (younger and older adults) were tested. In response time, focus-switch and task-switch costs as well as age-effects were strictly additive, indicating that focus switching and task switching chain in a serial fashion; age had differential effects on accuracy for focus switching and task switching, indicating at least partial independence of the two processes.

but the drop due to the task-switch process is not. This again suggests at least partial independence of the two processes.

More evidence for the independence of task switching and focus switching in this study was found in the parameters of the ex-Gaussian distribution. In this study, focus switching produced a substantial increase in each of the parameters, indicating that both the leading edge and the dispersion (including the skew) of the distribution was affected. Task switching produced an increase in *mu*, or the leading edge of the distribution, only. Thus, task switching has the effect of shifting the distribution along the horizontal axis, without changing its dispersion or skew. This is consistent with the insertion of a normally distributed process that does not interfere with the computational requirements of the continuous calculation task itself. The results for focus switching suggest either that an additional ex-Gaussian process is added to the original distribution, or that several of the component processes of the original distribution are slowed by a multiplicative factor. This result also suggests that exactly what parameters of the ex-Gaussian distribution will be subject to the focus-switch effect (more specifically, whether the Gaussian parameters will be affected or not) might be a function of the embedded task: Whereas our identify-judgment N-Back task did not lead to an increase in *mu* or *sigma*, the continuous-calculation task did. Perhaps the complexity of the embedded task is responsible for this difference.

Conclusion: the ins and outs of working memory

Many researchers have been interested in the static aspects of working memory, like the system's capacity and structure. Our studies have been more concerned with the dynamic aspects of working memory, the process that swaps items in and out of the focus of attention, the dynamics of retrieval and the relation between focus switching and other executive control processes.

In summary, our research supports the following conclusions. First, working memory contains at its core a zone of privileged access, the focus of attention. Second, depending on the task and on the allocation of resources (which is partially a function of experience with the task) this zone can hold between 1 and 4 items. Third, items within this zone appear to be retrieved through a parallel, limited-capacity search. Fourth, items stored in working memory beyond the focus of attention appear to be retrieved through a relatively slow, potentially serial search process, but can under ideal circumstances be accessed by direct, content-addressable retrieval. Fifth, the focus-switching cost cannot be attributed exclusively to the increase in memory load that may accompany the switch. Sixth, the focus-switching process is largely independent of other executive control processes operating on working memory – resistance to interference, updating, and task switching.

These conclusions are more tentative than we would like – the experiments are still too few. For instance, the extent to which our results will generalize to other experimental paradigms is not known. Another lapse in our knowledge concerns the determinants of the size of the focus-switch cost (Voigt and Hagendorf [2002] provided the first evidence for the influence of stimulus characteristics on focus switching; see also Zhang and Verhaeghen [2005]). Lastly, the role of focus-switching in standard working memory tasks, such as operation span, and in tasks involving multiple storage and processing demands, such as dual task coordination, needs to be elucidated.

Acknowledgments

This research was supported in part by grants from the National Institute on Aging (AG-16201 and AG–11451).

References

Baddeley, A (1996). Exploring the central executive. *Quarterly Journal of Experimental Psychology*, 49A, 5–28.

Basak, C (2005). Capacity limits of the focus of attention and dynamics of the focus switch cost in working memory. Unpublished doctoral dissertation, Syracuse University, Syracuse, New York.

Basak, C, Cerella, J and Verhaeghen, P (2004). Age-related differences in the expansion of focus of attention after extensive practice: Results from a columnized *N*-Back task. Poster presented at the Cognitive Aging Conference, Atlanta, GA, April.

Bopp, K (2003). Exploration of age-related differences in executive control processes of verbal and visuo-spatial working memory: Evidence from the repetition-detection paradigm. Unpublished doctoral dissertation, Syracuse University, Syracuse, New York.

Cowan, N (1995). *Attention and Memory: An integrated framework*. New York: Oxford University Press.

Cowan, N (1999). An embedded-processes model of working memory. In A. Miyake and P. Shah (eds), *Models of Working Memory: Mechanisms of active maintenance and executive control* (pp. 62–101). Cambridge: Cambridge University Press.

Cowan, N (2001). The magical number 4 in short-term memory: A reconsideration of mental storage capacity. *Behavioral and Brain Sciences, 24*, 87–185.

Dempster, FN and Corkill, AJ (1999). Individual differences in susceptibility to interference and general cognitive ability. *Acta Psychologica, 101*, 395–416.

Engle, RW, Tuholski, SW, Laughlin, JE and Conway, ARA (1999). Working memory, short-term memory, and general fluid intelligence: A latent-variable approach. *Journal of Experimental Psychology: General, 128*, 309–331.

Fisher, DL (1984). Central capacity limits in consistent mapping, visual search tasks: Four channels or more? *Cognitive Psychology, 16*, 449–484.

Garavan, H (1998). Serial attention within working memory. *Memory and Cognition, 26*, 263–276.

Hasher, L and Zacks, RT (1988). Working memory, comprehension, and aging: a review and a new view. In GH Bower (ed), *The Psychology of Learning and Motivation, Vol. 22* (pp. 193–225). San Diego, CA: Academic Press.

Hockley, WE (1984). Analysis of response time distributions in the study of cognitive processes. *Journal of Experimental Psychology: Learning, Memory and Cognition, 10*, 598–615.

Jersild, AT (1927). Mental set and shift. *Archives of Psychology, 89*.

Kahneman, D (1973). *Attention and Effort*. Englewood Cliffs, NJ: Prentice-Hall.

Kane, MJ and Engle, RW (2002). The role of prefrontal cortex in working-memory capacity, executive attention, and general fluid intelligence: An individual-differences perspective. *Psychonomic Bulletin and Review, 9*, 637–671.

McElree, B (1998). Attended and non-attended states in working memory: Accessing categorized structures. Journal of Memory and Language, *38*, 225–252.

McElree, B (2001). Working memory and focal attention. *Journal of Experimental Psychology: Learning, Memory, and Cognition, 27*, 817–835.

Miller, GA (1956). The magical number seven, plus or minus two: Some limits on our capacity for processing information. *Psychological Review, 63*, 81–97.

Miyake, A, Friedman, NP, Emerson, MJ, Witzki, AH and Howerter, A (2000). The unity and diversity of executive functions and their contributions to complex 'frontal lobe' tasks: A latent variable analysis. *Cognitive Psychology, 41*, 49–100.

Murdock, BB, Jr (1971). A parallel-processing model for scanning. *Perception and Psychophysics, 10*, 289–291.

Oberauer, K (2002). Access to information in working memory: Exploring the focus of attention. *Journal of Experimental Psychology: Learning, Memory, and Cognition, 28*, 411–421.

Oberauer, K, Süб, HM, Schulze, R, Wilhelm, O and Wittmann, WW (2000). Working memory capacity – facets of a cognitive ability construct. *Personality and Individual Differences, 29*, 1017–1045.

Ratcliff, R (1978). A theory of memory retrieval. *Psychological Review, 85*, 59–108.

Rogers RD and Monsell S (1995). Costs of a predictable switch between simple cognitive tasks. *Journal of Experimental Psychology: General, 124*, 207–231.

Sternberg, S (1966). High-speed scanning in human memory. *Science, 153*, 652–654.

Trick, L. M and Pylyshyn, ZW (1994). Why are small and large numbers enumerated differently? A limited-capacity preattentive stage in vision. *Psychological Review, 101*, 80–102.

Usher, M, Cohen, JD, Haarmann, HJ and Horn, D (2001). Neural mechanism for the magical number 4: competitive interactions and non-linear oscillations. *Behavioral and Brain Sciences, 24*, 151.

Van Zandt, T and Townsend, JT (1993). Self-terminating vs exhaustive processes in rapid visual, and memory search: An evaluative review. *Perception and Psychophysics*, *53*, 563–580.

Verhaeghen, P and Basak, C (2005). Aging and switching of the focus of attention in working memory: Results from a modified *N*-Back task. *Quarterly Journal of Experimental Psychology (A)*, *58*, 134–154.

Verhaeghen, P, Cerella, J and Basak, C (2004). A working memory workout: How to change to size of the focus of attention from one to four in ten hours or less. *Journals of Experimental Psychology: Learning, Memory, and Cognition*, *30*, 1322–1337.

Verhaeghen, P and Hoyer, WJ (2007). Aging, focus switching and task switching in a continuous calculation task: Evidence toward a new working memory control process. *Aging, Neuropsychology, and Cognition*, *14*, 22–39.

Voigt, S and Hagendorf, H (2002). The role of task context for component processes in focus switching. *Psychologische Beiträge*, *44*, 248–274.

Vogel, EK and Machizawa, MG (2004). Neural activity predicts individual differences in visual working memory capacity. *Nature*, *42*, 748–751.

Vogel, EK, McCollough, AW and Machizawa, MG (2005). Neural measures reveal individual differences in controlling access to working memory. *Nature*, *438*, 500–503.

Wickens, CD (1984). Processing resources in attention. In R Parasuraman and R Davies (eds), *Varieties of Attention* (pp. 61–101). New York: Academic Press.

Woltz, DJ, Bell, BG, Kyllonen, PC and Gardner, MK (1996). Memory for order of operations in the acquisition and transfer of sequential cognitive skills. *Journal of Experimental Psychology: Learning, Memory, and Cognition*, *22*, 438–457.

Zhang, YM and Verhaeghen, P (2005). *The effects of stimulus complexity on switching the focus of attention in visual working memory*. Poster presented at the CSAIL conference, Hood River, OR, August.

6

Neural bases of focusing attention in working memory
An fMRI study based on individual differences

Mariko Osaka and Naoyuki Osaka

Introduction

Working memory supports a variety of daily activities that require the storage and processing of information. When shopping, for example, we select an appropriate sweater while mentally reviewing the jackets currently in our wardrobe. We remember the color of a particular jacket and decide whether the sweater is appropriate to wear with that jacket. Most of our daily activities require the dual process of storing information, on the one hand, then processing information on the other.

This dual process often requires the person to focus attention by inhibiting other information that is unnecessary for the task being performed. In searching for a sweater to wear with a jacket, we sometimes compare the color, design and materials. When we search for the color, for instance, we need to focus attention on the color of the jacket and inhibit the material or other features of the jacket, and when we search for the design, as another instance, we focus attention on the material style, but inhibit the color. Thus, focusing and inhibiting attention are often required for the dual processing of information used in daily life.

This dual process is crucially required for higher cognitive brain functions, such as language comprehension. When we talk to each other or read text, focusing and inhibiting attention are also required. While reading a text, in order to comprehend the contents, readers likely search for the most important word, that is, the focus word, which provides an advantage during integration of the text. As well as focusing attention on the important word, the readers inhibit attention to other words not important to comprehending the sentence. Thus, while reading sentences, we continuously focus attention and inhibit attention in succession.

In this chapter, the neural substrates for focusing and shifting attention in executive function are described. Moreover, possible neural bases of focusing and shifting attention underlying individual differences between good and poor performers of a cognitive task are discussed.

Neural bases of working memory

Working memory serves the immediate brain processes involved in the simultaneous storage and processing of information and facilitates approaching the goals of cognitive function (Baddeley 1986; Just and Carpenter 1992).

Recent brain-imaging studies have attempted to identify the functional brain anatomy underlying working memory systems. It has been proposed that two types of working memory processes are subserved based on Baddeley's original model (Baddeley 1986): the one is modality-specific buffers, such as the phonological loop and visuospatial sketchpad; the other is the central executive system. Neuroimaging studies have explored the neural basis of these two types of working memory system (Kane and Engle 2002; Smith and Jonides 1999) and it was found that two types of working memory processes are subserved respectively by two distinct cortical structures. The retention of verbal information in the phonological loop evokes activation in the left ventrolateral prefrontal cortex (VLPFC), and that of visuospatial information in the right homologues (Awh, Jonides, Smith *et al.* 1996; Courtney Petit, Maisog *et al.* 1998; Jonides, Smith, Koeppe *et al.* 1993; Owen, Stern, Tracey *et al.* 1998; Paulesu, Frith and Frackowiak 1993; Smith, Jonides and Koeppe 1996).

As for the central executive system, it especially serves as an attention controller that allocates and coordinates attentional resources for cognitive tasks (Baddeley 1996; Engle, Tuholski, Laughlin *et al.* 1999; Baddeley and Logie 1999). Neuroimaging studies have explored the neural basis of this executive attention control system, and have suggested that the system is located in the prefrontal cortex, predominantly in the dorsolateral prefrontal cortex (DLPFC, BA9/46) and anterior cingulate cortex (ACC) (Bunge, Klinberg, Jacobson *et al.* 2000; Cohen, Perstein, Braver *et al.* 1997; D'Esposito, Detre, Alsop *et al.* 1995, D'Espostio, Aguirre, Zarahn *et al.* 1998, D'Esposito, Postle, Ballard *et al.* 1999; Kane and Engle 2003; Osaka, Osaka, Kondo *et al.* 2003, 2004; Owen, Evans and Petrides 1996; Smith and Jonides 1999; Smith, Geva, Jonides *et al.* 2001).

It has also been reported that brain activities in DLPFC increased with increases in working memory task demands (Braver, Cohen, Nystrom *et al.* 1997; Bunge *et al.* 2000; D'Esposito *et al.* 1995; Rypma, Prabhakaran, Desmond *et al.* 1999). D'Esposito *et al.* (1995) found that the DLPFC activation increased only during a dual task and not during single tasks. In their study, it was interesting that activation in DLPFC did not increase during single task even though the task difficulty was increased by a faster rate of stimulus presentation. The activation in DLPFC was also reported in Rypma *et al.* (1999). They compared activation in the DLPFC while subjects remembered one, three and six digits. While there was no activation when subjects remembered one or three digits, enhanced activation was found when they maintained six digits. Although three digits are easy enough for an adult to maintain (Cowan 2001), maintaining six digits exceeded the capacity of short-term memory. The subjects then needed the aid of executive attention control, which leads to activation increase in the DLPFC. According to these results, it is conceivable that the DLPFC plays a role in the attention control system of the executive function which required dual task performance or when the maintenance function exceeded the individual's short-term memory span.

The other critical area is ACC. It has been proposed that the anterior part of the cingulate cortex should be characterized as 'executive' in function, and the posterior parts characterized as 'evaluative' (Vogt, Finch and Olson 1992). Furthermore, the dorsal site of ACC is thought to be involved in cognitive activity, whereas the ventral site is an emotional division (Bush, Whalen, Rosen *et al.* 1998, Bush, Luu and Posner 2000). Additionally, increased ACC activation was reported to occur on error trials in high-conflict trials such as go/no-go, oddball, and two-alternative forced-choice selections (Barch, Braver, Nystrom *et al.* 1997; Braver *et al.* 2001; Bush *et al.* 1998; Carter, Braver, Barch *et al.* 1998). In these conflict situations, management of response conflict was required while facing two-response selection. Braver *et al.* (2001) reported a greater ACC response to error trials as opposed to high-conflict correct trials. Increased activation of the ACC was confirmed when subjects faced conflict situations, and considered inhibiting the interrupting response. It was also reported that ACC's signal intensity was significantly correlated with memory load using a delayed response task (Bunge, Oschner, Desmond *et al.* 2001).

Dissociation of ACC and DLPFC during cognitive task performance has been discussed by MacDonald, Cohen, Stenger *et al.* (2000) using a modified version of the Stroop paradigm. In their study, activation in ACC was found when subjects engaged in incongruent color-naming trials but not when engaged in congruent trials. However, activation was observed in the DLPFC even in congruent trials. According to these results, MacDonald *et al.* (2000) suggested that the ACC was subserved when control of attention needed to be strongly engaged to monitor performance during incongruent color-naming trials. The DLPFC, however, plays a role in providing top-down support of attention maintenance for task-appropriate behaviors. Smith and Jonides (1999) also proposed that the ACC mediates the inhibition of a preprogrammed response, that is, word reading, which occurs automatically in incongruent color-naming trials in Stroop task. In contrast, DLPFC reflected the operation of attention and inhibition in the processing sequences and both DLPFC and ACC play an executive role when performing working memory tasks.

Neural correlates of the span task

Since working memory resources available for both maintaining and processing are finite, there are individual differences in working memory capacity between people who effectively allocate portions of resources for maintaining or processing effectively. A reading span test (RST) was developed and implemented to behaviorally measure individual differences in verbal working memory capacity employed by processing and storage functions during reading sentences (Daneman and Carpenter 1980).

It is interesting that performance differences on RST can account for various aspects of language comprehension (Daneman and Carpenter 1980; Daneman and Merikle 1996; Just and Carpenter 1992). Daneman and Carpenter (1980) found a significant correlation between reading comprehension scores and RST span scores. Subjects with large working memory capacity were successful in maintaining target words, while subjects with small working memory capacity had difficulty due to insufficient working memory capacity during reading.

The functions or processes being measured during the span task are similar to executive control processes of the working memory system (Baddeley 1992; Just and Carpenter 1992). Then, resource allocation in RST must be controlled by the executive control system, which serves as an attention controller that allocates and coordinates attentional resources during reading and maintaining the representation of the target words.

Neural substrates of span tasks have been investigated by fMRI studies and increases in activation associated with task demands have been observed. Just, Carpenter and Keller (1996) found an activation increase in the left frontal and temporal language areas during RST as compared with a single reading task. In frontal regions, Bunge et al. (2000) found increased activation under the RST condition, suggesting that increased activation in this region is affected by dual task demands.

Using another kind of span task, that is operation span task (OST), in which subjects maintain the target words while performing arithmetic tasks, the neural bases of dual task were explored (Smith et al. 2001). They found activation in left DLPFC during OST, and it was also reported that activation in DLPFC occurred only in poor performers but not in good performers. It was suggested that the activation in DLPFC was affected by the level of task demand on subjects during the sequences of span task.

Following these findings, further questions arise concerning the neural bases attributable to the differences between high-span subjects and low-span subjects measured by the span task. What are the neural substrates of working memory resources and how do these relate to individual performance differences and which of these brain mechanisms are required to perform the span task?

Neural bases of individual differences

Although previous studies did not explore the neural bases on working memory capacity difference, Osaka et al. (2003, 2004a) investigated the neural substrates attributable to differences between two subject groups (high-span subjects (HSS) and low-span subjects (LSS) according to the span scores on the RST) during performance of a span task. The fMRI activity while subjects performed a listening span test (LST) in which subjects were required to both listen to sentences and remember the target words was compared with those during two single-task paradigms of maintaining the target words and listening to sentences. Significant activation was found mainly in three regions in comparison with resting control: left PFC, ACC and temporal language area. For both groups, the fMRI signal intensity increased in the left PFC during the LST condition compared to listening conditions. A group difference was found in the ACC region, specifically a significant increase in signal intensity was observed in ACC only for the HSS group but not for the LSS group (Osaka *et al.* 2003).

Figure 6.1 shows the activated areas on axial planes of the standard glass brain images under LST condition (Osaka *et al.* 2003). The figure on the left shows the activated areas averaged across HSS, that on the right those of LSS. To compare fMRI signal increases under LST or RST under single task condition, mean percentages of signal changes were calculated at the most activated voxels within each of the two regions of interest (ROIs), the left DLPFC and ACC. Figure 6.2 shows the mean time course of activated voxels in ACC and DLPFC while subjects performed LST in HSS (left figure) and LSS (right figure). The figure shows that the signal changes between two regions were more related for HSS compared with LSS.

While performing RST, significant activation was found mainly in three regions: ACC, left PFC and visual association area (Osaka *et al.* 2004a). For both groups, the fMRI signal intensity increased mainly in ACC and left PFC during the RST condition compared to the single reading condition. A group difference was also found in the ACC and left PFC region, specifically a significant increase of signal intensity was observed only for the HSS group but not for the LSS group.

Furthermore, in order to compare the possible functional connectivity between ACC and DLPFC, a separate mean time course was computed for the signal changes in HSS and LSS, respectively (Osaka *et al.* 2003, 2004a). The correlation coefficient between ACC and the DLPFC region was higher in HSS ($r = 0.82$) compared to that of LSS ($r = 0.69$) under LST condition (Osaka *et al.* 2003). Under RST condition, the correlation coefficient between ACC and the DLPFC region were also significantly higher in HSS ($r = 0.92$) compared to that in LSS ($r = 0.84$, Osaka *et al.* 2004a).

The correlation coefficient implies the similarity of voxel activation between the two regions. It is also possible to interpret that higher correlations across different cortical areas throughout the activation time course indicate increased functional connectivity (Diwadkar, Carpenter and Just 2000). From this suggestion, the relative functional connectivity between ACC and DLPFC on RST and LST appears stronger in HSS than in LSS. Behavioral data also showed that the performance was better in HSS than in LSS.

These findings indicate that executive function, especially the attention controlling system supported by ACC, is more effective in HSS than in LSS. Figure 6.3 shows network

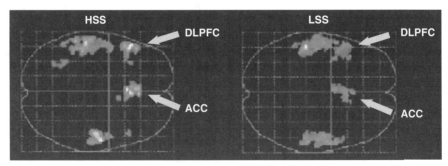

Figure 6.1 Activated areas on axial planes of the standard glass brain images (upper side of axial image shows left hemisphere). The figure on the left shows the activated areas averaged across eight HSS, while those on the right show those of LSS. Panels show the activated areas under the LST condition. See also color plate 1.

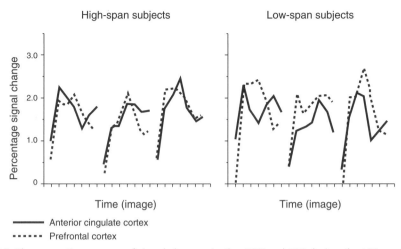

Figure 6.2 The mean time course of signal changes in the ACC and PFC during the LST condition. The left figure shows signal changes of HSS and the right those of LSS. Adapted with permission from Oasaka, M., Osaka, N., Kondo, H. et al. (2003). The neural basis of individual differences in working memory capacity: an fMRI study. *NeuroImage*, 18, 789–797, Elsevier Science.

differences in executive function between HSS and LSS groups. The dotted line shows the weak network of LSS between DLPFC and ACC. HSS engaged ACC more strongly than LSS. As a result, HSS were able to more effectively manipulate attentional control while monitoring their own performance compared to LSS, leading to a superior behavioral performance for HSS on the span task.

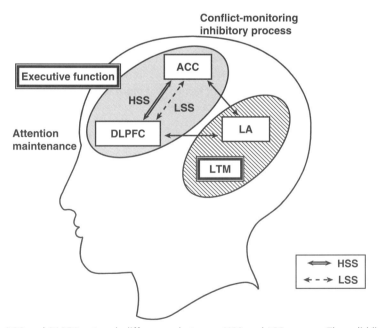

Figure 6.3 ACC and DLPFC network differences between HSS and LSS groups. The solid line shows the network for HSS and the dotted line that for LSS. The dotted line shows weak network of LSS between DLPFC and ACC.

Based on these findings, Osaka *et al.* (2003, 2004a) concluded that the ACC subserves attention control in working memory, allowing inhibition and monitoring in accordance with the DLPFC. While performing the span task such as LST and RST, the attention controller of the executive function was regulated by the DLPFC and ACC, which play roles in maintaining attention and inhibitory processes, respectively. As for capacity differences, it was found that activation differences between groups were also derived from differences in these two regions and high functional connectivity between ACC and DLPFC is constantly observed in HSS but not in LSS.

By applying structural equation modeling (SEM), we also identified the network system between DLPFC and ACC with empirical data using the OST (Kondo, Morishita, Osaka *et al.* 2004a). During OST, the subjects performed verification of arithmetic problems and retention of target words. Behavioral data showed that the performance was better in HSS than in LSS under OST, but there was no difference under two single-task conditions, that is, an arithmetic task and a word retention task.

Previous studies reported that the OST scores like RST scores are highly correlated with reading comprehension (Turner and Engle 1989). Engle *et al.* (1999) also suggested that predicted power of correlations between working memory tasks and cognitive tasks is derived from executive functioning using SEM. Then, we tested how activation of multiple brain areas is connected with working memory using SEM. We employed SEM to construct the best fitting neuronal network model that can account for time-series fMRI of ROIs.

The results showed that the ACC, left PFC and bilateral parietal cortex were activated for both groups. However, signal changes in the ACC were greater in the HSS than in the LSS under OST. SEM indicated that an estimate of effective connectivity from the ACC to the left PFC was positive (0.43) for the HSS while negative (−0.14) for the LSS, indicating that closer cooperation between the two brain areas was strongly related to working memory performance in HSS.

Using a spatial span task (SST), we also compared networks between ACC and DLPFC (Kondo, Osaka and Osaka. 2004b). In the SST, letter verification with mental rotation and retention of arrow orientations was performed. A significant positive correlation with signal change in the right DLPFC and right ACC (r = 0.49) was found under dual task. The rotation-arrow task is known to correlate with visuospatial processing (Shah and Miyake 1996). Right DLPFC activation was followed as the right brain plays a crucial role in visuo-spatial processing (Courtney *et al.* 1998; Jonides *et al.* 1993). We again confirmed that mean signal change was greater for the HSS than for the LSS under dual task, but not under either the rotation or arrow condition alone (single task). It was also found the effective connectivity between the right DLPFC and right ACC in the HSS but not in the LSS using SEM analysis.

These findings confirmed that executive function, i.e., attention controlling system, is more active in HSS than in LSS. These findings also suggest that there is a general neural basis for the central executive function in span tasks despite differences in modality-specific buffers that are employed by the phonological loop during RST, LST and OST or by visuospatial sketchpad during SST.

Focus and inhibitory processes

Little is known, however, regarding the neural bases of focusing attention during the span task. Focusing attention is extremely important for attentional control systems in executive function (Cowan 2001). The role of the central executive is related to the control and selection of the currently relevant portion of activated long-term memory representations, which was thought to be under the surveillance of the focus of attention (Cowan 1999, 2001). Cowan (2001) suggested that the focus of attention represents a capacity-limited part of working memory and that the focus of attention holds a restricted sets of items, that is, about four independent units.

Focusing attention is also important for language comprehension during reading or listening (Blutner and Sommer 1988; Carpenter and Just 1977; Hornby 1974; Osaka, Nishizaki, Komori et al. 2002). In text reading, Birch and Garnsey (1995) investigated the effect of focus on memory for words in sentences and found that focusing on a word enhances memory. They proposed that focus in the sentence facilitates the process of integrating information in sentences and is critical for creating a coherent understanding. Carpenter and Just (1977) also suggested that subjects direct their attention initially to the focus of a sentence and then focused constituents are easily comprehended during reading.

Thus, while reading a sentence, readers usually focus attention on the most critical word to facilitate comprehension of the sentence. Once readers make the mental representation with the focus word, the contents of the sentence may have been easily accessed via the mental representation. Thus, it became easier for the subjects to read and comprehend the sentences by using these mental representations.

Other researchers suggest the importance of an inhibitory mechanism in reading. Gernsbacher (1990) suggested that a deficit in the inhibitory mechanism is implicated in comprehension difficulty. In an experiment by Gernsbacher and Faust (1991), subjects were told to focus on either a picture or a word in the context display and to ignore the other. Then they were asked to indicate whether the probe word was related to the word in the context display. They found differences between skilled and less-skilled readers in terms of ignoring an irrelevant stimulus. The results suggested that the suppression mechanism of less-skilled readers is less efficient in suppressing the non-focused, ignored information than that of more skilled readers.

Similar suggestions have been made regarding deficits in inhibiting among those who perform poorly on the span task (Conway and Engle 1994; De Beni, Palladion, Pazzaglia et al. 1998; Engle, Conway, Tuholski et al. 1995; May, Hasher and Kane 1999). These studies showed that low performers in the span task have a deficit in inhibiting information irrelevant for the task. De Beni et al. (1998) presented random strings of words instead of sentences on the RST while requesting subjects to tap the hand when an animal noun appeared in the word strings. Then the subjects were required to recall the last word each set. The number of intrusion errors that subjects made when they recalled the target word were counted and compared between the two subject groups, identified as good comprehenders and poor comprehenders. The results showed that the intrusion errors when the subjects recalled the target words were larger for poor comprehenders than for good comprehenders. In addition, within the intrusion errors made by poor comprehenders, intrusions more frequently involved animal nouns than other non-target words. These results suggested that the low comprehenders had difficulty in inhibiting words that they had previously focused attention on.

Focused RST vs non focused RST

In order to confirm the importance of focusing attention in span task, Osaka et al. (2002) developed two kinds of RST, that is focused-RST (F-RST) and non-focused RST (NF-RST) and compared the performances between F-RST and NF-RST. In the F-RST, the target word to be maintained was a focus word of the sentence. In the NF-RST, however, the target word was not a focus word of the sentence.

The focus word was defined as the most critical word for comprehension of a sentence (Birch and Garnsey 1995; Halliday 1967), that is, the word with a core meaning necessary to integrate

Table 6.1 Sample of 'focus word' of a sentence and the target words of the focused and non-focused RST

The child dropped food on his jacket and made **stains**. *Focus word*
Focused RST
The child dropped food on his jacket and made **stains**. *Target word*
Non-focused RST
The child dropped **food** on his jacket and made stains. *Target word*

the sentence. To identify the focus word of each sentence, focus words were selected by students who evaluated the sentences in a preliminary investigation. These students were requested to identify which word of the sentence was the most important and critical to understanding the sentence. Focus words were adopted when more than 70 per cent of subjects selected the word as the focus word of the sentence, as the study by Birch and Garnsey (1995).

Table 6.1 shows sample sentences from both focused RST and non-focused RST. In the sentence 'The child dropped food on his jacket and made stains', the word 'stains' was chosen as the focus word by the preliminary investigation. Therefore, in the F-RST, 'stains' was selected as the target word, while in the NF-RST version, the non focus word 'food 'was selected as a target word. The non- focus word, that is 'food 'in NF-RST, was selected on 17 per cent of occasions as the most important word in the sentence.

As for the target position in the sentence of the Japanese version of RST, the target word occupied various positions in the sentence and was the underlined word in each sentence (Osaka and Osaka 1992, 1994). In studies of RST in English, the target word was the last word of each sentence (Daneman and Carpenter 1980). This difference of target position in our Japanese version was required because the last word of the sentence in Japanese is usually a verb. In addition, as a feature of Japanese syntactic mechanisms, the last word of a Japanese sentence is rarely a focus word (Kuno 1978), whereas in English, the last word of the sentence easily becomes the end focus word (Bolinger 1986).

With the difference of target position between Japanese-RST and English-RST, however, we found a significantly higher correlation between the Japanese-RST span scores and the English-RST span scores ($r = 0.84$, $p < 0.001$) (Osaka and Osaka 1992). Moreover, as in the English RST version, a high correlation was found between the Japanese RST span scores and reading comprehension test scores (Osaka and Osaka 1994).

Focusing attention and inhibitory processes in NF-RST

While reading a sentence in RST, subjects likely focus attention on the focus word of the sentence to comprehend it. However, in RST, two different functions are concurrently executed: reading the sentences and memorizing the target words. Because the goal of the RST is to recall target words, subjects are not likely to maintain attention on the focus word of the sentence.

Thus, when the 'target word' to be maintained coincides with the focus of attention ('focus word') in the sentence, word maintenance is likely to be easier. However, when the target word does not coincide with the focus word of the sentence, subjects have to shift attention from the focus word to another target word.

Figure 6.4 shows a diagram of attention-control during F-RST (left-hand side) and NF- RST (right-hand side). In F-RST, the focus of attention corresponds between the focus word 'stains' and target word 'stains'. However, in NF-RST (right-hand figure), the focus of attention does not correspond between the focus word 'stains' and target word 'food'. Then subjects have to shift

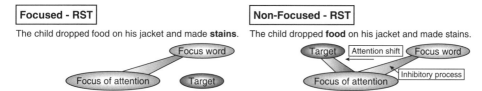

Figure 6.4 The diagram of attention control during both RST. The left diagram shows attention control under F-RST and the right that under NF-RST.

attention from the focus word 'stains' to the target word 'food'. Inhibition of attention on the focus word 'stains' is also required, because the focus of attention is capacity limited (Cowan 2001). Otherwise, subjects will be faced with a conflict between the target word and focus word.

In Osaka *et al.* (2002), span scores were significantly higher for F-RST compared to NF-RST. The number of intrusion errors was significantly higher in NF-RST than F-RST. In the NF-RST, intrusion errors were divided into two types. One was a focus-intrusion error in which subjects recalled the focus word 'stains' instead of the target word 'food', and the other was a non-focus-intrusion in which subjects recalled a word ('child' for example) other than the focus word. It was interesting that most of the intrusion errors in NF-RST were focus intrusion errors. The predominance of focus-intrusion errors in NF-RST suggests that subjects had difficulty inhibiting the focus word on which the subjects had previously focused attention.

Individual differences in focusing and shifting attention

Osaka *et al.* (2002) also compared performance on both F-and NF-RST between HSS and LSS. The results demonstrated a significant effect of focusing and shifting attention for LSS but not for HSS. Rates of intrusion errors were higher for LSS than for HSS. These findings indicated that LSS have deficits in their ability to shift attention and inhibit the irrelevant word. These results support previous studies that indicate LSS have a deficit in ability to inhibit information irrelevant for the task (May, Hasher and Kane 1999). It was also supported by other studies that indicate poor comprehenders make significantly more intrusion errors than good comprehenders (Gernsbacher 1990; Gernsbacher and Faust 1991).

However, the LSS in Osaka *et al.* (2002) made significantly more intrusion errors in the NF-RST condition than in F-RST. The theory by Gernsbacher (1990) that implicates a lack of inhibition of irrelevant stimuli for poor comprehenders would predict that intrusion errors on F-RST would be equal to that on NF-RST, because there were still irrelevant stimuli even in F-RST (child, food, jacket for example). It was interesting that among intrusion errors in NF-RST in LSS, the number of focus-intrusions was significantly larger than non-focus intrusion. In HSS, on the contrary, this difference was not found. These results suggest that LSS have more difficulty in inhibiting information, especially of the focus word. If LSS had difficulty in inhibiting any kind stimuli, they would have shown a worse performance on F-RST similar to that on NF-RST. Thus, it was not that LSS can not inhibit irrelevant information, but that they can not inhibit irrelevant information after having initially focused attention on it.

Following these findings, it could be possible that shifting attention does not function well for LSS after they have previously focused attention and built a mental focus.

Neural bases of focusing and shifting attention

In the following section, neural substrates for focusing and shifting attention in executive function will be discussed. In Osaka *et al.* (2004b, 2007), to examine the neural bases of focusing attention during RST, fMRI activations were compared between two kinds of RST conditions: F-RST and NF-RST. In addition, possible neural bases underlying group differences between HSS and LSS were examined.

fMRI activations were measured while subjects performed three kinds of experimental tasks: F-RST, NF-RST and READ. In READ condition, single reading of five sentences was required. Under RST conditions, subjects were required to read the sentence while concurrently remembering the target word in each sentence.

Figure 6.5 shows the experimental time course of RST and READ conditions. The lower left figure shows one block of the RST and the right shows the READ condition. Both conditions in reading phase consisted of five sentences.

Under both RST conditions, after the end of the reading phase, five probe stimuli appeared every 5 s in the recognition phase. The probe stimuli appeared in the same order as the stimulus sentences. Each probe stimulus consisted of two words and an X character. One of the probe words was the target word and other word was another word from the sentence. In F-RST, the target word was the focus word 'stains' of the sentence and in NF-RST, the target word was not the focus word of the sentence but rather a filler word 'food' was the target word. When the subject distinguished the target word between these two words, the subject pushed the key corresponding to the selected probe stimulus.

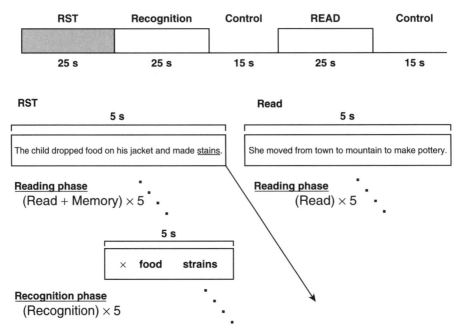

Figure 6.5 Time course of RST and READ conditions. The upper figure shows the block-design paradigm in fMRI study. The lower left figure shows one block of the RST and the right shows the READ condition. The reading phase under RST condition consisted on five sentences, which were presented at 5 s intervals. At the end of the five sentences under the RST condition, recognition stimuli appeared every 5 s during the recognition phase. Adapted with permission from Osaka, M., Komori, M., Morishita, M., & Osaka, N. (2007). Neural basis of focusing attention in working memory. *Cognitive, Affective & Behavioral Neuroscience*, In Press, The Psychonomic Society.

Behavioral data showed that the accuracy of the performance was better for F-RST than for NF- RST for both HSS and LSS. Moreover, in both RST, accuracy was better for HSS than LSS. The number of intrusion errors was also counted and the mean number of intrusion errors during NF-RST was larger than that during F-RST for only LSS. Moreover, there were more focus intrusions (subjects recalled 'stains' instead of the target word 'food' in NF-RST) for LSS than other non-focus intrusion (response X).

The fMRI data show activated areas included the left DLPFC and ACC under both RST conditions. In addition, enhanced activation was found in the left superior parietal lobule (SPL; BA7) during both reading phases.

Figure 6.6 upper panel shows significantly activated brain areas on sagittal plane of brain images (sliced, x = −26) for HSS during the reading phase under F-RST and NF-RST conditions relative to activations under the READ condition. The lower panel shows those for LSS. For HSS, increased activation was found in the left SPL under the NF-RST as compared with that under the F-RST (note the scale difference in the figure). For LSS, on the contrary, increased activation in the left SPL was scarcely found under the NF-RST compared with the F-RST condition.

To compare fMRI signal increases under the two RST conditions, mean percentages of signal changes were calculated at the most activated voxels within each of the three ROIs, left DLPFC, ACC and left SPL. The signal change was calculated separately for the two time phases in RST; the reading phase and recognition phase.

In the left SPL, significant activations were found for both RST compared to that under the single READ condition for both groups. Group differences were also found for the left SPL activation for both F-RST and NF-RST; HSS showed higher activity than LSS during both RST. Moreover, for HSS only, greater activation was seen during NF-RST than during F-RST.

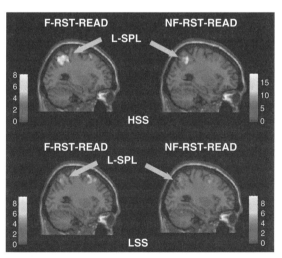

Figure 6.6 Activated areas on the sagittal plane of brain images (x = −26). Figures on the left side show activation areas under F-RST while those on the right side show activation areas under NF-RST condition relative to activations under READ condition. The upper panel shows the activated areas averaged across HSS and lower panel shows those across LSS. See also color plate 2.
Adapted with permission from Osaka, M., Komori, M., Morishita, M., and Osaka, N. (2007). Neural basis of focusing attention in working memory. *Cognitive, Affective & Behavioral Neuroscience*, In Press, The Psychonomic Society.

In the ACC, significantly greater signal increases were found during both RST than under the READ condition only for HSS. Group differences were also found for ACC activation. HSS showed higher activity than LSS during both types of RST. For the focusing effect, however, HSS displayed lower activation in the NF-RST than in the F-RST.

In the left DLPFC, signal changes increased significantly in both RST compared to the READ condition for HSS, but such increases were not found in the LSS group.

During the recognition phases, activated areas also included the left DLPFC, ACC and left SPL. Figure 6.7 shows significantly activated brain areas on sagittal plane of brain images (sliced, x = −4) during the recognition phase under the NF-RST condition. The left-hand figure shows the activation of HSS and right-hand side shows that of LSS. Figure 6.7 shows that dominant activation was found in the dorsal site of ACC under NF-recognition for LSS as compared with HSS. The mean percentages of signal changes were also calculated in the recognition phase. In ACC, a significant signal increase was found during non-focused recognition than during focused recognition for LSS only.

The role of ACC and DLPFC

Activation increases were found predominantly in three regions the left-DLPFC, ACC and SPL in both F-RST and NF-RST (Osaka *et al*. 2004a, 2007). Increased activation in the DLPFC and ACC confirmed previous reports of working memory demands (Bunge *et al*. 2000; D'Esposito *et al*. 1995; Cohen *et al*. 1997; Duncan and Owen 2000; Osaka *et al*. 2003, 2004b; Rypma 1999).

Regarding the role of the DLPFC, MacDonald *et al*. (2000) concluded that the DLPFC provides top-down support for task-appropriate behaviors. During reading phases in both F- and NF-RST, the subjects were required to remember the target word while they read sentences, thus maintaining attention on the target words was required. In both RST, increased activation in DLPFC was found only in HSS; thus, HSS could maintain attention to the target word. HSS showed superior maintenance of attention on the target words while reading sentences during the reading phase. The focusing effect, however, was not confirmed in left-DLPFC.

During the recognition phases, maintenance of attention on the target words was also needed while subjects determined whether the probe stimulus was identical to the target word. Because the filler probe word was the focus word in NF-RST, without attention maintenance to the target word, the subject could easily confuse target words with filler words. In non-focused recognition, increased activation in left-DLPFC was found only in HSS, thus HSS maintained attention on the target even in recognition phase.

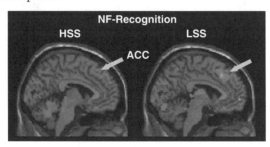

Figure 6.7 Activated areas on the sagittal plane of brain images (x = −4) in NF-recognition phase. Figures on the left show activation areas across HSS while those on the right show activation areas across LSS. See also color plate 3.
Adapted with permission from Osaka, M., Komori, M., Morishita, M., and Osaka, N. (2007). Neural basis of focusing attention in working memory. *Cognitive, Affective & Behavioral Neuroscience*, In Press, The Psychonomic Society.

Regarding ACC involvement, attention control mediates inhibition of preprogrammed responses as well as monitoring of task performance, leading to release conflict (MacDonald *et al.* 2000; Smith and Jonides 1999). During NF-RST, the subject must shift attention from the focus word to the target word and inhibition of the focus word is required. Then, activation of the ACC is considered to reflect the operation of inhibiting the focus word during the processing sequences. Increased activation of the ACC was found only in HSS, who were supposed to have a superior ability to shift attention from the focus word to the target word. For LSS, however, there was no increase in the activation of the ACC during either RST.

The focusing effect in ACC was not confirmed during the reading phase. On the contrary, significant signal decreases were found during NF-RST in HSS. During the recognition phase, conversely, the focusing effect was confirmed only in LSS, where significant signal increases were found during non-focused recognition compared to that during focused recognition.

Increased ACC activation was also reported to occur on error trials in high-conflict trials (Barch *et al.* 1997; Braver *et al.* 2001; Bush *et al.* 1998; Carter *et al.* 1998). In these conflict situations, management of response conflict was required when facing two-response selection. Increased activation of the ACC was confirmed when subjects faced conflict situations, and was considered to inhibit the interrupting response. In accordance with these findings, subjects in the NF-RST faced conflict between the target and the focus word during the recognition phase.

Figure 6.8 shows the diagram of attention control during the recognition phase in both RST. The left side diagram shows the recognition phase under F-RST and the right side diagram shows that of under NF-RST. Higher activations of the ACC in LSS in non-focused recognition were supposed to result from a conflict when they faced two potential conflict words, that is the target word and the focus word. Behavioral data of intrusion errors also confirmed this; intrusion errors in NF-RST increased not for HSS but for LSS.

In HSS, however, activation increases were not confirmed even during non-focused recognition. This is because HSS were released from conflict. HSS have already shifted attention to the target word in reading phases and could inhibit the unnecessary word during non-focused RST. Thus, HSS had no further conflict when facing the target and focus words in non-focused recognition.

SPL and focusing attention

Regarding SPL, increased activation in the left hemisphere was found during the reading phase in both RST. The SPL involving the lateral intraparietal area is generally related to attention and saccade-related eye movements (Cullan and Kanwisher 2001). Previous research also reported that the SPL and vicinity are activated during a mental rotation task (Carpenter *et al.* 1999).

Thus, SPL may potentially share the role of visual attention controller and serves to focus and shift attention together with executive functions in the ACC and DLPFC during the RST. A focusing effect in the left SPL was found only in HSS; HSS showed greater increases in activation during NF-RST compared with that during F-RST. In LSS, however, there was no detectable focusing effect.

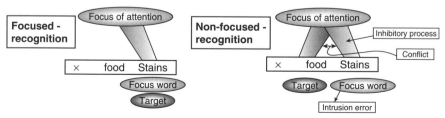

Figure 6.8 The diagram of attention control during the recognition phase under both RST. The left diagram shows F-RST and the right NF-RST.

It is also interesting that a reverse increase in ACC was found in HSS during the reading phase. This may be caused by the larger increase in SPL during the reading phase. When activity of the SPL increases to shift attention, subjects release the conflict between the focus word and target word. Then they had no further need to inhibit the focus word, and activity in the ACC decreased as a result. Thus, the SPL together with activation of the ACC plays a role in focusing and shifting attention.

Individual differences in focusing and shifting attention

The behavioral results, especially in intrusion errors, showed that the focus effect was more dominant for LSS than HSS. However, fMRI data showed that the focus effect was more dominant for HSS than LSS in the reading phase.

Activation increases in SPL during reading phases under NF-RST conditions were more pronounced in HSS than in LSS.

Figure 6.9 shows the neural bases of focusing attention on the executive control system. The solid line and dotted line also show neural network differences between HSS and LSS (dotted line indicates weak connectivity). Activation in SPL during the reading phase was accompanied by activation in the DLPFC and ACC in HSS.

For LSS, there were no detectable activation increases in SPL during reading phases under NF-RST conditions. In addition, activation in the DLPFC was insufficient to maintain attention on the target word. The limited activation in ACC during the reading phase confirmed that LSS were not sensitive to which word they focus attention on and for which one they inhibit attention.

This insensitivity of focusing attention leads LSS to face a strong conflict between the target word and focus word during the recognition phase. This conflict led LSS to greater activation of the ACC during the recognition phase in non-focused recognition. Moreover, the strong conflict caused an increase in intrusion errors for LSS during non-focused recognition.

Thus, in the recognition phases, fMRI activity in the ACC showed that the focus effect was more dominant for LSS than for HSS, leading to dominance of the focusing effect on behavioral results for LSS.

There are several possible arguments to explain the differences in focusing effect between HSS and LSS. One is that shifting attention contributed to a performance difference between the HSS and LSS. In NF-RST, the focus word interfered with the target word since the focus word had

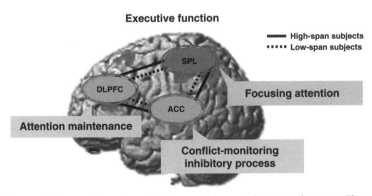

Figure 6.9 The neural bases of focusing attention on the executive control system. The solid line and dotted line also show neural network differences between HSS and LSS, respectively, (dotted line indicates weak connectivity). See also color plate 4.

already been activated during reading. Subjects would then have to decide which word was relevant to the goals of the task, i.e., the target word, and shift attention to the target word. With the aid of SPL, HSS shifted attention from the focus word to the target word immediately. LSS, however, with less aid from the SPL, had difficulty shifting attention from the focus word to the target word. Without shifting attention, it is likely that LSS are strongly affected by conflict between the focus word and the target word. This conflict between the two words is similar to the conflict in the Stroop task. As a result, LSS may lose track of what is required or what the goals of the task are. In addition, LSS have a deficit in monitoring system in the conflict situation, which disables their ability to keep track of the goals of the task or which word they should maintain.

Another argument is that LSS have a deficit in inhibiting their mental focus. LSS, however, can not inhibit irrelevant information, but they have difficulty in inhibiting information after having initially focused attention on it. The deficit in inhibiting mental focus coincided with previous findings reported by De Beni *et al.* (1998), which suggested that poor readers had difficulty in inhibiting words that required other forms of attention. In addition, as Gernsbacher and Faust (1991) reported that low comprehenders take a longer time to inhibit, LSS took a longer time to inhibit mental focus and this delay affected the shifting of attention to the target word.

A weak attention inhibition control system may account for LSS having difficulty in shifting attention to the target, thus facing a severe conflict situation. This conflict led LSS to greater activation of the ACC during the recognition phase especially in the non-focused recognition. Moreover, the strong conflict caused increased intrusion errors for LSS.

One last argument is that LSS have difficulty in focusing attention. In most research exploring the focus effect, the focus was defined by directing subjects to specific category, such as animal nouns, that they have to pay attention to (Gernsbacher and Faust 1991; De Beni *et al.* 1998), by the preceding question (Cutler and Fodor 1979; Blutner and Sommer 1988) or by controlling the sentence syntactically (Birch and Garnsey 1995). In the F- and NF-RST, the focus word was not presented by a question, nor was it stressed syntactically. Therefore, semantic processing was required for the subjects to find the focus word mentally. Establishing a mental focus requires information about word meaning, along with syntactic, pragmatic and semantic elaboration related to sentence processing. It is plausible to suggest that such an active search for a focus word, that is establishing a mental focus, can be accomplished more efficiently for HSS. This would be in agreement with Just and Carpenter (1992) and Turner and Engle (1989), who concluded that semantic or syntactic information must be activated efficiently in HSS.

Here, we consider that LSS have difficulty in the focusing and shifting attention and also inhibiting processes. The delay in establishing the focus word will precipitate a disturbance in the later shifting attention and inhibitory responses. Moreover, we suggest that HSS have an advantage in the ability to shifting attention aided by SPL compared to that of LSS, providing HSS with a more efficient attention control system supported by a network between DLPFC and ACC.

The important factor influencing the performance of subjects on span task, such as RST and LST, is how well they focusing attention while establishing a mental focus and then subsequently allocating this attention for shifting and inhibiting mental focus.

Attention control system in focusing and shifting attention is supported with the aid of SPL, and superior ability in inhibitory processes is supported by ACC. Those neural network systems supported with SPL, ACC and DLPFC facilitates smooth performance of tasks requiring higher cognitive brain function.

Moreover, theories implicating the role of attention control system in RST or LST can lend themselves to explanations of other span tasks such as the OST or SST task, which equally require the attention controller for the dual task performance.

Conclusion

The ability to focus attention arises from additive SPL activation, which plays a role in focusing and shifting attention and supports executive control of ACC and DLPFC. The neural substrates of executive function involve cooperative activations of the DLPFC, ACC and SPL. The DLPFC supports sufficient maintenance of attention on the target, and the ACC serves attention management, such as resolving conflict and inhibiting potential responses unnecessary for the goals of task performance. Focusing attention in the regulatory system of working memory is executed with the aid of the SPL and makes fine adjustments to cognitive brain function.

According to these findings, factors that contribute to individual differences on span task performance are related to the mental faculties of focusing, shifting and inhibiting attention. The neural bases of focusing attention that contribute to the differences between HSS and LSS are located in the SPL in cooperation with the ACC and DLPFC.

Acknowledgment

This work was supported by Grants from the Japan Society for the Promotion of Science #18330156 to MO, #16203037 and Nissan Science Foundation Grant (29th) to NO.

References

Awh, E, Jonides, J, Smith, EE, Schumacher, EH, Koeppe, RA and Katz, S (1996). Dissociation of storage and rehearsal in verbal working memory: Evidence from positron emission tomography. *Psychologiocal Science, 7*, 25–31.

Baddeley, AD (2003). Working memory: Looking back and looking forward. *Nature Review Neuroscience, 4*, 829–839.

Baddeley, AD (1986). *Working Memory*. Oxford: Oxford University Press.

Baddeley, AD (1992). Working memory. *Science 255*, 556–559.

Baddeley, AD (1996). Exploring the central executive. *Quarterly Journal of Experimental Psychology. 49A*, 5–28.

Baddeley, AD and Logie, RH (1999). Working memory: the multiple component model. In A Miyake and P Shah (eds), *Models of Working Memory: Mechanisms of active maintenance and executive control* (pp. 28–61).Cambridge: Cambridge University Press.

Barch, DM, Braver, TS, Nystrom, LE, Forman, SD, Noll, DC and Cohen, JD (1997). Dissociating working memory from task difficulty in human prefrontal cortex. *Neuropsychologia, 35*, 1373–1380.

Birch, S and Garnsey, S (1995). The effect of focus on memory for words in sentences. *Journal of Memory and Language, 34*, 232–267.

Blutner, R and Sommer, R (1988). Sentence processing and lexical access: The influence of the focus-identifying task. *Journal of Memory and Language, 27*, 359–367.

Bolinger, D (1986). *Intonation and its Parts*. Stanford, CA: Stanford University Press.

Braver, TS, Cohen, J, Nystrom, LE, Jonides, J, Smith, EE and Noll, DC (1997). A parametric study of prefrontal cortex involvement in human working memory. *NeuoImage, 5*, 49–62.

Braver, TS, Barch, DM, Gray, JR, Molfese, L and Snyder, A (2001). A parametric study of prefrontal cortex involvement in human working memory. *Cerebral Cortex, 11*, 825–836.

Bunge, SA, Klinberg, T, Jacobson, RB and Gabriel, JDE (2000). A resource model of the neural basis of executive working memory. *Proceedings of the National Academy of Science, 97*, 3573–3578.

Bunge, SA, Ochsner, KN, Desmond, JE, Glover, GH and Gabriel, JDE (2001). Prefrontal regions involved in keeping information in and out of mind. *Brain, 124*, 2072–2086.

Bush, G, Whalen, P, Rosen, BR, Jenike, M, McInerney, SC and Rauch, SL (1998). The counting stroop: an interference task specialized for functional neuroimaging validation study with functional MRI. *Human Brain Mapping, 6*, 70–282.

Bush, G, Luu, P and Posner, MI (2000). Cognitive and emotional influences in anterior cingulate cortex. *Trends in Cognitive Sciences, 4,* 215–222.

Carpenter, PA and Just, MA (1977). Integrative processes in comprehension. In P LaBerge and SJ Samuels (eds), *Basic Processes in Reading: Perception and comprehension* (pp. 217–241). Hillsdale, NJ: Erlbaum.

Carpenter, PA, Just, MA, Keller, TA, Eddy, W and Thulborn, K (1999). Graded functional activation in the visuospatial system with the amount of task demand. *Journal of Cognitive Neuroscience, 11,* 9–24.

Carter, CS, Braver, TS, Barch, D, Botvinick, MM, Noll, D and Cohen, JD (1998). Anterior cingulate cortex, error detection, and the online monitoring of performance. *Science, 280,* 747–749.

Cohen, JD, Peristein, WM, Braver, TS, Nystrom, LE, Noll, DC, Jonides, J and Smith, EE (1997). Temporal dynamics of brain activation during a working memory task. *Nature, 386,* 604–608.

Conway, ARA and Engle, RW (1994). Working memory and retrieval: A resource-dependent inhibition model. *Journal of Experimental Psychology: General, 123,* 354–373.

Courtney, SM, Petit, L, Maisog, JM, Ungerleider, LG and Haxby, JV (1998). An area specialized for spatial working memory in human frontal cortex. *Science, 279,* 1347–1350.

Cowan, N (1999). An embedded-processes model of working memory. In A Miyakeand P Shah (eds), *Models of Working Memory: Mechanisms of active maintenance and executive control* (pp. 62–101).Cambridge: Cambridge University Press.

Cowan, N (2001). The magical number 4 in short-term memory: A reconsideration of mental storage capacity. *Behavioral Brain Science, 24,* 87–185.

Culham, JC and Kanwisher, NG (2001). Neuroimaging of cognitive functions in human parietal cortex. *Current Opinion of Neurobiology, 11,* 157–163.

Cutler, A and Fodor, J (1979). Semantic focus and sentence comprehension. *Cognition, 7,* 49–59.

Daneman, M and Carpenter, PA (1980). Individual differences in working memory and reading. *Journal of Verbal Learning and Verbal Behavior, 19,* 450–466.

Daneman, M and Merikle, PM (1996). Working memory and language comprehension: A meta-analysis. *Psychonomic Bulletin and Review, 3,* 422–433.

De Beni, R, Palladino, P, Pazzaglia, F and Cornoldi, C (1998). Increases in intrusion errors and working memory deficit of poor comprehenders. *Quarterly Journal of Experimental Psychology, 51A,* 305–320.

D'Esposito, M, Detre, JA, Alsop, DC, Atlas, RK and Grossman, M (1995). The neural basis of the central executive system of working memory. *Nature, 378,* 279–281.

D'Esposito, M, Aguirre, GK, Zarahn, Ballard, D, Shin, RK and Leas, J (1998). Functional MRI studies of spatial and nonspatial working memory. *Cognitive Brain Research, 7,* 1–13.

D'Esposito, M, Postle, BR, Ballard, D and Lease, J (1999). Maintenance versus manipulation of information held in working memory. *Brain and Cognition, 41,* 66–86.

Diwadkar, VA, Carpenter, PA and Just, MA (2000). Collaborative activity between parietal and dorso-lateral prefrontal cortex in dynamic spatial working memory revealed by fMRI. *NeuroImage, 12,* 85–99.

Duncan, J and Owen, AM (2000). Common regions of the human frontal lobe recruited by diverse cognitive demands. *Trends in Neurosciences, 23,* 475–483.

Engle, RW, Conway, ARA, Tuholski, SW and Shisler, RJ (1995) A resource account of inhibition. *Psychological Science, 6,* 122–125.

Engle, RW, Tuholski, S, Laughlin, JE and Conway, ARA (1999). Working memory, short-term memory, and general fluid intelligence: A latent-variable approach. *Journal of Experimental Psychology, 128,* 309–331.

Gernsbacher, MA (1990). Less skilled readers have less efficient suppression mechanisms. *Psychological Science, 4,* 294–298.

Gernsbacher, MA and Faust, ME (1991). The mechanism of suppression: A component of general comprehension skill. *Journal of Experimental Psychology: Learning, Memory, and Cognition, 17,* 245–262.

Halliday, MAK (1967). Notes on transitivity and theme in English: Part 2. *Journal of Linguistics, 3,* 199–244.

Hornby, PA (1974). Surface structure and presupposition. *Journal of Verbal Learning and Verbal Behavior, 13,* 530–538.

Jonides, J, Smith, EE, Koeppe, RA, Awh, E, Minoshima, S and Mintun, MA (1993). Spatial working memory in humans as revealed by PET. *Nature, 363,* 623–625.

Just, MA and Carpenter, PA (1992). A capacity theory of comprehension: Individual differences in working memory. *Psychoogical Review, 99,* 122–149.

Just, MA, Carpenter, PA and Keller, T (1996). The capacity theory of comprehension: new frontiers of evidence and arguments. *Psychological Review, 103,* 773–780.

Kane, MJ and Engle, RW (2002). The role of prefrontal cortex in working-memory capacity, executive attention, and general fluid intelligence: An individual-differences perspective. *Psychonomic Bulletin and Review, 9,* 637–671.

Kane, MJ and Engle, RW (2003). Working-memory capacity and the control of attention: The contributions of goal neglect, response competition, and task set to Stroop interference. *Journal of Experimental Psychology: General, 132,* 47–70.

Kondo, H, Morishita, M, Osaka, N, Osaka, M, Fukuyama, H and Shibasaki, H (2004a). Functional roles of the cingulo-frontal network in performance on working memory. *NeuroImage 21,* 2–14.

Kondo, H, Osaka, N and Osaka, M (2004b). Cooperation of the anterior cingulated cortex and dorsolateral prefrontal cortex for attention shifting. *NeuroImage, 23,* 670–679.

Kuno, S (1978). *Discourse and Grammar.* Tokyo: Taishukan-syoten. (In Japanese).

MacDonald, III AW, Cohen, JD, Stenger, VA and Carter, CS (2000). Dissociating the role of the dorsolateral prefrontal and anterior cingulate cortex in cognitive control. *Science, 288,* 1835–1838.

May, CP, Hasher, L and Kane, MJ (1999). The role of interference in memory span. *Memory and Cognition, 27,* 759–767.

Osaka, M and Osaka, N (1992). Language-independent working memory as measured by Japanese and English reading span tests. *Bulletin of the Psychonomic Society, 30,* 287–289.

Osaka, M and Osaka, N (1994). Working memory capacity related to reading: Measurement with the Japanese version of reading span test. *Japanese Journal of Psychology, 65,* 339–345. (In Japanese with an English summary.)

Osaka, M, Nishizaki, Y, Komori, M and Osaka, N (2002). Effect of focus on verbal working memory: Critical role of the focus word in reading. *Memory and Cognition, 30,* 562–571.

Osaka, M, Osaka, N, Kondo, H, Morishita, M, Fukuyama, H, Aso, T and Shibasaki, H (2003). The neural basis of individual differences in working memory capacity: an fMRI study. *NeuroImage, 18,* 789–797.

Osaka, N, Osaka, M, Kondo, H, Morishita, M, Fukuyama, H and Shibasaki, H (2004). The neural basis of executive function in working memory: an fMRI study based on individual differences. *NeuroImage, 21,* 623–631.

Osaka, M, Komori, M, Morishita, M and Osaka, N (2004). Neural basis of focusing in executive function of working memory: Comparing focused- and non-focused- RST. Second *International Conference on Working Memory, Program and Abstract 16.*

Oaska, M, Komori, M, Morishita, M and Osaka, N (2007). Neural basis of focusing attention in working memory. *Cognitive, Affective and Behavioral Neuroscience,* In Press.

Owen, AM, Evans, AC and Petrides, M (1996). Evidence for a two-stage model of spatial working memory processing within the lateral frontal cortex: a positron emission tomography study. *Cerebral Cortex, 6,* 31–38.

Owen, AM, Stern, CE, Look, RB, Tracey, I, Rosen, BR and Petrides, M (1998). Functional organization of spatial and non-spatial working memory processing within the human lateral frontal cortex. *Proceedings of the National Academy of Science, 95,* 7721–7726.

Paulesu, E, Frith, CD and Frackowiak, RS (1993). The neural correlates of the verbal component of working memory. *Nature, 362,* 342–345.

Rypma, B, Prabhakaran, V, Desmond, JE, Glover, GH and Gablieli, JDE (1999). Load-dependent roles of frontal brain regions in the maintenance of working memory. *NeuroImage, 9,* 216–226.

Shah, P and Miyake, A (1996). The separability of working memory resources for spatial thinking and language processing: an individual differences approach. *Journal of Experimental Psychology: General, 125,* 4–27.

Smith, EE and Jonides, J (1999). Storage and executive processes in the frontal lobes. *Science*, *283*, 1657–1661.

Smith, EE, Jonides, J and Koeppe, RA (1996). Dissociating verbal and nonverbal working memory using PET. *Cerebral Cortex*, *6*, 11–20.

Smith, EE, Geva, A, Jonides, J, Miller, A, Reuter-Lorenz, P and Koeppe, RA (2001). The neural basis of task-switching in working memory: Effects of performance and aging. *Proceedings of the National Academy of Science*, *98*, 2095–2100.

Turner, ML and Engle, RW (1989). Is working memory capacity task dependent ? *Journal of Memory and Language*, *28*, 127–154.

Vogt, BA, Finch, DM and Olson, CR (1992). Functional heterogeneity in cingulate cortex: The anterior executive and posterior evaluative regions. *Cerebral Cortex*, *2*, 435–443.

7

Separating processing from storage in working memory operation span

Robert H. Logie and Simon C. Duff

Working memory refers to online cognitive processing and temporary storage in a wide range of tasks, and was originally viewed as a set of domain-specific components of cognition (Baddeley and Hitch 1974). This view has evolved using an experimental approach with both healthy and brain damaged individuals, and has identified several specific temporary memory systems and separate resources for supporting processing and multitask coordination (Baddeley and Logie 1999; Logie 2003).

An alternative view of working memory is as a domain-general cognitive resource supporting both processing and temporary storage within a single flexible system (e.g. Daneman and Carpenter 1980; Daneman and Hannon, this volume; Just and Carpenter 1992), or that the system might simply comprise the currently activated areas of long-term memory (e.g. Cowan 1999, 2005; Postle, this volume). The latter view has been driven by studies and theories of attention, suggesting that the current contents of working memory comprise the focus of attention. The former view has been driven by studies of individual differences in 'working memory span' (Daneman and Carpenter 1980), which involves, for example, processing a series of sentences or arithmetic problems, followed by a serial ordered retrieval of the final words in each sentence or the series of arithmetic totals. Retrieval performance is taken as a measure of working memory capacity, and the measure correlates highly with a range of cognitive tasks (e.g. Daneman and Merikle 1996; Daneman and Hannon, this volume; Engle, Kane and Tuholski 1999).

An important aspect of the debate concerning the nature of working memory is the contrast between approaches that explore the impact of different experimental conditions, and approaches that study the shared variance between measures of individual differences. If we were to find, using experimental manipulations, that working memory span reflects the operation of separate resources for processing and storage, this would not undermine the utility of working memory span as a predictor of cognitive performance (although see Miyake, Friedman, Rettinger *et al.* 2001). However, it would have implications for how the individual differences in working memory span are interpreted, as well as having implications for theories of the organization of working memory.

Working memory span involves a memory load in the context of processing material, and therefore involves at least two task components, although typically only the storage is measured. However, it is less clear whether the processing elements and the storage elements of working memory span tasks actually reflect the operation of the same system. For example, Caplan and Waters (1999; Waters and Caplan 1996) argued that evidence is sparse for a trade-off between sentence processing and memory storage, and that measures of processing do not correlate highly with measures of memory in working memory span tasks. Daneman and Hannon (this volume) show that processing speed for each of the sentences in a working memory span paradigm offers much less predictive power for general cognitive abilities than does the more widely used measure of memory for sentence-final items. Moreover, they report that speed of processing correlates poorly with memory for sentence-final items. However, the focus of their chapter is on those measures that best characterize the individual differences in working memory and that predict other cognitive abilities. In our own work, the focus has been on the assumptions that underlie the concept of a domain-general working memory system that supports both processing and storage – asking how does working memory work, rather than what drives the correlation between working memory span and general cognitive abilities.

Towse, Hitch and Hutton (2000, 2002) noted that working memory span involves interpolating processing between the items for recall, constituting a filled interitem delay that is not present in standard tests of memory span. Differences in working memory span may then reflect individual ability to retain material with a filled delay between the presentation of each item for recall. Also, performance may reflect the ability of individuals to switch between rehearsal of the memory items and processing of the sentences or arithmetic operations; the longer the sequence, the longer will be the filled delay between presentation of the earlier items in the list and recall of those items, and the longer that delay without rehearsal, the greater is the chance that items will be forgotten.

Barrouillet and Camos (2001; this volume; Barrouillet, Bernardin and Camos 2004) have proposed a time-based resource-sharing model that, like Towse *et al.* assumes that memory traces will decay over time unless rehearsed. Barrouillet further assumes that both rehearsal and processing requires the use of a limited attentional resource that can be alternately allocated to rehearsal, to retrieval, to sentence comprehension or to other aspects of the working memory span task. Indeed, they argue that retrieval processes are required for rehearsal to maintain items in an active state and to prevent decay. However, if one aspect of the task captures that attentional resource, then performance on other aspects will suffer. This model predicts that as long as attention is captured by one aspect of a task then there will be poorer performance elsewhere. However, longer processing times will not necessarily result in poorer recall of sentence-final items, if participants can covertly switch between processing and rehearsal. One potential difficulty with this theory is that we might know that attention has been captured by one aspect of the task only after we collect the data on performance levels. This would make the theory rather circular. However, Barrouillet and colleagues have shown that tasks involving significant time pressure for processing result in poorer performance on other aspects of the task. That is, the component of a task that is under time pressure for a response captures most or all of the attentional resource for extended periods of time, leaving very limited scope for that resource to be directed elsewhere, even for a short time.

On these arguments the Towse and Hitch approach makes a clear prediction that, for example, longer reading times for sentences will result in more forgetting and hence poorer recall of sentence final items in a working memory span task – a negative correlation between processing time and working memory span. In contrast, Barrouillet and colleagues might predict that a working memory span task that requires rapid and accurate processing will allow very little time for rehearsal of sentence final items, leading to poorer recall – a positive correlation between processing time and working memory span. In line with this prediction, they demonstrate that fast-paced presentation results in poorer recall than does slow-paced presentation.

Duff and Logie (2001) addressed the possible dissociation between memory and processing by assessing each component separately, and then combined within a working memory span procedure. They also examined the impact of systematically varying the pace at which participants had to respond. In one experiment, processing capacity was measured by the maximum number of sentences each participant could verify accurately within 10 seconds. The memory task involved serial recall of unrelated words. When combined, verification of sentences at an increasingly faster rate was followed by recall of the last word of each sentence. The maximum number of words recalled did not differ between the conditions of memory only and memory plus processing, nor was memory span affected by the pace at which processing was required in the combined condition. This was in contrast with the predictions of the Barrouillet model, indicating use of separate resource pools rather than a single shared attentional resource respectively for processing (sentence verification) and for maintenance of the words in temporary memory (word recall) rather than an attentional bottleneck. Similar results were obtained in a second experiment in which arithmetic verification was coupled with word recall: increasing the pace at which arithmetic sums had to be verified had no impact on recall of unrelated words that were presented along with each sum, compared with memory span for unrelated words in the absence of concurrent arithmetic. This lack of an impact of dual task demands has been shown in previous studies with healthy adults (e.g., Cocchini, Logie, Della Sala *et al.* 2002). Bayliss, Jarrold, Gunn *et al.* (2003) provided further support for the suggestion that processing and memory components of working memory span appear to draw on separate resource pools.

Although the results were clear in Duff and Logie (2001) it is possible that the lack of a trade-off between processing and storage arose because the memory items were distinctive relative to the processing requirements of the verification tasks. In Experiment 1, the final word (for recall) of each sentence (for processing) was not wholly determined by the text it followed; in Experiment 2, the words for recall were completely unrelated to the arithmetic sums for verification. The relative distinctiveness of the processing and memory tasks might have released some working memory capacity to focus on processing. Cowan (e.g. 2005) has argued that a lack of interference between memory tasks might arise because the contents for each task are quite distinct. Moreover, given the widely held assumptions of a trade-off in resource allocation between processing and storage in working memory span tasks, it is important to assess the generality of findings, such as those reported by Duff and Logie (2001), that are not consistent with these assumptions regarding resource allocation.

We approach the test of generality in two ways. First, we report two experiments that are direct analogies of the Duff and Logie (2001) studies, except that the working memory span tasks comprised arithmetic verification coupled with recall of two-digit totals for each sum to reduce the distinctiveness between the processing and storage elements of the task. Span levels for each participant were assessed separately for processing (by varying pace of required response) and for memory (by increasing list length of digit sequences) and then with both components performed together. In the verification task, the time available for processing each arithmetic sum decreased as the number of sums increased. This allowed us to ensure that sequence length had a minimal effect on presentation time. Experiment 2 followed a similar procedure except that the time available for rehearsal in the memory span only task was increased to assess the impact of rehearsal time on performance.

These two experiments are followed by a third study using a rather different approach, taking advantage of an opportunity to test very large numbers of participants (N = 24,630) via a web-based experiment in collaboration with the British Broadcasting Corporation (BBC). In this third study, a working memory processing plus storage sentence span task was presented with timing of response for processing each sentence and recording of memory performance using a serial reconstruction procedure. The intention was to examine the relationship between processing time and memory span. Barrouillet and colleagues might predict that people with very fast processing times would most likely have poorer recall than people who respond more slowly and have more time for rehearsal. Towse and Hitch might predict that slower response times will allow for more forgetting and therefore poorer memory spans. Compatible with this last prediction, a third possibility (e.g. Rabbitt 2005; personal communication) is that people who are generally of high mental ability will have both fast processing times and high levels of performance.

Experiment 1

Method

Participants Twenty undergraduate participants from the University of Bergen, Norway, were tested (16 female, 4 male, mean age 24 years, range 17 to 29 years).

Tasks

Memory task Participants were presented with lists of two-digit numbers appearing once per second in the centre of a computer screen and with a 0.5 s pause between stimuli. Following practice, the main task commenced with three trials of two different items per list. A tone prompted serial ordered oral recall of the preceding list. Successful recall on two of the three trials was followed by presentation of three lists, each with three items, followed in turn by four item lists and so on to a maximum of nine items per list. The procedure stopped after each participant failed to recall correctly two trials at a given list length. All participants received the same randomly generated order of two digit numbers. There was no duplication of numbers within any list, although some numbers appeared in more than one list.

Arithmetic verification task Participants were presented with single digit problems with two-digit solutions, half incorrect and half correct, e.g. $3 \times 6 = 16$; $8 + 7 = 17$; $9 \times 4 = 36$; $6 + 9 = 15$. The task was to respond on a computer keyboard whether the given solution was correct or incorrect ('M' for correct, 'Z' for incorrect). Only '+' and '×' were used and all operands were single digit numbers. Incorrect solutions were generated by adding two or subtracting two from the correct answer, maintaining a match in parity between the incorrect and the correct solution. Presentation orders of correct/incorrect and +/x were counterbalanced as closely as possible over each set of three trials. Following practice, participants received three trials with two problems per trial. A maximum of 5 s was permitted for response, followed by a 0.5 s delay before the next problem. Following successful completion of two trials participants were presented with three trials, each of three problems to be verified within 10 s (3.33 s per problem). Success at this stage led to three trials in which four problems had to be verified within ten seconds (2.5 s per problem). The number of problems to be verified within 10 s increased until the participant failed on two out of three trials. The time for each verification decreased from five seconds for each of two problems to 1.25 s for each of a maximum of eight problems. The 0.5 s delay between presentations did not contribute to the 10 s time limit. If participants failed to respond within the time limit, the next stimulus was presented and 'no response' recorded.

Combined task Here, lists of arithmetic sums to verify were followed by recall of the presented solutions for each sum in the serial order of presentation. Initially, lists of two sums were to be verified within 10 s, and 0.5s after each trial, a tone prompted participants to recall serially the presented solutions. List lengths increased as did the speed at which verification had to be completed for each problem, following the procedure for the single tasks. The stimuli used for the combined task were of the same type as, but different content from, the verification task. Participants continued to perform this task until they failed to perform successfully on two trials at a given level for both the verification and the memory components of the task.

Task order was counterbalanced for the single tasks, but the combined task was always performed last. All materials were presented in Norwegian. Each experimental session lasted approximately 30 minutes.

Results and discussion

Memory span was taken as the mean number of items correctly recalled from the last three accurate trials. For example, success at list length 4, but failure on two out of three lists at length 5, would result in a span of 4.33. Verification span was measured similarly as the mean number of sentences correctly verified, from the last three accurately verified trials within the ten second period.

Figure 7.1 shows mean memory span scores for component and combined task conditions. One-way ANOVA confirmed that combined task memory span was higher than single task, $F(1,19) = 7.92$; $MSE = 0.36$; $p <0.025$), and verification span was reduced under combined task conditions, $F(1,19) = 19.83$; $MSE = 0.81$; $p <0.001$).

An examination of whether processing and storage demands rely on separate or general-purpose cognitive resources would be further informed by examining the overall changes across both tasks between single and combined conditions. We calculated the mean percentage change in performance between conditions for each of the two component tasks for each participant as follows:

$$\text{Per cent change} = \frac{\text{Single task} - \text{Combined task} \times 100}{\text{Single task}}$$

Next, we calculated an overall measure of the percentage single task to combined task change by taking the median of the percentage change scores across the two tasks. The median and spread of scores from these derived measures are shown in Figure 7.2, which illustrates that the majority of participants (15) had equal or better memory span under combined task compared with single task conditions. Four participants also had equal or better verification span performance under combined task conditions. The overall measure of combined task performance was around 94 per cent of single task performance. This reinforces the case that combining

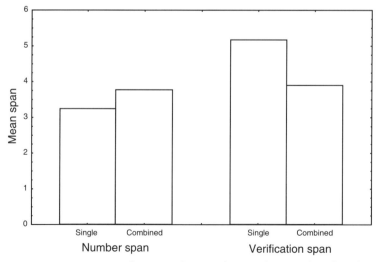

Figure 7.1 Mean memory span score from Experiment 1 for two digit numbers (number span) and mean arithmetic verification span score when performed as separate, single tasks or when combined within a single processing and storage task.

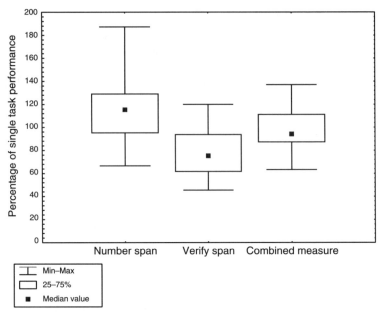

Figure 7.2 Median and range of scores from Experiment 1 for single task and for a combined measure of performance.

processing and memory proved to be not very much more demanding overall than performing each component task on its own.

These results cannot be attributed to a lack of power or sensitivity in the design. Each participant was performing at their own span level, and acted as their own control with combined task performance compared with single task performance at span. As such, performance levels were not at ceiling or at floor. These data would be very difficult to incorporate within a single flexible resource model or attention switching model of working memory. They also reinforce the view (e.g. Caplan and Waters 1999) that taking only a storage measure might provide a misleading picture of the capacity of working memory as a whole.

A possible caveat is that participants were somehow putting more 'cognitive effort' into the combined task condition, thereby effectively increasing the total resource available. This seems unlikely given that we adopted a span procedure that is widely used in assessments of working memory span as well as in measures of digit or word span.

A further possibility is that the one per second presentation rate for memory span single task might have been too rapid for two-digit numbers relative to the time available in the combined task condition. In this last condition, with two problems to verify within ten seconds, a participant might respond at a leisurely pace, allowing time to encode and rehearse presented totals. As the number of problems increased, the amount of time available for encoding each two-digit total would be reduced accordingly, but participants might have been strategic in their use of time-sharing between the tasks, allowing more time for the memory span combined task, thereby giving rise to the combined task improvement in span. In order to explore this possibility, we examined the verification response times in single and combined task conditions. If participants were indeed failing to use their full capacity in the single component task conditions, we might expect a different pattern of response times in the single and in the combined task conditions. Any trade-off in the combined task with participants taking advantage of time between sums for verification to focus on encoding and rehearsing the numbers should show up in slower response times for the verification component of the task.

Mean correct response times are illustrated in Figure 7.3 for two, three and four problems. There were too few correct responses for five or more problems. An ANOVA revealed no overall difference in response time between single and combined task, $F(1,18) < 1$. However there was a significant reduction in time as the number of problems increased, $F(2,36) = 18.42$; $MSE = 0.032$; $p < 0.001$, and a significant interaction, $F(2,36) = 11.18$; $MSE = 0.025$; $p < 0.001$. From Figure 7.3 it is clear that the reduction in correct response time occurred primarily in the single task condition; participants could improve their performance under single task conditions until they reached their span level. With the combined task, the response time function is largely flat. This indicates that participants may well be attempting to free up time in the combined task condition, possibly to switch between processing and rehearsal of the items for recall. This might offer a partial explanation for the slightly higher combined task memory span, but does not offer a complete account because the combined task memory span and verification span measures resulted from performance on the longer lists of problems when verification demands as well as storage demands were very high. However, it is possible that participants might have benefited from having longer for rehearsal under combined task conditions relative to single task conditions. Specifically, in the single task condition, the mean memory performance was 3.2 items (see Figure 7.1), with a rate of 1.5 s for presentation of each item, including interitem intervals. In the combined task condition, mean memory span was 3.8 items, and with a 11.5 s presentation time (10 s plus 3×0.5 s interstimulus intervals), this equates to around 3 s for each item.

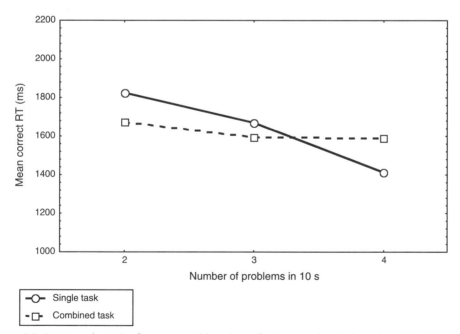

Figure 7.3 Response latencies for correct arithmetic verifications under single and combined task conditions in Experiment 1.

This additional time might have allowed for additional rehearsal in the combined task condition, although it would have had to incorporate verification of each sum as well as rehearsal. Nevertheless, it raises the possibility that single task memory demands were not wholly comparable with combined task memory span and the procedure was modified in Experiment 2 to examine this possibility.

Experiment 2

In Experiment 1, there was a suggestion that participants might have had effectively a longer period in which to encode and rehearse the numbers for recall for some of the trials in the combined task condition compared with the single task memory condition. Experiment 2 aimed to address this possibility by presenting the single task memory span materials at a slower rate. Moreover, given the lack of evidence for a trade-off between memory and verification components of the tasks, Experiment 2 also served to test the reliability of the findings from Experiment 1.

Method

Participants. Eighteen new participants were tested, all native Norwegian speakers from the University of Bergen, Norway. There were 9 males and 9 females (mean age 24 years, range 21 to 27 years).

Procedure. Tasks and procedure were as for Experiment 1, except that during the memory single task, items were displayed for 2 seconds each, with a 0.5 second interitem delay. The materials were those for Experiment 1 except that the arithmetic problems were allocated in a pseudo-random fashion to different lists, as were two-digit numbers for recall.

Results

One participant performed at floor on single task memory span, and these data were discarded. Span measures for the remaining 17 participants were calculated for both memory and verification during single and combined task procedures (Figure 7.4). An ANOVA confirmed that the memory span means did not differ between single and combined task conditions $F(1,16) <1$. Verification span combined task performance was poorer than single task performance by around 15 per cent and this difference was statistically reliable, $F(1,16) = 5.12$; $MSE = 0.692$; $p <0.05$).

The combined percentage change measure revealed that there was no overall combined task effect (98 per cent of single task performance). Like Experiment 1, participants were performing at their own span level and therefore this lack of an overall drop in performance cannot be attributed to performance levels being at floor or ceiling.

Mean correct verification times for two, three, and four problems in single and combined task conditions showed a very similar pattern to that for Experiment 1, with no overall difference in correct response time between single and combined task, $F(1,12) = 1.57$; $MSE = 0.056$; n.s., an effect of number of problems, $F(2,24) = 9.46$; $MSE = 0.030$; $p <0.001$, and an interaction, $F(2,24) = 11.49$; $MSE = 0.023$; $p <0.001$, with a reduction only in single task response time as the number of problems increased.

Mean memory scores under combined task conditions (Figure 7.4) show that participants averaged 3.3 items, or approximately 3.3 s per item, including any time for verification. Single task conditions involved presentation of an item once every 2.5 seconds, with no interpolated

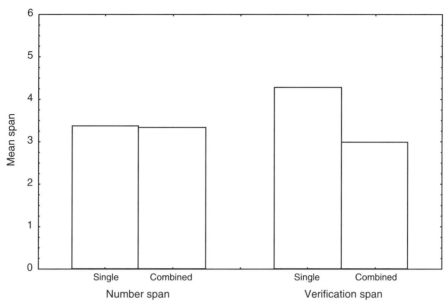

Figure 7.4 Mean memory span score in Experiment 2 for two digit numbers (number span) and mean arithmetic verification span score when performed as separate, single tasks or when combined within a single processing and storage task.

processing task, therefore allowing ample time for rehearsal. This makes it extremely unlikely that the protection of memory span performance resulted from increased rehearsal time in the combined task condition.

Discussion

The major impact of increasing single task exposure time for memory stimuli was that there was no combined task advantage for memory span. As in Experiment 1, there was no overall drop in performance resulting from combined task demands, and no evidence that memory span was being protected at the expense of verification or vice versa. Increased time for the memory task alone allowed the presentation time for single task and dual task span to be more comparable, but the total resource available for span as a single task appears to be the same when it is combined with arithmetic verification. The same interpretation broadly applies to the verification task. The dual task drop was significant, but it comprised a rather modest 15 per cent cost for performing verification (at span), and memory (at span) in combination.

The speeding of responses as the number of verification problems increased points to some deployment of additional resources as they are required within the single task condition until performance breaks down. As for Experiment 1, the lack of a reduction in response time under combined task conditions is consistent with participants switching between verification and rehearsal of the items for recall. The lack of an overall drop in performance between single and dual task conditions is not consistent with the use of a single flexible resource for both processing and storage, and is more consistent with the view that there are separate pools of resource available that can work in parallel for memory and for semantic processing.

Discussion of experiments 1 and 2

We set out to explore further a previous finding (Duff and Logie 2001) that separate cognitive resources might support respectively processing and temporary storage in working memory span tasks. Our new data are consistent with our previous findings and demonstrate that the apparent fractionation of processing and storage is unlikely to be due to distinctiveness in the codes used for retaining the items for recall relative to the processing task. Specifically, the cognitive demands of retaining a number sequence that is set at the limits of memory span for each individual participant appear to result in very little constraint on the ongoing processing when both memory and processing are task requirements. Likewise, demanding processing conditions appear not to constrain the ability of participants to retain as many items as they could when that processing demand was absent. Because the overall time for presenting the items in the combined task condition changed very little with the length of the sequence, our results are unlikely to be influenced by the length of time between item presentation and recall. The use of a longer single task presentation time for memory span in Experiment 2 demonstrated that the results of Experiment 1 are unlikely to be due to the amount of time for rehearsal in the combined task conditions.

The lack of evidence for a trade-off in performance between processing and storage demands is not compatible with the Barrouillet view that attention switching is required between the two task components, and suggests that maintenance of items for recall may continue even when participants are performing a highly demanding cognitive task. This points to the suggestion that there are separate cognitive resources for memory and for processing in the verification task, and that these can operate largely in parallel rather than relying on the switching of a single attentional resource between them. The notion of separate pools of attentional resource is not unprecedented (e.g. Hunt and Lansman 1981; Wickens 1984, Wickens and Liu 1988), in addition to evidence offered in more recent studies (e.g. Bayliss et al. 2003; Cocchini et al. 2002).

One further approach to investigating whether or not memory and processing components of working memory span are independent is to consider whether performance on the memory and processing measures tends to covary. Waters and Caplan (1996) reported low correlations between these measures in a sample of 94 participants who were mainly undergraduate students aged 18–37. They suggested that a combined measure of processing and of memory would provide a more reliable measure than would a memory score on its own. More recently, Waters and Caplan (2003) reported scores on a range of working memory measures derived from 139 participants spread across a wide age range (18–80+), with at least high school education. The working memory measures each had high internal consistency, but the tasks showed only modest intercorrelations. Moreover, test–retest reliability improved dramatically when combined scores for at least two different tests were used. The participant numbers in Experiments 1 and 2 were adequate for investigating the impact of experimental manipulations in task demands. However exploration of the processing and storage elements from an individual differences perspective would require rather larger numbers of participants that are more heterogeneous with respect to age and educational background. This was the aim of Experiment 3.

Experiment 3

In Experiment 3 we adopted an individual differences approach to explore the relationship between processing and storage in working memory span tasks. We took advantage of the opportunity to collect data via a web site in cooperation with the BBC. Collecting data via the internet has the major advantage that it allows for a diverse and very large sample of participants. Sample numbers are typically in the thousands and can be in the tens or even hundreds of thousands (e.g. Reimers, in press; Reimers and Maylor 2005), and both experimenter and demand effects are minimized. The problems associated with web-based experiments are now fairly well understood and there are documented procedures for maximizing the quality of the data obtained (e.g. Birnbaum 2004; Reips 2002). The experimental procedure can be standardized with control of presentation format and times, and of retention and response intervals, and allows for collection of real-time response times as well as accuracy data. Disadvantages include a lack of control of the conditions under which the test session is completed (e.g. background noise, time of day, illumination), and multiple attempts by the same individuals. The issue of multiple attempts can be handled by selecting for inclusion only the first attempt from any one computer, using a cookie system for recording previous attempts. The experimental environment will add noise to the data, but it is reasonable to assume that this is a random effect that will have little or no impact when set against the large numbers of participants. Dropout rate can be a serious problem if the experiment involves large numbers of trials or takes overly long to complete. This limits the range of measures and the number of data points per measure, but this again is compensated by having large numbers of participants so that between-participant designs can generate very substantial amounts of data across conditions.

The experiment reported here involved measuring working memory span via a BBC web site by means of sentence verification and recall of sentence-final words. Sentence verification times and accuracy were recorded and memory was tested using a serial reconstruction procedure. Working memory span was one of several measures of cognitive ability based on self report or on memory performance including digit span, visual pattern span, spatial orientation and binding of perceptual features in working memory.

Method

Participants. A total of 49,902 sets of data were collected via a BBC web site over a two-month period with participants drawn from a total of 150 countries. Of these, 41,917 comprised the first attempt from any particular computer. Each participant was asked to state their age, sex, the highest level of education they had reached – primary school, secondary or high school, technical or vocational college, other college, university graduate, postgraduate or professional degree, and to rate their general health – excellent, very good, good, moderate or poor. Participants who did not provide all four of these demographic details were excluded. Because the web site was in English, it is likely that most if not all participants were reasonably fluent in English even if it was a second language. However, given evidence that memory span may vary by language spoken and language fluency (e.g. Naveh-Benjamin and Ayres 1986) for the analysis reported here, only participants from countries for which the dominant language is English are included. This represented the majority of the total participants who provided demographic details and included Australia, Canada, Ireland, New Zealand, the United Kingdom and the United States. Information regarding first language was not requested, but this selection criterion should maximize the number of people for whom English is their native language. Finally, only participants reporting their age as between 16 and 60 years, and who rated their general health as good or better were included. Analyses of the complete data set will be reported elsewhere, and the experiment is ongoing at the time of writing, so the eventual data set may be much larger. However, the focus in this chapter is on the data for healthy adults without the possible impact of younger or older age, and the data patterns for the sample sizes reported here are unlikely to change with a larger sample. The resulting sample size was 24,630, with 14,955 female and 9675 male, mean age 31.73 years, SD = 11.56.

Web-based tests

All of the tests described below were programmed by BBC staff to function within Macromedia Flash, a system that allows the running of real time data collection via the Internet.

Working memory span involved presenting short sentences similar to those used by Baddeley, Logie, Nimmo Smith *et al.* (1985) for verification against semantic knowledge. Sentences were either typically true, e.g. 'flies are insects' or typically false, e.g. 'mobile phones are made of cheese'. Participants had to use their mouse to click on a 'true' or 'false' button on the screen as quickly as possible, and to remember the final word of the sentence. A second sentence was then presented for response and so on until the sequence of sentences was complete. At this stage, a set of 20 words was shown in a square array in the left two thirds of the screen, with the correct sentence final words given in random positions while the remaining words were unrelated foils. Participants had to click on each of the sentence final words that they could remember and drag them to boxes arranged vertically on the right of the screen in the order in which they were presented. There was no maximum time for a true/false response or for recalling the words. Sequences started with two sentences and increased to a maximum of six sentences, with two sequences for each sequence length. The test stopped if the participant was unable to recall all of the sentence final words for two successive sequences. Working memory span was taken as the average of the two longest sequences for which the sentence-final words were recalled correctly.

Digit span comprised presentation of random digit sequences of increasing length, with digits shown one at a time at a rate of one per second in the centre of the screen. At the end of the sequence, a blank box appeared in the centre of the screen and participants had to type in the digit sequence in the order shown. Sequence length started with three digits and increased to a maximum of nine with two sequences at each length. The test stopped if the participant was unable to correctly recall the digit sequence on two successive occasions. This test was originally devised by Jacobs (1887) but is included in most standard measures of mental ability and is widely used as a measure of short-term verbal memory capacity. Its correlations with other measures of cognitive ability such as reading comprehension tend to be rather lower than those reported for working memory span (e.g. Daneman and Hannon, this volume).

Visual pattern span was measured by presenting square matrix patterns with white and blue squares for immediate recall, based on a procedure from Logie and Pearson (1997; see also Della Sala, Gray, Baddeley *et al.* 1999; Wilson, Scott and Power 1987). Each pattern was shown for two seconds. It was then replaced with a blank matrix in the same location and participants were to click on the squares that had previously been filled in blue. The patterns started with 3×3 square, then 3×4 (5 blue squares for both), then 4×4 (8 blue squares) then 4×5 up to a maximum of 5×5 (9 squares blue for both), with two patterns at each level. The test stopped when participants failed to recall all of the squares correctly on two successive trials.

Spatial orientation involved presenting a male figure, arms outstretched with a blue ball in one hand and a white ball in the other. On any one trial, the figure was shown in one of four positions, namely facing the viewer and upright, with their back to the viewer and upright, facing the viewer and upside down or with their back to the viewer and upside down. The task was to click on the words 'left' or 'right' at the bottom of the screen to indicate in which hand the figure held the blue ball. Participants had to complete as many trials as possible in a period of 30 seconds. This task was based on the Manikin test used by Logie and Baddeley (1983).

Memory binding comprised presentation of colored shapes at one of four positions on the computer screen, top, right, bottom or left. The shapes appeared for 2 seconds for every shape shown, for example two shapes would have a total of four seconds display time. Following removal of the shapes, four colored patches appeared along the top of the screen, and four outlines of the shapes appeared down the left of the screen. The task was to recall the color, shape and position previously displayed, first by clicking on a color, then clicking on the shape shown in that color, and then clicking on the position in which that colored shape had been shown. No shape or color was repeated on any one trial. All three features had to be recalled correctly, thereby giving a measure of the binding in memory of the three features for each item shown on a given trial. The test started with one item for recall and increased to a maximum of four items. The test stopped if participants failed to recall all three features for an item on two successive trials. In all cases, the color of each item was drawn from the set red, yellow, green and blue, and no color was repeated on any one trial. Participants were randomly allocated to one of four conditions. In conditions one and two, participants were shown geometric shapes drawn from the set, square, circle, triangle, diamond. In conditions three and four, the shapes were of animals namely camel, penguin, elephant and pig, based on the Snodgrass and Vanderwart (1980) line drawings. In conditions one and three, for trials with two, three or four items, the items were shown simultaneously on the screen for respectively 4 seconds, 6 seconds and 8 seconds. In conditions two and four, the items were shown consecutively at a rate of 2 seconds per item. For each trial, the combination of shape, color and position for each item was allocated at random, and each trial involved different combinations. However, these combinations were identical for all participants in a given condition. A detailed analysis of these data will be reported elsewhere. For the purposes of this chapter, data were collapsed across conditions.

Results

The working memory span test generated two main scores, the average of the two longest sequences of sentence final words recalled, and the average time to respond to sentences when a response was recorded. Response times longer than nine seconds were not included in the analysis. Digit span was taken as the average of the two longest sequences correctly recalled. Visual pattern span was taken as the number of patterns correctly recalled out of a total of 10. The spatial orientation score comprised the total number of correct responses in 30 seconds. The memory binding score comprised the total number of stimuli for which shape, color and position combinations were correctly recalled.

The primary interest for this chapter is the pattern of correlations between working memory (WM) span and sentence verification time. We first present data on the internal consistency of each of the measures concerned and then some indication of the validity of our measure of working memory span. Table 7.1 shows the split half correlations for each of the measures included. For WM span, for verification time and for digit span, the split half correlations all exceeded 0.8. They were somewhat lower for the memory binding score and the visual patterns test but still indicate high internal reliability, particularly for this sample size. It is worth noting that with a sample size of over 24,000, correlations as low as $r = 0.05$ are statistically significant, although such relationships are unlikely to be meaningful. Split half-scores were not available for the spatial orientation test. Table 7.1 also shows the descriptive statistics, indicating that the data means and standard deviations were not dissimilar from those obtained with these tests under more tightly controlled laboratory settings (see the references above for each test).

Table 7.2 shows the intercorrelations among the measures reported here. For the purposes of this chapter, we only report and discuss the pattern of simple pairwise correlations relevant for working memory span, verification time and digit span, together with age. It is clear that working memory span correlated positively with other measures of working memory ability, notably digit span, visual pattern span and memory binding. It is also clear that, even with the relatively restricted age range, age correlated with verification time, as might be expected (e.g. Salthouse 1996), and correlated negatively with working memory time. We shall discuss these correlations in detail elsewhere, but the pattern shown here provides some validation that our measures of speed and of memory collected via the Internet are generating expected patterns of correlations with age.

Table 7.1 Means, standard deviations and split half reliability of web-based measures from Experiment 3.

	Mean	SD	Split half correlation
Variable			
WM span (0–6)	4.43	1.09	0.97
Verification time (seconds)	3.468	0.841	0.82
Digit span (3–9)	6.86	1.24	0.9
Visual matrix (1–5)	2.67	0.83	0.51
Spatial (Max correct in 30S)	8.89	3.31	–
Binding (0–20)	10.14	4.56	0.70

Turning to our main questions for this chapter, what is striking is that the correlation between working memory span and verification time is positive, and much lower than are the correlations among the memory scores. As discussed above, the Towse *et al.* (2000) model might predict that the slower people are in responding then the more time there is for memory decay before recall is required and the poorer will be their memory performance. This predicts a negative correlation between verification time and working memory span.

A model based on general mental ability would predict that people who have high general mental ability will have rapid responses and will also have a high working memory span, and this again would predict a negative correlation. If mental ability is driving overall performance levels on both aspects of the working memory span test, then we might expect that when the range of general ability is narrowed, the correlation between tests would be reduced. Taking highest educational level obtained as a proxy for general mental ability we examined the pattern of correlation at each educational level and found no systematic attenuation (or enhancement) of the correlation between working memory span and verification time. The one exception was for a relatively small number of people (N = 93), aged over 21 who declared that they completed only primary school education. In their case, the correlation was approximately zero.

Barrouillet and Camos' model (e.g. this volume) predicts that longer verification times would allow more time for switching between rehearsal and sentence processing and therefore a positive correlation, as has been obtained. However, the relationship between the two measures of performance within the working memory span test are considerably lower than are the correlations

Table 7.2 Correlations among web-based measures from Experiment 3.

	Age	Digit span	WM span	Verification time
Age	1.00	0.06	−0.13	0.20
Education	0.21	0.12	0.09	0.05
Spatial	−0.09	0.20	0.18	−0.17
Visual pattern	−0.31	0.17	0.23	−0.12
Digit span	0.06	1.00	0.28	−0.08
WM span	−0.13	0.28	1.00	0.11
Verification time	0.20	−0.08	0.11	1.00
Bind score	−0.22	0.22	0.26	−0.15

between the memory component and other memory measures. Verification time correlates most highly with the spatial orientation test, which is another speeded measure (number correct in 30 seconds hence a negative correlation), as well as with age. These results offer partial support for Barrouillet and Camos, but the observation that verification speed explains only 1.21 per cent of the variance in working memory span points to a much greater degree of independence between these components than is assumed by any of these models. They are highly consistent with our conclusion from Experiments 1 and 2, from Duff and Logie (2001), and from the conclusion by Bayliss *et al.* (2003) that separate pools of resource support verification and temporary memory. These results are also consistent with the poor correlation between verification time and working memory span reported by Daneman and Hannon (this volume).

Conclusions

At one level, the debate is about developing a theory of the nature and functional architecture of working memory. At another level, there is the discussion about the practical utility of working memory span – immediate memory in the context of processing – as a measure of individual ability (Daneman and Hannon, this volume), possibly akin to fluid intelligence (Engle *et al.* 1999; Kane and Engle 2002). There is no doubt that working memory span has been extremely successful in fulfilling its role as a measure of individual cognitive ability and our results offer no challenge to that success. However, we would argue that our approach directly assesses and our data question the assumption that working memory span reflects the operation of a single cognitive resource that is subject to trade-off in performance between processing and storage as suggested in the models of Towse *et al.* (2000, 2002) and Barrouillet and Camos (this volume). Our data also offer further support to the view expressed by Waters and Caplan (2003) that a combination of at least two different measures of working memory performance might offer a more powerful predictive tool than does the memory measure alone. In this sense, working memory span might encapsulate the operation of several different components of cognition. A related discussion about the so-called executive functions of working memory also has pointed to multiple factors (see e.g. Miyake, Friedman, Emerson *et al.* 2000; Collette *et al.* in press; Halford *et al.* this volume; Marklund and Nyberg, this volume). Our results seem to suggest that the same is likely to be true of the concept of processing and storage in working memory span.

Acknowledgments

The data collection for Experiments 1 and 2 was conducted while Simon Duff was employed and Robert Logie was a visiting professor at the University of Bergen, Norway. Experiment 3 was set up as a web-based experiment in collaboration with the British Broadcasting Company (BBC) in connection with a series of television and radio programmes on the topic of memory. Data reported here were collected worldwide via pages on the BBC web site over a period of two months prior to the broadcast of the television programme that described the tests on the web site. We are grateful to the Faculty of Psychology at the University of Bergen, and to staff in the Science Division of the BBC, particularly Becky Palmer and Stephen Mather, for their support.

References

Baddeley, AD and Hitch, GJ (1974). Working memory. In G. Bower (ed), *The Psychology of Learning and Motivation*, VIII, (pp. 47–90), New York: Academic Press.

Baddeley, AD and Logie, RH (1999). Working memory: The multiple component model. In A Miyake and P Shah (eds) *Models of Working Memory* (pp. 28–61). New York: Cambridge University Press.

Barrouillet, P, Bernardin, S and Camos, V (2004). Time constraints and resource sharing in adults' working memory spans. *Journal of Experimental Psychology: General, 133*, 83–100.

Barrouillet, P and Camos, V (2001). Developmental increase in working memory span: Resource sharing or temporal decay? *Journal of Memory and Language, 45*, 1–20.

Barrouillet, P and Camos, V (2007). The time-based resource-sharing model of working memory. In N Osaka, RH Logie and M D'Esposito (eds), *The Cognitive Neuroscience of Working Memory* (pp. 59–80). Oxford: Oxford University Press.

Bayliss, DM, Jarrold, C, Gunn, DM and Baddeley, AD (2003). The complexities of complex span: explaining individual differences in working memory in children and adults. *Journal of Experimental Psychology: General, 132*, 71–92.

Birnbaum, MH (2004). Human research and data collection via the Internet. *Annual Review of Psychology, 55*, 803–832.

Caplan, D and Waters, G (1999). Working memory and sentence comprehension. *Behavioral and Brain Sciences, 22*, 77–126.

Cocchini, G, Logie, RH, Della Sala, S, MacPherson, SE (2002). Concurrent performance of two memory tasks: evidence for domain-specific working memory systems. *Memory and Cognition, 30*, 1086–1095.

Collette, F, Van der Linden, M, Laureys, S, Arigoni, F, Delfiore, G, Degueldre, C, Luxen, A and Salmon, E (in press). Mapping the updating process: Common and specific brain activations across different versions of the running span task. *Cortex*.

Cowan, N (1999). An embedded-process model of working memory. In A Miyake and P Shah (eds), *Models of Working Memory: Mechanisms of active maintenance and executive control* (pp. 62–101). Cambridge: Cambridge University Press.

Cowan, N (2005). *Working Memory Capacity*. Hove: Psychology Press.

Daneman, M and Carpenter, PA (1980). Individual differences in working memory and reading. *Journal of Verbal Learning and Verbal Behavior, 19*, 450–466.

Daneman, M and Hannon, B (2007). What do working memory span tasks like reading span really measure? In N Osaka, RH Logie and M D'Esposito (eds), *The Cognitive Neuroscience of Working Memory* (pp. 21–42). Oxford: Oxford University Press.

Daneman, M and Merikle, PM (1996). Working memory and language comprehension: A meta-analysis. *Psychonomic Bulletin and Review, 3*, 422–433.

Della Sala, S, Gray, C, Baddeley, A, Allamano, N and Wilson, L (1999). Pattern span: A tool for unwelding visuo-spatial memory. *Neuropsychologia, 37*, 1189–1199.

Duff, SC and Logie, RH (2001). Processing and storage in working memory span. *Quarterly Journal of Experimental Psychology, 54A*, 31–48.

Engle, RW, Kane, MJ and Tuholski, AW (1999). Individual differences in working memory capacity and what they tell us about controlled attention, general fluid intelligence, and functions of the prefrontal cortex. In A Miyake and P Shah (eds), *Models of Working Memory*. (pp. 102–134). New York: Cambridge University Press.

Halford, GS, Phillips, S, Wilson, WH, McCredden, J, Andrews, G, Birney, D, Baker, R and Bain, JD (2007). Relational processing is fundamental to the central executive and it is limited to four variables. In N Osaka, RH Logie and M D'Esposito (eds), *The Cognitive Neuroscience of Working Memory* (pp. 261–280). Oxford: Oxford University Press.

Hunt, E and Lansman, M (1981). Individual differences in attention. In R Sternberg (ed), *Advances in the Psychology of Intelligence, Vol 1*. Hillsdale, NJ: Lawrence Erlbaum.

Jacobs, J (1887). Experiments on 'Prehension'. *Mind, 12* (45), 75–79.

Just, M and Carpenter, P (1992). A capacity theory of comprehension: Individual differences in working memory. *Psychological Review, 99*, 122–149.

Kane, MJ and Engle, RW (2002). The role of prefrontal cortex in working memory capacity, executive attention, and general fluid intelligence: An individual differences perspective. *Psychonomic Bulletin and Review, 9*, 637–671.

Logie, RH (2003). Spatial and visual working memory: A mental workspace. In D Irwin and B Ross (eds) *Cognitive Vision. A Volume of The Psychology of Learning and Motivation*, Vol. 42 (pp. 37–78). San Diego, CA: Academic Press.

Logie, RH and Baddeley, AD (1983) A trimix saturation dive to 660 metres: Studies of cognitive performance, mood and sleep quality. *Ergonomics*, *26* (4), 359–374.

Logie, RH and Pearson, DG (1997). The inner eye and the inner scribe of visuo-spatial working memory: Evidence from developmental fractionation. *European Journal of Cognitive Psychology*, *9*, 241–257.

Marklund, P and Nyberg, L (2007). Intersecting the divide between working memory and episodic memory: Evidence from sustained and transient brain activity patterns. In N Osaka, RH Logie and M D'Esposito (eds). *The Cognitive Neuroscience of Working Memory* (pp. 305–332). Oxford: Oxford University Press.

Miyake, A, Friedman, NP, Emerson, MJ, Witzki, AH and Howerter, A (2000). The unity and diversity of executive functions and their contributions to complex 'frontal lobe' tasks: a latent variable analysis. *Cognitive Psychology*, *41*, 49–100.

Miyake, A, Friedman, NP, Rettinger, D, Shah, P and Hegarty, M (2001). How are visuospatial working memory, executive functioning, and spatial abilities related? A latent variable analysis. *Journal of Experimental Psychology: General*, *130*, 621–640.

Naveh-Benjamin, M and Ayres, TJ (1986). Digit span, reading rate, and linguistic relativity. *Quarterly Journal of Experimental Psychology*, *38*, 739–751.

Postle, B (2007). "Activated long-term memory"? The bases of representation in working memory. In N Osaka, RH Logie and M D'Esposito (eds), *The Cognitive Neuroscience of Working Memory* (pp. 333–350). Oxford: Oxford University Press.

Rabbitt, PMA (2005). Cognitive gerontology: cognitive changes in old age. *Quarterly Journal of Experimental Psychology*, *58*, 1–4.

Reimers, S (in press). The BBC Internet Study: General methodology. *Archives of Sexual Behavior*.

Reimers, S and Maylor, EA (2005). Task switching across the life span: Effects of age on general and specific switch costs. *Developmental Psychology*, *41*, 661–671.

Reips, U-D (2002). Standards for Internet-based experimenting. *Experimental Psychology*, *49*, 243–256.

Salthouse, TA (1996). The processing speed theory of adult age differences in cognition. *Psychological Review*, *103*, 403–428.

Snodgrass, JG and Vanderwart, M (1980). A standardized set of 260 pictures: norms for name agreement, image agreement, familiarity, and visual complexity. *Journal of Experimental Psychology: Human Learning and Memory*, *6* (2), 174–215.

Towse, JN, Hitch, GJ and Hutton, U (2000). On the interpretation of working memory span in adults. *Memory and Cognition*, *28* (3), 341–348.

Towse, JN, Hitch, GJ and Hutton, U (2002). On the nature of the relationship between processing activity and item retention in children. *Journal of Experimental Child Psychology*, *82* (2), 156–184.

Waters, GS and Caplan, D (1996). The measurement of verbal working memory capacity and its relation to reading comprehension. *Quarterly Journal of Experimental Psychology*, *49A*, 51–79.

Waters, GS and Caplan, D (2003). The reliability and stability of verbal working memory measures. *Behavior Research Methods, Instruments and Computers*, *35*, 550–564.

Wickens, CD (1984). Processing resources in attention. In R Parasuraman and R Davies (eds), *Varieties of Attention* (pp. 63–101). New York: Academic Press.

Wilson, JTL, Scott, JJ and Power, G (1987). Developmental differences in the span of visual memory for pattern. *British Journal of Developmental Psychology*, *5*, 249–255.

8

The interpretation of temporal isolation effects

Stephan Lewandowsky, Tarryn Wright and
Gordon D. A. Brown

At first glance, there appears to be no doubt that time is an important determinant of memory. Whether time spans are measured in seconds, minutes, or years, the pervasive decline of performance with delay is obvious and nearly always inescapable (e.g., Brown and Chater 2001). Accordingly, the field abounds with theories that accord a central and causal role to time in memory (e.g., Brown, Neath and Chater 2002; Brown, Preece and Hulme 2000; Burgess and Hitch 1999; Page and Norris 1998). Here, we focus on one class of time-based theories known as 'distinctiveness models', according to which memory for events is determined by the extent to which they are temporally distinct from other items in memory (e.g., Bjork and Whitten 1974; Brown *et al.* 2000; Burgess and Hitch 1999; Crowder 1976; Glenberg and Swanson 1986; Neath 1993). Although there is considerable variation among implementations of the distinctiveness notion, the models share a crucial common prediction: all other things being equal, temporally isolated events in memory (e.g., where I parked my car in an unfamiliar car park in a strange city) are necessarily better remembered than events that are temporally crowded (e.g., where I parked my car today, as I do every other day, in the university car park outside the Psychology building). Temporal distinctiveness theories would have considerable difficulty accommodating the absence of a temporal isolation effect. This chapter examines the extent to which this core prediction holds in immediate memory for serial order, the hallmark paradigm of short-term memory research. To foreshadow our main conclusion, we find little support for a role of temporal distinctiveness in immediate memory for serial order.

The structure of this chapter is as follows: we begin by reviewing some of the existing evidence that has been advanced in support of temporal distinctiveness and argue that there are two non-temporal alternative explanations for the observed apparent temporal isolation effects; namely, rehearsal and selective encoding. We then present two experiments in which temporal gaps between list items were predictable and in which a temporal isolation effect was observed, such that recall was better for items that were surrounded by longer pauses, even when rehearsal was suppressed. This eliminates the first alternative explanation and suggests that rehearsal is not a major contributor to isolation effects. We next show by simulation that those results, like the outcomes of previous related studies, are nonetheless ambiguous and can be handled by the second alternative explanation, which assumes that people selectively encode those portions of the list that they know to be temporally well separated. We conclude the chapter by reviewing a number of recent studies in which both rehearsal and selective encoding strategies were eliminated, and which uniformly found that temporal isolation had no beneficial effect on immediate memory for serial order.

We close by drawing three principal conclusions:

1. Temporal separation at encoding need not play a role in short-term serial recall.

2. Previous experiments that purport to show effects of temporal isolation in serial recall are ambiguous.

3. Any known effects of temporal isolation at encoding can be ascribed to strategic effects such as selective encoding.

Although temporal distinctiveness models of free recall have enjoyed considerable empirical support (e.g., Bjork and Whitten 1974; Glenberg and Swanson 1986; Nairne, Neath, Serra, and Byun 1997), until recently only two studies extended the concept to serial recall by varying the temporal intervals between list items during presentation. Neath and Crowder (1996) systematically varied interitem intervals during rapid presentation of five-item lists of two-syllable words. In the two conditions of greatest interest, interitem intervals either increased or decreased consecutively across serial positions. In the increasing condition, the interitem interval increased from 50 (between the first two list items), to 100 (between items two and three), to 200, and then to 400 ms. The decreasing condition involved the reverse order of these intervals across serial position. In a third control condition, interitem intervals were a constant 50 ms.

The results supported the expectations of distinctiveness views, with serial recall performance for the last few items being significantly better for the increasing condition compared to the decreasing condition, whereas the reverse was true for the first few items. Performance on the constant-interval control list was in between these two conditions.

Similar results were reported by Welte and Laughery (1971) with slower presentation rates, suggesting that the results of Neath and Crowder (1996) were not tied to the use of very brief intervals. Welte and Laughery (1971) used lists of nine digits that were presented with either an increasing or a decreasing schedule of intervals. Intervals had a minimum duration of 500 ms with a uniform stepsize of 200 ms. The emphasis in Welte and Laughery's experiment was on examining the differences between serial recall and free recall. The results revealed the same beneficial pattern of temporal isolation for free recall as for serial recall, thus extending the generality of the finding by Neath and Crowder (1996). (See also Neath and Crowder 1990.)

At first glance, the studies by Neath and Crowder (1996) and Welte and Laughery (1971) provide strong support for the idea that temporal isolation benefits short-term memory for serial order. Irrespective of serial position, and with relevant variables such as retention interval and list length kept constant, recall was better for items that were widely separated from their neighbors than for items that were temporally crowded.

However, it turns out that the studies by Neath and Crowder (1996) and Welte and Laughery (1971) were characterized by two methodological features that prevent an unambiguous interpretation of the results and give rise to two alternative explanations. The first arises from the predictability of the list structure. On each list, the gap between the first two items predicted the duration of all following intervals: when the first interval was short, participants knew that the list would end with well-separated items, whereas when the first interval was long, participants knew that the list would end with items crowded together in time. This predictability may have encouraged participants to develop compensatory encoding strategies. For example, on an increasing list people may have chosen to await the well-separated terminal items for thorough encoding, and conversely on a decreasing list, they may have chosen to discontinue processing after encoding of the first few items. Any strategy of this type would also have given rise to the observed isolation effects, but of course it would have done so without any need to invoke the concept of temporal distinctiveness. We examine this potential alternative explanation further after presenting two experiments that addressed a second issue with the studies by Neath and Crowder (1996) and Welte and Laughery (1971).

This second problem is particularly obvious in the study by Welte and Laughery, in which participants could have readily used the moderately long interitem intervals to rehearse recently presented items. For example, on a list such as A.B..C. . .D. . . .E (where the letters represent arbitrary items and the dots represent units of time), people would have had considerably more opportunity to rehearse D than A.[1] Any strategy of this type would have produced the observed isolation effect; by implication, the potential presence of rehearsal renders the results of Welte and Laughery theoretically ambiguous. The problem of rehearsal was recognized by Neath and Crowder (1996), who sought to prevent rehearsal through the use of extremely brief intervals and short presentation durations (1100 ms for the entire list). However, for the word stimuli used by Neath and Crowder, articulation rates are known to be around three words per second (e.g., Hulme, Roodenrys, Brown *et al.* 1995), which implies that the longest interval (400 ms) in that study would have been sufficient for some limited rehearsal to take place. It follows that the possibility cannot be ruled out that rehearsal may have contributed to the isolation effects observed by Neath and Crowder.

We now present two experiments that resembled the studies by Neath and Crowder (1996) and Welte and Laughery (1971) but eliminated rehearsal by articulatory suppression (AS). AS is the repetitive vocalization of an irrelevant word by the participant during study and, by common agreement, is assumed to disrupt rehearsal (Saito 2000).

Experiment 1

Experiment 1 used increasing and decreasing presentation schedules in a quiet condition and with AS. It is known that AS significantly decreases performance without affecting the overall shape of the serial position curve (Anderson and Matessa 1997; Burgess and Hitch 1999; Hitch, Burgess, Towse *et al.* 1996). Temporal distinctiveness theories would expect the benefits of temporal isolation to be the same regardless of articulation, and would therefore expect both conditions to replicate the isolation effects just discussed. Alternatively, if the apparent effect of temporal distinctiveness found by Neath and Crowder and Welte and Laughery had been due to rehearsal during the intervals, then the effects of presentation schedule should be abolished by AS.

Method

Participants. Twenty-six first-year students from the University of Western Australia participated voluntarily in exchange for course credit. Two participants were removed from the analysis as they performed extremely poorly. This left 24 participants who were randomly allocated into either the AS or the quiet condition, 12 for each condition.

Design and materials. The experiment was computer controlled. Lists were constructed from 19 letters (all of the consonants except Q and Y) and items were randomly sampled without replacement for each list. The lists contained seven items and the total presentation duration was constant across all schedules. The increasing interitem intervals were set to 50, 100, 200, 400, 800 and 1200 ms, with the decreasing intervals in the reverse sequence and the interval in the constant presentation schedule set to 458 ms. Two independent variables were examined: presentation schedule (i.e., constant, increasing, or decreasing) was manipulated within participants, and articulation condition (either quiet or AS) was manipulated between participants.

---

[1] The term 'rehearsal' here is to be understood generically, to refer to any of a number of strategies that people may use during the gaps between items to consolidate already-presented information. For example, people might phonologically recode items (if they are visually presented); they might apply some mnemonic technique; or they might use the time for proper rehearsal.

Procedure. There were 40 trials for each presentation schedule, which were randomized into a contiguous sequence of 120 trials. Participants in the quiet condition quietly watched the presentation of the list, whereas participants in the AS condition repeated the word 'sugar' aloud during list presentation but not during recall. Participants' verbalizations were recorded to ensure that AS continued for the whole experiment.

Each trial commenced with a blank screen for 2000 ms, which was followed by the list with each item presented centrally for 300 ms. Items were separated by a blank screen for the time determined by the interval manipulation. After the last item, a blank screen of 100 ms and a mask of three asterisks appeared for 300 ms, which were followed by a '_' cursor to prompt recall via the keyboard. Responses remained on the screen until all items were entered but correction was not possible. The computer also recorded the latency of responses.

Participants were instructed to recall all of the items in the list in their presented order as accurately and as quickly as possible. Participants were instructed to guess if necessary or alternatively use the spacebar to indicate an omission. Emphasis was placed on ensuring that items were recalled in the correct position.

Results

Responses were scored as correct only if the item was recalled in its correct position. Performance of individual participants in both groups ranged from 0.21 to 0.78 (averaged across serial positions).

Figure 8.1 shows the serial position curves for both conditions and all presentation schedules. The figure suggests that an effect of presentation schedule was obtained for both the quiet and the AS group, with performance at early serial positions being better in the decreasing than the increasing conditions, and with a reverse difference between conditions at later serial positions.

A $2 \times 3 \times 7$ (Condition $\times$ Presentation schedule $\times$ Serial position) between-within subjects ANOVA revealed main effects of condition, $F(1, 22) = 15.99$, MSe $= 0.33$, $p < 0.001$; presentation

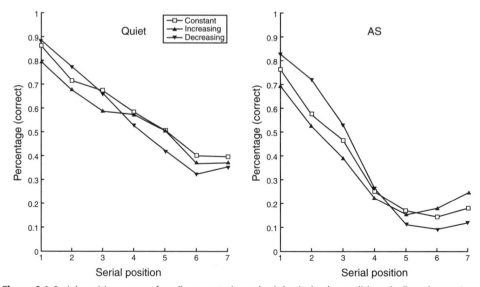

Figure 8.1 Serial position curves for all presentation schedules in both conditions in Experiment 1.

schedule, $F(2, 44) = 3.66$, MSe $= 0.01$, $p < 0.05$; and serial position, $F(6, 132) = 132.87$, MSe $= 0.024$, $p < 0.0001$. Serial position also interacted with condition, $F(6, 132) = 6.31$, MSe $= 0.024$, $p < 0.0001$, and, crucially, with presentation schedule, $F(12, 264) = 9.59$, MSe$= 0.006$, $p < 0.0001$. No other interactions, including the overarching three-way interaction between all variables, were significant.

The interaction between serial position and presentation schedule was further explored by two separate within-subjects Presentation schedule × Serial position ANOVAs for the quiet and AS condition, respectively. The interaction between presentation schedule and serial position condition was significant for the quiet condition, $F(12, 132) = 2.84$, MSe $= 0.007$, $p < 0.002$, as well as for the AS condition, $F(12, 132) = 8.53$, MSe $= 0.006$, $p < 0.0001$.

Discussion

The results of Experiment 1 are consonant with the predictions of temporal distinctiveness theories: irrespective of their serial position, items that were widely separated in time were remembered better than items that were temporally crowded. Experiment 1 thus replicated the results of Neath and Crowder (1996) and additionally extended their findings to longer lists (seven instead of five items), to a closed vocabulary set (letters instead of words), to significantly longer presentation durations and interitem intervals, and to situations when rehearsal at encoding was prevented by articulatory suppression.

The first experiment thus provided evidence against a possible role of rehearsal in producing temporal isolation effects. Moreover, contrary to the expectations of a rehearsal view, the magnitude of the isolation effect at early serial positions appeared to be greater in the AS condition than in the quiet condition. Figure 8.1 shows that performance at early serial positions for the decreasing schedule in the quiet condition was arguably close to ceiling, and this may have prevented the isolation effect from exhibiting its true magnitude. Experiment 2 explored this possibility by inserting a brief distractor task between list presentation and recall in the quiet condition.

Experiment 2

Experiment 2 was identical to the first study except for a brief distractor task between study and retrieval in the quiet condition. In addition, the constant presentation schedule was omitted, and participants were queried about their encoding strategies after completion of the experiment.

Method

Participants. Fourteen first-year students from the University of Western Australia participated voluntarily in exchange for course credit. Three participants were removed due to poor performance and one because the participant took almost three times as long as anyone else to complete the task. This left 10 participants, an equal number of whom were randomly assigned to the AS and quiet conditions.

Design and procedure. Lists were constructed in the same manner as for Experiment 1, except that the constant condition was not included. There were 40 trials of each presentation condition; increasing or decreasing. Presentation schedules were randomly intermixed.

In the quiet condition, participants repeated out aloud a random 3-digit number that was presented immediately after the list for 2,000 ms. In the AS condition, a blank screen of 100 ms followed by a mask of asterisks for 300 ms separated the last study item from the recall phase. After completion of the experiment, participants were queried about what strategies they used to perform the experiment.

Results

Correct-in-position performance for individual participants in both groups ranged from 0.24 to 0.48 (averaged across serial positions). The serial position curves for both conditions and both presentation schedules are presented in Figure 8.2.

A $2 \times 2 \times 7$ (Condition $\times$ Presentation schedule $\times$ Serial position) between-within ANOVA revealed a significant main effect of presentation schedule, $F(1, 8) = 5.50$, $p < 0.05$, MSe = 0.019, and serial position, $F(6, 48) = 29.10$, $p < 0.0001$, MSe = 0.03. In addition, the interaction of presentation schedule and serial position was significant, $F(6, 48) = 7.81$, $p < 0.0001$, MSe = 0.008. No other effects reached significance.

Two separate 2×7 (Presentation schedule $\times$ Serial position) within-subjects ANOVAs within each condition confirmed the presence of the crucial presentation schedule $\times$ serial position interaction for the quiet condition, $F(6, 24) = 3.34$, $p < 0.02$, MSe = 0.01, as well as the AS condition, $F(6, 24) = 5.28$, $p < 0.002$, MSe = 0.006.

As for Experiment 1, the benefits for the decreasing interval were found at the beginning of the list for the first three serial positions, whereas the fifth and sixth serial positions benefited in the increasing condition. The crossover at serial position four is at roughly the same point as in Experiment 1 (see Figures 8.1 and 8.2). The apparent lack of difference between the decreasing and increasing condition for the terminal item in the quiet condition probably resulted from a suffix effect induced by the requirement to pronounce a random number at the end of the list. Suffix effects are a standard finding in serial recall (e.g., Greene and Crowder 1988; Hitch, Burgess, Towse *et al.* 1996) and this result is therefore not surprising.

The interview at the end of testing revealed that participants used a consistent encoding strategy. All participants, regardless of articulatory condition, reported that with decreasing presentation schedules they focused on remembering only the first three to four items. With increasing presentation schedules, all but two participants (both in the quiet condition) likewise reported that they focused only on the last three or four items during list presentation.

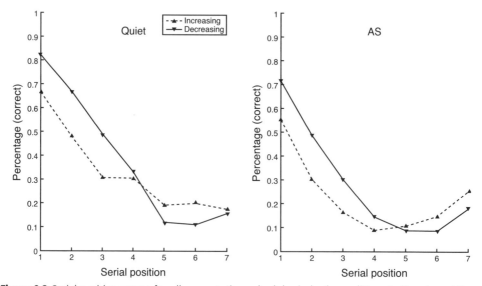

Figure 8.2 Serial position curves for all presentation schedules in both conditions in Experiment 2.

Discussion

Experiment 2 replicated the results of the first study even though performance in the quiet condition, including the first list item, could no longer be considered to be anywhere near ceiling. The results further weaken a rehearsal-based explanation for temporal isolation effects, and we give it no further consideration as a viable alternative explanation.[2]

The recall data are therefore compatible with a temporal distinctiveness notion, although the verbal reports by participants are supportive of the other alternative account of the data advanced at the outset; namely, that the predictability of intervals engendered selective encoding strategies. On this account, it was not temporal distinctiveness per se that produced the isolation effects at retrieval, but people's choice to memorize well-separated items at the expense of others that they found more difficult to encode. In order to confirm the viability of this alternative explanation, we now model the data from the first two experiments in two ways; within a conventional temporal distinctiveness framework and within a nontemporal account augmented by selective encoding.

Temporal distinctiveness vs selective encoding: the SIMPLE theory

A powerful recent instantiation of the temporal distinctiveness hypothesis is the SIMPLE theory (*Scale Invariant Memory, Perception, and LEarning*) of Brown *et al.* (2002). At an intuitive level, SIMPLE postulates that the confusability between any two memory traces is related to the ratio of the time that has elapsed between their encoding and the time of recall. The lower that ratio, the lower the confusability among items and hence the more likely it is that an item is recalled correctly. This mechanism favors recent items over more distant events. For example, items that were encoded 1 s and 2 s ago are less confusable (ratio of 0.5) than are items from 5 and 6 seconds ago (0.83). The mechanism also favors items that were separated in time over others that occurred in close succession. For example, items that occurred 5 s and 10 s ago (ratio 0.5) are less confusable than items that occurred 7 s and 8 s ago (0.88), notwithstanding the fact that the average retention interval is equal for both pairs of items. It follows that items from further in the past, and items that occurred near each other in time, will be more difficult to recall (see Brown *et al.* 2002 for further details).

More formally, SIMPLE rests on three principal assumptions:

1. Items are represented by their position within a potentially multidimensional psychological space, with one of those dimensions necessarily devoted to representing time. Here, the temporal dimension was accompanied by a second, positional dimension that corresponded to the list position of items.

2. The similarity between any two items in memory is a declining function of the distance separating them in psychological space.

3. The probability of recalling an item is inversely proportional to that item's summed similarity to all other response alternatives, as just illustrated by the ratios between elapsed times of item pairs.

The SIMPLE architecture

Encoding in multidimensional space. Memory representations are organized along a primary temporal dimension that reflects the (logarithmically transformed) time since encoding. Retrieval can

---

[2] This conclusion stands in contrast to our interpretation of an earlier study (Lewandowsky and Brown 2005), in which we ascribed an apparent isolation effect to rehearsal. Upon reexamination, that effect was more likely to be the product of a grouping strategy, similar to the strategic explanation advanced here for the present experiments. See Lewandowsky, Brown, Wright *et al.* (2006) for details.

be cued by the remembered location of an item along this dimension. In the present case, a second dimension represents within-list position, coded by ordinal numbers (i.e., position 1, 2,...). There is ample evidence that positional information – which can be decoupled from elapsed time – is relevant in serial recall (Henson 1999; Ng and Maybery 2002).

To illustrate, consider the representation of a two-item list after a 6 s retention interval (with items being separated by 1 s on the list): the two items would be in locations {log(7), 1} and {log(6), 2}, respectively, in the {time, position} space. The relative importance of the two dimensions at retrieval is determined by the parameter wt, which is the attentional weight paid to the temporal dimension. The weight given to the positional dimension is given by $1-wt$, and therefore:

$$d_{i,j} = wt \left| Log(T_i) - Log(T_j) \right| + (1 - wt) \left| P_i - P_j \right|$$

where $d_{i,j}$ is the psychological distance between stimulus i and stimulus j, T_i is the temporal distance of stimulus i from the time of retrieval (logarithmically transformed to capture the fact that temporally distant events are more compressed than recent ones), and P_i is the ordinal position of item i. The attentional parameter wt (see, e.g., Nosofsky 1992) can be thought of as stretching (shrinking) the psychological space along the most (least) important dimension. In the present case, if wt is unity, the simulations implement an exclusively time-based representation (for the earlier two-item list, the representation reduces to {log(7)} and {log(6)}). Conversely, as wt approaches zero, the representation is no longer time-based but positional and the representation of the list becomes {1} and {2}.

Similarity-distance metric. Following much precedent in the categorization literature, SIMPLE assumes that the similarity of any two items in memory is a reducing exponential function of the distance between them in psychological space:

$$\eta_{i,j} = e^{-c d_{i,j}}$$

where $\eta_{i,j}$ is the similarity between items i and j and $d_{i,j}$ the distance between them. It follows that items that are very close have a similarity approaching unity, whereas items that are more psychologically distant have a similarity that, in the extreme, approaches zero. The parameter c governs the rate of decline of similarity with distance. In conjunction with the logarithmic transformation of time, this similarity metric gives rise to the distinctiveness ratios mentioned earlier.

Similarity determines recall. The third assumption is that the probability of recalling item i is inversely proportional to the summed similarity of that item to every other potentially recallable item. Specifically, the discriminability of the memory trace for item i, D_i, is given by:

$$D_i = \frac{1}{\sum_{k=1}^{n} (\eta_{i,k})}$$

where n is the number of available response alternatives, which in the present case is assumed to be equal to the number of list items.

Discriminability translates into recall probability by taking into account the possibility of omissions. Omissions arise from thresholding of low retrieval probabilities by a sigmoid function: if D_i is the discriminability given by the preceding equation, the recall probability P_i is derived as:

$$P_i = \frac{1}{1 + e^{-s(D_i - t)}}$$

where t is the threshold and s the slope (or noisiness) of the transforming function. Any D_i that falls below the threshold engenders an omission.

Model parameters. For the present simulations, we used a basic version of SIMPLE that did not incorporate mechanisms for extra-list intrusions or response suppression and that ignored possible phonological or semantic similarity between items. All of these mechanisms are necessary for modeling of a wider range of paradigms; however, they are not needed for (and indeed could potentially obscure) the core predictions that are of interest here.

The present basic version of SIMPLE thus has five free parameters:

1. c governs the rate at which the psychological similarity of two items decreases as a function of the distance between them in psychological space.

2. wt specifies the amount of attention paid to the temporal dimension (at the expense of attention paid to the positional dimension).

3. s (for 'slope') and

4. t (for 'threshold') relate to omissions as described above.

5. An additional parameter o is required to accommodate output interference. It is assumed that the memories of to-be-recalled items become progressively less distinctive as recall proceeds due to interference caused be each successive recall. The output interference parameter, o, reduces the value of c for the nth item recalled by multiplying it by o^{n-1}. Thus with $o = 1$, there is no output interference; as o reduces below 1 there is increasing output interference.

Two rival accounts for the data

All simulations implemented the exact presentation regime of the experiment(s) being modeled, using the experimental presentation duration, interitem intervals, and retention intervals. The best-fitting parameter estimates and R^2 values for all simulations reported in this article are summarized in Table 8.1.

Time-based account. The time-based account for Experiment 2 was straightforward, with the parameters being estimated from the data using the experimental presentation regime. Parameter values were estimated separately for the quiet and suppression conditions, but were held constant for the increasing and decreasing schedules within each articulation condition. The results are shown in the left panel of Figure 8.3, where it is evident that a good fit was obtained. Moreover, the parameter estimates were meaningful and consistent with a time-based interpretation of the

Table 8.1 SIMPLE parameter values used in all simulations

Experiment	Cond	c	wt	o	t	s	R^2
One	Quiet	9.37	0.74	0.75	0.56	3.79	0.960
(temporal)	Suppress	9.16	0.73	0.84	0.83	9.45	0.992
Two	Quiet	12.1	0.86	0.79	0.74	5.45	0.978
(temporal)	Suppress	5.49	0.67	0.91	0.84	9.78	0.988
One	Quiet	15.6	0	0.21	0.01	2.79	1.00
(encoding)	Suppress	9.87	0	0.40	0.68	21.0	0.990
Two	Quiet	5.36	0	0.50	0.61	4.18	0.990
(encoding)	Suppress	2.78	0	0.85	0.85	11.1	0.991

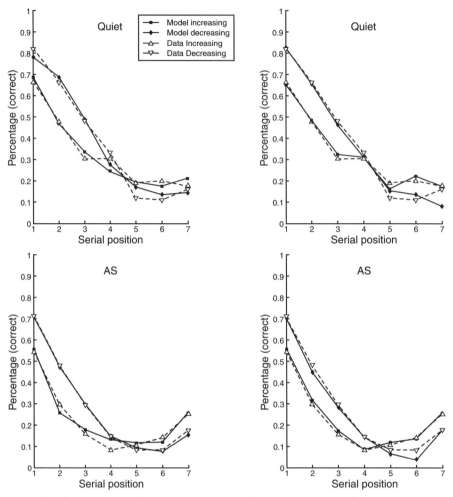

Figure 8.3 Fits of two versions of SIMPLE to the data of Experiment 2. The left panel shows the predictions of the time-based account and the right panel shows predictions of the event-based selective-encoding account. See text for explanation.

results (e.g., the distinctiveness parameter c was lower in the suppression condition). Of particular interest, the estimated weight on the temporal dimension, wt, was substantially greater than zero in both conditions, confirming that the model gives attentional weight to the temporal dimension in order to capture the effects of presentation schedule. Overall, then, the results are consistent with a time-based interpretation of the effects of increasing and decreasing presentation schedules, and with the Neath-Crowder interpretation.[3]

Selective-encoding account. For the alternative account based on selective encoding, the wt parameter was set to zero, which ensured that only position, and not time, played a role in memory. In addition, the probability of encoding of an item was hypothesized to be a function of its total

---

[3] Further simulations confirmed that the same temporal model could fit the data from Experiment 1; parameter and R^2 values are shown in Table 8.1.

temporal isolation, such that terminal (early) list items in the decreasing (increasing) condition had little chance of being encoded, and conversely, early (terminal) items were certain to be encoded.[4] On each particular simulated trial, SIMPLE was presented with a list of only those items that were chosen for encoding according to those probabilities. In consequence, encoded lists were rarely of length seven and contained a variable number of items, with the majority of encoded items being those that were surrounded by longer intervals on the list. This encoding regime was thought to implement the strategies that participants in Experiment 2 reported during debriefing.

Because scoring of recall was with respect to the full seven-item lists, this mechanism necessarily produced a disadvantage for temporally crowded items. We estimated the encoding-probability parameter separately for each serial position, and then examined whether the resulting parameter estimates conformed to the prediction that encoding was less likely for items with reduced temporal isolation. Although the number of parameters is large compared to the number of data points, thus facilitating a good fit, the modeling strategy allows a test of the variable-encoding probability hypothesis without the need to make assumptions about exactly how encoding probability would change with temporal isolation.

The results, based on 5,000 replications in each case, are shown in the right panel of Figure 8.3. As expected, good fits were obtained.[5] Of greater interest is the set of estimated parameter values. For the middle five items (end items were not considered because they have only one neighbor), estimated encoding probabilities increased monotonically with temporal isolation, with the average estimates across conditions ranging from 0.56 and 0.57 for temporal isolations of 150 and 300 ms to 0.66, 0.68 and 0.70 for isolations 600, 1200 and 2000 ms, respectively. These estimates suggest that a total surrounding time of 0.5 s or greater substantially increased the probability that an item would be encoded.

Conclusions from modeling

The main role of the modeling was not to flesh out the particulars of each account, but to show that the data of Experiment 2 – and, by implication, the results of related precedents – are ambiguous and can be explained in two ways. Accordingly, we modeled the data in two ways with virtually equal quantitative precision: first, with a temporal-distinctiveness account as suggested by Neath and Crowder (1996), and second, with a selective-encoding account as suggested by the reports of our participants.

Although one may question the specific assumptions underlying our selective-encoding account, on the basis of the modeling there can be little doubt that predictable presentation schedules cannot provide unambiguous support for the role of temporal distinctiveness in short-term serial recall. Support for the notion of distinctiveness can only be drawn from studies in which selective encoding is disabled. An obvious way to disable selective encoding is by rendering

---

[4] Although we present this account by referring to selective *encoding*, we remain theoretically neutral as to whether the selectivity applies strictly to initial encoding or may involve some type of directed forgetting after initial registration of the stimulus. There is ample evidence that people can choose to discard information from memory after its initial registration (e.g., MacLeod 1998). Within SIMPLE, the two notions are indistinguishable and both converge on the representations that are being simulated here.

[5] The simulations required a very large amount of CPU time and in some cases it was necessary to terminate them when an R^2 value of 0.99 was reached. Further simulations confirmed that the same model could fit the data from Experiment 1; parameter and R^2 values are shown in Table 8.1.

the interitem intervals within each list unpredictable. With unpredictable intervals, participants have no way of predicting whether particular serial positions will be well separated or crowded in time, thus preventing application of selective-encoding strategies. We next review a number of recent studies that have examined the role of temporal isolation with unpredictable intervals.

Unpredictable temporal isolation

Suppose a participant is presented with the list A. . . . .B. . .C. .D.E . . . .F, where the dots again correspond to units of time. According to a temporal distinctiveness theory, such as SIMPLE, recall of B should be better than recall of D because the former item is more temporally isolated than the latter. Suppose that list was followed by another one, such as A.B..C. . . ..D. . .E. . . .F, in which the intervals were unpredictably different. Again, the most isolated item should be recalled better than any of the others, even though the participant has no way of knowing ahead of time what interval to expect between items, thus precluding a strategic focus on well-separated portions of the list. A number of recent studies have used this paradigm in search of a temporal distinctiveness effect.

For example, Lewandowsky, Brown, Wright *et al.* (2006) used a methodology in their first study that was identical in most respects to the method of the present Experiment 1, except that participants were exposed to a different unique permutation of the six possible interitem intervals on each trial. In consequence, across replications, items in each serial position were preceded and followed by all possible intervals an equal number of times, thus permitting an unconfounded assessment of the effects of temporal isolation at each serial position. The results were quite clear: as shown by a regression analysis with interitem interval as the independent variable, performance generally did not improve with temporal isolation. Table 8.2 shows the estimated regression parameters, broken down by serial position and whether the interval in question preceded ('pre') or followed ('post') the item whose performance was predicted. The table also shows the range of intervals (in this case 50–1200 ms) by which items were separated. It will be noted that isolation did have an effect at serial position four; further analysis revealed that this effect was due to people's subjective grouping of the seven-item list with the item in position four at the group boundary. Only those participants who were identified by independent means as grouping the list contributed to the effect whereas those who did not group the list also did not show an isolation effect in position four.

Lewandowsky *et al.* reported a second experiment that also used unpredictable intervals, but in which participants on each trial were probed to recall only one randomly chosen item. This probed-recall procedure was used to eliminate output interference, which might have overshadowed any small effects of isolation in their first study. As shown in Table 8.2 (which also summarizes all remaining experiments), the elimination of output interference did not lead to the emergence of an isolation effect; performance continued to be unaffected by temporal isolation.

The intervals used by Lewandowsky *et al.* ranged from 50 to 1200 ms. Although the present experiments confirm that this range was sufficiently large to create a reliable effect of isolation when intervals are predictable, the range may have been too constrained to permit an effect to emerge when intervals were unpredictable. Nimmo and Lewandowsky (2005) addressed this possibility in a study with intervals spanning the range 50 ms through 4000 ms. Again, no effect of temporal isolation was observed; an item that was followed by a blank interval of 4 s was recalled as well as an item that was followed 50 ms later by another study item.

There is some suggestion that temporal isolation effects are larger when material is presented auditorily than when it is presented visually (e.g., Glenberg and Swanson 1986). Although this

Table 8.2 Regression estimates for the effects of temporal isolation in studies with unpredictable interitem intervals

Studya	Experiment/ condition	Intervals (ms)	Serial position	Parameter estimate	
				Pre	Post
LBWN	1/Quiet	50–1200	2	−0.0003	−0.0003
			4	−0.025	0.054*
			6	−0.014	−0.0008
	1/AS	50–1200	2	0.028	0.009
			4	0.060*	0.056*
			6	0.006	0.014
LBWN	2	50–1200	all	0.005	
NandL1	Quiet	50–4000	2	−0.003	−0.004
			4	−0.000	0.013
			6	−0.017	0.002
	AS	50–4000	2	−0.016	0.019
			4	0.05	0.019
			6	0.022	0.004
NandL2	1/Auditory	450–1600	all	0.016	0.018
	1/Auditory	450–4400	all	0.010	0.003
	2/Auditory	125–4000	all	0.003	0.008*
	2/Visual	125–4000	all	0.001	0.005
PKD	Auditory verbal	50–950	all	−0.36	0.11
	Spatial nonverbal	50–950	all	−0.27	−0.02
Average (SD)				−0.0289 (0.1036)	0.0165 (0.0289)

* $p < 0.05$.

[a] LBWN = Lewandowsky, Brown, Wright et al. (2006); NandL1 = Nimmo and Lewandowsky (2005); NandL2 = Nimmo and Lewandowsky (2006); PKD = Parmentier et al. (2006).

modality difference remains contentious because it is not supported by all available evidence (e.g., Crowder and Greene 1987; Neath and Crowder 1990), it must be noted that the present experiments and all studies reviewed this far have exclusively used visual presentation. Nimmo and Lewandowsky (2006) addressed this issue by comparing auditory and visual presentation in several experiments with unpredictable interitem intervals. In neither study was there any difference between modalities: temporal isolation had no substantial effect on recall (although one of the experiments by Nimmo and Lewandowsky was powerful enough to detect an effect of the post interval with auditory presentation whose magnitude was 0.8 of a per cent performance improvement per second isolation. We do not consider this effect to be sufficiently large to provide strong support for the notion of distinctiveness).

The finding by Nimmo and Lewandowsky that temporal isolation has no effect even when stimulus presentation is auditory was replicated by Parmentier, King and Dennis (2006).

The study by Parmentier *et al.* also differed from related precedents in two important ways: first, they used a reconstruction task in all conditions. In a reconstruction task, the list items are re-presented in random order at retrieval, thus eliminating the need for item memory, and participants merely indicate (e.g., by mouse click) the order in which items were originally presented. Second, in one of their conditions, lists consisted not of verbal material but of short bursts of white noise that were presented in different spatial locations. Participants had to reconstruct the order of those locations, and performance was again found to be impervious to temporal isolation.

Overall, there is now considerable and wide-ranging evidence that temporal isolation does not benefit short-term memory for serial order. This conclusion holds regardless of modality (auditory vs visual); material (letters vs digits vs bursts of noise); type of retrieval task (serial recall vs probed recall vs reconstruction); and across a wide range of intervals (from 50 ms through 4.4 seconds). To provide a quantitative impression of this conclusion, Table 8.2 also reports the average estimates, across all analyses, of the regression parameters for the pre and post intervals together with their standard deviations. Although this average is not sensitive to variables such as sample size and other slight differences between experiments, it provides a useful summary of the results overall and provides a guide to the magnitude of the effect. In particular, the summary clarifies that there is no reason to suspect that a large and theoretically important effect of temporal isolation might be lurking underneath the repeated report of individual null results: if the overall estimates for pre and post are in turn averaged to provide a single index of the effect of temporal isolation, that index differs trivially (and negatively) from zero.

Conclusions

We close by drawing three principal conclusions:

1. A brief review of the recent relevant literature shows that temporal isolation does not play a role in memory for serial order over the short term.

2. Modeling using SIMPLE confirmed that previous experiments that purport to show effects of temporal isolation in serial recall are ambiguous, even though we report two studies that undermine the case for rehearsal as an alternative explanation of isolation effects.

3. On the basis of a comparison between the present studies and others in which intervals are unpredictable, we suggest that any existing effects of temporal isolation at encoding can be ascribed to strategic effects such as selective encoding.

The three preceding conclusions have associated with them at least one clear boundary condition: they are limited to situations in which memory for the order among items is important and in which participants have no control over the order in which items are reported. That is, all the material reviewed here involved either serial recall, in which items must be reported from the beginning of the list to its end, probed recall in which a single item must be reported in response to a cue (i.e., the preceding list item), or serial reconstruction in which people have to select items for report in the order in which they were initially presented. We make no claim that the observed absence of isolation effects would also occur in paradigms such as free recall, in which people are free to report items in any order. When report order is free, additional opportunities arise for isolation to have a beneficial effect. For example, people may choose to report isolated items first, thus protecting them against the effects of prolonged output interference. Given the rather large literature on isolation effects in free recall, there is every possibility that report order may turn out to be an important variable that determines whether or not temporal isolation benefits memory.

Acknowledgments

Preparation of this paper was facilitated by a Discovery Grant from the Australian Research Council to the first author, by two Linkage International Grants from the Australian Research Council to the first third author, and by ESRC (UK) Grant RES000231038 to the third author. Address correspondence to the first author at the School of Psychology, University of Western Australia, Crawley, W.A. 6009, Australia. Electronic mail may be sent to lewan@psy.uwa.edu.au. Personal web page: http://www.psy.uwa.edu.au/user/ lewan/.

We gratefully acknowledge assistance from Leo Roberts at all stages of manuscript preparation.

References

Anderson, JR and Matessa, M (1997). A production system theory of serial memory. *Psychological Review*, *104*, 728–748.

Bjork, RA and Whitten, WB (1974). Recency-sensitive retrieval processes in long-term free recall. *Cognitive Psychology*, *6*, 173–189.

Brown, GDA and Chater, N (2001). The chronological organization of memory: Common psychological foundations for remembering and timing. In C Hoerl and T McCormack (eds), *Time and Memory: Issues in philosophy and psychology* (pp. 77–110). Oxford: Oxford University Press.

Brown, GDA, Neath, I and Chater, N (2002). SIMPLE: A local distinctiveness model of scale invariant memory and perceptual identification.Unpublished manuscript.

Brown, GDA, Preece, T and Hulme, C (2000). Oscillator-based memory for serial order. *Psychological Review*, *107*, 127–181.

Burgess, N and Hitch, GJ (1999). Memory for serial order: A network model of the phonological loop and its timing. *Psychological Review*, *106*, 551–581.

Crowder, RG (1976). *Principles of Learning and Memory*, xiii edn. Hillsdale, NJ: Lawrence Erlbaum.

Crowder, RG and Greene, RL (1987). On the remembrance of times past: The irregular list technique. *Journal of Experimental Psychology: General*, *116*, 265–278.

Glenberg, AM and Swanson, NG (1986). A temporal distinctiveness theory of recency and modality effects. *Journal of Experimental Psychology: Learning, Memory, and Cognition*, *12*, 3–15.

Greene, RL and Crowder, RG (1988). Memory for serial position: Effects of spacing, vocalization, and stimulus suffixes. *Journal of Experimental Psychology: Learning, Memory, and Cognition*, *14*, 740–748.

Henson, RNA (1999). Positional information in short-term memory: Relative or absolute? *Memory and Cognition*, *27*, 915–927.

Hitch, GJ, Burgess, N, Towse, JN and Culpin, V (1996). Temporal grouping effects in immediate recall: A working memory analysis. *The Quarterly Journal of Experimental Psychology*, *49A*, 116–139.

Hulme, C, Roodenrys, S, Brown, GDA and Mercer, R (1995). The role of long-term memory mechanisms in memory span. *British Journal of Psychology*, *86*, 527–536.

Lewandowsky, S and Brown, GDA (2005). Serial recall and presentation schedule: A micro-analysis of local distinctiveness. *Memory*, *13*, 283–292.

Lewandowsky, S, Brown, GDA, Wright, T and Nimmo, LM (2006). Timeless memory: Evidence against temporal distinctiveness models of short-term memory for serial order. *Journal of memory and language*, *54*, 20–38.

MacLeod, CM (1998). Directed forgetting. In JM Golding and CM MacLeod (eds), *Intentional forgetting: Interdisciplinary approaches*. (pp. 1–57). New Jersey: Lawrence Erlbaum Associates.

Nairne, JS, Neath, I, Serra, M and Byun, E (1997). Positional distinctiveness and the ratio rule in free recall. *Journal of Memory and Language*, *37*, 155–166.

Neath, I (1993). Distinctiveness and serial position effects in recognition. *Memory and Cognition*, *21*, 689–698.

Neath, I and Crowder, RG (1990). Schedules of presentation and temporal distinctiveness in human memory. *Journal of Experimental Psychology: Learning, Memory, and Cognition, 16*, 316–327.

Neath, I and Crowder, RG (1996). Distinctiveness and very short-term serial position effects. *Memory, 4*, 225–242.

Ng, HLH and Maybery, MT (2002). Grouping in short-term verbal memory: Is position coded temporally? *Quarterly Journal of Experimental Psychology, 55A*, 391–424.

Nimmo, LM and Lewandowsky, S (2006). Distinctiveness revisited: Unpredictable temporal isolation does not benefit short-term serial recall of heard or seen events. *Memory and Cognition, 34,* 1368–1375.

Nimmo, LM and Lewandowsky, S (2005). From brief gaps to very long pauses: Temporal isolation does not benefit serial recall. *Psychonomic Bulletin and Review, 12,* 999–1004.

Nosofsky, RM (1992). Similarity scaling and cognitive process models. *Annual Review of Psychology, 43*, 25–53.

Page, MPA and Norris, D (1998). The primacy model: A new model of immediate serial recall. *Psychological Review, 105*, 761–781.

Parmentier, FBR, King, S and Dennis, I (2006). Local temporal distinctiveness does not benefit auditory verbal and spatial serial recall. *Psychonomic Bulletin and Review, 13*, 458–465.

Saito, S (2000). Effects of articulatory suppression on immediate serial recall of temporally grouped and intonated lists. *Psychologia, 41*, 95–101.

Welte, J and Laughery, K (1971). Short-term memory: The effects of interitem time distribution and recall procedure. *Canadian Journal of Psychology, 25*, 436–442.

9

Working memory and short-term memory storage
What does backward recall tell us?

Gerald Tehan and Kaye Mills

One of the recent issues for those interested in working memory is the distinction between what have become to be known as simple span and complex span tasks. This distinction is made because some have argued that the different tasks rely upon different storage mechanisms (Baddeley 1986; Brainerd and Kingma 1985, Swanson 1996). The current research continues the exploration of the grounds for such a distinction. It also deals with a second issue, that of the direction of recall. Almost all of the research into working memory has involved forward serial recall and many sophisticated formal models of serial recall exist (Burgess and Hitch 1999; Henson 1998; Farrell and Lewandowsky 2002, Page and Norris 1998). In contrast, no such models of backward recall exist. Moreover, there is no agreement as how to conceptualize backward recall: while there are some clear similarities between forward and backward recall in simple span tasks, there are also many differences. Those who focus upon the differences argue for different retrieval mechanisms in backward recall to those in forward recall. The current research combines the common storage and direction of recall issues by examining backward recall of simple, complex and delayed memory tasks.

Common storage

The distinction between short-term memory and working memory has generally been based upon the assumption that short-term memory tasks are primarily tasks that focus upon storage capacity. In working memory tasks, however, processing issues are seen as just as important as storage issues. To that extent a common definition of a working memory task is one in which small amounts of information must be kept highly active and available for later use during cognitive processing of some other information. For example, in the operations span task devised by Engle and his colleagues (Engle, Kane and Tuholski 1999), words must be kept in memory for future recall while simultaneously processing of maths problems. Clearly, both simple and complex tasks require the storage of items for later recall. The dispute has been about whether different stores underlie the different tasks.

Exploring differences between short-term memory (STM) and working memory tasks has largely been conducted using individual differences methodologies. The basis for the exploration is that working memory tasks appear to be better predictors of other complex cognitive tasks (e.g. measures of fluid intelligence) than short-term memory tasks, and it is often argued that this relationship reflects the common processing demands of working memory and complex cognitive tasks rather than storage issues. The individual differences approach, however, is complicated by the fact that short-term memory tasks often correlate with the complex cognitive tasks (although not as strongly as the working memory tasks) and more importantly short-term memory and working memory tasks correlate quite highly with each other. This high correlation is the basis for the common storage assumption. In short, an individual differences approach highlights the fact that short-term memory and working memory tasks have much in common. In fact, the collinearity problem has often made it extremely difficult to tease apart storage and processing components of the two types of tasks.

A less frequent approach to the common storage issue has involved experimental techniques. Here factors that are known to affect performance on a simple span task are also applied to working memory tasks. For present purposes, an experiment by Tehan, Hendry and Koscinski (2001) illustrates this. In their experiment they examined word length and phonological similarity effects across immediate serial recall, operation span and Brown–Peterson tasks. It is well documented that in immediate serial recall (simple span, STM task) short words are better recalled than long words, and phonologically similar items are less well recalled than phonologically dissimilar items. Tehan *et al.* wanted to know if these same factors would influence recall in a working memory task (operations span) and a long-term memory task (Brown–Peterson) task. It emerged that all three tasks produced robust word length and phonological similarity effects. In spite of theoretical reasons why one might expect different outcomes across the three tasks, the only thing that differentiated performance on the three tasks was absolute levels of recall. There was little support for the notion that the underlying processes for the three tasks differed.

In sum, a distinction between short-term memory, working memory and to a lesser extent long-term memory appears consistently in the literature. The empirical evidence for such a distinction is not quite so compelling. Instead, both the individual differences and experimental literature indicate that most short-term retention tasks, be they simple span, operations span or delayed recall, share much in common and that it is extremely difficult to distinguish between such tasks.

Backward recall

Backward serial recall has not been as extensively or as systematically studied as forward recall. In contrast to forward recall there are no formal mathematical models of how the task is done. Where the issue has been addressed, the assumption is often made that backward recall is simply repeated serial forward recall (Page and Norris 1998). That is, in order to recall the last word in the list participants use forward recall to get to the last item, they output it, and then start forward serial recall through the list again until they get to the second from last item, they output it and then commence the same process again and again until only the first item has to be recalled. This explanation does have some empirical support in that response latencies differ for backward and forward recall, and that the pattern of latencies for backward recall is consistent with the notion of repeated cycles of forward recall (Thomas, Milner and Haberlandt 2003).

There are two interesting corollaries of such an explanation. First, describing simple backward recall in such a way seems to qualify the task as a working memory task. That is, participants need to continually keep hold of where they are in a list while forward recalling to that point. Secondly, if backward recall is nothing more than repeated forward recall, the factors that are known to influence forward recall should have a similar impact upon backward recall. As it turns out, there are factors that have similar influences on backward and forward recall, but there are others that have differential effects.

The current research centers on two factors that are know to have robust influences forward recall: phonological similarity and word length. In immediate forward serial recall similar-sounding words are less well recalled than dissimilar-sounding words and short words are better recalled than long words. As mentioned above, these effects also generalize to working memory and delayed memory tasks (Tehan *et al.* 2000). While the effects are readily observed in forward recall, there is some contention as to their effects in backward recall.

Forward and backward recall seem to be differentially affected by verbal and visual distractor activity, and this has led to the proposition that forward recall relies upon phonological coding, but backward recall does not. The genesis of this debate can be found in Li and Lewandowsky's (1993, 1995) findings that verbal distractors disrupted forward but not backward recall, whereas visuospatial activity adversely affected backward but not forward recall. Hulme *et al.* (1997) also suggested that participants did not rely upon a phonological strategy in order to explain their finding that word frequency effects had little impact on backward recall. Farrand and Jones (1996) provided counter evidence to the Li and Lewandowsky conclusion, but probably the most direct test of the phonological coding assumption is in a study by Rosen and Engle (1997) where they directly examined the phonological similarity effect in immediate forward and backward recall. Phonological similarity effects were observed for each direction. The logical conclusion from this study was that, at least for immediate recall, both forward and backward recall were supported by phonological representations.

With respect to word length, there have been a number of studies that have explored word length effects in backward recall with the general outcome that word length effects are present but weaker than with forward recall (Cowan, Wood and Borne 1994; Walker and Hulme 1999). For example, Cowan *et al.* (1994) looked at differences between immediate recall and continuous distractor tasks on backward recall. The study involved mixed and pure lists of short and long words, that is lists varied as to whether short and long words occurred early or late in a sequence, with some beginning with long words and ending in short words (LS) or vice versa (SL), and others in which all were short (SS) or all were long (LL). Results showed that the typical short word advantage was present on the immediate backward recall task. However, on the continuous distractor task, a long word advantage emerged. Cowan *et al.* concluded that this result was prima facie evidence for the need to distinguish a short-term store from a long-term store.

The current study

The current study is motivated primarily by the finding that when it comes to phonological similarity and word length effects in forward recall, it is not possible to distinguish between short-term memory, working memory or delayed recall tasks. The above review suggests that the pattern may be different with backward recall. With respect to word length, Cowan's results lead to the conclusion that differences in word length effects can be observed between immediate recall and long-term memory tasks. Word length effects on backward recall of complex span tasks remains untested. With respect to phonological similarity effects, the similarity decrement can be observed with immediate recall, but given Li and Lewandowsky's results when interlist distraction is employed as is the case with complex span and delayed memory tests, the potential is there for the similarity effects to be attenuated.

Experiment 1

In the first experiment word length effects were examined in three tasks that required the backward recall of four-word lists. The simple version of the task involved the recall of the four words in reverse order immediately after presentation. The complex span version of the task was similar to that used by Tehan *et al.* (2001, Experiment 1B) in that four maths equations that required shadowing were interleaved with four words on each trial. In the delayed task the four words

were presented and followed by 12 seconds of distractor activity prior to recall. If we are to replicate Cowan *et al.*, word length effects should be present on the immediate test, they should be
attenuated or reversed on the delayed memory task. Given that the complex span task is a mini
version of the continuous distractor task used by Cowan *et al.*, one might expect that word length
effect would be attenuated or reversed.

Method

Participants. Twenty adults volunteered to participate in the experiment. All participants were
tested individually in sessions averaging 30 minutes' duration.

Materials. The long and short words used in this experiment were taken from the MRC linguistic database (Coltheart 1981). A pool of 96 words made up of seven phonemes (two and three-
syllable words) and 96 words made up of three phonemes (one-syllable words) was selected. The
word pools were matched for word frequency using the Kucera and Francis (1967) norms. The
mean frequency of the short words was 8.22 words per million (SD = 8.14) and that of the long
words was 7.79 words per million (SD = 10.43). The words were also matched for concreteness.
The mean for short words was 564.86 (SD = 64.84) and the mean for long words was 550.40
(SD = 52.74). The word pool was supplemented by a pool of 128 maths equations constructed
following the procedures used by LaPointe and Engle (1990). They consisted of either a product
or dividend, followed by either a simple addition or subtraction, then an answer that was either
true or false (e.g., $10/2 - 1 = 4$). Half the problems had correct answers and half had incorrect
answers. These were randomly assigned to blocks of four for each trial excluding the immediate
serial recall trials.

Participants studied 48 trials and on each trial were requested to remember the four words in
reverse order. For 24 of the trials the four words were randomly sampled from the pool of short
words and for the other 24 trials they were randomly sampled from the long word pool. Eight
each of the short and long lists were randomly allocated to the immediate recall condition (e.g.,
thong dew maze vine), eight each were randomly allocated to the operations span condition and
eight each were randomly allocated to the delayed recall condition. Each trial was created by following the procedures used by Tehan *et al.* (2001). To create each trial for the operations span
task, four maths equations were randomly selected from the pool and these were interleaved with
the four words (e.g., *stair*: $(12/4) + 1 = 4$ *peg*: $(2 \times 5) + 3 = 13$ *bib*: $(8/4) + 3 = 4$ *ham*: $(8/4) + 3 = 4$.
To create each delayed trial, four maths equations were randomly selected from the pool and
placed after the four words (e.g., *keg lung babe lute* $(2 \times 5) - 3 = 7$ $(3 \times 4) - 2 = 10$ $(2 \times 4) - 5 = 4$
$(8/2) - 1 = 1$. The order of the 48 trials was then randomized. This procedure was conducted for
each participant and 20 different sets of trials were generated.

Procedure. Participants were given printed instructions detailing the different tasks and the
requirement to recall the four words verbally in reverse order They then completed standard consent forms and practice trials for each type of task. Participants' questions were answered and
they were seated in front of a computer with a monochrome screen. Each trial started with an
auditory beep and ended with a row of question marks. The stimulus items were presented one at
a time in black lowercase type in the centre of the screen. When the row of question marks
appeared on the screen the participants were requested to recall the four words in reverse order
and to say "something" or "pass" if they could not recall a word, in order to preserve the serial
order of the remaining recalled words. In all trials participants had 15 seconds to recall the four
items in reverse order before the next trial began.

Immediate recall task. The immediate recall lists contained word stimuli presented at a rate
of one word per second. Participants were instructed to read each word aloud as it appeared

on the screen and to recall the four words in reverse order immediately after the row of question marks.

Delayed recall task. The delayed lists contained words that were again presented at a rate of one word per second. The four words were immediately followed by four maths equations presented at a rate of one equation every three seconds. Participants were instructed to read each word and the digits of each maths equation aloud as they appeared on the screen. Participants did not have to solve the maths problems: All they had to do was to read the four or five digits involved in the problem. Verbal shadowing is a typical means of distractor activity in the Brown–Peterson task, upon which the current task is modelled. A row of question marks again appeared three seconds after presentation of the final equation as a cue to commence reverse recall.

Operations span task. On the operations span trials, a word and a maths equation appeared simultaneously on the screen. The four word-equation pairs were presented at a rate of one pair every four seconds. Participants were instructed to read each word and the digits in the corresponding maths equation aloud as they appeared on the screen. The recall cue was presented four seconds after the final list item. The request to read the digits, rather than solve the maths problems, deviates from the typical working memory task where solution is often requested. Tehan *et al.* (2001) demonstrated that shadowing led to exactly the same outcomes as solving the problems, which is not all that surprising given that both are designed to prevent the rehearsal of the to-be-remembered items.

Results

Scoring. Recall performance was scored in three ways. A response was scored as correct if the correct word was reported in the appropriate serial position. This is the traditional measure used in short-term memory experiments. Secondly, an item was scored correct if it appeared somewhere in the recall protocol regardless of what position it was recalled in. This form of scoring has been widely used in complex span tasks (La Pointe and Engle 1990; Tehan *et al.* 2001). Thirdly, recall accuracy was scored by dividing the number of items recalled correctly in position by the total number of items recalled (Fallon, Groves and Tehan 1999; Poirier and Saint-Aubin 1995). Unless stated, an alpha level of 0.05 was used to determine statistical reliability.

Correct in position. The mean number of words correctly recalled in their appropriate serial position is shown in the upper section of Table 9.1. A 3×2 repeated measures ANOVA with word length and type of task as factors revealed a significant main effect for type of task, $F (2,38) = 88$, $Mse = 24.44$. Performance on the immediate recall task differed significantly from the operations span task, $t (19) = 2.96$, and performance on both tasks differed significantly from the delayed recall task, $t (19) = 12.98$, and $t (19) = 9.57$, respectively. The main effect of word length and the interaction between word length and task were not significant, $F (1,19) = 1.37$, $Mse = 19.72$, and, $F (2,38) = 0.40$, $Mse = 9.37$.

Item recall. The mean number of words correctly recalled irrespective of the order they were recalled is shown in the middle panel of Table 9.1. A repeated measures ANOVA again revealed a main effect for task type, $F (2,38) = 134.40$, $Mse = 8.35$; performance on the immediate recall task differed significantly from the operations span task, $t (19) = 5.88$, and performance on both tasks differed significantly from the delayed recall task, $t (19) = 13.88$, and $t (19) = 11.13$. The main effect of word length and the interaction between word length and task was not significant, $F (1,19) = 4.02$, $Mse = 10.17$, and, $F (2,38) = 0.11$, $Mse = 5.94$.

Order accuracy. Order accuracy is shown at the bottom of Table 9.1. A repeated measures ANOVA again revealed a main effect of task type, $F (2,38) = 44.81$, $Mse = 0.03$; performance on the immediate recall task did not differ significantly from the operations span task, $t (19) = 1.06$,

Table 9.1 Mean backward serial recall performance (and SD) for short and long words across recall tasks

	Simple span	**Task Operation span**	**Delayed recall**
Correct in position			
Short	24.70 (5.81)	21.30 (4.64)	10.10 (6.63)
Long	23.30 (4.49)	20.10 (5.20)	9.85 (6.45)
Item recall			
Short	29.95 (1.82)	26.60 (2.66)	19.45 (4.88)
Long	28.50 (2.28)	25.65 (2.76)	18.35 (4.52)
Order accuracy			
Short	0.82 (0.18)	0.80 (0.13)	0.49 (0.23)
Long	0.81 (0.12)	0.78 (0.15)	0.52 (0.23)

but performance on both tasks differed significantly from performance on the delayed recall task, t (19) = 8.10, and t (19) = 7.09. The main effect of word length and the interaction between word length and task were not significant, F (1,19) = 0.00, Mse = 0.02, and, F (2,38) = 0.54, Mse = 0.01.

Discussion

The present experiment has failed to find evidence of word length effects in backward recall. This was the case across all three tasks and regardless of scoring procedure. Experiment 1 also revealed a significant decrement in performance across the three tasks when correct in position and item recall scoring was used. The immediate recall and operations span tasks were not significantly different when order errors were scored.

Obviously the most contentious issue here is the fact that Cowan *et al.*'s (1994) results have not been replicated on an immediate test. In Cowan *et al.*'s experiment recall of six words from a closed set was required, whereas here the four words on each trial were taken from an open set. List length should not be an issue, but it quite possible that the use of an open versus closed set may. Such differences have emerged in other instances. One other way in which the experiments differed is that in the Cowan *et al.* (1994) experiment the rate of recall was controlled. Participants were not allowed to recall the items at their own rate. This was not an issue, however, in the Walker and Hulme (1999) study where word length effects were obtained albeit in a weaker form than with forward recall. However, Walker and Hulme again used a closed set which may have been problematic.

One possible explanation is that our manipulation of word length is not as sensitive as possible, in that our short words were monosyllables and our long words were two or three syllables, whereas in other research the comparison has involved monosyllables versus four or five- syllable words. The argument against this notion is that robust word length effects with forward recall of one versus two and three-syllable words have been found (Tolan and Tehan 2005). Power is a potential problem in that there are only eight trials of each type. Again, we would argue that this is unlikely to be the case given that word length effects can be observed on the first trial of a session (Tehan and Turcotte 2002).

A strategy explanation is also possible for the discrepant findings. In the current experiments the three types of tasks were randomly intermixed. In a blocked presentation, participants on an immediate test may well adopt rehearsal as the means of maintaining the items in memory and may well adopt a repeated forward recall output strategy. With intermixed trials, it may well be the case that participants abandon both rehearsal and repeated forward serial recall, with a resultant attenuation of the word length effect.

The present experiment failed to find evidence of a word length effect in three forms of backward recall. If one accepts that finding as real, the results suggest a common storage system across all three tasks, as was the case in the Tehan *et al.* (2001) research. However, the absence of word length effects suggests that backward recall is not just repeated forward serial recall. If it were, robust word length effects should have emerged in the way that they do with forward recall across the three tasks (Tehan *et al.* 2001).

Experiment 2

The current experiment addresses the second point of contention, the degree to which backward recall is based upon phonological coding. As indicated earlier there is some debate over this issue. Li and Lewandowsky have suggested that while forward recall is based upon phonological codes, backward recall relies more upon visual codes. In contrast, Rosen and Engle (1997) found robust phonological similarity effects in both forward and backward simple span tasks. The question is, will backward complex and delayed recall exhibit the same effects?

Method

Participants. Twenty adults volunteered to participate in the experiment. All participants were tested individually in sessions averaging 30 minutes' duration.

Materials. Four single-syllable instances were selected without replacement from each of 48 different rhyme categories from the University of South Florida rhyme category norms (Walling, McEvoy, Oth *et al.* 1984). For each participant, 48 four-item lists were assembled and randomly assigned to two groups of 24. For the 24 rhyming lists the four rhyming items within each category were randomized in order (e.g., *smoke soak broke coke*). For the dissimilar condition, the remaining 24 lists were pooled and the resulting 96 words were randomly assigned to dissimilar four-item lists with the restriction that no two rhyming words were in the same list (e.g., *fill tusk lark fine*). Eight each of the dissimilar and rhyming lists were randomly allocated to the immediate recall condition, operations span condition or the delayed recall condition. The latter two types of trials were constructed in the same way as for Experiment 1. The order of the 48 trials was also randomized for each participant.

Procedure. The procedure was identical to that used in Experiment 1.

Results

Correct in position. The mean number of words correctly recalled in their appropriate serial position is shown in the upper section of Table 9.2. Dissimilar words were better recalled than rhyming words in the immediate recall task but not the operations span or delayed recall tasks. The data were submitted to a 3 × 2 repeated measures ANOVA with phonological similarity and type of task as factors. There was a main effect for type of task, $F(2,38) = 127.75$, $Mse = 15.03$; performance on the immediate recall task did not differ significantly from the operations span task, $t(19) = 1.92$, but performance on both tasks differed significantly from performance on the delayed recall task, $t(19) = 12.32$, and $t(19) = 15.18$. The main effect of phonological similarity and the interaction between phonological similarity and task were not significant, $F(1,19) = 0.71$, $Mse = 8.60$, and, $F(2,38) = 2.29$, $Mse = 7.47$.

Table 9.2 Mean backward serial recall performance (and SD) for dissimilar and rhyming words across recall tasks

	Simple span	Task Operation span	Delayed recall
Correct in position			
Dissimilar	21.50 (5.81)	18.90 (4.39)	7.60 (4.60)
Rhyming	20.45 (3.85)	19.95 (3.03)	8.95 (3.91)
Item recall			
Dissimilar	27.70 (2.90)	22.95 (2.84)	12.95 (4.51)
Rhyming	29.05 (1.82)	26.95 (2.42)	22.55 (3.72)
Order accuracy			
Dissimilar	0.77 (0.16)	0.82 (0.13)	0.56 (0.22)
Rhyming	0.70 (0.12)	0.74 (0.09)	0.39 (0.15)

Item recall. The mean number of words correctly recalled irrespective of the order they were recalled is shown in the middle panel of Table 9.2. A 3×2 repeated measures ANOVA indicated that rhyming words were better recalled than dissimilar words, $F(1,19) = 132.10$, $Mse = 5.64$. There were differences in recall across tasks, $F(2,38) = 32.49$, $Mse = 7.20$; performance on the immediate recall task differed significantly from the operations span task, $t(19) = 7.70$, and performance on both tasks differed significantly from the delayed recall task, $t(19) = 15.42$, and $t(19) = 11.28$. The interaction of task type with phonemic information was also significant, $F(2,38) = 32.49$, $Mse = 5.46$. More rhyming than dissimilar words were recalled on the operations span and delayed recall tasks, $t(19) = 5.87$, and $t(19) = 10.08$, but not the immediate recall task, $t(19) = 2.53$.

Order accuracy. As can be seen in Table 9.2, accuracy was better for dissimilar words than rhyming words, $F(1,19) = 21.87$, $Mse = 0.02$. There were also differences among tasks, $F(2,38) = 72.30$, $Mse = 0.02$; order accuracy on the immediate recall task did not differ significantly from the operations span task, $t(19) = 1.94$, but performance on both tasks differed significantly from performance on the delayed recall task, $t(19) = 8$, and $t(19) = 11.66$. The interaction between phonological similarity and task was not significant, $F(2,38) = 2.39$, $Mse = 0.02$.

Discussion

The results of this experiment show that there is no significant effect of phonological similarity when correct-in-position scoring is used. When items are scored as correct if they are recalled anywhere in the recall protocol, significantly more rhyming than dissimilar words were recalled on the operations span and the delayed recall tasks. However, across all three tasks more order errors were made on the rhyming lists than the dissimilar lists. These results are similar to those obtained by Tehan *et al.* (2001) when participants recall in the forward direction. That is, in both cases, the item scoring advantage for rhyming words was offset by a disadvantage in order accuracy, which resulted in a null effect when combined into a correct-in-position score. Consequently, we are confident that the three forms of backward recall used here are all based upon phonological representations, as is the case with forward recall. The only caveat to this conclusion its the absence of an item advantage for rhyming lists on the immediate recall task. This is likely to reflect a ceiling effect rather than a fundamental difference in processing.

The presence of phonological similarity across all three backward recall tasks suggests that phonological information can be maintained in working memory for at least 12 seconds and possibly longer. Phonological codes are not as transient as has often previously been assumed. Moreover, these results also imply that backward recall relies on phonological coding and not visuospatial representation of the study material as suggested by Li and Lewandowsky (1995).

General Discussion

The current research was motivated by two questions. Is it possible to distinguish between simple, complex and delayed recall tasks in any other way besides absolute levels of recall? Secondly, is backward recall in any fundamental sense different to forward recall?

With respect to the first question, the results in both experiments, using any scoring procedure, indicate that there is little to distinguish performance across the three tasks. Word length effects and phonological similarity effects were identical (save for one instance where ceiling effects were in force). These results parallel those of Tehan *et al.* (2001) where with forward recall, word length and phonological similarity effects were equivalent across simple, complex and delayed recall tasks. The current experimental approach complements the individual differences litera-ture in that both are converging on the notion that it is hard to distinguish between tasks. It seems as though a common store is being used in all tasks.

With respect to the second issue we first replicate the Turner and Engle (1997) findings that phonological similarity effects can be found in backward recall of simple span tasks. We extend these findings by showing that phonological similarity effects generalize to complex and delayed span tasks. Performance across all three tasks appears to be supported, at least in part, by phono-logical representations of the list items. The common memory store appears to be phonological in nature. Is this store the phonological loop? We would argue that this is not the case. The decre-ment in absolute levels of performance in the delayed recall case at least, indicates that the dis-tractor activity has been effective in preventing rehearsal (assuming that rehearsal is an effective means of preparing for backward recall). Given that phonological representations in the phono-logical store are supposed to decay rapidly in the absence of rehearsal, a 12 second retention interval should be sufficient for such traces to decay. We would conclude that contrary to Li and Lewandowsky's conclusion, backward recall in any short-term memory task is underpinned by phonological codes.

The current results have produced one novel set of findings and that is that word length effects were not present in any of our backward recall conditions. The parameters for the current study are almost identical to those used by Tehan *et al.* (2001); all that differed was the direction of recall. With forward recall there were robust word length effects across all tasks. However, with backward recall, word length effects failed to emerge. The absence of word length effects question the assertion that backward recall is simply repeated forward recall. However, it is difficult to indicate what the absence of word length effects does mean, given that rehearsal accounts of the word length effect are no longer tenable (Nairne 2002) and that no alternative explanation has been widely accepted. The current results would, of course, inform alternative explanations.

In conclusion, it seems that recall across simple span, complex span and delayed recall tasks is supported by phonological codes. While the stored representations may be the same for forward and backward recall, our data point to one clear difference. Word length effects are readily observable in forward recall but they are severely attenuated in backward recall. We cannot at this stage say why this is the case.

References

Baddeley, AD (1986). *Working Memory*. London: Oxford University Press.

Brainerd, CJ and Kingma, J (1985). On the independence of short-term memory and working memory in cognitive development. *Cognitive Psychology*, *17*, 210–247.

Burgess, N and Hitch, GJ (1999). Memory for serial order: A network model of the phonological loop and its timing. *Psychological Review*, *106*, 551–581.

Coltheart, M (1981). The MRC psycholinguistic data base. *Quarterly Journal of Experimental Psychology*, *33A*, 532–505.

Cowan, N, Wood, N and Borne, D (1994). Reconfirmation of the short-term storage concept. *Psychological Science*, *5*, 103–107.

Enlge, RW, Kane, MJ and Tuholski, SW (1999). Individual differences in working memory capacity and what they tell us about controlled attention, general fluid intelligence, and functions of the prefrontal cortex. In A Miyake and P Shah (eds), *Models of Working Memroy: Mechanisms of active maintenance and executive control* (pp. 102–134). New York: Cambridge University Press.

Fallon, AB, Groves, K and Tehan, G (1999). Phonological similarity and trace degradation in the serial recall task: when CAT helps RAT, but not MAN. *International Journal of Psychology*, *34*, 301–308.

Farrand, P and Jones, D (1996). Direction of report in spatial and verbal serial short term memory. *Quarterly Journal of Experimental Psychology*, *49A*, 140–158.

Farrell, S and Lewandowsky, S (2002). An endogenous distributed model of ordering in serial recall. *Psychonomic Bulletin and Review*, *9*, 59–79.

Henson, RNA (1998). Short-term memory for serial order: The start-end model. *Cognitive Psychology*, *36*, 73–137.

Hulme, C, Roodenrys, S, Schweickert, R, Brown, GDA, Martin, S and Stuart, G (1997). Word frequency effects on short-term memory tasks: evidence for a multinomial processing tree model of immediate serial recall. *Journal of Experimental Psychology: Learning, Memory, and Cognition*, *23*, 1217–1232.

Kucera, H and Francis, WN (1967). *Computational Analysis of Present-day American English*. Providence, RI: Brown University Press.

LaPointe, LB and Engle, RW (1990). Simple and complex word spans as measures of working memory capacity. *Journal of Experimental Psychology: Learning, Memory, and Cognition*, *16*, 1128–1133.

Li, S-C and Lewandowsky, S (1993). Intralist distractors and recall direction: Constraints on models of memory for serial order. *Journal of Experimental Psychology: Learning, Memory, and Cognition*, *19*, 895–908.

Li, S-C and Lewandowsky, S (1995). Forward and backward recall: Different retrieval processes. *Journal of Experimental Psychology: Learning, Memory and Cognition*, *21*, 837–847.

Nairne, JS (2002). Remembering over the short term: the case against the standard model. *Annual Review of Psychology*, *53*, 53–81.

Page, MPA and Norris, D (1998). The primacy model: A new model of immediate serial recall. *Psychological Review*, *105*, 761–781.

Poirier, M and Saint-Aubin, J (1995). Memory for related and unrelated words: Further evidence of the influence of semantic factors in immediate serial recall. *Quarterly Journal of Experimental Psychology*, *48A*, 384–404.

Rosen, V and Engle, RW (1997). Forward and backward serial recall. *Intelligence*, *25*, 37–47.

Swanson, HL (1996). Individual differences in children's working memory. *Memory and Cognition*, *24*, 70–82.

Tehan, G and Turcotte, J (2002). Word length effects are not due to proactive interference. *Memory*, *10*, 139–150.

Tehan, G, Hendry, L and Kocinski, D (2001). Word length and phonological similarity effects in simple, complex and delayed serial recall task: Implications for working memory. *Memory*, 9, 333–348.

Thomas, JG, Milner, HR and Haberlandt, KF (2003). Forward and backward recall: Different response time patterns, same retrieval order. *Psychological Science*, 14, 169–174.

Tolan, GA and Tehan, G (2005). Is spoken duration a sufficient explanation of the word length effect? *Memory*, 13, 372–379.

Turner, M and Engle, RW (1989). Is working memory capacity task dependent? *Journal of Memory and Language*, 28, 127–154.

Walker, I and Hulme, C (1999). Concrete words are easier to recall than abstract: evidence for a semantic contribution to short-term serial recall. *Journal of Experimental Psychology: Learning, Memory and Cognition*, 25, 1256–1271.

Walling, JR, McEvoy, CL, Oth, JE and Nelson, DL (1984). *The University of South Florida Rhyme category norms*. Unpublished manuscript, University of South Florida.

10

Accounting for age-related differences in working memory using the feature model

Ian Neath and Aimée M. Surprenant

The phonological loop, part of the working memory framework, was originally developed to account for four memory phenomena: the word length effect, the acoustic confusion effect, the irrelevant speech effect and the concurrent articulation effect (Baddeley 1986, 1992). There are numerous studies that have examined these effects in traditional populations (i.e., college-age people) and many studies that include other populations, including children and people with a variety of neurological disorders. One population that has not received much sustained attention in terms of these four basic effects consists of healthy adults over the age of 65. Given the central importance of these effects to the theory, it is perhaps surprising that there is relatively little conclusive data on whether younger and older adults show similar or different patterns of behavior. Furthermore, substantial declines in immediate memory performance from early to late adulthood are well documented (Salthouse 1985; Verhaeghen, Marcoen and Goossens 1993) and age-related declines in immediate recall have serious consequences for episodic recall, fluid intelligence and language comprehension and production (Verhaeghen and Salthouse 1997). In this chapter, we summarize the data that do exist and then consider how any age-related differences that are found could be modeled using a simulation model, the Feature Model (Nairne 1990), developed to account for a variety of immediate memory phenomena in young adults.

The effects

Irrelevant speech effect

The irrelevant speech effect refers to the finding that performance on an immediate serial recall task is worse when presentation of the list is accompanied by irrelevant speech than when presentation occurs with no accompanying irrelevant auditory information (Colle and Welsh 1976). According to the phonological loop hypothesis, irrelevant speech reduces recall because phonemes from the irrelevant stream interfere with phonemes of the to-be-remembered items that are in the phonological store (Baddeley 1986). Thus, it does not matter whether the irrelevant auditory information is in a language spoken by the subject or whether it is nonsense and it does not matter whether the irrelevant speech is loud or soft (e.g., between 76 dB(A) or 40 dB(A); see Neath 2000 for a detailed review). However, the phonological similarity of the to-be-remembered items and the irrelevant items is also irrelevant (Jones and Macken 1995), a problem for the phonological loop view that is still not fully resolved (Baddeley 2000). One variable that does affect the magnitude of the irrelevant speech effect is the degree to which the irrelevant auditory information changes (e.g., Jones, Madden and Miles 1992).

The effects of irrelevant speech have been less studied with children and other populations than word length and acoustic confusion effects. However, Elliott (2002) reported that the effects of irrelevant speech decreased as a function of the age of the child, particularly in conditions that required more attentional control. She interpreted this as suggesting that the locus of the irrelevant speech effect is due, in part, to distraction from the competing materials. As far as we can determine the irrelevant speech effect has not been explored in clinical populations.

Concurrent articulation effect

Concurrent articulation (e.g., saying the digits '1, 2, 3, 4' out loud over and over during list presentation) also reduces overall recall relative to a control condition (Murray 1968). According to the phonological loop hypothesis, this concurrent articulation prevents rehearsal; indeed, the manipulation is usually known as articulatory suppression. We prefer the term 'concurrent articulation' as it does not presume that all articulatory activity is suppressed; rather, it describes what the subject is asked to do.

Concurrent articulation has an effect on memory in children but only those who have begun to rehearse to-be-remembered items verbally. The effect gradually increases as children grow older and is identical to that of adults by the age of about eleven years old (Halliday, Hitch, Lennon *et al.* 1990). Research using patient populations has made it clear that overt articulation is not necessary for this effect or for recoding written stimuli into a phonological form. For example, patients suffering from dyarthric impairments preventing them from normal speech production show normal word length and acoustic confusion effects (Baddeley and Wilson 1998; Vallar and Cappa 1987). In contrast, patients with a higher-level impairment of speech motor planning, called apraxia, appear to act as if they are performing a concurrent articulation task (Waters, Rochon and Caplan 1992).

Word length effect

The word length effect refers to the finding that lists of shorter words are recalled better than otherwise comparable lists of longer words (Baddeley, Thomson and Buchanan 1975). There are two different versions of this effect. The time-based word length effect requires that the only difference between the short and long items is pronunciation time; the items have the same number of phonemes, syllables, etc. This finding, it has been argued, is obtainable only with a limited set of stimuli (see Neath, Bireta and Surprenant 2003). The syllable-based word length effect, in contrast, allows the words to vary in both pronunciation time and the number of syllables and/or phonemes and is observable with numerous different stimulus sets, although the particular pattern of results may also depend on the particular stimulus set used (Bireta, Neath and Surprenant 2006).

According to the phonological loop hypothesis, word length effects arise because of the trade-off between decay within the phonological store and rehearsal via the articulatory control process. Because longer items take more time to rehearse, fewer can be refreshed in a given amount of time. Word length effects are observable in children who have begun to rehearse (Hulme, Thomson, Muir *et al.* 1984) and are sometimes absent in patients suffering from damage to certain left-hemisphere areas of the brain known to be involved in articulation (Vallar and Baddeley 1984).

Acoustic confusion effect

The acoustic confusion effect refers to the finding that lists of items that sound similar are harder to recall in order than lists of otherwise comparable items that sound different from one another (Conrad 1964). Although often referred to as the phonological similarity effect, the key is whether the items rhyme: one can have phonologically similar items that do not rhyme and that do not result in reduced recall. Thus, a more accurate term is the acoustic confusion effect. This effect is found not only for items that have been heard, but also for items that have been seen. According to the phonological loop hypothesis, the acoustic confusion effect is due to confusion within the phonological store. In order to observe an acoustic confusion effect with visually presented items, the visual items must be recoded via the articulatory control process. Because recoding using articulatory mechanisms is necessary for visual items to be encoded into the phonological store, the acoustic confusion effect disappears in the presence of concurrent articulation for visual, but not auditory, presentation (Baddeley, Lewis and Vallar 1984; but see Jones, Macken and Nichols 2004).

Children who are poor readers tend to show smaller acoustic confusion effects than good readers, suggesting that the poor readers are not coding the to-be-remembered items in a phonological form as well as the good readers (Shankweiler, Liberman, Marks *et al.* 1979). Furthermore, the acoustic confusion effect can be absent in certain neuropsychological patients who show very poor reading and spelling skills along with deficits in other phonological processing tasks. It is important to note that these patients' general level of intelligence and memory for non-phonological materials is completely intact (e.g., Campbell and Butterworth 1985).

In addition to the main effects described above, these manipulations produce particular interactions when combined (see Neath and Surprenant 2003, Chapter 4, for a review).

Issues with difference scores

For many immediate memory tasks, there is no difficulty in assessing whether there are age-related differences. For example, memory span is, on average, shorter in older as compared to younger populations (Grégoire and Van der Linden 1997; Myerson, Emery, White *et al.* 2003) but this is easy to measure as scores drop from eight to seven to six and so on. For the four benchmark phenomena of the phonological loop, however, the comparison is of two difference scores. The difference between memory for short and long words, for example, in older adults is compared to the difference between memory for short and long words in younger adults. Because of this, one issue is how best to measure any differences in difference scores that might exist between young and old subjects.

An illustration will help make this issue more clear. Table 10.1 shows a hypothetical situation in which younger and older subjects receive two conditions, control and experimental. These could be short and long words, or dissimilar and similar items, or quiet and concurrent articulation, or absence of and presence of irrelevant speech. The last two columns show two ways of measuring the difference in performance in the two conditions. 'Absolute difference' is simply the numerical difference in performance in the two conditions. 'Relative difference' is the difference between the conditions relative to performance in the control condition (i.e., (X-Y)/X; cf. Logie, Della Sala, Laiacona *et al.* 1996). The first two rows show the same absolute difference for younger and older adults and would result, in an analysis of variance, in no significant age by condition interaction. In contrast, the relative measure suggests an interaction in that the older subjects are (relatively) more affected by the manipulation than the younger subjects.

Similarly, the last two rows show a larger absolute difference for younger than for older adults, and there would be a significant age by condition interaction. However, the last column shows an identical relative difference, suggesting similar effect sizes. This issue is not unique to this particular topic (see, for example, the discussion of forgetting by Wixted 1990), but it is likely to make comparisons between groups complex. If the researcher uses the same length lists for both younger and older subjects, then the two groups are likely to differ in performance on the control condition. Therefore, any differential difference in the experimental condition needs to be interpreted with care. Since there is not an easy resolution of this problem (equating for span causes its own difficulties), we suggest that researchers report at least two measures, one based on the absolute difference

Table 10.1 Hypothetical example of the difficulty in comparing performance of younger and older subjects when performance in the control condition differs.

	Control	Experimental	Absolute difference	Relative difference
Younger	0.9	0.6	0.30	0.33
Older	0.5	0.2	0.30	0.60
Younger	0.9	0.36	0.54	0.60
Older	0.5	0.2	0.30	0.60

and one, such as the relative difference score used here, that takes into account differences relative to performance in the control condition.

Aging and working memory phenomena

Irrelevant speech effect

The most well-established age-related result of the four benchmark phenomena of working memory is the apparent lack of an age-related difference in the irrelevant speech effect (Beaman 2005; Belleville, Rouleau, Van der Linden *et al.* 2003; Rouleau and Belleville 1996), at least when using absolute difference measures. In two of these studies (Beaman 2005; Belleville *et al.* 2003), the younger and older subjects did not differ in performance in the quiet condition. For both experiments, the absolute and relative difference measures tell the same story: For Beaman's data, the absolute difference was 0.09 for the younger subjects and 0.11 for the older subjects; the respective values for the relative differences were 0.11 and 0.13. For the study of Belleville *et al.*, the absolute differences were 0.11 and 0.10 and the relative differences were 0.13 and 0.12.

In the third study on aging and the irrelevant speech effect, Rouleau and Belleville (1996) found that the younger and older subjects did differ in their performance in the quiet condition, 0.88 and 0.59 respectively. When measured by absolute difference, irrelevant speech had the same effect for both groups, a decrement of 0.13. When measured by relative difference, the irrelevant speech had a smaller effect on younger subjects (0.15) than on older subjects (0.23).

Concurrent articulation effect

Rouleau and Belleville (1996) also included a manipulation of concurrent articulation. In the control condition, the mean proportion correct was 0.88 for the younger subjects compared to 0.59 for the older subjects. The absolute difference was 0.42 for the younger subjects compared to 0.33 for the older, whereas the relative difference was 0.47 and 0.47. The results might be compromised by floor effects for the older subjects in the concurrent articulation condition, in which the overall proportion correct was only 0.25 for a list of seven digits. However, Fradet, Gil, and Gaonac'h (1996) also found a greater effect of concurrent articulation on younger subjects using a span task. Younger subjects had a slightly larger span on the control list (4.5 vs 4.3) but older subjects had slightly larger spans with concurrent articulation (3.5 vs 3.6). The younger subjects showed larger effects of concurrent articulation by an absolute measure (0.98 and 0.70) but the values for the relative measure (0.22 and 0.16) were quite similar.

Acoustic confusion effect

Belleville *et al.* (1996) presented lists of dissimilar and similar sounding letters at each subject's span. With auditory presentation, the younger subjects had a higher span than older subjects (4.11 and 3.46) and both the absolute difference measure (1.86 and 2.75 for younger and older subjects, respectively) and the relative difference measure (0.45 and 0.80) show a larger acoustic confusion effect for older subjects. With visual presentation, the older subjects showed a smaller effect, both by the absolute measure (1.67 and 1.43) and by the relative measure (0.42 and 0.34). A similar pattern was reported by Belleville *et al.* (2003), although the numeric differences were far smaller: a larger acoustic confusion effect for older adults for auditory presentation by both the absolute (0.05 and 0.09) and relative (0.09 and 0.14) measures and a smaller acoustic confusion effect by both the absolute (0.08 and 0.07) and relative (0.11 and 0.08) measures.

Word length effect

Belleville, Peretz and Malenfant (1996) used one- and four-syllable words as stimuli. With auditory presentation, the younger and older subjects had similar spans with the short words, 3.99 and 3.81. The older subjects had approximately equivalent effects of word length as the younger subjects by both the absolute (1.77 and 1.63) and relative (0.44 and 0.43) measures. In contrast, with visual presentation, the younger subjects had slightly lower spans than older subjects for short words, 3.74 and 3.99. The younger subjects had larger effects of word length by both the absolute (2.33 and 1.56) and relative (0.62 and 0.39) measures. Given that the older subjects did better in the 'control' condition, however, this latter result is difficult to interpret.

Summary

Given the paucity of research on these topics, this summary should be taken as a tentative first statement and the reader is cautioned that additional research is needed to confirm the following assessment. Furthermore, these statements are made primarily on the basis of the relative difference measure. Any account of basic working memory phenomena should be able to explain why, relative to younger adults, older adults show (1) an equivalent effect of irrelevant speech; (2) an equivalent effect of concurrent articulation; (3) a larger acoustic confusion effect for auditory items but a smaller acoustic confusion effect for visual items; and (4) an equivalent effect of word length for auditory items and an unknown effect for visual items.

Modeling age-related differences in memory

Much of the work on cognitive aging has taken either a psychometric or 'macro' approach or an experimental or 'micro' approach (Salthouse 2000). The macro approach focuses on a broad range of cognitive processing abilities that differ as a function of age and generally utilizes correlational or psychometric techniques. Typically, researchers adopting this method analyze their data using multivariate analyses, including alternative structural equation models with hierarchical structures, and test to see how much variance can be accounted for by common versus specific influences of age on each test and/or latent variable. Using such designs one can identify the number of age-related influences that operate on the cognitive variables being measured. Mediating variables that interact with the latent variables can also be identified (e.g., Salthouse and Ferrer-Caja 2003). These types of studies have provided valuable insights into the differences and similarities among a constellation of abilities in both older and younger adults, and how they relate and depend on one another.

In contrast, the micro approach focuses on describing specific tasks and processes that differ as a function of age and generally utilizes an experimental manipulation of independent variables. This type of approach lends itself naturally to an experimental design in which the experimenter varies the parameters of a single task to try to determine effects of aging on each aspect of the task.

Both types of designs have their advantages and disadvantages (see Hertzog 1996 for a review). One advantage of the 'micro' approach for exploring the locus of age-related differences in memory performance is that one can use formal quantitative models that have been developed to account for specific patterns of errors in memory performance in young adults to fit the data from the older adults. Such simulation models have recently become increasingly sophisticated, predicting not just overall errors but patterns of omissions, transpositions, movements, and intrusions (e.g., Farrell and Lewandowsky 2003; Henson, Norris, Page *et al.* 1996; Brown, Neath and Chater 2002; Brown, Preece and Hulme 2000). One advantage of a formal model is that it allows for the exploration of higher-order interactions that simply could not be worked through with a verbal model. A full analysis of errors provides a far richer and more detailed picture of performance than one based solely on overall per cent correct or mean response time. In addition, clear and testable predictions can be made from a formal model in which psychologically plausible parameters are mapped on to particular human processes. Thus formal predictions can be made such that by manipulating a process (or combination of processes) a particular outcome will be observed. These advantages are particularly important for a field such as cognitive aging in which multiple changes occur to various extents in each individual. The model can be set such that it simulates performance with distorted input, fewer processing resources, slowed processing, etc. or any combination thereof.

One difficulty with these modeling efforts is that they are almost too good: it is not easy to find critical areas in which the various models differ. However, a stringent test of any model would be whether it can be extended to populations of individuals other than young adults. The challenge is to find data within these alternate populations that are sufficient for modeling purposes. Although there are many experimental studies that show overall differences in measures of accuracy or latency in certain types of working memory tasks as a function of age, there have been very few detailed analyses of error patterns. The few exceptions to this rule are summarized below.

In one of the first investigations of its kind, Balota, Duchek and Paullin (1989) used Estes' (1955, 1959) stimulus fluctuation model to fit data on spacing, lag and retention interval for both young and old adults. They showed that the pattern of results was similar for both old and young although the level of performance was lower in every case for the older adults. In order to fit the data from the older adults, two parameters, those representing probability of encoding an element from the context and the rate at which elements from the context fluctuate over time, needed to be varied. Thus, one could conclude that older adults encoded fewer contextual elements and the context changed more slowly for the older adults.

Another experiment that was used for formal quantitative modeling of age-related differences in memory is reported by Maylor, Vousden and Brown (1999). They compared a group of young college-age individuals and an older group (M age = 65) on immediate serial recall of lists of acoustically confusable (i.e., all the items in the list rhymed when pronounced) or acoustically nonconfusable (i.e., each item had a unique rhyme) nonsense syllables. They also manipulated list length from six to seven items. In addition to measuring overall performance, they examined order errors, omissions and intrusions. Importantly, they found not just quantitative differences (older adults made more errors of every type), but also qualitative differences: even after an age-related increase in response threshold had been ruled out, the majority of the older adults' errors were omissions. Maylor *et al.* (1999) fit the data using OSCAR (Brown *et al.* 2000), an oscillator-based model of memory. After fitting the younger subjects' data, they found the model could not be made to fit the older subjects' data when only one parameter was changed. Thus, no single factor was able to account for the difference in performance between younger and older subjects. Rather, a good fit required a change of two parameters, one of which reflected context quality and the other output forgetting.

In OSCAR, the context quality parameter provides distinctive temporal cues for neighboring items in a sequence of events. When the cues are less specific, the pattern of errors mimics that of the older adults. Output forgetting could either be due to greater interference or slowed responses that could map on to processing speed. Maylor *et al.* (1999) did not report acoustic confusion errors.

This type of analysis is very valuable in furthering our understanding of the multiple interactions among factors that may underlie the difference between younger and older adults. They provide a way of testing the possible impact that different input and output parameters might have on memory performance. These simulation modeling efforts have complemented the data reported from the psychometric approach and emphasize the value of looking for converging operations from multiple paradigms (e.g., Garner, Hake and Eriksen 1956; Bromley 1990; Hertzog 1996; Salthouse 2000). The idea is that to the extent that one finds a similar pattern of results using a number of different perspectives, the results are less likely to be due to the adoption of one particular method.

The Feature Model

The Feature Model (Nairne 1990) was developed to account for the major effects observed when memory is tested by immediate serial recall, including the basic serial position function, modality and suffix effects, grouping effects, acoustic confusion effects and concurrent articulation effects and interactions among these variables. Subsequent extensions have shown how the model explains word length effects (Neath and Nairne 1995) and irrelevant speech effects (Neath 2000). Thus, the Feature Model addresses all four core memory phenomena that serve as the basis of the phonological loop hypothesis. Its major strength for present purposes is that it allows direct manipulation of the quality of sensory and perceptual coding, represented in the model as modality-dependent features, independently from the higher-level coding, represented in the model as modality-independent features. Thus, it can readily implement the idea that perceptual deficits might result in higher level cognitive deficits (e.g., Schneider and Pichora-Fuller 2000).

In the Feature Model modality-dependent features represent the perceptual aspects of the stimulus unique to the modality of presentation, whereas modality-independent features represent the nature of the item itself and are generated through internal processes, such as categorization and identification. This follows a distinction, proposed by the broad class of dual coding models, between an abstract form of representation and a form that more closely represents the physical characteristics (see Surpranant and Neath 1996). The Feature Model distinguishes between primary and secondary memory. Primary memory has no capacity limits, and items in primary memory do not decay. Rather, the major function of primary memory is to construct and maintain cues that may indicate which items were recently presented. Order information is encoded as a point in multidimensional space and is stored with the cues in primary memory. For each cue, this point can drift (or perturb) along the various relevant dimensions, based on Estes' (1972, 1997) perturbation theory.

Within the context of the Feature Model, it is assumed that perturbations in either direction are equally likely and that an item cannot perturb past the bounds imposed by the task (e.g., an item cannot perturb to position $n + 1$ in a list of n items). The probability that a cue's encoded representation will perturb along the position dimension during a particular time interval is given by *theta*. This is held constant at 0.05 and is not considered a free parameter. The probability that a cue for item I will indicate the item occupies a particular position, p, during the next time interval, $t+1$, is given by

$$I_{p,t+1} = (1 - \theta) I_{p,t} + \frac{\theta}{2} I_{p-1,t} + \frac{\theta}{2} I_{p+1,t} \qquad 1$$

For the end positions, a slightly different equation is used, which takes into account the limit that perturbation can occur in only one direction. For position 1,

$$I_{1,t+1} = 1 - \frac{\theta}{2}I_{1,t} + \frac{\theta}{2}I_{2,t} \qquad 2$$

and for position n

$$I_{n,t+1} = 1 - \frac{\theta}{2}I_{n,t} + \frac{\theta}{2}I_{n-1,t} \qquad 3$$

Recall begins with the cue in primary memory that has the highest probability of being the cue for the first item. The probability of sampling (P_s) a particular secondary memory item, SM_j, given a particular primary memory cue, PM_i, depends of the ratio of the similarity of the cue and target relative to the similarity of the cue to all other possible responses:

$$P_S(SM_j|PM_i) = \frac{s(i,j)}{\sum_{k=1}^{n} s(i,k)} \qquad 4$$

In this equation, n is the number of potential responses and the similarity between the cue and the secondary memory item, $s(i,j)$, is given by

$$s(i,j) = e^{-d_{ij}} \qquad 5$$

In Equation 5, distance, d, is based on the number of mismatching features, M, divided by the number of compared features, N:

$$d_{ij} = \frac{a\sum M_k}{N} \qquad 6$$

The value M_k is the number of times the feature at position k in the cue does not match the feature at position k in the secondary memory item. The parameter a is a scaling parameter that can be mapped onto the overall level of attention or available resources.

After an item has been sampled, it still might not be output. The probability of outputting an item, P_o, depends on the number of times it has been previously recalled, r, as well as a scale constant, c

$$P_0 = e^{-cr} \qquad 7$$

Simulations

Given the relative lack of data, some simplifying assumptions will be made for the purpose of fitting the data. First, all simulations will use the same list length rather than simulating span-adjusted lengths. Secondly, it is assumed that older subjects will always recall slightly less in the 'control' condition (i.e., short words, dissimilar letters, quiet condition) than younger subjects. Third, the key measure will be relative difference, given the built-in absolute difference in the control conditions. Thus, the five results to be simulated are the following: Relative to younger adults, older adults show (1) an equivalent effect of irrelevant speech; (2) an equivalent effect of concurrent articulation; (3) a larger acoustic confusion effect for auditory items but (4) a smaller acoustic confusion effect for visual items; and (5) an equivalent effect of word length for auditory items (the effect for visual items is unknown).

The basic strategy, as in other simulations with the Feature Model, is to begin with a standard set of parameters (see Table 10.2) to produce the simulated data for the young subjects, and then change only those parameters directly tied to the hypothesized difference between younger and older subjects to fit the data of the older adults. Thus, we start by simulating immediate serial recall of six item lists by younger subjects. To fit the data of the older subjects, we change two parameters. First, the probability of correctly encoding a particular modality-independent feature is reduced from 1.0 (for young adults) to 0.66 (for older adults). The idea is that the representations of older adults are noisier or less clear. Second, when auditory presentation is used, the probability of encoding a particular modality-dependent feature is reduced from 1.0 (for young adults) to 0.66 (for older adults). This reflects the common finding that most older adults have some degree of hearing loss relative to young adults. When visual presentation is being modeled, the probability of encoding a particular modality-dependent feature remains at 1.0, as most older adults have similar visual abilities as younger adults. Note that there is an overall difference in recall in all of the simulations below, and that this is due to the assumed worse modality-independent representation in the older subjects.

Irrelevant speech effect

The Feature Model offers a different explanation than that given by working memory for the four phenomena that are the focus of this chapter. The effects of irrelevant speech and concurrent

Table 10.2 Standard parameters for the simulations.

	Young	Old
List length	6	6
Probability of encoding each MI feature	1.0	0.66
Probability of encoding each visual MD feature	1.0	1.0
Probability of encoding each auditory MD feature	1.0	0.66
Number of MI features	20	20
Number of MD features: visual	2	2
Number of MD features: auditory	20	20
Number of similar MI features	0	0
Number of similar MD features	0	0
Attention (a)	12.0	12.0
Probability of overwriting (F)	1.0	1.0
Recovery constant (c)	2.0	2.0
Number of perturbations	3	3
Perturbation probability (theta)	0.05	0.05
Number of simulations	5000	5000

Table 10.3 Relative effect (Control–Experimental)/Control, for young and old subjects and simulation results from the feature model.

Source	Young	Old
Irrelevant speech effect		
Belleville *et al.* (2003)	0.13	0.12
Model	0.222	0.215
Concurrent articulation effect		
Rouleau and Belleville (1996)	0.47	0.47
Model	0.450	0.461
Acoustic confusion effect (auditory)		
Belleville *et al.* (1996)	0.45	0.80
Model	0.397	0.559
Acoustic confusion effect (visual)		
Belleville *et al.* (1996)	0.42	0.34
Model	0.414	0.419
Word length effect (auditory)		
Belleville *et al.* (1996)	0.44	0.43
Model	0.095	0.086
Word length effect (visual)		
Model	0.196	0.181

articulation are seen as being due to the same fundamental cause (Neath, Farley and Surprenant 2003). Each results in a process called feature adoption, in which a modality-independent feature of the irrelevant auditory information is incorporated into the representation of the to-be-remembered item. This reduces the similarity of the cue in primary memory to the undegraded trace in secondary memory, and so results in a decrease in the likelihood of sampling the correct item. The difference between irrelevant speech and concurrent articulation is one of degree, in that it takes less effort or attention to passively hear irrelevant speech than to articulate.

The simulation follows those described in more detail by Neath (2000). In particular, the simulated data for young subjects is produced in exactly the way described previously. The sole difference between the younger and older adults is the reduction in the probability of encoding each modality independent feature from 1.0 to 0.66 for both the quiet and irrelevant speech conditions.

The mean proportion correct for the young subjects was 0.616 in the quiet condition compared to 0.442 in the irrelevant speech condition, a relative effect of 0.222. For the older subjects, the values were 0.542 and 0.426, a relative effect of 0.215. Thus, the model produces the same qualitative pattern as observed in the data: equivalent disruption by irrelevant speech for both age groups. The reason that there is no age-related difference in the model is that irrelevant speech affects modality independent features and the difference between older and younger subjects is also modeled by affecting the modality independent features. Thus, some of the features changed by the feature adoption process will actually be already affected by the reduction in the probability of encoding. In the Feature Model, all that matters is a mismatch; if the same feature is affected twice, it mismatches just as much as if it mismatches once.

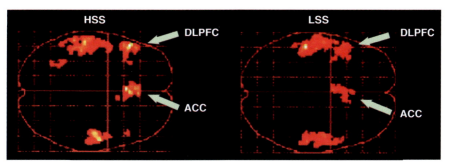

Plate 1 Activated areas on axial planes of the standard glass brain images (upper side of axial image shows left hemisphere). The figure on the left shows the activated areas averaged across eight HSS, while those on the right show those of LSS. Panels show the activated areas under the LST condition. See also figure 6.1, page 102.

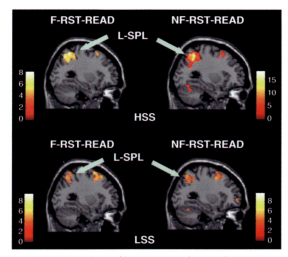

Plate 2 Activated areas on the sagittal plane of brain images (x = −26). Figures on the left side show activation areas under F-RST while those on the right side show activation areas under NF-RST condition relative to activations under READ condition. The upper panel shows the activated areas averaged across HSS and lower panel shows those across LSS. Adapted with permission from Osaka, M., Komori, M., Morishita, M., and Osaka, N. (2007). Neural basis of focusing attention in working memory. *Cognitive, Affective & Behavioral Neuroscience*, In Press, The Psychonomic Society. See also figure 6.6, page 109.

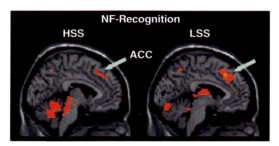

Plate 3 Activated areas on the sagittal plane of brain images (x = −4) in NF-recognition phase. Figures on the left show activation areas across HSS while those on the right show activation areas across LSS. Adapted with permission from Osaka, M., Komori, M., Morishita, M., and Osaka, N. (2007). Neural basis of focusing attention in working memory. *Cognitive, Affective & Behavioral Neuroscience*, In Press, The Psychonomic Society. See also figure 6.7, page 110.

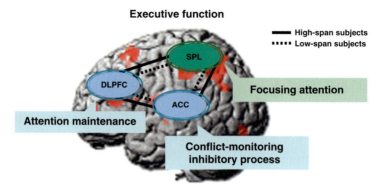

Plate 4 The neural bases of focusing attention on the executive control system. The solid line and dotted line also show neural network differences between HSS and LSS, respectively, (dotted line indicates weak connectivley). See also figure 6.9, page 112.

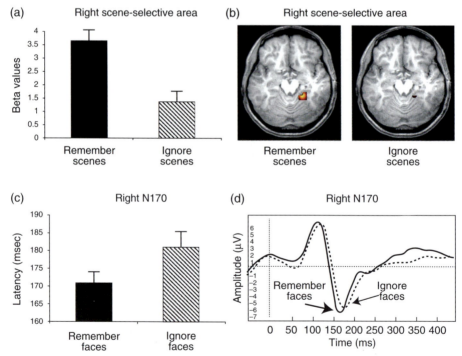

Plate 5 Activity data for *Remember* and *Ignore* conditions: fMRI and ERP. (a) Group data: Average beta values in the scene selective area revealing greater activity in Remember scenes vs Ignore scenes condition. (b) A representative subject demonstrating the BOLD signal level within the masked scene selective in Remember scenes vs Ignore scenes condition. (c) Group data: Average peak latency for the right N170 in PO8 electrode revealing earlier latency for Remember faces vs Ignore faces. (d) Grand-averaged waveforms of the time-locked ERPs to face stimuli revealing earlier latency for Remember faces vs Ignore faces. Error bars indicate standard error of the mean. (Adapted from Gazzaley *et al.* (2005a) *J Cogn Neurosci, 17* (3), 507–517.) See also figure 12.2, page 201.

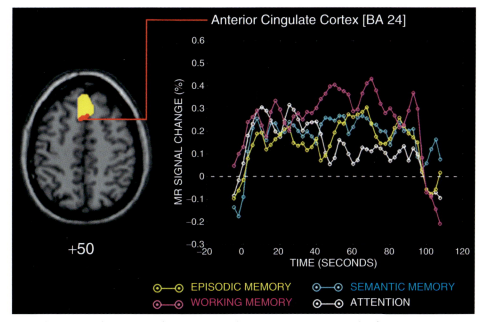

Plate 6 Illustration of a common frontal sustained activation increase. See also figure 18.2, page 312.

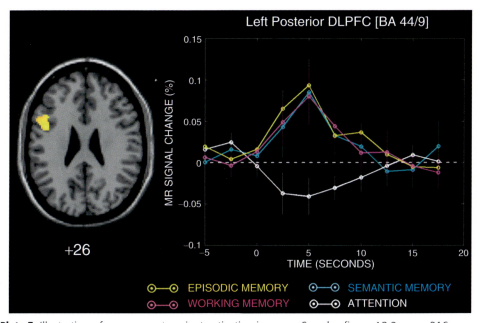

Plate 7 Illustration of a common transient activation increase. See also figure 18.3, page 316.

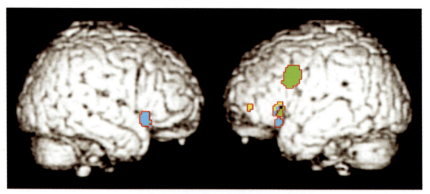

Plate 8 Schematic illustration of common lateral PFC sites for sustained or transient modulations during working memory and episodic memory (blue = common sustained activity increases for attention, long-term memory and working memory; yellow = common sustained activity increases for long-term memory and working memory; green = common transient activity increases for long-term memory and working memory). See also figure 18.4, page 324.

(a)

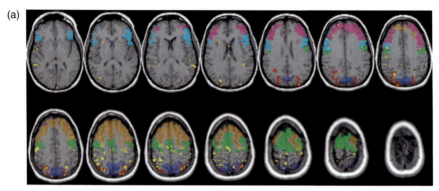

Plate 9 fMRI correlates of attention-based rehearsal of locations in working memory. The data illustrated here correspond to a delayed-location discrimination task in which subjects, while fixating centrally, judged whether a probe stimulus was closer to or further from central fixation than had been a target stimulus that had been presented 7 s previously. The delay period was unfilled. (a) illustrates the delay-evoked activity in a representative participant. Structural regions of interest (ROIs) are identified by translucent colors – superior parietal lobule (SPL; dark blue), intraparietal sulcus (IPL; red), premotor cortex (PMC; green), frontal eye fields (FEF; red), superior frontal cortex (SFC; orange), dorsolateral PFC (DLPFC; fuchsia), ventrolateral PFC (VLPFC; light blue) – and are overlaid by delay-responsive voxels, which appear yellow and orange.

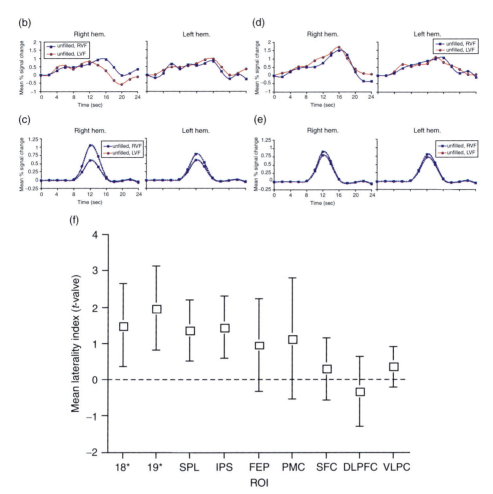

Plate 9 (*continued*) (b) illustrates trial-averaged fMRI data, by hemisphere, from the SPL delay-responsive voxels of the participant illustrated in (a). (c) illustrates quantitatively the delay effects (delay-epoch covariates scaled by their parameter estimates) estimated by the statistical analysis of the data illustrated in (b). (d) illustrates trial-averaged fMRI data, by hemisphere, from the IPS voxels illustrated in (a). (e) illustrates quantitatively the delay effects estimated by the statistical analysis of the data illustrated in (d). (f) illustrates the group results (mean and 95 percent confidence interval, n = 9) from this study, which indicate that the contralateral bias (referred to on vertical axis as the 'Laterality Index') of delay-period activity was significantly different from 0 in Brodmann Areas (BA) 18 and 19 of the occipital cortex, and in IPS and SPL, but not in any of the frontal cortical ROIs. This contralateral bias is an operationalization of an attention-based rehearsal effect. For complete details, see Postle, Awh, Jonides et al. (2004). See also figure 19.1, page 336–7.

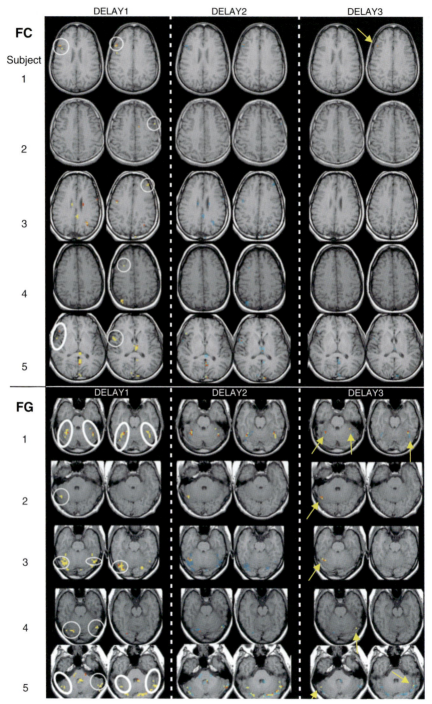

Plate 10 fMRI results from a multi-step delayed face-recognition task (behavioral task described in the text, and in Postle, Druzgal, and D'Esposito, 2003). The Delay 1 column illustrates the statistical maps identifying voxels in frontal cortex (FC) and fusiform gyrus (FG) with Delay 1-specific activity (critical voxels are circled). Delay 1 activity in FC was located in: right hemisphere middle frontal

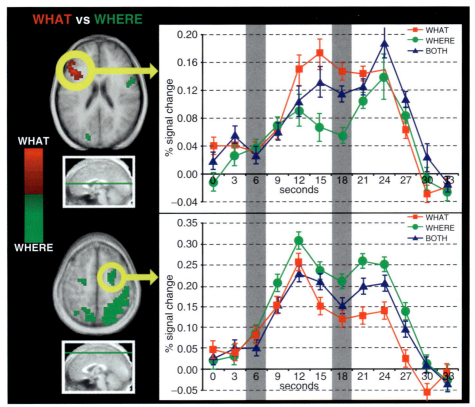

Plate 11 FMRI activation patterns during working memory for fractal-like patterns ('WHAT'), the locations of those patterns ('WHERE'), or both the patterns and their locations ('BOTH'). There is a dorsal/ventral spatial/nonspatial topography for the what-only and where-only tasks, but the activation for the BOTH task is in between the levels of activation for the preferred and non-preferred information types, consistent with a more selective representation for an object-in-its-location, involving fewer cells than are active during maintenance of the preferred information, but with those cells more highly active than during maintenance of the non-preferred information. Reprinted with permission from Sala and Courtney (2007). See also figure 21.1, page 374.

gyrus (MFG, Brodmann's area [BA] 9/46) and inferior frontal gyrus (IFG, BA 44) in subject 1; left MFG (BA 8) in subject 2; left MFG (BA 9/46) in subject 3; right superior frontal sulcus (BA 8) in subject 4; and IFG (BA 44) and premotor cortex (BA 6) in subject 5. FG Delay 1 activity was located bilaterally in subjects 1, 3, 4 and 5, and in right hemisphere in subject 2. The Delay 2 column illustrates the statistical maps identifying voxels in FC and FG with Delay 2-specific activity within the search space comprising the voxels that had been identified in the Delay 1 column (translucent blue). The Delay 3 column illustrates the statistical maps identifying voxels in FC and FG with Delay 3-specific activity within the search space comprising the voxels that had been identified in the Delay 2 column (translucent blue). This Delay 3 activity can be interpreted as a candidate neural correlate of the STR of face information. Such activity, identified with arrows, was seen in FC only in subject 1 (right MFG [BA 9/46]), and in FG bilaterally in subjects 1 and 5, in right hemisphere in subjects 2 and 3, and in left hemisphere in subject 4. See also figure 19.3, page 340.

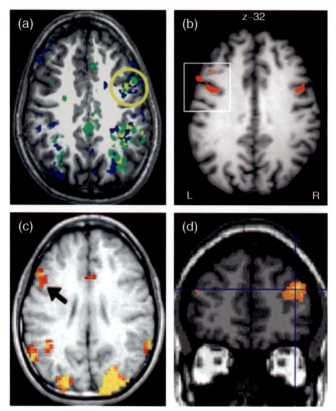

Plate 12 Activation of middle frontal cortex (possibly Brodmann's Area 46) in several studies involving the prioritization of one type of information over another: (a) Updating (in green),
WM maintenance (blue), and their overlap (yellow) (reprinted with permission from Roth et al. 2006),
(b) Common activation for task-switching, Stroop task, and n-back working memory task (reprinted with permission from Derrfuss et al. 2004), (c) Refreshing of just-seen information (reprinted with permission from Johnson et al. 2003), (d) Interference-resistant WM maintenance (reprinted with permission from Sakai et al. 2002). See also figure 21.2, page 377.

Concurrent articulation effect

As already noted, the Feature Model views concurrent articulation and irrelevant speech as being due to the same fundamental cause, feature adoption. Indeed, the only difference is that concurrent articulation requires more attention or resources than does irrelevant speech. The same simulation described above was rerun, except that there was less overall attention (see Neath 2000, for details). The mean proportion correct for the young subjects in the quiet condition was 0.609 compared to 0.335 in the concurrent articulation condition, a relative effect of 0.450. For the older subjects, the values were 0.549 and 0.296, a relative effect of 0.461. Note that even though the effect of concurrent articulation is approximately twice as large as that of irrelevant speech within the model, there are still equivalent relative effects just as observed in the data. The reason is the same as for the lack of an age-related difference in the magnitude of the irrelevant speech effect: the older adults have already had modality independent features encoded incorrectly, so the adoption of features from the material that is being articulated will have no additional effect.

Acoustic confusion effect

The acoustic confusion effect, according to the Feature Model, is due to the fact that similar items will share more features than dissimilar items. The more features in common, the larger the value of the denominator in equation 4 and thus the lower the sampling probability. As with previous simulations (e.g., Nairne 1990), there were 20 modality-dependent features for auditory presentation and 2 modality-dependent features for visual presentation. The total absolute number of features is not important (see the simulation reported in Chapter 4 of Neath and Surprenant 2003). To represent similar items, 10 modality-independent and 10 (auditory) or 1 (visual) modality-dependent features were set to the same value. The values of the remaining features were determined randomly, as usual. The only difference between young and older subjects was again the probability of encoding both modality-independent and dependent features (auditory simulation) or just modality-independent features (visual simulation).

For auditory presentation with young subjects, the mean proportion correct in the dissimilar condition was 0.651 compared to 0.392 in the similar condition, a relative effect of 0.397. For the older adults, the values were 0.577 and 0.254, a relative effect of 0.559. This is the same pattern as observed in the data discussed above: a larger effect for older subjects when the items are acoustically confusable. The reason, in the Feature Model, that older adults show a larger acoustic confusion effect with auditory presentation than younger adults is that they suffer from a more impoverished representation, relative to younger adults. These representations are all more similar in the dissimilar case, and the result is compounded when the to-be-remembered stimuli are acoustically similar. Thus, not only is there less information available from the modality-independent features, but also less information from the modality-dependent features.

For visual presentation with young subjects, the mean proportion correct in the dissimilar condition was 0.618 compared to 0.362 in the similar condition, a relative effect of 0.415. For the older adults, the values were 0.553 and 0.321, a relative effect of 0.420. Unlike other simulations reported so far, this is different from the data in which there is a smaller effect for older adults. Over repeated simulations, the two relative values were always quite close but no reversal occurred. Unlike with the auditory case, there was no additional loss of modality-dependent information in the visual (to be consistent with the other simulations that use visual presentation). Thus, the older adults do not have an additional source of information loss, and therefore the effects are of comparable magnitude.

Word length effect

According to the Feature Model, the word length effect is analogous to a list length effect. Words are made up of segments (which could correspond to phonemes or syllables) that need to be assembled prior to output. Long words have (by definition) more segments than short words. Assuming a given probability of assembling one segment incorrectly, there is more chance of an assembly error for a long word than for an otherwise comparable short word (Neath and Nairne 1995). As in the earlier simulations, the probability of a segment error is the same for short and long items (0.10) but long items are assumed to have more segments (10) than short items (1).

As when simulating the acoustic confusion effect with auditory items, the simulation of the word length effect with auditory items set the probability of encoding both modality-independent and modality-dependent features to 0.66. With auditory presentation for young subjects, the mean proportion correct was 0.658 for the short words compared to 0.595 for the long words, a relative effect of 0.095. For the older subjects, the values were 0.573 and 0.524, a relative effect of 0.086. As with the data, there was an equivalent effect of word length. The reason in the model is that when an error occurs in assembling an item for recall, it results in setting half of the modality independent features to 0 to reflect missing information. The older adults already have some of these feature values missing, so the additional change does not cause the mismatch to be any greater.

With visual presentation for young subjects, the mean proportion correct was 0.615 for short words and 0.494 for long words, a relative effect of 0.196. For the older adults, the values were 0.532 and 0.435, a relative effect of 0.182. The model predicts equivalent relative differences for the same reason as with the auditory case. Although the data are not clear on whether older adults show a similar relative effect of word length with visual presentation, the larger word length effect observed in the model with visual compared auditory presentation does reflect the pattern observed in data from younger subjects (see also Watkins and Watkins 1973). The reason for the larger effect of word length with visual presentation (for both age groups) is that a segment assembly error affects only modality-independent features. Auditory presentation entails more modality-dependent features than visual presentation, and thus a larger proportion of overall features is affected by a segment assembly error with visual than with auditory presentation.

Evaluation of simulations

Overall, the simulations produce the appropriate qualitative pattern of age-related differences for four cases for which there is fairly good data available: irrelevant speech, concurrent articulation, acoustic confusion with auditory presentation and word length with auditory presentation. The model made an incorrect prediction for acoustic confusion with visual presentation; for the final case, word length with visual presentation, the data are not sufficiently clear to judge whether the prediction of the model is correct.

To minimize the number of differences between the simulations, we assumed a fixed list length (six items) and also kept all parameters identical except for those explicitly related to the effect being simulation. In contrast, in the available data there were many variations in design, list length, scoring methodology, etc., which could play a role in the overall magnitude of the various effects. It should not be surprising, therefore, to find that although the relative effect size predicted was comparable in magnitude to that observed in the data in approximately half of the simulations, the magnitudes were substantially different in some of the simulations. Specifically, the model predicted a much smaller relative effect of word length than found in the data and a larger effect of irrelevant speech. Closer fits are possible, but were not pursued.

Interestingly, an additional prediction may be derived from the model: older adults should show a larger relative modality effect than younger adults. Although there is not much data on this, what data do exist suggest an accurate prediction (e.g., Raanaas, Nordby and Magnussen 2002). The reason, according to the simulations run, is that older adults have perceptual deficits that result in impoverished modality-dependent features.

Note that the particular implementation of the effect of 'aging' here allows, in principle, fitting gradual declines in people as they age from 20 to 30 to 40 to 50 and so on. In each case, one can simply decrease the probability of correctly encoding each modality-independent feature. The result is a gradual overall decline in performance. Moreover, this implementation allows for quite substantial individual differences among older subjects. For example, it is predicted that those individuals with fewer perceptual deficits will have better memory than those with more perceptual deficits, especially those related to auditory processing.

Summary and conclusions

Given the central importance of the effects of irrelevant speech, concurrent articulation, acoustic confusion, and word length to the development of the phonological loop component of working memory, it is perhaps surprising that there are relatively little data on how these phenomena might by affected by age. For the data that are available, it is revealing that older subjects show a similar magnitude relative effect except for the auditory acoustic confusion effect (where the relative effect is larger than for young subjects) and for the visual acoustic confusion effect (where the relative effect is smaller than for young subjects). Clearly, more data are needed in order to confirm these findings, and studies that focus on the interaction of these phenomena (e.g., concurrent articulation and word length) would be particularly useful.

Given the relative paucity of data, we made several simplifying assumptions when modeling the qualitative pattern of results. With the assumption that older adults have, on average, noisier or less clear representations than younger adults, the Feature Model produced the appropriate pattern of results in all but one case. The model was also found to predict a larger relative modality effect for older adults than younger adults, as has been reported. Although by no means a complete explanation of age-related differences in working memory or even of age-related differences in these four basic effects, the account offered by the Feature Model is quite precise about the cause and the effect of the difference. It is still an open question as to why the modality independent representations in memory might not be so clear older adults: our preferred view is that at least part of this is due to perceptual difficulties that accompany normal aging, but it is also consistent with some versions of the speed of processing and other accounts.

There exist several implementations of the phonological loop (e.g., Burgess and Hitch 1999; Page and Norris 1998), and it would be informative to see whether those models are capable of accounting for the data discussed in this chapter. Neither has such a direct manipulation of sensory/perceptual information that is separate from abstract/conceptual information, but perhaps a similar idea could be implemented by changes in the representations of the phonological information.

The effects of aging on cognition are extremely complex and it seems likely that age-related differences are due to multiple interactions among factors. Simulation models have several notable advantages over purely verbal theories, including a confirmation on reasoning that examines higher-order interactions. In addition, although only briefly mentioned in this paper, intermediate states and individual differences can be explained by different weights on the parameters. Clear and testable predictions can be made from a formal model in which psychologically plausible parameters are mapped on to particular human processes. The drawback to computational modeling, of course, is that it is merely an existence proof; it shows that if we manipulate the parameters in such a way, the appropriate pattern of data emerges. If the parameters do not map on to real properties of the organism, it can become merely an exercise in fitting data.

The present demonstration, then, is meant to illustrate the utility of using simulation models to help identify the loci of the differences between older and younger adults in immediate memory. It is a first step towards using the insights and lessons learned from simulation modeling to help understand the multiple origins of age-related differences in immediate memory.

Acknowledgments

Preparation of this chapter was sponsored by National Institute on Aging Grant AG021071 awarded to both authors. Portions of this chapter were written while the authors were Visiting Fellows at the Department of Psychology, City University, London, UK. Correspondence may be addressed to either author.

References

Baddeley, AD (1986). *Working Memory*. Oxford University Press, New York.

Baddeley, AD (1992). Is working memory working? *Quarterly Journal of Experimental Psychology, 44A*, 1–31.

Baddeley, AD (2000). The phonological loop and the irrelevant speech effect: Some comments on Neath. *Psychonomic Bulletin and Review, 7*, 544–549.

Baddeley, AD and Wilson, B (1985). Phonological coding and short-term memory in patients without speech. *Journal of Memory and Language, 24*, 490–502.

Baddeley, AD Lewis, VJ and Vallar, G (1984). Exploring the articulatory loop. *Quarterly Journal of Experimental Psychology, 36*, 233–252.

Baddeley, AD Thomson, N and Buchanan, M (1975). Word length and the structure of short-term memory. *Journal of Verbal Learning and Verbal Behavior, 14*, 575–589.

Balota, DA Duchek, JM and Paullin, R (1989). Age-related differences in the impact of spacing, lag, and retention interval. *Psychology and Aging, 4*, 3–9.

Beaman, CP (2005). Irrelevant sound effects amongst younger and older adults: Objective findings and subjective insights. *European Journal of Cognitive Psychology, 17*, 241–265.

Belleville, S, Peretz, I and Malenfant, D (1996). Examination of the working memory components in normal aging and in dementia of the Alzheimer type. *Neuropsychologia, 34*, 195–207.

Belleville, S, Rouleau, N, Van der Linden, M and Collette, F (2003). Effect of manipulation and irrelevant noise on working memory capacity of patients with Alzheimer's dementia. *Neuropsychology, 17*, 69–81.

Bireta, TJ, Neath, I and Surprenant, AM (2006). The syllable-based word length effect and stimulus set specificity. *Psychonomic Bulletin and Review, 13*, 434–438.

Bromley, DB (1990). *Behavioural Gerontology: Central issues in the psychology of ageing*. John Wiley and Sons, Chichester, UK.

Brown, GDA, Neath, I and Chater, N (2002). A ratio model of scale-invariant memory and identification. Unpublished manuscript.

Brown, GDA, Preece, T and Hulme, C (2000). Oscillator-based memory and serial order. *Psychological Review, 107*, 127–181.

Burgess, N and Hitch, GJ (1999). Memory for serial order: A network model of the phonological loop and its timing. *Psychological Review, 106*, 551–581

Campbell, R and Butterworth, B (1985). Phonological dyslexia and dysgraphia in highly literate subjects: A developmental case with associated deficits of phonemic processing and awareness. *Quarterly Journal of Experimental Psychology, 37A*, 435–476.

Colle, HA and Welsh, A (1976). Acoustic masking in primary memory. *Journal of Verbal Learning and Verbal Behavior, 15*, 17–32.

Conrad, R (1964). Acoustic confusions in immediate memory. *British Journal of Psychology, 55*, 75–84.

Elliott, EM (2002). The irrelevant-speech effect and children: Theoretical implications of developmental change. *Memory and Cognition, 30*, 478–487.

Estes, WK (1955). Statistical theory of spontaneous recovery and regression. *Psychological Review*, *62*, 145–154.

Estes, WK (1959). The statistical approach to learning theory. In S Koch (ed), *Psychology: A study of a science* (pp. 380–491). McGraw-Hill, New York.

Estes, WK (1972). An associative basis for coding and organization in memory. In AW Melton and E Martin (eds), *Coding Processes in Human Memory* (pp. 151–190). Washington, DC: Winston.

Estes, WK (1997). Processes of memory loss, recovery, and distortion. *Psychological Review*, *104*, 148–169.

Farrell, S and Lewandowsky, S (2003). Dissimilar items benefit from phonological similarity in serial recall. *Journal of Experimental Psychology: Learning, Memory, and Cognition*, *29*, 838–849.

Fradet, A, Gil, R and Gaonac'h, D (1996). Codages phonologique et semantique en memoire a court terme chez des sujets adultes jeunes ou ages. [Phonological and semantic coding in short-term memory in young and older adults] *Revue de Neuropsychologie*, *6*, 53–81.

Garner, WR, Hake, HW and Eriksen, CW (1956). Operationism and the concept of perception. *Psychological Review*, *63*, 149–158.

Grégoire, J and Van der Linden, M (1997). Effect of age on forward and backward digit spans. *Aging, Neuropsychology, and Cognition*, *4*, 140–149.

Halliday, MS, Hitch, GJ, Lennon, B and Pettifer, C (1990). Verbal short-term memory in children: the role of the articulatory loop. *European Journal of Cognitive Psychology*, *2*, 23–38.

Henson, RNA, Norris, DG, Page, MPA and Baddeley, AD (1996). Unchained memory: Error patterns rule out chaining models of immediate serial recall. *Quarterly Journal of Experimental Psychology: Human Experimental Psychology*, *49A*, 80–115.

Hertzog, C (1996). Research design in studies of aging and cognition. In JE Birren and KW Schaie (eds), *Handbook of the Psychology of Aging*, 4th edn (pp. 24–37). San Diego, CA: Academic Press.

Hulme, C, Thomson, N, Muir, C and Lawrence, A (1984). Speech rate and the development of short-term memory span. *Journal of Experimental Child Psychology*, *38*, 241–253.

Jones, DM and Macken, WJ (1995). Phonological similarity in the irrelevant speech effect: Within-or between-stream similarity? *Journal of Experimental Psychology: Learning, Memory, and Cognition*, *21*, 103–115.

Jones, DM, Macken, WJ and Nichols, AP (2004). The phonological store of working memory: Is it phonological and is it a store? *Journal of Experimental Psychology: Learning, Memory and Cognition*, *30*, 656–674.

Jones, DM, Madden, C and Miles, C (1992). Privileged access by irrelevant speech to short-term memory: The role of changing state. *Quarterly Journal of Experimental Psychology*, *44A*, 645–669.

Logie, RH, Della Sala, S, Laiacona, M, Chalmers, P and Wynn, V (1996). Group aggregates and individual reliability: The case of verbal short-term memory. *Memory and Cognition*, *24*, 305–321.

Maylor, EA, Vousden, JI and Brown, GDA (1999). Adult age differences in short-term memory for serial order: Data and a model. *Psychology and Aging*, *14*, 572–594.

Murray, DJ (1968). Articulation and acoustic confusability in short-term memory. *Journal of Experimental Psychology*, *78*, 679–684.

Myerson, J, Emery, L, White, DA and Hale, S (2003). Effects of age, domain, and processing demands on memory span: Evidence for differential decline. *Aging, Neuropsychology, and Cognition*, *10*, 20–27.

Nairne, JS (1990). A feature model of immediate memory. *Memory and Cognition*, *18*, 251–269.

Neath, I (1999). Modelling the disruptive effects of irrelevant speech on order information. *International Journal of Psychology*, *34*, 410–418.

Neath, I (2000). Modeling the effects of irrelevant speech on memory. *Psychonomic Bulletin and Review*, *7*, 403–423.

Neath, I and Nairne, JS (1995). Word-Length effects in immediate memory: Overwriting trace decay theory. *Psychonomic Bulletin and Review*, *2*, 429–441.

Neath, I and Surprenant, AM (2003). *Human Memory: An introduction to research, data, and theory*, 2nd edn. Belmont, CA: Wadsworth.

Neath, I, Bireta, TJ and Surprenant, AM (2003). The time-based word length effect and stimulus set specificity. *Psychonomic Bulletin and Review, 10*, 430–434.

Neath, I, Farley, LA and Surprenant, AM (2003). Directly assessing the relationship between irrelevant speech and articulatory suppression. *Quarterly Journal of Experimental Psychology, 56A*, 1269–1278.

Page, MPA and Norris, D (1998). The Primacy Model: A new model of immediate serial recall. *Psychological Review, 105*, 761–781.

Raanaas, RK, Nordby, K and Magnussen, S (2002). The expanding telephone number Part 2: Age variations in immediate memory for multiple-digit numbers. *Behaviour and Information Technology, 21*, 39–45.

Rouleau, N and Belleville, S (1996). Irrelevant speech effect in aging: An assessment of inhibitory processes in working memory. *Journals of Gerontology: Series B: Psychological Sciences and Social Sciences, 51B*, P356–P363.

Salthouse, TA (1985). *A Theory of Cognitive Aging.* Amsterdam: North-Holland.

Salthouse, TA (2000). Methodological assumptions in cognitive aging research. In FIM Craik and TA Salthouse, eds *The Handbook of Aging and Cognition, 2nd edn* (pp. 467–498). Mawah, NJ: Lawrence Erlbaum Associates.

Salthouse, TA and Ferrer-Caja, E (2003). What needs to be explained to account for age-related effects on multiple cognitive variables? *Psychology and Aging, 18*, 91–110.

Shankweiler, D, Liberman, IY, Marks, LS, Fowler, CA and Fischer, FW (1979). The speech code and learning to read. *Journal of Experimental Psychology: Human Learning and Memory, 5*, 531–545.

Schneider, BA and Pichora-Fuller, MK (2000). Implications of perceptual deterioration for cognitive aging research. In FIM Craik and TA Salthouse (eds), *The Handbook of Aging and Cognition, 2nd edn* (pp. 155–219). Mawah, NJ: Erlbaum.

Surprenant, AM and Neath, I (1996). The relation between discriminability and memory for vowels, consonants, and silent-center vowels. *Memory and Cognition, 24*, 356–366.

Vallar, G and Baddeley, AD (1984). Fractionation of working memory: Neuropsychological evidence for a short-term store. *Journal of Verbal Learning and Verbal Behavior, 23*, 151–161.

Vallar, G and Cappa, SF (1987). Articulation and verbal short-term memory: Evidence from anarthria. *Cognitive Psychology, 4*, 55–78.

Verhaeghen, P and Salthouse, TA (1997). Meta-analyses of age-cognition relations in adulthood: Estimates of linear and nonlinear age effects and structural models. *Psychological Bulletin, 122*, 231–249.

Verhaeghen, P, Marcoen, A and Goossens, L (1993). Facts and fiction about memory aging: A quantitative integration of research findings. *Journals of Gerontology, 48*, P157–P171.

Waters, GS, Rochon, E and Caplan, D (1992). The role of high-level speech planning in rehearsal: evidence from patients with apraxia of speech. *Journal of Memory and Language, 31*, 54–73.

Watkins, MJ and Watkins, OC (1973). The postcategorical status of the modality effect in serial recall. *Journal of Experimental Psychology, 99*, 226–230.

Wixted, JT (1990). Analyzing the empirical course of forgetting. *Journal of Experimental Psychology: Learning, Memory, and Cognition, 16*, 927–935.

11

Implications from cognitive neuropsychology for models of short-term and working memory

Randi C. Martin and A. Cris Hamilton

Beginning in the nineteenth century, some of the most profound insights into cognition have originated with observations of individuals suffering brain damage. Since this time, particularly within the past 25 years, cognitive neuropsychology has evolved into a subdiscipline of cognitive psychology with a rigorous methodology based on the examination of individuals who have sustained brain damage. Many of these data form the foundation of theories of cognition in areas such language, memory, reading and attention.

In this chapter we present findings from research with brain-damaged patients that we believe point to important issues germane to the current working memory literature. First, we provide a brief overview of our methodology, its advantages and shortcomings, and the role of single case studies (and patient data in general) in the field of cognitive psychology and cognitive neuroscience. Secondly, we provide a brief review of some often overlooked studies of patients with short-term memory deficits. Finally, we present a summary of our own work examining short-term memory, language processing and (more recently) executive control processes and discuss the implications of these data for some contemporary models of working memory, including the four-component model proposed by Baddeley (2000).

Cognitive neuropsychology

Excellent introductions to cognitive neuropsychology can be found in Rapp (2001) and Ellis and Young (1988). Below we outline a few points that we feel are particularly relevant to the current volume.

Cognitive neuropsychology attempts to explain patterns of impaired and intact cognitive performance seen in individuals with brain damage. Ultimately, careful testing of impaired and intact capabilities seen in brain-injured patients are used to make inferences regarding the functional organization of human cognition (Ellis and Young 1988).

Cognitive neuropsychology has three objectives (McCloskey 2001), although researchers vary in terms of their emphasis of each. The principle goal is to gain insight into the structure and function of normal cognition. The second is to provide data regarding the localization of cognitive functions in the brain. Relevant to this second point, it is important to acknowledge that some cognitive neuropsychologists do not feel that localization in any way constrains implications for cognitive function (see Coltheart 2004 for a recent discussion). Finally, the third objective is to understand the various cognitive deficits that result from brain damage in order to advance knowledge needed for diagnosis and ultimate treatment.

Much of the literature in cognitive neuropsychology is formed around the demonstration of dissociations in cognitive function. That is, based on a model of function in a given cognitive domain, the patient is tested on a number of tasks that presumably tap different cognitive components of the model. If a patient successfully performs a variety of tasks that are hypothesized to draw on one cognitive mechanism, but is impaired on tasks that tap another, then the data provide evidence supporting the independence of the mechanisms. It should be emphasized that demonstrating a mere dissociation between two *tasks* is not considered sufficient evidence to make valid inferences about a hypothesized cognitive model – patient performance on multiple tasks should converge on the same conclusion. Of course, other explanations for such dissociations must be ruled out.

Traditionally, a 'double dissociation' constitutes even more persuasive evidence. For example, if one patient is impaired on component A, but unimpaired on component B, while another patient shows the reverse pattern, then explanations based on relative difficulty of the tasks drawing on the two components can be ruled out. McCloskey (2001), however, argues that requiring double dissociations is overly conservative and may not be possible in certain architectural configurations where the output of component A serves as the input to component B. Moreover, McCloskey points out that in addressing the 'resource artifact' objection, data from healthy age- and education-matched control subjects is often instructive. That is, claims of differences in task difficulty can often be addressed by appealing to the control subjects' data. If no such differences exist, this objection carries little weight.

Cognitive neuropsychology typically employs careful analysis of data from a single patient or a small series of case studies to make these inferences. Case studies may seem conspicuously suspect to many cognitive psychologists accustomed to running large groups of healthy undergraduate students and statistically demonstrating some effect or another. However, cognitive neuropsychology considers case studies using single patients or a small number of patients to be preferable to using larger groups of patients selected for one or another diagnostic syndromes or lesion localization. Several papers have presented the logic for single case studies (Caramazza 1984, 1986; McCloskey 1993), so we will not address the issue fully here. Importantly, however, it should be pointed out that cognitive neuropsychologists are not attempting to form novel models of cognition based on a single patient. Instead, we attempt to integrate inferences made from a single patient's data with the literature using any number of other methodologies – both from cognitive psychology and cognitive neuroscience as well as other reports of brain-damaged patients.

Several variables conspire to complicate the interpretation of data obtained from patients with brain damage (see Ellis and Young 1998, for a discussion). For example, given normal variability in task performance even among healthy subjects, one must sufficiently demonstrate that a particular patient performs well below the range of normal performance as defined by a representative sample of age- and education-matched control subjects and does so on a number of tasks that tap the same component. The greater the convergence of evidence for damage to a component (and the sparing of others), the lower the likelihood that the results are due to random variation.

Another popular criticism, often voiced by those working outside cognitive neuropsychology, is that the pattern of performance may reflect the patient's efforts to compensate for their deficits in cognition rather than the operation of the normal system in the absence of one or more components. Often, however, such comments come without any suggestion as to what a plausible compensatory strategy might be that could accommodate the results. To the extent that a testable hypothesis is offered, compensatory strategies could be tested empirically. Furthermore, to the extent that the patients' performance reflects the adoption of some strategy not employed by those with intact cognitive systems, the cognitive system hypothesized on the patient data should fail to converge with that hypothesized on the basis of the data from other patients or neurally intact subjects, and consequently, the findings may eventually be discounted. Compensatory effects undoubtedly do occur. For example, as Ellis and Young (1988) point out, some patients with a particular type of acquired reading disorder, termed 'letter-by-letter' readers, learn to circumvent damage to the normal reading system by reading aloud the letters in the word and then recognizing the spelling. In this case, it seems unlikely that one would be tempted to postulate that the procedures engaged by these patients are part of the normal reading system or that any evidence would be forthcoming from normal subjects to support such a claim. Of course, more subtle strategies may be used by patients in other domains; however, erroneous assumptions about cognitive structure based on strategy should be undermined by evidence from other sources.

While these 'experiments of nature' have inherent shortcomings, they also possess advantages over other methodologies. Specifically, where localization of cognitive processes is concerned, patient data can offer stronger evidence (relative to neuroimaging data) for claims of necessity – that is, that a particular brain area is necessary for a certain cognitive process. Patient data has thus proved to be a valuable source of data that motivate hypotheses regarding both functional and cortical organization of cognitive processes. In turn, these hypotheses may be tested using a number of other methodologies.[1] In our own research program, we have attempted to corroborate patient data regarding the functional organization and localization of separable semantic and phonological short-term memory capacities using functional magnetic resonance imaging (Martin, Wu, Freedman *et al.* 2003; Martin, Burton and Hamilton 2005).

Cognitive neuropsychology and short-term/working memory

In 1974, Baddeley and Hitch proposed their influential model of working memory. Working memory was assumed to handle the temporary storage and manipulation of information required for complex cognition, including language processing. The original formulation of Baddeley and Hitch's (1974) model included three components – the phonological loop, the visuospatial sketchpad and the central executive. The phonological loop was subsequently divided into two subcomponents, a storage system which maintains information over a few seconds and a second component involved in the subvocal rehearsal. The subvocal rehearsal component is employed to refresh and maintain information in working memory. In addition, the visuospatial sketchpad was proposed as a mechanism to integrate, store and manipulate spatial and visual information. Finally, the central executive was conceived as an attentional controller that coordinated information held by the phonological loop and visuospatial sketchpad. Neuroanatomically, it has been proposed that the storage component of the phonological loop is represented in BA 40 and the rehearsal component is BA 44 and 6, while the visuospatial sketchpad is localized to the right hemisphere, including the occipital, parietal and frontal areas (Baddeley and Wilson 2002; Vallar and Papagno 1995). The central executive is commonly assumed to be related to the function of the frontal lobes.

---

[1] Despite shortcomings in inferential power, principally the correlational nature of the data, functional neuroimaging is the preeminent methodology in cognitive neuroscience. A recent review of the literature by Fellows *et al.* (2005) found that neuroimaging studies were cited three times more often than studies principally employing brain-damaged patients. Fellows *et al.* also found that neuroimaging studies more often appear in higher impact journals. Neuroimaging articles were less likely to cite patient data than patient studies were to evoke neuroimaging data. Given the emphasis on converging operations in cognitive neuroscience, this seems quite surprising.

From the outset, research made appeals to patient data to corroborate theoretical models of short-term and working memory. It was widely assumed that short-term memory was crucial for sentence comprehension (Clark and Clark 1977; Frazier and Fodor 1978). Thus, if a patient had a short-term memory deficit, as measured by a very limited span in short-term recall, this patient should show deficits in sentence comprehension. Initial studies of patients did in fact seem to provide evidence that a phonological short-term store was important in the comprehension of sentences when verbatim content was necessary to extract meaning. For example, Vallar and Baddeley (1984) reported patient PV, who was described as having a phonological short-term store deficit, did show deficits in comprehension for very long sentences, although she performed normally for shorter sentences, even if verbatim retention of information was required. Similar cases were reported by Caramazza, Basili, Koller *et al.* (1981), Caramazza Berndt and Basili (1983) and Saffran and Marin (1983).

However, in the 25 years since the Baddeley and Hitch (1974) model was introduced, several shortcoming of the original model have emerged. Perhaps one of the most conspicuous challenges for Baddeley's working memory model is the much better recall of words presented in the context of sensible prose when compared to unrelated lists of words. For example, while healthy subjects can recall a list of up to six unrelated words, they can successfully recall meaningful sentences comprised of up to 16 words (Baddeley 2000). The discrepancy between unrelated word lists and prose was assumed to be attributable to a role of LTM. However, recent data casts doubt on this hypothesis. Specifically, Baddeley and Wilson (2002) tested amnesic patients on immediate and delayed recall of prose. These amnesic patients, who have profoundly impaired long-term memory, were not impaired in the immediate recall of prose. Obviously, these data suggest LTM is not necessary for immediate recall.

As for the role of working memory in language comprehension, this assumption was also eventually undermined by patient data. Several patients with severely impaired short-term memory have been reported, who nevertheless have intact sentence comprehension, even for very complex sentences commonly assumed to make demands of short-term memory. For example, Butterworth, Campbell and Howard (1986) reported patient RE, who had a severely impaired short-term memory capacity. Despite this deficit, patient RE had little difficulty in parsing and understanding sentences even with complex syntactic structures. Moreover, patient RE could judge grammaticality of sentences that she could not repeat verbatim. Thus, Butterworth *et al.* concluded that the phonological short-term store was not necessary for sentence comprehension. Another example, patient BO, reported by Waters, Caplan and Hildebrandt (1991), who had a memory span of only two or three items, nevertheless performed normally on comprehension tasks with even very complex syntactic constructions. Patient BO even performed well on complex garden path sentences for which one might have expected reanalysis to depend on storage of a phonological representation.

Additional data from our own lab also suggests that normal language comprehension is possible for individuals with severely impaired short-term memory. Hanten and Martin (2001) reported patient BS, a developmental case of phonological short-term memory deficit, who nonetheless showed no difficulty in making anomaly judgments on sentences containing center-embedded relative clauses. These data undermine the hypothesis that phonological short-term memory is necessary for language comprehension. Despite these cases, many still commonly assume that short-term memory, particularly the phonological store, is crucial for language comprehension.

To address the shortcomings of the original Baddeley and Hitch (1974) working memory model, Baddeley has proposed an additional component to the model – the 'episodic buffer'. The episodic buffer, as proposed by Baddeley (2000), is a limited-capacity temporary storage system that integrates information from a number of sources across space and time. The episodic buffer is assumed to be dissociable from LTM, but introduces information into, and retrieves information from, long-term memory. Thus, the episodic buffer serves as an interface to integrate representations from a number of systems using a 'common multidimensional code'. More speculatively, Baddeley (2000) proposed that the episodic buffer serves as an interface between memory and conscious awareness.

Meanwhile, our lab has proposed an alternative approach to address the inconsistent association of STM and language comprehension. Martin, Shelton and Yaffee (1994) and Martin and Romani (1994) proposed a multiple capacities model in which there exist separable semantic and phonological components in short-term memory. This model was motivated principally to address the apparent inconsistencies in the relationship between short-term/working memory and language processing illuminated by patient data in cognitive neuropschology.

A multiple capacities model of short-term memory

Again, while some patients with short-term memory deficits remarkably do not show deficits in sentence comprehension, there do still exist cases that represent associations of short-term memory impairment and difficulty with language comprehension (for example, Vallar and Baddeley 1984). How are we to reconcile this apparent inconsistency?

Over the past twenty years, our lab has been examining this relationship among short-term memory, language production and comprehension. In doing so, we have proposed a novel model of STM in which there exist dissociable semantic and phonological components, each of which have unique relationships with language processing. Below, we briefly review our previous findings on short-term memory and language processing. Finally, we discuss recent experiments examining control processes that may be particularly important in deficits of semantic short-term memory.

We have reported data from a number of experiments with several brain-damaged patients that demonstrate a distinction between semantic and phonological STM deficits (Martin, Shelton and Yaffee 1994; Martin and He 2004). In addition, several neuroimaging studies support this dissociation (Martin, Wu, Freedman et al. 2003; Shivde and Thompson-Schill 2003). Based on the patient and neuroimaging data, we have proposed that maintenance of semantic representations is supported by left frontal areas, while phonological maintenance can be localized to more posterior areas such as the inferior parietal lobe.

We have also found that deficits of semantic and phonological short-term memory have very different consequences for language processing. Unlike some of the patients with phonological STM deficits, patients with semantic short-term memory deficits do have difficulty in the comprehension of some types of sentences – particularly, sentences that require maintenance of multiple semantic representations (Martin and Romani 1994; Martin and He 2004). Specifically, patients with semantic short-term memory deficits have difficulty detecting semantic anomalies embedded in sentences in which three adjectives precede a noun ('She saw the *green*, *bright*, *shining* sun, which pleased her'). When three adjectives followed the noun, as in the sentence, 'The sun was *bright*, *shining* and *green*, which pleased her', these patients performed within the range of normal healthy control subjects. Crucially, patients with semantic short-term memory deficits had no such difficulty detecting semantic anomalies when only one adjective appeared before a noun ('She saw the *green* sun, which pleased her'). Normal performance when a single anomalous adjective precedes the noun suggests that these patients do not have difficulty making semantic anomaly judgments; rather, their difficulty is with maintenance of multiple semantic representations. Moreover, Martin and Romani (1994) found that patients with phonological short-term memory deficits do not show this pattern of performance on this task.

Patients with semantic STM deficits show a similar pattern of performance in the *production* of phrases. Using a picture naming task which presented three pictures of a single object (such as 'hair') that differed in three dimensions (i.e., short vs long, blonde vs black, curly vs straight), Martin and Freedman (2001) reported that semantic short-term memory patients had great difficulty producing adjective noun phrases such as 'short, curly, blonde hair'. However, these patients were not impaired in producing shorter phrases such as 'short hair', 'curly hair' or 'blonde hair'.

Assuming a phrasal scope of planning (Smith and Wheeldon 1999), Martin *et al.* hypothesized that subjects must activate and maintain all of the lexical–semantic representations in a phrase in a lexical–semantic buffer prior to the initiation of the utterance. Presumably, patients with a semantic STM deficit are unable to maintain these representations simultaneously due to the damaged semantic STM buffer. Consequently, they place content words in separate phrases, in a piecemeal fashion, such as 'short hair … curly hair … short, curly …'. Thus in our model of short-term memory, elaborated by Martin and Freedman (2001), semantic short-term memory is important in both the comprehension and production of language. Again, semantic STM is particularly important when multiple lexical–semantic representations are to be maintained simultaneously. Additional evidence for a shared semantic buffer involved in both comprehension and production comes from recent fMRI data from our lab. We have found that the same brain areas in the left frontal lobe are recruited for both production and comprehension of adjective noun phrases like those described above (Martin, Burton and Hamilton 2005).

Executive/control processes in short-term and working memory

Until recently, we have assumed that the production and comprehension difficulties observed among semantic short-term memory patients are attributable to abnormally rapid decay of semantic representations in a semantic short-term memory buffer. Semantic short-term memory patients are thought to have better maintenance of phonological representations, at least relative to semantic retention. In contrast, we have assumed phonological short-term memory patients were plagued by rapid decay of phonological representations in short-term memory with relatively preserved semantic maintenance. Rapid decay of phonological representations was thought to have less severe implications for language production and comprehension. However, several findings have prompted us to reconsider the role of rapid decay, particularly for semantic STM deficits.

One such finding is that semantic STM patients show exaggerated interference effects when producing conjoined noun phrases in a picture naming task (Freedman, Martin and Biegler 2004). While healthy control subjects typically show interference effects when given two semantically related pictures that must be named in a single phrase (i.e., saying 'duck and swan' when presented a single display with pictures of a duck and swan), semantic STM patients showed greatly exaggerated interference effects (interference effects are calculated by comparing related picture pairs to unrelated picture pairs). Patients with phonological STM deficits did not show this effect. Importantly, both semantic and phonological short-term memory patients had similar onset latencies in naming single pictures. These exaggerated effects for the semantic STM deficit patients are thought to stem from difficulty in selecting between two semantically related representations that must be maintained in order to produce a single utterance. Evidence for this hypothesis comes from presentation of written words instead of pictures. Using written words, the interference effect for semantic relatedness disappeared for control participants and both types of patients showed only small, nonsignificant differences in onset latencies when comparing related vs unrelated pairs of words. Naming pictures requires access to and maintenance of semantic information while reading words aloud does not.

Martin and Lesch (1994) also presented data that, in some respects, are problematic for an account which emphasizes rapid decay as being the principle mechanism in semantic short-term memory deficits. Specifically, although these patients with semantic STM deficits had great difficulty recalling lists of even three words, they nevertheless produced intrusions of words from previously presented lists. In other words, these patients seemed to be extremely susceptible to effects of proactive interference. These interference effects are problematic for an account of short-term memory deficits in which failures to maintain semantic representations are attributable to rapid decay. This led us to begin a series of experiments to examine the role of proactive interference and inhibition in semantic short-term memory deficits.

Of course, inhibition and interference resolution are prominent features in several contemporary models of short-term/working memory, particularly the models of Hasher and colleagues and Engle and colleagues. Hasher and colleagues (see May, Hasher and Kane 1999) have proposed that a component of both attentional and short-term memory processes is the ability to inhibit irrelevant information. They enumerated three functions for an inhibitory mechanism 1.) it restricts access into WM to only relevant information, 2) it deletes items that were once relevant but are no longer relevant and 3.) it restrains the production of prepotent or highly probable responses until they can be adequately evaluated.

Similarly, Kane and Engle (2003) proposed that 'information maintenance in the face of interference is the critical function of working memory capacity'. Engle and colleagues have reported several tasks (Stroop, antisaccade, dichotic listening and proactive interference tasks), most seemingly unrelated to working memory, that nonetheless correlate with working memory performance. These correlations are thought to be attributable to the necessary engagement of controlled attention in all of the tasks.

Given that patients with semantic short-term memory deficits appear to be extremely sensitive to proactive interference (Martin and Lesch 1996), we asked whether one such patient would be impaired on a number of other tasks thought to require inhibition.

Proactive interference and semantic STM

We examined proactive interference and semantic short-term memory deficits in a series of experiments with Patient ML, a patient previously identified as having a semantic short-term memory deficit (see Martin and He 2004). Patient ML was tested on a number of variations of the recent negatives task, a task designed to elicit proactive interference in short-term memory (Hamilton and Martin 2005, 2007). The recent negatives task (Monsell 1978) presents a list of items serially, followed by a probe. Subjects respond 'yes' or 'no', indicating whether the probe appeared in the list. In one-half of the negative trials, the probe did not appear in the present list, but appeared in the immediately preceding list. These trials are called 'recent negatives'. For the nonrecent negative trials, the negative probe did not appear in the previous two lists. The same manipulation was applied to the positive probes – a recent positive trial included a probe that appeared in the present list as well the previous list. In a nonrecent positive trial, the probe appeared in the present list but not the previous two lists. Interference effects were calculated using the contrast of recent negative vs nonrecent negative trials – reaction times were expected to be longer and accuracy lower for the recent negatives than for the nonrecent negatives.

If ML's deficit is due to rapid decay of representations in short-term memory, then one would predict reduced or absent interference effects. However, if ML experiences an abnormal persistence of representations in short-term memory, as suggested by his performance on several other tasks, then an exaggerated interference effect would be predicted.

Data from this experiment appear in Table 11.1. As predicted by his intrusions during serial recall, ML demonstrated an exaggerated proactive interference effect in reaction time for

Table 11.1 Reaction time and accuracy for recent-negatives task controls and patient ML (from Hamilton and Martin, 2005)

	Recent negatives	Non-recent negatives	Recent positives	Non-recent positives	Interference (Recent/ non-recent negatives)
Reaction time					
Controls	1006	915	873	872	91
Patient ML	2905	2174	1474	1416	731
Accuracy (% Correct)					
Controls	94.7	98.9	98.9	98.9	4.2
Patient ML	62.5	87.5	100	96	25

recent vs nonrecent negatives (731ms)[2]. Relative to control subjects, ML's accuracy was much worse on recent negative trials (62.5 per cent) than on nonrecent negative trials (87.5 per cent). This 25 per cent difference was statistically significant ($p = 0.046$) and far outside the range for controls. ML's interference effect was 5.9 standard deviations above the mean interference effect for controls and substantially outside their range. Data from this experiment are not easily accommodated by assuming abnormally rapid decay of representations in short-term memory. In fact, given this data, the most parsimonious explanation of ML's deficit is that he has an abnormal *persistence* of activations in short-term memory. Interestingly, ML also shows exaggerated interference effects even when probes are only semantically or phonologically related to previously presented list items (see Hamilton and Martin, 2007).

Other tasks of interference and control processes

Hamilton and Martin (2005) also tested patient ML on a number of other verbal and nonverbal tasks assumed to require inhibition. Unlike the recent negatives task, none of these tasks make any obvious demands of short-term or working memory. All of these tasks are commonly considered to be tasks involving executive function. Most of these tasks were included in a factor analytic study of executive function by Miyake *et al.* (2000). Two of these tasks (the antisaccade and the Stroop tasks) loaded on an inhibition factor in the Miayke *et al.* (2000) study. Two verbal and two nonverbal tasks were selected, allowing us to determine if ML had difficulty in both the verbal and nonverbal domain. In addition to the previously described recent negatives task, a verbal and nonverbal Stroop task and the antisaccade task were administered to ML. We were especially interested in the antisaccade task, as performance on the antisaccade task and working memory measures are reported to correlate (Roberts, Hager and Heron 1994; Kane, Bleckley, Conway *et al.* 2001).

Verbal and nonverbal Stroop task. The Stroop task is widely considered the quintessential measure of inhibitory control. In the Stroop experiment, subjects name the color of the stimulus presented

2 Given common objections (see Verhaeghen and De Meersman 1998) to the use of difference scores to compare interference effects (such as when calculating interference effects using a comparison of 'incongruent' vs 'neutral' trials) for subjects showing large differences in mean reaction times (such as comparing neurologically impaired subjects vs healthy control subjects), we also calculated interference using log transformations. The log transformation minimizes the influence of outliers and the difference between logarithms (used to calculate interference effects) is equivalent to a ratio (Meiran 1996).

on the screen. Stimuli were either color words (red, green, blue, orange, yellow or purple) or rows of asterisks. The interference effect is characterized by longer onset latencies when naming the color on incongruent trials (the word RED appearing in a blue font) than when naming the color of neutral trials (a row of asterisks, *****, appearing in a blue font).

Data from the Stroop task appear in Table 11.2. While control subjects demonstrated the typical Stroop interference effect (197 ms), ML showed remarkably greater interference (969 ms). ML's interference effect was 12.4 standard deviations above the mean interference effect for controls and well outside the range of controls (101–279 ms).

Another task was designed to be analogous to the Stroop task with nonverbal stimuli. This 'nonverbal Stroop task' requires the resolution of interference when the local direction of an arrow and spatial position of the same arrow conflict. For example, when presented a right-pointing arrow on the left half of a display, participants have to indicate which direction the arrow is pointing.

Arrows pointing either to the left or right were presented on a computer display in one of three positions – either at the left of the display, at the right of the display or directly at the center of the display. Subjects were asked to press a key corresponding to the direction the arrow was pointing, regardless of the arrow's position. There were congruent trials (a right pointing arrow on the right side of the display), neutral trials (either right or left pointing arrows appearing in the middle of the display) and incongruent trials (a left pointing arrow appearing on the right side of the display). Analogous to the traditional Stroop task, interference was calculated by subtracting reaction times of neutral trials from reaction times to incongruent trials.

Patient ML's significant interference effect (106 ms) was well within the range of 15 control participants (27–29 ms). Data from the non-verbal Stroop task appear in Table 11.3. ML's mean reaction time for both incongruent and neutral trials were also within the range of healthy controls and there were no differences in accuracy for either controls or ML.

Thus, patient ML appears to be impaired on a task requiring resolution of interference with verbal materials, while being normal on an analogous task with nonverbal materials. Although one may argue that our nonverbal Stroop task differs fundamentally from the classic verbal Stroop paradigm, similar tasks have traditionally been considered to represent a variation of Stroop interference (see MacLeod 1991, for a review).

Given ML's normal performance on the nonverbal Stroop task and greatly exaggerated interference effects on both the verbal Stroop and recent negatives task, we tested the possibility that ML's deficit in inhibition was limited to the verbal domain. In order to test this possibility, we also

Table 11.2 Reaction times (RT), Interference (in ms) and accuracy (% correct) on Stroop task for controls and patient ML

	Congruent	Neutral	Incongruent	Interference
	Reaction time			
Controls	828	777	974	197*
Patient ML	1889	2470	3449	969*
	Accuracy			
Controls	98	100	93.7	
Patient ML	92	89	87	

* $p < 0.001$

Table 11.3 Reaction times (RT), Interference (in ms) and accuracy (% correct) on non-verbal Stroop task for controls and patient ML

	Congruent	Neutral	Incongruent	Interference
	Reaction time			
Controls	593	611	686	75
Patient ML	585	556	662	106

tested ML on the antisaccade task. The antisaccade task is a difficult task, with even healthy undergraduate subjects reaching accuracy in the range of 79–88 per cent (Roberts *et al.* 1994). Thus data from the antisaccade task allows us to address whether ML's difference in performance on verbal and nonverbal Stroop inhibition tasks was attributable merely to task difficulty.

Antisaccade task. The antisaccade task requires subjects to inhibit reflexive eye movements to sudden onsets of stimuli presented in the periphery of the visual field. After withholding an eye movement to the sudden onset of a cue stimulus, subjects are asked to make an eye movement in the opposite direction, where a target is briefly presented (for 150 ms) on the other side of the display. Although this task has no obvious short-term or working memory requirements, performance on the antisaccade task has been reported to correlate with working memory ability (Kane *et al.* 2001; Mitchell, Macrae and Gilchrist 2002; Roberts *et al.* 1994).

Each trial began with a fixation point followed by a cue briefly presented on either the left or right side of the display, 3.4″ from fixation, for 175 ms. The cue was followed by a target that appeared on the opposite side of the screen, 3.4″ from fixation, for 150 ms. The cue was a small black square, while the target was an arrow that pointed to the left, up or right. After 150 ms the target was replaced by cross-hatching to mask any after-images which might aid subjects in identifying the target. Correct identification of the target required the participant to press one of three keys corresponding to left, right, and up. Participants must resist making a reflexive saccade to the initial cue in order to detect the target on the opposite side of the screen. Given the brief presentation of the target, the target is difficult, if not impossible, to identify if the participant makes an initial saccade to the cue.

Data from the antisaccade task appear in Table 11.4. ML's accuracy (80 per cent) was actually higher than the mean for controls (72 per cent, range = 59–94 per cent). His mean reaction time (724 ms) was below controls (771 ms) and was well within the range of the controls 492–1394ms).

Thus, ML performed normally on the antisaccade task. ML's normal level of performance on the antisaccade task would seem contrary to findings from normal participants, indicating a relation between antisaccade performance and working memory capacity (Kane *et al.* 2001).

Table 11.4 Reaction times (RT, in ms), interference and accuracy (% correct) on anstisaccade task

	Prosaccade	Antisaccade
	Reaction time	
Controls	485	771
Patient ML	521	724
	Accuracy	
Controls	97	72
Patient ML	93	80

Discussion

In this chapter we have discussed several models of short-term or working memory and their ability to accommodate data from both cognitive neuropsychology and cognitive psychology. We have briefly outlined the influential Baddeley and Hitch (1974) model of working memory and the more recent iteration of the model proposed by Baddeley (2000). The more recent model has added a fourth component, the episodic buffer, to address several shortcomings of the original model. Our lab has taken a different approach and proposed a multiple capacities model of short-term memory, in which there exist dissociable semantic and phonological retention components. This model has been developed to address the relationship between short-term memory and language processing. Control processes or executive functions are thought to be important for both components, although they may be particularly important for semantic short-term memory. However, in anticipation of an obvious question, could we also explain these data by simply assuming that these patients have deficits localized to the episodic buffer (Baddeley 2000)?

One set of data that are problematic for an episodic buffer account is ML's poorer comprehension of phrases in which several adjectives precede a noun, such as 'green, bright, shining sun' compared to when the same adjectives follow the noun as in 'sun was shining, bright and green'? In the current formulation of the episodic buffer (Baddeley 2000, 2003), there is no a priori reason to expect that a patient with an episodic buffer deficit would have greater difficulty when three adjectives appear before a noun than when the adjectives appear after a noun. Given that the episodic buffer is recruited when the task demands presumably exceed the capacity of the phonological loop, why would one construction be more difficult than the other?

Even more problematic for an episodic buffer account is the excellent memory for prose demonstrated by patients with semantic short-term memory deficits. Romani and Martin (1999) compared a patient with a semantic short-term memory deficit, patient AB, with two amnesic patients on several tasks of long-term memory and learning. These tasks included both verbal and nonverbal stimuli. Patient AB performed normally on long-term memory tasks in which pictures or shapes were presented, but was very impaired on paired-associates tasks and repeated-list learning consisting of words. Remarkably, however, AB had no difficulty with long-term retention of prose (assessed by a yes/no and multiple choice questions). Similar results were obtained with patient ML, who also scored within the normal on long-term memory for prose.3 Given that one of the principle motivations for proposing the episodic buffer was the better recall of prose than unrelated words, these data from AB and ML are particularly problematic for this model.

In addition to the episodic buffer, Baddeley and Wilson (2002) and Baddeley (2003) have also proposed that the episodic buffer 'depends heavily' on executive processes for the combination of words, phrases and semantic representations during prose comprehension. Again relevant to this point is the data of patient ML, another semantic short-term memory patient whom, like patient AB reported by Romani and Martin (1999), also shows normal prose comprehension despite a semantic short-term memory impairment. This is notable, because as summarized above and reported by Hamilton and Martin (2005), ML is greatly impaired on some tasks tapping 'executive processes'. Specifically, ML is impaired on tasks consisting of verbal stimuli that require

---

3 Similar results were obtained for patient ML. On story memory tests where a 45-minute filled interval intervened between story presentation and test, ML scored 66 per cent correct on narrative stories (control range: 63–84 per cent), 71 per cent correct on descriptive stories (control range: 69–81 per cent), and 82 per cent on a mixed set of stories (control range: 72–100 per cent). See Romani and Martin (1999) for details on materials and procedure.

resolution of interference (e.g., Stroop task and a proactive interference task), but performs normally on nonverbal tasks that demand interference resolution (e.g., antisaccade task, nonverbal Stroop task). The presence of intact prose comprehension with greatly impaired executive control processes would not be predicted by the Baddeley (2000) model in its present formulation.

Similarly, it is not obvious how Baddeley's (2000) revised model of working memory would accommodate the verbal vs nonverbal dissociations in tasks of executive control reported by Hamilton and Martin (2005). Given that the episodic buffer and central executive is claimed to coordinate the manipulation of representations or codes from multiple systems (Baddeley 2000, p. 421), it is presently unclear why ML would show a deficit for tasks that require resolution of interference only in verbal tasks.

We also believe that the data we have presented here have implications for other models of working memory that emphasize the role of controlled attention. Some may raise the objection that ML may indeed have a short-term memory impairment, but not necessarily a *working memory* deficit. From this perspective, ML's normal performance on the antisaccade task may not be deemed relevant to claims about working memory as his span deficit could be attributed purely to a STM deficit rather than to a working memory deficit. For example, in the model postulated by Engle, Tuholski, Laughlin and Conway (1999), working memory is composed of STM storage plus central executive function. Thus, patient ML's deficit might be considered restricted to the STM storage component. However given ML's performance on the Stroop task and recent negatives task, it seems certain that ML should be considered as having deficient attentional control.

The dissociation between Stroop and antisaccade performance challenges many of the individual differences studies examining controlled attention and working memory with healthy subjects. For example, Kane and Engle (2003) proposed that a single mechanism, localized to the dorsolateral prefrontal cortex, is involved in performance of the antisaccade task, Stroop task and resolution of proactive interference. Here, we have presented a patient with a deficit of short-term memory (he is unable to reliably recall even three items during serial recall), who performs very poorly on the Stroop task as well as tasks that promote proactive interference, but nevertheless has no difficulty with the antisaccade task. Such a pattern of performance would seem to indicate that these three tasks do not involve the same brain region. Moreover, these tasks loaded on a single factor in the factor analytic studies (Miyake *et al.* 2000, Friedman and Miyake 2004).

If tasks dissociate in a brain-damaged patient, how are we to explain the correlations among these tasks found in experiments conducted with healthy undergraduate subjects? As argued in Hamilton and Martin (2005), it may be that correlations among these tasks in neurally intact individuals result from the activity of catecholamines. Catecholamines are a family of neurotransmitters that include dopamine, norepinephrine, and epinephrine. Indeed, it has been known for over two decades that catecholamines influence working memory performance. Excellent reviews of this literature appear in Arnsten and Robbins (2002) and Arnsten and Li (2005). In general, low doses of dopamine agonists (which generally serve to increase the availability of dopamine in the brain) improve working memory and attention performance. This literature is of course complicated by a number of dopamine subreceptors, many of which may have different neuromodulatory influences and pharmacological agents with differing affinities for each subreceptor.

Another catecholamine, norepinephrine, has also been implicated in executive function and control processes. For example, administration of guanfacine, an α-2A-adrenoceptor agonist, is reported to improve working memory performance and increases resistance to distractability in monkeys (Arnsten and Li 2005). Similarly, Steere and Arnsten (1997) reported that administration of guanfacine improved performance on a 'reversal of visual object discrimination task'.

In this task, monkeys were presented with three objects, only one of which was associated with a food reward. Objects were drawn from a pool of over 2000 objects that differed in shape and color. Once monkeys reached a criterion level of performance (successfully choosing the stimulus associated with food award), the contingencies were reversed and the object least preferred by the monkey in previous sessions now became the rewarded object (the object associated with a food reward). Thus, this task is analogous to many tasks of 'executive function', in that the monkeys have to inhibit or suppress no longer relevant information in order to perform a subsequent task.

Of course, dopamine has also been implicated in a number of conditions in which deficits of executive function are considered a cardinal feature. Parkinson's disease, schizophrenia and attention deficit hyperactivity disorder have all been related to dysfunction of dopaminergic systems and are also associated with deficits of working memory and executive function. Administration of dopaminergic drugs such as methylphenidate to healthy subjects does appear to improve performance on some working memory tasks and memory retrieval functions. However, these drugs may actually impair performance on other tasks (see Arnsten and Robbins 2002, for a review of both facilitative and detrimental effects).

Thus, although the data from Hamilton and Martin (2005) suggest that different brain regions may be involved in inhibition tasks, these regions may be modulated by relatively few neuro-transmitter mechanisms. To the extent that there exists individual differences and variability in the function of these neuromodulatory systems among individuals, these systems may represent an explanation of the individual differences and factor analytic studies reported by Engle and colleagues and Miyake *et al.* (2000).

Conclusions

In this chapter we have attempted to illustrate how careful testing of single case studies may provide valuable data with implications for theories of working and short-term memory. Data obtained from patients with deficits of short-term memory have revealed several interesting insights. First, although it would seem intuitively likely that deficits of short-term memory might necessarily be associated with deficits in language comprehension, this does not appear to be the case. Several patients with deficits of phonological short-term memory, whom nonetheless have completely intact language comprehension, even for syntactically complex sentence structures, have been reported. To address this discrepancy, Martin and colleagues have proposed dissociable phonological and semantic short-term memory buffers. Testing of patients with semantic short-term memory deficits has revealed that they do have difficulty with sentence comprehension and production, specifically when successful comprehension or production requires maintenance of multiple semantic representations. We have also found that patients with phonological short-term memory deficits do not have these deficits in language processing.

Another area of inquiry is the role of executive control processes in semantic short-term memory and language processing in general (also see Novick, Trueswell and Thompson-Schill 2005). Hamilton and Martin (2005) found that difficulty with verbal tasks of inhibition may be associated with semantic short-term memory deficits. However, future research is needed to replicate this association. Moreover, it was discovered that tasks reported to correlate in healthy subjects (Stroop, antisaccade and susceptibility to proactive interference) are, in fact, dissociable in patient ML. This suggests that the correlations may not be attributable to a common neural substrate (i.e., the dorsolateral prefrontal cortex), but instead to some other variable. We propose that the neuromodulatory influences of various catecholamines may be responsible for the shared variance among these tasks.

Acknowledgment

Preparation of this manuscript was supported in part by NIH grant DC-00218 to Rice University.

References

Arnsten, AFT and Li, B-M (2005). Neurobiology of executive functions: Catecholamine influences on prefrontal cortical functions. *Biological Psychiatry*, *57*, 1377–1384.

Arnsten, AFT and Robbins, TW (2002). Neurochemical modulation of prefrontal cortical function in humans and animals. In DT Stuss and RT Knight (eds), *Principles of Frontal Lobe Function*. New York: Oxford University Press.

Baddeley, A (2000). The episodic buffer: a new component of working memory? *Trends in Cognitive Sciences*, *4*(11), 417–423.

Baddeley, A (2003). Working memory and language: an overview. *Journal of Communication Disorders*, *36*, 189–208.

Baddeley, AD and Hitch, GJ (1974). Working memory. In GH Bower (ed), *The Psychology of Learning and Motivation*, *Vol. 8* (pp. 47–90). London: Academic Press.

Baddeley, A and Wilson, BA (2002). Prose recall and amnesia: implications for the structure of working memory. *Neuropsychologia*, *40*(2), 1737–1743.

Butterworth, B, Campbell, R and Howard, D (1986). The uses of short-term memory: A case study. *The Quarterly Journal of Experimental Psychology*, *38A*, 705–737.

Caramazza, A (1984). The logic of neuropsychological research and the problem of patient classification in aphasia. *Brain and Language*, *21*, 9–20.

Caramazza, A (1986). On drawing inferences about the structure of normal cognitive systems from the analysis of patterns of impaired performance: The case for single-patient studies. *Brain and Cognition*, *5*, 41–66.

Caramazza, A, Basili, AG, Koller, JJ and Berndt, RS (1981). An investigation of repetition and language processing in a case of conduction aphasia. *Brain and Language*, *14*, 235–275.

Caramazza, A, Berndt, RS and Basili, AG (1983). The selective impairment of phonological processing: A case study. *Brain and Language*, *18*, 128–174.

Clark, HH and Clark, EV (1977). *Psychology and Language: An introduction to psycholinguistics*. New York: Harcourt Brace Jovanovich.

Coltheart, M (2004). Brain imaging, connectionism, and cognitive neuropsychology. *Cognitive Neuropsychology*, *21*(1), 21–25.

Ellis, AW and Young, AW (1988). *Human Cognitive Neuropsychology*. Hove: Lawrence Erlbaum Associates, Ltd.

Engle, RW and Kane, MJ (2004). Executive attention, working memory capacity and a two-factor theory of cognitive control. *The Psychology of Learning and Motivation*, *44*, 145–199.

Engle, RW, Tuholski, SW, Laughlin, JE and Conway, AR (1999). Working memory, short-term memory, and general fluid intelligence: a latent-variable approach. *Journal of Experimental Psychology: General*, *128*(3), 309–331.

Fellows, LK, Heberlein, AS, Morales, DA, Shivde, G, Waller, S and Wu, DH (2005). Method matters: An empirical study of impact in cognitive neuroscience, *Journal of Cognitive of Neuroscience*, *17*(6), 850–858.

Frazier, L and Fodor, JD (1978). The sausage machine: A new two-stage parsing model. *Cognition*, *6*, 291–325.

Freedman, M, Martin, R and Biegler, K (2004). Semantic relatedness effects in conjoined noun phrase production: Implications for the role of short-term memory. *Cognitive Neuropsychology*, *21*(2–4), 245–265.

Friedman, NP and Miyake, A (2004). The relations among inhibition and interference control functions: A latent variable analysis. *Journal of Experimental Psychology: General*, *133*, 101–135.

Hamilton, AC and Martin, RC (2005). Dissociations among tasks involving inhibition: A single-case study. *Cognitive, Affective and Behavioral Neuroscience*, *5*(1), 1–13.

Hamilton, AC and Martin, RC (2007). Proactive interference in a semantic short-term memory deficit: Role of semantic and phonological relatedness. *Cortex, 43,* 112–23.

Hanten, G and Martin, R (2001). A developmental short-term memory deficit: A case study. *Brain and Cognition, 45,* 164–188.

Kane, MJ, Bleckley, MK, Conway, ARA and Engle, RW (2001). A controlled-attention view of working-memory capacity. *Journal of Experimental Psychology: General, 130*(2), 169–183.

Kane, MJ and Engle, RW (2003). Working memory capacity and the control of attention: The contributions of goal neglect, response competition, and task set to Stroop interference. *Journal of Experimental Psychology: General, 132,* 47–70.

MacLeod, CM (1991). Half a century of research on the Stroop effect: An integrative review. *Psychonomic Bulletin, 109,* 163–203.

Martin, RC, Burton, PC and Hamilton, AC (2005). Left inferior frontal involvement in semantic retention during phrase comprehension and production: Evidence from functional neuroimaging. *Brain and Language, 95,* 249–250.

Martin, RC and Freedman, ML (2001). Short-term retention of lexical-semantic representations: Implications for speech production. *Memory, 9*(4/5/6), 261–280.

Martin, RC and He, T (2004). Semantic short-term memory and its role in sentence processing: a replication. *Brain and Language, 89*(1), 76–82.

Martin, RC and Lesch, MF (1996). Associations and dissociations between language impairment and list recall: Implications for models of short-term memory. In S Gathercole (ed), *Models of Short-term Memory* (pp. 149–178). Hove, UK: Lawrence Erlbaum Associates Ltd.

Martin, RC and Romani, C (1994). Verbal working memory and sentence comprehension: A multiple-components view. *Neuropsychology, 8*(4), 506–523.

Martin, RC, Shelton, JR and Yaffee, LS (1994). Language processing and working memory: Neuropsychological evidence for separate phonological and semantic capacities. *Journal of Memory and Language, 33*(1), 83–111.

Martin, RC, Wu, D, Freedman, M, Jackson, EF and Lesch, M (2003). An event-related fMRI investigation of phonological versus semantic short-term memory. *Journal of Neurolinguistics. Special Issue: Functional neuroimaging contributions to neurolinguistics, 16*(4–5), 341–360.

May, CP, Hasher, L and Kane, MJ (1999). The role of interference in memory span. *Memory and Cognition, 27,* 759–767.

McCloskey, M (1993). Theory and evidence in cognitive neuropsychology: A 'radical' response to Robertson, Knight, Rafal, and Shimamura (1993). *Journal of Experimental Psychology: Learning, Memory, and Cognition, 19*(3), 718–734.

McCloskey, M (2001). The future of cognitive neuropsychology. In B Rapp (ed), *The Handbook of Cognitive Neuropsychology*. Philadelphia, PA: Taylor and Francis.

Meiran, N (1996). Reconfiguration of processing mode prior to task performance. *Journal of Experimental Psychology: Learning, Memory and Cognition, 22,* 1423–1442.

Mitchell, JP, Macrae, CN and Gilchrist, ID (2002). Working memory and suppression of reflexive saccades. *Journal of Cognitive Neuroscience, 14,* 95–103.

Miyake, A, Friedman, NP, Emerson, MJ, Witzki, AH, Howerter, A and Wager, TD (2000). The unity and diversity of executive functions and their contributions to complex 'Frontal Lobe' tasks: a latent variable analysis. *Cognitive Psychology, 41*(1), 49–100.

Monsell, S (1978). Recency, immediate recognition memory, and reaction time. *Cognitive Psychology, 10,* 465–501.

Novick, JM, Trueswell, JC and Thompson-Schill, SL (2005). Cognitive control and parsing: Reexamining the role of Broca's area in sentence comprehension. *Cognitive, Affective, and Behavioral Neuroscience, 5*(3), 263–281.

Rapp, B (2001). *The Handbook of Cognitive Neuropsychology: What deficits reveal about the human mind.* Philadelphia, PA: Psychology Press.

Roberts, RJ, Hager, LD and Heron C (1994). Prefrontal cognitive processes: Working memory and inhibition in the antisaccade task. *Journal of Experimental Psychology: General, 123*, 374–393.

Romani, C and Martin, RC (1999). A deficit in the short-term retention of lexical-semantic information: Forgetting words, but remembering a story. *Journal of Experimental Psychology: General, 128*, 56–77.

Saffran, E and Marin, OSM (1975). Immediate memory for word lists and sentences in a patient with deficient auditory short-term memory. *Brain and Language, 2*, 420–433.

Shivde, G and Thompson-Schill, S (2004). Dissociating semantic and phonological maintenance using fMRI. *Cognitive, Affective and Behavioral Neuroscience, 4*(1), 10–19.

Smith, M and Wheeldon, LR (1999). High level processing scope in spoken sentence production. *Cognition, 73*, 205–246.

Steere, JC and Arnsten, AFT (1997). The α–2A noradrenergic receptor agonist guanfacine improves visual object discrimination reversal performance in aged rhesus monkeys. *Behavioral Neuroscience, 111*(5), 883–891.

Vallar, G and Baddeley, AD (1984). Phonological short-term store, phonological processing and sentence comprehension: A neuropsychological case study. *Cognitive Neuropsychology, 1*(2), 121–141.

Vallar, G and Papagno, C (1995). Neuropsychological impairments of short-term memory. In A Baddeley, B Wilson, F Watts (eds), *Handbook of Memory Disorders*, (pp. 135–165). New York: Wiley.

Verhaeghen, P and De Meersman, L (1998). Aging and Stroop effect: A meta-analysis. *Psychology and Aging, 13*, 120–126.

Wanner, E and Maratsos, M (1978). An ATN approach to comprehension. In M Halle, J Bresnan, and GA Miller (eds), *Linguistic Theory and Psychological Reality* (pp. 119–161). Cambridge, MA: MIT Press.

Waters, G, Caplan, D and Hildebrandt, N (1991). On the structure and function role of auditory-verbal short-term memory in sentence comprehension: A case study. *Cognitive Neuropsychology, 2*, 81–126.

12

Top-down modulation in visual working memory

Adam Gazzaley and Mark D'Esposito

Working memory (WM) is a construct that encompasses our ability to temporarily maintain and manipulate information that is no longer accessible in the environment for a brief period of time in order to guide subsequent behavior (Baddeley 1986). A majority of the research over the last thirty years directed at understanding the neural basis of WM has focused on characterizing the pattern of neural activity that occurs when active representations of recently presented information are maintained prior to an action guided by these maintained representations. This focus was launched with physiology studies that first discovered persistent activity in prefrontal cortex (PFC) neurons in monkeys during this processing stage (Fuster and Alexander 1971; Kubota and Niki 1971), and has continued to thrive with dozens of single unit recording studies in experimental animals (Chafee and Goldman-Rakic 1998; Funahashi, Bruce and Goldman-Rakic 1989; Fuster 1990; Miller, Li and Desimone 1991; Niki, Sakai and Kubota 1972; Watanabe and Niki 1985; Wilson, Scalaidhe and Goldman-Rakic 1993) and functional imaging studies utilizing WM paradigms in human subjects (Courtney, Ungerleider, Keil *et al.* 1997; D'Esposito, Postle and Rypma 2000; Jha and McCarthy 2000; Postle, Druzgal and D'Esposito 2003; Ranganath and D'Esposito 2001).

Recently, our laboratory has investigated the neural mechanisms underlying encoding processes, that is, the processes that influence what information is actively maintained, and what is not. It is clear that ability to actively maintain relevant information will depend critically on how well such representations are generated during encoding. Furthermore, active representations are susceptible to interference by distracting information (Miller, Erickson and Desimone 1996). In the real world, as compared to the artificial environment of WM tasks, multiple streams of information reach our awareness, some of it relevant, some not for the task at hand. Given the inherent capacity limitations of WM (Luck and Vogel 1997), it is essential that only representations of task-relevant information are generated and maintained in the first place. Thus, an important aspect of goal-directed behavior is understanding the neural mechanisms underlying how task-relevant versus task-irrelevant information is differentially processed.

To investigate the neural mechanisms underlying goal-directed behavior, we have focused on the process of *top-down modulation*. Human interaction with our environment involves a fluid integration of externally driven perceptual information that demands attention based on stimulus salience or novelty (bottom-up processes) and internally driven, goal-directed decisions concerning external stimuli or stored representations (top-down modulation) (Bar 2003; Frith 2001). Top-down modulation has been described both when a stimulus is present in the environment – e.g., selective attention and memory encoding (Bar 2003; Pessoa, Kastner and Ungerleider 2003; Treue and Martinez Trujillo 1999; Wojciulik, Kanwisher and Driver 1998) – and when a stimulus is absent – e.g., mental imagery, working memory maintenance and anticipation (Fuster 1990; Ishai, Haxby and Ungerleider 2002; Kastner, Pinsk, De Weerd *et al.* 1999; Miller,

Li and Desimone 1993). It underlies our ability to selectively focus on relevant stimuli and ignore distracting stimuli, establishing a foundation for attention and memory. Understanding the cognitive and neural mechanisms of top-down modulation are important for reconciling the large body of literature that exists for both attention and memory processes. It has long been acknowledged that these processes, especially WM and selective attention, are similar conceptually, but have traditionally been classified separately and studied independently. It is only recently that the mechanistic overlap of these processes has become the subject of a concerted research focus (Awh and Jonides 2001; de Fockert, Rees, Frith *et al.* 2001; Desimone 1996; LaBar, Gitelman, Parrish *et al.* 1999). Evidence has revealed that selective attention is necessary to restrict the contents of capacity-limited memory networks to task-relevant representations (Rainer, Asaad and Miller 1998), thus favoring successful memory performance by limiting interference from task-irrelevant representations (Ploner *et al.* 2001).

The theoretical framework of the neural basis of top-down modulation relies on extensive evidence from single-cell physiology, functional neuroimaging and EEG data, revealing increased activity in specialized posterior cortical regions – the presumed sites of neural representation – when attention is directed toward a stimulus or stimulus attribute (Barcelo, Suwazono and Knight 2000; Corbetta, Miezin, Dobmeyer *et al.* 1990; Kastner and Ungerleider 2001; Moran and Desimone 1985; Pessoa, Kastner and Ungerleider 2003). Descriptions of top-down modulation of activity magnitude has been described for the auditory (Hillyard, Hink, Schwent *et al.* 1973), olfactory (Zelano *et al.* 2005) and somatosensory (Seminowicz, Mikulis and Davis 2004) systems, but the modality most studied has been vision. Physiological and neuroimaging studies have revealed that neural activity is enhanced in the visual association cortex (VAC) for behaviorally relevant visual stimuli (Duncan, Humphreys and Ward 1997; Fuster 1990; Hopfinger, Buonocore and Mangun 2000; Kanwisher and Wojciulik 2000). Reciprocal *suppression* of activity in visual regions that encode non-relevant stimuli has also been reported (Duncan, Humphreys and Ward 1997; Kastner, De Weerd, Desimone *et al.* 1998; Kastner and Ungerleider 2001). In this *biased competition model*, suppression occurs due to competition of multiple stimuli for limited visual processing resources (Desimone and Duncan 1995).

Enhancement and suppression: defining neural measures

Our recent experiments have focused on studying top-down enhancement and suppression of neural activity while a stimulus is being presented in a WM task. Experimental paradigms directed at understanding the neural mechanisms of WM maintenance are often delay tasks, designed to temporally isolate WM component processes. In a typical delayed recognition trial, the subject is first required to remember a stimulus presented during a 'cue' period and then maintain this information for a brief 'delay' interval when the stimulus is absent. Lastly, the subject responds to a 'probe' stimulus to determine whether the information was successfully retained. Thus, the cognitive stages are segregated in time and can be investigated in relative isolation by recording during these distinct stages with microelectrodes in animals and event-related fMRI in human participants. We have modified the classic delayed-recognition task to study the processes of enhancement and suppression directly. We identify distinct measures of top-down enhancement and suppression by utilizing a paradigm we developed consisting of three tasks in which aspects of visual information are held constant while task-demands are manipulated (Figure 12.1) (Gazzaley, Cooney, McEvoy *et al.* 2005a). During each trial, participants observe sequences of two faces and two natural scenes presented in a randomized order. The tasks differ in the instructions informing the participants how to process the stimuli: (1) *Remember faces and ignore scenes*, (2) *Remember scenes and ignore faces*, or (3) *Passively view*

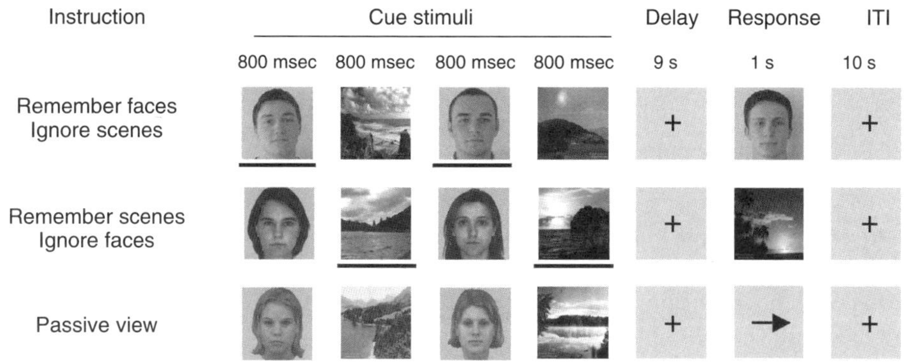

Figure 12.1 Experimental design of the selective working memory task. Tasks differed in the instructions given at the beginning of each run and in the response requirements. Participants were instructed to (1) Remember faces and ignore scenes, (2) Remember scenes and ignore faces, and (3) Passively view both faces and scenes – with no attempt to remember or evaluate them. In the memory trials response period, a face or scene stimulus was presented (depending upon the condition), and participants were required to report with a button press whether the stimulus matched one of the previously presented stimuli. During the response period of the Passive view task, an arrow was presented and participants were required to make a button press indicating the direction of the arrow. (Adapted from Gazzaley et al. (2005a) J Cogn Neurosci, 17(3), 507–517.)

faces and scenes without attempting to remember them. In each task, the period in which the cue stimuli are presented is balanced for bottom-up visual information, thus allowing us to probe the influence of goal-directed behavior on neural activity (top-down modulation). In the two memory tasks, the encoding of the task-relevant stimuli requires selective attention and thus permits the dissociation of physiological measures of enhancement and suppression relative to the passive baseline. For example, measures of neural activity above passive baseline reflect enhancement, and activity below baseline is suppression. Also in the memory tasks, after a 9 s delay, the participants are tested on their ability to recognize a probe stimulus as being one of the task-relevant cues, yielding a behavioral measure of WM performance. In addition, a post-experiment surprise recognition memory enables us to evaluate incidental long-term memory of the stimuli.

The experiments we performed using this paradigm employed both event-related functional MRI (fMRI) and electroencephalography (EEG) on counterbalanced sessions to record correlates of neural activity while the participants performed the task. This allowed us capitalize on the high spatial resolution achievable with the fMRI Blood Oxygen Level Dependent (BOLD) signal and the high temporal resolution attained when recording electrical activity with EEG. Although both measures are thought to reflect cortical activity driven by local cortical processing and the summation of postsynaptic potentials on synchronously active, large ensembles of neurons (Chawla, Lumer and Friston 1999; Logothetis, Pauls, Augath et al. 2001; Silva 1991), changes in BOLD signal can be localized to cortical regions separated by millimeters and EEG can resolve activity changes in the millisecond range. Thus these techniques offer complementary but unique information to study the modulation of activity at the neuronal population level.

Our original research focus was to identify neural measures of both the enhancement and suppression of neural activity associated with task-relevant and task-irrelevant information, respectively. Inherent to theories of top-down modulation is the concept that neural activity is modulated relative to a level of activity generated when a stimulus is passively viewed and no goal-directed decisions are performed, i.e. its bottom-up, perceptual influence. Neural activity in response to viewing a stimulus may be differentially enhanced or suppressed relative to this level of activity if it is respectively attended or ignored. Despite this logic, modulation relative to a stimulus-present, neutral baseline has rarely been evaluated and comparisons are usually made between attend and ignore tasks or relative to a resting baseline without visual stimulation (Eimer 2000; Holmes, Vuilleumier and Eimer 2003; O'Craven, Downing and Kanwisher 1999; Pinsk, Doniger and Kastner 2004; Rees, Frith and Lavie 1997; Vuilleumier, Armony, Driver *et al.* 2001; Wojciulik, Kanwisher and Driver 1998). Without establishing a perceptual baseline level of activity, it is not possible to interpret top-down influences as representing enhancement or suppression. While modulation both above and below a perceptual baseline has not yet been reported with neuroimaging data, the presence of enhancement and suppression has been suggested in EEG studies of spatial attention documenting a decreased amplitude of the P1 component for ignored locations and increased amplitude of the N1 component for attended locations, both relative to a baseline obtained with 'neutral' trials when attention was unfocused or broadly focused (Luck and Hillyard 1995; Luck *et al.* 1994). The passive viewing task utilized in our experiment established a perceptual, bottom-up baseline from which activity in the remember tasks could be compared.

We chose to focus our first study on activity measures of enhancement and suppression obtained from visual association cortex of young healthy participants. For fMRI, we used an independent functional localizer to identify both stimulus-selective *face* regions and *scene* regions in the fusiform gyrus and the parahippocampal/lingual gyrus, respectively. For the purpose of this chapter, we will focus on the fMRI data from the left scene-selective region since it yielded the most robust measures of top-down modulation. For EEG, we utilized a face-selective event-related potential (ERP), the N170, a component localized to posterior occipital electrodes and reflecting visual association cortex activity with face specificity (Bentin, Allison, Puce *et al.* 1996). Our fMRI and EEG data revealed top-down modulation of both activity magnitude and processing speed occur above and below a perceptual baseline depending on task instruction (Figure 12.2). Modulation of the processing speed as reflected by a shift in the latency of the N170 was a novel finding that revealed another aspect of top-down modulation. It suggested that in addition to modifying activity magnitude, top-down influences can modulate the time-course of neural activity, as reflected by a shorter time to reach maximal synchronized neural activity (Silva 1991). It has been proposed that amplification of activity magnitude improves signal/noise ratio, allowing more information to be extracted from relevant stimuli (Hillyard, Vogel and Luck 1998). Likewise, faster processing speed reflects an augmentation in the efficiency of neural processing, further facilitating information extraction.

It is well documented that the nervous system utilizes interleaved inhibitory and excitatory mechanisms throughout the neuroaxis (e.g., spinal reflexes, cerebellar outputs and basal ganglia movement control networks). It is thus not surprising that top-down modulation would utilize both enhancement and suppression to control the impact of sensory information on neural activity, providing a powerful contrast for sculpting these neural processes (Knight, Staines, Swick *et al.* Chao 1999; Shimamura 1997). Thus, by generating contrast via enhancing and suppressing activity magnitude and processing speed, top-down signals bias the likelihood of successful representation of relevant information in a competitive system.

A unique aspect of this study was that the relevant and irrelevant stimuli were presented sequentially. Most selective attention studies that have assessed activity modulation have used tasks in which multiple stimuli were presented *simultaneously* (O'Craven, Downing and Kanwisher 1999; Vuilleumier, Armony, Driver *et al.* 2001; Wojciulik, Kanwisher and Driver 1998), and so modulation was considered to be driven by competition for limited perceptual processing resources. In contrast, our findings reveal that modulation of activity magnitude can occur based

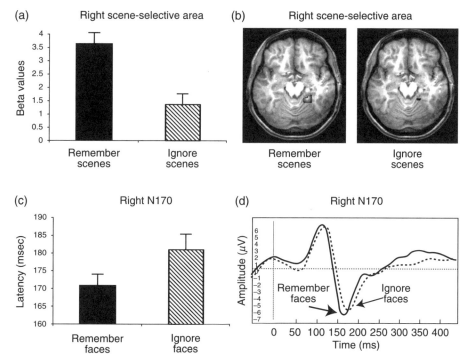

Figure 12.2 Activity data for *Remember* and *Ignore* conditions: fMRI and ERP. (a) Group data: Average beta values in the scene selective area revealing greater activity in Remember scenes vs Ignore scenes condition. (b) A representative subject demonstrating the BOLD signal level within the masked scene selective in Remember scenes vs Ignore scenes condition. (c) Group data: Average peak latency for the right N170 in PO8 electrode revealing earlier latency for Remember faces vs Ignore faces. (d) Grand-averaged waveforms of the time-locked ERPs to face stimuli revealing earlier latency for Remember faces vs Ignore faces. Error bars indicate standard error of the mean. (Adapted from Gazzaley *et al.* (2005a) *J Cogn Neurosci*, *17* (3), 507–517.) See also color plate 5.

on task-relevancy that directs differential attention to *sequentially* presented stimuli, without competition for perceptual processing resources. Thus, we inferred that modulation was needed to resolve competition for limited working memory resources. This finding supports a more general model of top-down modulation in which goal-directed decisions modulate activity levels to resolve competition for limitations in cognitive resources, whether perceptual or mnemonic (Ranganath, DeGutis and D'Esposito 2004).

Enhancement and suppression: dissociable processes?

Using the selective WM paradigm we developed, we are able to generate distinct measures of top-down enhancement and suppression by calculating the fMRI BOLD magnitude and ERP component amplitude or latency difference between the remember condition and passive view (enhancement), or between passive view and the ignore condition (suppression). An important question that emerged was whether or not these two processes are mechanistically dissociable? If they have independent control processes, either anatomically or neurochemically, then they might be differentially affected by aging or disease. Our first attempt at addressing this was to study top-down modulation using this paradigm in a population of healthy older participants (Gazzaley, Cooney, Rissman *et al.* 2005b). In this population, we predicted that we would see a shift in the balance between enhancement and suppression. It is well-established that many aspects of cognition decline with normal aging (Craik and Salthouse 2000). However, behavioural evidence exploring the interaction between attention and WM in aging suggests that age-related WM impairments are associated with increased sensitivity to interference from task-irrelevant information (Hasher and Zacks 1988; May, Hasher and Kane 1999; West 1999). We hypothesized that the older individuals may have a selective deficit in their ability to suppress task-irrelevant information. Such a select deficit would provide evidence for dissociable mechanisms of enhancement and suppression.

In a recent publication, we compared the fMRI BOLD signal magnitude between the tasks within each group of younger (n = 17, 19–30 years of age) and older participants (n = 16, 60–77 years of age) (Figure 12.3). Direct comparisons of BOLD signal across age groups revealed a significantly greater signal magnitude within the scene-selective region in the older group than in the younger group in the Ignore scenes condition (*p* <0.005), while no age-related differences existed between the Remember scenes (*p* = 0.37) or Passive view conditions (*p* = 0.96). These comparisons reveal the presence of a selective age-related deficit in the suppression of task-irrelevant information. To further compare across age groups, we calculated three modulation indices: overall modulation index (Remember scenes – Ignore scenes), enhancement index (Remember scenes – Passive view) and suppression index (Passive view – Ignore scenes). The use of these indices enabled across-group comparisons to be performed without directly contrasting BOLD signal magnitude between populations that might have vascular responsivity differences

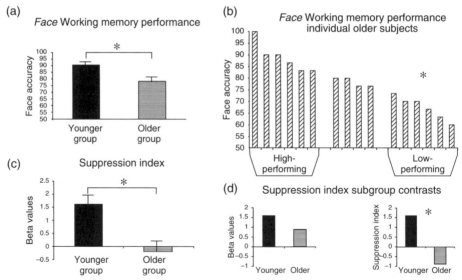

Figure 12.3 Relationship of suppression deficit and WM deficit. (a) and (c) Across-group comparisons of (a) Face WM accuracy (* *p* = 0.001) and (c) Suppression indices (* *p*< 0.005). (b) Subgroups of the six high performing and six low performing older individuals (**p*<10–5) on the Remember faces condition. (d) A significant suppression deficit is only present in the low performing older subgroup (* *p*<0.05). Error bars indicate standard error of the mean. (Adapted from Gazzaley *et al.* (2005b) *Nat Neurosci*, 8(10), 1298–1300.)

(D'Esposito, Deouell and Gazzaley 2003). This analysis confirmed an age-related decrease in the degree of overall modulation ($p <0.05$). Critically, this age-related decrease in modulation can be attributed to a selective decrease in the subcomponent process of suppression ($p <0.005$), as there was no significant difference in the enhancement subcomponent ($p = 0.27$).

Furthermore, we determined that only the subpopulation of older adults with a significant WM deficit on the task had a significant suppression deficit. This subpopulation also rated the scenes that were viewed during the Ignore scenes task as significantly more familiar than the younger participants rated them on the surprise post-experiment recognition test, revealing increased incidental long-term memory of distracting information and supporting our neural data that task-irrelevant scenes were not suppressed. This established the relationship between an age-related deficit in selective attention (specifically the suppression of task-irrelevant information), incidental long-term memory encoding and interference during the WM task. This finding, in addition to yielding important information about normal aging, revealed that enhancement and suppression, as defined by our measures, are dissociable processes.

To further explore the dissociation between the neural mechanisms of enhancement and suppression, we have begun experiments to manipulate the cognitive demands of the task and evaluate its effect on these measures. In one experiment, we are attempting to determine if having participants perform a nonverbal working memory task concurrently with the visual selective attention working memory task will differentially affect enhancement and suppression measures. At the beginning of each trial, participants were presented auditorily with six digits to memorize. On half of the trials the digit sequence was random (*high load*); on the other half the digit sequence was '1, 2, 3, 4, 5, 6' (*low load*). After hearing the digits, the participants then performed the face/scene WM paradigm as previously described. Preliminary results revealed that the high digit load did not alter the participants' ability to enhance activity levels in the scene-selective region during the Remember scenes task, but did result in increased BOLD signal associated with the irrelevant scenes in the Ignore scenes task (Rissman, Gazzaley and D'Esposito 2005). The fact that increased WM load in younger adults produced a selective suppression deficit similar to that seen in older adults suggests that age-related changes in top-down modulation may, in part, result from decreased WM resources with age.

These data and the findings on older participants converge to suggest that enhancement and suppression processes are dissociable. In these studies, only the measure of suppression was influenced by aging and increasing memory load, while the enhancement index was unchanged. This suggests that they are differentially regulated and thus may have different anatomical and neurotransmitter control systems.

Where is the top?

Identification of distinct and dissociable measures of top-down enhancement and suppression in visual association cortex raises the important question of which brain regions drive top-down modulation? It has been suggested that the top-down modulation is not an intrinsic property of sensory cortices, but rather is achieved by intricate neural connections subserving dynamic interactions between brain regions, or neural networks. Tract-tracing studies in monkeys reveal an intricate anatomic network of reciprocal corticocortical connections between regions in the prefrontal cortex (PFC) and parietal cortex and the visual association cortex (Cavada and Goldman-Rakic 1989; Petrides and Pandya 1999, 2002; Ungerleider, Gaffan and Pelak 1989; Webster, Bachevalier and Ungerleider 1994). Several of these pathways have also been described in humans with post-mortem dissection (Heimer 1983) and more recently with *in vivo* diffusion tensor magnetic resonance imaging (Makris *et al.* 2004). These anatomically defined networks establish the structural basis by which the PFC may exert control over diverse cognitive processes, and there is also accumulating neurophysiological evidence of PFC networks and their role in control processes. Neuronal recordings and neuroimaging data have revealed that top-down modulation of visual processing involves simultaneous activation of these regions (Corbetta 1998; D'Esposito *et al.* 1998; E. K. Miller, Li, and Desimone 1993; Moran and Desimone 1985; Ungerleider, Courtney and Haxby 1998). In addition, we observe increased BOLD signal in pre-frontal and parietal regions in the memory tasks of our paradigm relative to the passive view task, suggesting a role of these regions as a 'top' in the visual association cortex activity modulation. It is important to note that the majority of these studies, including our own, reveal indirect evidence of functional interaction between these areas based on univariate statistics, which measure the activity in brain regions independently of other regions.

A noninvasive approach to evaluate interactions between regions with preserved structure and function is via multivariate analysis, a statistical method that used to generate maps of functional connectivity between brain regions during different cognitive processes (Buchel and Friston 2000; Friston, Phillips, Chawla *et al.* 2000; K. J. Friston, Frith, Liddle *et al.* 1993; Lin *et al.* 2003; McIntosh 1998; Penny, Stephan, Mechelli *et al.* 2004; Sun, Miller and D'Esposito 2004). Multivariate analyses generate functional and effective connectivity maps of interacting brain regions by measuring the activity relationship between anatomically connected regions and the cognitive processes being performed. We have recently developed a new multivariate method, designed specifically to characterize functional connectivity in an event-related fMRI dataset and measure interregional correlations during the individual stages of a multistage cognitive task (Rissman, Gazzaley and D'Esposito 2004). The method, beta series correlations, employs a standard general linear model (GLM) approach as do most univariate analyses for estimating stage-specific activity (Friston *et al.* 1995), but adapts the model such that distinct parameter estimates are computed for each trial and then used as the dependent data in a correlation analysis. Another important aspect of the technique is the use of a 'seed' region to explore the network correlated with a selected region and thus associated with a particular cognitive process. We have recently validated this method as a suitable measure of functional connectivity (Rissman, Gazzaley and D'Esposito 2004) and characterized the brain regions that revealed significant correlation with a visual association cortex seed during the maintenance period of a WM task (Gazzaley, Rissman and Desposito 2004). This maintenance network included the dorsolateral and ventrolateral PFC, premotor cortex, intraparietal sulcus, caudate nucleus, thalamus, hippocampus and occipitotemporal regions. These findings support the notion that the coordinated functional interaction between nodes of a widely distributed network underlies the active maintenance of a perceptual representation.

We are now in the process of performing a comparable functional connectivity analysis on the encoding phase of the selective working memory task we have described. Preliminary evidence has revealed regions of robust functional connectivity between the PFC and visual association cortex seeds during the encoding period, further supporting the role of the prefrontal cortex as a control region. However, there are only minimal differences between the connectivity patterns in the PFC associated with enhancement versus suppression. Using this dataset and the beta series correlation analysis, we have further revealed that functional connectivity between a visual association cortex seed and both the hippocampus and a region of the PFC, the inferior frontal gyrus, correlated with incidental long-term memory recognition when evaluated across subjects: thus establishing the utility of connectivity measures to predict cognitive performance (Siebert, Gazzaley, Rutman *et al.* 2005).

Although there is accumulating evidence that the PFC mediates its influence over diverse mental processes by modulating the magnitude of neural activity in distant brain regions via the long-range projections, the majority of the evidence, including most multivariate analyses, are correlational. These studies only support the engagement of PFC in these cognitive processes and do not establish the casual relationship between PFC and control via top-down modulation. An optimal experimental design to directly assess the mechanism of PFC control involves the disruption of PFC afferents and physiological recordings of distant brain regions while the subject is engaged in a control task. There have been several studies that have implemented such a lesion-physiology design on experimental animals and humans. These studies support the conclusion that top-down modulation, utilizing both enhancement and suppression, is a mechanism of PFC control over diverse cognitive processes.

Research on experimental animals provided the first direct electophysiological evidence of a PFC role in modulating activity in sensory cortices. It was observed that cooling the PFC in cats results in increased amplitudes of evoked electrophysiological responses recorded from the primary cortex for all sensory modalities (Skinner and Yingling 1977). Conversely, stimulation of specific regions of the thalamus that surround the sensory relay thalamic nuclei (i.e. nucleus reticularis thalami) results in modality specific suppression of activity in primary sensory (Yingling and Skinner 1977). Thus, these findings suggest the presence of an inhibitory pathway from PFC that regulates the flow of sensory information via thalamic relay nuclei. This prefrontal-thalamic inhibitory system provides a mechanism for modality specific suppression of irrelevant inputs at an early stage of sensory processing.

In nonhuman primates, PFC mediated top-down modulation during a WM task was studied by coupling single-cell recordings and cortical cooling in monkeys (Fuster, Bauer and Jervey 1985). This experiment revealed that PFC cooling results in both augmentation and diminution of spontaneous and task-specific activity in inferotemporal neurons during the encoding (stimulus-present modulation) and delay period (stimulus-absent modulation) of a visual delayed-response task, suggesting the presence of both enhancing and suppressive PFC influences. Furthermore, cooling was accompanied by WM performance deficits, thus establishing a link between PFC-mediated top-down modulation and cognition. These findings have been complemented by the elegant callosal lesion-physiology study of Tomita *et al.* (1999), which revealed that top-down enhancement signals from the PFC to inferior temporal cortex during visual memory recall are mediated not by subcortical pathways, but front-temporal corticocortical projections and that this modulatory influence is necessary for successful memory recall. This supports the assertion that representations are stored in posterior sensory regions and top-down signals from the PFC trigger the activation of these memory representations (Miyashita 2004). Coupled with the results of lesion-behavior studies (Hasegawa, Fukushima, Ihara *et al.* 1998) and functional neuroimaging studies (Lee *et al.* 2002; Ranganath, Johnson and D'Esposito 2003), these results establish a role of PFC-mediated top-down modulation in long-term memory. Recent lesion-physiology studies in rodents have also revealed the presence of modulatory PFC influences on the activity of hippocampal place cells (Kyd and Bilkey 2003) and perirhinal neurons during a spatial delayed-response task (Zironi, Iacovelli, Aicardi *et al.* 2001).

In humans, combined lesion-ERP studies have provided evidence of PFC-dependent top-down enhancement of visual association cortex activity occurring in the first few hundred milliseconds of the visual processing for selectively attended stimuli (Barcelo, Suwazono and Knight 2000). Moreover, electrophysiological alterations accompanying PFC lesions were associated with deficits in visual detection ability. Comparable findings of PFC-mediated ERP enhancement and performance dependence have been obtained during a selective attention auditory task (Knight, Hillyard, Woods *et al.* 1981). There is also evidence in humans that the PFC exhibits suppressive control over distant cortical regions. For example, ERP studies in patients with focal PFC damage have revealed that auditory (Knight, Scabini and Woods 1989) and somatosensory

(Yamaguchi and Knight 1990) evoked responses are enhanced, suggesting disinhibition of sensory flow to these regions. These suppressive influences have also been extended to emotionally salient stimuli, as was recently demonstrated by enhanced ERPs recorded in response to mildly aversive stimuli in patients with orbitofrontal lesions (Rule, Shimamura and Knight 2002). Furthermore, there is evidence that PFC-mediated suppression extends to selectively ignored auditory stimuli (Chao and Knight 1998; Knight *et al.* 1981).

We are currently evaluating the causal role of the PFC in top-down modulation of activity in the visual association cortex by using the same selective working memory visual task in patients that have had a stroke to different regions of their frontal cortex. Although still preliminary, in comparison to control subjects, patients with damage to the left or right middle frontal gyrus, or to projections connecting the MFG with posterior regions, exhibit impaired top-down modulation of visual processing (Cooney, Gazzaley and D'Esposito 2005). In contrast, a patient with intact MFG exhibited robust top-down modulation despite damage to left insula, inferior frontal gyrus and premotor areas. These data suggest a direct role of the middle frontal gyrus in the visual cortex activity modulation we have recently characterized. Due to the limitations of this lesion technique, in terms of inability to control the anatomical localization of the lesions and the potential for plasticity in response to a chronic lesion, we have now completed a pilot study to evaluate the potential of using transcranial magnetic stimulation (TMS) to study the PFC role in top-down modulation. The goal of this experiment was to utilize repetitive TMS (rTMS) to transiently disrupt neural activity in prefrontal areas identified with fMRI in young adults performing our cognitive task, and then to evaluate cognitive performance and neural electrical measures in distant visual association cortex with EEG during the period of disruption, thus allowing the direct evaluation of prefrontal pathways in top-down modulation and cognition. The pilot experiment performed on four subjects revealed that transient disruption of fMRI identified regions in the middle frontal gyrus resulted in an alteration of distant neural measures of top-down modulation (amplitude increase of the p300 in the remember condition), as well as a significant reduction in speed of the response time on the working memory task. A complete study is now underway to directly evaluate the causal role of the PFC in goal-directed modulation of visual cortex activity (Miller, Gazzaley, McEvoy *et al.* 2005).

Conclusions

In summary, it is likely that such parallel enhancement/suppression control entails large-scale neural networks (Knight 1997), including an inhibitory PFC-thalamic gating network and a direct excitatory PFC projection to specific cortical regions. Alternatively, suppression might entail long-range excitatory prefrontal-cortical projections that then activate local inhibitory neurons (Carr and Sesack 1998), or perhaps involves the withdrawal of excitatory influences by the reallocation of resources. For a review of computational models of inhibitory control, see Houghton and Tipper (1996). Clearly more empirical research is needed to further our understanding of the mechanisms of top-down enhancement and suppression, as well as place these modulatory control mechanisms within the framework of PFC functional architecture and associated neural networks.

References

Awh, E and Jonides, J (2001). Overlapping mechanisms of attention and spatial working memory. *Trends Cogn Sci*, 5(3), 119–126.

Baddeley, A (1986). *Working Memory*. Oxford: Oxford University Press.

Bar, M (2003). A cortical mechanism for triggering top-down facilitation in visual object recognition. *J Cogn Neurosci, 15*(4), 600–609.

Barcelo, F, Suwazono, S and Knight, RT (2000). Prefrontal modulation of visual processing in humans. *Nat Neurosci, 3*(4), 399–403.

Bentin, S, Allison, T, Puce, A, Perez, E and McCarthy, G (1996). Electrophysiological studies of face perception in humans. *J Cogn Neurosci, 8*(6), 551–565.

Buchel, C and Friston, K (2000). Assessing interactions among neuronal systems using functional neuroimaging. *Neural Netw, 13*(8–9), 871–882.

Carr, DB and Sesack, SR (1998). Callosal terminals in the rat prefrontal cortex: synaptic targets and association with GABA-immunoreactive structures. *Synapse, 29*(3), 193–205.

Cavada, C and Goldman-Rakic, PS (1989). Posterior parietal cortex in rhesus monkey: II. Evidence for segregated corticocortical networks linking sensory and limbic areas with the frontal lobe. *J Comp Neurol, 287*(4), 422–445.

Chafee, MV and Goldman-Rakic, PS (1998). Matching patterns of activity in primate prefrontal area 8a and parietal area 7ip neurons during a spatial working memory task. *J Neurophysiol, 79*(6), 2919–2940.

Chao, LL and Knight, RT (1998). Contribution of human prefrontal cortex to delay performance. *J Cogn Neurosci, 10*(2), 167–177.

Chawla, D, Lumer, ED and Friston, KJ (1999). The relationship between synchronization among neuronal populations and their mean activity levels. *Neural Comput, 11*(6), 1389–1411.

Cooney, JW, Gazzaley, A and D'Esposito, M (2005). Frontal lobe strokes impair top-down modulation of visual processing: fMRI evidence. *Society for Neuroscience Abstracts.*

Corbetta, M (1998). Frontoparietal cortical networks for directing attention and the eye to visual locations: identical, independent, or overlapping neural systems? *Proc Natl Acad Sci USA, 95*(3), 831–838.

Corbetta, M, Miezin, FM, Dobmeyer, S, Shulman, GL and Petersen, SE (1990). Attentional modulation of neural processing of shape, color, and velocity in humans. *Science, 248*(4962), 1556–1559.

Courtney, SM, Ungerleider, LG, Keil, K and Haxby, JV (1997). Transient and sustained activity in a distributed neural system for human working memory. *Nature, 386*(6625), 608–611.

Craik, FI and Salthouse, TA (2000). *Handbook of Aging and Cogntion II.* Mahwah, NJ: Erlbaum.

D'Esposito, M, Aguirre, GK, Zarahn, E, Ballard, D, Shin, RK and Lease, J (1998). Functional MRI studies of spatial and nonspatial working memory. *Brain Res Cogn Brain Res, 7*(1), 1–13.

D'Esposito, M, Deouell, LY and Gazzaley, A (2003). Alterations in the BOLD fMRI signal with ageing and disease: a challenge for neuroimaging. *Nat Rev Neurosci, 4*(11), 863–872.

D'Esposito, M, Postle, BR and Rypma, B (2000). Prefrontal cortical contributions to working memory: evidence from event-related fMRI studies. *Exp Brain Res, 133*(1), 3–11.

de Fockert, JW, Rees, G, Frith, CD and Lavie, N (2001). The role of working memory in visual selective attention. *Science, 291*(5509), 1803–1806.

Desimone, R (1996). Neural mechanisms for visual memory and their role in attention. *Proc Natl Acad Sci USA, 93*(24), 13494–13499.

Desimone, R and Duncan, J (1995). Neural mechanisms of selective visual attention. *Annu Rev Neurosci, 18*, 193–222.

Duncan, J, Humphreys, G and Ward, R (1997). Competitive brain activity in visual attention. *Curr Opin Neurobiol, 7*(2), 255–261.

Eimer, M (2000). Attentional modualtions of event-related brain potentials sensitive to faces. *Cognitive Neuropsychology, 17*, 103–116.

Friston, K, Phillips, J, Chawla, D and Buchel, C (2000). Nonlinear PCA: characterizing interactions between modes of brain activity. *Philos Trans R Soc Lond B Biol Sci, 355*(1393), 135–146.

Friston, KJ, Frith, CD, Liddle, PF and Frackowiak, RS (1993). Functional connectivity: the principal-component analysis of large (PET) data sets. *J Cereb Blood Flow Metab, 13*(1), 5–14.

Friston, KJ, Holmes, AP, Worsley, KJ, Poline, JP, Frith, CD and Frackowiak, RSJ (1995). Statistical parametric maps in functional imaging: A general linear approach. *Human Brain Mapping, 2,* 189–210.

Frith, C (2001). A framework for studying the neural basis of attention. *Neuropsychologia, 39*(12), 1367–1371.

Funahashi, S, Bruce, CJ and Goldman-Rakic, PS (1989). Mnemonic coding of visual space in the monkey's dorsolateral prefrontal cortex. *J Neurophysiol, 61*(2), 331–349.

Fuster, JM (1990). Inferotemporal units in selective visual attention and short-term memory. *J Neurophysiol, 64*(3), 681–697.

Fuster, JM and Alexander, GE (1971). Neuron activity related to short-term memory. *Science, 173*(997), 652–654.

Fuster, JM, Bauer, RH and Jervey, JP (1985). Functional interactions between inferotemporal and prefrontal cortex in a cognitive task. *Brain Res, 330*(2), 299–307.

Gazzaley, A, Cooney, JW, McEvoy, K, Knight, RT and D'Esposito, M (2005a). Top-down enhancement and suppression of the magnitude and speed of neural activity. *J Cogn Neurosci, 17*(3), 507–517.

Gazzaley, A, Cooney, JW, Rissman, J and D'Esposito, M (2005b). Top-down suppression deficit underlies working memory impairment in normal aging. *Nat Neurosci, 8*(10), 1298–1300.

Gazzaley, A, Rissman, J and D'Esposito, M (2004). Functional connectivity during working memory maintenance. *Cogn Affect Behav Neurosci, 4*(4), 580–599.

Hasegawa, I, Fukushima, T, Ihara, T and Miyashita, Y (1998). Callosal window between prefrontal cortices: cognitive interaction to retrieve long-term memory. *Science, 281*(5378), 814–818.

Hasher, L and Zacks, RT (1988). Working memory, comprehension and aging: A review and a new view. In GH Bower (ed), *The Psychology of Learning and Motivation, Vol. 22* (pp. 193–225). New York, NY: Academic Press.

Heimer, L (1983). *The Human Brain and Spinal Cord: Functional neuroanatomy and dissection guide.* New York: Springer Verlag.

Hillyard, SA, Hink, RF, Schwent, VL and Picton, TW (1973). Electrical signs of selective attention in the human brain. *Science, 182*(4108), 177–179.

Hillyard, SA, Vogel, EK and Luck, SJ (1998). Sensory gain control (amplification) as a mechanism of selective attention: electrophysiological and neuroimaging evidence. *Philos Trans R Soc Lond B Biol Sci, 353*(1373), 1257–1270.

Holmes, A, Vuilleumier, P and Eimer, M (2003). The processing of emotional facial expression is gated by spatial attention: evidence from event-related brain potentials. *Brain Res Cogn Brain Res, 16*(2), 174–184.

Hopfinger, JB, Buonocore, MH and Mangun, GR (2000). The neural mechanisms of top-down attentional control. *Nat Neurosci, 3*(3), 284–291.

Houghton, G and Tipper, SP (1996). Inhibitory mechanisms of neural and cognitive control: applications to selective attention and sequential action. *Brain and Cognition, 30* (1), 20–43.

Ishai, A, Haxby, JV and Ungerleider, LG (2002). Visual imagery of famous faces: effects of memory and attention revealed by fMRI. *Neuroimage, 17*(4), 1729–1741.

Jha, AP and McCarthy, G (2000). The influence of memory load upon delay-interval activity in a working-memory task: an event-related functional MRI study. *J Cogn Neurosci, 12* (Suppl 2), 90–105.

Kanwisher, N and Wojciulik, E (2000). Visual attention: insights from brain imaging. *Nat Rev Neurosci, 1*(2), 91–100.

Kastner, S, De Weerd, P, Desimone, R and Ungerleider, LG (1998). Mechanisms of directed attention in the human extrastriate cortex as revealed by functional MRI. *Science, 282*(5386), 108–111.

Kastner, S, Pinsk, MA, De Weerd, P, Desimone, R and Ungerleider, LG (1999). Increased activity in human visual cortex during directed attention in the absence of visual stimulation. *Neuron, 22*(4), 751–761.

Kastner, S and Ungerleider, LG (2001). The neural basis of biased competition in human visual cortex. *Neuropsychologia, 39*(12), 1263–1276.

Knight, RT (1997). Distributed cortical network for visual attention. *Journal of Cognitive Neuroscience*, *9*(1), 75–91.

Knight, RT, Hillyard, SA, Woods, DL and Neville, HJ (1981). The effects of frontal cortex lesions on event-related potentials during auditory selective attention. *Electroencephalography and Clinical Neurophysiology*, *52*(6), 571–582.

Knight, RT, Scabini, D and Woods, DL (1989). Prefrontal cortex gating of auditory transmission in humans. *Brain Res*, *504*(2), 338–342.

Knight, RT, Staines, WR, Swick, D and Chao, LL (1999). Prefrontal cortex regulates inhibition and excitation in distributed neural networks. *Acta Psychol (Amst)*, *101*(2–3), 159–178.

Kubota, K and Niki, H (1971). Prefrontal cortical unit activity and delayed alternation performance in monkeys. *J Neurophysiol*, *34*(3), 337–347.

Kyd, RJ and Bilkey, DK (2003). Prefrontal cortex lesions modify the spatial properties of hippocampal place cells. *Cereb Cortex*, *13*(5), 444–451.

LaBar, KS, Gitelman, DR, Parrish, TB and Mesulam, M (1999). Neuroanatomic overlap of working memory and spatial attention networks: a functional MRI comparison within subjects. *Neuroimage*, *10*(6), 695–704.

Lee, AC, Robbins, TW, Smith, S, Calvert, GA, Tracey, I, Matthews, P *et al.* (2002). Evidence for asymmetric frontal-lobe involvement in episodic memory from functional magnetic resonance imaging and patients with unilateral frontal-lobe excisions. *Neuropsychologia*, *40*(13), 2420–2437.

Lin, FH, McIntosh, AR, Agnew, JA, Eden, GF, Zeffiro, TA and Belliveau, JW (2003). Multivariate analysis of neuronal interactions in the generalized partial least squares framework: simulations and empirical studies. *Neuroimage*, *20*(2), 625–642.

Logothetis, NK, Pauls, J, Augath, M, Trinath, T and Oeltermann, A (2001). Neurophysiological investigation of the basis of the fMRI signal. *Nature*, *412*(6843), 150–157.

Luck, SJ and Hillyard, SA (1995). The role of attention in feature detection and conjunction discrimination: an electrophysiological analysis. *Int J Neurosci*, *80*(1–4), 281–297.

Luck, SJ, Hillyard, SA, Mouloua, M, Woldorff, MG, Clark, VP and Hawkins, H L. (1994). Effects of spatial cuing on luminance detectability: psychophysical and electrophysiological evidence for early selection. *J Exp Psychol Hum Percept Perform*, *20*(4), 887–904.

Luck, SJ and Vogel, EK (1997). The capacity of visual working memory for features and conjunctions. *Nature*, *390*(6657), 279–281.

Makris, N, Kennedy, DN, McInerney S, Sorensen, AG, Wang, R, Caviness, V S, Jr *et al.* (2004). Segmentation of subcomponents within the superior longitudinal fascicle in humans: A quantitative, *in vivo*, DT-MRI study. *Cereb Cortex*.

May, CP, Hasher, L and Kane, MJ (1999). The role of interference in memory span. *Mem Cognit*, *27*(5), 759–767.

McIntosh, AR (1998). Understanding neural interactions in learning and memory using functional neuroimaging. *Ann N Y Acad Sci*, *855*, 556–571.

Miller, BT, Gazzaley, A, McEvoy, K, Knight, RT and D'Esposito, M (2005). Functional deactivation of the prefrontal cortex disrupts posterior physiological signals: Joint TMS/EEG evidence for PFC-mediated top-down modulation. *Society for Neuroscience Abstracts*.

Miller, EK, Erickson, CA and Desimone, R (1996). Neural mechanisms of visual working memory in prefrontal cortex of the macaque. *J Neurosci*, *16*(16), 5154–5167.

Miller, EK, Li, L and Desimone, R (1991). A neural mechanism for working and recognition memory in inferior temporal cortex. *Science*, *254*(5036), 1377–1379.

Miller, EK, Li, L and Desimone, R (1993). Activity of neurons in anterior inferior temporal cortex during a short-term memory task. *J Neurosci*, *13*(4), 1460–1478.

Miyashita, Y (2004). Cognitive memory: cellular and network machineries and their top-down control. *Science*, *306*(5695), 435–440.

Moran, J and Desimone, R (1985). Selective attention gates visual processing in the extrastriate cortex. *Science*, *229*(4715), 782–784.

Niki, H, Sakai, M and Kubota, K (1972). Delayed alternation performance and unit activity of the caudate head and medial orbitofrontal gyrus in the monkey. *Brain Res*, *38*(2), 343–353.

O'Craven, KM, Downing, PE and Kanwisher, N (1999). fMRI evidence for objects as the units of attentional selection. *Nature*, *401*(6753), 584–587.

Penny, WD, Stephan, KE, Mechelli, A and Friston, KJ (2004). Comparing dynamic causal models. *Neuroimage*, *22*(3), 1157–1172.

Pessoa, L, Kastner, S and Ungerleider, LG (2003). Neuroimaging studies of attention: from modulation of sensory processing to top-down control. *J Neurosci*, *23*(10), 3990–3998.

Petrides, M and Pandya, DN (1999). Dorsolateral prefrontal cortex: comparative cytoarchitectonic analysis in the human and the macaque brain and corticocortical connection patterns. *Eur J Neurosci*, *11*(3), 1011–1036.

Petrides, M and Pandya, DN (2002). Comparative cytoarchitectonic analysis of the human and the macaque ventrolateral prefrontal cortex and corticocortical connection patterns in the monkey. *Eur J Neurosci*, *16*(2), 291–310.

Pinsk, MA, Doniger, GM and Kastner, S (2004). Push-pull mechanism of selective attention in human extrastriate cortex. *J Neurophysiol*, *92*(1), 622–629.

Ploner, CJ, Ostendorf, F, Brandt, SA, Gaymard, BM, Rivaud-Pechoux, S, Ploner, M *et al.* (2001). Behavioural relevance modulates access to spatial working memory in humans. *Eur J Neurosci*, *13*(2), 357–363.

Postle, BR, Druzgal, TJ and D'Esposito, M (2003). Seeking the neural substrates of visual working memory storage. *Cortex*, *39*(4–5), 927–946.

Rainer, G, Asaad, WF and Miller, EK (1998). Selective representation of relevant information by neurons in the primate prefrontal cortex. *Nature*, *393*(6685), 577–579.

Ranganath, C and D'Esposito, M (2001). Medial temporal lobe activity associated with active maintenance of novel information. *Neuron*, *31*(5), 865–873.

Ranganath, C, DeGutis, J and D'Esposito, M (2004). Category-specific modulation of inferior temporal activity during working memory encoding and maintenance. *Brain Res Cogn Brain Res*, *20*(1), 37–45.

Ranganath, C, Johnson, MK and D'Esposito, M (2003). Prefrontal activity associated with working memory and episodic long-term memory. *Neuropsychologia*, *41*(3), 378–389.

Rees, G, Frith, CD and Lavie, N (1997). Modulating irrelevant motion perception by varying attentional load in an unrelated task. *Science*, *278*(5343), 1616–1619.

Rissman, J, Gazzaley, A and D'Esposito, M (2004). Measuring functional connectivity during distinct stages of a cognitive task. *Neuroimage*, *23*(2), 752–763.

Rissman, J, Gazzaley, A and D'Esposito, M (2005). The effect of phonological working memory load on top-down enhancement and suppression of visual processing. *Society for Neuroscience Abstracts*.

Rule, RR, Shimamura, AP and Knight, RT (2002). Orbitofrontal cortex and dynamic filtering of emotional stimuli. *Cogn Affect Behav Neurosci*, *2*(3), 264–270.

Seminowicz, DA, Mikulis, DJ and Davis, KD (2004). Cognitive modulation of pain-related brain responses depends on behavioral strategy. *Pain*, *112*(1–2), 48–58.

Shimamura, AP (1997). The role of the prefrontal cortex in dynamic filtering. *Psychobiology*, *28*(2), 207–218.

Siebert, TM, Gazzaley, A, Rutman, AM and D'Esposito, M (2005). Top-down enhancement of hippocampal-visual association cortex interactions underlies incidental long-term memory. *Society for Neuroscience Abstracts*.

Silva, L d (1991). Neural mechanisms underlying brain waves: from neural membranes to networks. *Electroencephalog Clin Neurophysiol*, *79*, 81–93.

Skinner, J and Yingling, C (1977). Central gating mechanisms that regulate event-related potentials and behavior. In J Desmedt (ed), *Progress in Clinical Neurophysiology, Vol. 1* (pp. 30–69). Basel: S Karger.

Sun, FT, Miller, LM and D'Esposito, M (2004). Measuring interregional functional connectivity using coherence and partial coherence analyses of fMRI data. *Neuroimage*, *21*(2), 647–658.

Tomita, H, Ohbayashi, M, Nakahara, K, Hasegawa, I and Miyashita, Y (1999). Top-down signal from prefrontal cortex in executive control of memory retrieval. *Nature*, *401*(6754), 699–703.

Treue, S and Martinez Trujillo, JC (1999). Feature-based attention influences motion processing gain in macaque visual cortex. *Nature*, *399*(6736), 575–579.

Ungerleider, LG, Courtney, SM and Haxby, JV (1998). A neural system for human visual working memory. *Proc Natl Acad Sci USA*, *95*(3), 883–890.

Ungerleider, LG, Gaffan, D and Pelak, VS (1989). Projections from inferior temporal cortex to prefrontal cortex via the uncinate fascicle in rhesus monkeys. *Exp Brain Res*, *76*(3), 473–484.

Vuilleumier, P, Armony, JL, Driver, J and Dolan, RJ (2001). Effects of attention and emotion on face processing in the human brain: an event-related fMRI study. *Neuron*, *30*(3), 829–841.

Watanabe, T and Niki, H (1985). Hippocampal unit activity and delayed response in the monkey. *Brain Res*, *325*(1–2), 241–254.

Webster, MJ, Bachevalier, J and Ungerleider, LG (1994). Connections of inferior temporal areas TEO and TE with parietal and frontal cortex in macaque monkeys. *Cereb Cortex*, *4*(5), 470–483.

West, R (1999). Visual distraction, working memory, and aging. *Mem Cognit*, *27*(6), 1064–1072.

Wilson, FA, Scalaidhe, SP and Goldman-Rakic, PS (1993). Dissociation of object and spatial processing domains in primate prefrontal cortex. *Science*, *260*(5116), 1955–1958.

Wojciulik, E, Kanwisher, N and Driver, J (1998). Covert visual attention modulates face-specific activity in the human fusiform gyrus: fMRI study. *J Neurophysiol*, *79*(3), 1574–1578.

Yamaguchi, S and Knight, RT (1990). Gating of somatosensory input by human prefrontal cortex. *Brain Res*, *521*(1–2), 281–288.

Yingling, C and Skinner, J (1977). Gating of thalamic input to cerebral cortex by nucleus reticularis thalami. In J Desmedt (ed), *Progress in Clinical Neurophysiology, Vol. 1*. Basel: S. Karger.

Zelano, C, Bensafi, M, Porter, J, Mainland, J, Johnson, B, Bremner, E *et al.* (2005). Attentional modulation in human primary olfactory cortex. *Nat Neurosci*, *8*(1), 114–120.

Zironi, I, Iacovelli, P, Aicardi, G, Liu, P and Bilkey, DK (2001). Prefrontal cortex lesions augment the location-related firing properties of area TE/perirhinal cortex neurons in a working memory task. *Cereb Cortex*, *11*(11), 1093–1100.

13

The general-purpose working memory system and functions of the dorsolateral prefrontal cortex

Shintaro Funahashi

Introduction

Working memory has been described as a system which includes mechanisms for temporary maintenance as well as manipulation and processing of information. Baddeley and Logie (1999) described working memory as a mechanism to

> allow humans to comprehend and mentally represent their immediate environment, to retain information about their immediate past experience, to support the acquisition of new knowledge, to solve problems, and to formulate, relate, and act on current goals.
>
> Baddeley and Logie (1999)

Kieras *et al.* (1999) described working memory as a mechanism to 'encompass the entire ensemble of temporary stored codes, knowledge representations, and procedures whereby information is maintained, updated, and applied for performing perceptual-motor and cognitive tasks'. Further, Miyake and Shah (1999) described working memory as 'mechanisms or processes that are involved in the control, regulation, and active maintenance of task-relevant information in the service of complex cognition, including novel as well as familiar, skilled tasks'. Thus working memory is an important concept for understanding mechanisms to perform higher cognitive functions such as thinking, planning, reasoning, decision-making and language comprehension.

Several models of working memory have been proposed (see for example Miyake and Shah 1999). The most influential model of working memory is the one proposed by Baddeley and Hitch (1974) and Baddeley (1986). Baddeley (2000) recently proposed his revised model of working memory, which includes one master component (the central executive) and three slave components (the visuospatial sketchpad, the phonological loop and the episodic buffer). The phonological loop is a system for speech perception and language comprehension and includes mechanisms for temporary maintenance of speech-based information by subvocal rehearsal. The visuospatial sketchpad is a system for processing visuospatial information as well as information that cannot be processed by language. The visuospatial sketchpad includes mechanisms for temporarily maintaining information as visual images. The episodic buffer is a temporary storage buffer with a limited capacity to integrate information from a variety of sources, including long-term memory, as 'chunks'. The central executive is the master component and considered to be an attentional system with a limited capacity of memory. The central executive is to select appropriate control processes or strategies for performing current tasks. Thus, the central executive supervises the performance of three slave components.

The models of working memory proposed by Baddeley and Hitch (1974) and Baddeley (2000) are abstract models. As Baddeley himself stated (Baddeley 1986), in general, none of the four components of working memory that he proposed correspond to any particular brain structure. However, when we consider how working memory is executed in the brain, how each component of working memory carries out its function, and how the central executive manages slave components, a process-based model rather than an abstract model would be useful. The kind of information processed in each slave component is different from other slave components. However, all slave components include neural mechanisms for maintaining and processing information. Therefore, these neural mechanisms must be basic common mechanisms among slave components. In addition, neural mechanisms for maintaining and processing information could also be included in the central executive, and these mechanisms must play significant roles in the central executive. Therefore, to understand how working memory is executed in the brain, it would be useful to work out basic common neural mechanisms of working memory, such as neural mechanisms for maintaining and processing information.

A process-based model of working memory

Goldman-Rakic (1987) has proposed that working memory is an important concept for understanding prefrontal functions, especially the functions of the dorsolateral prefrontal cortex (DLPFC), in both humans and animals. Since then, the DLPFC has come to be understood as important brain area for neural mechanisms of working memory. The importance of the DLPFC in working memory has been supported by a variety of experiments including lesion studies (see reviews by Fuster 1997; Goldman-Rakic 1987; Petrides 1994), neurophysiological studies using nonhuman primates (see reviews by Funahashi and Kubota 1994; Funahashi and Takeda 2002; Fuster 1997; Goldman-Rakic 1998), and brain imaging studies using human subjects (see Stuss and Knight 2002). Close relationships between working memory and functions of the DLPFC indicate that neurophysiological investigations in the DLPFC could provide important clues for common neural mechanisms of working memory, for example, how active maintenance of information is achieved and how information-processing is performed.

In fact, neurophysiological studies have shown that many neurons in the DLPFC exhibit tonic sustained activation (delay-period activity) during the delay period of spatial working memory tasks (e.g., an oculomotor delayed-response task) (Funahashi *et al.* 1989; Hasegawa *et al.* 1998; Joseph and Barone 1987; Sawaguchi and Goldman-Rakic 1994). Most of this delay-period activity was observed only when the visual cue was presented in a particular area within the visual field (directional selectivity). Delay-period activity was observed only when the subject performed correct movements (e.g., saccadic eye movements). In addition, the duration that delay-period activity was maintained was prolonged or shortened depending on the length of the delay-period. Therefore, delay-period activity observed during performance of working memory tasks has been considered to be a neural correlate of the mechanism for temporarily active maintenance of information (Funahashi 2001; Funahashi and Takeda 2002; Fuster 1997; Goldman-Rakic 1987). It has also been shown that information processing in the DLPFC can be seen as a temporal change of the information represented by a population of neural activities using a population vector analysis (Takeda and Funahashi 2004). Functional interactions among DLPFC neurons have been shown by cross-correlation analysis of simultaneously recorded pairs of neural activities (Constantinidis *et al.* 2001; Funahashi and Inoue 2000). Therefore, these interactions could play an essential role in a temporal change of the information represented by a population of neural activities. Functional interactions among neurons exhibiting different kinds of task-related activity or neurons exhibiting different preferences in task-related activity could be a mechanism for information-processing.

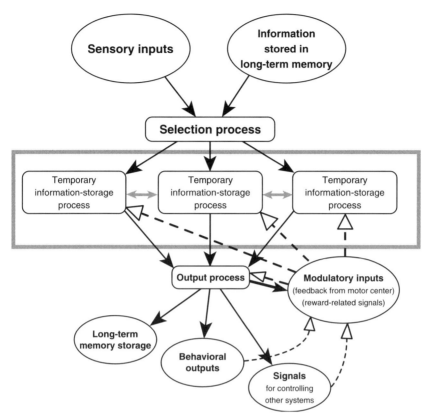

Figure 13.1 A process-based model for explaining working memory processes in the dorsolateral prefrontal cortex.

Based on these findings, we proposed a process-based model to understand how working memory is performed in the DLPFC (Funahashi 2001). As shown in Figure 13.1, this model includes four neural processes: a selection process, a temporary information-storage process, an output process and modulatory inputs. Since the DLPFC is included in the multimodal association areas (Mesulam 2000), the DLPFC receives a variety of information including sensory, motor, motivational, and emotional information from other cortical and subcortical areas. In addition, in order for the DLPFC to perform such higher cognitive functions as thinking, reasoning, decision-making and language comprehension, the DLPFC not only receives a variety of information from cortical and subcortical areas but also sends a variety of information to those areas. Although the DLPFC receives a variety of information, the information temporarily maintained and processed in the DLPFC would be the information necessary to achieve a current goal. To maintain and process the necessary information to achieve a current goal, a neural process for selecting essential information among a variety of information (selection process) would be required. The temporary information-storage process is another essential component of the neural mechanism of working memory in the DLPFC. This neural process would temporarily maintain the information which is selected by the selection process. In addition, by interacting among temporary information-storage processes and other processes, maintained information would be processed, replaced and updated. Therefore, interactions among temporary information-storage processes and other processes can be considered a mechanism for dynamic information processing and a mechanism for creating new information. The output process would send out maintained information to the brain areas where the information is utilized. Target areas of the output process would be the areas related to motor outputs, the areas related to long-term memory, and the areas where the DLPFC is monitoring their operation. The modulatory input is a signal or information to modulate the information maintained in the temporary information-storage processes. The modulatory input can be created within the DLPFC or sent to the DLPFC from other brain areas. The modulatory input includes feedback information from motor centers, motivational or emotional information from the limbic areas (Barbas 1992), or modulatory signals by catecholaminergic or monoaminergic inputs (Arnsten 1998; Sawaguchi 1998; Sawaguchi and Goldman-Rakic 1994; Wang *et al.* 2004; Williams and Goldman-Rakic 1995).

In this model, we hypothesized dynamic and flexible modulation in the strength of functional interactions among different processes and among temporary information-storage processes. Dynamic and flexible modulation in the strength of functional interactions between neurons has been observed in the DLPFC depending on the context of the behavioral task (Funahashi 2001; Vaadia *et al.* 1995). In addition to the interactions among temporary information-storage processes, modulatory inputs sent from other brain areas could also play a significant role in modifying or updating the information maintained in temporary information-storage processes. Thus, information processing in working memory could be explained as a change of the information represented in temporary information-storage processes caused by dynamic interactions among these processes.

Temporary information-storage process

Delay-period activity, most of which is tonic sustained activation observed during an imposed delay period, has been considered to be a neural correlate of temporary information-storage processes (Funahashi 2001; Funahashi and Kubota 1994; Funahashi and Takeda 2002; Fuster 1997; Goldman-Rakic 1987; Miller 2000). Neurophysiological studies using spatial working memory tasks such as the delayed-response task have revealed that many neurons in the DLPFC exhibit delay-period activity (Funahashi *et al.* 1989; Fuster 1973; Kojima and Goldman-Rakic 1982; Niki 1974; Niki and Watanabe 1976). The duration of delay-period activity is prolonged or shortened depending on the length of the delay period (Funahashi *et al.* 1989; Fuster 1973; Kojima and Goldman-Rakic 1982). This activity is observed only when monkeys perform correct behavioral responses (Funahashi *et al.* 1989; Fuster 1973). If the monkey made an error, delay-period activity was truncated or not observed. A great majority of delay-period activity exhibits a directional or positional preference (Funahashi *et al.* 1989), such that delay-period activity was observed only when a visual cue was presented at a particular area in the visual field. Many DLPFC neurons exhibited directional delay-period activity, and preferred directions of this activity differed from neuron to neuron. Based on these observations, it has been proposed that neurons having directional delay-period activity have mnemonic receptive fields (memory fields) regarding visual cues in the visual field (Funahashi *et al.* 1989; Rainer *et al.* 1998). In addition, using delayed pro- and antisaccade tasks, it has been shown that the great majority (about 70 per cent) of delay-period activity represented information regarding the position of the visual cue, whereas the minority represented information regarding the direction of the saccade (Funahashi *et al.* 1993). Similar results have been observed by Niki and Watanabe (1976) using a manual delayed-response task and a conditional position task and by Takeda and Funahashi (2002) using conventional and rotatory versions of the oculomotor delayed-response (ODR) task. Thus, delay-period activity represents either retrospective or prospective information, although the majority of delay-period activity represents retrospective information in the DLPFC.

Experiments using nonspatial working memory tasks (e.g., delayed matching-to-sample tasks and delayed conditional tasks) have revealed that delay-period activity also represents the active retention of nonspatial information, including faces (O'Scalaidhe *et al.* 1997; Wilson *et al.* 1993), object shapes, patterns, or colors (Asaad *et al.* 1998; Freedman *et al.* 2002; Miller *et al.* 1996; Rainer *et al.* 1999; Rao *et al.* 1997; Sakagami and Niki 1994). Romo *et al.* (1999) showed that the magnitude of delay-period activity varied as a monotonic function of the base stimulus frequency in a somatosensory discrimination task, in which monkeys were required to discriminate the difference of frequency between two mechanical vibrations (the base stimulus and the test stimulus) applied to the fingertips. Based on this result, Romo *et al.* (1999) concluded that this monotonic stimulus encoding may be a fundamental representation of one-dimensional sensory stimulus quality in working memory. In addition, White and Wise (1999) found rule-dependent neuronal activity in the DLPFC. They reported that one-third to one half of task-related neurons showed statistically significant differences in task-related activity depending on the task rule (either a conditional or a spatial rule), indicating that these neurons retained rules of behavioral tasks by modulating the magnitude of task-related activity. Similar rule-dependent activity has also been reported by Wallis *et al.* (2001). Further, it has been shown that delay-period activity represents reward information (Hikosaka and Watanabe 2000; Kobayashi *et al.* 2002; Wallis and Miller 2003; Watanabe 1996).

Thus, delay-period activity observed in the DLPFC can be considered a neural correlate of the temporary information-storage process (Funahashi 2001; Funahashi and Kubota 1994; Funahashi and Takeda 2002; Fuster 1997; Goldman-Rakic 1998; Miller 2000). A wide variety of information is temporarily maintained in this process, including visuospatial information, nonspatial visual features, quality and quantity differences in one stimulus modality, motor outputs, or task rules. Regional differences have been proposed in processing information. For example, Goldman-Rakic proposed that the mid-dorsolateral sector mainly participates in visuospatial information processing, whereas the mid-ventrolateral sector mainly participates in information processing of nonspatial visual features (Wilson *et al.* 1993; O'Scalaidhe *et al.* 1997; Goldman-Rakic 1998). Hoshi (2006) also suggests that at least two distinct subregions (dorsal sector and ventral sector) can be identified based on region-specific neural activity within the DLPFC. However, neurons having various task-related activities and various spatial and nonspatial features of task-related activity were widely distributed within the DLPFC with substantial overlap (Carlson *et al.* 1997; Quintana and Fuster 1999; Rainer *et al.* 1999; Sakagami and Tsutsui 1999). A number of neurons exhibited task-related activity in both spatial and nonspatial working memory tasks (Rao *et al.* 1997). These observations indicate that neurons in the DLPFC can maintain a variety of information, although each neuron's preferred information seems to be different from neuron to neuron, and that neurons representing different information are intermingled in the DLPFC.

Information processing

Information processing in working memory could be described as a change of the information represented in temporary information-storage processes caused by dynamic interactions among these and other processes. Neurophysiological studies have revealed evidence for manipulating or integrating information by interactions among processes in the DLPFC. One example is observed in the interaction between neurons having delay-period activity and neurons having post-saccadic activity. It has been shown that many DLPFC neurons exhibit saccade-related activity when saccadic eye movements are used as behavioral responses (Boch and Goldberg 1989, Funahashi *et al.* 1991; Takeda and Funahashi 2002). Most of saccade-related activity was post-saccadic in the DLPFC (Funahashi *et al.* 1991; Takeda and Funahashi 2002). Since post-saccadic activity started after the initiation of the saccadic eye movement, this activity is not directly related to the initiation as well as the control of the eye movement. However, most of this activity exhibited directional selectivity, such that post-saccadic activity was observed only when the monkey made a saccade toward a particular direction. Therefore, post-saccadic activity can be considered as feedback signals from oculomotor centers which directly participate in the initiation and the control of the eye movement (Funahashi et al. 1991). On the other hand, it has been shown that delay-period activity terminated soon after the subject performed a response behavior. A comparison of temporal profiles between the initiation of post-saccadic activity and the termination of delay-period activity revealed that the termination of delay-period activity coincided with the initiation of post-saccadic activity, suggesting that post-saccadic activity controls the timing of the termination of delay-period activity (Funahashi and Kubota 1994; Funahashi and Takeda 2002; Goldman-Rakic et al. 1990). Erasing unnecessary information from the temporary information-storage process is an important action of working memory. Therefore, post-saccadic activity or feedback inputs from motor centers could serve as a signal to erase unnecessary information from the temporary information-storage process by terminating delay-period activity.

Further evidence for processing and integrating information by interactions among neurons having delay-period activity has been shown by experiments using delayed-response tasks with sequential movements (Funahashi et al. 1997; Inoue and Funahashi 2002). These studies showed that delay-period activity represented composite information when monkeys performed delayed-response tasks combined with sequential hand-reaching behavior (Funahashi et al. 1997) or sequential saccades (Barone and Joseph 1989; Inoue and Funahashi 2002). These include delay-period activity representing a pair of different spatial positions, delay-period activity representing the temporal order of the presentation of multiple cues, and delay-period activity representing a pair of different spatial positions of the visual cues as well as the temporal order of their presentation (Barone and Joseph 1989; Funahashi et al. 1997; Inoue and Funahashi 2002). When activities were recorded during a conventional delayed-response task in which a single spatial cue was presented in each trial, most of these neurons exhibited delay-period activity with simple and monotonic directional selectivity (Funahashi et al. 1997; Inoue and Funahashi 2002). Therefore, delay-period activity representing composite information might be created by interactions among neighboring neurons representing different spatial features.

Several studies have shown that the information represented by prefrontal activity changes with the progress of the task. For example, using a delayed paired association task, Rainer et al. (1999) showed that although prefrontal activity primarily represented characteristics of the sample stimuli (sensory-related coding) during the early phase of the delay period, this activity began to represent characteristics of anticipated targets (prospective coding) toward the end of the delay period. Similarly, using a spatial delayed matching-to-sample task, Sawaguchi and Yamane (1999) showed that spatial information was tuned broadly by delay-period activity in the early phase of the delay period. However, the proportion of neurons exhibiting sharper spatial tuning and high spatial discriminability increased in the later phase of the delay period. Further, Asaad et al. (1998) showed that neural activity conveyed the direction of the impending eye movement progressively earlier along successive trials while monkeys performed arbitrary cue-response association tasks. Quintana and Fuster (1999) observed DLPFC neurons attuned to the cue color and neurons attuned to response directions while monkeys performed working memory tasks using color cues. They found that the discharge of neurons attuned to the cue color gradually diminished during the delay period, whereas the discharge of neurons attuned to response directions gradually increased. These results indicate that the modulation of the temporal pattern of neural discharges reflects the change of the information represented by the neuron and that the information represented by the temporal pattern of the firing of a neuron or an assembly of neurons alters gradually as the trial progresses.

Takeda and Funahashi (2002) examined DLPFC activity using two kinds of oculomotor delayed-response tasks (ODR and R-ODR tasks). In the ODR task, the monkey was required to make a saccade to the direction where the visual cue was presented, whereas in the R-ODR task, the monkey was required to make a saccade 90° clockwise from the direction where the visual cue was presented. They showed that the majority of delay-period activity represented the direction of the visual cue, whereas the minority of delay-period activity and the majority of response-period activity represented the direction of the saccade. These results suggest that the transformation from visuospatial information to motor information is carried out in the DLPFC. Since both visuospatial information and motor information can be depicted as directional preference of neural activity, transformation from visual information to motor information could be demonstrated as the temporal change of the preferred direction of neural activity along trials of ODR and R-ODR tasks. Takeda and Funahashi (2004) used population vectors to demonstrate the temporal change of the preferred direction of a population of DLPFC activities with the progress of a trial of the ODR task and the R-ODR task. Figure 13.2a shows population vectors calculated by a population of DLPFC activities at the 180° trial of the ODR task. Population vectors were mostly directed toward the 180° direction. Since the direction of the visual cue and the direction of the saccade were the same in the ODR task, this result indicates that the same directional information is maintained along the delay period (see Figure 13.2c). Figure 13.2b shows

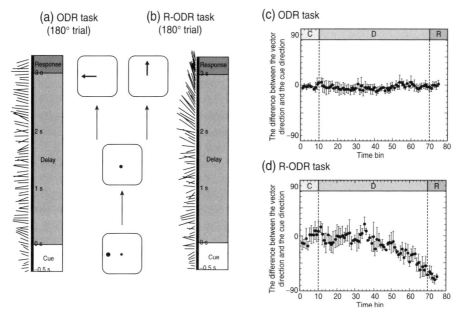

Figure 13.2 (a) Temporal change of the directions of population vectors along the 180° trial of the ODR task. Most of population vectors were directed toward the 180° direction. (b) Temporal change of the directions of population vectors along the 180° trial of the R-ODR task. The direction of the population vector gradually rotated from the 180° direction to the 90°; direction during the delay period. (c) The difference between the vector direction and the cue direction along the ODR trial. The population vector was directed toward the cue direction during the delay period. (d) The difference between the vector direction and the cue direction along the R-ODR trial. The direction of the population vector gradually rotated from the cue direction to the saccade direction during the delay period.

population vectors calculated by a population of DLPFC activities at the 180° trial of the R-ODR task, in which the visual cue was presented at the 180° direction and the direction of the correct saccade was the 90° direction. Population vectors were directed toward the 180° direction at the beginning of the delay period. However, population vectors began to rotate in the middle of the delay period, continued to rotate slowly from the 180° direction to the 90° direction during the late half of the delay period, and finally directed toward the 90° direction at the response period (see Figure 13. 2d). This result indicates that the information represented by a population of DLPFC activities changes during the delay period. Fuster (1997) had proposed that the mediation of cross-temporal contingency is an important function of the DLPFC. He stated that the delay period is the period for the cross-temporal bridging of sensory-to-motor information transformation, which is a dynamic process for internal transfer of information as well as a process of cross-temporal matching. The present result supports the notion that the DLPFC plays a significant role for mediating the cross-temporal contingency. This result also suggests that delay-period activity observed in the DLPFC contributes significantly to the dynamic process related to internal information transfer.

Interactions among prefrontal neurons

Takeda and Funahashi (2006) showed the presence of the information flow from neurons having cue-period activity to neurons having oculomotor activity through neurons having delay-period activity in the DLPFC. While monkeys performed ODR tasks, cue- (C), delay- (D), or response-period (R) activities or their combinations (CD, CR, DR, CDR) were observed in DLPFC neurons. They characterized each neuron based on which task-related activity was exhibited and which information (*cue location* or *saccade direction*) each task-related activity represented, then classified these neurons into nine groups (C, D*cue*, D*sac*, CD*cue*, D*cue*R*cue*, D*sac*R*sac*, D*cue*R*sac*, CD*cue*R*cue* and CD*cue*R*sac*). Preferred directions were similar between cue- and delay-period activities in groups of CD*cue*, CD*cue*R*cue* and CD*cue*R*sac*, all of which represented visual information, indicating that the directional selectivity of delay-period activity was affected by the directional selectivity of cue-period activity for each neuron. Preferred directions were also similar between delay- and response-period activities in groups of D*cue*R*cue*, CD*cue*R*cue* and D*sac*R*sac*, indicating that the directional selectivity of delay-period activity affects the directional selectivity of response-period activity in these neurons. By the comparison of temporal profiles of delay-period activity among these groups, they found (1) cue-period activity of C, CD*cue* and CD*cue*R*cue* groups might contribute to the initiation and the maintenance of delay-period activity of CD*cue*, CD*cue*R*cue*, D*cue* and D*cue*R*cue* groups, and (2) saccade-related activity of D*sac*R*sac* could be affected by delay-period activity of D*sac* and D*sac*R*sac* groups. Thus, while monkeys performed the ODR tasks, the information flow from neurons having cue-period activity to neurons having oculomotor activity through neurons having delay-period activity is present in the DLPFC. Information processing could be performed during this information flow process.

Dynamic and flexible changes in functional interaction among temporary information-storage processes would be a key component to understand neuronal mechanisms of information processing. In the DLPFC, Wilson *et al.* (1994) showed that types of responses (excitatory or inhibitory) of pyramidal and nonpyramidal neurons were often inverted (e.g., pyramidal neurons exhibited excitatory responses while nonpyramidal neurons exhibited inhibitory responses) and that the timing of excitatory and inhibitory responses appear to be phased. This result suggests the presence of functional interactions between pyramidal and nonpyramidal neurons. Rao *et al.* (1999) used a cross-correlation analysis to examine functional interactions between pyramidal and nonpyramidal neurons in the DLPFC and found inhibitory interactions between pyramidal neurons and adjacent nonpyramidal interneurons. Funahashi and Inoue (2000) also applied a cross-correlation analysis to simultaneously isolated pairs of prefrontal activities during ODR performances and examined functional interactions between task-related DLPFC neurons. When both neurons of examined pairs exhibited delay-period activity, these neurons tended to show excitatory interactions and to show similar directional preferences. Interactions between task-related neurons with different directional preferences increased with the progress of the trial. Excitatory interactions among neurons having delay-period activity were frequently observed in the DLPFC, suggesting that the information stored in temporary information-storage processes may be transformed from one form of representation to another or integrated to represent more complex information (e.g., delay-period activity representing a combination of visual cue positions and the temporal order of their presentation) by these interactions.

Each neuron changes the magnitude of activity depending on the trial conditions (e.g., difference in the position where the visual cue was presented or the direction where the saccade was directed), the temporal context of the trial and trial events. Therefore, the strength of functional interactions could be changed depending on the trial conditions or the temporal context of the trial. In fact, the height of the peak of the cross-correlogram changed depending on the cue conditions. This modulation of the peak height in the cross-correlogram was observed in most of the neuron pairs examined in the DLPFC. These results suggest that, although many DLPFC neurons have functional interaction with neurons exhibiting same or different kinds of task-related activity, the strength of the interaction may change dynamically depending on the conditions of the trials. Thus, dynamic and flexible changes of functional interactions among temporary information-storage processes could be an important element in understanding neural mechanisms of information processing.

Two working memory systems

A process-based model of working memory in the DLPFC was explained in the previous section. However, a similar system is also necessary in the brain areas where sensory or motor information are processed. Temporary maintenance of information and processing information could be ubiquitous processes for any kind of information processing in the brain. In fact, tonic sustained delay-period activity has been observed not only in the DLPFC, but also in the frontal eye field (Funahashi *et al.* 1989; Lawrence *et al.* 2005; Roesch and Olson 2005), the inferior temporal cortex (Fuster 1990; Fuster and Jervey 1982; Miller *et al.* 1993; Miyashita and Chang 1988; Naya *et al.* 1996), the posterior parietal cortex (Chafee and Goldman-Rakic 1998; Murata *et al.* 1996; Pesaran *et al.* 2002; Sereno and Amador 2006; Zhang and Barash 2004), and the premotor cortex (Crammond and Kalaska 2000; Kurata and Wise 1988; Obayashi *et al.* 2003; Weinrich and Wise 1982;). Thus, the process-based model of working memory that we proposed is not just for the model to explain functions of the DLPFC but may be a ubiquitous system in the brain.

The specific feature of working memory system operating in the DLPFC would be that this system is not for information processing of specific purpose, such as only for visual information processing, only for control of limb movements, or only for speech comprehension, but rather is general purpose and is an essential element for a variety of information processing that the DLPFC participates in. The DLPFC is located in the best position to monitor the functional state of the posterior association cortices and to control their functions by sending command signals (or top-down signals), since the DLPFC has heavy anatomical connections, mostly reciprocal connections, with the posterior association cortices. On the other hand, working memory systems must be present in the modality-specific cortical areas, such as the sensory system, as well as the motor system. In these modality-specific cortical areas, temporary maintenance and processing of information are also essential processes. Therefore, working memory systems can be divided into two types: a general-purpose working memory system and a modality-specific working memory system.

A modality-specific working memory system is a mechanism for temporary maintenance and processing of certain types of information, such as sensory, linguistic, or motor information. Modality-specific working memory systems will be present in cortical and subcortical areas which participate mostly in sensory and motor information processing. On the other hand, a general-purpose working memory system is a mechanism to maintain or process a variety of information including the behavioral context to perform various cognitive tasks or control signals (e.g., top-down signals) to monitor or regulate operations of other cortical and subcortical areas. The contents of a general-purpose working memory system would affect or regulate the contents of modality-specific working memory systems and lead information processing operated in modality-specific working memory system to necessary directions.

Cohen and others (Cohen and Servan-Schreiber 1992; Cohen *et al*. 1996; Miller and Cohen 2001) explained prefrontal executive functions by computational architectures with the connectionist framework. They hypothesized that the DLPFC represents the context information, which corresponds to the goal representation in the computational architecture of the production system. Context information can be defined as the information necessary to mediate an appropriate behavioral response, and includes a set of task instructions, a specific prior stimulus, or the result of processing a sequence of prior stimuli (Cohen *et al*. 1996). To accomplish a particular goal, some brain region needs to maintain an internal representation of the goal, to suppress unnecessary behaviors and to temporally coordinate series of behaviors. Cohen *et al*. (1996) considered the DLPFC as this cortical region. In this regard, prefrontal executive functions that Cohen and others proposed are similar to the functions of the general-purpose working memory system.

Interactions between the DLPFC and other cortical areas

To understand how the DLPFC acts as the general-purpose working memory system, it is important to consider dynamic and flexible functional interactions between the DLPFC and other cortical and subcortical areas. Corticocortical and corticosubcortical anatomical connections with the DLPFC have been examined extensively – see reviews by Fuster (1997), Petrides (1994), Petrides and Pandya (2002). The DLPFC has reciprocal connections with the posterior parietal cortex, the inferior temporal cortex, the superior temporal polysensory areas, the anterior cingulate, the retrosplenial cortex and the parahippocampal gyrus. The DLPFC also has strong reciprocal connections with the mediodorsal nucleus of the thalamus (Ray and Price 1993; Siwek and Pandya 1991). In addition, the DLPFC has connections with the frontal eye field, the presupplementary motor area, the premotor cortex, and the caudate nucleus (Miyachi *et al*. 2005). Morris *et al*. (1999) reported that the mid-dorsolateral prefrontal cortex (areas 46 and 9) projects to the retrosplenial area 30 and the posterior presubiculum, and suggested that this system could be the anatomical substrate of functional interaction between the DLPFC and the hippocampus. Thus, the DLPFC has anatomical connections with various cortical and subcortical areas, especially sensory and motor association areas and the limbic brain areas. Most of these connections are reciprocal. These observations indicate that the DLPFC can receive various kinds of information including sensory, motor, and emotional information as well as information stored in long-term memory, and is located in a good position to monitor both internal and external environment. These observations also indicate that the DLPFC can send various kinds of information and signals to various brain areas, and is again located in a good position to coordinate information processing operated in various brain regions and direct these operations to a particular goal. Strong reciprocal connections between the DLPFC and various brain areas are the anatomical basis of dynamic and flexible interactions between the general-purpose working memory system and the modality-specific working memory systems.

Noninvasive brain imaging studies have also revealed dynamic and flexible functional interactions between the DLPFC and other cortical areas. n-back tasks have often been used as working memory tasks. Bilateral DLPFC has been shown to be activated in visuospatial n-back tasks (Cohen *et al.* 1997; Smith and Jonides 1997, 1998). The magnitude of the activation in the DLPFC depended on the memory load required to perform the task (Callicott *et al.* 1999; Carlson *et al.* 1998). However, working memory tasks like n-back tasks are composed of numerous elementary neural processes. Based on the analysis using evoked potentials, McEvoy *et al.* (1998) showed that, although some of these neural processes were affected by the type of information (verbal or spatial), the neural processes associated with frontal and parietal slow waves were affected not by the type of information, but by the amount of information being retained. McEvoy *et al.* (1998) suggested that working memory is operating by dynamic cortical networks of information-specific processes (e.g., modality-specific working memory system) and nonspecific, capacity-limited, higher-order processes (e.g., general-purpose working memory system).

Dynamic cortical networks including the DLPFC have been shown directly by correlation analyses in functional brain imaging studies as well as by covariance and correlation analyses of event-related potentials. Using a working memory task of faces, McIntosh *et al.* (1996) examined functional interactions among different cortical regions by an anatomy-based covariance structural equation model. As a result, they found that different functional interactions among different cortical areas were observed in different task conditions (e.g., different delay lengths) and that a top-down interaction from the DLPFC to the temporal and occipital cortices was observed in a long delay condition. McIntosh *et al.* (1999) also showed that only aware subjects exhibited learning-related modulations of brain activation in the left DLPFC during an associative learning task and that a correlation analysis of this modulation revealed significant functional connectivity among bilateral DLPFC, the sensory association cortices and the cerebellum. In addition, evidence for homotopic interaction or coactivation of the bilateral DLPFC has been reported (Klingberg *et al.* 1997; McGuire *et al.* 1991). Klingberg *et al.* (1997) reported the increase of bilateral coactivation of the DLPFC and the inferior parietal cortex in association with the increase of task difficulty. They also found that the inferior parietal cortex was often coactivated with the DLPFC in working memory tasks and tasks involving planning. Further, Huettel *et al.* (2005) showed that the degree of uncertainty on decision making influenced the magnitude of activation of both prefrontal and parietal cortices. Collette *et al.* (2005) showed activation of both the prefrontal and the inferior parietal cortex in dual-task performance. Thus, all of these results indicate the importance of functional interactions as well as coactivation between the DLPFC and other cortical and subcortical areas when subjects perform cognitive tasks. These results also indicate that functional interactions and coactivation between the DLPFC and other cortical and subcortical areas are dynamically and flexibly modulated depending on the context of the cognitive task.

Evidence of top-down modulatory effects by the DLPFC have also been shown. Using visual associative memory tasks, Hasegawa *et al.* (1998) showed that retrieval of visual images from long-term memory was under the executive control of the DLPFC by an experiment using partial split-brain monkeys. In addition, by neurophysiological experiments using monkeys having resection of the corpus callosum, Tomita *et al.* (1999) showed that top-down signals from the DLPFC regulated retrieval of associative memory in inferior temporal neurons. These observations indicate that the DLPFC can control information processing in other cortical areas by sending top-down signals (Miyashita 2005). Lumer and Rees (1999) showed by fMRI that covariation of activation was observed in multiple extrastriate areas, the parietal cortex, and the prefrontal cortex in bistable viewing conditions. Coordinated activation of these areas was not linked to either sensory or motor events, but rather reflected perceptual events or internal changes of perception. Therefore, they concluded that functional interactions between visual areas and the prefrontal cortex are important for conscious vision. On the other hand, either enhancement or suppression of the visual response was observed in inferior temporal neurons when two visual stimuli (one preferred and the other nonpreferred) were presented simultaneously in the neuron's receptive field. Chelazzi *et al.* (1998) proposed that this phenomenon can be explained by a 'biased competition' model of attention. Based on this model, simultaneously presented objects in the visual receptive field would compete with others for representation within the cortex. They suggested that this competition could be biased by 'top-down' feedback signals from brain structures involved in working memory. Based on the results by Hasegawa *et al.* (1998), Tomita *et al.* (1999), and Lumer and Rees (1999), it would be reasonable to think that top-down signals from the DLPFC bias the magnitude of the activity in the visual system. These results indicate the presence and importance of top-down modulatory effects by the DLPFC to perform cognitive tasks. These results also suggest that top-down modulatory effects by the DLPFC affect a wide variety of cognitive activities including sensory perception, directed attention, episodic memory encoding and retrieval through dynamic and flexible functional interactions. This could be the typical function of the DLPFC as the general-purpose working memory system.

Conclusions

In this manuscript, we proposed a general-purpose working memory system to explain how the DLPFC performs executive control. This general-purpose working memory system can (1) represent and process various kinds of information, (2) access various systems (e.g., modality-specific working memory systems) to obtain any kind of necessary information and monitor their operations, and (3) send appropriate information and signals (e.g., top-down signals) to various systems to control their operations. To represent and process various kinds of information in the general-purpose working memory system, this system needs to integrate following four processes: a selection process, a temporary information-storage process, an output process and modulatory signals. We also proposed the presence of extensive functional interactions among temporary information-storage processes for information processing. The dynamic and flexible nature of these interactions is an essential feature of the general-purpose working memory system. In addition, dynamic and flexible interactions between the general-purpose working memory system and the modality-specific working memory systems are also essential to consider the function of the general-purpose working memory system as well as the functions of the DLPFC. However, it is not known how the selection process selects necessary information from a variety of information in a variety of brain areas, how the DLPFC creates appropriate top-down signals, how the DLPFC sends appropriate information and top-down signals to the exact systems or exact brain areas to control their operations, and how the DLPFC can manage a variety of functions efficiently. Therefore, we need further experiments to solve these questions and to understand functions of the DLPFC as the general-purpose working memory system.

Acknowledgment

This work was supported by a Grant-in-Aid for Scientific Research (No. 17021022, 17300103, 17650101) from the Japanese Ministry of Education, Culture, Sports, Science, and Technology (MEXT). This work was also supported by the 21st Century COE Program (D-2 to Kyoto University) by the MEXT.

References

Arnsten, AFT (1998). Catecholamine modulation of prefrontal cortical cognitive function. *Trends in Cognitive Sciences, 2,* 436–447.

Asaad, WF, Rainer, G and Miller, EK (1998). Neural activity in the primate prefrontal cortex during associative learning. *Neuron, 21,* 1399–1407.

Baddeley, A (1986). *Working Memory.* Oxford: Oxford University Press.

Baddeley, A (2000). The episodic buffer: a new component of working memory? *Trends in Cognitive Science, 4,* 417–423.

Baddeley, A and Hitch, GJ (1974). Working memory. In GH Bower (ed), *The Psychology of Learning and Motivation, Vol. 8* (pp. 47–89). New York: Academic Press.

Baddeley, A and Logie, RH (1999). Working memory: the multiple-component model. In A Miyake and P Shah (eds), *Models of Working Memory: Mechanisms of active maintenance and executive control* (pp. 28–61). Cambridge: Cambridge University Press.

Barbas, H (1992). Architecture and cortical connections of the prefrontal cortex in the rhesus monkey. In AV Chauvel *et al.* (eds), *Advances in Neurology, Vol. 57* (pp. 91–115). New York: Raven Press.

Barone, P and Joseph, JP (1989). Prefrontal cortex and spatial sequencing in macaque monkey. *Experimental Brain Research, 78,* 447–464.

Boch, RA and Goldberg, ME (1989). Participation of prefrontal neurons in the preparation of visually guided eye movements in the rhesus monkey. *Journal of Neurophysiology, 61,* 1064–1084.

Callicott, JH, Mattay, VS, Bertolino, A, Finn, K, Coppola, R, Frank, JA, Goldberg, TE and Weinberger, DR (1999). Physiological characteristics of capacity constraints in working memory as revealed by functional MRI. *Cerebral Cortex, 9,* 20–26.

Carlson, S, Martinkauppi, S, Rama, P, Salli, E, Korvenoja, A and Aronen, HJ (1998). Distribution of cortical activation during visuospatial n-back tasks as revealed by functional magnetic resonance imaging. *Cerebral Cortex, 8,* 743–752.

Carlson, S, Rama, P, Tanila, H, Linnankoski, I and Mansikka, H (1997). Dissociation of mnemonic coding and other functional neuronal processing in the monkey prefrontal cortex. *Journal of Neurophysiology, 77,* 761–774.

Chafee, MV and Goldman-Rakic, PS (1998). Matching patterns of activity in primate prefrontal area 8a and parietal area 7ip neurons during a spatial working memory task. *Journal of Neurophysiology, 79,* 2919–2940.

Chelazzi, L, Duncan, J, Miller, EK and Desimone, R (1998). Responses of neurons in inferior temporal cortex during memory-guided visual search. *Journal of Neurophysiology, 80,* 2918–2940.

Cohen, JD, Braver, TS and O'Reilly, RC (1996). A computational approach to prefrontal cortex, cognitive control and schizophrenia: recent developments and current challenges. *Philosophical Transactions of Royal Society of London, B, 351,* 1515–1527.

Cohen, JD, Peristein, WM, Braver, TS, Nystrom, LE, Noll, DC, Jonides, J and Smith, EE (1997). Temporal dynamics of brain activation during a working memory task. *Nature, 386,* 604–607.

Cohen, JD and Servan-Schreiber, D (1992). Context, cortex, and dopamine: a connectionist approach to behavior and biology in schizophrenia. *Psychological Review, 99,* 45–77.

Collette, F, Olivier, L, Van der Linden, M, Laureys, S, Delfiore, G, Luxen, A and Salmon, E (2005). Involvement of both prefrontal and inferior parietal cortex in dual-task performance. *Cognitive Brain Research, 24,* 237–251.

Constantinidis, C, Franowicz, MN and Goldman-Rakic, PS (2001). Coding specificity in cortical microcircuits: a multiple-electrode analysis of primate prefrontal cortex. *Journal of Neuroscience, 21,* 3646–3655.

Crammond, DJ and Kalaska, JF (2000). Prior information in motor and premotor cortex: activity during the delay period and effect on pre-movement activity. *Journal of Neurophysiology, 84,* 986–1005.

Freedman, DJ, Riesenhuber, M, Poggio, T and Miller, EK (2002). Visual categorization and the primate prefrontal cortex: neurophysiology and behavior. *Journal of Neurophysiology, 88,* 929–941.

Funahashi, S (2001). Neuronal mechanisms of executive control by the prefrontal cortex. *Neuroscience Research*, *39*, 147–165.

Funahashi, S, Bruce, CJ and Goldman-Rakic, PS (1989). Mnemonic coding of visual space in the monkey's dorsolateral prefrontal cortex. *Journal of Neurophysiology*, *61*, 331–349.

Funahashi, S, Bruce, CJ and Goldman-Rakic, PS (1991). Neuronal activity related to saccadic eye movements in the monkey's dorsolateral prefrontal cortex. *Journal of Neurophysiology*, *65*, 1464–1483.

Funahashi, S, Chafee, MV and Goldman-Rakic, PS (1993). Prefrontal neuronal activity in rhesus monkeys performing a delayed anti-saccade task. *Nature*, *365*, 753–756.

Funahashi, S and Inoue, M (2000). Neuronal interactions related to working memory processes in the primate prefrontal cortex revealed by cross-correlation analysis. *Cerebral Cortex*, *10*, 535–551.

Funahashi, S, Inoue, M and Kubota, K (1997). Delay-period activity in the primate prefrontal cortex encoding multiple spatial positions and their order of presentation. *Behavioural Brain Research*, *84*, 203–223.

Funahashi, S and Kubota, K (1994). Working memory and prefrontal cortex. *Neuroscience Research*, *21*, 1–11.

Funahashi, S and Takeda, K (2002). Information processes in the primate prefrontal cortex in relation to working memory processes. *Reviews in the Neurosciences*, *13*, 313–346.

Fuster, JM (1973). Unit activity in prefrontal cortex during delayed-response performance: neuronal correlates of transient memory. *Journal of Neurophysiology*, *36*, 61–78.

Fuster, JM (1990). Inferotemporal units in selective visual attention and short-term memory. *Journal of Neurophysiology*, *64*, 681–697.

Fuster, JM (1997). *The Prefrontal Cortex: Anatomy, physiology, and neuropsychology of the frontal lobe*, 3rd edn, Philadelphia, PA: Lippincott-Raven.

Fuster, JM and Jervey, JP (1982). Neuronal firing in the inferotemporal cortex of the monkey in a visual memory task. *Journal of Neuroscience*, *2*, 361–375.

Goldman-Rakic, PS (1987). Circuitry of primate prefrontal cortex and regulation of behavior by representational memory. In F Plum (ed), *Higher Functions of the Brain, Part 1, Handbook of Physiology, Section 1: The Nervous System, Vol. V.*pp. 373–417). Bethesda, MD: American Physiological Society.

Goldman-Rakic, PS (1998). The prefrontal landscape: implications of functional architecture for understanding human mentation and the central executive. In AC Roberts, TW Robbins and L Weiskrantz (eds), *The Prefrontal Cortex: Executive and cognitive functions* (pp. 87–102). Oxford: Oxford University Press.

Goldman-Rakic, PS, Funahashi, S and Bruce, CJ (1990). Neocortical memory circuits. *Cold Spring Harbor Symposium Quantitative Biology*, *55*, 1025–1038.

Hasegawa, I, Fukushima, T, Ihara, T and Miyashita, Y (1998). Callosal window between prefrontal cortices: cognitive interaction to retrieve long-term memory. *Science*, *281*, 814–818.

Hasegawa, R, Sawaguchi, T and Kubota, K (1998). Monkey prefrontal neuronal activity coding the forthcoming saccade in an oculomotor delayed matching-to-sample task. *Journal of Neurophysiology*, *79*, 322–333.

Hikosaka, K and Watanabe, M (2000). Delay activity of orbital and lateral prefrontal neurons of the monkey varying with different rewards. *Cerebral Cortex*, *10*, 263–271.

Hoshi, E (2006). Functional specialization within the dorsolateral prefrontal cortex: a review of anatomical and physiological studies of non-human primates. *Neuroscience Research*, *54*, 73–84.

Huettel, SA, Song, AW and McCarthy, G (2005). Decisions under uncertainty: probabilistic context in fluences activation of prefrontal and parietal cortices. *Journal of Neuroscience*, *25*, 3304–3311.

Inoue, M and Funahashi, S (2002). Prefrontal delay-period activity is affected by visual cues presented outside the memory field. *NeuroReport*, *13*, 2097–2101.

Joseph, JP and Barone, P (1987). Prefrontal unit activity during a delayed oculomotor task in the monkey. *Experimental Brain Research*, *67*, 460–468.

Kieras, DE, Meyer, DE, Mueller, S and Seymour, T (1999). Insights into working memory from the perspective of the EPIC architecture for modeling skilled perceptual-motor and cognitive human performance. In A Miyake and P Shah (eds), *Models of Working Memory: Mechanisms of active maintenance and executive control* (pp. 183–223). Cambridge: Cambridge University Press.

Klingberg, T, O'Sullivan, BT and Roland, PE (1997). Bilateral activation of fronto-parietal networks by incrementing demand in a working memory task. *Cerebral Cortex*, *7*, 465–471.

Kobayashi, S, Lauwereyns, J, Koizumi, M, Sakagami, M and Hikosaka, O (2002). Influence of reward expectation on visuospatial processing in macaque lateral prefrontal cortex. *Journal of Neurophysiology*, *87*, 1488–1498.

Kojima, S and Goldman-Rakic, PS (1982). Delay-related activity of prefrontal neurons in rhesus monkeys performing delayed response. *Brain Research*, *248*, 43–49.

Kurata, K and Wise, SP (1988). Premotor cortex of rhesus monkeys: set-related activity during two conditional motor tasks. *Experimental Brain Research*, *69*, 327–343.

Lawrence, BM, White, III RL and Snyder, LH (2005). Delay-period activity in visual, visuomovement, and movement neurons in the frontal eye field. *Journal of Neurophysiology*, *94*, 1498–1508.

Lumer, ED and Rees, G (1999). Covariation of activity in visual and prefrontal cortex associated with subjective visual perception. *Proceedings of National Academy of Science USA*, *96*, 1669–1673.

McEvoy, LK, Smith, ME and Gevins, A (1998). Dynamic cortical networks of verbal and spatial working memory: effects of memory load and task practice. *Cerebral Cortex*, *8*, 563–574.

McGuire, PK, Bates, JF and Goldman-Rakic, PS (1991). Interhemispheric integration: I. Symmetry and convergence of the corticocortical connections of the left and the right principal sulcus (PS) and the left and the right supplementary motor area (SMA) in the rhesus monkey. *Cerebral Cortex*, *1*, 390–407.

McIntosh, AR, Grady, CL, Haxby, JV, Ungerleider, LG and Horwitz, B (1996). Changes in limbic and prefrontal functional interactions in a working memory task for faces. *Cerebral Cortex*, *6*, 571–584.

McIntosh, AR, Rajah, MN and Lobaugh, NJ (1999). Interactions of prefrontal cortex in relation to awareness in sensory learning. *Science*, *284*, 1531–1533.

Mesulam, MM (2000). *Priniciples of Behavioral and Cognitive Neurology*. 2nd edn, New York: Oxford University Press.

Miller, EK (2000). The prefrontal cortex and cognitive control. *Nature Reviews Neuroscience*, *1*, 59–65.

Miller, EK and Cohen, JD (2001). An integrative theory of prefrontal cortex function. *Annual Review of Neuroscience*, *24*, 167–202.

Miller, EK, Erickson, CA and Desimone, R (1996). Neural mechanisms of visual working memory in prefrontal cortex of the macaque. *Journal of Neuroscience*, *16*, 5154–5167.

Miller, EK, Lin, L and Desimone, R (1993). Activity of neurons in anterior inferior temporal cortex during a short-term memory task. *Journal of Neuroscience*, *13*, 1460–1478.

Miyachi, S, Lu, X, Inoue, S, Iwasaki, T, Koike, S, Nambu, A and Takada, M (2005). Organization of multisynaptic inputs from prefrontal cortex to primary motor cortex as revealed by retrograde transneuronal transport of rabies virus. *Journal of Neuroscience*, *25*, 2547–2556.

Miyake, A and Shah, P (1999). Toward unified theories of working memory: emerging general consensus, unresolved theoretical issues, and future research directions. In A Miyake and P Shah (eds), *Models of Working Memory: Mechanisms of active maintenance and executive control* (pp. 442–481). Cambridge: Cambridge University Press.

Miyashita, Y (2005). Cognitive memory: cellular and network machineries and their top-down control. *Science*, *306*, 435–440.

Miyashita, Y and Chang, HS (1988). Neuronal correlate of pictorial short-term memory in the primate temporal cortex. *Nature*, *331*, 68–70.

Morris, R, Pandya, DN and Petrides, M (1999). Fiber system linking the mid-dorsolateral frontal cortex with the retrosplenial/presubicular region in the rhesus monkey. *Journal of Comparative Neurology*, *407*, 183–192.

Murata, A, Gallese, V, Kaseda, M and Sakata, H (1996). Parietal neurons related to memory-guided hand manipulation. *Journal of Neurophysiology*, *75*, 2180–2186.

Naya, Y, Sakai, K and Miyashita, Y (1996). Activity of primate inferotemporal neurons related to a sought target in pair-association task. *Proceedings of National Academy of Science USA*, *93*, 2664–2669.

Niki, H (1974). Differential activity of prefrontal units during right and left delayed response trials. *Brain Research*, *70*, 346–349.

Niki, H and Watanabe, M (1976). Prefrontal unit activity and delayed response: relation to cue location versus direction of response. *Brain Research*, *105*, 79–88.

Obayashi, M, Ohki, K and Miyashita, Y (2003). Conversion of working memory to motor sequence in the monkey premotor cortex. *Science*, *301*, 233–236.

O'Scalaidhe, SP, Wilson, FAW and Goldman-Rakic, PS (1997). Areal segregation of face-processing neurons in prefrontal cortex. *Science*, *278*, 1135–1138.

Pesaran, B, Pezaris, JS, Sahani, M, Mitra, PP and Andersen, RA (2002). Temporal structure in neuronal activity during working memory in macaque parietal cortex. *Nature Neuroscience*, *5*, 805–811.

Petrides, M (1994). Frontal lobes and working memory: evidence from investigations of the effects of cortical excisions in nonhuman primates. In F Boller, H Spinnler and JA Hendler (eds), *Handbook of Neuropsychology, Vol. 9.* (pp. 17–58). Amsterdam: Elsevier.

Petrides, M and Pandya, DN (2002). Association pathways of the prefrontal cortex and functional observations. In DT Stuss and RT Knight (eds), *Principles of Frontal Lobe Function* (pp. 31–50). New York: Oxford University Press.

Quintana, J and Fuster, JM (1999). From perception to action: temporal integrative functions of prefrontal and parietal neurons. *Cerebral Cortex*, *9*, 213–221.

Rainer, G, Asaad, WF and Miller, EK (1998). Memory fields of neurons in the primate prefrontal cortex. *Proceedings of National Academy of Science USA*, *95*, 15008–15013.

Rainer, G, Rao, SC and Miller, EK (1999). Prospective coding for objects in primate prefrontal cortex. *Journal of Neuroscience*, *19*, 5493–5505.

Rao, SC, Rainer, G and Miller, EK (1997). Integration of what and where in the primate prefrontal cortex. *Science*, *276*, 821–824.

Rao, SG, Williams, GV and Goldman-Rakic, PS (1999). Isodirectional tuning of adjacent interneurons and pyramidal cells during working memory: evidence for microcolumnar organization in PFC. *Journal of Neurophysiology*, *81*, 1903–1916.

Ray, JP and Price, JL (1993). The organization of projections from the mediodorsal nucleus of the thalamus to orbital and medial prefrontal cortex in macaque monkeys. *Journal of Comparative Neurology*, *337*, 1–31.

Roesch, MR and Olson, CR (2005). Neuronal activity dependent on anticipated and elapsed delay in macaque prefrontal cortex, frontal and supplementary eye fields, and premotor cortex. *Journal of Neurophysiology*, *94*, 1469–1497.

Romo, R, Brody, CD, Hernandez, A and Lemus, L (1999). Neuronal correlates of parametric working memory in the prefrontal cortex. *Nature*, *399*, 470–473.

Sakagami, M and Niki, H (1994). Encoding of behavioral significance of visual stimuli by primate prefrontal neurons: relation to relevant task conditions. *Experimental Brain Research*, *97*, 423–436.

Sakagami, M and Tsutsui, K (1999). The hierarchical organization of decision making in the primate prefrontal cortex. *Neuroscience Research*, *34*, 79–89.

Sawaguchi, T (1998). Attenuation of delay-period activity of monkey prefrontal neurons by an alpha2-adrenergic antagonist during an oculomotor delayed-response task. *Journal of Neurophysiology*, *80*, 2200–2205.

Sawaguchi, T and Goldman-Rakic, PS (1994). The role of D1-dopamine receptor in working memory: local injections of dopamine antagonists into the prefrontal cortex of rhesus monkeys performing an oculomotor delayed-response task. *Journal of Neurophysiology*, *71*, 515–528.

Sawaguchi, T and Yamane, I (1999). Properties of delay-period neuronal activity in the monkey dorsolateral prefrontal cortex during a spatial delayed matching-to-sample task. *Journal of Neurophysiology*, *82*, 2070–2080.

Sereno, AB and Amador, SC (2006). Attention and memory-related responses of neurons in the lateral intraparietal area during spatial and shape-delayed match-to-sample tasks. *Journal of Neurophysiology*, *95*, 1078–1098.

Siwek, DF and Pandya, DN (1991). Prefrontal projections to the mediodorsal nucleus of the thalamus in the rhesus monkey. *Journal of Comparative Neurology*, *312*, 509–524.

Smith, EE and Jonides, J (1997). Working memory: a review from neuroimaging. *Cognitive Psychology*, *33*, 5–42.

Smith, EE and Jonides, J (1998). Neuroimaging analyses of human working memory. *Proceedings of National Academy of Science USA*, *95*, 12061–12068.

Stuss, DT and Knight, RT (2002). *Principles of Frontal Lobe Function*. New York: Oxford University Press.

Takeda, K and Funahashi, S (2002). Prefrontal task-related activity representing visual cue location or saccade direction in spatial working memory tasks. *Journal of Neurophysiology*, *87*, 567–588.

Takeda, K and Funahashi, S (2004). Population vector analysis of primate prefrontal activity during spatial working memory. *Cerebral Cortex*, *14*, 1328–1339.

Takeda, K and Funahashi, S (2007). Relationship between prefrontal task-related activity and information flow during spatial working memory performances. *Cortex 43*, 38–52.

Tomita, H, Ohbayashi, M, Nakahara, K, Hasegawa, I and Miyashita, Y (1999). Top-down signal from prefrontal cortex in executive control of memory retrieval. *Nature*, *401*, 699–703.

Vaadia, E, Haalman, I, Abeles, M, Bergman, H, Prut, Y, Slovin, H and Aertsen, A (1995). Dynamics of neuronal interactions in monkey cortex in relation to behavioral events. *Nature*, *373*, 515–518.

Wallis, JD and Miller, EK (2003). Neuronal activity in primate dorsolateral and orbital prefrontal cortex during performance of a reward preference task. *European Journal of Neuroscience*, *18*, 2069–2081.

Wallis, JD, Anderson, KC and Miller, EK (2001). Single neurons in prefrontal cortex encode abstract rules. *Nature*, *411*, 953–956.

Wang, M, Vijayraghavan, S and Goldman-Rakic, PS (2004). Selective D2 receptor actions on the functional circuitry of working memory. *Science*, *303*, 853–856.

Watanabe, M (1996). Reward expectancy in primate prefrontal neurons. *Nature*, *382*, 629–632.

Weinrich, M and Wise, SP (1982). The premotor cortex of the monkey. *Journal of Neuroscience*, *2*, 1329–1345.

White, IM and Wise, SP (1999). Rule-dependent neuronal activity in the prefrontal cortex. *Experimental Brain Research*, *126*, 315–335.

Williams, GV and Goldman-Rakic, PS (1995). Modulation of memory fields by dopamine D1 receptors in prefrontal cortex. *Nature*, *376*, 572–575.

Wilson, FAW, O'Scalaidhe, SP and Goldman-Rakic, PS (1993). Dissociation of object and spatial processing domains in primate prefrontal cortex. *Science*, *260*, 1955–1958.

Wilson, FAW, O'Scalaidhe, SP and Goldman-Rakic, PS (1994). Functional synergism between putative gamma-aminobutyrate-containing neurons and pyramidal neurons in prefrontal cortex. *Proceedings of National Academy of Science USA*, *91*, 4009–4013.

Zhang, M and Barash, S (2004). Persistent LIP activity in memory antisaccades: working memory for a sensorimotor transformation. *Journal of Neurophysiology*, *91*, 1424–1441.

14

Visuospatial rehearsal processes in working memory

David G. Pearson

The concept of an active rehearsal mechanism that maintains material within short-term memory has been an integral feature of theoretical modeling in the thirty years since the publication of Baddeley and Hitch's multicomponent model of working memory (Baddeley and Hitch 1974). The majority of research on the topic has focused on the maintenance of verbal material, and a well-documented account of verbal rehearsal has developed in which an active articulatory mechanism revives auditory memory traces stored within a temporary phonological store (Baddeley 1986, 2000). In contrast, accounts of rehearsal processes within visuospatial working memory have been less well developed (Pearson 2001, 2006). This chapter will review recent research that has focused on the rehearsal of visual and spatial material within working memory, including both serially presented spatial locations and memory for dynamic spatial displays that occur during multiple-target tracking. Although the research literatures on target tracking and serial spatial recall have developed separately, with relatively little cross-referencing, there are several areas of overlap in terms of the theoretical issues being addressed. I will argue that a consideration of the findings from both research areas can be very informative in terms of understanding how visuospatial rehearsal processes might operate within working memory.

Oculomotor processes and spatial working memory

An early series of studies conducted by Idzikowski and colleagues proposed that processes associated with eye movements might act as a rehearsal mechanism within the visuospatial domain (reported in Baddeley 1986; see also Postle, Idzikowski, Della Sala *et al.* 2006). They examined the effect on verbal and spatial working memory of asking participants to track a sinusoidally moving target with their eyes. Their results showed that concurrent eye movements produced a significant decline in spatial working memory in comparison to a verbal control and a condition in which the background to the target moved while the eyes remained stationary. In addition, Idzikowski *et al.* found that the interference effect occurred during both the encoding and/or retrieval of the spatial material. Baddeley (1986) concluded from these findings that rehearsal in visuospatial working memory might occur via an active process linked to oculomotor control that refreshed visuospatial material represented within a passive perceptual input store. This proposed structure mirrored the relationship between a phonological store and an articulatory loop that had already been proposed to account for rehearsal within verbal working memory (Baddeley and Lewis 1981, Baddeley 1986).

However, later studies demonstrated that both the sequential tapping of keys (Smyth, Pearson and Pendleton 1988; Smyth and Pendleton 1989; Logie and Marchetti 1991; Pearson, Logie and Gilhooly 1999) and arm movements across an unseen matrix (Quinn and Ralston 1986; Quinn 1991) could produce interference in spatial working memory even in the absence of related eye movements. Johnson (1982) also found that simply asking participants to imagine making an arm movement was enough to disrupt temporary memory for location, implying that the cognitive planning of movement alone was sufficient to produce interference even if the actual movement itself was not physically enacted. This potential overlap between a spatial rehearsal mechanism and processes underlying the planning and production of movement forms the basis of a model of visuospatial working memory proposed by Logie (1995). The model consists of an active spatial "inner scribe" mechanism which extracts information from a passive visual cache system to allow for targeted movement. A direct prediction of Logie's model is that the production of physical movement, or even simply planned production without overt movement, should significantly interfere with any task that also requires the operation of the inner scribe, which includes the temporary retention of sequential locations or movements (Logie 1995).

However, the extent to which actual explicit or implicit motor processes might be involved during the operation of visuospatial working memory remains controversial, particularly regarding temporary memory for serially presented sequences of spatial locations. Smyth and Scholey (1994) demonstrated that spatial recall span could be significantly impaired if participants were exposed to visual or auditory signals appearing in different spatial locations. The level of impairment was increased further if participants were required to point to the location of the signal or make left/right categorical judgments. A follow-up study that controlled for eye movements confirmed that it was covert shifts in attention alone that were significantly disrupting spatial span, in the clear absence of any overt movement of the eyes or limbs (Smyth 1996). Smyth and colleagues interpreted these results as providing evidence that the rehearsal of location in spatial working memory was based on shifts of spatial attention rather than the operation of implicit motor processes. The interference produced by concurrent eye or limb movements could therefore be accounted for in terms of related shifts in spatial attention rather than the planning and production of the actual movement itself.

A more detailed model of attention-based spatial rehearsal has been proposed by Awh and colleagues (Awh, Anllo-Vento and Hillyard 2000; Awh and Jonides 2001). They have argued that spatial rehearsal invokes a frontal-parietal system that actively maintains spatial information via focal shifts of spatial attention to memorized locations held within working memory. Awh, Jonides and Reuter-Lorenz (1998) found that asking participants to hold a specified location in working memory facilitated visual processing of stimuli appearing in that location in comparison to control stimuli appearing in nonmemorized locations. Awh et al. (1998) also found that disrupting the focus of spatial location during a retention interval significantly interfered with participants' accuracy on a spatial memory task in comparison to a condition in which the focus of attention was kept static. On the basis of such findings Awh and colleagues have argued that the process of visual selection is a key component of rehearsal within spatial working memory, with the cognitive mechanisms involved during spatial selective attention also being used to provide functional markers for location-specific representations in working memory (Awh and Jonides 2001; Awh, Sgarlata and Kliestik 2005).

The account of spatial rehearsal offered by Awh and colleagues assumes a supramodel basis for attention, in which covert shifts in spatial attention involve processes that are functionally independent from those that mediate oculomotor programming (Awh, Jonides and Reuter-Lorenz 1998; Awh, Anllo-Vento and Hillyard 2000). However, a study conducted by myself and Arash Sahraie suggests that oculomotor control processes may play a significant role during rehearsal within visuospatial working memory (Pearson and Sahraie 2003). In a series of experiments we contrasted the effect of concurrent eye movements, limb movements and covert shifts in attention on participants' working memory for sequentially presented spatial locations. Participants' spatial span was assessed using a computerized version of the Corsi blocks task illustrated in Figure 14.1. All conditions that required participants to move their eyes during a retention interval resulted in

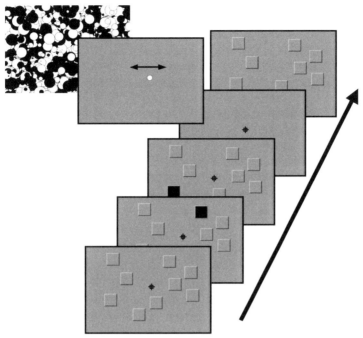

Figure 14.1 Diagram of screenshots depicting the order and timing of events in a computerized Corsi blocks procedure. The example shown depicts a two-location trial. Events run in the direction of the arrow and represent (1) initial presentation of array of blocks, (2) presentation of first location, (3) presentation of second location, (4) five-second retention interval with presentation of uniform field and fixation point (screenshots from conditions with continuous pursuit eye movements and visual noise also illustrated), (5) block array reappears and participants indicate position and order of presented locations using the PC mouse. Reproduced from Pearson and Sahraie (2003).

a significantly greater reduction in span than comparable conditions in which covert attention shifts or limb movements occurred while the eyes remained fixated (Figure 14.2). The type of eye movement performed during the retention interval was also found to be important, with saccadic eye movements producing significantly greater interference than continuous smooth pursuit of a moving target. Finally, analysis of the type of recall errors committed by participants showed that both saccadic and smooth pursuit eye movements produced a significantly greater proportion of spatial location errors (i.e., selecting a location that was not part of the presented sequence) than temporal order errors (i.e., selecting a presented location in the incorrect serial order) in comparison with non-eye movement conditions.

An earlier study conducted by Lawrence, Myerson, Oonk *et al.* (2001) had proposed that all spatially directed movement produces similar effects within visuospatial working memory. In contrast, Pearson and Sahraie (2003) found that concurrent eye movement produces significantly greater levels of interference than other spatially directed disruptors, and that the strength of interference can be modulated by the type of eye movement being executed. On the basis of these findings it was argued that eye movements can act as a unique form of disrupter for the temporary memory of sequentially presented spatial locations. However, no evidence was found to suggest that participants were using overt eye movements as a rehearsal strategy to retain a sequence of serially presented locations. Participants made no consistent eye movements during

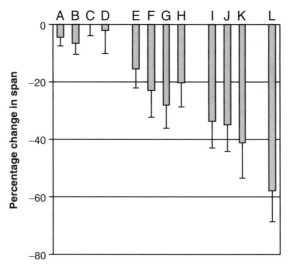

Figure 14.2 Illustration of the percentage change in baseline for: (a) Free eye movement; (b) Eyes shut with no movement; (c) Visual noise; (d) Articulatory suppression; (e) Continuous covert attention shifts; (f) Continuous covert attention shift plus color change monitoring and report; (g) Discrete covert attention shifts; (h) Spatial tapping; (i) Smooth pursuit eye movement; (j) Smooth pursuit eye movement plus color change monitoring and report; (k) Saccadic eye movement with eyes shut; (l) Saccadic eye movement with eyes open. Reproduced from Pearson and Sahraie (2003).

a retention interval in which they were free to move their eyes in any way they wished, and spatial recall span was not significantly different from conditions in which their eyes had to remain fixated. When questioned, participants reported initially expecting that overt eye movements would be beneficial, but in practice they found that such movements appeared to hinder their performance. Some participants reported consciously trying to keep their eyes as still as possible while rehearsing the presented spatial sequences. This suggests that overt eye movements may actually be ineffective as a rehearsal strategy for maintaining sequentially-presented visuospatial information, particularly under circumstances in which sequence-lengths longer than one or two locations need to be maintained. Some previous studies using the Corsi blocks procedure have argued that overt pointing to one location during recall may interfere with memory representations held in working memory for later responses (Smyth and Scholey 1994; Hale, Myerson, Rhee *et al.* 1996). It is possible that a retention strategy based on overt eye movement might result in eye movements to locations presented early in a sequence producing interference with the representation of locations presented later in a sequence. However, the issue of the usefulness of eye movements as a retention strategy requires greater study, as it is equally possible that the participants reported by Pearson and Sahraie were simply too highly practised at having to perform the spatial memory task while keeping their eyes fixated (e.g., Laeng and Teodorescu 2002).

In the theory of spatial rehearsal proposed by Awh and colleagues (Awh *et al.* 1998, 2000, 2005, Awh and Jonides 2001) spatial representations are actively maintained by focal shifts of attention to memorized locations held in working memory. It has been well-established that, while in the majority of cases attention shifts are accompanied by corresponding movement of the eyes or limbs, focal attention can also be dissociated from the direction of gaze (James 1890/1905; see also Posner 1980; Umiltà 1988). In addition, the preparation of an eye movement towards a location appears to automatically induce a concurrent shift of attention towards the same location

(Chelazzi, Biscaldi, Corbetta *et al.* 1995; Shepherd, Findlay and Hockey 1986). Therefore, while voluntarily produced eye movements are always accompanied by a corresponding overt shift in attention (Hoffman and Subramaniam 1995; Rizzolatti, Riggio, Dascola *et al.* 1987), covert attention shifts can also be carried out independently of eye movements.

While previous studies have shown that covert attention shifts alone can disrupt temporary memory for spatial location (Smyth and Scholey 1994; Smyth 1996; Awh *et al.* 1998), the results of Pearson and Sahraie (2003) show that this disruption is significantly less than that produced by equivalent eye movements. These findings could be accounted for by an attention-based theory of spatial rehearsal if it is assumed that the attention shift associated with a voluntary eye movement is substantially larger than a covert attention shift carried out while the gaze remains fixated. Alternatively, separate processes could underlie both effects. Considering the close integration of attentional and oculomotor processes at the neural level, it may be misleading to consider the temporary maintenance of spatial information in terms of a supramodel model of attention, in which the control of focal attention is viewed as being independent of the processes involved during oculomotor control (Posner 1980; Klein 1980; Klein, Kingstone and Pontefract 1992). As an alternative, Rizzolatti and colleagues have put forward a premotor account of attention which proposes that spatial attention is derived from the operation of maps used to code space for programming eye movements, rather than as a consequence of specific attentional circuits (Rizzolatti 1983; Rizzolatti, Riggio, Dascola *et al.*1987, 1994; Sheliga, Riggio and Rizzolatti 1995; Umiltà, Mucignat, Riggio *et al.* 1994). Support for this view is provided by an fMRI study conducted by Beauchamp *et al.* (Beauchamp, Petit, Ellmore *et al.* 2001). They found that covert attention shifts to a target location were produced by moderate degrees of activation in oculomotor control areas, which were sufficient to orient the focus of spatial attention to a target without generating a corresponding eye movement. This suggests that covert attention shifts are mediated by the same processes that mediate oculomotor programming.

Pearson and Sahraie (2003) concluded that the disruption of spatial working memory caused by concurrent eye movement and covert attention shifts were produced by interference in an oculomotor control network rather than a more general attention-based rehearsal mechanism. This can be related to the work of Brockmole and colleagues, who have proposed that visual processing involves an integration between visual percepts and representations stored in visual short-term memory (Brockmole, Irwin and Wang 2003; Brockmole and Wang 2003; Brockmole, Wang and Irwin 2002). Recently Brockmole and Irwin (2005) have examined the role of eye movements during the consolidation and maintenance of information in visual short-term memory. Their participants were required to integrate together two sequentially presented visual arrays that appeared either in the same or different spatial locations. When the spatial location of both arrays remained constant, there was little evidence that overt eye movements were necessary for integration to occur. However, when the position of the second array was different to that of the first, participants made systematic eye movements to the spatial position of the original array during integration. This finding is consistent with previous research which suggests that eye movements may play a functional role in linking together mental and retinal images (Hebb 1968; Brandt and Stark 1997; Spivey and Geng 2001).

Such temporal integration is a key feature of procedures such as the Corsi blocks paradigm (Corsi 1972; Berch, Krikorian, and Huha 1998), in which a series of sequentially presented locations must be integrated together into a single continuous path or movement sequence. A number of previous studies have demonstrated that serial memory for a sequence of locations is affected not just by the absolute number of locations presented, but also by the characteristics of the order in which the locations are presented (Smirni, Villardita and Zappala 1983; Helstrup 1999; Kemps 2001). Parmentier, Elford and Maybery (2005) have recently examined in detail how serial memory for a sequence of locations can be affected by different characteristics of a presented sequence. The number of path crossings, path length and mean angular variation of a sequence were all found to significantly affect participants' serial recall accuracy. Parmentier *et al.* characterize these factors as representing transitional information, and argue that their influence on serial recall of locations bears similarity to the effect of transitional information on order memory for verbal material (Murray and Jones 2002; Stuart and Hulme 2000).

Whilst visuospatial working memory lacks the type of formal models for serial memory which have been proposed for verbal material (e.g., Henson 1998; Burgess and Hitch 1992), empirical data such as that collected by Paramentier *et al.* can be seen to represent an essential step in establishing such models. However, while such models may prove valuable in reaching a greater understanding of serial memory than that known for verbal stimuli, their usefulness in terms of a general understanding of visuospatial working memory may be more limited. The development of visuospatial memory procedures such as the Corsi blocks task were strongly influenced by serial recall techniques developed to study verbal short-term memory (e.g., Ebbinghaus 1885/1913; Wickelgren 1965). However, while serial recall of verbal stimuli arguably captures important functional characteristics of verbal short-term memory, the same need not be true of the serial recall of visuospatial material. Auditory input is inherently serial in nature, and accurate representation of serial order forms an essential aspect of the comprehension and recall of linguistic information. In contrast there is much greater variety in terms of visuospatial input, where the same series of locations can be presented either sequentially or simultaneously (Logie and Pearson 1997; Pickering, Gathercole, Hall *et al.* 2001; Rudkin, Pearson and Logie, 2007). The functional value of preserving serial order outside the artificial constraints of experimental learning paradigms is considerably weaker for visuospatial working memory than that established for verbal working memory. Parmentier *et al.* (2005) have argued that participants' performance on serial visuospatial tasks should be considered as a problem-solving exercise. They note that, in contrast to verbal tasks, visuospatial serial recall does not seem to benefit from a well-practiced rehearsal strategy such as subvocal rehearsal, nor does it involve well-established preexisting representations in long-term memory. This view is consistent with studies which have shown a heavy executive involvement in visuospatial short-term memory (Baddeley, Cocchini, Della Sala *et al.* 2007), as well as recent data which shows greater executive involvement in serial sequential visuospatial tasks than simultaneous tasks that do not require serial recall (Rudkin, Pearson and Logie, 2007). If this is accepted, however, it raises the issue of whether there may be alternative paradigms that better capture how visuospatial working memory might operate under more naturalistic settings. The second half of this chapter will concentrate on one such alternative: multiple-target tracking.

Working memory involvement during multiple-target tracking

In addition to the limitations of focusing on serial recall, paradigms such as Corsi blocks or similar variants only present participants with static target locations that, although they may become occluded during a retention period, do not change spatial position relative to the viewer. Such procedures seem poorly equipped to capture the dynamic nature of the environment we live in. Navigation through a complex three-dimensional environment requires a coordination of movements with a number of objects that may themselves also be in motion. This will require some form of real-time cognitive ability that can simultaneously keep track of a number of moving targets (Allen, McGeorge, Pearson *et al.* 2004, 2006).

A highly influential account of multiple-target tracking is the spatial index theory proposed by Pylyshyn and colleagues (McKeever and Pylyshyn 1993; Pylyshyn 1994, 2001; Pylyshyn *et al.* 1994; Pylyshyn and Storm 1988; Sears and Pylyshyn 2000; Trick and Pylyshyn 1989, 1993).

The theory proposes that multiple-target tracking is dependent on a limited number of preattentive indexes that can be attracted to targets as they appear within the visual field. Once an index has been assigned it will continue to point to the target even if it moves, thereby drawing attentional processes to its location. This spatial index model was first proposed by Pylyshyn and Storm (1988) who studied participants' ability to track a number of visual targets amongst a set of distractors. They were required to respond accurately to the onset of a probe which could appear over a target or over a distractor. Their results showed that participants could successfully keep track of up to five targets from a set of ten. However, participants' accuracy and reaction times declined gradually as the number of targets increased rather than failing catastrophically, which was more consistent with a resource-limited rather than preattentive process. Pylyshyn and Storm argued that this could be due to the operation of a resource-limited serial process which cycled through indexed targets in order to determine which one had been probed.

However, Yantis (1992) provides an alternative explanation. Yantis argues that, prior to the commencement of tracking, targets are grouped together into a single, higher-order virtual object to which attention is then directed – a "virtual polygon" (Yantis 1992, p. 301). Once established this virtual object is then monitored and updated by comparing it with the stimulus input throughout the objects' motion. Unlike the initial preattentive assignment of indexes to targets, this updating process is dependent upon attentional resources. The points at which the sides of the virtual polygon meet define the moment-by-moment locations of the targets being tracked. Therefore the size, shape, orientation and position of the virtual polygon will change continuously as the individual targets move.

A common feature of the explanations for multiple-target tracking offered by Pylyshyn and Yantis is that both divide the tracking task into two distinct phases: a target acquisition phase, followed by a tracking phase concerned with the maintenance and/or identification of the indexed targets. Where the explanations diverge is in terms of the stage of tracking at which attentional resources become involved. According to Yantis, attentional involvement is vital for the initial formation of the virtual object prior to the commencement of tracking. In contrast, Pylyshyn argues that attention is engaged during the tracking phase, but is not involved during initial target acquisition.

Within the multicomponent working memory framework established by Baddeley, Hitch and colleagues, it would seem reasonable to expect that the visual, spatial and executive components could all make some form of contribution during performance of multiple-target tracking. However, although both Pylyshyn and Yantis propose a tracking phase that requires the temporary maintenance and updating of targets after initial acquisition, the cognitive processes within short-term memory that are responsible have not been clearly specified. Yantis' description of the formation of a virtual polygon in particular could be viewed as an example of 'chunking' phenomena, in which separate items in short-term memory are organized into combined units (Miller 1956; Cowan 2001). Yantis (1992) found that participants who were presented targets in a canonical configuration (thereby providing visual clues about virtual polygon formation) performed better than participants presented with a random display of targets. However, this advantage disappeared after the initial stages of the experiment. Yantis suggested that this was due to participants in the random condition discovering a grouping strategy for themselves. This implies that parts of the target acquisition process could be subject to conscious strategic influences that might engage the resources of the central executive component.

A series of studies conducted by Allen and colleagues have examined the potential role played by working memory during multiple target tracking (Allen, McGeorge, Pearson *et al.* 2004, 2006). Allen *et al.* (2004) contrasted multiple target tracking ability in groups of professional radar operators and undergraduate students. The radar operators where classified as experts in tracking because of their presumed skill at dynamic spatial tasks, while the undergraduates were classified as novices. All participants completed the tracking task (Figure 14.3) together with a concurrent digit categorization task that took place either before or after the target acquisition stage. Results showed that executive resources appeared to make a contribution to target tracking for both novice and expert groups, but only the novice group showed greater disruption from the categorization task if it occurred during target acquisition. The expert group also outperformed the novice group on the tracking task in all conditions, suggesting that performance may improve given sufficient practice in related spatial tasks. Recently Trick, Jaspers-Fayer and Sethi (2005) have examined tracking performance in children aged from six to nineteen years of age using a modified

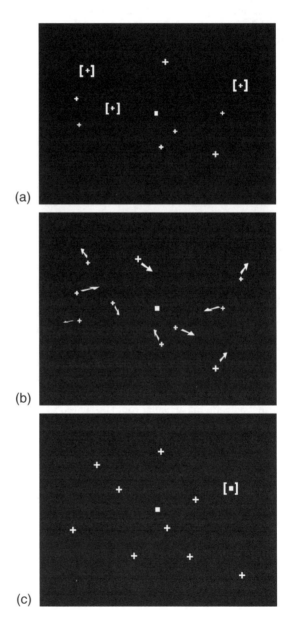

(a)

(b)

Figure 14.3 (a) Target acquisition phase (objects in brackets are flashing on and off). (b) Target tracking phase (objects no longer flashing and all are moving at random). (c) Probe (the probed object is briefly transformed into a square). Reproduced from Allen, McGeorge, Pearson, and Milne (2006).

(c)

version of the Pylyshyn and Storm (1988) procedure called "Catch the Spies". They found that children who regularly played action-oriented video games performed significantly better than children who did not. Of course, with results such as these it is unclear whether practice improves performance, or whether individuals with inherently better tracking ability are more likely to participate in such activities than individuals with poorer ability. However, a study conducted by Green and Bavelier (2003) has suggested that practice with a spatially themed video game can improve ability to allocate attention during perception after as little as ten hours of playing.

Allen *et al*.'s (2004) results also indicated that tracking performance was affected by the number of targets being tracked, as participants' ability to track the targets decreased as the number of targets increased. While Pylyshyn and colleagues have argued that the initial assignment of spatial indexes is preattentive, they have also suggested several potential roles for attentional processes during multiple-target tracking. These include checking whether or not a target has been probed (Pylyshyn and Storm 1988) or maintaining an index against the effects of decay or interference (Burkell and Pylyshyn 1997). Yantis (1992) has also argued that attentional processes are involved during the maintenance of a virtual object during tracking. Allen *et al*.'s (2004) finding that both experts and novices display a decrement in tracking performance with a concurrent categorization task is consistent with an involvement of executive resources.

Allen *et al*. (2004) also found that the novice group showed a greater decrement when the concurrent task was performed during target acquisition, but that this was not the case for the expert group. This implies that the attentional demands of the categorization task interfered with novices' ability to find or apply an appropriate encoding strategy during target acquisition. In contrast, for radar operators the strategic elements of target acquisition appeared to be either more automatic or require less attentional resources. A follow-up study conducted by Allen *et al*. has examined in more detail the impact on tracking performance of articulatory suppression and spatial tapping as well as executive visual/verbal and auditory/verbal digit categorization tasks (Allen, McGeorge, Pearson *et al*. 2006). They found that tracking performance declined as cognitive load increased, which is consistent with the involvement of a resource-limited system such as the central executive. In all dual-task conditions participants displayed longer response times and significantly poorer ability to discriminate targets from distractors in comparison to single task conditions. In addition, both the visual/verbal digit categorization and spatial tapping tasks produced a significant decrement in participants' target/distractor trial discrimination performance. These decrements occurred during the target acquisition phase when participants are believed to be consciously developing a tracking strategy (Yantis 1992). This suggests that the formation of a virtual polygon that connects individual targets may implicate specific visuospatial processes within working memory.

The results of Allen *et al*. (2006) are consistent with Pylyshyn and Storm's (1988) original proposal that targets appearing in the visual field are tagged by indexes for subsequent attentional processing. The notion of preattentive processing followed by attentional input is also central to descriptions of the operation of "object files" during perception (Kahneman, Treisman and Gibb 1992; Wolfe and Bennett 1997). Kahneman *et al*. have proposed that a critical feature of object tracking is the establishment and use of temporary episodic representations called "object files" that emerge as the main end product of perceptual processing of a stationary scene (1992, p. 178). Along similar lines, Wolfe and Bennett (1997) have argued that during the early stages of perceptual processing the visual array is preattentively subdivided into object-like perceptual entities, although these would appear to relate to earlier processing stages than those discussed by Kahneman *et al*.

In terms of multiple-target tracking, the initial grouping into a virtual object would reflect a static scene that could be encoded as an attentional object file. Visuospatial working memory, if involved during tracking, would most likely be active during the formation of such object files. During target acquisition each indexed target could be encapsulated within a separate preattentive object file. Following this the application of a tracking strategy as proposed by Yantis (1992) could result in individual targets being "chunked" together to form a single attentional object file. Such an action would be consistent with Wolfe and Bennett's (1997) proposal that attentional resources play a key role during the binding of preattentive information during perception. After this initial phase, visuospatial working memory could be involved in incorporating the necessary spatial and relational information to establish the indexed targets' arrangement in an initially static scene (Kahneman *et al.* 1992). The central executive could also be expected to play a role during the moment-to-moment comparisons of object files that occur during the tracking process itself.

Pylyshyn and Storm (1988) originally argued that the tracking of multiple targets requires only a single focus of attention that can cycle rapidly through all indexed locations, returning to the first index before the target has moved too far from its original location. Similarly, the strategy of grouping targets into a virtual object suggested by Yantis (1992) also only requires a single focus for attention. In contrast, Cavanagh and Alvarez (2005) have recently proposed that tracking may instead be dependent on multifocal attention. They argue that attention has a fixed bandwidth available for target selection which can be shared across multiple input channels or targets if necessary (thereby resulting in limited capacity for encoding in each channel), or alternatively allocated solely to a single channel or target (thereby providing the maximum capacity for encoding). If such a multifocal attentional process exists, Cavanagh and Alvarez argue that the control processes necessary to deploy and position multiple input channels would be significantly greater than those necessary for deployment of a single focus for attention. Again, there is a potential link here to the notion of the involvement of executive working memory processes during the tracking of multiple targets or objects, assuming that the control and coordination of such multiple input channels would engage executive resources.

Summary and conclusions

This chapter has briefly reviewed work in two research literatures; one concerned with cognitive processes involved in maintaining a series of sequentially presented locations, the other with processes involved in tracking multiple moving targets and distinguishing them from distractors. Although both of these literatures have developed with little direct relation to each other, I would argue that there are substantial areas of overlap, particularly regarding the potential involvement of working memory processes.

In his proposal for an episodic buffer Baddeley (2000) commented that there was little evidence for a specific output process in visuospatial working memory that was equivalent to the subvocal rehearsal of verbal and auditory material. However, since then a number of studies have demonstrated the importance of factors associated with eye movements, although the extent to which they might constitute an active rehearsal mechanism remains unresolved. Pearson and Sahraie (2003) have argued that concurrent eye movements produce a unique form of interference in spatial working memory, and that an oculomotor control network plays a crucial role during the short-term rehearsal of location-specific representations. The work of Brockmole and Irwin (2005) also demonstrates that eye movements appear to play a functional role during the integration of mental and retinal images within working memory. During a discussion of how distractor items are excluded during visual selection, Awh *et al.* have suggested that regular changes in eye position produce multiple retinotopic maps that support an attentional mechanism for controlling distractor exclusion (Awh, Sgarlata and Kliestik 2005). Requiring participants who are performing the Corsi blocks task to produce a series of task-unrelated eye movements during a retention interval may generate extraneous retinotopic maps that interfere with the encoded representations of presented locations in working memory (Pearson and Sahraie 2003).

Another important factor relevant to visuospatial rehearsal processes is how differential strategy selection may impact on spatial span performance. Parmentier, Elford and Maybery (2005) have identified the number of path crossings, path length and mean angular variation of a sequence as factors that can all significantly affect participants' serial recall accuracy. They suggest that performance of serial spatial recall may be better characterized as a problem-solving exercise in contrast to a highly automated process such as subvocal rehearsal. However, a potential limiting factor of many studies of spatial working memory is too great an emphasis on serial recall, which may not provide a naturalistic test of how visuospatial working memory operates in a majority of everyday cognitive situations.

In the case of multiple-target tracking, research has shown that tracking performance can be separated into two distinct phases; a target acquisition phase followed by a target tracking phase. The work of Allen *et al.* (2004, 2006) suggests that after targets within the visual field have been preattentively indexed, conscious processes are then used to develop a tracking strategy prior to target movement. This conscious strategy formation is vulnerable to secondary task interference from concurrent visual and spatial tasks. Once random movement of targets commences the central executive component of working memory becomes involved in keeping track of indexed locations, perhaps by repeatedly comparing a succession of target object files and inhibiting the creation of new object files (Allen *et al.* 2006).

A key issue that needs to be addressed in future studies in these areas is the extent to which working memory processes involved during the retention of sequentially presented locations are also involved during multiple target tracking. It is possible that "the very notion of object files may be synonymous with the activities of the visuo-spatial sketchpad" (Allen *et al.* 2006, p. 1114), in which case the limitation on the number of objects that can be tracked may reflect the general resource-limited capacity of working memory (Cowan 2001). It has not yet been established whether a spatial indexing process such as that proposed by Pylyshyn and colleagues could also play a role during the encoding of locations during a Corsi blocks-style procedure. In principle any target appearing within the visual field should be capable of attracting an index. The work of Scholl and Pylyshyn (1999) suggests that indexes can only persist during a retention interval if it is treated as an episode of occlusion rather than of a target disappearing and reappearing. However, if target acquisition is followed by a much more strategic conscious process, it is not clear how this would adapt in a situation in which targets are absent during an interval but do not change their spatial position. The image-based tracking strategy suggested by Yantis (1992) could be viewed as synonymous with similar image-based retention strategies that have been proposed for the retention of sequence of locations or movements (Parmentier *et al.* 2005; Kemps 2001; Helstrup 1999; Berch *et al.* 1998), with visuospatial working memory performing a similar type of function across both forms of task.

In conclusion, visuospatial rehearsal processes within working memory are clearly more complex than comparable rehearsal processes that may operate for verbal material, and appear to engage both modality-specific and more general attentional resources. Despite this additional complexity, I would argue that real progress has been made in establishing the cognitive processes that underlie the encoding and maintenance of visuospatial information in working memory. Future progress will be enriched further by taking a perspective on visuospatial working memory that extends beyond focusing primarily on understanding issues related to serial recall, and also by combining together findings and experimental paradigms from different literatures in psychology and vision research, and working to establish commonalities in theoretical issues and problems being addressed.

References

Allen, R, McGeorge, P, Pearson, DG and Milne, AB (2006). Multiple-target tracking: A role for working memory? *Quarterly Journal of Experimental Psychology*, *59*(6), 1101–1116.

Allen, R, McGeorge, P, Pearson, D and Milne, AB (2004). Attention and expertise in multiple target tracking. *Applied Cognitive Psychology*, *18*, 337–347.

Awh, E, Anllo-Vento, L and Hillyard, SA (2000). The role of spatial selective attention in working memory for locations: Evidence from event-related potentials. *Journal of Cognitive Neuroscience*, *12*(5), 840–847.

Awh, E and Jonides, J (2001). Overlapping mechanisms of attention and spatial working memory. *Trends in Cognitive Sciences*, *5*(3), 119–126.

Awh, E, Jonides, J and Reuter-Lorenz, PA (1998). Rehearsal in spatial working memory. *Journal of Experimental Psychology: Human Perception and Performance*, *24*, 780–790.

Awh, E, Sgarlata, AM and Kliestik, J (2005). Resolving visual interference during covert spatial orienting: Online attentional control through static records of prior visual experience. *Journal of Experimental Psychology: General*, *134*(2), 192–206.

Baddeley, AD (1986). *Working Memory*. Oxford: Oxford University Press.

Baddeley, AD (2000). The episodic buffer: a new component of working memory? *Trends in Cognitive Sciences*, *4*(11), 417–423.

Baddeley, AD, Cocchini, G, Della Sala, S, Logie, RH and Spinnler, H (1999). Working memory and vigilance: Evidence from normal aging and Alzheimer's disease. *Brain and Cognition*, *41*, 87–108.

Baddeley, AD and Hitch, GJ (1974). Working Memory. In G Bower (ed), *The Psychology of Learning and Motivation* (pp. 47–89). New York: Academic Press

Baddeley, AD and Lewis, VJ (1981). Inner active processes in reading: The inner voice, the inner ear and the inner eye. In AM Lesgold and CA Perfetti (eds), *Interactive Processes in Reading* (pp. 107–129). Hillsdale, NJ: LEA.

Beauchamp, MS, Petit, L, Ellmore, TM, Ingeholm, J and Haxby, JV (2001). A parametric fMRI study of overt and covert shifts of visuospatial attention. *NeuroImage*, *14*, 310–321.

Berch, DB, Krikorian, R and Huha, EM (1998). The Corsi block-tapping task: Methodological and theoretical considerations. *Brain and Cognition*, *38*(3), 317–338.

Brandt, SA and Stark, LW (1997). Spontaneous eye movements during visual imagery reflect the content of the visual scene. *Journal of Cognitive Neuroscience*, *9*, 27–38.

Brockmole, JR and Irwin, DE (2005). Eye movements and the integration of visual memory and visual perception. *Perception and Psychophysics*, *67*(3), 495–512.

Brockmole, JR, Irwin, DE and Wang, RF (2003). The locus of spatial attention during the temporal integration of visual memories and visual percepts. *Psychonomic Bulletin and Review*, *10*, 510–515.

Brockmole, JR and Wang, RF (2003). Integrating visual images and visual percepts across time and space. *Visual Cognition*, *10*, 853–874.

Brockmole, JR, Wang, RF and Irwin, DE (2002). Temporal integration between visual images and visual percepts. *Journal of Experimental Psychology: Human Perception and Performance*, *28*, 315–334.

Burgess, N and GJ Hitch (1992). Towards a network model of the articulatory loop. *Journal of Memory and Language*, *31*(4), 429–460.

Burkell, J. A. and Pylyshyn, Z. W. (1997). Searching through subsets: a test of the visual indexing hypothesis. *Spatial Vision*, *11*(2), 225–258.

Cavanagh, P and Alvarez, GA (2005). Tracking multiple targets with multifocal attention. *Trends in Cognitive Sciences*, *9*(7), 349–354.

Chelazzi, L, Biscaldi, M, Corbetta, M, Peru, A and Berlucchi, G (1995). Oculomotor activity and visual spatial attention. *Behavioural and Brain Research*, *71*, 81–88.

Corsi, PM (1972). Human memory and the medial temporal region of the brain. Doctoral dissertation, McGill University, Montreal.

Cowan, N (2001). The magic number 4 in short-term memory: A reconsideration of mental storage capacity. *Behavioral and Brain Sciences*, *24*, 87–185.

Ebbinghaus, H (1885). Uber das Gedachtnis. Leipzig: Dunker. (Translation by H Ruyer and CE Bussenius, (1913), *Memory*. New York: Teachers College, Columbia University.

Green, CS and Bavelier, D (2003). Action video game modifies visual selective attention. *Nature*, *423*(6939), 534–537.

Hale, S, Myerson, J, Rhee, SH, Weiss, CS and Abrams, RA (1996). Selective interference with the maintenance of location information in working memory. *Neuropsychology*, *10*, 228–240.

Hebb, DO (1968). Concerning imagery. *Psychological Review*, *75*, 466–477.

Helstrup, T (1999). Visuo-spatial encoding of movement patterns. *European Journal of Cognitive Psychology*, *11*(3), 357–371.

Henson, RNA (1998). Short-term memory for serial order: the start-end model. *Cognitive Psychology*, *36*, 73–137.

Hoffman, JE and Subramaniam, B (1995). The role of visual attention in saccadic eye movements. *Perception and Psychophysics*, *57*, 787–795.

James, W (1890). *Principles of Psychology, Vol. 1.* (1905 edn). London: Methuen and Co.

Johnson, P (1982). The functional equivalence of imagery and movement. *Quarterly Journal of Experimental Psychology*, *34*(A), 349–365.

Kahneman, D, Treisman, A and Gibb, B J (1992). The reviewing of object files – object-specific integration of information. *Cognitive Psychology, 24*(2), 175–219.

Kemps, E (2001). Complexity effects in visuo-spatial working memory: Implications for the role of long-term memory. *Memory*, *9*(1), 13–27.

Klein, R (1980). Does oculomotor readiness mediate cognitive control of visual attention? In RS Nicerson (ed), *Attention and Performance VII* (pp. 259–276). Hillsdale, NJ: Erlbaum.

Klein, RM, Kingstone, A and Pontefract, A (1992). Orienting of visual attention. In K Rayner (ed), *Eye Movements and Visual Cognition: Scene perception and reading* (pp. 46–65). New York: Springer.

Laeng, B and Teodorescu, D (2002). Eye scanpaths during visual imagery re-enact those of perception of the same visual scene. *Cognitive Science*, *26*, 207–231.

Lawrence, BM, Myerson, J, Oonk, HM and Abrams, RA (2001). The effects of eye and limb movements on working memory. *Memory*, *9*(4–6), 433–444.

Logie, RH (1995). *Visuo-spatial Working Memory*. Hove: LEA.

Logie, RH and Marchetti, C. (1991). Visuo-spatial working memory: Visual, spatial, or central executive? In RH Logie and M Denis (eds), *Mental Images in Human Cognition* (pp. 105–115). Amsterdam: North Holland Press.

Logie, RH and Pearson, DG (1997). The inner eye and the inner scribe of visuospatial working memory: Evidence from developmental fractionation. *European Journal of Cognitive Psychology*, *9*(3), 241–257.

McKeever, P and Pylyshyn, Z (1993). *Nontarget numerosity and identity maintenance with FINSTs: A two component account of multiple target tracking.* Centre for Cognitive Science, University of Western Ontario, Technical Report: Cogmem 65.

Miller, GA (1956). The magical number seven, plus or minus two: Some limits on our capacity for processing information. *Psychological Review*, *63*, 81–97.

Murray, A and Jones, DM (2002). Articulatory complexity at item boundaries in serial recall: The case of Welsh and English digit span. *Journal of Experimental Psychology: Learning, Memory and Cognition*, *28*, 594–598.

Parmentier, FB, Elford, G and Maybery, M (2005). Transitional information in spatial serial memory: Path characteristics affect recall performance. *Journal of Experimental Psychology: Learning, memory and cognition*, *31*(3), 412–427.

Pearson, DG (2001). Imagery and the visuo-spatial sketchpad. In J Andrade (ed), *Working Memory in Perspective*. Hove, UK: Psychology Press.

Pearson, DG (2006). The episodic buffer: Implications and connections with visuo-spatial research. In T Vecchi and G Bottini (eds), *Imagery and Spatial Cognition: Methods, models and cognitive assessment,* pp. 139–53. Amsterdam: John Benjamins Publishing Company.

Pearson, DG, Logie, RH and Gilhooly, K (1999). Verbal representations and spatial manipulation during mental synthesis. *European Journal of Cognitive Psychology, 11*(3), 295–314.

Pearson, DG and Sahraie, A (2003). Oculomotor control and the maintenance of spatially and temporally distributed events in visuo-spatial working memory. *Quarterly Journal of Experimental Psychology, 56A*(7), 1089–1111.

Pickering SJ, Gathercole SE, Hall, M and Lloyd SA (2001). Development of memory for pattern and path: Further evidence for the fractionation of visuo-patial memory. *Quarterly Journal of Experimental Psychology, 54A*(4), 397–420.

Posner, MI (1980). Orienting of attention. *Quarterly Journal of Experimental* Psychology, *32,* 3–25.

Postle, BR, Idzikowski, C, Della Sala, S, Logie, RH and Baddeley, AD (2006). The selective disruption of spatial working memory by eye movements. *Quarterly Journal of Experimental Psychology, 59*(1), 100–120.

Pylyshyn, Z (1994). Some Primitive Mechanisms of Spatial Attention. *Cognition, 50*(1–3), 363–384.

Pylyshyn, ZW (2001). Visual indexes, preconceptual objects and situated vision. *Cognition, 80*(1–2), 127–158.

Pylyshyn, Z, Burkell, J, Fisher, B, Sears, C, Schmidt, W and Trick, L (1994). Multiple parallel access in visual-attention. *Canadian Journal of Experimental Psychology-Revue Canadienne De Psychologie Experimentale, 48*(2), 260–283.

Pylyshyn, Z and Storm, RW (1988). Tracking multiple independent targets: Evidence for a parallel tracking mechanism. *Spatial Vision, 3*(3), 179–197.

Quinn, JG (1991). Towards a clarification of spatial processing. *Quarterly Journal of Experimental Psychology, 47A,* 465–480.

Quinn, JG and Ralston, GE (1986). Movement and attention in visual working memory. *Quarterly Journal of Experimental Psychology, 38*(A), 689–703.

Rizzolatti, G (1983). Mechanisms of selective attention in mammals. In JP Ewert, RR Capranica and DJ Ingle (eds), *Advances in Vertebrate Neuroethology* (pp. 261–297). London: Plenum Press.

Rizzolatti, G, Riggio, L, Dascola, I and Umilta, C (1987). Reorienting attention across the horizontal and vertical meridians: Evidence in favor of a premotor theory of attention. *Neuropsychologia, 25,* 31–40.

Rizzolatti, G, Riggio, L and Sheliga, BM (1994). Space and selective attention. In C Umilta and M Moscovitch (eds), *Attention and Performance XV* (pp. 231–265). Cambridge, MA: MIT Press.

Rudkin, SJ, Pearson, DG and Logie, RH (2007). Executive processes in visual and spatial working memory tasks. *Quarterly Journal of Experimental Psychology, 60,* 79–100.

Sears, CR and Pylyshyn, ZW (2000). Multiple object tracking and attentional processing. *Canadian Journal of Experimental Psychology-Revue Canadienne De Psychologie Experimentale, 54*(1), 1–14.

Scholl, BJ and Pylyshyn, ZW (1999). Tracking multiple items through occlusion: Clues to visual objecthood. *Cognitive Psychology, 38*(2), 259–290.

Sheliga, BM, Riggio, L and Rizzolatti, G (1995). Spatial attention and eye movements. *Experimental Brain Research, 105,* 261–275.

Shepherd, M, Findlay, J and Hockey, R (1986). The relationship between eye movements and spatial attention. *Quarterly Journal of Experimental Psychology, 38A,* 475–491.

Smirni, P, Villardita, C and Zappala, G (1983). Influence of different paths on spatial memory performance in the block-tapping test. *Journal of Clinical Neuropsychology, 5,* 355–359.

Smyth, MM (1996). Interference with rehearsal in spatial working memory in the absence of eye movements. *Quarterly Journal of Experimental Psychology, 49*(A4), 940–949.

Smyth, MM, Pearson, NA and Pendleton, LR (1988). Movement and working memory: Patterns and positions in space. *Quarterly Journal of Experimental Psychology, 40*(A), 497–514.

Smyth, MM and Pendleton, LR (1989). Working memory for movements. *Quarterly Journal of Experimental Psychology, 41*(A), 235–250.

Smyth, MM and Scholey, KA (1994). Interference in spatial immediate memory. *Memory and Cognition,* *22,* 1–13.

Spivey, MJ and Geng, JJ (2001). Oculomotor mechanisms activated by imagery and memory: Eye movements to absent objects. *Psychological Research, 65,* 235–241.

Stuart, G and Hulme, C (2000). The effects of word co-occurrence on short-term memory: Associative links in long-term memory affect short-term performance. *Journal of Experimental Psychology: Learning, Memory and Cognition, 26,* 796–802.

Stuyven, E, Van der Goten, K, Vandierendonck, A, Claeys, K and Crevits, L (2000). The effect of cognitive load on saccadic eye movements. *Acta Psychologica, 104,* 69–85.

Trick, LM, Jaspers-Fayer, F and Sethi, N (2005). Multiple-object tracking in children: The "Catch the Spies" task. *Cognitive Development, 20*(3), 373–387.

Trick, L and Pylyshyn, Z (1989). Subitizing and the finst spatial index model. *Bulletin of the Psychonomic Society, 27*(6), 490–490.

Trick, L and Pylyshyn, Z (1993). What enumeration studies can show us about spatial attention – evidence for limited capacity preattentive processing. *Journal of Experimental Psychology-Human Perception and Performance, 19*(2), 331–351.

Umiltà, C (1988). Orienting of attention. In F Boller and J Grafman (eds), *Handbook of Neuropsychology, Vol. 1* (pp. 175–193). Elsevier: Amsterdam.

Umiltà, C, Mucignat, C, Riggio, L, Barbieri, C and Rizzolatti, G (1994). Programming shifts of spatial attention. *European Journal of Cognitive Psychology, 6,* 23–41.

Wickelgren, WA (1965). Short-term memory for phonemically similar lists. *American Journal of Psychology, 78,* 657–574.

Wolfe, J M and Bennett, S C (1997). Preattentive object files: Shapeless bundles of basic features. *Vision Research, 37*(1), 25–43.

Yantis, S (1992). Multielement visual tracking: Attention and perceptual organization. *Cognitive Psychology, 24*(3), 295–340.

15

Towards a multicomponent view of executive control

The case of response selection

André Vandierendonck, Arnaud Szmalec,
Maud Deschuyteneer and Ann Depoorter

When Baddeley and Hitch (1974) first proposed their working memory model, the *central executive* constituted the core of the model. While it was initially not clear what exactly the functions of this executive system were, over the years it evolved into a ragbag of everything in working memory that was not easily explained by means of modality-specific slave systems (the phonological loop and the visuospatial sketch pad). By identifying the central executive with the supervisory attentional system (SAS) in the model of Norman and Shallice (1986), Baddeley (1986) tried to provide a more disciplined definition of the central executive. By doing this, the relationship between the notions of central executive and *executive functions* in the domain of neuropsychology became more transparent.

Today, notions akin to the central executive are present in many subfields of cognitive psychology, and the labels used may vary from executive functions, over executive processes to executive control (sometimes also called cognitive or attentional control). While all these concepts have been introduced, in order to get rid of prescientific terms such as *volition*, it is as yet not clear whether these new labels provide a better scientific service than the layman's terms that they are supposed to replace. The concepts of central executive, executive function and cognitive control are not less vague, neither less circular than the prescientific vocabulary is. Therefore, we argue that starting from an acceptable definition of executive control, there is a need for a different approach in which processes or processing components are identified that can explain behavioral effects which are usually associated with qualifications such as 'controlled' or 'executive', so that executive control *emerges* as a property of the interaction of processes in the system. While most views developed thus far assume that there is some cognitive agency responsible for cognitive control, in the present approach, cognitive control is believed to be the result of interactions in the cognitive system between task goal representations in working memory and activations of long-term memory representations. This proposal derives from our view that executive or cognitive control concerns the flexible guiding of behavior towards the achievement of particular goals (cf. Courtney 2004; Nieuwenhuis *et al.* 2004). Taking this starting point, in the present chapter we shall develop an approach based on the assumption that so-called 'controlled' or goal-directed behavior emerges from an interaction between representations of the task goal (and more generally, the task-set) maintained in temporary storage on the one hand and automatically triggered processes on the other hand. We shall argue that this interaction is present even at the level of such elementary processes as response selection. We will further develop the thesis that in a typical working memory context, this competition is amplified because the requirement to remember information (as in a complex span task) adds a simultaneous task, with its own specific task-set.

Findings from a number of recent studies will be presented to show that these interactions do indeed occur at the level of response selection.

Executive control

Every task we perform starts from a representation of what is to be achieved and the conditions that constrain achievement of the goal. The representation of a task goal in working memory is considered to be part of a task-set (as in research on task-switching, cf. Rogers and Monsell 1995). Basically, a task-set is a representation comprising several elements, such as a task intention and a task context. The task intention or task goal represents the state to be achieved on completion of the task. The task context is a collection of parameters that specify particular constraints and restrictions on the task execution. Typically, these parameters relate to the task modality (oral response, manual response, …) and, if applicable, to the way the task outcomes are mapped on the possible (allowable) response alternatives.

As an example, consider a magnitude judgment (decide whether a digit is smaller or larger than 5). In the context of an experiment, participants are instructed to perform this task as fast and as accurately as possible. This gives rise to a goal representation (e.g., magnitude). The instructions at the start of the experiment also provide other information that is relevant to be kept in the task-set. For example, the participants are told that the numbers have to be categorized as smaller (left) or larger than 5 (right response) and the response is to be given by pressing the keys on a response box with the index fingers of both hands. All this information specifies a modality constraint (manual responses on a response box) and an outcome-response mapping. All this information is bound together in a task-set representation (goal, modality, outcome-response mapping) that is maintained in short-term storage as long as the task remains valid.

On each trial, a stimulus is presented which must be categorized. The digit presented (e.g., 8) automatically accesses a semantic representation (a rather broad segment of the mental number line, see Dehaene 2003). This semantic activation is propagated in a network of representations to 'large' (8 is larger than 5). From there on the activation may also be propagated to a representation of the responses. On the basis of the evidence with respect to the spatial-numeric association of response codes (SNARC) effect, the large representation automatically favours the route to the right response (see e.g. Gevers et al. 2006). Even though the correct response (right) is favored by this automatically triggered processing route, without a modulating effect from the task-set, there is no guarantee that a correct response will be produced. Figure 15.1 shows how the presentation of the stimulus propagates via different representation layers (semantic representation, stimulus–response mappings) towards the response.

Several elements in the task-set intervene to modulate processing via this route. The *task goal representation* will modulate the excitability of the magnitude representation. As a consequence, the automatically triggered route via the magnitude node will be facilitated while the route to other competing representations (e.g., parity) will be suppressed. This will result in a stronger activation of the 'large' node than of the other (competing) nodes. Furthermore, the *mapping information* represented in the task-set will also play a modulating role. Since in such a task there are two possible mappings, the large-right link should be facilitated in the context of the present example and this can be achieved by changing the excitability of the responses in agreement with the correct mapping. These two modulating effects originating from the task-set representation are also shown in Figure 15.1 by means of the dashed arrows starting at the working memory (WM) layer.

Although the different elements represented in the task-set may thus modulate different aspects of the stimulus–response processing stream, the judgment task will still not be performed correctly all the time. The reason for this is that even though the task-set parameters can modulate

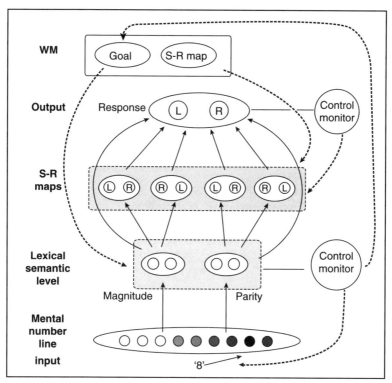

Figure 15.1 Propagation of activation from input to response (thin lines), and task-set related processes modulating bottom-up processing. The box WM shows task-set representation in working memory. The goal representation modulates activation propagation at the task level (semantic layer). The mapping representation modulates activation propagation at the level of the S–R mappings. Furthermore, conflict sensitive controls at the different levels show modulation of propagation at anterior levels.

the automatic processing route, this modulation will not always be powerful enough. Therefore, on some occasions, the response performed may be the one propagated via the automatic route. Sometimes, this will be the correct response, but at other times the response will be incorrect because of stimulus–response compatibility (as observed in the Simon effect, the SNARC effect, etc.) or because the stimulus–response association is a particularly strong one (e.g., a prepotent response). For a completely rational system, this implies that other interactions will be necessary to maximize correct performance.

Several authors have explored the idea that neural structures within the anterior cingulate cortex monitor the presence of response conflict, i.e., a situation in which one response is not favored over another one (see Botvinick *et al.* 2004). When such a conflict is detected, the attentional selectivity on the input is changed, which in its turn results in an adjustment of the activation of the response alternatives. Although a very interesting idea, conflict detection only at the level of response choice (output level in Figure 15.1) does not seem to be enough when there are several task parameters that may affect the response activations (as also suggested by Botvinick *et al.* 2004). In the example we have been considering thus far, response conflict is only partially informative, because it is the product of several information processing routes that are at work. However, the idea may be extended by assuming that conflicts may occur at different processing stages and that all these conflicts may be monitored. This leads to the propagation of a signal that may be used to modulate processing. In particular, we propose that a conflict may also occur at the semantic level. Basically, at this level, two kinds of conflicts may be distinguished. First, it may be argued that at this level a kind of implicit response is required in the categorization of the inputs. In the example of Figure 15.1, a digit has to be categorized as large or small. If the activations of the two categories conflict (are rather similar), then a conflict arises that may be detected and used for further adaptations. Second, it is also possible that the amount of activation for the relevant task (magnitude judgment in our example) conflicts with activations in nodes associated with other, probably irrelevant, tasks. If the activations accrued for an irrelevant task compete with the activation in the relevant task stream, there is again a conflict that may be detected and counteracted by biasing processing towards the relevant task.

This extension of the conflict-monitoring hypothesis is displayed in Figure 15.1. A conflict monitoring unit is present in this figure not only at the level of response choice, but also at the level of stimulus categorization. In both cases, the output of the conflict monitoring unit feeds a signal to the task-set representation in working memory. More specifically, the conflict detected at the output level is propagated to the stimulus–response mapping configuration, so that via this connection adaptations can be initiated directed to the mapping layer. By biasing the activations towards the relevant stimulus–response mapping, it may be possible to reduce the conflict. Similarly, the conflict detected at the semantic level propagates a signal to the goal representation in the task-set and from there the activations leading to stimulus categorization may be modulated. The figure shows one of the possible streams, namely to bias the activations towards the relevant task.

Occasionally, conflict detection will not suffice to bias the system towards the appropriate response. This may result in the selection of an incorrect response. While this happens, the cycle of conflict monitoring and subsequent adjustments may still be operative, so that it becomes possible to detect that there is a mismatch between the response being executed and the one that should have been selected. This mechanism is then at the basis of the detection of an error. As the cycle is continuing to produce adjustments, this will lead to an increase of the response threshold with a subsequent slower responding on the following trial (e.g., Gratton *et al.* 1992).

It should be clear from this explanation that response selection is based on an interaction of bottom-up routes (from stimulus to response) and top-down modulations based on the signal provided by conflict detection units and propagated further on by mediation of the currently active task-set. In this proposal, conflict is monitored at two different stages of information processing and the modulations based on these conflicts are also mediated by different components within the task-set representation. At present, the number of stages at which conflict monitoring may be needed is not clear at all. However, we have argued that such monitoring occurs at least at two levels.

The stimulus–response translation processes described here seem to fit well with the traditional distinction between three processing stages, namely perception or stimulus identification (the lowest two levels in Figure 15.1), response selection (semantic to output levels), and response execution. One possible view is that the response selection stage is capacity limited so that only one response selection can be performed at any time. This central bottleneck hypothesis has been proposed to explain the psychological refractory period (PRP), a response delay which occurs when the stimulus for a second task follows very shortly (0–300 ms) after the onset of the stimulus for the first task (e.g., Pashler 1984; Ruthruff *et al.* 2001). This bottleneck hypothesis has been challenged, however, by the observation of cross-talk between the two tasks in the backward compatibility design (e.g., Hommel 1998). Without abandoning the idea that response selection is capacity-limited, the latter findings can be explained by distinguishing four, instead of three processing stages. After stimulus identification and before response selection, there is a stage of response activation which is not capacity-limited and in which the possible response alternatives are activated prior to the selection being made (cf. Lien and Proctor 2002). With reference to Figure 15.1, response activation concerns the bottom-up processing of the incoming stimulus up to the output level. Response selection itself comes into play when the detected conflicts lead to a modulating signal that is propagated via the active task-set in working memory. In the first of these two stages (response activation), the activations of the incoming information are quasi-automatically propagated through the network. In the second stage, the propagation of information is modulated by information propagated from the working memory representation.

A number of neuroimaging studies support such a distinction between response activation and response selection stages of processing. Bunge *et al.* (2002) report an event-related fMRI study in which healthy adults performed a flanker task. On the basis of appropriate comparisons, the authors could conclude that the parietal cortex is involved in the activation of possible responses and that areas in the prefrontal cortex, in particular, the lateral prefrontal and rostral anterior cingulate cortices, are recruited when a selection between competing responses is needed (see also the review by Bunge 2004).

The mechanisms discussed thus far cover an important part of executive control, namely that part which is involved in the selection of an appropriate response. We have described a system from which goal-directed behavior emerges because there is a task-set representation modulating the activations that are propagated from stimulus to response. The system is also capable of error monitoring, because on error trials, there is a heightened conflict at some processing stages. The monitor being sensitive to such conflict propagates this back to the task-set representation in working memory, which in its turn modulates propagation of the activation from stimulus to response. The (part of the) system as described here explains that response selection, rather than response activation, recruits the relevant task-set representation in the capacity-limited working memory system.

Dual-task coordination and response selection

The question may now be raised how such a system explains the trade-offs observed in dual-task situations typical of working memory research. Actually, two different situations must be distinguished. A first type of dual-task situation concerns the execution of two processing tasks concurrently. The second type concerns combinations of storage and processing as in the complex memory span tasks.

When two tasks must be performed concurrently, the task-sets for both tasks must be configured and maintained in working memory. At each time one of the two task-sets is more activated than the other one. The most active task-set is considered to be dominant in that it currently governs controlled processing and behaviour, because only this task-set can send signals to modulate processing. When the activation for the competing task-set increases so that this one becomes dominant, then only this task-set can affect information processing in agreement with the task goals and task constraints. This constitutes a bottleneck on control. This bottleneck is functional, rather than structural, because the fact that there is a bottleneck depends on the fact that there are two independent tasks. If after extensive practice the two tasks are coordinated into a single task, the processing limitation is no longer effective.

If two tasks are performed concurrently, and both tasks require the selection of an appropriate response, then both tasks will also require controlling signals forwarded from the task-set representation. However, only the signals coming from the dominant task-set will be propagated and have an effect on resolving the conflict at the semantic or the response level. If meanwhile the nodes activated for the second task require also resolution of a conflict, the processing of the conflict adaptation will be delayed until the second task-set becomes dominant. As a consequence, responding to the second task will be delayed and in some cases, the delay may cause the conflict to be resolved by bottom-up propagation of activation, occasionally resulting in an error. Hence, the competition between the two tasks will lead to delayed responding and an increase in errors. These delays will not be restricted to one task. Sometimes, the 'second' task will be the dominant one, and the first one will have to wait. In sum, on the basis of this view it is expected that when both tasks require the selection of an appropriate response among two or more alternatives, both tasks will be slowed down and will be more error-prone in comparison to the same tasks performed in single-task conditions.

The second kind of dual-task design involves a trade-off between maintenance of information and processing. In order to clarify this trade-off, we shall start from the example of a working memory span task, also known as complex span task. In the operation span task (Turner and Engle 1989), for example, participants have to memorize a sequence of words while performing a series of calculations. A trial starts with a rather complex arithmetical operation that must be solved; after that, a word is presented for later recall. Then another operation is given and another word is presented. After such a sequence of 2–6 operations/words, the participant is required to recall the words in the correct order. Trials start with a sequence length of two and continue as long as the participant is able to respond correctly to the majority of the trials of a given length. A better variant of the task reverses the two components in each trial by first presenting a word to-be-remembered followed by an operation to be performed (see Barrouillet and Camos 2001). This procedure ensures that from the very start of a trial, a memory load is present.

This is clearly a dual-task design; it requires the participant to achieve two task goals. On the one hand, it is necessary to remember all the words in the presentation order. On the other hand, it is necessary to perform well on the calculation task. Hence, the participant must configure two task-sets that are kept active during the entire test procedure. The first task requires maintenance in memory of the sequence of words in the correct order. To achieve this goal, the memory traces must be reactivated before they fade away. Without the presence of a calculation task, memory maintenance can be achieved by subvocal rehearsal so as to keep the phonological word forms active (in the phonological loop). However, it is quite likely that both the passive phonological storage and the articulatory rehearsal loop are also used to solve the rather complex equations (maintenance of subgoals of the calculation, interim results, whether or not a carry is needed, etc.). In other words, to maintain the words in (short-term) memory, attention has to be paid to the words and meanwhile the numbers for the calculation task are presented and now the participants have to execute the appropriate operations to produce the correct answer.

How can the participants succeed in both tasks of such a dual-task set-up? Probably the control mechanisms will be involved in both tasks. These mechanisms are part of different processing routes (word memorization and calculation) and work independently from each other. They propagate signals to the respective task-sets stored in working memory. Our assumption is that only one task-set governs behavior at any one time (cf. supra). Consequently, the signal from the control mechanism from only one task at a time can be handled to modulate processing and this depends on the task-set presently active (or dominant). This way, a functional bottleneck arises at the level of the controlling or adjusting working memory representation. While the signal of one of the tasks is processed, the other task has to wait and as a consequence, processing is delayed. At times the delay may be so large that errors occur. Hence, the dual-task situation leads to performance being slower and/or less accurate. Similarly, when the memorization task is kept on hold, it may become impossible to access the stored element and at the end of the series, recall is incomplete.

To sum up, if our view is correct, response selection plays an important role in dual-task situations as well with a memory and a processing task as with two concurrent stimulus–response tasks.

The reasons for this are (a) that the task-set components send controlling signals to modulate ongoing processing and (b) that only the most active or dominant task-set can exert this kind of control. The result of this is that in a situation with two stimululs–response (S–R) tasks, both tasks are impaired (slower and possibly less accurate), and that in a situation with competing storage demands and an S–R task, similarly, maintenance of stored information and performance on the S–R task will suffer.

Control at the level of response selection

Since the view elaborated here strongly depends on the presence of response selection in the S–R tasks, the question arises as to what happens if only one of both tasks involves response selection. It is known that a simple reaction-time task does not involve a response selection (Schubert 1999). Although such a task may still need some form of control for its proper execution, no choice requirements must be met. No semantic categorization of the stimulus is required, as it suffices to detect the presence of a stimulus to emit the response. Therefore no conflict is expected to occur at either the semantic level or the output level, and there will be no requirement to modulate processing so as to resolve these conflicts. These expectations are supported by an event-related potentials (ERP) study of Szmalec *et al.* (submitted). These authors found a large N2 component, which is considered to be a marker of cognitive conflict, for a choice reaction time (RT) task but no N2 for a simple RT task.

Also at the behavioral level, the role of response selection can be estimated by comparing the effects of a choice RT task to the effect of a simple RT task. This yields a simple and straightforward methodology to test the prediction that the presence of response selection in a dual-task setting where the other task involves either memory maintenance or another choice task will result in impaired task performance. This implication concerning response selection was tested in a series of behavioral studies. In the remainder of the current section we present a brief overview of these studies and the obtained results, in saccade control, in verbal fluency, in mental arithmetic and in working memory tasks involving the slave systems.

Control of saccades

A distinction is made between the fast saccades (sudden eye-movements) towards a peripheral stimulus (prosaccades) and the slower eye-movements away from the peripheral stimulus (antisaccades). The standard view is that prosaccades are faster because they are triggered rather automatically by the exogenous cue (Hallett 1978; Roberts *et al.* 1994) even though they can be stopped (Logan and Irwin 2000) or changed when necessary. This view also proposes that antisaccades are slower because they are controlled eye-movements. According to some authors, for the execution of an antisaccade, first the automatically triggered prosaccade must be suppressed and a saccade in the opposite direction must be programmed (see Findlay and Walker, 1999), whereas other authors defend the position that some form of competition occurs between the automatically triggered prosaccade and the planned antisaccade (Massen 2004).

In addition to a vast and growing literature about the difficulties of antisaccade performance in certain patients groups, dual-task studies with normal participants have shown that antisaccades, but not prosaccades are delayed and more error-prone under a working memory or executive load (e.g., Roberts *et al.* 1994; Stuyven *et al.* 2000). In view of the thesis advocated in the present chapter, it may be argued that a prosaccade can be performed and controlled with a minimal configuration of the task-set representation in working memory. The stimulus–response mapping must not be configured because the target location is present as part of the stimulus. For an antisaccade, on the contrary, all elements of the task-set must be filled in, because the normal

S–R mapping is reversed. The consequence of this is that the prosaccade can be performed without any intervention based on conflict detection because only one response alternative is activated and no selection or only a minimal one is required. In an antisaccade task, however, a stimulus–response mapping is required and the incorrect and correct response alternatives are both activated. Conflict monitoring and task-set mediated adjustment is now required before a response can be selected.

Summarizing and simplifying, antisaccades but not prosaccades require conflict monitoring and adjustments for their execution. This implies that in a dual-task situation with a secondary task requiring response selection, the antisaccades will be impaired more than the prosaccades. If, on the contrary, the secondary task does not involve response selection, then prosaccades and antisaccades will be impaired to a similar but small degree. We tested these predictions by implementing a dual-task design with concurrent execution of a saccade task and a continuous reaction time task (Vandierendonck et al., in press). The reaction time task was either a choice-reaction task or a simple reaction task. While the former involves response selection by definition, the latter does not call on response selection (Schubert 1999). In a first experiment, the prosaccade task was combined with either continuous choice reactions or continuous simple reactions. As predicted, there were no differences in latency or error of the prosaccades as a function of the kind of secondary task. In the second experiment, the same design was used with the antisaccade task. Again, the prediction was confirmed: with the choice reaction task as secondary task saccades were slowed down significantly. Clearly, only when both tasks involved a response selection, saccade performance was slowed down.

Response selection and verbal fluency

It may be argued that the control of saccades constitutes a fairly 'low' level of control and that the mechanisms involved may be different from those at work in tasks that are typically used to diagnose executive dysfunction. To refute this interpretation, an experiment was designed in which the role of the same secondary tasks (simple and choice reaction) in verbal fluency was studied. Verbal fluency tasks belong to the tests used to diagnose executive dysfunction (Phillips 1997). A design was implemented (Szmalec et al. 2005, Experiment 3) in which different kinds of fluency tasks were performed either under single-task conditions (fluency alone) or under dual-task conditions (with simple or with choice RT). The rationale of this experiment was that among other things, verbal fluency requires retrieval from long-term memory. In addition to the spontaneous retrieval that may be triggered by the task ('name vegetables'), the retrieval itself requires control (one must check to emit vegetable names and not something else) and moreover, it is also necessary to keep track of which words have been produced already. In other words, verbal fluency consists of a stream of response selections. If there is a simultaneous task also requiring response selection, performance on the fluency task will suffer. Indeed, in comparison to the single-task fluency condition, a significantly smaller amount of words were produced when a continuous choice reaction task had to be performed concurrently. The condition with a continuous simple reaction task did not impair performance at all. So, also when the primary task involves 'higher' levels of control, performance is impaired when concurrently a task involving response selection must be performed.

Response selection and mental arithmetic

Another cognitive task relying strongly on executive control is mental arithmetic. Whether it concerns simple problems (such as 4 + 3 or 6 × 5) or complex problems (such as 235 + 72), executive control seems to be always involved (see review by DeStefano and LeFevre 2004). In fact, the available evidence suggests that in reference to the working model of Baddeley and Hitch (1974), only the central executive is involved in solving simple sums and products (e.g., De Rammelaere *et al.* 2001; Seitz and Schumann-Hengsteler 2000, 2002).

Whether simple sums are solved by a direct retrieval from memory (for addition and multiplication, by far the most frequent strategy) or by application of a transformation procedure (e.g., $8 + 7 = 8 + 2 + 5 = 10 + 5 = 15$), always one or more retrievals from memory are required. As already argued, retrieval requires the conflict control mechanism which is also required for a response selection. Consequently, it is expected that in a dual-task set-up the presence of response selection will impair performance on these simple arithmetic problems.

This prediction was tested by Deschuyteneer and Vandierendonck (2005a) for simple sums and by Deschuyteneer and Vandierendonck (2005b) for simple multiplications. Participants were required to solve all possible sums with digits between two and nine in a single-task control condition and in conditions with either a continuous simple reaction task or a continuous choice reaction task. In the experiments with the sums, the problems were solved much slower when the secondary task required a response selection (1028 vs 928 ms). Similarly, in the experiments with multiplications, the presence of response selection in the secondary task slowed solutions by 114 ms. Further research with subtractions and divisions, basically revealed the same pattern of results: a slowing of respectively 191 and 200 ms (Deschuyteneer *et al.* submitted).

These findings confirm our hypothesis. One could expect even stronger results. The literature on simple arithmetic has shown the presence of a problem size effect (Ashcraft 1995): problems with a smaller sum are solved faster than those with a larger sum. It could be argued that the problems with a larger sum will more often be solved by a transformation strategy while for those with a smaller outcome, a direct retrieval from memory will occur. This prediction was tested but not confirmed. In fact, 80–90 per cent of the problems were solved by direct memory retrieval, so that the data were not sensitive enough for a proper test of this additional prediction.

Dissociations

The findings reviewed thus far were concerned with primary tasks that are known to rely heavily on cognitive control. It is also interesting to look at tasks that can be impaired by operations affecting memory storage as well as by operations changing the load on executive control. Short-term memory tasks, and in particular the memory span task, forms a case in point. Operations that affect processing of information in the phonological loop (phonological similarity, irrelevant speech, word length and articulatory suppression) lead to performance decrements in verbal span tasks (Baddeley 1986). These effects are achieved without any intervention of controlled processing. However, loads on executive control can also impair performance on the memory span task (e.g., Vandierendonck *et al.* 1998a, 1998b). Even though this state of affairs makes it more difficult to test hypotheses about factors affecting memory performance, it is possible to realize a dissociation. If the memory task is made more difficult by increasing its executive requirements, then it is expected that operations affecting executive control will have a larger effect on the more difficult version, while no such difference is expected for the operations affecting processing in the slave system.

Taking advantage of this particular possibility Szmalec *et al.* (2005, Experiment 1) designed a verbal memory experiment in which the executive difficulty of the memory task was manipulated by comparing performance when instructed for normal (forward) order recall with performance when instructed to recall the elements in the reversed (backward) order. With the latter instruction, the task becomes more difficult because more mental operations have to be performed in coding and recall (see e.g., Rosen and Engle, 1997). On this basis, the authors expected a larger interference from a task requiring response selection, while the impairments due to articulatory suppression would not differ between the two task versions, in a design with secondary tasks present only during the presentation of the to-be-remembered elements and not during recall. The findings corroborated the author's hypotheses. Articulatory suppression strongly impaired memory performance but the degree of impairment did not differ between the forward and the backward recall condition. In contrast, the secondary task condition with response selection had a larger disrupting effect in the backward than in the forward recall condition.

The authors applied the same logic for a visuospatial working memory span task, the Corsi blocks tapping task. Previous research has shown that this task calls indeed on the visuospatial slave system as defined within the model of Baddeley and Hitch (1974), but it also seems to load quite heavily on the central executive (Vandierendonck *et al.* 2004). While there is no evidence for a performance difference between backward and forward recall in this task, it can still be argued that the backward version of the task engages a higher cognitive load. There are some indications that in normal conditions, this disadvantage is overruled by better possibilities for binding order and locations (see e.g., Vandierendonck and Szmalec 2004). On these bases it can be predicted that the effects of recall instruction (mediated by executive control) and a task disrupting spatial codes (matrix tapping; mediated by the visuospatial sketch pad) will be dissociated. Indeed on the basis of previous findings, it was expected that matrix tapping would interfere less with the backward than with the forward recall condition. It was also expected that the presence of a concurrent task involving response selection would not result in an advantage for backward recall. The findings confirmed these predictions, so that also for visuospatial short-term memory a dissociation was found between the two manipulations.

Summary

All the studies reviewed here tested the influence of the presence of response selection in a secondary task on performance on a primary task. The results of these experiments are very clear. When both the primary task and the secondary task require the selection of a response among alternatives, then the primary task is clearly impaired. That was the case for antisaccades, for verbal fluency and for simple mental arithmetic. When the primary task does not engage response selection, then the effects of a secondary task with response selection are not different from those of a simple reaction time task. In particular, this was observed with the prosaccade task as primary task. Finally, we also presented evidence showing that the effects of response selection are dissociated from the effects of task intended to interfere with refreshment of the contents of the two slave systems. Together these observations constitute a pretty strong case in favor of the thesis that response selection involves controlled processing.

Conclusions

In this chapter, we defended the view that executive or cognitive control emerges from interactions between stimulus-driven and working-memory based processing streams. More specifically, we proposed (a) that the currently dominant task-set representation in working memory biases the propagation of activations from stimulus to response, and (b) that conflict detection at a number of processing levels (in particular, the semantic level and the output level) is propagated to the working memory task-set representation which mediates further modulations on the stimulus-driven processing stream. We argued that these task-set based and conflict monitoring mechanisms are invoked when an appropriate response has to be selected. This led to three predictions that were all corroborated by empirical findings. The first prediction entails that dual-task situations in which both tasks require a response selection will result in slower and more error-prone performance (this was confirmed in antisaccades, in verbal fluency, and in mental arithmetic). The second prediction implies that no such performance deterioration will occur in dual-task situations in which only one task involves response selection (confirmed in prosaccades, in verbal fluency with simple reaction tasks as secondary task). A third prediction states that the effects of response selection in dual-task designs are dissociable from effects produced at the modality-specific slave systems in the working memory model of Baddeley and Hitch (1974). Although these findings are encouraging, we must be aware that we are only beginning to understand the way response selection is involved in executive control. The scheme proposed here will have to be further elaborated in future research.

This chapter focused on the relationship between executive control and response selection and ignored the many other components that are involved in cognitive control. We believe that our view, which characterizes cognitive control as a property emerging from the interaction between top-down and bottom-up processes, can be extended towards these other components of cognitive control. Without going into details and without claiming an exhaustive overview, evidence is being accumulated in favor of such an extension. Our group has, for example, already made some effort to clarify the role of conflict monitoring in changing attentional biases in the context of *input monitoring* (e.g., Deschuyteneer and Vandierendonck, 2005a, 2005b, Deschuyteneer *et al.* submitted). Although often neglected, this is an important aspect of executive control, as it provides a possible link between control of actions (the typical meaning of executive control) and control of perceptions by selective attention.

Given the focus on task-set representation, also the extension to *task switching* is straightforward and some first results from our group are available (e.g. Liefooghe *et al.* 2007). *Interference control* constitutes another important aspect, because it is at the heart of controlling and monitoring conflicts between activations. Currently, our research on interference control follows two different angles. On the one hand, we have used the stop-signal paradigm to investigate the commonalities between different tasks and situations that involve some form of inhibition, such as Stroop and flanker tasks, negative priming, etc. (see e.g., Verbruggen *et al.* 2004; Verbruggen *et al.* 2005a, 2005b). On the other hand, we are exploring variations on *memory updating* paradigms, such as running span and n-back tasks, to disentangle controlled changes to memory representations and interference between new and old information that have to be maintained in memory.

Besides these few, many more components of cognitive control, such as planning, troubleshooting, error detection, etc., should also be addressed. In our opinion, the view defended here can be developed into a framework in which all components of cognitive control can be reformulated. Much more theoretical, methodological and empirical development will be needed to achieve a more elaborated and more precise theory of executive control. Most importantly, the view elaborated here consists of a first step towards a dismissal of the homunculus.

Acknowledgments

The research reported in this chapter was supported by grant no. 10251101 of the Special Research Fund of Ghent University to the first author.

References

Ashcraft MH (1995). Cognitive psychology and simple arithmetic: A review and summary of new directions. *Mathematical Cognition*, *1*, 3–34.

Baddeley, A (1986). *Working Memory*. Oxford: Oxford University Press.

Baddeley AD and Hitch G (1974). Working memory. In GH Bower (ed), *The Psychology of Learning and Motivation*, Vol. 8, (pp. 47–89). New York: Academic Press.

Barrouillet P and Camos V (2001). Developmental increase in working memory span: Resource sharing or temporal decay? *Journal of Memory and Language*, *45*, 1–20.

Botvinick MM, Cohen JD and Carter CS (2004). Conflict monitoring and anterior cingulate cortex: an update. *Trends in Cognitive Science*, 8, 539–546.

Bunge SA (2004). How we use rules to select actions: A review of evidence from cognitive neuroscience. *Cognitive, Affective, and Behavioral Neuroscience*, 4, 564–579.

Bunge SA, Hazeltine E, Scanlon MD, Rosen AC and Gabrieli JDE (2002). Dissociable contributions of prefrontal and parietal cortices to response selection. *NeuroImage*, 17, 1562–1571.

Courtney SM (2004). Attention and cognitive control as emergent properties of information representation in working memory. *Cognitive, Affective, and Behavioral Neuroscience*, 4, 501–516.

De Rammelaere S, Stuyven E and Vandierendonck A (2001). Verifying simple arithmetic sums and products: Are the phonological loop and the central executive involved? *Memory and Cognition*, 29, 267–274.

Dehaene S (2003). The neural basis of the Weber-Fechner law: a logarithmic mental number line. *Trends in Cognitive Sciences*, 7, 145–147.

Deschuyteneer M and Vandierendonck A (2005a). Are 'input monitoring' and 'response selection' involved in solving simple mental additions. *European Journal of Cognitive Psychology*, 17, 343–370.

Deschuyteneer M and Vandierendonck A (2005b). The role of 'response selection' and 'input monitoring' in solving simple arithmetical products. *Memory and Cognition*, 33, 1472–1483.

DeStefano D and LeFevre J-A (2004). The role of working memory in mental arithmetic. *European Journal of Cognitive Psychology*, 16, 353–386.

Findlay JM and Walker R (1999). A model of saccade generation based on parallel processing and competitive inhibition. *Behavioral and Brain Sciences*, 22, 661–721.

Gevers W, Verguts T, Reynvoet B, Caessens B, and Fias W (2006). Numbers and space: A computational model of the SNARC effect. *Journal of Experimental Psychology: Human Perception and Performance*, 32, 32–44.

Gratton G, Coles MG and Donchin E (1992). Optimizing the use of information: strategic control of activation of responses. *Journal of Experimental Psychology: General*, 121, 480–506.

Hallett PE (1978). Primary and secondary saccades to goals defined by instructions. *Vision Research*, 18, 1279–1296.

Hommel B (1998). Automatic stimulus–Response translation in dual-task performance. *Journal of Experimental Psychology: Human Perception and Performance*, 24, 1368–1384.

Liefooghe B, Verbruggen F, Vandierendonck A, Fias W and Gevers W (2007). Task switching and across-trial distance priming are independent. *European Journal of Cognitive Psychology*, 19, 1–16.

Lien M-C and Proctor RW (2002). Stimulus–Response compatibility and psychological refractory period effects: Implication for response selection. *Psychonomic Bulletin and Review*, 9, 212–238.

Logan GD and Irwin DE (2000). Don't look! Don't touch! Inhibitory control of eye and hand movements. *Psychonomic Bulletin and Review*, 7, 107–112.

Massen C (2004). Parallel programming of exogenous and endogenous components in the anti-saccade task. *Quarterly Journal of Experimental Psychology*, 57A, 475–498.

Nieuwenhuis S, Broerse A, Nielen MMA and de Jong R (2004). A goal activation approach to the study of executive function: An application to anti-saccade tasks. *Brain and Cognition*, 56, 198–214.

Norman DA and Shallice T (1986). Attention to action: Willed and automatic control of behavior. In RJ Davidson, GE Schwarts and D Shapiro (eds), *Consciousness and Self-regulation, Vol. 4*, (pp. 1–18). New York: Plenum Press.

Pashler H (1984). Processing stages in overlapping tasks: Evidence for a central bottleneck. *Journal of Experimental Psychology: Human Perception and Performance*, 10, 358–377.

Phillips LH (1997). Do 'frontal tests' measure executive function? Issues of assessment and evidence from fluency tests. In P Rabbitt (ed), *Methodology of Frontal and Executive Function* (pp. 191–213). Hove: Psychology Press.

Roberts RJ, Jr Hager LD and Heron C (1994). Prefrontal cognitive processes: Working memory and inhibition in the anti-saccade task. *Journal of Experimental Psychology: General*, 123, 374–393.

Rogers RD and Monsell S (1995). Costs of a predictable switch between simple cognitive tasks. *Journal of Experimental Psychology: General*, *124*, 207–231.

Rosen VM and Engle RW (1997). Forward and backward serial recall. *Intelligence*, *25*, 37–47.

Ruthruff E, Pashler HE and Klaassen A (2001). Processing bottlenecks in dual-task performance: Structural limitation or strategic postponement? *Psychonomic Bulletin and Review*, *8*, 73–80.

Schubert T (1999). Processing differences between simple and choice reactions affect bottleneck localization in overlapping tasks. *Journal of Experimental Psychology: Human Perception and Performance*, *25*, 408–425.

Seitz K and Schumann-Hengsteler R (2000). Mental multiplication and working memory. *European Journal of Cognitive Psychology*, *12*, 552–570.

Seitz K and Schumann-Hengsteler R (2002). Phonological loop and central executive processes in mental addition and multiplication. *Psychologische Beiträge*, *44*, 275–302.

Stuyven E, Van der Goten K, Vandierendonck A, Claeys K, and Crevits L (2000). Saccadic eye movements under conditions of cognitive load. *Acta Psychologica*, *104*, 69–85.

Szmalec A, Vandierendonck A and Kemps E (2005). Response selection involves executive control: Evidence from the selective interference paradigm. *Memory and Cognition*, *33*, 531–541.

Turner ML and Engle RW (1989). Is working memory capacity task dependent? *Journal of Memory and Language*, *28*, 127–154.

Vandierendonck A, Deschuyteneer M, Depoorter M, and Drieghe D (in press). Input monitoring and response selection as components of executive control in pro-saccades and anti-saccades. *Psychological Research*.

Vandierendonck A, De Vooght G and Van der Goten K (1998a). Does random time interval generation interfere with working memory executive functions? *European Journal of Cognitive Psychology*, *10*, 413–442.

Vandierendonck A, De Vooght G and Van der Goten K (1998b). Interfering with the central executive by means of a random interval repetition task. *Quarterly Journal of Experimental Psychology*, *51A*, 197–218.

Vandierendonck A, Kemps E, Fastame C and Szmalec A (2004). Working memory components in the Corsi blocks task. *British Journal of Psychology*, *95*, 57–79.

Vandierendonck A and Szmalec A (2004). An asymmetry in the visuospatial demands of forward and backward recall in the Corsi blocks task. *Imagination, Cognition and Personality*, *23*, 225–231.

Verbruggen F, Liefooghe B and Vandierendonck A (2004). The interaction between stop-signal inhibition and distractor interference in the flanker and stroop task. *Acta Psychologica*, *116*, 21–37.

Verbruggen F, Liefooghe B, Szmalec, A. and Vandierendonck A (2005a). Inhibiting when switching: Does it matter? *Experimental Psychology*, *52*, 125–130.

Verbruggen F, Liefooghe B and Vandierendonck A (2005b). On the difference between response inhibition and negative priming: Evidence from simple and selective stopping. *Psychological Research*, *69*, 262–271.

16

Relational processing is fundamental to the central executive and is limited to four variables

Graeme S. Halford, Steven Phillips, William H. Wilson, Julie McCredden, Glenda Andrews, Damian Birney, Rosemary Baker and John D. Bain

In this chapter we want to address two broad questions. The first is: What sort of information is processed by the central executive? And the second question is: What limits the information processing capacity of the central executive?

In answer to the first question we propose that the central executive is specialized to some extent to process relational information. Although there has been a considerable amount of research on executive functions (Zelazo *et al.* 2003) they are not well defined, and it is not clear whether the various functions reflect distinct cognitive processes (Birney, Bowman and Pallier 2006; Blair 2006) or how central they are to working memory (Birney, Bowman and Bui, 2006). With this caveat in mind, we will make a cautious attempt to define some of the processes that are common to executive functions, drawing on relational knowledge theories (Goodwin and Johnson-Laird 2005; Halford *et al.* 1998; Phillips *et al.* 1995).

Executive functions that are used in problem-solving require a cognitive map, or mental model, of the structure of the task. This mental model has to represent relations between the entities in the task, because relations are the defining property of structure. In its most basic form, it has to represent the links between the current situation, a set of actions or operators, and a goal or outcome. This representation has to be created by the central executive in such a way that it is accessible to other cognitive processes so that it can be used to plan actions, to select the best actions to achieve particular goals in given circumstances, to make inferences, and to perform the many functions of higher cognition. Controlled planning and strategy development require representation of structure to determine which actions or operators will achieve specific goals in particular situations. Goals must be maintained in such a way that relations between the current state, actions and goal states are explicitly represented. Switching between rules is a comparison of relations, and requires choosing the best one to achieve a particular goal. Inhibitory control involves relational processing because inhibition of any process requires that an alternative be represented, and a representation of the relation between alternatives is needed. Relational complexity has been shown to fit data from some tasks that are usually attributed to inhibitory control (Andrews *et al.* 2003). Inferences require representation of relations between variables.

One powerful reasoning process is analogical reasoning. Analogy can be said to be at the core of executive functions (Grafman and Litvan 1999) because analogy is fundamental to higher cognitive processes (Binet and Simon 1905/1980; Halford 1990, 1993; Hofstadter 2001; Piaget 1950), and mental models, which are important to some theories of human reasoning (Johnson-Laird 1983;

Johnson-Laird and Byrne 1991; Polk and Newell 1995) are essentially analogs. Analogy is a structural correspondence between two cognitive representations, one called a source, the other a target, both being comprised of representations of relations (Gentner 1983; Gentner *et al.* 2001; Holland *et al.* 1986).

The structural correspondence between source and target permits a possible mechanism for representation of variables, which are also basic to higher cognition. Analogical mappings align representational entities using corresponding slots in relations, which effectively function as variables. For example, the relation older-than(-,-) has two slots, one for an older entity and one for a younger entity. These can be instantiated in a variety of ways such as older-than (Tom, John), older-than (Frank, Peter), older-than (Tom, Paul). In the proportional analogy, Tom is to Frank as John is to whom?, the common relation allows the slots for the older entity to be aligned (Tom = Frank), and similarly for the slots for the younger entity (John = Peter), so as to discover the solution to the problem. To perform this set of relational manipulations, the central executive needs to:

1. Represent relations,
2. Mark slots and assign fillers,
3. Align the instances of the common relation,
4. Use the alignment to find the missing element as the solution.

Therefore ability to process relations is at the core of analogical reasoning and of many other higher cognitive processes.

Neuroscience evidence of relational processing

Recent results from neuroscience support our claim that relational processing is basic to the functions of the central executive. The prefrontal cortex is generally thought to support executive functions such as working memory, preparatory set, and inhibitory control (Fuster 1997). A number of reviews have also highlighted functional differences within this region. For example, Cabeza and Nyberg (2000) have provided a broad classification of brain regions and memory types, allocating working memory to bilateral regions in frontal, as well as parietal and temporal lobes. Tekin and Cummings (2002) describe the dorsolateral prefrontal cortex as being mainly involved in tasks like planning ahead, regulating actions according to the environmental stimuli, shifting behavioral sets appropriately, and temporal ordering of recent events. In addition, Ridderinkhof *et al.* (2004) assign performance monitoring to medial frontal cortex and subsequent adjustment to lateral and orbitofrontal cortex. Most relevant for our purposes is the review by Robin and Holyoak (1995), proposing that the frontal lobes also specialize in relational processing.

A number of brain imaging studies have investigated changes in activity on tasks that exercise relational processing capacity (Andrews and Halford 2002), including fluid intelligence tests (Duncan *et al.* 2000), mathematical operations (Prabhakaran *et al.* 2001), transitive inference (Goel *et al.* 2004; Heckers *et al.* 2004; Nagode and Pardo 2002), Raven's Progressive Matrices (Christoff *et al.* 2001; Kroger *et al.* 2002; Prabhakaran *et al.* 1997); and pair recognition (Phillips and Niki 2002, 2003). Differences in regional activity that are correlated with changes in the amount of relational processing have repeatedly been observed in prefrontal, parietal and temporal lobes.

Phillips and Niki (2002, 2003) have interpreted their results in terms of maintaining the role or positional information that affords access (i.e., an index) to a relational set. Frontal and parietal lobe activity often coactivate in relationally difficult tasks, but repetitive transcranial magnetic stimulation (rTMS) revealed differences in terms of maintenance (parietal and prefrontal) and retrieval (prefrontal only) (Koch *et al.* 2005). Whereas frontal and parietal regions often coactivate in relationally difficult tasks, rTMS has revealed differences in terms of their working memory functions.

The picture emerging from such brain imaging studies is one where prefrontal, parietal and temporal regions contribute to various components of relational processing. Tentatively, prefrontal regions are involved in the retrieval and monitoring of relational information, the parietal regions are involved in the maintenance of relational structures (i.e., the explicit dimensions over which the relations are defined), and the temporal regions are involved in the formation of bindings between related items.

The neuroscience evidence we have considered in this brief review supports the claim that the frontal lobes are involved in processing relations, and evidence is accumulating of involvement of specific regions within the prefrontal cortex. Given that the frontal lobes are involved in executive functions, this supports the claim that relational processing is an important function of the central executive. There is also evidence that specifically links frontal processing to the complexity of relations. We will consider this evidence after we outline our proposals on relational complexity.

Limits to the cognitive complexity of the central executive

Our second major claim is that the information processing capacity of the central executive is limited in the complexity of the relational structures that it can process. A number of cognitive complexity metrics have been proposed, and those that were designed to account for cognitive development have been reviewed by Halford (2002). There are two metrics that are being used in contemporary research. The first is the cognitive complexity and control (CCC) metric (Frye and Zelazo 1998) that has been employed in cognitive development, and the second is the relational complexity (RC) theory (Halford *et al.* 1998) that has been employed in child and adult cognition, and in animal cognition. These metrics developed in parallel and have significant common ground.

Cognitive Complexity and Control (CCC) theory (Zelazo and Frye 1998) proposes that complexity can be defined by the number of levels in a hierarchy of rules. For example, preschoolers can adequately represent simple 'if-then' rules, allowing effective representation of relations between antecedent and consequent conditions, but it is not until about five years that children can embed rules under higher order rules, thereby forming a hierarchy of rules. However the complexity of a rule hierarchy can also be accounted for by the complexity of relations, because each additional level of a hierarchy entails another variable. Halford *et al.* (1998) have accounted for the complexity of the Tower of Hanoi puzzle, which entails a hierarchy of goals, in terms of relational complexity. Thus CCC theory can be subsumed within RC theory, described below.

Relational Complexity (RC) theory (Andrews and Halford 2002; Halford *et al.* 1998) argues that task complexity is a function of the number of related variables required to be processed in parallel. Each argument or slot of a relation corresponds to a variable. For example, the binary relation 'larger-than', with instances such as larger-than (elephant, horse), larger-than (dog, mouse), has two arguments or slots. Each slot can be filled in a variety of ways, as these examples illustrate, and therefore constitutes a dimension or variable. Relations vary in the number of dimensions that they entail. An *n*-ary relation is a set of points in *n*-dimensional space, so a unary relation represents one dimension, a binary relation links elements in two dimensions, and so on. Relational complexity theory proposes that more complex relations impose higher processing loads, and that humans are limited in the complexity of relations that can be processed in any one representation. We suggest that due to these limitations, humans try to reduce the complexity of a task using two main cognitive heuristics, as follows.

Conceptual chunking involves recoding concepts into less complex relations. For instance, speed as a function of distance/time is a ternary relation but can be reduced to a unary representation, e.g., speed (80kph). This strategy reduces processing load but relations between chunked variables become inaccessible. For example, questions such as 'How would speed change if we were to cover the same distance in a third of the time?' can no longer be answered under the unary representation of speed. Therefore conceptual chunking cannot be used when the interaction between variables needs to be made explicit.

Segmentation involves dividing tasks into less complex subtasks that can be processed serially. For example, segmentation occurs in comprehension of English when sentences are parsed into constituents that are processed sequentially. While segmentation reduces processing load, relations between variables in different segments will not be accessible in the representations of the segments, and some overarching representation is needed.

Together, conceptual chunking and segmentation permit complex, hierarchical structures to be handled by processing one level at a time (Wilson *et al.* 2001). Taking into account the human tendency to use these strategies, we have devised a set of principles, called the Method for Analysis of Relational Complexity (MARC), for measuring the complexity of any given cognitive task. The most important MARC principle is that variables can be chunked or segmented only if relations between them do not need to be processed.

Using MARC principles to define complexity, we have investigated how performance on various cognitive tasks changes as complexity increases. Relational complexity effects have been observed in studies involving adults. The domains included comprehension of relative clause sentences (Andrews *et al.* 2006), the n-back task (Zielinski 2006), and reasoning on the knights and knaves (Birney and Halford 2002), latin square (Birney *et al.* 2006), Tower of Hanoi (Loveday 1995) and categorical syllogisms tasks (Zielinski 2006).

Our conclusion from this section is that limitations to working memory can be well defined by the complexity of relations that can be processed. It remains, however, to provide a reasonably definitive assessment of working memory capacity, and it is to this that we turn next.

Quantifying processing capacity

The study by Halford *et al.* (2005) was designed to determine limits to human information processing capacity, using the relational complexity metric. There have been theoretical estimates of working memory capacity (Hummel and Holyoak 2003; Miller 1956), there is a review by Cowan (2001), and there is an estimate of the capacity of visual short-term memory (Luck and Vogel 1997; but see also Davis and Holmes 2005). However there did not appear to have been an empirical determination of the number of variables humans can process, and this is vital to the central executive.

Empirical determination of processing capacity required that chunking and segmentation strategies for overcoming capacity limitations be constrained within the experiment, based on the MARC principles above. We found that this could be achieved by using statistical interactions for the problem domain, because these problems cannot be decomposed into subproblems (e.g., we cannot interpret main effects without taking account of the interactions in which they participate).

We therefore developed a problem domain where participants were asked to interpret graphical presentations of two-, three- and four-way interactions based on fictitious data on one of six everyday topics (e.g., cars, cakes, houses). Participants were presented with a set of verbal descriptions corresponding to graphical depiction of two-, three- and four-way interactions (an example is shown in Figures 16.1 and 16.2). The graphs were very carefully designed so that the configurations of bars were consistent across problem types, so that height differences could be discerned visually, and so that simplification strategies would be unlikely to be used. To optimize expertise for the task, participants were 30 academic staff and graduate students from Psychology and Computer Science, who had experience in interpreting the type of data presented.

(a) People prefer **fresh** cakes to **frozen** cakes. The difference depends on the flavor (**chocolate** vs **carrot**).

Left half (black)

             ○ greater

The diference between **fresh** and **frozen** is   for **chocolate** cakes than for **carrot** cakes.

             ○ smaller

Right half (gray)

             ○ greater

The diference between **fresh** and **frozen** is   for **chocolate** cakes than for **carrot** cakes.

             ○ smaller

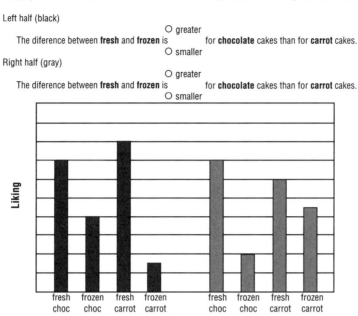

(b) People prefer **fresh** cakes to **frozen** cakes. The difference depends on the flavor (**chocolate** vs **carrot**) and the type (iced vs plain).

The difference between **fresh** and **frozen** increases from **chocolate** cakes to **carrot** cakes.

             ○ greater

This increase is   for **iced** cakes than for **plain** cakes.

             ○ smaller

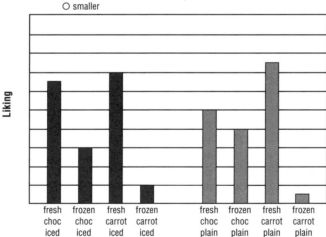

Figure 16.1 Example problems (8 bars). Graphs were presented in blue and yellow, represented here by black and gray, respectively. (a) 2 × 2-way. Answers: smaller, greater. (b) Three-way. Answer: smaller. Adapted from Figure 1 in Halford, GS, Baker R, McCredden , JE and Bain, JD (2005) How many variables can humans process? *Psychological Science, 16*(1), 70–76.

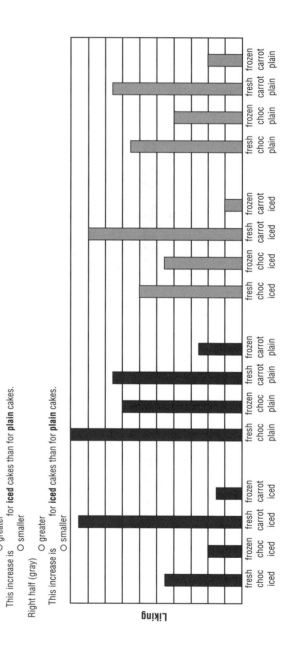

(a) People prefer **fresh** cakes to **frozen** cakes. The difference depends on the flavor (**chocolate** vs **carrot**) and the type (**iced** vs **plain**).

The difference between **fresh** and **frozen** increases from **chocolate** cakes to **carrot** cakes.

Left half (black)

This increase is ○ greater ○ smaller for **iced** cakes than for **plain** cakes.

Right half (gray)

This increase is ○ greater ○ smaller for **iced** cakes than for **plain** cakes.

(b) People prefer **fresh** cakes to **frozen** cakes. The difference depends on the flavor (**chocolate** vs **carrot**), the type (**iced** vs **plain**) and the richness (**rich** vs **low-fat**).

The difference between **fresh** and **frozen** increases from **chocolate** cakes to **carrot** cakes.

This increase is greater for **iced** cakes than for **plain** cakes.

There is a ○ greater
change in the size of the increase for **rich** cakes than for **low-fat** cakes.
○ smaller

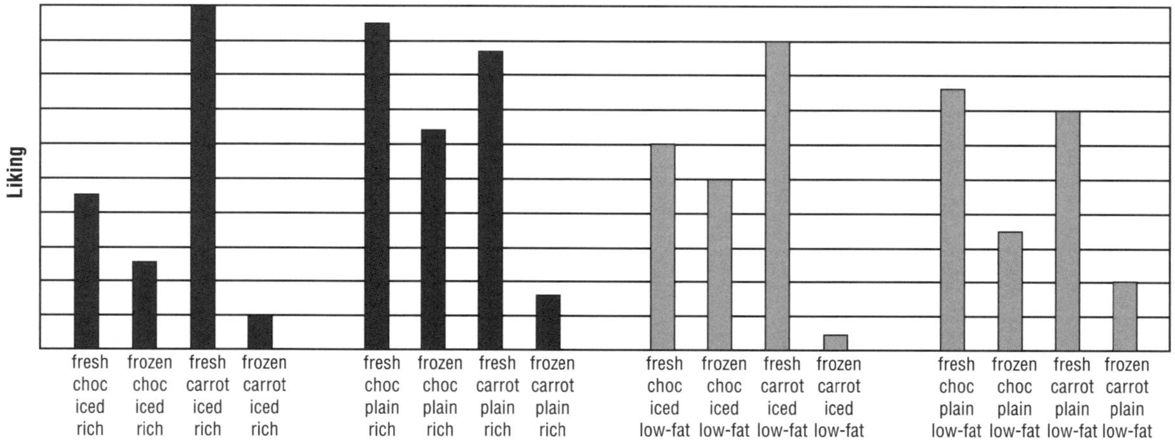

Figure 16.2 Example problems (16 bars). Graphs were presented in blue and yellow, represented here by black and gray, respectively. (a) 2 × 3-way. Answers: greater; greater. (b) Four-way. Answer: smaller. Adapted from Figure 2 in Halford, GS, Baker R, McCredden, JE and Bain, JD (2005) How many variables can humans process? *Psychological Science, 16*(1), 70–76.

Table 16.1 Number of participants answering neither, one, or both problems of each type correctly (n = 30)

Score	Problem type			
	2 × 2-way	3-way	2 × 3-way	4-way
Both correct	30	26	23	13
One incorrect	0	4	7	13
Both incorrect	0	0	0	4

In the experiment, the verbal description of an interaction containing two possible directions for the interaction (greater or smaller) was presented at the top of the screen. A graph was then displayed below the text, initially using equal bar heights, while the participant read the verbal description and came to terms with how the descriptor variables mapped onto the corresponding bar labels in the graph. When the participants were ready, they pressed two keys which caused the graph to be transformed into a full figure, illustrating the interaction.

The experiment was designed to compare processing loads when task complexity increased, while holding memory load constant. Thus, two two-way interactions were compared with a three-way interaction (both using 8 bars) as shown in Figures 16.1a and b, and two three-way interactions were compared with a four-way interaction (both using 16 bars), as shown in Figures 16.2a and b. Each participant received two problems of each type for each of these two main comparisons. Solution times were recorded for the problem-solving phase (i.e., while the bars were unequal length). In addition, participants rated their confidence level for each answer.

Table 16.1 shows that as the complexity of the interaction increased, the number of participants answering one or more problems correctly decreased. Figure 16.3 shows that as task complexity increased, speed and confidence also both decreased, particularly between the 2 × 3-way and four-way problems. A supplementary experiment showed that performance on a five-way problem was no better than chance.

Overall, the results showed that a four-way interaction is difficult even for experienced adults to process without external aids. A soft limit to capacity to process information was indicated by the decline from three- to four-way interactions, with five-way being performed no better than chance. Our findings suggest that a structure defined on four variables is at the limit of human processing capacity, as a four-way interaction requires four variables to be integrated within a single concept. Representations based on four variables would coordinate well with visual and short-term memory capacities of four items, and are consistent with predictions from symbolic connectionist models, to be considered in a later section.

Neuroscience evidence for relational complexity

There is some evidence that specifically links relational complexity to processing in the frontal lobes. Waltz *et al.* (1999) contrasted two levels of relational complexity in participants with either prefrontal or anterior temporal lobe damage. The tasks used were transitive inference and modified Raven's Progressive Matrices. In the one-relation condition, premises were presented in order, such as 'Sam taller than Nate, Nate taller than Roy.' This task can be segmented by processing one premise at a time, the order (Sam, Nate) being determined first, with Roy being concatenated to it, creating the ordered triple (Sam, Nate, Roy). This requires one binary relation to be

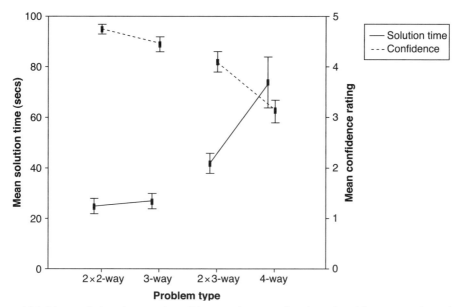

Figure 16.3 Mean solution times and confidence ratings as a function of problem type. Adapted from Figure 3 in Halford GS, Baker R, McCredden JE and Bain JD (2005) How many variables can humans process? *Psychological Science, 16*(1), 70–76.

processed at each step. In the two relations condition, premises were presented in scrambled order, such as 'Beth taller than Tina, Amy taller than Beth.' In this case, the premises have to be considered jointly to determine the order of the three elements. Processing 'Beth taller than Tina' only shows that Beth goes into first or second condition, and 'Amy taller than Beth' must be processed to determine that Amy is first and Beth second. Neither premise alone is sufficient to uniquely determine the ordinal position of an element. Using both premises to construct the ordered triple monotonically taller (Amy, Beth, Tina) entails processing a ternary relation, which entails a higher level of complexity.

Waltz *et al.* (1999) found a double dissociation, so that prefrontal patients were impaired in processing complex relations, but were unimpaired in recall from semantic memory, whereas anterior temporal lobe damage was associated with impairment in semantic memory but not with impairment in relational processing. Furthermore, the groups did not differ in IQ, indicating that the effects reflected prefrontal involvement in processing complex relations, rather than a general factor of task difficulty.

Using a similar modification of Raven's task to that used by Waltz *et al.* (1999), Christoff *et al.* (2001) observed greater activity in middle frontal gyrus (Brodmann area 10) for the two-relation condition than for the one or zero relation conditions, in a contrast analysis of fMRI (functional magnetic resonance imaging) data. Other studies (Kroger *et al.* 2002; Prabhakaran *et al.* 1997) found similarly increased activity in this and other prefrontal regions, as well as in the parietal lobes. Christoff and Gabrieli (2000) proposed a hierarchical model of the prefrontal cortex in relational processing, consisting of three functions: storage (ventrolateral); manipulation (dorsolateral); and evaluation (frontopolar). That is, processes in dorsolateral PFC operate on relations stored in ventrolateral PFC, and processes in frontopolar PFC evaluate the results of those operations.

Further evidence for changes in cortical activity with changes in relational complexity has been found. Contrasts of activity during retention of binary (two roles) versus unary (one role) indexed lists revealed greater parietal and prefrontal activity for a variety of materials (Phillips and Niki 2002). Activity during the retention period for two binary lists was greater than for two unary lists for a region in the superior parietal lobule, dorsal to the occipitoparietal sulcus.

Developmental studies

The relational complexity metric has also been applied to a number of topics in cognitive development. Andrews and Halford (2002) conducted complexity analyses of tasks from six content domains: transitive inference, class inclusion, comprehension of relative clause sentences, cardinality, hypothesis testing and hierarchical classification. These analyses suggested that the tasks that cause difficulty for young children entail ternary relations, whereas the tasks mastered by young children are less complex. These complexity analyses were supported by a large-scale empirical study involving 241 children aged from 3 to 8 years. Children completed tasks in the six content domains, and relational complexity was manipulated in five of these. The items differed in complexity (binary- and ternary-relational) but were comparable in all other respects. Significant effects of relational complexity were observed in each domain. The ternary-relational items were more difficult, and were mastered later in development than the binary-relational items. Comparable ages of attainment were observed for tasks at the same complexity level in different domains. All tasks loaded on a single factor and factor scores were correlated with age ($r = 0.80$) fluid intelligence ($r = 0.79$) and working memory capacity (Listening span, $r = 0.66$). These results suggest that cognitive development is constrained by children's capacity to process complex relations.

The relational complexity metric has been used to integrate findings from different paradigms and to resolve some long-standing paradoxes within the developmental literature. For example, category induction is attained by three years of age (Gelman and Markman 1987), when children can infer that a property attributed to one instance of a category is more likely to belong with other members of the same category than with members of a different category, independent of appearance (Deak and Bauer 1996; Gelman and Markman 1986, 1987; Gelman and O'Reilly 1988; Lopez *et al.* 1992). By contrast, children have difficulty making valid inferences about hierarchically structured categories until they are five years or older (Hodkin 1987; Inhelder and Piaget 1964; Winer 1980). For example, if they are shown a display depicting three bananas and five apples and are asked, 'Are there more apples or more fruit?', children under five or six years typically say, 'More apples'. This apparent paradox has been resolved by relational complexity analysis. When both category induction and hierarchical classification were assessed using a common methodology (property inference tasks), the earlier development of category induction was shown to be due to its complexity being binary-relational, whereas hierarchical classification is ternary-relational. This was confirmed by the finding that hierarchical classification assessed using the property inference procedure corresponded in age of attainment to other ternary-relational tasks, transitivity and class inclusion assessed using the traditional procedure (Halford, Andrews and Jensen 2002).

The theory has generated many predictions beyond those that can be determined intuitively. Theory of mind provides an example. Theory of mind is typically assessed using false belief and appearance reality tasks, both of which are difficult for children younger than four to five years (Wellman *et al.* 2001). Relational complexity analyses indicated that these tasks are ternary-relational, therefore a structural complexity effect was predicted by Halford (1993). This has since been confirmed (Andrews *et al.* 2003). These authors devised binary-relational items that were closely matched in other respects to standard false belief and appearance-reality items. Mastery of these binary-relational items was demonstrated by three-year-olds, whereas mastery of the ternary-relational items occurred later (four to five years).

Ternary-relational scores in the domains of transitivity, class inclusion, hierarchical classification and cardinality accounted for a high proportion of the variance in theory of mind scores, before and after controlling for age and performance on the binary-relational items in the same domains. Combined with the relational complexity effects, these results provide support for the role of relational complexity as a contributor to children's theory of mind.

Predictions about children's balance scale reasoning were also made ahead of data. It was predicted (Halford 1993) that two-year-olds would give correct judgments about a beam balance outcome when the decision could be based on weight information alone or distance information alone, because these are binary-relational. However children would not integrate weight and distance information until they could process ternary relations. These predictions were confirmed by Halford, Andrews, Dalton *et al.* (2002).

The above review demonstrates an accumulating body of research indicating that the capacity to process complex relations increases with age during childhood. Evidence obtained so far suggests that child cognitive development progresses through four levels of complexity. Unary relations are processed at a median age of one year. Children of this age appear to understand class membership, for example, dog (Fido). Binary relations, such as larger (elephant, mouse), are attained by about 1½–2 years of age. Ternary relations are processed at a median age of five years. Quaternary relations such as proportion (e.g., 2/4 = 4/8) emerge later, at around 11 years. That complexity effects are observed in a wide range of content domains indicates that the relational complexity metric is domain general in its application. There is also evidence for cross-domain consistency within individuals during early and middle childhood (Andrews and Halford 2002). The literature is consistent with an interpretation of the attainments of younger children, including some that have been regarded as precocious, as reflecting less complex processes than those of older children (Halford and Andrews 2006).

Working memory boundary conditions

The limitations of the central executive do not apply to all tasks, and it is essential to distinguish those cognitive processes that are subject to capacity limitations from those that are not. Lack of criteria for this can only lead to confusions and intractable issues. Three factors that distinguish cognitive tasks that are not capacity limited are automaticity, modularity and implicit processing. Automaticity develops through extended practice under constant mapping conditions (Hasher and Zacks 1979; Logan 1979; Logan 2005; Shiffrin and Schneider 1977) and is a well-known way of reducing processing loads. While constant mapping conditions of practice are maintained, tasks will be relatively free of capacity limitations, though the limitations will recur if mappings become varied.

Modular processes are also known not to impose processing loads on working memory. Modular processes are distinguished by the fact that they tend to be rapid, automatic, relatively unmodifiable, domain-specific and informationally encapsulated (Anderson 1992; Fodor 1983; Pylyshyn 1999). The distinction between implicit and explicit processes (Karmiloff-Smith 1992) is also relevant to identification of capacity limitations, because implicit processes tend to make low processing demands. They typically reflect a relatively early stage of development of acquisition of a concept, and are characterized by lack of strategic modifiability, so that performance tends to follow established or stereotyped procedures (Clark and Karmiloff-Smith 1993). The implicit–explicit distinction bears some correspondence to the distinction between associative and relational processes (Phillips *et al.* 1995).

Symbolic processes and neural net representation of relations

We conceptualize the central executive as being specialized for processing relations, so we aim to demonstrate that relations can be represented in a neural network framework, along with processes for operating on the representation. There are two major approaches to neural net modeling of relational knowledge and, while there is some controversy, the common ground between the approaches provides useful insight into basic requirements for relational processing, and also provides possible explanations for capacity limitations in the central executive.

One approach to modeling relational knowledge uses role-filler bindings (Hummel and Holyoak 2003; Shastri and Ajjanagadde 1993). With this approach, *loves* (*John, Mary*) would be represented by binding *John* to the agent role of *loves,* and *Mary* to the patient role. This has limitations when multiple relational instances are to be represented (Halford *et al.* 1998, Sections 4.1.1.1 and 4.1.3; but see also Doumas and Hummel 2005).

The other major approach is to use symbol-argument bindings (Halford *et al.* 1998). That is, to represent *loves* (*John, Mary*), we bind the relation symbol *loves* simultaneously to *John* and to *Mary*. Structural alignment is used to maintain correspondence between instances, so if we have a second instance *loves* (*Tom, Wendy*), the two instances of *loves* are aligned, as are *John* and *Tom, Mary* and *Wendy*.

Bindings are implemented in two main ways. One way is based on synchronous activation (Hummel and Holyoak 2003; Shastri and Ajjanagadde 1993). Shastri and Ajjanagadde make units representing a role oscillate in phase (i.e., synchronously) with units representing the filler bound to that role, and out of phase with units representing other roles and fillers. This is a form of role-filler binding (see Figure 16.4).

Binding by simultaneous oscillation supports capacity limitations as follows, given that:

◆ a neural substrate is envisaged for this model

◆ biological neurons have a maximum rate at which they can oscillate (fire)

◆ cognition requires an (unspecified) minimum oscillation frequency, or cognitive responses become too slow, and

◆ oscillation frequencies must be sufficiently different, in order to be discriminable.

This means there must be a limited number of frequency 'slots' at which bound concepts can oscillate. This limits the number of concepts that can be represented simultaneously in a synchronous oscillation system.

The other approach to binding is based on a product operation, such as the tensor product, or outer product (Halford *et al.* 1998; Smolensky 1990) or circular convolution (Plate 1995). In the Structured Tensor Analogical Reasoning (STAR) model (Halford *et al.* 1998; Wilson *et al.* 2001; Wilson *et al.* 1995) the relation symbol and arguments are each represented by vectors, and the binding is represented by the outer product of these vectors. Thus the relational instance

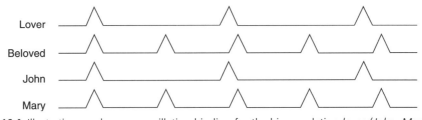

Figure 16.4 Illustrating synchronous oscillation binding for the binary relation *loves* (*John, Mary*).

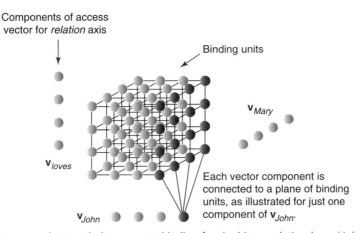

Figure 16.5 Tensor product symbol-arguments binding for the binary relation *loves* (*John, Mary*).

loves (*John, Mary*) would be represented by $v_{loves} \otimes v_{John} \otimes v_{Mary}$, as shown in Figure 16.5. More generally, the relational instance $r(a_1, ..., a_n)$ would be represented in a tensor product space $V_r \otimes V_1 \otimes ... \otimes V_n$. Thus one axis of the tensor represents the relation symbol, and each of the remaining axes corresponds to an argument (role) of the relation (see Figure 16.5). Thus there is a natural correspondence between the mathematical properties of a relation and its representation in symbol-argument tensor product neural nets. At the neural network level, there is a group of units for each tensor axis (relation symbol or argument) connected to a group of binding units, as shown in Figure 16.5. Representations of relational instances can be superimposed. For example, *loves* (*John, Mary*) and *loves* (*Cathy, Tom*) would be represented as $v_{loves} \otimes v_{John} \otimes v_{Mary} + v_{loves} \otimes v_{Cathy} \otimes v_{Tom}$. This adds considerably to the power of the representation. Both synchronous oscillation and tensor product models capture the basic properties of higher cognition (Halford *et al.* 1998; Shastri and Ajjanagadde 1993).

In a more practical system, there would be many more than four vector components in each vector.

Tensor product binding supports capacity limitations as follows: the number of binding units in a tensor product network grows exponentially with the rank of the tensor product, that is, the number of concepts involved – three in *loves* (*John, Mary*), four in *gives* (*John, Mary, chocolates*). Given that there is a limit to the number of binding units that can be allocated to the tensor product network, there is a limit on the rank of the tensor product network, or its equivalent in a biological neural system. This limits the number of concepts that can be represented simultaneously in a tensor product binding system.

These symbolic neural net models have been demonstrated to have some properties of higher cognition, including determining the truth value of a proposition (Halford *et al.* 1998, Section 4.2.2; Humphreys *et al.* 1989), processing higher-order relations (Halford *et al.* 1998, Section 4.2.5), increased processing load with higher relational complexity (Halford *et al.* 1998, Section 5.2), and analogical reasoning (Gray 2003; Halford *et al.* 1994).

Integration with relational complexity metric: representational rank

In this section we want to integrate the relational complexity metric with simpler levels of processing that do not entail processing relations. We do this by defining the concept of representational rank.

In general, representational rank can be defined as the number of identifiable components bound into a structured representation, such that the components satisfy the constraints imposed by the structure. An example would be a cognitive representation of the binary relations 'more-than' and 'less-than' defined on a finite set of positive integers, such as > (3, 2), > (5, 4) and < (2, 5), < (3, 7). There are constraints between the components, so that for the relation '>', the integer in the first position (first slot) of each pair must be greater than the integer in the second position (with a corresponding constraint for '<'). There is further constraint so that, for example, given (3, 2), the relation must be '>'. Each instance, such as > (3, 2), of a binary relation has three components, '>', '3', and '2' so this representation would be Rank 3. Representational rank is one more than the arity of a relation, so a binary relation is Rank 3, a ternary relation is Rank 4, and so on.

The representational rank metric comprises levels 0 to 6, as shown in Figure 16.6. An elemental association between an input and output, without any internal symbol, has rank 0. At the next level are representations that have an internal representation, but these are rank 1 because the representation functions in a holistic fashion. Even if there is more than one element in the representation, the elements are not composed into a structure. A good example of this level of processing would be the representations in the hidden layer of many three-layered net models. The units of the hidden layer represent a property that is computed from two or more input units, modified by connection weights, but no compositions of the hidden layer units are defined. For example, there is nothing equivalent to the relational representations shown in Figures 16.4 or 16.5 for symbolic neural net models. Ranks 2–6 correspond to unary to quinary relations, respectively. Figure 16.6 shows Ranks 0 to 6, with a schematic illustration of the symbolic connectionist representation based on tensor product theory of relational representations. Also shown are examples of the concepts belonging to each rank.

The representational rank metric has been applied to various cognitive tasks in order to make predictions about human capacity to deal with these tasks. Rank 0 can be performed by all animals with nervous systems, and tasks that can be identified with Rank 1 can be performed by many species of vertebrates (e.g. Fagot *et al.* 2001) and even some invertebrates (Giurfa *et al.* 2001). Apes have been demonstrated to perform Rank 3 tasks such as the binary-relational match-to-sample task and proportional analogies (Halford *et al.* 1998; Thompson *et al.* 1997) but only humans have been demonstrated to perform ranks 4–6. The norms for cognitive development indicate that Ranks 3, 4, and 5 are attained at median ages of 2, 5, and 11 years, respectively (Andrews and Halford 2002; Halford 1993), while Rank 6 is believed to be attained by a minority of adults.

Both the symbolic model of relations and the representational rank metric provide a way of investigating the representation and manipulation of relations in human working memory, and they have generated a considerable amount of empirical work that we have briefly reviewed. The model of executive functions based on relational processing gives some conceptual underpinning to this complex and diverse set of processes. Relational processes correspond to established mathematical concepts, and conceptual complexity can be defined by the *arity*, or number of arguments bound into a relational representation. Objective rules for complexity analyses are defined in the Method for Analysis of Relational Complexity. The representational rank metric provides a way of ordering cognitive functions according to their conceptual complexity, such that the lower ranks will evolve and develop earlier than the higher ranks. The representational rank metric has potential to bring more order to our conceptualisation of human problem-solving and reasoning.

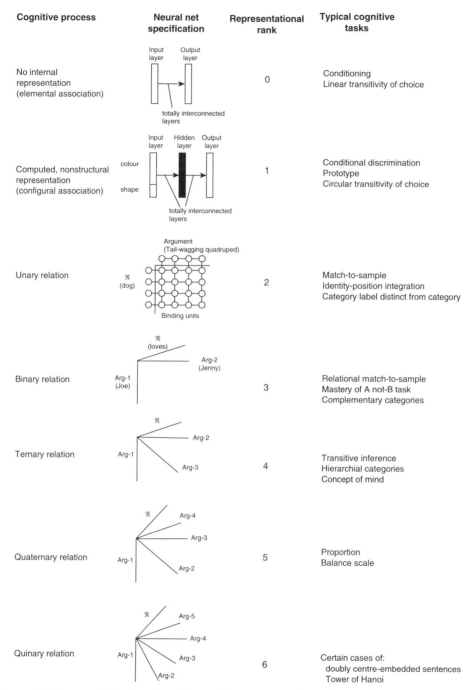

Figure 16.6 Representational ranks with cognitive processes, schematic neural nets and typical cognitive tasks.

Summary and conclusion

In this chapter we have outlined the following propositions:

- The central executive processes relational information that is used in planning, reasoning, and language comprehension.

- Cognitive complexity can be defined by the number of variables that have to be related in a single representation.

- Humans are generally limited to relating four variables in a cognitive representation, though a minority of adults can relate five variables.

- Complex tasks can be performed by conceptual chunking and segmentation, thereby making the best use of limited processing capacity.

- Tasks that are automatic, or modular, or depend on implicit processing, impose lower loads and are not subject to the capacity limitations outlined above.

- There is mounting neurocortical evidence for frontal-parietal activity in representing and processing relations and this activity seems to be related to relational complexity.

- The representational rank metric integrates all levels of cognitive complexity into seven levels from subsymbolic (Rank 0) to the highest levels of symbolic representation (Rank 6).

References

Anderson, M (1992). *Intelligence and Development: A cognitive theory*. Oxford: Blackwell.

Andrews, G, Birney, DP and Halford, GS (2006). Relational processing and working memory in the comprehension of complex relative clause sentences. *Memory and Cognition*, 34, 1325–1340.

Andrews, G and Halford, GS (2002). A cognitive complexity metric applied to cognitive development. *Cognitive Psychology*, 45, 153–219.

Andrews, G, Halford, GS, Bunch, KM, Bowden, D and Jones, T (2003). Theory of mind and relational complexity. *Child Development*, 74, 1476–1499.

Binet, A and Simon, T (1905/1980). *The Development of Intelligence in Children*. Nashville, TN: Williams Printing Co.

Birney, D. P., Bowman, D. B., and Bui, M. (2006, July 16–21). *Working-memory as 'g', or Gf, or, EF, or .?* Paper presented at the Fourth International Conference on Memory, University of New South Wales.

Birney, DP, Andrews, G and Halford, GS (2006). The influence of relational complexity on reasoning: The development of the Latin Square Task. *Educational and Psychological Measurement*, 66, 146–171.

Birney, DP, Bowman, DB and Pallier, G (2006). Prior to paradigm integration, the task is to resolve construct definitions of gF and WM. *Behavioral and Brain Sciences*, 29, 127 .

Birney, DP and Halford, GS (2002). Cognitive complexity of suppositional reasoning: An application of the relational complexity metric to the knight-knave task. *Thinking and Reasoning*, 8, 109–134.

Blair, C (2006). How similar are fluid cognition and general intelligence? A developmental neuroscience perspective on fluid cognition as an aspect of human cognitive ability. *Behavioral and Brain Sciences*, 29, 109–160.

Cabeza, R and Nyberg, L (2000). Neural bases of learning and memory: Functional neuroimaging evidence. *Current Opinion in Neurology*, 13, 415–421.

Christoff, K and Gabrieli, JDE (2000). The frontopolar cortex and human cognition: Evidence for a rostrocaudal hierarchical organization within the human prefrontal cortex. *Psychobiology*, 28, 168–186.

Christoff, K, Prabhakaran, V, Dorfman, J *et al.* (2001). Rostrolateral prefrontal cortex involvement in relational integration during reasoning. *Neuroimage*, 14, 1136–1149.

Clark, A and Karmiloff-Smith, A (1993). The cognizer's innards: A psychological and philosophical perspective on the development of thought. *Mind and Language*, 8, 487–519.

Cowan, N (2001). The magical number 4 in short-term memory: A reconsideration of mental storage capacity. *Behavioral and Brain Sciences*, *24*, 87–185.

Davis, G and Holmes, A (2005). The capacity of visual short-term memory is not a fixed number of objects. *Memory and Cognition*, *33*, 185–195.

Deak, GO and Bauer, PJ (1996). The dynamics of preschoolers' categorization choices. *Child Development*, *67*, 740–767.

Doumas, LAA and Hummel, JE (2005). Approaches to modeling human mental representations: What works, what doesn't, and why. In KJ Holyoak and RG Morrison (eds), *Cambridge Handbook of Thinking and Reasoning* (pp. 73–93). Cambridge University Press, New York.

Duncan, J, Seitz, RJ, Kolodny, J *et al.* (2000). A neural basis for general intelligence. *Science*, *289*, 457–460.

Fagot, J, Wasserman, EA and Young, ME (2001). Discriminating the relation between relations: The role of entropy in abstract conceptualization by baboons (Papio papio) and humans (Homo sapiens). *Journal of Experimental Psychology: Animal Behavior Processes*, *27*, 316–328.

Fodor, JA (1983). *Modularity of Mind: An essay on faculty psychology*. Cambridge, MA: MIT Press.

Frye, D and Zelazo, PD (1998). Complexity: From formal analysis to final action. *Behavioral and Brain Sciences*, *21*, 836–837.

Fuster, JM (1997). *The Prefrontal Cortex: Anatomy, physiology, and neuropsychology of the frontal lobe*. Philadelphia, PA: Lippincott-Raven.

Gelman, SA and Markman, EM (1986). Categories and induction in young children. *Cognition*, *23*, 183–209.

Gelman, SA and Markman, EM (1987). Young children's inductions from natural kinds: The role of categories and appearances. *Child Development*, *58*, 1532–1541.

Gelman, SA and O'Reilly, AW (1988). Children's inductive inferences within superordinate categories: The role of language and category structure. *Child Development*, *59*, 876–887.

Gentner, D (1983). Structure-mapping: A theoretical framework for analogy. *Cognitive Science*, *7*, 155–170.

Gentner, D, Holyoak, KJ and Kokinov, B (eds) (2001). *The Analogical Mind: Perspectives from cognitive science*. Cambridge, MA: MIT Press.

Giurfa, M, Zhang, S, Jenett, A, Menzel, R and Srinivasan, MV (2001). The concepts of 'sameness' and 'difference' in an insect. *Nature*, *410*, 930–933.

Goel, V, Makale, M and Grafman, J (2004). The hippocampal system mediates logical reasoning about familiar spatial environments. *Journal of Cognitive Neuroscience*, *16*, 654–664.

Goodwin, GP and Johnson-Laird, PN (2005). Reasoning about relations. *Psychological Review*, *112*, 468–493.

Grafman, J and Litvan, I (1999). Importance of deficits in executive functions. *The Lancet*, *354*, 1921–1923.

Gray, B (2003). Relational models of feature based concept formation, theory-based concept formation and analogical retrieval/mapping. Unpublished PhD Thesis, University of Queensland, Brisbane.

Halford, GS (1990). Is childrens' reasoning logical or analogical? Further comments on Piagetian cognitive developmental psychology. *Human Development*, *33*, 356–361.

Halford, GS (1993). *Children's Understanding: The development of mental models*. Hillsdale, NJ: Erlbaum.

Halford, GS (2002). Information processing models of cognitive development. In U Goswami (ed), *Blackwell Handbook of Childhood Cognitive Development* (pp. 555–574). Oxford: Blackwell.

Halford, GS and Andrews, G (2006). Reasoning and problem solving. In D Kuhn and R Siegler (eds), *Handbook of Child Psychology: Volume 2. Cognitive, language and perceptual development*. Hoboken, NJ: Wiley.

Halford, GS, Andrews, G, Dalton, C, Boag, C and Zielinski, T (2002). Young children's performance on the balance scale: The influence of relational complexity. *Journal of Experimental Child Psychology*, *81*, 417–445.

Halford, GS, Andrews, G and Jensen, I (2002). Integration of category induction and hierarchical classification: One paradigm at two levels of complexity. *Journal of Cognition and Development*, *3*, 143–177.

Halford, GS, Baker, R, McCredden, JE and Bain, JD (2005). How many variables can humans process? *Psychological Science, 16*, 70–76.

Halford, GS, Wilson, WH, Guo, J, Gayler, RW, Wiles, J and Stewart,, JEM (1994). Connectionist implications for processing capacity limitations in analogies. In KJ Holyoak and J Barnden (eds), *Advances in Connectionist and Neural Computation Theory: Vol 2. Analogical connections* (pp. 363–415). Norwood, NJ: Ablex.

Halford, GS, Wilson, WH and Phillips, S (1998). Processing capacity defined by relational complexity: Implications for comparative, developmental, and cognitive psychology. *Behavioral and Brain Sciences, 21*, 803–831.

Hasher, L and Zacks, RT (1979). Automatic and effortful processes in memory. *Journal of Experimental Psychology: General, 108*, 356–388.

Heckers, S, Zalesak, M, Weiss, AP and Titone, D (2004). Hippocampal activation during transitive inference in humans. *Hippocampus, 14*, 153–162.

Hodkin, B (1987). Performance model analysis in class inclusion: An illustration with two language conditions. *Developmental Psychology, 23*, 683–689.

Hofstadter, DR (2001). Analogy as the core of cognition. In D Gentner, KJ Holyoak and BN Kokinov (eds), *The Analogical Mind: Perspectives from cognitive science* (pp. 499–538). MIT Press, Cambridge.

Holland, JH, Holyoak, KJ, Nisbett, RE and Thagard, PR (1986). *Induction: Processes of inference, learning and discovery*. Cambridge, MA: MIT Press.

Hummel,, JE and Holyoak, KJ (2003). A symbolic-connectionist theory of relational inference and generalization. *Psychological Review, 110*, 220–264.

Humphreys, MS, Bain, JD and Pike, R (1989). Different ways to cue a coherent memory system: A theory for episodic, semantic and procedural tasks. *Psychological Review, 96*, 208–233.

Inhelder, B and Piaget, J (1964). *The Early Growth of Logic in the Child*. London: Routledge and Kegan Paul.

Johnson-Laird, PN (1983). *Mental Models*. Cambridge: Cambridge University Press.

Johnson-Laird, PN and Byrne RMJ (1991). *Deduction*. Hillsdale, NJ: Erlbaum.

Karmiloff-Smith, A (1992). *Beyond Modularity: A developmental perspective on cognitive science*. Cambridge, MA: MIT Press.

Koch, G, Oliveri, M, Torriero, S, Carlesimo, GA, Turriziani, P and Caltagirone, C (2005). rTMS evidence of different delay and decision processes in a fronto-parietal neuronal network activated during spatial working memory. *Neuroimage, 24*, 34–39.

Kroger, J, Sabb, FW, Fales, C, Bookheimer, SY, Cohen, MS and Holyoak, K (2002). Recruitment of anterior dorsolateral prefrontal cortex in human reasoning: A parametric study of relational complexity. *Cerebral Cortex, 12*, 477–485.

Logan, GD (1979). On the use of a concurrent memory load to measure attention and automaticity. *Journal of Experimental Psychology: Human Perception and Performance, 5*, 189–207.

Logan, GD (2005). Attention, automaticity, and executive control. In AF Healy (ed), *Experimental Cognitive Psychology and its Applications* (pp. 129–139). Washington, DC: American Psychological Association.

Lopez, A, Gelman, SA, Gutheil, G and Smith, EE (1992). The development of category-based induction. *Child Development, 63*, 1070–1090.

Loveday, W (1995). The effect of complexity on planning in the Tower of Hanoi problem. Unpublished Honours Thesis, University of Queensland, Brisbane, Australia.

Luck, SJ and Vogel, EK (1997). The capacity of visual working memory for features and conjunctions. *Nature, 390*, 279–281.

Miller, GA (1956). The magical number seven, plus or minus two: Some limits on our capacity for processing information. *Psychological Review, 63*, 81–97.

Nagode, JC and Pardo, JV (2002). Human hippocampal activation during transitive inference. *NeuroReport, 13*, 939–944.

Phillips, S, Halford, GS and Wilson, WH (1995). The processing of associations versus the processing of relations and symbols: A systematic comparison. In JD Moore and JF Lehman (eds), *Proceedings of the Seventeenth Annual Conference of the Cognitive Science Society* (pp. 688–691). Pittsburgh, PA: Lawrence Erlbaum.

Phillips, S and Niki, K (2002). Separating relational from item load effects in paired recognition: Temporoparietal and middle frontal gyral activity with increased associates, but not items during encoding and retention. *NeuroImage, 17*, 1031–1055.

Phillips, S and Niki, K (2003). Increased bilateral occipitoparietal activity for retention of binary versus unary indexed lists in pair recognition. *NeuroImage, 20*, 1226–1235.

Piaget, J (1950). *The Psychology of Intelligence*, translate by M Piercy and DE Berlyne. London: Routledge and Kegan Paul. (Original work published 1947.)

Plate, TA (1995). Holographic reduced representations. *IEEE Transactions on Neural Networks, 6*, 623–641.

Polk, TA and Newell, A (1995). Deduction as verbal reasoning. *Pychological Review, 102*, 533–566.

Prabhakaran, V, Rypma, B and Gabrieli, JD (2001). Neural substrates of mathematical reasoning: A functional magnetic resonance imaging study of neocortical activation during performance of the necessary arithmetic operations test. *Neuropsychology, 15*, 115–127.

Prabhakaran, V, Smith, JA, Desmond, JE, Glover, GH and Gabrieli, JD (1997). Neural substrates of fluid reasoning: an fMRI study of neocortical activation during performance of the Raven's Progressive Matrices Test. *Cognitive Psychology, 33*, 43–63.

Pylyshyn, ZW (1999). Is vision continuous with cognition? The case for cognitive penetrability of visual perception. *Behavioural and Brain Sciences, 22*, 341–423.

Ridderinkhof, KR, van den Wildenberg, WP, Segalowitz, SJ and Carter, CS (2004). Neurocognitive mechanisms of cognitive control: The role of prefrontal cortex in action selection, response inhibition, performance monitoring, and reward-based learning. *Brain and Cognition, 56*, 129–40.

Robin, N and Holyoak, KJ (1995). Relational complexity and the functions of prefrontal cortex. In MS Gazzaniga (ed), *The Cognitive Neurosciences* (pp. 987–997). Cambridge, MA: MIT Press.

Shastri, L and Ajjanagadde, V (1993). From simple associations to systematic reasoning: A connectionist representation of rules, variables, and dynamic bindings using temporal synchrony. *Behavioral and Brain Sciences, 16*, 417–94.

Shiffrin, RM and Schneider, W (1977). Controlled and automatic human information processing: II. Perceptual learning, automatic attending, and a general theory. *Psychological Review, 84*, 127–90.

Smolensky, P (1990). Tensor product variable binding and the representation of symbolic structures in connectionist systems. *Artificial Intelligence, 46*, 159–216.

Tekin, S and Cummings, JL (2002). Frontal-subcortical neuronal circuits and clinical neuropsychiatry: An update. *Journal of Psychosomatic Research, 53*, 647–54.

Thompson, RKR, Oden, DL and Boysen, ST (1997). Language-naive chimpanzees (Pan troglodytes) judge relations between relations in a conceptual matching-to-sample task. *Journal of Experimental Psychology: Animal Behavior Processes, 23*, 31–43.

Waltz, JA, Knowlton, BJ, Holyoak, KJ *et al.* (1999). A system for relational reasoning in human prefrontal cortex. *Psychological Science, 10*, 119–125.

Wellman, HM, Cross, D and Watson, J (2001). Meta-analysis of theory-of-mind development: The truth about false belief. *Child Development, 72*, 655–684.

Wilson, WH, Halford, GS, Gray, B and Phillips, S (2001). The STAR-2 model for mapping hierarchically structured analogs. In D Gentner, K Holyoak and B Kokinov (eds), *The Analogical Mind: Perspectives from cognitive science* (pp. 125–159). Cambridge, MA: MIT Press.

Wilson, WH, Street, DJ and Halford, GS (1995). Solving proportional analogy problems using tensor product networks with random representations. Paper presented at the *IEEE International Conference on Neural Networks Proceedings, Perth, Australia*.

Winer, GA (1980). Class-inclusion reasoning in children: A review of the empirical literature. *Child Development*, 51, 309–328.

Zelazo, PD and Frye, D (1998). Cognitive complexity and control: II. The development of executive function in childhood. *Current Directions in Psychological Science*, 7, 121–126.

Zelazo, PD, Muller, U, Frye, D and Marcovitch, S (2003). The development of executive function in early childhood. *Monographs of the Society for Research in Child Development*, 68(3), Serial No. 274.

Zielinski, TA (2006). Performance of aging subjects on tasks varying in relational complexity. Unpublished PhD thesis, University of Queensland, Brisbane.

17

A neural efficiency hypothesis of age-related changes in human working memory performance

Bart Rypma

Since its inception, cognitive aging research has indicated that increasing age is associated with lower performance on a broad range of cognitive tasks (e.g., Foster and Taylor 1920; Jones and Conrad 1933). These changes are mediated by deterioration of the physiological mechanisms that give rise to information processing capabilities. Indeed, the entire stream of information processing, from peripheral perceptual processes to central cognitive processes, appears to undergo profound age-related change. In this chapter I will present evidence to support the notion that the cognitive consequences of age-associated changes to peripheral and central nervous system structures is a reduction in the efficiency of information processing.

Structural changes in the periphery and their relations to cognitive aging

Perceptually, auditory and visual deficits increase with age. Hearing loss is among the most prevalent and disabling symptoms that older adults encounter. Changes in the human cochlear structure lead to age-related hearing impairment. Focal inner hair cell loss in the basilar membrane leads to diminution of sensitivity to higher frequencies while diffuse outer hair cell loss in the basilar membrane leads to reduced processing of low frequencies. Age-related changes to auditory brainstem lead to more profound changes in frequency discrimination, temporal discrimination, localization and speech perception (e.g., Willot 1991; Hellstrom and Schmeidt 1991; Schneider 1997; Schneider and Pichora-Fuller 2000).

As with the auditory apparatus, the human visual system also exhibits age-related changes that lead to information processing difficulties. Changes to the cornea, iris, lens and vitreous and aqueous humors adversely affect the quality of the image projected to the retina (e.g., Michaels 1993). These structural changes lead to increases in retinal blurring, light-scatter that decreases retinal contrast (Sloane, Owsley and Jackson 1988). Reductions in contrast sensitivity have been associated with age-related changes in object recognition performance (Owsley and Sloane 1987).

Second and third order brain regions in the visual pathway appear to be less affected by aging. Structural studies of lateral geniculate nucleus (LGN) suggest age-equivalent neuron density and minimal changes in size. Functional studies suggest minimal age changes in LGN-cell response properties (Ahmad and Spear 1993; Spear *et al.* 1994). Striate cortex similarly undergoes minimal age-related structural changes in neuron density or cellular response properties (Haug *et al.* 1984; Vincent, Peters and Tigges 1989). The apparent sparing of these higher-order visual structures implicates reduced functions in the visual periphery as a causal factor in age-related performance changes.

A number of investigators have explored the effects of peripheral function changes on age-related changes in cognitive performance. In one study, for instance, Salthouse and colleagues (1998) demonstrated that changes in visual acuity accounted for around one-half of the age-related variance in cognitive measures. Similarly about one-third of age-related variance in Raven Advanced Progressive Matrices performance may be accounted for by visual acuity. Results from several large-scale studies support the notion that age-related changes in sensory acuity are intimately related to changes in higher cognitive functions. In one study of 516 70–103 year-olds, threshold measures of visual and auditory acuity accounted for 93 per cent of the age-related variance in intellectual functioning as measured by a comprehensive battery of 14 tests (Lindenberger and Baltes 1994). Subsequent work has tied changes in visual acuity to a fundamental index of cognitive efficiency, processing speed (Salthouse *et al.* 1996).

Central structural changes and their relations to cognitive aging

In addition to peripheral visual structures, central brain regions undergo progressive age-related tissue loss. This loss is marked by neocortical atrophy, widening sulci and ventricular dilation. Progressive tissue volume decrease culminates in brain mass shrinkage by as much as 10 per cent by 80 years of age (Minckler and Boyd 1968; Wisniewski and Terry 1976). Tissue loss is not evenly distributed across the cortex. Disproportionate tissue decline has been observed in prefrontal cortex, as compared to other structures in both humans and primates (e.g., Haug and Eggers 1991; Corsellis 1976; Raz *et al.* 1997; Raz 2000).

There has been considerable controversy concerning the relative contributions of gray and white brain matter to such deterioration. Gray matter is comprised of neural cell bodies in the cortex and in subcortical structures. White matter is comprised of tightly packed axons that connect neurons to each other in the cortex and that connect cortical neurons to the periphery. Studies across species suggest a primary role for white-matter changes in human and primate brain-aging, possibly especially in prefrontal cortex (PFC Peters 2002; Peters and Sethares 2002, 2004; Madden *et al.* 2004). Further, age-related white matter loss without axonal loss suggests that the observed changes may be related specifically to decreases in nonneural cells, particularly myelinating oligodendroglia (Sim *et al.* 2002; Franklin, Zhao and Sim 2002; Tang *et al.* 1997). These changes could lead to disruptions of transcortical information flow and suggest a plausible neural mechanism for processing-efficiency models of age-related cognitive slowing.

Other research has suggested that age-related brain volume changes may result from gray-matter degeneration. Early brain aging hypotheses maintained that cortical atrophy resulted from widespread neuron loss (e.g., Brody 1955) in adulthood and senescence (Turlejski and Djavadian 2002; Kemper 2002). Recent studies in humans using voxel-based morphometric analysis are in agreement with these early hypotheses in suggesting that age-related changes result more from *gray* matter tissue loss, than white matter, although evidence for white matter change is sometimes also observed in these studies. Tisserand and colleagues (2002) reported a significant age-associated decline in gray matter volume with VBM, but they did not evaluate white matter and only analyzed anterior regions. Good and colleagues (2001) examined grey matter, white matter and cerebrospinal fluid (CSF) volumes in 465 adults with age ranges 18–79 years. They found linear age-related declines in gray matter volume concentrated in several regions. These regions included the parietal, anterior cingulate and middle frontal gyri corresponding to dorsal PFC. Other aging studies have revealed selective gray matter decline in the absence of white matter (Taki *et al.* 2004; Tisserand *et al.* 2004). Resnick *et al.* (2000) longitudinally examined gray and white matter changes in older adults (59–85 years old). Total gray and white matter volume loss was approximately 5.4 cm^3 and 2.4 cm^3, respectively. The greatest changes were observed in frontal and parietal lobes (see also Resnick *et al.* 2004).

Precise relationships between age-related anatomical changes and age-related cognitive decline are not yet well understood. On one hand, anatomical, histological, neurochemical and neuroimaging data implicate principally white-matter change with relative sparing of gray matter. On the other hand, voxel-based morphometric studies implicate either mainly gray matter, or both gray and white matter changes. Presently, the weight of evidence supports the notion that brain volume loss is predominantly due to white matter changes with relative sparing of gray matter. Future research will be required to disentangle the differences between these studies and what effect different measurement techniques have on these discrepant results.

The evidence reviewed above indicates that, while many brain regions suffer deleterious aging effects, prefrontal cortex may be especially susceptible to such effects. Histological studies have shown the greatest age-related decrements in cortical volume within PFC as compared to other brain regions (Haug and Eggers 1991). MRI studies have found the greatest age-related structural decline in PFC that correlates with executive task impairment Raz *et al.* 1997, 1998, 2000; West 1996). PET studies in old subjects have found reduced metabolism within PFC (e.g., Kuhl *et al.* 1982). Finally, neuropsychological tests show that older adults are more impaired on tasks that depend upon PFC function than other brain regions (West 1996). Together, these results suggest that those cognitive processes that depend on prefrontal function are especially susceptible to deleterious aging effects. One such process, working memory (WM), is considered essential to many higher intellectual functions that are known to be adversely affected by age.

Neural mediators of age-related changes in working memory

WM can be defined as the cognitive apparatus that allows individuals to temporarily maintain and manipulate information in mind. Because WM is considered fundamental to many higher cognitive processes (e.g., reasoning, text comprehension, problem-solving), findings of age-related WM changes may plausibly explain the performance changes observed across a broad array of such higher cognitive tasks. There are several theoretical conceptions of WM but one prominent theory holds that it can be divided into separate components. "Slave system" buffers mediate the short-term retention of small amounts of information. An additional "supervisory attentional system" or "central executive" controls allocation of attention to the slave system buffers (Baddeley 1986; Norman and Shallice 1980; Baddley and Hitch 1974). Neuropsychological studies in humans and unit-recording studies in monkeys have indicated an intimate connection between prefrontal cortex function and WM performance (e.g., Kubota and Niki 1971; Goldman-Rakic 1987; Fuster and Alexander 1971; Goldman-Rakic and Friedman 1991; Funahashi, Bruce and Goldman-Rakic 1989). Single cell recordings of monkey brains have shown persistent activity in dorsolateral PFC cells during delay period of a delayed-match-to-sample task. Moreover, monkeys with principal sulcus lesions show location specific deficits in delayed response performance (Goldman-Rakic and Friedman 1991).

Age-related behavioral changes in working memory

Evidence from behavioral research with animals and humans indicates declines in WM with advancing age. The observation of these declines is considered critical to an understanding of the broadspread cognitive changes that accompany human aging because much evidence from a variety of research domains suggest that WM function is central to many human cognitive functions including reasoning, planning and problem-solving (Baddeley 1986; Norman and Shallice 1980). Behavioral studies with older monkeys show performance deficits compared to their younger counterparts on delayed response WM tasks (e.g., Presty *et al.* 1987; Bachevalier, *et al.* 1991; Bartus, Dean and Fleming 1979).

Similar to older monkeys, older humans show behavioral deficits in WM. Age-related performance differences are often observed in delayed-response WM tasks. Moreover, greater performance declines are observed with increasing delay intervals (e.g., Craik 1977; Smith 1975; Poon and Fozard 1980; Nielsen-Bohlman and Knight 1995). The amount of information that must be held in mind (i.e., memory load) also exacerbates age-related differences in WM performance. A number of studies examining the effects of varying memory loads on delayed-response task performance have shown greater age differences with higher than with lower memory loads (Anders, Fozard and Lillyqist 1972; Eriksen, Hamlin and Daye 1973; Anders and Fozard 1973; Marsh 1975). Anders, Fozard and Lillyquist (1972), for instance, examined age-differential performance when subjects had to remember various numbers of digits across an unfilled delay interval. They observed increasing age differences in performance with increasing memory load, indicating faster memory retrieval rates in younger than in older participants. Other studies using similar designs have not observed age differences in memory retrieval rate (e.g., Kirsner 1972; Boaz and Denney 1993).

The factors that mediate age-differential or age-equivalent WM performance are not yet clearly understood. Such variance may be related to task factors that vary between studies. Indeed, compared to memory tasks that involve delays of at least several seconds, those with minimal delays often show minimal age-related performance differences. One such task is digit span, in which participants recall a digit string immediately following presentation. Performance on this task often appears unaffected by healthy aging (Gilbert 1941;Bromley 1958; Craik, 968; Kriauciunas 1968; Gilbert and Levee 1971; Drachman and Leavitt 1972; Botwinick and Storandt 1974; Friedman 1974; Taub 1973).

The observation of greater age-differences with increases in delay time or memory load suggests that different components of WM may be differentially susceptible to the deleterious effects of advancing age. It may be that WM slave systems, that allow maintenance of lower memory loads at shorter intervals, are relatively unaffected by aging. Executive WM mechanisms, those believed to facilitate maintenance of higher memory loads over long delay intervals, may be differentially affected by advancing age.

Age-related changes in neural activity: data and theories

The advent of functional neuroimaging techniques has permitted testing of hypotheses of age-related brain changes, developed through behavioral comparisons of younger and older adults, and older normal adults with older neurological patients (such as those with Alzheimer's or Parkinson's disease and focal brain injury; e.g., Gabrieli 1991, 1996). These hypotheses may now be further tested and extended by observation of the intact human brain (Prull, Bunge and Gabrieli 2000; Raz 2000; Rypma and Gabrieli 2000).

Patterns of neural activity do appear to change with age. Regions of increased activity in older adults, relative to younger adults, have been observed in a number of studies using PET and fMRI (e.g., Grady *et al.* 1992; Cabeza *et al.* 1997; Madden *et al.* 1999; Reuter-Lorenz *et al.* 2000; Rypma, Prabhakaran, Desmond *et al.* 2000).

A number of "compensation" hypotheses have been advanced to account for these patterns of results. One form of this hypothesis may be referred to as a "brain-compensation" hypothesis. In this view, the older brain "compensates" for affected regions with presumably less-affected regions that, in a sense, "take over" the functions of the affected regions. Support for the hypothesis that relatively intact regions can assume the functions of regions that suffer from deterioration or trauma comes from studies showing functional plasticity in the face of traumatic injury (Finger, Buckner and Buckingham 2003; Buckner *et al.* 1996). The observation that high-demand tasks involve brain regions that do not appear to be active in low-demand forms of these tasks also supports compensation hypotheses (e.g., Awh *et al.* 1996; Rypma *et al.* 1999; Rypma and D'Esposito 1999, 2002; Manoach *et al.* 1997). Problems with age related compensation hypotheses arise from observations that activation increases and decreases do not appear to be systematically related. That is, age-related activation increases are not consistently accompanied by decreases in those regions activated in younger adults. More generally, activation decreases are not consistently accompanied by increases in other regions. Thus, while brain compensation is advanced as a general principal to explain age-related differences in neural activity, the data do not support a specific mechanism by which such a process might occur.

Another form of compensation hypothesis with clearer behavioral implications may be referred to as "cognitive compensation". In this view, older adults cognitively "compensate" by using strategies that are different from those they used as young adults. This strategic shift presumably accommodates age-related changes to the "wet-ware" platform that yields the "young" strategies untenable.

Observations of increasing age-related performance differences with memory-load increases and age related activation differences with increases in memory-load in dorsal PFC may reflect differences in the susceptibility of slave-system WM components and executive components to the deleterious effects of age. The notion that rehearsal mechanisms are engaged by low-memory demand tasks and that additional memory mechanisms are engaged by high-memory demands to compress or "chunk" to-be-maintained information has been supported in a number of studies of short-term memory capacity (e.g., Waugh and Norman 1965; Baddeley and Hitch 1974; Glanzer and Razel 1974). These behavioral results, coupled with findings of load-related increases in dorsal PFC (e.g., Rypma *et al.* 1999; Rypma and D'Esposito 1999, 2002) suggest (1) that activation increases in this region reflect cognitive strategy changes aimed at accommodation of supracapacity memory demand (i.e., recruitment of executive processes) and (2) that the age-related changes in this region may reflect age-related differences in the cognitive strategies employed by younger and older adults under conditions of supracapacity memory demand. Indeed, the observation of age-related increases in other PFC regions in the Rypma *et al.* (1999) study further suggests that this difference may reflect age-related strategy differences (cf. Cabeza 2002; Grady *et al.* 1994, 2002).

Problems with these hypotheses arise from observations that debriefing protocols and analyses of errors show minimal evidence for age-related strategy differences. In addition, age-related activation increases have not been consistently linked to performance improvements, a prediction that the "cognitive compensation" hypothesis would seem to predict. Reuter-Lorenz (2001) reviewed studies that show age-related increases in activity that have been accompanied by age-equivalent performance in some cases (Cabeza *et al.* 1997), and age-differential performances in others (Reuter-Lorenz *et al.* 2000, 2001). She and her colleagues (Jonides, Marshuetz, Smith *et al.* 2000) have observed still a third relationship between performance and neural activity, age-related reductions in PET activation associated with reduced cognitive performance in elderly relative to young. Finally, in tasks that restrict the available strategies, age-related activation differences are still observed (for instance by limiting the task to simple visual search; e.g., McIntosh 1999; Eldreth *et al.* 2004).

Age-related brain–behavior changes – an individual differences approach

The literature reviewed above suggests that, although they are intuitively appealing, compensation hypotheses may not account well for the observed patterns of age-related changes in neural activity. Moreover, there is little evidence to suggest that they provide any insight regarding age-related performance changes. One feature of compensation hypotheses is that most of the evidence used to support them is based on mean or median observations of age-related performance changes in neural activity. It may be that a better understanding of the age-changes in complex brain–behavior relationships may be gained by more closely examining the relationship between neural activity and performance at the level of individual subjects. That is to say, understanding the neural factors that underlie age-related changes in performance may best be approached by the study of individual differences in brain-behavior relationships. Support for this notion comes from fMRI studies that use event-related methods. Event-related methodology has the advantage of permitting analyses that emphasize relationships between individual subjects' performance and their neural activity (Rypma and D'Esposito 2001).

In one event-related study, Rypma and D'Esposito (2000) sought to determine possible sources of age-related differences in activation using an event-related fMRI methodology in which age-differences in activation could be isolated to the encoding, maintenance and retrieval portions of a delayed-response item-recognition task. Their results suggest that the age-related activation differences in dorsal PFC were isolated to memory retrieval. In their experiments, subjects were required to (1) encode either two or six letters, (2) maintain them over an unfilled delay interval and (3) determine if a simple letter was or was not part of the memory-set. The results of their studies indicated age-equivalent load-dependent effects in the Encoding and Delay periods of the task. In the Retrieval period, however, large and significant differences in PFC activation were observed only in dorsal regions. These results indicated that PFC mechanisms related to encoding and maintenance of WM may be relatively robust to the deleterious effects of age. Those PFC mechanisms that mediate WM executive processes related to memory retrieval, however, may suffer in the aging process.

In addition to these region- and task-period-dependent age-related effects, Rypma and D'Eposito noticed that there was a considerable role for subject factors in explaining the variability of fMRI data. When they tested the relationship between subjects' performance and PFC activation in all task periods and PFC regions, they observed that individual subjects' reaction times accounted for most of the variability in fMRI data only in dorsal PFC regions and only during the response period. Specifically, for younger subjects, response period activation showed a significant positive correlation between individual subjects' RT and dorsal PFC activity that accounted for 71 per cent of the variance. In contrast, for older subjects, response period activation showed a significant negative correlation between individual subjects' RT and dorsal PFC activation that accounted for 72 per cent of the variance.

These results suggest an alternative explanation to the notion that age-related activation changes reflect some form of compensation. One possibility suggested by these data is that age-related activation increases may be related to differences in the efficiency of transmission mechanisms that are required for the implementation of cognitive processes. Thus decreased speed of information processing may be related to increases in activation in younger adults, but to decreases in activation in older adults. One model that could account for such a pattern of activation-performance relationships is based on findings of overall age-related reductions in baseline levels of activation in humans (e.g., De Santi *et al.* 1995; Eberling et al. 1995; Moeller *et al.* 1996; Rypma and D'Esposito 2000). For instance, Moeller and his colleagues examined age-related changes in "metabolic topography" using PET. In a sample of 130 adults ranging in age from 21–90 years of age, they observed relative frontal hypometabolism in the brains of older, as compared to younger, adults. Such overall activation reductions could alter the relationship between neural activation and response probability. This relationship is known to be sigmoid in nature; middle ranges of neural activation result in optimal performance while increases above or below this optimal range result in performance-level decrements, i.e., a shift in the bias parameter of the sigmoid function (Servan-Schreiber, Printz and Cohen 1990; Kimberg, D'Esposito and Farah 1997: Rypma and D'Esposito 2000).

In summary, findings of age-differential PFC activation patterns, and age-differential functions relating PFC activation-levels to performance, suggest two possible hypotheses to explain age-related increases in neural activity during WM performance. The first hypothesis suggests that the age-related differences in patterns of PFC activation reflect differences in the cognitive strategies employed by younger and older adults. The second hypothesis suggests that age-related differences in patterns of PFC activation reflect changes in the neural integrity of direct processing links between nodes that must make contact for WM processing to occur. Such changes lead to age-related differences in the optimal neural activation level require for optimal task performance.

In one study we sought to test the hypothesis of age-related differences in strategy by comparing PFC activation levels of younger and older adults performing a WM task with a broad range(1–8 letters) of memory-demand levels. Findings of age-related differences in the functions relating PFC activation tomemory demand would suggest a fundamental shift in the strategies used by younger and older adults during WM task performance. Additionally, we sought to test the hypothesis of age-related differences in neural efficiency by comparing PFC activation across performance levels of younger and older adults performing a delayed response item recognition task (Rypma, Berger, Genova *et al.* 2005).

Strategy differences or efficiency differences? Studies of age-related cerebral activity changes during delayed-response task performance.

For this study eight right-handed young subjects and six right-handed older, community-dwelling subjects (age range = 55–83; 2 men) were recruited. Subjects were excluded if they had any medical, neurological or psychiatric illness or if they were taking any type of prescription medication. All subjects gave informed consent. Older subjects showed no symptoms of premorbid dementia or depression (all scores on Mini-Mental Status Exam greater than 26; all Beck Depression inventory scores less than 10).

To start each trial, letter strings, ranging in length from 1 to 8, were presented simultaneously in pseudo-random order for 4 s followed by a 12 s unfilled delay. A probe letter then appeared for 2 s during which the subject pressed a button with their right thumb if the prove item was part of the memory set or with their left thumb if the probe item was not part the memory set. Following these behavioral events there was a 16 second intertrial interval (ITI). The total time from trial onset to trial offset was 34 seconds. This design allowed us to examine neural activity associated with stimulus encoding, 4 s and 8 s into the delay period, and response. Subjects viewed a backlit projection screen from within the magnet bore through a mirror mounted on the head coil.

All subjects completed 8 runs of 10 trials each. A total of 136 gradient-echo echoplanar images in time were obtained per slice in each 340 sec run. Thus, a total of 1360 observations were obtained for each voxel in the brain for each subject, giving us considerable power to detect effects within subjects. Subjects performed the task while lying in a 1.5T SIGNA scanner (GE Medical Systems) equipped with a fast gradient system for echoplanar imaging. A standard radio frequency head coil was used with foam padding to comfortably restrict head motion. We collected high resolution saggital and axial T1-weighted images from every subject. While subjects performed the task, a gradient echo, echoplanar pulse sequence was used to acquire data sensitive to the BOLD signal.

The data were analyzed using event-related methods in which fMRI signal changes that occurred during particular temporal periods of the behavioral trials were modeled with covariates comprised of shifted, BOLD hemodynamic response functions (HRFs), the fMRI response resulting from a brief pulse of neural activity (Zarahn *et al.* 1997; Postle, Zarahn and D'Esposito 2000). Changes in BOLD signal associated with the Encoding, Delay and Response periods of the behavioral task were tested with covariates that modeled the expected BOLD signal response in the event of an increase in neural activity (relative to the ITI) occurring in each of the task periods.

To examine activity in specific regions of PFC, dorsal PFC regions of interest (ROIs) were drawn to include middle and superior frontal gyri, corresponding to Brodmann's Areas (BAs) 9 and 46, according to the Talairach and Tournoux (1988) atlas on standard T1 axial slices in the axial plane. A similar procedure was used to draw ventral PFC ROIs to include inferior frontal gyrus corresponding to BAs 44, 4 and 47. These ROIs were then normalized to each subject's T1 axial images using a 12 parameter affine transformation (Friston *et al.* 1995) with a nonlinear deformation routine (Ashburner and Friston 1996).

Relationships with each task period and the ITI were assessed by contrasts (yielding t-statistics with –1195 df) involving the parameter estimates that corresponded to covariates that modeled each task period. Note that three covariates modeled each 4 s of the delay period. The first 4 s period would be contaminated by hemodynamic activity from the Encoding Period. Thus only the second 4 s interval (designated as Delay Period 1) and third 4 s interval of the delay period designated as Delay Period 2) are considered in the analyses. The false positive rate was controlled at = 0.05 by Bonferroni correction for the number of voxels per region of interest (ROI; approximately 400 voxels; t ~ 3.7).

Because we have observed reliable age differences in the noise component of fMRI signal (which could lead to spurious inferences of age differences in intensity of neural activity; D'Esposito, Zarahn, Aguirre *et al.* 1999), we assessed cortical activation in each subject's dorsal and ventral PFC in the Encoding, Delay and Response periods in each of the eight memory load conditions (i.e., 1 to 8 letters) using the parameter estimates (non-thresholded) for the covariates that modeled each task-period, in each memory-load condition. Hypotheses of linear changes in cortical activity over all subjects were assessed using distribution-free tests for ordered alternatives. Hypotheses of age-related linear changes in cortical activity with increasing memory load

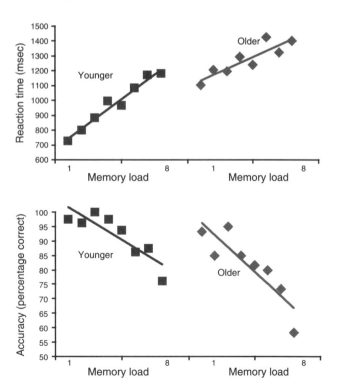

Figure 17.1 (a) Reaction time across memory-load conditions for younger subjects (squares) and older subjects (diamonds). (b) Accuracy rate across memory-load conditions for younger subjects (squares) and older subjects (diamonds).

were assessed using nonparametric Kolmogorov–Smirnov (K–S) tests, distribution-free tests for general differences in two populations (Hollander and Wolfe 1999).

Analyses of the behavioral data from the experiment indicated that, overall, younger subjects (976.5 msec) performed faster than older subjects (1276.0 msec), $F(1, 12) = 15.5$, $p < 0.002$ 9130.7 (see Figure 17.1a). For RT data, the interaction of age-group and memory set-size was significant, $F(7. 84) = 3.2$, $p < 0.005$. Overall, older subjects performed less accurately than younger subjects, $F(1, 12) = 10.8$, $p < 0.007$ and performance accuracy decreased with increasing memory-set size $F (97, 84) = 13.9$, $0 < 0.0001$, MSE = 67.3 (see Figure 17.1b). For accuracy data, the age-group by memory-set size interaction was not significant, $F < 1$.

fMRI signal: tests of age-related strategy differences

Tests of strategy differences between the two subject-groups involved examination of differences in neural activity between memory-load conditions across individual subjects, in each task period. To examine the relationship between PFC activation and memory-load in each of the age-groups, we determined, for each subject, the extent of activation change in each task period, by determining the regional mean parameter estimate in each memory-load condition. Figure 17.2 shows the regional mean parameter estimates of younger and older subjects plotted against memory-load in each task period.

Dorsal PFC

Activation in each memory-load condition and task-period, for each group in dorsal PFC, (based on median parameter estimates) can be observed in Figure 17.2. First, we performed tests for monotonic changes in this region with increasing memory-load across all subjects. No significant changes were found in the Encoding period ($p = 0.26$) but significant increases in activation with increasing memory-load were found in the first Delay period ($p = 0.03$), in the second Delay period, ($p = 0.003$) and in the Retrieval period ($p = 0.003$). Next, we performed tests to assess whether the pattern of changes in PFC activation across different memory loads differed between age groups. Visual inspection of the slope functions plotted in Figure 17.2 indicated minimal age-related differences. Formal testing confirmed this observation; K–S tests were non-significant in the Encoding ($p = 0.19$), the first Delay period ($p = 0.86$); the second Delay period ($p = 0.50$), and in the Response period ($p = 0.99$).

Ventral PFC

Activation in each memory-load condition and task-period, for each group in ventral PFC, (based on median parameter estimates) can be observed in Figure 17.2. Tests of monotonic activation changes in this region with increasing memory-load across all subjects were significant in all task periods. In the Encoding period there were significant decreases in activation with increasing memory load ($p = 0.007$) whereas in the first Delay period ($p = 0.05$), second Delay period ($p = 0.03$) and Retrieval period ($p = 0.003$) there were significant increases. Visual inspection of the slope functions plotted in Figure 17.2 indicated minimal age-related differences. These observations were supported by K–S tests in the Encoding period ($p = 0.27$), the first Delay period ($p = 0.94$), second Delay period ($p = 0.50$), and in the Response period ($p = 0.76$).

Tests of age-related efficiency differences

Tests of efficiency differences between the two subject groups involved examination of differences in activation-performance relationships between individual subjects across memory-load conditions,

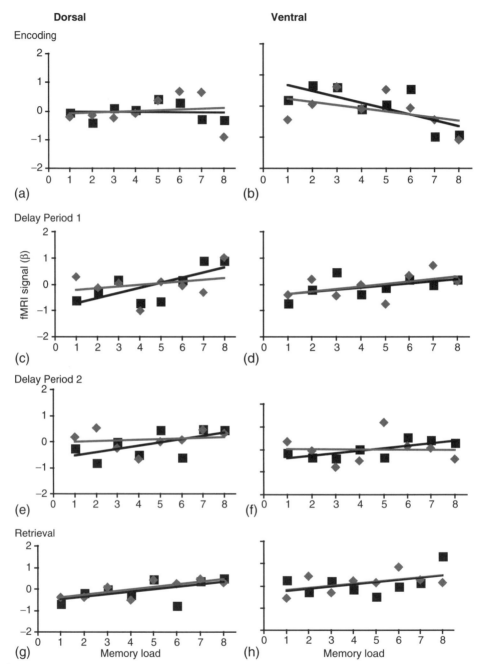

Figure 17.2 fMRI signal plotted against memory-load for each task period in (a) dorsal PFC for Encoding, (b) ventral PFC Encoding, (c) dorsal PFC Delay Period 1, (d) ventral PFC for Delay period 1, (e) dorsal PFC for Delay period 2, (f) ventral PFC for Delay period 2, (g) dorsal PFC for Response period, (h) ventral PFC for Response period.

Table 17.1 Individual subjects' performance scores

Subject	Performance score	Subject	Performance score
BB	1.58	ME	2.49
BH	1.00	JO	1.35
NO	0.27	DA	0.33
MP	0.11	PU	−0.61
JL	−0.40	SP	−1.45
TW	−0.52	WH	−2.94
IT	−0.59		
HL	−1.46		

Note: Higher performance scores correspond to better performance. Younger subjects are in the left-hand columns, older subjects are in the right-hand columns.

in each task period. To characterize the performance of individual subjects, we computed a performance composite score for each subject that was comprised of the subject's z-standardized RT subtracted from their standardized accuracy scores. Thus, high performance composite scores corresponded to high accuracy and low RT. Table 17.1 shows subjects' performance scores by rank. To characterize each subject's activation level we determined, for each subject, the extent of activation in each task period, independent of memory-load, by determining the regional mean parameter estimate averaged over memory load. We could infer age-related differences in neural efficiency to the extent that we could observe interactions between Age-group, Performance score on activation. Thus, to test for age-differences in performance activation relationships, we performed analyses of variance in each task period, with age-group, performance score and activation as between-subjects factors.

Dorsal prefrontal cortex

Table 17.2 shows the standardized regression coefficients that characterize the relationship between performance-composite scores and regional activation in dorsal PFC, and the results of the F-test for the interaction of Age-group and Performance-score on activation. Examination of Table 17.2 indicates that the regression coefficients for younger subjects were negative, indicating *decreases* in activation with increasing performance-composite scores whereas regression coefficients for older subjects were positive, indicating *increases* in activation with increasing performance-composite scores for older adults. The observation of opposite linear trends between the younger and older subjects was confirmed, in the Encoding and Response periods, by significant interactions of Age-group and Performance score in these task periods (Encoding: $F(1,10) = 10.88$, $p < 0.008$, MSe = 0.003; Response: $F(1,10) = 5.30$, $p < 0.04$, MSe = 0.005). In general, more modest regression slopes were observed in the Delay periods. No other main effects or interactions were significant.

Ventral prefrontal cortex

Table 17.3 shows the standardized regression coefficients that characterize the relationship between performance-composite scores and regional activation in ventral PFC, and the results of the F-test for the interaction of Age-group and Performance score on activation. Examination of Table 17.3 indicates that the regression coefficients for younger subjects were negative, indicating *decreases* in activation with increasing performance-composite scores whereas regression

Table 17.2 Dorsal PFC

Regression of activation and performance composite				
Task period	Slope	r^2	F(1, 10)	P
Encoding				
Younger	−0.96	0.91	10.88	0.008*
Older	0.71	0.50		
Delay 1				
Younger	−0.05	0.003	0.784	0.40
Older	0.43	0.19		
Delay 2				
Younger	−0.44	0.19	0.948	0.35
Older	0.56	0.32		
Response				
Younger	−0.75	0.56	5.30	0.04*
Older	0.65	0.42		

Note: Asterix denotes statistical significance.

Table 17.3 Ventral PFC

Regression of activation and performance composite				
Task period	Slope	r^2	F(1, 10)	P
Encoding				
Younger	−0.72	0.52	6.81	0.03*
Older	0.37	0.14		
Delay 1				
Younger	−0.48	0.23	0.82	0.39
Older	0.04	0.001		
Delay 2				
Younger	−0.57	0.32	7.60	0.02*
Older	0.82	0.67		
Response				
Younger	−0.45	0.20	1.14	0.31
Older	0.11	0.01		

Note: Asterix denotes statistical significance.

coefficients for older subjects were positive, indicating *increases* in activation with increasing performance-composite scores for older adults. The regression analyses indicated that best-fitting slopes occurred in the Encoding and Late delay periods. In the Encoding period, there was no effect of Age-group on activation (F<1). The main effect of Performance score was not significant, $F(1, 10) = 3.25$, $p < 0.10$, MSe = 0.004. The interaction of Age-group and performance score was significant $F(1, 10) = 6.81$, $p < 0.03$. In Delay period 1, there were minimal effects of Age-group and

Performance-score or their interaction, Fs<1. In Delay period 2, there was a significant effect of Age-group F(1, 10) = 8.47, p <0.02, MSe = 0.001. There was no effect of Performance score, F<1. The interaction of Age-group and performance score was significant, F(1, 10) = 7.60, p <0.02. In the Response period, there was a minimal effect of Age-group, F(1, 10) = 1.34, p <0.27, MSe = 0.011. There was no effect of Performance score, F<1. The Age-group X performance score interaction was not significant, F(1, 10) = 1.14, p <0.31.

The results of these analyses indicate PFC activity that, for younger subjects, decreased with increasing performance while the opposite effect was observed for older subjects. These results replicate earlier findings from our laboratory showing age-differential activation-performance relationships that were limited to dorsal PFC in the Retrieval task-period (see Figure 17.3). However we also observed such age-differential relationships in the Encoding period and in ventral PFC.

The present results suggest that these effects may be more widespread than our previous results indicated (e.g., Rypma and D'Esposito 2000). To gain some understanding of this result, we performed further analyses in which we decomposed the performance-composite score into its accuracy and RT components. We then regressed the parameter estimates against accuracy and RT separately, in each task period and ROI. In ventral PFC, the only significant result was the interaction of Age group accuracy on Activation in delay period 2 (F(1, 10) = 9.16, p <0.01, MSe = 0.003). In dorsal PFC, the only significant results were the interactions of Age group, and Accuracy on activation in the encoding period (F(1, 10) = 4.95, p <0.05, MSe = 0.005), and

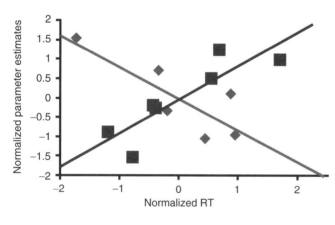

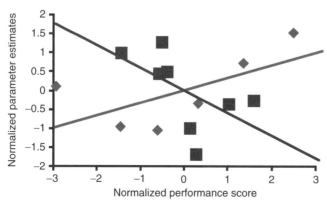

Figure 17.3 Scatterplots of normalized regional mean parameter estimates during the response period in dorsal PFC from (a) an earlier study, plotted against normalized RT for younger subjects (squares; slope = 0.87, r^2 = 0.76) and older subjects (diamonds; slope = −0.82, r^2 = 0.68; Rypma and D'Esposito, 2000, 2001) and (b) from the present study plotted against normalized performance scores (for younger, slope = −0.75, r^2 = 0.56; for older, slope = 0.65, r^2 = 0.42).

the interaction Age group and RT on Activation in the response period (F(1, 10) = 4.95, p <0.05, MSe = 0.005). Thus, the performance-activation interaction at Encoding was due mainly to age-differences in the relationship between performance *accuracy* and fMRI activation whereas the performance-activation interaction we observed at Response was due to age-differences in the relationship of individual subjects' performance *speed* and fMRI activation.

We observed large and significant age-related differences in the nature of the relationship between performance and activation in both dorsal and ventral PFC. These results suggest that the mechanisms underlying the observation of age-related differences in neural activity are related to age-related reductions in the efficiency of WM-critical PFC mechanisms.

In dorsal PFC, there were significant interactions of age, performance and fMRI activation in the Encoding and the Response periods. In ventral PFC such interactions also occurred in the Encoding period and during the second Delay period. Decomposition of the Performance score indicated that the performance-activation interaction at Encoding was due mainly to age-differences in the relationship between performance *accuracy* and fMRI activation. This decomposition analysis also indicated that the performance-activation interaction we observed in the Response period was mainly due to age-differences in the relationship of individual subjects' performance *speed* and fMRI activation.

These results are consistent with previous reports of performance-activation relationships in our laboratory (Rypma and D'Esposito 2000, 2001; Rypma, Berger and D'Esposito 2002) and the laboratories of others (Grady, McIntosh and Craik 2002; Mattay *et al*. 2000; Kosslyn *et al*. 1996; Haier *et al*. 1992).

Age-related strategy differences

Both subject groups showed increases in dorsal PFC activation with increasing memory-load. These results are consistent with earlier studies showing increasing fMRI signal in dorsal PFC with increases in mnemonic demand. For example in an fMRI study using a blocked design (i.e., signal collapsed across all task periods), Rypma *et al*. (1999) observed increasing activation in dorsal and ventral PFC with increasing memory loads. They proposed that ventral PFC is involved in maintenance of subcapacity WM loads but when WM loads exceed memory-capacity, dorsal PFC may be additionally recruited to mediate strategic processes necessary for maintenance of high WM loads. The present results are consistent with this proposal and suggest that both younger and older subjects utilize manipulation functions of dorsal PFC to implement strategic data-compression or "chunking" operations (e.g., Miller 1956; Cowan 2001; Bor, Duncan, Wiseman *et al*. 2003) for maintenance of large amounts of information (e.g., Rypma and Gabrieli 2001; Rypma and D'Esposito 1999). In the current study too we found increasing activation in dorsal PFC with increasing load, but in contrast to our earlier studies which examined only two memory set sizes (Rypma and D'Esposito 1999, 2000), these load-dependent activation increases occurred later in the task, during the retention and retrieval periods. One possible reason for this difference may be the increased and more varied memory-load requirements of the present task compared to those used in previous studies (Rypma and D'Esposito 2002). Indeed, strategic organization and strategy-shifting may be among the processes mediated by dorsal PFC (Prabhakaran *et al*. 1997; Prabhakaran *et al*. 2001; Jenkins *et al*. 1994; Deiber *et al*. 1991).

Ventral PFC, which is proposed to mediate maintenance/rehearsal processes (Awh *et al*. 1996; Paulesu *et al*. 1993; Rypma *et al*. 1999; D'Esposito *et al*. 1999), showed decreases in activation with increasing memory-demand during encoding, suggesting that it may play a larger role in memory encoding with subcapacity memory loads than with supracapacity memory loads.

Ventral PFC may play an increasingly limited role in WM encoding functions with increasing memory loads, given its limited capacity. The qualitative difference between this activation pattern and those observed in dorsal PFC is consistent with proposals suggesting distinct roles for dorsal and ventral PFC in WM (e.g., D'Esposito *et al.* 1995, 1999; Rypma *et al.* 1999; Rypma and D'Esposito 1999, 2003; D'Esposito, Postle and Rypma 2000). In other task periods, ventral PFC showed increases in activation with increasing memory-load. This result is consistent with some earlier results (Rypma *et al.* 1999) but inconsistent with others (Rypma and D'Esposito 1999). Further research will be required to determine when, and under what task conditions, ventral PFC is sensitive to memory-load effects.

Conclusions about similarities and differences between two groups depend upon sufficient power to detect statistical effects. The relatively small number of participants in the present study could raise concerns about statistical power. There was, however, sufficient power to detect statistically significant interactions of age-group and performance on PFC activation. These results indicate that there was sufficient power to detect age related effects in the present study (Grady *et al.* 1995). Nonetheless, conclusions made on the basis of null effects are tenuous; the small age-differences in memory-load effects on fMRI signal may represent meaningful age-related processing differences. Future research will certainly be required to determine the circumstances under which age-related activation differences occur with increases in memory demand.

In summary, the present results indicate minimal age-related differences in the relationship between PFC activation and memory-load. Thus, they provide little support for the notion that younger and older adults bring fundamentally different strategies to the task of encoding, maintaining or retrieving sub- or suprathreshold loads of information.

Age-related neural efficiency differences

Results of our regression analyses indicated that the age-equivalent load-dependent effects described above were imbedded within a pattern age-differential activation-performance patterns. These analyses suggested that, for younger subjects, dorsal and ventral PFC activation was greater during the Encoding, Maintenance and Retrieval periods for those who performed more slowly and less accurately relative to those who performed faster and more accurately. For older adults, we observed the opposite pattern. Specifically, dorsal and ventral PFC activation was reduced during the Encoding, Maintenance and Retrieval periods for those who performed more slowly and less accurately than those who performed faster and more accurately.

These results replicate earlier results from our laboratory showing less PFC activation for faster and more accurate young adults during memory retrieval. These results also replicate earlier results from our laboratory showing more PFC activation for faster and more accurate older adults during memory retrieval (Rypma and D'Esposito 1999, 2000, 2001; see Figure 17.3). They are at variance, however, with our previous results indicating that relationships between activation and performance were limited to dorsal regions of PFC and to retrieval periods of delayed-response WM tasks.

The disparity between this result and our earlier results is important because it suggests that where (i.e., in which brain regions), and when (i.e., in which WM-task subcomponents), age-related differences in neural efficiency exert their effects depends on the relative importance of the WM-subcomponent and the brain-region to the task. Thus it may be that the current task taxed the encoding functions of dorsal PFC relatively more than the limited extreme-conditions designs we have previously employed. Similar variations in task complexity have been shown to influence neural activity in previous research (e.g., Schacter *et al.* 1996; Johnson *et al.* 1997).

An important implication of the present findings, therefore, is that differences in task-structure play a vital, albeit poorly understood, role in neuroimaging results. A critical task for future research will be to more precisely identify the nature of neural processes underlying these differences.

Finally, these data provide further support for a model of age-related changes in brain–behavior relationships that we have proposed and tested earlier. The persistence of this pattern of results, both in our own laboratory (Rypma and D'Esposito 1999, 2000, 2001, 2002; Rypma, Eldreth and Rebbechi 2007) and in the laboratories of others (Mattay *et al.* 2002; Grady, McIntosh and Craik 2002) suggest that the pervasive age-related slowing observed across many different kinds of behavioral tasks (e.g., Myerson, Hale, Wagstaff *et al.* 1990; Salthouse 1996) may result from a fundamental change in brain-behavior relationships with age.

A model of age-related changes in brain–behavior relationships

Our proposal is that age-related behavioral changes result from age-related decreases in neural efficiency. Reductions in neural efficiency may begin with reductions in the quality of information relayed to central structures from peripheral structures. Subsequent deterioration of central structures, most notably PFC, could exacerbate slowing of central cognitive processes, including the speed with which information can be activated in WM. Slower WM activation may lead to degradation in the quality of information that is encoded, maintained and available for memory retrieval.

Our proposed model of the age-related brain–behavior differences observed in this and other studies is an extension of models of performance based on the sigmoid (S-shaped) relationship between a neuron's input activation and its firing probability. Some researchers have proposed that this relationship influences performance (Kimberg and Farah 1993; Kimberg, D'Esposito and Farah 1997; Servan-Schreiber, Printz and Cohen 1990). In these models, response selection is characterized as a signal detection mechanism in which the probability of a given response is determined by the relative strength of signal between representations in memory. Middle ranges of neural activation result in large differences in signal between representations and easy discrimination between potential responses. As neural activation levels move above or below this range, these signal differences become less discriminable and response selection becomes more difficult (Rypma and D'Esposito 2000, 2001).

This model proposes that aging may result in baseline reductions in PFC activation levels (e.g., Moeller *et al.* 1996). One consequence of this reduced neural activity may be that higher activation levels are required to optimally encode, maintain and retrieve information from WM. That is, the sigmoid function relating neural activation to optimal performance may require a higher level of activation for older adults to achieve optimal performance. Relative to older adults, younger adults function with higher baseline activation levels. Thus they require relatively less activation to achieve optimal performance. This proposal is consistent with our observation that increased activation is associated with performance improvements for older adults but to decrements for younger adults (see also Rypma and D'Esposito 2000, 2001). The effects of these age-related changes in the sigmoid functions relating neural activity to performance may be implemented in transactions between nodes (possibly representing functional cell assemblies; Hebb, 1949) in a system such as that proposed by Cerella (1990).

These results shed light on the neural basis of age-related changes in WM performance. Younger and older adults may bring similar strategies to the task of retaining varying amounts of information over delay periods. Age-related changes in neural activity observed in these and other studies may result from age-related efficiency decreases in the interaction of neural cell assemblies during WM performance.

References

Aguirre, GK, Zarahn, E and D'Esposito, M (1998). The variability of the human BOLD hemodynamic responses. *NeuroImage*, *8*, 360–369.

Ahmad, A and Spear, PD (1993). Effects of aging on the size, density, and number of rhesus monkey lateral genicualte neurons. *Journal of Comparative Neurology*, *334*, 631–643.

Anders, TR and Fozard, JL (1973). Effects of age upon retrieval from primary and secondary memory. *Developmental Psychology*, *9*, 411–415.

Anders, TR, Fozard, JL and Lillyquist, TD (1972). Effects of age upon retrieval from short-term memory. *Developmental Psychology*, *6*, 214–217.

Ashburner, J and Friston, K (1996). Fully three-dimensional nonlinear spatial normalization: A new approach. *NeuroImage*, *3*, S111.

Awh, E, Jonides, J, Smith, EE, Schumacher, E, Koeppe, R and Katz, S (1996). Dissociation of storage and rehearsal in working memory: Evidence from positron emission tomography. *Psychological Science*, *7*, 25–31.

Baddeley, A (1986). *Working Memory*. New York: Oxford University Press.

Baddeley, A and Hitch, GJ (1974). Working memory. In G Bower (ed), *Recent Advances in Learning and Motivation*, Vol. 8 (pp. 47–89). New York: Academic Press.

Bachevalier, JL, Landis, S, Walker, LC, Brickson, M, Mishkin, M, Price, DL and Cork, LC (1991). Aged monkeys exhibit behavioral deficits indicative of widespread cerebral dysfunction. *Neurobiology of Aging*, *12*, 99–111.

Bartus, RT, Dean, RL III and Fleming, DL (1979). Aging in the rhesus monkey: Effects on visual discrimination learning and reversal learning. *Journal of Gerontology*, *34*, 209–219.

Boaz, TL and Denney, DR (1993). Speed of scanning in primary memory in persons with dementia of the Alzheimer type. *Psychology and Aging*, *2*, 294–300.

Bor, D, Duncan, J, Wiseman, RJ and Owen, A (2003). Encoding strategies dissociate prefrontal activity from working memory demand. *Neuron*, *37*, 361–367.

Botwinick, J and Storandt, M (1974). *Memory, Related Functions, and Age*. Springfield, IL: Charles C. Thomas.

Brody, H (1955). Organization of the cerebral cortex: 3. A study of aging in the human cerebral cortex. *Journal of comparative neurology*, *102*, 511–556.

Bromley, J (1958). Some effects of age on short-term learning and memory. *Journal of Gerontology*, *13*, 12–21.

Buckner, RL, Corbetta, M, Schatz, J, Raichle, ME and Petersen, SE (1996). Preserved speech abilities and compensation following prefrontal damage. *Proceedings of the National Academy of Sciences of the United States of America*, *93*, 1249–1253.

Cabeza, R (2002). Hemispheric asymmetry reduction in older adults: The HAROLD model. *Psychology and Aging*, *17*, 85–100.

Cabeza, R, Grady, CL, Nyberg, L, McIntosh, AR, Tulving, E, Kapur, S, Jennings, JM and Craik, FIM (1997). Age-related differences in neural activity during memory encoding and retrieval: A positron emission tomography study. *Journal of Neuroscience*, *17*, 391–400.

Cerella, J (1990). Aging and information processing rate. In JE Birren and KW Schaie (eds), *Handbook of the Psychology of Aging* (pp. 201–221). San Diego, CA: Academic Press.

Corsellis, JAW (1976). Some observations on the Purkinje cell population and on brain volume in human aging. In RD Terry and S Gershon (eds), *Neurobiology of Aging* (pp. 205–209).

Cowan, N (2001). The magical number 4 in short-term memory: A reconsideration of mental storage capacity. *Behavioral and Brain Sciences*, *24*, 87–185.

Craik, FIM (1968). Short-term memory and the aging process. In GA Talland (ed), *Human Aging and Behavior* (pp. 131–168). New York: Academic Press.

Craik, FIM (1977). Age differences in human memory. In JE Birren and KW Schaie (eds), *Handbook of the Psychology of Aging* (pp. 384–420). New York: Van Nostrand Reinhold (1977).

Deiber, MP, Passingham, RE, Colebatch, JG, Friston, KJ, Nixon, PD and Frackowiak, RS (1991). Cortical areas and the selection of movement: A study with positron emission tomography *Experimental Brain Research*, *84*, 393–402.

D'Esposito, M, Aguirre, GK, Zarahn, E, Ballard, D, Shin, RK (1998). Functional MRI studies of spatial and non-spatial working memory. *Cognitive Brain Research*, *7*, 1–13.

D'Esposito, M, Detre, JA, Alsop, DC, Shin, RK, Atlas, S and Grossman, M (1995). The neural basis of the central executive system of working memory. *Nature*, *378*, 279–281.

D'Esposito, M, Postle, BR, Ballard, D and Lease, J (1999). Maintenance versus manipulation of information held in working memory: An event-related fMRI study. *Brain and Cognition*, *41*, 66–86 (1999).

D'Esposito, M, Postle, BR and Rypma, B (2000). Prefrontal cortical contributions to working memory: Evidence from event-related fMRI studies. *Experimental Brain Research*, *33*, 3–11.

D'Esposito, M, Zarahn, E, Aguirre, GK and Rypma, B (1999). The effect of normal aging on the coupling of neural activity to the BOLD hemodynamic response. *NeuroImage*, *10*, 6–14.

Drachman, D and Leavitt, J (1972). Memory impairment in the aged: Storage versus retrieval deficit. *Journal of Experimental Psychology*, *93*, 302–308.

Duncan, J, Seitz, RJ, Kolodny, J, Bor, D, Herzog, H, Ahmed, A, Newell, FN and Emslie, H (2000). A neural basis for general intelligence. *Science*, *289*, 457–460.

Erikson, CW, Hamlin, RM and Daye, C (1973). Aging adults and rate of memory scan. *Bulletin of the Psychonomic Society*, *1*, 259–260.

Finger, S, Buckner, RL and Buckingham, H (2003). Does the right hemisphere take over after damage to Broca's area? The Barlow case of 1877 and its history. *Brain and Language*, *85*, 385–395.

Foster, JC and Taylor, GA (1920). The applicability of mental tests to persons over 50. *Journal of Applied Psychology*, *4*, 39–58.

Franklin, RJ Zhao, C and Sim FJ (2002). Ageing and CNS remyelination. *Neuroreport, 13*, 923–8

Friedman, H (1974). Interrelation of two types of immediate memory in the aged. *Journal of Psychology*, *87*, 177–181.

Friston, KJ, Ashburner, J, Frith, CD, Poline, J-B, Heather, JD and Frackowiak, RSJ (1995). Spatial registration and normalization of images. *Human Brain Mapping*, *2*, 165–189.

Fuster, JM and Alexander, GE (1971). Neuron activity related to short-term memory. *Science*, *173*, 652–654.

Gabrieli, JDE (1991). Brain basis of changes in memory performance in aging and Alzheimer's disease. *Experimental Aging Research*, *17*, 96–97.

Gabrieli, JDE (1996). Memory systems analysis of mnemonic disorders in aging and age-related diseases. *Proceedings of the National Academy of Sciences of the United States of America*, *93*, 13534–13540.

Gilbert, JG (1941). Memory loss in senescence. *Journal of Abnormal and Social Psychology*, *36*, 73–86.

Gilbert, JG and Levee, RF (1971). Patterns of declining memory. *Journal of Gerontology*, *26*, 70–75.

Glanzer, M and Razel, M (1974). The size of the unit in short-term storage. *Journal of Verbal Learning and Verbal Behavior*, *13*, 114–131.

Goldman-Rakic, PS (1987). Circuitry of primate prefrontal cortex and regulation of behavior by representational memory. In F Plum (ed), *Handbook of Physiology – the nervous system V* (pp. 373–417). New York: Oxford University Press.

Goldman-Rakic, PS and Friedman, H. (1991). Circuitry of the prefrontal cortex and the regulation of behavior by representational memory. In H Levin, H Eisenberg and A Benton (eds), *Frontal Lobe Function and Dysfunction* (pp. 72–91). New York: Oxford University Press.

Good, CD, Johnsrude, IS, Ashburner, J, Henson, RN, Friston, KJ and Frackowiak, RS (2001). A voxel-based morphometric study of ageing in 465 normal adult human brains. *Neuroimage*, *14*, 21–36.

Grady, CL, Haxby, JV, Horwitz, B, Schapiro, MB, Rapoport, SI, Ungerleider, LG, Mishkin, M, Carson, RE and Herscovitch, P (1992). Dissociation of object and spatial vision in human extrastriate cortex: Age-related changes in activation of regional cerebral blood flow measured with 15O water and positron emission tomography. *Journal of Cognitive Neuroscience*, *4*, 23–34.

Grady, CL, McIntosh, AR and Craik, FIM (2003). Age-related differences in the functional connectivity of the hippocampus during memory encoding. *Hippocampus*, *13*, 572–586.

Grady, CL, McIntosh, AR, Horwitz, B, Maisog, JM, Ungerleider, LG, Mentis, MJ, Pietrini, P, Schapiro, MB and Haxby, JV (1995). Age-related reductions in human recognition memory due to impaired encoding. *Science*, *269*, 218–220.

Haier, RJ, Siegel, B, Tang, C, Abel, L and Buchsbaum, MS (1992). Intelligence and changes in regional cerebral glucose metabolic-rate following learning. *Intelligence*, *16*, 415–426.

Haug, H and Eggers, R (1991). Morphometry of the human cortex cerebri and corpus striatum during aging. *Neurobiology of Aging*, *12*, 336–338.

Haug, H, Kuhl, S, Mecke, E, Sass, N-L and Wasner, K (1984). The significance of morphometric procedures in the investigation of age changes in cytoarchitectonic structures of human brain. *Journal fur Hirnforschung*, *25*, 353–374.

Hebb, DO (1949). *The Organization of Behavior*. New York: John Wiley.

Hellstrom, LI and Schmeidt, RA (1990). Compound action potential input/output functions in young and quiet-aged gerbils. *Hearing Research*, *50*, 163–174.

Hollander, M and Wolfe, DA (1999). *Nonparametric Statistical Methods*. New York: John Wiley and Sons.

Jenkins, IH, Brooks, DJ, Nixon, PD, Frackowiak, RSJ and Passingham, RE (1994). Motor sequence learning: A study with positron emission tomography. *Journal of Neuroscience*, *14*, 3774–3790.

Johnson, MK, Nolde, SF, Mather, TEM, Kounios, J, Schacter, DL and Curran, T (1997). Mental agendas can affect the similarity associated with true and false recognition memory. *Psychological Science*, *8*, 250–257.

Jonides, J, Marshuetz, C, Smith, EE, Reuter-Lorenz, PA, Koeppe, RA and Hartley, A (2000). Brain activation reveals changes with age in resolving interference in verbal working memory. *Journal of Cognitive Neuroscience*, *12*, 188–196.

Jones, HE and Conrad, H (1933). A study of a homogeneous group between the ages of ten and sixty. *Genetic Psychological Monographs*, *13*, 223–298.

Kemper, TL (2002). Neuroanatomical and neuropathological changes during aging and in dementia. In ML Albert and EJE Knoepfel (eds), *Clinical Neurology of Aging*, 2nd edn (pp. 3–67). New York: Oxford University Press.

Kimberg, DY and Farah, MT (1993). A unified account of cognitive impairments following frontal lobe damage: The role of working memory in complex organized behavior. *Journal of Experimental Psychology: General*, *122*, 411–428.

Kimberg, DY, D'Esposito, M and Farah, MT (1997). Effects of bromocriptine on human subjects depend on working meory capacity. *Neuroreport*, *8*, 3581–3585.

Kirsner, K (1972). Developmental changes in short-term recognition memory. *British Journal of Psychology*, *63*, 109–117.

Kosslyn, SM, Thompson, WL, Kim, IJ, Rauch, SL and Alpert, NM (1996). Individual differences in cerebral blood flow in area 17 predict the time to evaluate visualized letters. *Journal of Cognitive Neuroscience*, *8*, 78–82.

Kubota, K and Niki, H (1971). Prefrontal cortical unit activity and delayed alternation performance in monkeys. *Journal of Neurophysiology*, *34*, 337–347.

Kuhl, DE, Metter, EJ, Riege, WH and Phelps, ME (1982). Effect of human aging on patterns of local cerebral glucose utilization determined by 18-F-fluorodeoxyglucose method. *Journal of Cerebral Blood Flow and Metabolism*, *2*, 163–171.

Leung, HC, Gore, JC and Goldman-Rakic, PS (2002). Sustained mnemonic response in the human middle frontal gyrus ding on-line storage of spatial memoranda. *Journal of Cognitive Neuroscience*, *14*, 659–671.

Lindenberger, U and Baltes, PB (1994). Sensory functioning and intelligence in old age: A strong connection. *Psychology and Aging, 9,* 339–355.

Madden, DJ, Turkington, TG, Provenzale, JM, Denny, LL, Hawk, TC, Gottlob, LR and Coleman, RE (1999). Adult age differences in functional neuroanatomy of verbal recognition memory. *Human Brain Mapping, 7,* 115–135.

Madden, DJ, Whiting, WL, Huettel, SA, White, LE, MacFall, JR and Provenzale, JM (2004). Diffusion tensor imaging of adult age differences in cerebral white matter: Relation to response time. *NeuroImage, 21,* 1174–1181.

Manoach, DS, Schlaug, G, Siewert, B, Darby, DG, Bly, BM, Benfield, A, Edelman, RR and Warach, S (1997). Prefrontal cortex fMRI signal changes are correlated with working memory load. *Neuroreport, 8,* 545–549.

Marsh, GR (1975). Age differences in evoked potential correlates of a memory scanning process. *Experimental Aging Research, 1,* 3–16.

Mattay, VS, Callicott, JH, Bertolino, A, Heaton, I, Frank, JA, Coppola, R, Berman, KF, Goldberg, TE and Weinberger, DR (2000). Effects of dextroamphetamine on cognitive performance and cortical activation. *NeuroImage, 12,* 268–275.

McIntosh, AR, Sekuler, AB, Penpeci, C, Rajah, MN, Grady, CL, Sekuler R and Bennett PJ (1999). Recruitment of unique neural systems to support visual memory in normal aging. *Current Biology, 9,* 1275–1278.

Miller, G (1956). The magical number seven, plus or minus two: Some limits on our capacity for processing information. *Psychological Review, 63,* 81–97.

Moeller, JR, Ishikawa, T, Dhawan, V, Spetsieris, P, Mandel, F, Alexander, GE, Grady, C, Pietrini, P and Eidelberg, D (1996). The metabolic topography of normal aging. *Journal of Cerebral Blood Flow and Metabolism, 16,* 385–398.

Michaels, DD (1993). Ocular disease in the elderly. In A.A. Rosenbloom and MW Morgan (eds), *Vision and Aging* (pp. 111–159). Butterworth Heineman.

Minckler, TM and Boyd, E (1968). Physical growth. In J Minckler (ed), *Pathology of the Nervous System* (pp. 98–122). New York: McGraw-Hill.

Myerson, J, Hale, S, Wagstaff, D, Poon, LW and Smith, GA (1990). The information-loss model: A mathematical theory of age-related cognitive slowing. *Psychological Review, 97,* 475–487.

Nielsen-Bohlman, L and Knight, RT (1995). Prefrontal alterations during memory processing in aging. *Cerebral Cortex, 5,* 541–549.

Norman, D and Shallice, T (1980). Attention to action: Willed automatic control of behavior. University of California CHIP Report 99.

Ogawa, S, Lee, T-M, Nayak, AS, Glynn, P (1990). Oxygenation-sensitive contrast in magnetic resonance image of rodent brain at high magnetic fields. *Magnetic Resonance in Medicine, 14,* 68–78.

Ogawa, S, Tank, DW, Menon, R, Elermann, JM, Merkle, H and Ugurbil, K (1992). Intrinsic signal changes accompanying sensory stimulation: functional brain mapping using magnetic resonance imaging. *Proceedings of the.National Academy of Sciences (USA), 89,* 5951–5955.

Owsley, C and Sloane, ME (1987). Coi..rast sensitivity, acuity and the perception of 'real world' targets. *British Journal of Opthalmology, 71,* 791–796.

Park, DC, Lautenschlager, G, Hedden, T, Davidson, NS, Smith, AD and Smith, PK (2002). Models of visuospatial and verbal working memory across the adult life span. *Psychology and Aging, 17,* 299–320.

Paulesu, E, Frith, C and Frackowiak, R (1993). The neural correlates of the verbal component of working memory. *Nature, 362,* 342–345.

Persson J, Sylvester CY, Nelson JK, Welsh KM, Jonides J and Reuter-Lorenz PA (2004). Selection requirements during verb generation: Differential recruitment in older and younger adults. *Neuroimage, 23,* 1382–1390.

Peters, A (2002). The effects of normal aging on myelin and nerve fibers: A review. *Journal of Neurocytology, 8–9,* 581–593.

Peters, A and Sethares, C (2002). Aging and the myelinated fibers in prefrontal cortex and corpus of the monkey. *Journal of Computational Neurology*, *442*, 277–91.

Peters, A and Sethares, C (2004). Oligodendrocytes, their progenitors, and other neuroglial cells in the aging primate cortex. *Cerebral Cortex*, *14*, 995–1007.

Poon, LW and Fozard, JL (1980). Age and word frequency effects in continuous recognition memory. *Journal of Gerontology*, *35*, 77–86.

Postle, BR, Zarahn, E and D'Esposito, M (2000). Using event-related fMRI to assess delay-period activity during performance of saptial and nonspatial working memory tasks. *Brain Research Protocols*, *5*, 57–66.

Prabhakaran, V, Smith, JAL, Desmond, JE, Glover, GH and Gabrieli, JDE (1997). Neural substrates of fluid reasoning: An fMRI study of neocortical activation during performance of the Raven's Progressive Matrices Test. *Cognitive Psychology*, *33*, 43–63.

Prabhakaran, V, Rypma, B and Gabrieli, JDE (2001). Neural substrates of mathematical reasoning: an fMRI study of neocortical activation during performance of the Necessary Arithmetic Operations Test. *Neuropsychology*, *15*, 115–127.

Presty, SK, Bachevalier, J, Walker, LC, Struble, RG, Price, DL, Mishkin, M and Cork, LC (1987). Age differences in recognition memory of the rhesus monkey (Macaca mulatta). *Neurobiology of Aging*, *8*, 435–440.

Prull, M, Bunge, S and Gabrieli, JDE (2000). In FIM Craik and TA Salthouse (Eds), *Handbook of Aging and Cognition*. Mahwah, NJ: Erlbaum.

Raz, N, Gunning, FM, Head, DP, Dupuis, JH, McQuain, JM, Briggs, SD, Thornton, AE, Loken, WJ and Acker, JD (1997). Selective aging of human cerebral cortex observed *in vivo*: Differential vulnerability of the prefrontal gray matter. *Cerebral Cortex*, *7*, 268–282.

Raz, N (2000). Aging of the brain and its impact on cognitive performance: Integration of structural and functional findings. In FIM Craik and TA Salthouse, TA (eds) *The Handbook of Aging and Cognition*. Mahwah, NJ: Lawrence Erlbaum Associates.

Resnick, SM, Goldszal, AF, Davatzikos, C, Golski, S, Kraut, MA, Metter, EJ, Bryan, RN and Zonderman, AB (2000). One-year age changes in MRI brain volumes in older adults. *Cereb Cortex*, *10*, 464–472.

Resnick, SM, Pham, DL, Kraut, MA, Zonderman, AB and Davatzikos, C (2003). Longitudinal magnetic resonance imaging studies of older adults: a shrinking brain. *Journal of Neuroscience*, *23*, 3295–3301.

Reuter-Lorenz, PA, Jonides, J, Smith, E, Hartley, A, Miller, A, Marshuetz, C and Koeppe, R (2000). Age differences in the frontal lateralization of verbal and spatial working memory revealed by PET. *Journal of Cognitive Neuroscience*, *12*, 174–187.

Reuter-Lorenz, PA, Marshuetz, C, Jonides, J, Smith, EE, Hartley, A and Koeppe, R (2001). Neurocognitive aging and storage of executive processes. In U Mayr, DH Spieler and R Kliegl (eds), *Ageing and Executive Control* (pp.). Hove, UK: Psychology Press.

Rypma, B, Berger, JS, Genova, HM, Rebecchi, DM and D'Esposito, M (2005). Dissociating age-related changes in cognitive strategy and neural efficiency using event-related fMRI. *Cortex*, *41*, 582–594.

Rypma, B, Eldreth, DA and Rebbechi, D (2007). Age-related differences in activation performance relations in delayed-response tasks: A multiple component analysis. *Cortex*, 65–76.

Rypma, B, Berger, JS and D'Esposito, M (2002). The influence of working-memory demand and subject performance on prefrontal cortical activity. *Journal of Cognitive Neuroscience*, *14*, 721–731.

Rypma, B, Prabhakaran, V, Desmond, JE and Gabrieli, JDE (2001). Age differences in prefrontal cortical activity in working memory. *Psychology and Aging*, *16*, 371–384.

Rypma, B, Prabhakaran, V, Desmond, JE, Glover, GH and Gabrieli, JDE (1999). Load-dependent roles of prefrontal cortical regions in the maintenance of working memory. *NeuroImage*, *9*, 216–226.

Rypma, B and D'Esposito, M (1999). The roles of prefrontal brain regions in components of working memory: Effects of memory load and individual differences. *Proceedings of the National Academy of Sciences of the United States of America*, *96*, 6558–6563.

Rypma, B and D'Esposito, M (2000). Isolating the neural mechanisms of age-related changes in human working memory. *Nature-Neuroscience*, *3*, 509–515.

Rypma, B and Gabrieli, JDE (2000). Functional neuroimaging of short-term memory: The neural mechanisms of mental storage. *Behavioral and Brain Sciences, 24,* 87–185.

Rypma, B and D'Esposito, M (2001). Age-related changes in brain-behavior relationships: Evidence from event-related functional MRI studies. *European Journal of Cognitive Psychology, 13,* 235–256.

Salthouse, TA (1996). The processing speed theory of adult age differences in cognition. *Psychological Review, 103,* 403–428.

Salthouse, TA, Hancock, HE, Meinz, EJ and Hambrick, DZ (1996). Interrelations of age, visual acuity, and cognitive functioning. *Journal of Gerontology: Psychological Sciences, 51B,* P317–P330.

Salthouse, TA, Hambrick, DZ and McGuthry, KE (1998). Shared age-related influences on cognitive and non-cognitive variables. *Psychology and Aging, 13,* 486–500.

Schacter, DL, Reiman, E, Curran, T, Yun, LS, Bandy, D, McDermott, KB and Roediger, IH (1996). Neuroanatomical correlates of veridical and illusory recognition memory: Evidence from positron emission tomography. *Neuron, 17,* 267–274.

Schneider, BA (1997). Psychoacoustics and aging: Implications for everyday listening. *Journal of Speech-language Pathology and Audiology, 21,* 111–124.

Schneider, BA and Pichora-Fuller, MK (2000). Implications of perceptual deterioration for cognitive aging research. In Craik, FIM and Salthouse, TA (eds), *Handbook of Aging and Cognition* (pp. 155–219), Mahwah, NJ: Lawrence Erlbaum.

Servan-Schreiber, D, Printz, H and Cohen, JD (1990). A network model of catecholamine effects: gain, signal to noise ratio, and behavior. *Science, 249,* 892–895.

Sim, FJ, Zhao, C, Pendaris, J, Franklin, RJ (2002). The age-related decrease in CNS remyelination efficiency is attributable to an impairment of both oligodendrocyte progenitor recruitment and differentiation. *Journal of Neuroscience, 22,* 2451–2459.

Sloane, ME, Owsley, C and Jackson, CA (1988). Aging and luminance-adaptation effects on spatial contrast sensitivity. *Journal of the Optical Society of America, 5,* 2181–2190.

Smith, AD (1975). Aging and interference with memory. *Journal of Gerontology, 30,* 319–325.

Spear, PD (1993). Neural bases of visual deficits during aging. *Vision Research, 33,* 2589–2609.

Sternberg, S (1966). High-speed scanning in human memory. *Science, 153,* 652–654.

Taki, Y, Goto, R, Evans, A, Zijdenbos, A, Neelin, P, Lerch, J, Sato, K, Ono, S, Kinomura, S, Nakagawa, M, Sugiura, M, Watanabe, J, Kawashima, R and Fukuda, H (2004). Voxel-based morphometry of human brain with age and cerebrovascular risk factors. *Neurobiol Aging, 25,* 455–463.

Talairach, J and Tournoux, P (1988). *A Co-planar Stereotaxic Atlas of the Human Brain: An approach to medical cerebral imaging.* New York: Thieme Medical Publishers.

Tang, Y, Nyengaard, JR, Pakkenberg, B and Gundersen, HJ (1997). Age-induced white matter changes in the human brain: A stereological investigation. *Neurobiology of Aging, 18,* 609–615.

Taub, HA (1973). Memory span, practice and aging. *Journal of Gerontology, 28,* 335–338.

Tisserand, DJ, Pruessner, JC, Sanz, Arigita, EJ, van Boxtel, MP, Evans, AC and Jolles, J (2002). Regional frontal cortical volumes decrease differentially in aging: An fMRI study to compare volumetric approaches and voxel-based morphometry. *NeuroImage, 17,* 657–669.

Tisserand, DJ, van Boxtel, MP, Pruessner, JC, Hofman, P, Evans, AC and Jolles, J (2004). A voxel-based morphometric study to determine individual differences in gray matter density associated with age and cognitive change over time. *CerebCortex, 14,* (pp. 966–73).

Turlejski, K and Djavadian, R (2002). Life-long stability of neurons: a century of research on neurogenesis, neuronal death and neuron quantification in adult CNS. *Progress in Brain Research, 136,* 39–65.

Vincent, SL, Peters, A and Tigges, J (1989). Effects of aging on the neurons within Area 17 of rhesus monkey cerebral cortex. *Anatomical Record, 223,* 329–341.

Waugh, NC and Norman, DA (1965). Primary memory. *Psychological Review, 72,* 89–104.

West, RL (1996). An application of prefrontal cortex function theory to cognitive aging. *Psychological Bulletin, 2,* 272–292.

Willott, JF (1991). *Aging and the Auditory System: Anatomy, physiology, and psychophysics*. San Diego, CA: Singular Press.

Wisniewski, HM and Terry, RD (1976). Neuropathology of the aging brain. In RD Terry and S Gershon (eds), *Neurobiology of Aging* (pp. 65–78). New York: Raven Press.

Worsley, KJ and Friston, KJ (1995). Analysis of fMRI time-series revisited-Again. *NeuroImage*, *2*, 173–182.

Zarahn, E, Aguirre, GK and D'Esposito, M (1997). Empirical analyses of BOLD fMRI statistics I. Spatially unsmoothed data collected under null-hypothesis conditions. *NeuroImage*, *5*, 179–195.

18

Intersecting the divide between working memory and episodic memory
Evidence from sustained and transient brain activity patterns

Petter Marklund and Lars Nyberg

Introduction

Functional brain mapping investigations of human working memory have revealed findings that corroborate and extend prior evidence from cognitive neuropsychology (Smith and Jonides 1996) and single-unit recordings in nonhuman primates (Fuster and Alexander 1971; Funahashi *et al.* 1989) by implicating regions within the prefrontal cortex (PFC) in various working memory processes (D'Esposito *et al.* 1998; Smith and Jonides 1999). Much work has focused on identifying and characterizing neuroanatomical correlates of the different subcomponents in the influential working memory model proposed by Baddeley and Hitch (1974). Tasks entailing temporary maintenance of verbal information within working memory over a delay typically evoke neural activity in regions of the left ventrolateral part of PFC (VLPFC) (BA 44/45/47), involving activation at or adjacent to Broca's area as well as premotor regions. The activation of these areas has been taken to reflect the operation of active subvocal rote rehearsal within the phonological loop (Smith and Jonides 1999). Temporary retention of visual or spatial information, on the other hand, has been associated with a separate short-term buffer, the visuospatial sketchpad (Baddeley and Hitch 1974; Baddeley 1986), the neural correlates of which appear to involve homologue PFC areas in the right hemisphere (Owen *et al.* 1998). Moreover, the central executive component of working memory, postulated to mediate higher-level control operations, has been posited to involve dorsolateral regions of PFC (DLPFC; BA 9/46) (D'Esposito *et al.* 1999; Smith and Jonides 1999).

It should be emphasized that no single brain region is considered to be solely responsible for any higher-order function, such as the overarching and supervisory functions associated with the 'central executive'. Rather, results from functional neuroimaging studies that have focused on isolating the neural substrates of putative subcomponents of executive control suggest that these functions are not exclusively related to the frontal lobes (Collette and Van der Linden 2002). Instead, they seem to be mediated by distributed large-scale networks involving regions of both the PFC and posterior neocortical areas as well as subcortical structures, with rather specific network nodes being activated as a function of the particular executive requirements of a given task (Funahashi 2001). Accordingly, to reconcile such findings with the functional concept of a 'unitary' central executive, Baddeley emphasized the need for its fractionation (e.g., Baddeley 1996). Today, there is emerging consensus that the mechanisms underlying the central executive might correspond to the dynamic and flexible interactions among multiple control processes of (relative) functional independence (Andrés 2003). Thus, taken as a whole, extant imaging data have substantiated the widely held view of the frontal lobes as a key structure for working memory and executive control.

More recently, neuroimaging studies have revealed that various long-term memory processes also engage PFC (for review, see Cabeza and Nyberg 2000), including subregions that previously were thought to be rather specific for working memory and executive control (Wagner 2002). The discussion in this chapter will revolve around functional brain imaging findings of commonalities in PFC activation patterns during working memory and episodic memory. We will base our discussion on imaging data from a recent fMRI study that assessed patterns of sustained and transient neural activity across tests of working memory, episodic and semantic long-term memory and attention. Finally, we will attempt to relate our findings to the views of (1) working memory as the activated subset of long-term memory, and (2) executive control mechanisms as the common denominator of human memory functions.

Episodic memory and frontal lobe damage

It has been shown that patients with frontal lobe lesions exhibit disproportionate impairment on long-term memory tests that require access to the source of memorized information (Schacter 1987). Moreover, patients with PFC damage display moderate but consistent impairments in free recall (Incisa della Rochetta and Milner 1993). In contrast, frontal lobe patients tend to perform within the normal range on basic item recognition tests, although some investigators have found even recognition to be associated with a small but significant deficit (Wheeler *et al.* 1995). Thus, memory traces of episodic information are apparently stored in long-term memory despite compromised PFC function, although the subsequently retrieved episodic information appears to lack the contextual information that specifies memories along the spatiotemporal dimension (i.e., the key signature denoting episodic memory). Taken at face value, this observation would strongly suggest that processes necessary for the actualization of conscious recollection or 'ecphory' (Tulving 1983) critically depend on the integrity of the frontal lobes. In congruence with this seemingly disproportionate impairment on source memory tests, patients with PFC damage also exhibit impairments on recency judgments (Milner *et al.* 1991) and memory tests that require temporal organization of events, both in the short- and long-term (Shimamura *et al.* 1990). However, rather than postulating a selective deficit for certain aspects of episodic memory functioning, it has been suggested that the mechanisms underlying these deficits in frontal patients may more accurately relate to more general functions of the frontal lobes, i.e., those same executive control functions posited to be subserved by the central executive (Baddeley 1986, see above). Patients with PFC damage are particularly characterized by dysfunctional executive processes, as evidenced by their impaired performance on neuropsychological tests indexing cognitive control; planning, reasoning, problem-solving and working memory (Shallice and Burgess 1991). Even though these patients are capable of verbalizing the appropriate task rules (which clearly indicates that the rules are stored in memory) they appear to be incapable of retrieving and implementing currently context-relevant rules (Shallice and Burgess 1991). Taken together, several of the impairments observed in frontal patients might be associated with deficiencies related to endogenous control processes underlying goal setting and task-set maintenance (Duncan *et al.* 1996). Such a process-general interpretation predicts similarities in brain activity for tasks assessing working memory and episodic memory.

Episodic memory and PFC brain activity

Brain imaging of the various component processes contributing to episodic memory retrieval or remembering has consistently revealed PFC activity. Initial evidence for a link between PFC and human long-term memory abilities came from two early positron emission tomography (PET) investigations of episodic memory (Shallice *et al.* 1994; Tulving *et al.* 1994a). In parallel, these studies revealed pronounced frontal lobe activity during the performance of episodic encoding and retrieval: an unpredicted discovery, since clinical observations of frontal patients typically reported neuropsychological performance to be largely spared on standard tests of episodic memory (cf. above). Even more intriguing was the lateralization effect regarding the pattern of PFC activity shown between memory acquisition and subsequent retrieval (Shallice *et al.* 1994; Tulving *et al.* 1994a). In both studies it was shown that right PFC was preferentially engaged during episodic retrieval, whereas left PFC was preferentially engaged during encoding (Nyberg *et al.* 1996). The right PFC involvement in episodic retrieval typically involves a posterior region of VLPFC (BA 45) and a region in the anteriormost extent of PFC termed the frontopolar cortex (BA 10) (Nyberg 1998). Moreover, a mid-frontal region in the dorsal section of the anterior cingulate cortex (ACC) (BA 24/32) was also found to be generally activated during various episodic retrieval tasks (Nyberg 1998).

Exploring the points of intersection

As more and more studies of increasingly more specific cognitive component processes have been published, the need for seeing the 'whole picture', or at least to take a broader perspective, has become apparent. That is, the degree to which brain activation patterns evoked by different cognitive functions exhibit regional commonalities has become a question on its own. Inherent in this more global analysis is the question of what the appropriate functional interpretation(s) of intersecting sites of activation in terms of cognitive component processes should be.

In a large-scale meta-analysis involving 275 PET and fMRI studies from several different cognitive domains, both similarities and differences in activation patterns were considered (Cabeza and Nyberg 2000). The data set included studies of attention, perception, working memory, semantic memory retrieval, episodic memory encoding and episodic retrieval across verbal, object and spatial stimulus materials. Although specific activation patterns were identified for each cognitive function, the aggregated activation data also revealed a high degree of overlap in regional cerebral recruitment across diverse arrays of cognitive tasks, including tasks of working memory and episodic memory (Cabeza and Nyberg 2000). The most consistent site of across-function similarities was the frontal lobes.

Concerning the generality of PFC involvement in different working memory and long-term memory processes, other meta-analyses and reviews were specifically conducted to evaluate the extent to which distinct subregions within PFC could be identified as commonly recruited across forms of memory (Christoff and Gabrieli 2000; Duncan and Owen 2000; Fletcher and Henson 2001). In a survey of between-study similarities associated with encoding and retrieval aspects of working memory and episodic long-term memory, a selective set of PFC areas including VLPFC, DLPFC and anterior PFC were indicated to be commonly engaged (Fletcher and Henson 2001). Another meta-analysis highlighted task-general recruitment in regions of VLPFC, DLPFC and ACC across multiple cognitive domains, encompassing five different cognitive demands; response conflict, novelty, working memory load, working memory delay and perceptual difficulty (Duncan and Owen 2000). Collectively, the various meta-analyses point to regions in VLPFC (BA 44/45/47), DLPFC (9/46), frontopolar cortex (BA 10) and ACC (BA 24/32) as generic to different mnemonic demands.

These across-study findings were soon complemented by studies that compared brain activity associated with episodic long-term memory and working memory within the same set of subjects (Braver *et al.* 2001; Cabeza *et al.* 2002; Nyberg *et al.* 2003; Ranganath *et al.* 2003). The findings of such within-study experiments confirmed the meta-analyses by revealing a high degree of over-lapping activation patterns across tasks. For example, across two PET experiments conducted by Nyberg and colleagues (2003), three different working memory tasks along with three different episodic retrieval tasks evoked a general pattern of increased activity in a set of four distinct regions within the frontal lobes. The common activations were located in the VLPFC, DLPFC, and frontopolar cortex in the left hemisphere, and the dorsal part of ACC.

Theoretical models of the relationship between working memory and long-term memory

Findings of overlapping activation patterns for working memory and episodic memory raises the intriguing question as to whether these two functions should be considered to constitute separate systems, or whether working memory may be conceived of as the temporary activation of a subset of long-term memory content. There is support from theoretical models for both views. The influential working memory model proposed by Baddeley and Hitch (1974) postulates a multi-component system of working memory that comprise two limited-capacity retention stores (harboring verbal and visuospatial representations, respectively) under the supervisory and operational control of a central executive processing mechanism. According to this view, the processes and stores implicated within the working memory system are considered to be functionally and anatomically separate from declarative (episodic and semantic) long-term memory systems (Baddeley and Logie 1999).

On the other hand, so-called processing or 'proceduralist-activation' models propose an opposing view as to the structural and functional relationship between working memory (i.e., short-term memory storage and retention) and long-term memory. According to this view the temporary retention of information in working memory is 'simply' accomplished by the prolonged, selective activation of already existing long-term memory representations reflecting or corresponding to the recently encountered and to-be-retained sensory input(s) (Cowan 1999; Ruchkin *et al.* 2003). Two basic principles pertaining to this idea have been captured by Fuster and Crowder, respectively, stating that

> essentially, working memory is attention focused on an internal representation, that is, on a representation stored in long-term memory that, at a given time, has been activated and updated for the performance of a particular task or sequence of acts

(Fuster 2003, p. 737)

and that stored long-term memory representations reside 'in the same neural units that processed the information at the time of original acquisition' (Crowder 1993, p. 143). In proceduralist models, the role of a central executive is principally related to the control and selection of the currently relevant portion of activated long-term memory representations (Cowan 1999). The selected part of the activated representations denotes the information that is under direct surveillance of the 'focus of attention' which represents the capacity-limited part of working memory and may hold only restricted sets of items at any given time (i.e., about four independent representational units) (Cowan 2001).

Baddeley has hypothetically speculated on a 'general retrieval system' run by the central executive, which 'should be able to encode and retrieve information both from the slave systems and temporarily activated components of long-term memory' (Baddeley 1996). In so doing, he expressed the notion that the relationship between working memory and long-term memory processes might involve interplay via shared neuroanatomical mechanisms related to common control processes. As was discussed above, shared patterns of PFC activity between working memory and episodic memory have encouraged some authors to posit general control and/or mnemonic control processes to serve purposes applicable to both memory functions (Wagner 1999). Proposed candidate roles for these prefrontally mediated control processes have involved controlled selection of task-relevant information (Fletcher and Henson 2001) and top-down biasing functions that facilitate processing of context-relevant representations in posterior neo-cortical association areas (Miller and Cohen 2001). These ideas might be bundled together and discussed as representing a general framework that primarily regards the commonalities that bridge working memory and long-term memory as related to executive control functions.

The present chapter

In the next sections we will address four topics that speak to the relationship between working memory and episodic memory in terms of similarities and differences:

1. To what extent might sustained PFC activity reflect generic executive mechanisms that subserve task-set maintenance and state-related control processes shared between working memory and episodic memory?

2. To what degree might working memory and episodic memory elicit selective patterns of sustained PFC activity and what component processes could be reflected in such patterns?

3. To what extent might working memory and episodic memory exhibit overlap in stimulus-locked transient PFC activity and what component processes could be inferred from such commonalities?

4. To what degree might selective transient PFC activity dissociate working memory and episodic memory and what domain-specific component processes might be implicated in such responses?

These issues were empirically addressed by using a so-called 'mixed' (or 'hybrid') blocked/event-related fMRI design, and before we turn to present some findings from a recent fMRI study, we will briefly consider some key methodological aspects of the mixed design.

The mixed fMRI design

The logic behind the mixed design approach rests upon the assumption that performance on any conceivable experimental task can be decomposed into two fundamental and complementary cognitive components:

1. 'Cognitive state' assigned to task-set configuration and maintenance, which relates to state-related control processes that provide the neural and cognitive context within which task-specific cognitive operations are to be implemented in terms of

2. Stimulus-locked item processes that operate in concordance with the given context.

These two processes are superimposed on each other and they are concurrently interacting dynamically throughout task performance. At the core of performance on any given task resides what constitute the cognitive state of the experimental subject, which is induced by task instructions and involves mechanisms that instantiate and maintain task-set (i.e., intentional representation of 'what to do' during a specific task, including, but not limited to, stimulus-response mappings) (Allport and Wylie 2000). Theories have proposed that task-set governs the orchestration of item-specific cognitive processes (i.e., processes that become operative on a trial-by-trial basis) by means of biasing processing in favor of currently context-relevant cognitive operations for the duration of task performance (Miller and Cohen 2001). Hence, maintenance of task-set should depend on state-related control mechanisms, the neural implementation of which should

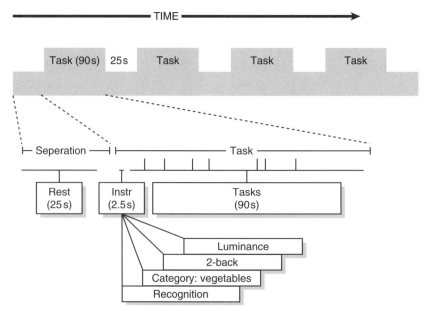

Figure 18.1 Illustration of implementation of the mixed blocked/event-related fMRI design.

exhibit sustained activation changes throughout an entire task. Item-related processes on the other hand implicate the cognitive operations that are triggered by the individual events within a task (e.g., stimulus presentation). As these processes are engaged in a stimulus-synchronous manner the brain activity they evoke should be transient in nature, and distinct from the prolonged changes in the neural responses that reflect state-related control processes and task-set maintenance.

Mixed fMRI designs combine standard event-related fMRI procedures that explicitly measure the temporally isolated and transient brain signals evoked by individual items, with epoch-related blocked procedures that index the average brain activity changes that occur throughout the duration of task performance as compared to the brain activity measured during control blocks. Importantly, mixed designs allow the simultaneous assessment of these temporally independent brain responses. Generally, mixed paradigms alternate task blocks of cognitive performance with control blocks comprising periods of some low-level baselines (e.g., resting) (see Figure 18.1). A critical feature of the mixed design is that the interstimulus-intervals (ISIs) that are interspersed between stimulus presentations must be of varying time duration or 'jittered' including some prolonged ISIs approximating 20 s, in order to keep the correlation between the state and item regressors reasonably low which is a prerequisite to separate the sustained and transient fMRI signals. To date several studies have successfully utilized mixed fMRI designs to measure sustained and transient brain activity separately (Donaldson *et al.* 2001; Braver *et al.* 2003).

Dividing lines and intersecting points: dissociable and common activation patterns for working memory and episodic memory

To elucidate the functional-anatomic relationship between working memory and episodic memory, we have conducted a mixed blocked/event-related fMRI experiment in which sustained and transient brain activity patterns were first separated within each of four tasks (working memory, episodic memory, semantic memory and attention) and then compared across tasks (Marklund *et al.* 2007). By analyzing sustained state-related neural responses and transient stimulus-locked neural responses separately across tasks we were able to demonstrate patterns of regional activation commonalities that differed as to the temporal signature of the underlying neural modulation. In keeping with previous cross-function imaging studies that incorporated tasks of working memory and episodic memory for direct within-study comparisons (Braver *et al.* 2001; Cabeza *et al.* 2002; Nyberg *et al.* 2002; Ranganath *et al.* 2003), common activations were found in a distributed network of brain areas, with the most salient points of intersection occurring within the frontal lobes. However, prior studies investigating these two memory functions or 'systems' together have focused exclusively either on comparisons based on the neural activity triggered by distinct types of events (event-related designs), or comparisons based on the average relative change in neural activity evoked by the total number of trials (including the ISIs) within running blocks of continuous task performance (blocked designs). The neural mechanisms and different component processes evoked during performance of cognitive tasks are arguably represented throughout a spectrum of different time scales. Investigations using either a blocked or event-related design cannot provide measures of item-specific transient responses or temporally extended state responses, respectively, because the former confounds the two types of responses, while the latter selectively index transient changes. Mixed fMRI designs such as the one utilized here are unique because they allow researchers to dissociate and concurrently measure transient item-related responses induced on a trial by trial basis within tasks *and* item-independent sustained neural activity that occur throughout entire task blocks (Donaldson *et al.* 2001).

In the next sections we consider the implications of overlapping PFC activity between working memory and episodic memory with respect to underlying temporal profiles and the degree to which commonalities further overlap with the activation patterns associated with semantic memory and attention/vigilance, respectively. We start by considering the PFC regions that exhibited common sustained activity in working memory and episodic memory and tentatively propose hypotheses as to the candidate component processes that may be attributable to each of the implicated areas. The results of our mixed fMRI study will also be considered with respect to other relevant brain imaging studies, neuropsychological studies and electrophysiological findings.

Overlapping sustained neural activity: common control processes related to maintenance of an attentive state and task-set representation

Compared to a low-level resting baseline, sustained activity that was common for working memory and episodic memory was manifested within a network of primarily frontal and parietal cortices. The areas of commonality within PFC included bilateral ventrolateral PFC (BA 47/45), anterior PFC (i.e., frontopolar cortex; BA 10), and a midline portion of frontal cortex encompassing parts of dorsal ACC (BA 32) and the pre-supplementary motor area (pre-SMA) (BA 6) (for an example, see Figure 18.2). Beyond PFC, both tasks additionally exhibited shared activation with a sustained temporal profile in the left parietal cortex (BA 40/39), and left temporal cortex (BA 21). The sustained activation pattern shared by working memory and episodic memory involved three out of four PFC regions that were identified in a previous study by Nyberg and colleagues (2003) to show common recruitment in two large-scale PET experiments that together comprised multiple tasks indexing working memory, episodic memory and semantic memory, respectively. These common frontal lobe regions involved left VLPFC, frontopolar cortex and the dorsal ACC, all of which (in particular VLPFC and ACC, and to a lesser degree frontopolar cortex) have been

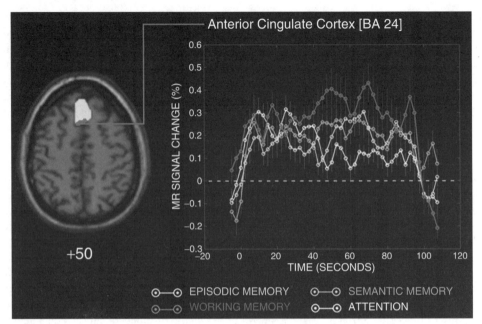

Figure 18.2 Illustration of a common frontal sustained activation increase. See also color plate 6.

highlighted in a number of comprehensive reviews of across-study similarities in PFC activity (Cabeza and Nyberg 2000; Christoff and Gabrieli 2000; Duncan and Owen 2000; Fletcher and Henson 2001; Ramnani and Owen 2004), which further corroborate the generality of their involvement in a wide spectrum of memory tasks and other cognitive challenges. Despite extensive research, it remains unclear how to best characterize the precise functional contribution of these regions, although several candidate processes have thus far been proposed. Nevertheless, many prior accounts regarding the nature of the component processes mediated by these commonly recruited regions (i.e., theories that posit item-related transient processes) cannot account for the current data, as our analysis clearly demonstrated item-independent sustained activity within these areas, and predominantly no transient neural activity changes.

In the overall task comparison both the right VLPFC (BA 47) and medial PFC/ACC (BA 6/32) regions were found to yield a similar state-related effect across all four tasks relative to a low-level baseline (resting while maintaining the gaze upon a small circle in the center of the visual field), which suggested a generic role in basic attentional processes such as maintaining an attentive state throughout task performance and an enhanced level of alertness in comparison with baseline. The right lateralization of the VLPFC response associated with attention converge with prior imaging studies that have found right hemisphere PFC regions to be engaged in vigilance tasks (Pardo *et al.* 1991). Another closely related interpretation would be that these areas may play a role in the apprehension of upcoming events, a feature pertaining to all tasks. Such a notion concurs with the consistent findings of activation in right VLPFC/anterior insula and medial PFC in association with task preparation and attention in studies that have employed different kinds of cueing paradigms (Brass and von Cramon 2002; Luks *et al.* 2002; Curtis *et al.* 2004). All of these processes may be partly or entirely subserved by a common attention network (Pashler *et al.* 2001), and ACC has for a long time been proposed to play a key role in an anterior attentional system (Posner and Petersen 1990). In contrast to the regions in right VLPFC and ACC, the frontopolar regions (BA 10) which was found to exhibit common sustained activity in working memory and episodic memory elicited no significant response during attention/vigilance. In the literature, the frontopolar area has been intimately linked with episodic memory, and more specifically, the instantiation and maintenance of retrieval mode, which reflects a specific cognitive state or task-set that supports recovery of episodic event information (Tulving 1983; Lepage *et al.* 2000). Although this account fits well with the sustained temporal signature of the observed frontopolar activity, it cannot explain our findings of parallel effects in both working memory and semantic memory. The common sustained effect obtained across all memory tasks (but not attention/vigilance), clearly indicate that this region of anterior PFC may play a more general role in state-related control than endorsed by the retrieval mode hypothesis, which putatively correspond to what in the literature has been referred to as task-set maintenance or context representation (Braver *et al.* 1999; Allport and Wylie 2000). Some authors have considered such control processes to correspond to a procedural working memory: however, in our view such accounts merely encompasses a subset of the high-level control processes that subserve task-set maintenance. Task-set or 'task-set configuration' refers to the task goal, strategic and procedural directives and constraints, stimulus-response mappings, and an abstract model of the appropriate set of operational component processes to be utilized in order to achieve the goal. Importantly, task-set representations can be defined as schemas in its most abstract form. This implicates very fundamental control mechanisms that should be engaged in the service of performance on practically any type of experimental task, even very simple tasks, although the complexity of the task-set representation and required top-down modulations would differ. However, it should be emphasized that we posit that the task-set processes represented by the anterior-most section of PFC may diverge from those being exploited in very basic tasks contexts (e.g., attention/vigilance tasks). In congruence with the cognitive control theory put forward by Braver, Cohen and Barch (2002) in which context representations (i.e., task-sets) are contingent upon sustained neural implementation, the neural mechanisms of the frontopolar control processes presumed to subserve task-set maintenance in all memory tasks appear to operate throughout the duration of task performance as indicated by the sustained neural activity. Frontopolar cortex allegedly maintains a mental state of tonic intentionality and anticipation related to current and future goal states.

Theories concerning the brain mechanisms that underlie cognitive control related to representing and maintaining contextual information and the exertion of top-down modulation in the service of goal-directed behavior have typically focused on the DLPFC (BA 9/46) as the principal brain structure responsible for such higher-order control processes (Braver *et al.* 2002; Curtis and D'Esposito 2003). A primary influence to this strong emphasis on DLPFC in contemporary theories of cognitive control and working memory comes from experimental studies of nonhuman primates (e.g., Funahashi *et al.* 1993).

Human neuropsychological studies of patients with selective damage to the DLPFC have not always been able to establish a similarly strong link between DLPFC and working memory/executive processes (Müller *et al.* 2002). These results would suggest that the working memory or executive processes (e.g., manipulation and monitoring) often specifically assigned to DLPFC in many theoretical models of PFC function may not be strictly dependent on this area. (A cautionary note: based on evidence of compensatory neuroplasticity suffice to functional reorganization in the human brain [Buckner *et al.* 1996] it could be argued that, since all DLPFC lesions were unilateral, critical operations subserved by the damaged area might be transferred contralaterally, whereby the operational responsibilities could be adopted by the intact homologous area in that hemisphere). Only lesions comprising both DLPFC and VLPFC were associated with impaired performance in all tasks (most severely in the two-back tasks), including simple one-back tasks.

Nevertheless, we do not question the critical role subserved by DLPFC in diverse executive control processes, although we posit that the specific control processes associated with task-set maintenance might be subserved by the frontopolar cortex.

As previously mentioned prior imaging studies have noted prominent activity in the right frontopolar cortex in tasks of episodic retrieval (Tulving *et al.* 1994b; Cabeza and Nyberg 2000; Lepage *et al.* 2000), seemingly independent of level of retrieval success, which served to inspire the attribution of this consistent pattern to the adoption and maintenance of retrieval mode (e.g., Lepage *et al.* 2000). However, as noted above, the retrieval mode hypothesis cannot account for the equivalent state effects associated with semantic categorization and working memory in the current study (Marklund *et al.* 2007). Prior imaging literature has reported instances of anterior PFC activation in working memory tasks (Braver and Bongiolatti 2002; Cabeza *et al.* 2002; Nyberg *et al.* 2002), the compliance of which appears to depend intrinsically on whether tasks entail subgoals embedded within working memory tasks or not (Braver and Bongiolatti 2002). Activations of frontopolar cortex have also been demonstrated in semantic monitoring (MacLeod *et al.* 1998), cognitive branching (Koechlin *et al.* 1999) and prospective memory (Burgess *et al.* 2003). Prior suggestive evidence for a frontopolar role in task-set maintenance was obtained in a recent event-related fMRI study by Sakai and Passingham (2003) that aimed to investigate preparatory neural activity evoked before the onset of upcoming working memory tasks. Frontopolar cortex was found to be activated in a sustained manner over a delay interval following the short presentation of a pre-task cue that merely informed participants of what specific task they were about to perform. This finding was taken to reflect the sustained engagement of frontopolar cortex to subserve the establishment and maintenance of task-set configurations and control processes related to task preparation (Sakai and Passingham 2003). In a mixed fMRI study that explored the temporal dynamics underlying task switching right frontopolar cortex demonstrated selective sustained activity during mixed-task blocks (i.e., not in single-task blocks) which was interpreted as reflecting augmented demand on cognitive control mechanisms to regulate the need for flexibility and keeping in mind multiple tasks (Braver *et al.* 2003). Finally, two previous mixed fMRI studies of episodic retrieval both reported sustained frontopolar activity, although a hemispheric asymmetry in the brain responses was revealed between the studies (Donaldson *et al.* 2001; Velanova *et al.* 2003). In one of these episodic memory investigations the anterior PFC showed left lateralized sustained recruitment in a simple item-recognition task (Donaldson *et al.* 2001), whereas in the other episodic study two discrete frontopolar sites elicited right lateralized sustained activity that modulated with increased amount of controlled processing required during retrieval (Velanova *et al.* 2003). None of the regions demonstrated any transient effects. Collectively, the current data and prior literature clearly indicate state-related processes, rather than item-related processes to encompass the functional contributions of the anteriormost portion of PFC (BA 10). Ramnani and Owen (2004) have proposed that anterior PFC is engaged in task context processing when there is demand to integrate the outcome of two or more different cognitive operations in a coordinated fashion to meet task requirements. However, this view cannot readily explain the general finding of sustained frontopolar activity in simple item recognition tasks and semantic categorization.

On the basis of current findings and prior data we propose that state-related control processes subserved by anterior PFC (BA 10) appear to be recruited in task situations that require the integration of a predefined type of internal representation not externally accessible (e.g., conceptual knowledge, episodic memoranda, working memory content), with some anticipated aspect of the immediate or intermediate future (e.g., upcoming item stimuli such as retrieval cues) via a discrete set of cognitive operators or computational maneuvers (e.g., classification, memory search, matching, updating, selection processes), in accordance with a given set of 'if-then' rules given by the task instructions (i.e., task-set configuration including stimulus-to-response mappings). In other words, right frontopolar cortex is posited to play a critical role in task-set control processes that might be preferentially engaged in tasks that involve working memory, and episodic and semantic long-term memory. This would imply a putatively distinct conception of a particular kind of task-set configuration that might be referred to as a 'general retrieval mode'.

Selective sustained neural activity: distinct processes related to active maintenance and monitoring within working memory

As would be expected, there was a set of prefrontal areas that exhibited sustained neural activity during delay-intervals in the two-back working memory task, in the absence of corresponding state-related effects in the episodic memory task. These regions involved the left mid-DLPFC (BA 9), right posterior DLPFC (BA 6) and the medial frontal cortex including dorsal ACC (BA 6/32). Conversely, no region was selectively engaged in association with maintenance of the task-set assumed to be uniquely devoted to retrieval mode (see above). It should be noted, though, that the apparent lack of process-specificity in the state-related activation pattern associated with the episodic retrieval task might be eloquently linked to the pertinent differences in processing load across the two functions. Taking into consideration system-specific neurocognitive component processes generally found to evoke sustained neural activity in respective task, the episodic task concur principally with retrieval mode related to the cognitive state of directed remembering of things past, whereas the two-back working memory task involve constant online processing related to active maintenance and continuous monitoring of the two most recently presented items. Hence, with respect to processing demands, the ISIs in the episodic retrieval task as compared to the two-back task must be considered relatively process vacant. Although state-related neural activity was found in regions classically associated with retrieval mode (e.g., right-lateralized frontopolar and VLPFC activations), they were also activated in the two-back task. Prior imaging studies of working memory have also reported significant activity in frontopolar areas, although not invariantly so (Braver and Bongiolatti 2002).

A quite unexpected result was the finding that the state-related pattern of sustained activity associated with semantic categorization showed such an extensive overlap with the activation pattern exhibited by working memory. Only the region of left hemispheric mid-DLPFC (BA 9) prevailed as selective to working memory after taking into account or disregarding sustained activity that was shared with the semantic memory task. Although the type of semantic task employed inherently involves working memory in order to retain the specific category instance given in the task cue (we used four different categories, the specific target category being presented in the task cue immediately before each of four task blocks) and that all non-target items belonged to a strongly related category (e.g., fruit vs vegetables), it was surprising that only the left DLPFC (BA 9) region turned out to be selectively engaged in the two-back task.

The functional contributions ascribed to this area appear closely linked to the type of control operations generally associated with the central executive (e.g., D'Esposito *et al.* 1998). Two major perspectives related to DLPFC functions can be distinguished in the imaging literature. One view holds that DLPFC is preferentially involved with the mechanisms underlying active maintenance of task-relevant information within working memory (e.g., Fuster 1995; Goldman-Rakic 1995), whereas the other view postulates a broader role of DLPFC in subserving multiple executive control processes that monitor, coordinate and manipulate/act upon representations held online within working memory while attributing active maintenance processes to the VLPFC (D'Esposito *et al.* 1998; Smith and Jonides 1997). Brain imaging studies specifically designed to dissociate the brain regions involved in maintenance versus manipulation processes have reported inconsistent findings (Veltman *et al.* 2003). Successful two-back task performance requires the combined deployment of processes underlying maintenance and manipulation/monitoring. Regarding the selective sustained activation that we observed, there are a number of distinct task properties of the two-back paradigm that differentiate it from the other tasks with respect to control processes expected to operate throughout the ISIs. Specific requirements involve the need to constantly hold in memory the two most recent items and keep track of which item was most recently presented. These specific task demands are assumed to engage processes of active maintenance and monitoring of item information (representations of item identity and their interrelational order), both of which generally engage the DLPFC (Owen *et al.* 1996).

Overlapping transient neural activity: shared control processes related to response selection and context-integrative item coding into transiently internalized representations

Similarities in transient item-related activity between working memory and episodic memory were assessed after first controlling for sensory and motor activity by subtracting out transient responses elicited by target detection in the attention/vigilance task. Overlapping transient activity was found in three frontal sites including left posterior DLPFC (BA 44/9), a small area of left VLPFC (BA 47), and medial PFC involving ACC/pre-SMA (BA 32/6). Other areas exhibiting shared transient engagement were located in left superior parietal cortex (BA 7) and medial cerebellum. In comparison with the item effects observed in the semantic memory task, it was found that all of the transiently activated regions that were shared between working memory and episodic memory also exhibited similar transient activity in the semantic memory task. The finding of shared involvement across all memory tasks in a region of left posterior DLPFC (approximating an area at the conjunction of BA 44/9) was of special interest (see Figure 18.3).

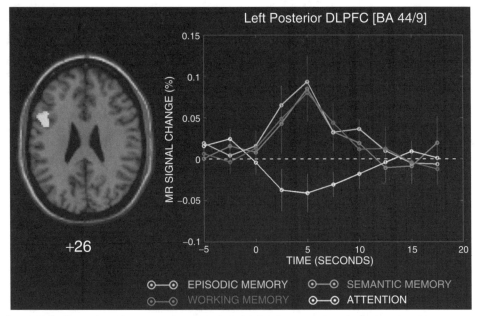

Figure 18.3 Illustration of a common transient activation increase. See also color plate 7.

Noteworthy, this frontal area is identical to an area of commonality that was observed in a previous analysis assessing the prevalence of overlapping activation patterns across two PET experiments that together comprised nine different memory tasks (i.e., triplets of tasks were included for working memory, episodic memory and semantic memory) (Nyberg *et al.* 2003). However, since PET data (and blocked designs in general) do not permit inferences with respect to differential temporal properties of neural activity changes, this former analysis made detailed functional interpretations of the reported common DLPFC activity problematic.

As discussed in the prior section on overlapping sustained neural activity, several authors have considered DLPFC to represent an area of central importance in the service of different aspects of higher-order cognitive control and executive functions (Braver *et al.* 2002). Reminiscent of the functions ascribed to the 'supervisory attentional system' in Norman and Shallice's model (1986), the DLPFC has been posited to influence the level of activation within multiple other brain systems via sustained (excitatory and/or inhibitory) top-down modulations to bolster context-appropriate processing pathways and goal-oriented behavior (Cohen and Servan-Schreiber 1992). Although certainly a most prevalent region of activation in functional brain imaging investigations of the brain systems engaged in demanding working memory tasks and other executive tasks, the precise role of DLPFC in executive processing remains controversial. In the view of DLPFC as a sort of 'task-process coordinator' that represents and maintains context-relevant information in the service of exerting top-down modulatory influence on the neural processing throughout the cortex to promote efficient and accurate task performance, this area should be expected to exhibit sustained activation (Curtis and D'Esposito 2003).

The response selection hypothesis

An opposing view holds that DLPFC is preferentially concerned with memory-guided short-term control processes that act in the service of response selection, rather than maintenance processes (Frith 2000). Several recent imaging studies have provided evidence that supports this claim (e.g. Schumacher and D'Esposito 2002). For example, in an fMRI study of spatial working memory, where the task was explicitly designed to assure that selection of the relevant information held online in working memory could not be carried out until the trial was terminated (i.e., with the onset of a test probe) (Rowe *et al.* 2000), DLPFC was found to exhibit significant transient activity in association with the response phase, while showing no sustained activity during the maintenance phase. Consequently, it has been argued that brain imaging findings of persistent delay period activity in DLPFC may be attributable to control processes related to response preparation that may occur only to the extent that the employed experimental task design allows for response selection to take place during delays, i.e., in advance of its execution (Curtis *et al.* 2004).

According to the selection account, DLPFC should be expected to evoke transient neural activity associated with control processes that may help to resolve response competition (e.g., evaluating the relevance of active internal representations with respect to task goal). The current data converge with this account by demonstrating common transient activity in left posterior DLPFC across working memory and episodic memory in the absence of concurrent sustained activity. We also note that the present activation foci in the left posterior DLPFC (two peaks corresponding to the x, y, z coordinates −46, 6, 30 and −44, 16, 26) are more caudal and ventral as compared to the mid-DLPFC (BA 46/9) area that has previously been proposed as a prime candidate for higher-order control processes linked with the central executive (Curtis and D'Esposito 2003). However, our general transient activation focus in posterior DLPFC is in complete concordance with the focus of a previous event-related fMRI study that also examined working memory and episodic memory together (Cabeza *et al.* 2002). This cross-study overlap of common activation foci applied only to the retrieval phase of the working memory and episodic memory tasks, whereas no significant effect was found in relation to either the encoding or maintenance phase in the study by Cabeza and colleagues (2002). Hence, across two independent within-study comparisons of working memory and episodic memory, retrieval was associated with a topographically identical overlap in transient left posterior DLPFC activity. However, our mixed study additionally revealed a similar transient activation for the semantic categorization task, which together with previously reported data (e.g., Nyberg *et al.* 2003) further implicate a rather domain-independent functional role of this region (at least with respect to a variety of mnemonic retrieval demands).

Brain imaging of episodic retrieval has previously shown increased transient activity in the left posterior DLPFC as a function of the executive requirements associated with memory search (Cabeza *et al.* 2003; Velanova *et al.* 2003; Wheeler and Buckner 2003), which might entail auxiliary increases on selection control processes. For example, the study by Wheeler and Buckner (2003) demonstrated significantly greater activity in the left posterior DLPFC for retrieval trials involving items studied only once as compared to retrieval trials involving either extensively studied 'overlearned' items or 'new' items. The observed transient effects related to episodic memory retrieval tasks that require executive control during retrieval may conceivably be accounted for by the (response) selection hypothesis, in that more elaborative evaluation would be required before a memory judgment could be decided upon for items that only received shallow encoding (items studied once) as opposed to those receiving deeper encoding (items repetitively studied) (Craik and Lockhart 1972).

Returning to the item effects obtained in our study, it was found that the PFC regions commonly recruited across working memory and episodic retrieval also exhibited similar item-related activity during semantic categorization. Both the left posterior DLPFC (BA 44/9) and left VLPFC (BA 47) have in numerous previous studies been strongly linked with controlled retrieval and selection of information from semantic memory (Badre and Wagner 2002) and corresponding left PFC regions have been proposed to subserve semantic working memory processes (Gabrieli *et al.* 1998)). With respect to such 'narrow' and domain-specific interpretations, which are typically inferred from studies of single cognitive functions in isolation, our results point to the value of employing multiple tasks of different cognitive functions for cross-comparisons within the same 'within-subjects' study.

However, a more general account of left PFC function has been proposed by Thompson-Schill (2003), who argues that regions within the left VLPFC (approximating BA 47/45/44), although representing the most replicated area of activation in semantic tasks (together with inferior temporal cortex), do not serve controlled semantic processing per se, but may rather mediate a general control mechanism supporting selection processes independent of cognitive domain. This account fits well with the previously discussed response selection hypothesis.

Context-integrative item coding

It should be noted that the shared recruitment of left DLPFC may contribute to transient component processes other than selection mechanisms. Courtney and co-workers have pointed out that 'activation of the same areas by both long-term retrieval and working memory is consistent with the idea that retrieval produces an active representation of the recalled material much like the active representation of material held during working memory delay' (Courtney *et al.* 1997, p. 610). Extending this notion, it might likewise be argued that externally presented stimulus items, especially in tasks that involve judgments based on mnemonic information (e.g., retrieval cues), need to be transiently (en)coded/maintained in a working-with memory state (Moscovitch 1992) to provide a comparison template for matching purposes while context-relevant item attributes are evaluated with regard to stored representations. In addition to item coding for identity, such transiently maintained item representations might also encompass more context-integrative dimensions such as intentional purpose (e.g., matching the current item to the item presented n-back or a previously memorized list of items or a semantic category) and relevant stimulus-response associations. It is this conception of context-integration with respect to purposeful and intentional stimulus-to-response processing that distinguishes and constrains the type of item coding processes proposed here from, for example, perceptual coding processes involved in passive word reading (although multiple coding elements undeniably overlap between the two).

On the basis of our data and relevant prior imaging studies of various cognitive domains showing a general pattern of item activation within the left posterior DLPFC, we tentatively propose this area to play a role in item-generic control processes related to the operative integration of (1) code-specification of items, (2) transferring of salient cues (extracted during code-specification) to designated processing systems, and (3) linking computational outcome to stimulus-response associations and corresponding motor output. The running implementation of these item processes is assumed to produce a transiently coded internal representation that should enter into a working-with memory state. These control processes serve to implement task-set 'intentions' during each trial by enhancing context-salient item properties for the coding of transient internal representations optimized for current context-appropriate type of cognitive operations. Depending on the time required for completion of adequate item processing on each trial, the engagement of retention systems might become necessary, even though most tasks typically finalize item-related perceptual input-motor output cycles very quick leading to rapid decay of the transient unitized code unless effortful biasing is exerted to prolong the maintenance of the representation (Ruchkin *et al.* 2003).

This aspect relates to the idea that encoding processes mediated by left posterior DLPFC/VLPFC might entail working memory processes that enable access to and maintenance of item-specific phonological and semantic codes as well as associative connections, the only difference to 'traditional' working memory maintenance being the briefer engagement of those processes during item encoding (Wagner 1999). Findings of positive correlations between the time an item is maintained in working memory via rote rehearsal and subsequent recognition performance seem to parallel this hypothesis (Davachi *et al.* 2001). However, the cognitive mechanisms hypothesized to subserve the transient item coding processes are assumed to be independent from the working memory mechanisms that support active maintenance, by contributing primarily to the operations involved in the encoding and retrieval aspects of working memory tasks in a fashion that generalize to episodic and semantic long-term memory tasks, (and possibly non-mnemonic tasks as well). Accordingly, studies directly comparing brain activity between encoding and retrieval tasks have consistently reported similar transient recruitment of the posterior DLPFC area during item processing across encoding and retrieval (Wagner *et al.* 1998; McDermott *et al.* 1999; Ranganath *et al.* 2000), which has been taken to reflect incidentally evoked encoding processes during the active retrieval (attempts) of items (McDermott *et al.* 1999). The incidental encoding effects associated with active processing of episodic retrieval cues have also been explicitly demonstrated by Buckner and co-workers (Buckner *et al.* 2001). Indeed, active retrieval mechanisms that involve elaborative search for item-salient memory traces might incidentally recruit semantic processes during the strategic probing and evaluation of associative information presumably generated during the initial encoding. In fact, it might be argued that all episodic retrieval attempts involve an interaction between active mnemonic control operations in PFC and stored semantic information such as item-specific feature representations and their associative links held in posterior cortex. As already mentioned, the left posterior DLPFC/VLPFC has consistently been activated in tasks that require controlled retrieval of semantic associations (Badre and Wagner 2002).

However, an intriguing finding not consistent with a role of left posterior DLPFC in context-integrative coding processes specific to memory functions in general comes from an fMRI study that assessed the neural effects of increased task difficulty in non-mnemonic tasks of response selection (complex vs simple response-stimulus mapping rules) and perceptual discrimination (fine vs coarse line length) (Jiang and Kanwisher 2003). A closely located region in left posterior DLPFC showed increased neural activity with increased difficulty across both task manipulations. Moreover, this common effect was also seen in other contrasts of high versus low task difficulty, including tasks of color discrimination and lexico-semantic classification (Jiang and Kanwisher 2003). This would seem to implicate a more general and broader functional contribution of the left posterior DLPFC extending beyond memory tasks. Possibly, left posterior DLPFC participates in many domains of information to implement context-integration of stimulus-to-response processing on an item to item basis, whereas in tasks that involve mnemonic or lexico- semantic coding of items the left VLPFC is engaged in tandem with left posterior DLPFC.

If the common function reflected in the shared recruitment of posterior DLPFC would be attributable to cognitive efficiency with respect to the implementation of context-relevant item processing in a general sense, the magnitude of the neural response in this area should be positively correlated with behavioral indices of task performance. A practical means to obtain relevant measures for this type of assessment in the context of episodic memory is to use the subsequent memory paradigm (Wagner *et al.* 1999). The set-up of this design allows event-related neural activity elicited during item encoding to be partitioned as to whether each item is later remembered or forgotten in an ensuing recognition test, which provides an excellent index of the neural correlates of encoding efficacy. Several studies using this design have indeed demonstrated significantly greater neural response in the area of left posterior DLPFC during encoding of those items that were subsequently remembered than those that were forgotten (e.g. Otten *et al.* 2001). Viewed from the perspective that posterior DLPFC mediates top-down control to optimize context-contingent item processing these findings would be expected, in that the certified implementation of task-set goals in the context of intentional encoding should indeed entail elaborative and successful encoding promoting higher levels of recovery for those items endorsed by transient activity increases in this area as opposed to items that did not afford an equal degree of context-integrative control. A more recent fMRI study manipulated an incidental study phase as to produce intermixed deep (semantic judgments) versus shallow (orthographic judgments) encoding and measured brain activity on an item by item basis during both encoding and retrieval phases (Henson *et al.* 2005). Of the relevant comparisons conducted in this study, only a single contrast showed a transient increase in the left posterior DLPFC. This selective activation reflected shallow encoding associated with subsequent hits relative to subsequent misses, which was attributed to familiarity-based recognition processes. By contrast, bilateral VLPFC (BA 47) activity associated with subsequent hits following deep encoding relative to shallow encoding was assumed to reflect processes underlying recollection memory (Henson *et al.* 2005). However, it might equally well be reasoned that more elaborative conceptual processing as compared to shallow processing at encoding should increase the relative degree of familiarity-based memory rather than recollection-based memory. Particularly so, as the study by Henson and colleagues employed a simple yes-no recognition test without the explicit demand on recovery of contextual detail. The conclusion by Henson and colleagues appears to be at odds with other imaging evidence.

For example, this is the case in an fMRI study that examined the effects of divided attention on the activation patterns associated with encoding and retrieval, by using secondary tasks to be performed concurrently with encoding (Kensinger *et al.* 2003). Two levels of secondary task difficulty were used to manipulate the attentional resources available for encoding operations. It was found that the encoding-related neural activity in the left posterior DLPFC was reduced by concurrent performance of the 'difficult' as compared to the 'easy' distraction task, as revealed by a significantly greater response evoked in the 'easy' encoding condition. This could be taken to reflect a greater detrimental impact of the harder concurrent task on the capability to integrate the component processes required for successful encoding. Accordingly, adequate context-integration during item processing is hampered to the extent that the secondary task impinges upon control systems otherwise engaged in encoding. Unfortunately, for the analysis of subsequent memory effects, the authors reported the stereotactic coordinates for only one of two observed left PFC regions associated with greater activation for remembered items than for missed items. These two left prefrontal regions (the reported region being located in the left VLPFC (BA 45/47) showed a response magnitude predictive only of successful retrieval of items encoded during the easy secondary task. On the other hand, the analysis of brain activity associated with the retrieval task found the left posterior DLPFC (BA 9/44) and left VLPFC (BA 45) to exhibit greater transient activity for items that were encoded in the easy as opposed to the hard condition (Kensinger *et al.* 2003). By using a 'remember-know' recognition paradigm, it could be determined that encoding during the easy secondary task produced a greater amount of 'remember' or recollection responses than encoding during the hard secondary task. In contrast to the interpretation by Henson and colleagues (2005), the findings of Kensinger and colleagues (2003) clearly indicated that the left posterior DLPFC was associated with recollection and retrieval of contextually detailed information. These results support the idea of interdependent functional roles being subserved by left posterior DLPFC and VLPFC in the service of context-integration and evaluation of conceptual associations during item coding operations in both encoding and retrieval tasks, which contributes to recollective processing and the activation of relevant representations of long-term memory.

Other studies have also focused on the activation patterns associated with episodic retrieval processes following either shallow or deep encoding, measuring brain activity in the subsequent recognition tests (e.g., Buckner *et al.* 1998). In an early blocked fMRI experiment, the left posterior DLPFC (BA 44/9) was found to elicit greater activation for retrieval processing following shallow encoding (co-occurring with low retrieval success) as compared to deep encoding (co-occurring with high retrieval success) (Buckner *et al.* 1998). However, since those results were obtained from blocked recognition conditions that comprised either items of shallow or deep encoding, the differential activation could relate to differences regarding effortful retrieval attempts and/or behavioral strategies adapted for low/high confidence memory judgments. However, in more recent studies using event-related and mixed fMRI studies (Wheeler and Buckner 2003, Velanova *et al.* 2003) which allow individual retrieval attempts to be divided into successful recovery, correct rejection, false alarm and miss, it was found that the region in left posterior DLPFC was preferentially activated during controlled retrieval of shallowly encoded items. The utilization of strategic retrieval processes presumably required in such instances would entail the type of context-integrative control processes suggested to be implemented by the left posterior DLPFC (BA 44/9), and the subsequent memory effects associated with this area similarly agree with such hypothesis with respect to the mechanisms underlying elaborative encoding.

Imaging evidence from working memory studies appear to parallel the above findings from long-term memory by suggesting that task difficulty and increased load in working memory tasks is associated with increased activity in DLPFC during strategic encoding of items but not maintenance (Rypma and D'Esposito 1999). In an early fMRI study, Courtney and colleagues (1997) employed an event-related design to index the neural correlates of face working memory in order to separate patterns of brain activity into distinct temporal phases of the task corresponding to encoding and maintenance operations. Their analysis revealed a neural response profile in keeping with a predominantly transient encoding-related recruitment of posterior DLPFC. Across three prefrontal activation sites reported in the study (DLPFC, VLPFC and anterior PFC) the posterior DLPFC area showed the relatively strongest transient effect for encoding, combined with the relatively weakest sustained effect for active maintenance (Courtney *et al.* 1997).

Taken together, several previous fMRI findings may be interpreted as to confer with the idea that left posterior DLPFC (BA 44/9) might play an integrative role in contextual top-down biasing of initial perceptual processes that link input of currently relevant stimulus dimensions via a transiently coded internal representation to appropriate processing pathways in posterior cortical circuitry while accessing stimulus-to-response mapping rules (and related motor response set) presumably held in parietal cortex in anticipation of computational feedback. In line with the assumption that this area exert biasing of perceptual processing, Carter and colleagues (Carter *et al.* 2000) found bilateral posterior DLPFC to exhibit transient activity showing a very early peak response as opposed to ACC which was assumed to reflect strategic item-by-item selection demands that was stronger for unexpected congruent trials than other trials in a stroop color task. Although this region was located a bit more caudal than the current focus, the fact that its activation also came before a co-occurring transient activation of extrastriate cortex (BA 18/19) seems to suggest that DLPFC and ACC may interact to modulate posterior visual areas. The common posterior DLPFC activation observed in the current study actually contained two peak foci (x, y, z-coordinates; −46, 6, 30 and −44, 16, 26), the more caudal area presumably linking the item directly with context-relevant representations for integrative coding to be carried out, while the more rostral area may promote context-biasing on the processes exercised in the caudal area by facilitating access to relevant stored information and suppressing irrelevant information (Brass and von Cramon 2004).

A common requirement across the tasks of working memory, episodic retrieval and semantic categorization comprises the need to compare external stimulus material with internal mnemonic information. This comparison process should to varying degrees require retrieval processes that actively probe internally stored information, retained in working memory or long-term memory. In keeping with a number of prior theories on control of memory (Buckner 2003), we propose that such matching and evaluation processes are subserved by left VLPFC regions which act to disambiguate item saliency by exerting top-down biasing on processing in posterior cortical areas that contain the actual subset of long-term memory representations required to be reactivated and recovered. Regions in VLPFC have been postulated to entail item-related control processes underlying active retrieval, intentional encoding and decision making related to the evaluation of mnemonic information held in working memory or stored in long-term memory (Petrides 2005).

Pertaining to the generic context-integrative and/or selection control functions we propose to be subserved by the regions of posterior DLPFC and VLPFC, their anatomical locations are quite fitting; being situated in the principal sulcus of frontal cortex, they (especially the more caudal foci of DLPFC and VLPFC) are deemed 'the initial recipients of information from posterior association areas and are the locus of the initial interaction of executive processing with short-term memory for modality-specific and multimodal information' (Petrides 1994). The posterior DLPFC has been suggested to be optimally situated to integrate premotor, PFC, and verbal information (Brass and von Cramon 2004). The close structural relationship further indicates that the control mechanisms subserved by left posterior DLPFC and VLPFC are intimately intertwined as to their role in selecting, coordinating and certifying the internal integration of stimulus input, appropriate cognitive processing, response selection and motor output.

Selective transient neural activity: updating and temporal coding of working memory items versus active long-term memory probing for episodic traces

Numerous prior event-related fMRI studies have investigated the differential functional activation patterns associated with working memory and episodic memory. In convergence with these studies, the current experiment revealed selective transient activity in the left DLPFC (BA 9) for working memory and the right VLPFC (BA 47) for episodic memory. The activation of the left DLPFC region is more dorsal as compared to the DLPFC region that evoked common transient activation. With regard to item-specific component processes whose contribution should be of critical importance to performance in two-back tasks an obvious candidate is updating. Updating refers to the executive mechanism by which the working memory content is successively refreshed and modified in accord with the most recently encountered items and 'refreshing' actually refers to a specific control process postulated to be mediated by left DLPFC (Johnson *et al.* 2003). However, two-back task performance arguably necessitates complementary executive control processes. For instance, selective inhibition might serve to facilitate the updating process by disambiguating the two item representations held online to ensure that the correct item is discarded from memory.

Another item-related control process claimed to be mandatory in the two-back task promotes temporal 'tagging' of items, which may be referred to as the operation by which the encoding of each item integrates representation of identity with temporal code-specification (Smith and Jonides 1997). Such temporal coding has been explicitly related to activity in the left DLPFC (Smith and Jonides 1997). An alternative account of the processes underlying coding of temporal order in two-back tasks proposes spatial recoding of this interrelational information (cf. Courtney 2004), which could explain the transient DLPFC recruitment in accordance with theories of the functional organization within PFC that postulate dorsal parts to predominantly engage in spatial processes and ventral parts to predominantly engage in nonspatial processes (e.g., Levy and Goldman-Rakic 2000). Generally, activation of DLPFC is the most frequently reported finding in brain imaging studies that have assessed diverse control processes considered to be dependent upon the central executive (Smith and Jonides 1999). A possible interpretation would be that the key operational characteristics of the transient control effect seen in left DLPFC may relate to the effective coordination of other more specific computational units that promote the attainment of the implicated executive functions. With respect to the episodic memory task the selective activation of the right VLPFC (BA 47) involving frontal operculum in the vicinity of the anterior insula may be considered as 'prototypical' for episodic retrieval. It has previously been hypothesized that right VLPFC is part of a network of regions responsible for establishing and maintaining 'retrieval mode' during the performance in episodic tasks (Lepage *et al.* 2000). In line with such accounts, the current data revealed a concurrent role of right frontal operculum in state-related processing by demonstrating both transient *and* sustained activity. The observation of this co-occurring pattern of item and state-related activation in this particular PFC region is in fact a replication of the findings of a previous mixed fMRI study that employed a highly similar recognition task in which an identical area in right (bilateral) frontal operculum showed the same combination of transient and sustained effects (Donaldson *et al.* 2001). Since our mixed fMRI experiment incorporated multiple tasks within the same study protocol in order to identify common neural mechanisms across different tasks we were able to show that the state-related activity in right VLPFC was not specific to episodic memory. This result suggests that the domain-specificity ascribed to 'retrieval mode' may be in need for re-consideration as our analysis showed similar levels of sustained activity across working memory, semantic memory and attention.

An alternative possibility, however, that might account for the observed transient right PFC activity in terms of retrieval mode relates to a feature of the mixed design used in the study. A prerequisite for the extraction of sustained and transient neural responses in this type of design is the obligatory use of a temporally jittered stimulus presentation, i.e., varying length of time intervals between stimuli within task blocks, including a few rather extended time periods. This is necessary in order to increase the variance of signal magnitude in the activation data within respective task blocks (the same procedure is used for rapid event-related fMRI designs) and thus decorrelate the state- and item regressors. Hence, within each task block quite long periods without the occurrence of items are inserted, during which the 'retrieval mode' tentatively might be turned off or at least diminish its influence on task-irrelevant processing (i.e., task-unrelated spontaneous thought processes become disinhibited) until the next item appears. According to this hypothesis, 'retrieval mode' might be attained in a more item-selective manner, in case of which a transient neural response should be observed.

A tentative hierarchical cognitive architecture of identified common control components

The current data and the neuroimaging literature reviewed here demonstrate the consistent recruitment of a common prefrontal network with a distinct set of subregions across a wide range of memory processes (i.e., working memory, episodic memory and semantic memory tasks) (Nyberg *et al.* 2003) and other cognitive abilities and challenges (Duncan and Owen 2000). In this chapter we have presented an attempt to delineate the functional characteristics of common regions of PFC activation in terms of putatively shared component processes. Using a mixed fMRI design we were able to dissociate overlapping neural activity with respect to the temporal dynamics of the underlying neural modulations. In this section we will present the outline of a hierarchical cognitive architecture of PFC in which the functional organization pertains to different levels of control among the distinguished common regions and associated component processes (cf. Nyberg 2006).

At the most fundamental and general cognitive task level we posit regions of VLPFC (BA 45/47) (see Figure 18.4) and medial PFC (BA 6) including a portion of the dorsal ACC (BA 32) to mediate

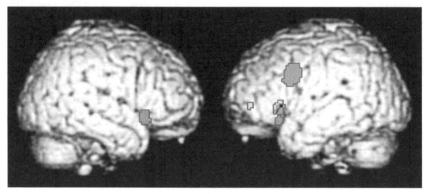

Figure 18.4 Schematic illustration of common lateral PFC sites for sustained or transient modulations during working memory and episodic memory (blue = common sustained activity increases for attention, long-term memory and working memory; yellow = common sustained activity increases for long-term memory and working memory; green = common transient activity increases for long-term memory and working memory). See also color plate 8.

shared component processes related to domain-independent basic attentional processes such as maintaining a preparatory attentive state throughout task performance. These general attentional control mechanisms are associated with sustained neural activity and should be engaged in practically all types of task contexts, even though the degree of recruitment may be modulated with factors such as level of expertise and task difficulty (Dehaene *et al.* 1998). More specifically, ACC has been related to continuous performance monitoring that index and signal the need for control adjustments (MacDonald *et al.* 2000) and is considered to be an integral part of an anterior attentional network (Posner and Peterson 1990).

The common pattern of prefrontal sustained activation showed a more selective recruitment in a region of frontopolar cortex (BA 10) (see Figure 18.4). This state-related effect was seen in all memory tasks, but not in the attention/vigilance task, which implicate frontopolar contributions to another form of fundamental control processes by which task-set is implemented and maintained throughout task performance. As opposed to the above defined attention/vigilance mechanisms that promote a general state of focused attention in any given task situation (in a fashion presumably independent of the specific task-context and content, although typically modulating with task difficulty) the mechanisms that enable task-set configuration support the maintenance of currently relevant context representations including task goals (Braver *et al.* 1999). Task-set constitutes more abstract types of information (e.g., instructions, intentions, motivation, strategies) as compared to more item-specific information such as stimulus features which are actively maintained in more 'classical' working memory buffers after removal of sensory input (Courtney 2004). Task-set may be defined as abstract means-end representations by which the specific cognitive operations to be performed on the stimulus input are specified (Gallese 2003). The current data and prior imaging findings (e.g., Nyberg *et al.* 2003) furthermore indicate a potentially selective role of frontopolar cortex in what could be termed a 'general retrieval mode', subserving state-related control processes among tasks that require some type of mnemonic representation to be accessed and evaluated in order to generate the context-appropriate behavioral output, including information stored in working memory, episodic and semantic long-term memory.

The proposed hierarchical cognitive model of PFC organization also constitutes control mechanisms that operate within the task-set-biased sustained cognitive and neural context in terms of stimulus-locked item processes which are associated with transient activation changes. Common transient neural effects were elicited in left posterior DLPFC (BA 44/9, and also left VLPFC, BA 47) across all types of mnemonic operations associated with item-related processing (i.e., working memory, episodic retrieval and semantic categorization after subtracting out target detection activity in the attention/vigilance task; see Figure 18.4). We propose that the contribution of left posterior DLPFC might relate to an early frontal ERP component thought to be 'elicited by items that can be represented in a unitized code, a format that represents an item within a particular domain of processing and by which it can be integrated in a task context' (Mecklinger 2000, p. 568), which resonates well with our purported role of this area in transient control of context-salient code-specification and stimulus-to-response integration. The transiently coded representation of such items might encompass multiple associative links in long-term memory, the activation of which may predispose recognition (Weiskrantz 1997). An important line of evidence supporting this conjecture comes from a recent event-related fMRI study of working memory (Mitchell *et al.* 2004), where it was found that left posterior DLPFC was activated when task demands required activation of specific attributes pertaining to items that were maintained within working memory before a correct response could be given. This transient item effect was of equal magnitude in both immediate trials (items still actively maintained) and long delay trials that were assumed to require reactivation of item representations before responding (Mitchell *et al.* 2004). In a similar vein, another fMRI study demonstrated left posterior DLPFC to exhibit a significantly greater event-related response for frequency judgments that required detailed analysis of perceptual traits/contextual item information as opposed to judgments merely requiring familiarity assessment (Dobbins *et al.* 2004). Both of these findings converge with the view that left posterior DLPFC contributes to controlled context-integrative coding processes.

Interestingly, an equivalent event-related effect is generally not observed for spatial location stimuli in either episodic retrieval tasks (Penney *et al.* 2000) or working memory tasks (Sala *et al.* 2003). The typically less pronounced item modulation in left posterior DLPFC for spatial information is allegedly tied to a format which precludes representation along the conceptual dimension and requires instead a visual-structural representation format (Mecklinger 2000). Accordingly, only certain types of materials such as objects, pictures and words, but not spatial locations seem to entail contextual relationships embedded in their transiently coded internal representation.

Conclusions

In the present chapter we have explored similarities and differences between the concepts of working memory and episodic memory and their neural underpinnings. Based on our own findings and an overview of the available extant empirical data, we conclude that executive control mediated by PFC is a common neural denominator across tasks of episodic and working memory. Findings of regional commonalities in brain activity between working memory and long-term memory might have theoretical implications for the way we classify human memory functions (Cabeza and Nyberg 2000; Fletcher and Henson 2001). That is, to further advance our understanding of the relative interdependence between working memory and long-term memory processes, it is important to identify and characterize the neural substrates and component processes that are shared by these 'systems' (Baddeley 2000). Such similarities seem to involve the structural basis of representational codes and shared purpose-general neural and cognitive control mechanisms. In a broader perspective, all coherent forms of cognition may involve constant interactions between different forms of memory, the coordination of which may depend on temporally dynamic prefrontal control mechanisms for biasing the working memory processes that select, activate and integrate multiple currently relevant representations of long-term memory for input to the focus of attention.

References

Allport, A and Wylie, G (2000). Task switching, stimulus-response bindings, and negative priming. In S Monsell and J Driver (eds), *Control of Cognitive Processes. Attention and Performance XVIII* (pp. 35–70). London: A Bradford Book.

Andrés, P (2003). Frontal cortex as the central executive of working memory: time to revise our view. *Cortex*, *39*, 871–895.

Baddeley, AD (1986). *Working Memory*. Oxford: Oxford University Press.

Baddeley, AD (1996). Exploring the central executive. *The Quarterly Journal of Experimental Psychology*, *49A*, 5–28.

Baddeley, AD (2000). The episodic buffer: a new component of working memory? *Trends in Cognitive Sciences*, *20*, 417–423.

Baddeley, AD and Hitch, GJ (1974). Working memory. In GA Bower (ed), *Recent Advances in Learning and Motivation* (pp. 47–89). New York, Academic Press.

Baddeley, AD and Logie, RH (1999). Working memory: The multiple component model. In A Miyake and P Shah (eds), *Models of Working Memory: Mechanisms of active maintenance and executive control* (pp. 28–61). New York: Cambridge University Press.

Badre, D and Wagner, AD (2002). Semantic retrieval, mnemonic control, and prefrontal cortex. *Behavioural Cognitive Neuroscience Reviews, 1*, 206–218.

Brass, M and von Cramon, DY (2002). The role of the frontal cortex in task preparation. *Cerebral Cortex, 12*, 908–914.

Brass, M and von Cramon, DY (2004). Decomposing components of task preparation with functional magnetic resonance imaging. *Journal of Cognitive Neuroscience, 16*, 609–620.

Braver, TS, Barch, DM and Cohen, JD (1999). *Mechanisms of Cognitive Control: Active memory, inhibition, and the prefrontal cortex.* (Technical Report PDP.CNS.99.1). Pittsburgh, PA: Carnegie Mellon University.

Braver, TS, Barch, DM, Kelley, WM, Buckner, RL, Cohen, NJ, Miezin, NF, Ollinger, JM, Akbudak, E, Conturo, TE and Petersen, SE (2001). Direct comparison of prefrontal cortex regions engaged by working and long-term memory tasks. *NeuroImage, 14*, 48–59.

Braver, TS and Bongiolatti, SR (2002). The role of the frontopolar prefrontal cortex in subgoal processing during working memory. *NeuroImage, 16*, 317–330.

Braver, TS, Cohen, JD and Barch, DM (2002). The role of prefrontal cortex in normal and disordered cognitive control: a cognitive neuroscience perspective. In DT Stuss and RT Knight (eds), *Principles of Frontal Lobe Function* (pp. 428–447). New York: Oxford University Press.

Braver, TS, Reynolds, JR and Donaldson, DI (2003). Neural mechanisms of transient and sustained cognitive control during task switching. *Neuron, 39*, 713–726.

Buckner, RL (2003). Functional-anatomic correlates of control processes in memory. *Journal of Neuroscience, 23*, 3999–4004.

Buckner, RL, Corbetta, M, Schatz, J, Raichle, ME and Petersen, SE (1996). Preserved speech abilities and compensation following prefrontal damage. *Proceedings of the National Academy of Science in the USA, 93*, 1249–1253.

Buckner, RL, Koustaal, W, Shachter, DL, Wagner, AD and Rosen, B (1998). Functional-anatomic study of episodic retrieval using fMRI: I. Retrieval effort vs retrieval success. *NeuroImage, 7*, 151–162.

Buckner, RL, Wheeler, ME and Sheridan, MA (2001). Encoding processes during retrieval tasks. *Journal of Cognitive Neuroscience, 13*(3), 406–416.

Burgess, PW, Scott, SK and Frith, CD (2003). The role of the rostral frontal cortex (area 10) in prospective memory: a lateral versus medial dissociation. *Neuropsychologia, 41*, 906–918.

Cabeza, R, Dolcos, F, Graham, R and Nyberg, L (2002). Similarities and differences in the neural correlates of episodic memory retrieval and working memory. *NeuroImage, 16*, 317–330.

Cabeza, R, Locantore, JK and Anderson, ND (2003). Lateralization of prefrontal activity during episodic memory retrieval: evidence for the production-monitoring hypothesis. *Journal of Cognitive Neuroscience, 15*, 249–259.

Cabeza, R and Nyberg, L (2000). Imaging cognition II: empirical review of 275 PET and fMRI studies. *Journal of Cognitive Neuroscience, 12*, 1–47.

Carter, CS, MacDonald, AW, Botvinick, M, Ross, LL, Stenger, VA, Noll, D and Cohen, JD (2000). Parsing executive processes: strategic vs evaluative functions of the anterior cingulate cortex. *Proceedings of the National Academy of Science in the USA, 97*, 1944–1948.

Christoff, K and Gabrieli, JDE (2000). The frontopolar cortex and human cognition: evidence for a rostro-caudal hierarchical organization within the human prefrontal cortex. *Psychobiology, 28*, 168–186.

Cohen, JD and Servan-Schreiber, D (1992). Context, cortex and dopamine: a connectionist approach to behaviour and biology in schizophrenia. *Psychology Review, 99*, 45–77.

Collette, F and Van der Linden, M (2002). Brain imaging of the central executive component of working memory. *Neuroscience and Biobehavioral Reviews, 26*, 105–125.

Courtney, SM (2004). Attention and cognitive control as emergent properties of information representation in working memory. *Cognitive, Affective, and Behavioral Neuroscience, 4*, 501–516.

Courtney, SM, Ungerleider, LG, Keil, K and Haxby, JV (1997). Transient and sustained activity in a distributed neural system for human working memory. *Nature, 386*, 608–612.

Cowan, N (1999). An embedded-processes model of working memory. In A Miyake and P Shah (eds), *Models of Working Memory: Mechanisms of active maintenance and executive control* (pp. 62–101). New York: Cambridge University Press:.

Cowan, N (2001). The magical number 4 in short-term memory: a reconsideration of mental storage capacity. *Behavioral and Brain Sciences, 24,* 87–185.

Craik, FIM and Lockhart, RS (1972). Levels of processing: a framework for memory research. *Journal of Verbal Learning and Verbal Behavior, 11,* 671–684.

Crowder, RG (1993). Short-term memory: where do we stand? *Memory and Cognition, 21,* 142–145.

Curtis, CE and D'Esposito, M (2003). Persistent activity in the prefrontal cortex during working memory. *Trends in Cognitive Sciences, 7,* 415–423.

Curtis, CE, Rao, VY and D'Esposito, M (2004). Maintenance of spatial and motor codes during oculomotor delayed response tasks. *Journal of Neuroscience, 24,* 3944–3952.

D'Esposito, M, Aguirre, GK, Zarahn, E and Ballard, D (1998). Functional MRI studies of spatial and nonspatial working memory. *Cognitive Brain Research, 7,* 1–13.

D'Esposito, M, Postle, BR, Ballard, D and Lease, J (1999). Maintenance versus manipulation of information held in working memory. *Brain and Cognition, 41,* 66–86.

Davachi, L, Maril, A and Wagner, AD (2001). When keeping in mind supports later bringing to mind: neural markers of phonological rehearsal predict subsequent remembering. *Journal of Cognitive Neuroscience, 13,* 1059–1070.

Dehaene, S, Kerszberg, M and Changeux, JP (1998). A neuronal model of a global workspace in effortful cognitive tasks. *Proceedings of the National Academy of Science in the USA, 24,* 14529–14534.

Dobbins, IG, Simons, JS and Schacter, DL(2004). fMRI evidence for separable and lateralized prefrontal memory monitoring processes. *Journal of Cognitive Neuroscience, 16,* 908–920.

Donaldson, DI, Petersen, SE, Ollinger, JM and Buckner, RL (2001). Dissociating state and item components of recognition memory using fMRI. *NeuroImage, 13,* 129–142.

Duncan, J, Emslie, H Williams, P, Johnson, R and Freer, C (1996). Intelligence and the frontal lobe: the organization of goal-directed behavior. *Cognitive Psychology, 30,* 257–303.

Duncan, J and Owen, AM (2000). Common regions of the human frontal lobe recruited by diverse cognitive demands. *Trends in Neurosciences, 23,* 475–483.

Fletcher, PC and Henson, R (2001). Frontal lobes and human memory: Insights from functional neuroimaging. *Brain, 124,* 849–881.

Frith, CD (2000). The role of the dorsolateral prefrontal cortex in the selection of action. In S Monsell and J Driver (eds), *Control of Cognitive Processes. Attention and performance XVIII* (pp. 549–564). Cambridge, MA: MIT Press.

Funahashi, S (2001). Neuronal mechanisms of executive control by the prefrontal cortex. *Neuroscience Research, 39,* 147–165.

Funahashi, S, Bruce, CJ and Goldman-Rakic, PS (1989). Mnemonic coding of visual space in the monkey's dorsolateral prefrontal cortex. *Journal of Neurophysiology, 61,* 331–349.

Funahashi, S, Bruce, CJ and Goldman-Rakic, PS (1993). Dorsolateral prefrontal lesions and oculomotor delayed-response performance: evidence for mnemonic 'scotomas'. *Journal of Neuroscience, 13,* 1479–1497.

Fuster, JM (1995). *Memory in the Cerebral Cortex: An empirical approach to neural networks in the human and nonhuman primate.* Cambridge, MA: MIT Press.

Fuster, JM (2003). More than working memory rides on long-term memory. *Behavioral and Brain Sciences, 26,* 737.

Fuster, JM and Alexander, GE (1971). Neuron activity related to short-term memory. *Science, 173,* 652–654.

Gabrieli, JDE, Poldrack, RA and Desmond, JE (1998). The role of left refrontal cortex in language and memory. *Proceedings of the National Academy of Science in the USA, 95,* 906–913.

Gallese, V (2003). A neuroscientific grasp of concepts: from control to representation. *Philosophical Transactions of the Royal Society in London: Series B, 358,* 1231–1240.

Goldman-Rakic, PS (1995). Architecture of the prefrontal cortex and the central executive. *Annals of the New York Academy of Sciences, 769*, 71–83.

Henson, RNA, Hornberger, M and Rugg, MD (2005). Further dissociating the processes involved in recognition memory: an fMRI study. *Journal of Cognitive Neuroscience, 17*, 1058–1073.

Incisa della Rochetta, A and Milner, B (1993). Strategic search and retrieval initiation: The role of the frontal lobes. *Neuropsychologia, 31*, 503–524.

Jiang, Y and Kanwisher, N (2003). Common neural mechanisms for response selection and perceptual processing. *Journal of Cognitive Neuroscience, 15*, 1095–1110.

Johnson, MK, Raye, CI, Mitchell, KJ, Greene, EJ and Anderson, AW (2003). fMRI evidence for an organization of prefrontal cortex by both type of process and type of information. *Cerebral Cortex, 13*, 265–273.

Kensinger, EA, Clarke, RJ and Corkin, S (2003). What neural correlates underlie successful encoding and retrieval? A functional magnetic resonance imaging study using a divided attention paradigm. *Journal of Neuroscience, 23*, 2407–2415.

Koechlin, E, Basso, G, Pietrini, P, Panzer, S and Grafman, J (1999). The role of the anterior prefrontal cortex in human cognition. *Nature, 399*, 148–151.

Lepage, M, Ghaffar, O, Nyberg, L and Tulving, E (2000). Prefrontal cortex and episodic memory retrieval mode. *Proceedings of the National Academy of Science in the USA, 97*(1), 506–511.

Levy, R and Goldman-Rakic, PS (2000). Segregation of working memory functions within the dorsolateral prefrontal cortex. *Experimental Brain Research, 233*, 23–32.

Luks, TL, Simpson, GV, Feiwell, RJ and Miller, WL (2002). Evidence for anterior cingulate cortex involvement in monitoring preparatory attentional set. *NeuroImage, 17*, 792–802.

MacDonald, AW, Cohen, JD, Stenger, VA and Carter, CS (2000). Dissociating the role of the dorsolateral prefrontal and anterior cingulate cortex in cognitive control. *Science, 288*, 1835–1838.

MacLeod, AK, Buckner, RL, Miezin, FM and Petersen, SE (1998). Right anterior prefrontal cortex activation during semantic monitoring and working memory. *NeuroImage, 7*, 41–48.

Marklund, P, Fransson, P, Cabeza, R, Petersson, KM, Ingvar, M and Nyberg, L (2007). Sustained and transient neural modulations in prefrontal cortex related to declarative long-term memory, working memory, and attention. *Cortex, 43*, 22–37.

McDermott, KB, Buckner, RL, Petersen, SE, Kelley, WM and Sanders, AL (1999). Set- and code-specific activation in the frontal cortex: an fMRI study of encoding and retrieval of faces and words. *Journal of Cognitive Neuroscience, 11*, 631–640.

McDermott, KB, Ojemann, JG, Petersen, SE, Ollinger, JM, Snyder, AZ, Akbudak, E, Conturo, TE and Raichle, ME (1999). Direct comparison of episodic encoding and retrieval of words: an event-related fMRI study. *Memory, 7*, 661–678.

Mecklinger, A (2000). Interfacing mind and brain: a neurocognitive model of recognition memory. *Psychophysiology, 37*, 565–582.

Miller, EK and Cohen, JD (2001). An integrative theory of prefrontal cortex function. *Annual Review of Neuroscience, 24*, 167–202.

Milner, B, Corsi, P and Leonard, G (1991). Frontal-lobe contribution to recency judgments. *Neuropsychology, 29*, 601–618.

Mitchell, KJ, Johnson, MK, Raye, CI and Greene, EJ (2004). Prefrontal cortex activity associated with source monitoring in a working memory task. *Journal of Cognitive Neuroscience, 16*, 921–934.

Moscovitch, M (1992). Memory and working-with-memory: a component process model based on modules and central systems. *Journal of Cognitive Neuroscience, 4*, 257–267.

Müller, NG, Machado, L and Knight, RT (2002). Contributions of subregions of the prefrontal cortex to working memory: evidence from brain lesions in humans. *Journal of Cognitive Neuroscience, 14*, 673–686.

Nyberg, L (1998). Mapping episodic memory. *Behavioral Brain Research, 90*, 107–114.

Nyberg, L (2006). Imaging cognition: recent developments and a tentative hierarchical cognitive model. In Q Jing, MR Rosenzweig, G d'Ydewalle, H Zhang, H-C Chen and K Zhang (eds), *Progress in Psychological*

Science Around the World. Volume 1. Neural, Cognitive and Developmental Issues: Proceedings of the 28th International Congress of Psychology (pp. 163–176). Hove: Psychology Press.

Nyberg, L, Cabeza, R and Tulving, E (1996). PET studies of encoding and retrieval: the HERA model. *Psychonomic Bulletin and Review, 3*, 135–148.

Nyberg, L, Forkstam, C, Petersson, KM, Cabeza, R and Ingvar, M (2002). Brain imaging of human memory systems: between-systems similarities and within-system differences. *Cognitive Brain Research, 13*, 281–292.

Nyberg, L, Marklund, P, Persson, J, Cabeza, R, Forkstam, C, Petersson, KM and M. Ingvar, M (2003). Common prefrontal activations during working memory, episodic memory, and semantic memory. *Neuropsychologia, 41*, 371–377.

Otten, LJ, Henson, RN and Rugg, MD (2001). Depth of processing effects on neural correlates of memory encoding: relationship between findings from across- and within-task comparisons. *Brain, 124*, 399–412.

Owen, AM, Evans, AC and Petrides, M (1996). Evidence for a two-stage model of spatial working memory processing within the lateral frontal cortex: a positron emission tomography study. *Cerebral Cortex, 6*, 31–38.

Owen, AM, Stern, CE, Look, RB, Tracey, I, Rosen, BR and Petrides, M (1998). Functional organization of spatial and nonspatial working memory processing within the human lateral frontal cortex. *Proceedings of the National Academy of Science in the USA, 95*, 7721–7726.

Pardo, JV, Fox, PT and Raichle, ME (1991). Localization of a human system for sustained attention by positron emission tomography. *Nature, 349*, 61–64.

Pashler, H, Johnston, J and Ruthruff, E (2001). Attention and performance. *Annual Review of Psychology, 52*, 629–651.

Penney, TB, Mecklinger, A, Hilton, HJ and Cooper, LA (2000). Priming and recognition of novel 3D objects: guidance from event-related potentials. *Cognitive Science Quarterly, 1*, 67–90.

Petrides, M (1994). Frontal lobes and behavior. *Current Opinion in Neurobiology, 4*, 207–211.

Petrides, M (2005). Lateral prefrontal cortex: architectonic and functional organization. *Philosophical Transactions of the Royal Society in London: Series B, 360*, 781–795.

Posner, MI and. Petersen, SE (1990). The attention system in the human brain. *Annual Review of Neuroscience, 13*, 25–42.

Ramnani, N and Owen, M (2004). Anterior prefrontal cortex: insights into function from anatomy and neuroimaging. *Nature Reviews Neuroscience, 5*, 184–194.

Ranganath, C, Johnson, MK and D'Esposito, M (2000). Left anterior prefrontal activation increases with demands to recall specific perceptual information. *Journal of Neuroscience, 20*, RC108.

Ranganath, C, Johnson, MK and D'Esposito, M (2003). Prefrontal activity associated with working memory and episodic long-term memory. *Neuropsychologia, 41*, 378–389.

Rowe, JB, Toni, I, Josephs, O Frackowiak, RSJ and Passingham, RE (2000). The prefrontal cortex: Response selection or maintenance within working memory? *Science, 288*, 1656–1660.

Ruchkin, DS, Grafman, J, Cameron, K and Berndt, RS (2003). Working memory retention systems: a state of activated long-term memory. *Behavioral and Brain Sciences, 26*, 709–777.

Rypma, B and D'Esposito, M (1999). The roles of prefrontal brain regions in components of working memory: effects of memory load and individual differences. *Proceedings of the National Academy of Science in the USA, 96*, 6558–6563.

Sakai, K and Passingham, RE (2003). Prefrontal interactions reflect future task operations. *Nature Neuoscience, 6*, 75–81.

Sala, JB, Rama, P and Courtney, SM (2003). Functional topography of a distributed neural system for spatial and nonspatial information maintenance in working memory. *Neuropsychologia, 41*, 341–356.

Schacter, D (1987). Memory, amnesia and frontal lobe dysfunction: a critique and interpretation. *Psychobiology, 15*, 21–36.

Schumacher, EH and D'Esposito, M (2002). Neural implementation of response selection in humans as revealed by localized effects of stimulus-response compatibility on brain activation. *Human Brain Mapping*, *17*, 193–201.

Shallice, T and Burgess, PW (1991). Deficits in strategy application following frontal lobe damage in man. *Brain*, *114*, 727–741.

Shallice, T, Fletcher, P, Frith, CD, Grasby, P, Frackowiak, RSJ and Dolan, RJ (1994). Brain regions associated with acquisition and retrieval of verbal episodic memory. *Nature*, *368*, 633–635.

Shimamura, AP, Janowsky, JS and Squire, LR (1990). Memory for the temporal order of events in patients with frontal lobe lesions and amnesic patients. *Neuropsychologia*, *28*, 803–813.

Smith, EE and Jonides, J (1996). Working memory in humans: neuropsychological evidence. In M Gazzaniga (ed), *The Cognitive Neurosciences* (pp. 1009–1020). Cambridge, MA: MIT Press.

Smith, EE and Jonides, J (1997). Working memory: a view from neuroimaging. *Cognitive Psychology*, *33*, 5–42.

Smith, EE and Jonides, J (1999). Storage and executive processes in the frontal lobes. *Science*, *283*, 1657–1661.

Thompson-Schill, SL (2003). Neuroimaging studies of semantic memory: inferring 'how' from 'where'. *Neuropsychologia*, *41*, 280–292.

Tulving, E (1983). *Elements of Episodic Memory*. New York: Oxford University Press.

Tulving, E, Kapur, S, Craik, FIM, Moscovitch, M and Houle, S (1994a). Hemispheric encoding/retrieval asymmetry in episodic memory: positron emission tomography findings. *Proceedings of the National Academy of Science in the USA*, *91*, 2016–2020.

Tulving, E, Kapur, S, Craik, FIM, Moscovitch, M and Houle, S (1994b). Neuroanatomical correlates of retrieval in episodic memory: auditory sentence recognition. *Proceedings of the National Academy of Science in the USA*, *91*, 2012–2015.

Wagner, AD (1999). Working memory contributions to human learning and remembering. *Neuron*, *22*, 19–22.

Wagner, AD (2002). Cognitive control and episodic memory. In L R Squire and D Schacter (eds), *Neuropsychology of Memory* (pp. 174–192). New York, The Guilford Press.

Wagner, AD, Koutstaal, W and Schacter, DL (1999). When encoding yields remembering: insights from event-related neuroimaging. *Philosophical Transactions of the Royal Society in London: Series B*, *354*, 1307–1324.

Wagner, AD, Poldrack, RA, Eldridge, LL, Desmond, JE, Glover, GH and Gabrieli, JDE (1998). Material-specific lateralization of prefrontal activation during episodic encoding and retrieval. *Neuroreport*, *9*, 3711–3717.

Weiskrantz, L (1997). Fragments of memory. *Neuropsychologia*, *35*, 1051–1057.

Velanova, K, Jacoby, LL, Wheeler, ME, McAvoy, MP, Petersen, SE and Buckner, RL (2003). Functional-anatomic correlates of sustained and transient processing components engaged during controlled retrieval. *Journal of Neuroscience*, *23*, 8460–8470.

Veltman, DJ, Rombouts, SA and Dolan, RJ (2003). Maintenance versus manipulation in verbal working memory revisited: an fMRI study. *NeuroImage*, *18*, 247–256.

Wheeler, MA and Buckner, RL (2003). Functional dissociation among components of remembering: control, perceived oldness, and content. *Journal of Neuroscience*, *23*, 3869–3880.

Wheeler, MA, Stuss, D and Tulving, E (1995). Frontal lobe damage produces episodic memory impairment. *Journal of International Neuropsychological Society*, *1*, 525–536.

19

Activated long-term memory?

The bases of representation in working memory

Bradley R. Postle

This chapter will advance the argument, built largely on evidence from neuroimaging, neuro-physiology, and neuropsychology, that the short-term retention (STR) of information during working memory tasks is accomplished via sustained activity in brain regions whose primary function is not working memory (nor short-term memory). Rather, the critical brain areas are the very same as those that are necessary for the 'primary' processing of the information in question. Thus, for example, the STR of the precise direction of a field of moving dots is supported by activity in the neurons of visual area MT/V5 that are required for the *perception* of motion direction. The STR of a spoken sentence depends on sustained activity in the networks responsible for *perceiving* and *recognizing* the lexical content and syntax of the sentence (as well as the volume, timbre, and identity of the talker's voice), on sustained activity in the networks responsible for *understanding* the meaning of the sentence, and on covertly activating the speech production routines required for the *rehearsal* of the sentence. Thus, although it might be said that working memory depends on *sustained activation of portions of long-term memory* (as proposed, for example, by Anderson 1983; Cowan 1995; Oberauer 2002; Ruchkin, Grafman, Cameron *et al.* 2003), this idea is most accurate if one construes 'long-term memory' in the broadest of senses. (This is because perceiving, recognizing, understanding and rehearsing are all abilities that we have acquired and refined as a result of extensive experience, and that can thus be construed as the products of long-term memory. For a related view, see Fuster [2003].) A second important property of working memory that will be emphasized in this chapter is that, just as with real-time perception, the STR of information in working memory is not restricted to the channel or channels by which this information enters the nervous system. Although this *multiple encoding* property complicates the evaluation of the representational bases of working memory, it also addresses some of the concerns that might be raised by the concept of activated long-term memory as the basis of storage in working memory.

Since the early 1970s, the dominant view of working memory has held it to be supported by a cognitive system of domain-specific memory buffers that effect the storage of information, making it available for manipulation, for interaction with other cognitive systems, and/or for the guidance of behavior (Baddeley 2000; Baddeley and Hitch 1974; Baddeley and Logie 1999). Complementarily, many of those who have studied the brain bases of working memory have argued that these cognitive systems are instantiated in working-memory brain systems located in the prefrontal cortex (PFC) (Courtney 2004; Goldman-Rakic 1990). Recently, however, a growing body of data has prompted an alternative view that calls into question the existence of specialized working memory systems in either mind or brain. Instead, it suggests that working memory is better understood as an emergent property produced by sustained attention to information represented in systems that have evolved to perform perception-, representation-, or action-related functions (e.g., Postle 2006). This chapter will summarize evidence that the STR of information in working memory tasks is supported by sustained activity in the same nonPFC brain regions that process this information in situations that do not require memory. Examples will be drawn from experimental psychology and psychophysics, human and monkey neuropsychology, human and monkey electrophysiology and human neuroimaging. Complementary reviews that focus in greater detail on just one or another of these sources of data can be found in Jonides *et al.* (2005), Pasternak and Greenlee (2005) and Slotnick (2005). The sections that follow will be organized by domain of information to be remembered: spatial/kinetic; object identity; and linguistic.

Spatial location and kinetic features

Working memory is often studied with delay tasks in which the presentation of one or more memoranda is followed by a delay period, during which information related to the presentation event is presumably retained in an active state, followed by a response epoch. Depending on the procedure, the response-eliciting cue typically requires either recall or recognition. (Spatial delayed response can be thought of as an example of the former.) Regardless of the procedural specifics, elevated, sustained activity during the delay period of such tasks is often interpreted as a neural correlate of the retention of information in working or short-term memory (Courtney, Ungerleider, Keil *et al.* 1997; Curtis and D'Esposito 2003; Funahashi, Bruce and Goldman-Rakic 1989; Fuster and Alexander 1971; Zarahn, Aguirre and D'Esposito 1997).

Studies of spatial delayed response in the monkey find delay-period activity in several regions, including in a region of the lateral intraparietal sulcus known as LIP (e.g., Constantinides and Steinmetz 1996; Gnadt and Andersen 1988; Gnadt, Bracewell and Andersen 1991; Goldberg, Bisley, Powell *et al.* 2002), in the frontal eye fields (FEF – a region of frontal cortex at the border between premotor and frontal areas) (Balan and Ferrera 2003a, b), and in PFC, particularly in the vicinity of the caudal third of the principle sulcus (e.g., Funahashi, Bruce and Goldman-Rakic 1989; Funahashi, Chafee and Goldman-Rakic 1993; Fuster 1973; Fuster and Alexander 1971). Interpretation of delay-period activity from the spatial delayed-response task can be difficult to interpret, however, because this task can be solved either by maintaining a (retrospective) sensory representation of the target location, or a (prospective) representation of the motor plan that will be implemented at the end of the trial. In particular, the precise function of PFC delay-period activity in this task is controversial. Initial reports typically emphasized a STR function (e.g., Constantinides and Steinmetz 1996; Funahashi, Bruce and Goldman-Rakic 1989; Funahashi, Chafee and Goldman-Rakic 1993; Fuster and Alexander 1971; Wilson, O'Scalaidhe and Goldman-Rakic 1993), whereas several recent analyses suggest that it may represent attention- or control-related processes, rather than information storage per se (e.g., Lebedev, Messinger, Kralik *et al.* 2004; Passingham and Sakai 2004; Rose and Colombo 2005). More conclusive are studies that combine physiological measurements with stimulation and disruptive techniques. For example, Bisley and colleagues (2001) have recorded in area MT of the monkey to determine the precise direction of movement for which a column of neurons is tuned. They next established the causal role of these neurons in the perception of movement by demonstrating that stimulating these neurons while the monkey views a display biases its percept in a manner concordant with the tuning of these cells. Comparable stimulation during the delay period of a delayed-recognition of motion direction task disrupted performance, indicating that activity in this station of the dorsal (aka 'where') stream makes a necessary contribution to the working-memory retention of motion information. Complementarily, unilateral lesions to MT disrupted task performance in systematic and predictable ways (Bisley and Pasternak 2000). Here, then, is a concrete example that the STR of a specific feature of the visual scene – direction of visually perceived motion – depends on contributions from the same mental process(es) and from the same brain area that are necessary for the real-time perceptual analysis of this feature. Behavioral and physiological data relating to the STR of other, analogous perceptual features and their related neural activity – from vision, for example vernier spacing, contrast, orientation, spatial frequency and speed (Kahana and Sekuler 2002; Magnussen 2000; Magnussen and Greenlee 1999; Magnussen, Greenlee, Asplund and Dyrnes 1991), from audition, for example pitch, loudness and location (Anourova *et al.* 1999; Clement, Demany and Semal 1999; Deutsch 1972), and from somatosensation, for example flutter frequency and texture discrimination (Romo and Salinas 2003; Zhou and Fuster 1996) – suggest that the same principle may generalize to many other types of perceivable information (Pasternak and Greenlee 2005).

When evaluating the STR of location information in the human, accounting for the prospective vs retrospective strategies afforded by working memory tasks remains important. Regarding the mechanistic bases of the retrospective STR of location information, Awh and colleagues have produced convincing behavioral evidence for *attention-based rehearsal*, the rehearsal of spatial information via covert shifts of spatial selective attention to memorized locations (Awh and Jonides 2001; Awh, Vogel and Oh 2005). This hypothesized mechanism does not depend on a specialized memory buffer. Instead, it operates via the allocation of attention (under the control of the frontal eye fields (e.g., Corbetta *et al.* 1998) and parietal attention centers (e.g., Yantis *et al.* 2002)) to regions of extrastriate and parietal cortex responsible for the perception and analysis of location. Data consistent with this hypothesis have been provided by neuroimaging and electrophysiological studies showing attention-like biasing of delay-period activity in regions of occipital and parietal cortex that are also active during stimulus encoding (see Figure 19.1 and Awh, Anllo-Vento and Hillyard 2000; Awh *et al.* 1999; Jha 2002; Postle, Awh, Jonides *et al.* 2004). This model also fits with the considerable evidence that spatial working memory and spatial selective attention recruit largely overlapping regions of a 'frontoparietal attentional network' including the FEF, supplementary eye fields (SEF), lateral regions of the premotor cortex (PMC), and superior parietal lobule and intraparietal sulcus (e.g., Chelazzi and Corbetta 2000; Corbetta, Kincade and Shulman 2002; LaBar, Gitelman, Parrish *et al.* 1999; Smith and Jonides 1999). Thus, the attention-based rehearsal mechanism of spatial working memory depends on sustained activity in areas whose primary functions can be said to be perceptual, motoric, and/or attentional. (It is also important to note that we have found no evidence for activity consistent with attention-based rehearsal in PFC: see Figure 19.1 and Postle, Awh, Jonides, Smith and D'Esposito [2004].)

Prospective motor coding, a second hypothesized mechanism for the STR of location information, can be implemented when a target location can be represented with a motor plan. It can be accomplished by transforming vision-based coordinates into a motor plan, retaining this motor plan throughout the delay period, and using it either to guide the response (in the case of delayed response) or to evaluate the validity of the memory probe (in the case of delayed recognition). Consistent with the prospective motor coding idea is the fact that working memory for locations is disrupted by concurrent motor activity with any of a number of effectors, including the eyes (Baddeley 1986; Hale, Myerson, Rhee *et al.* 1996; Lawrence, Myerson, Oonk *et al.* 2001; Pearson and Sahraie 2003; Postle, Idzikowski, Della Salla *et al.* 2006), fingers (Farmer, Berman and Fletcher 1986; Salway and Logie 1995; Smyth, Pearson and Pendleton 1988), hands (Cheffi, Allport and Woodin 1999), arms (Baddeley and Lieberman 1980; Lawrence, Myerson, Oonk *et al.* 2001; Logie and Marchetti 1991; Quinn and Ralston 1986), fingers, hands, and arms together (when pointing, Hale, Myerson, Rhee *et al.* 1996), and feet (Cheffi, Allport and Woodin 1999). fMRI studies of humans and electrophysiological studies of monkeys that have induced a prospective motor coding strategy by manipulating either spatial frame of reference of target stimuli (Postle and D'Esposito 2003) or the degree to which the target predicted the metrics of

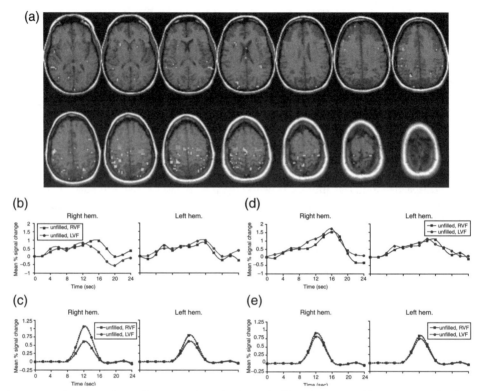

Figure 19.1 fMRI correlates of attention-based rehearsal of locations in working memory. The data illustrated here correspond to a delayed-location discrimination task in which subjects, while fixating centrally, judged whether a probe stimulus was closer to or further from central fixation than had been a target stimulus that had been presented 7 s previously. The delay period was unfilled. (a) illustrates the delay-evoked activity in a representative participant. Structural regions of interest (ROIs) are identified by translucent colors – superior parietal lobule (SPL; dark blue), intraparietal sulcus (IPL; red), premotor cortex (PMC; green), frontal eye fields (FEF; red), superior frontal cortex (SFC; orange), dorsolateral PFC (DLPFC; fuchsia), ventrolateral PFC (VLPFC; light blue) – and are overlaid by delay-responsive voxels, which appear yellow and orange. (b) illustrates trial-averaged fMRI data, by hemisphere, from the SPL delay-responsive voxels of the participant illustrated in (a). (c) illustrates quantitatively the delay effects (delay-epoch covariates scaled by their parameter estimates) estimated by the statistical analysis of the data illustrated in (b). (d) illustrates trial-averaged fMRI data, by hemisphere, from the IPS voxels illustrated in (a). (e) illustrates quantitatively the delay effects estimated by the statistical analysis of the data illustrated in (d). See also color plate 9.

the impending saccade (Curtis, Rao and D'Esposito 2004; Quintana and Fuster 1992; Takeda and Funahashi 2002, 2004) have found prospective motor coding-related activity in the caudate nucleus, the premotor cortex (including FEF), and dorsolateral PFC. Neurons of the dorsolateral PFC also register updates of the trial-ending saccade metrics when these are changed during the trial (Fukushima, Hasegawa and Miyashita 2004). These brain systems are likely involved in the sensory-motor coordinate transformation necessary for creating a prospective motor code, and/or in the STR of the motor plan itself.

Although attention-based rehearsal and prospective motor coding are summarized here as distinct mechanisms, each may simply represent a different point along a single sensorimotor continuum.

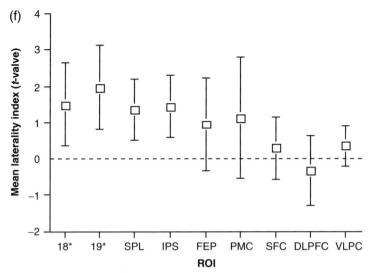

Figure 19.1 (*continued*) (f) illustrates the group results (mean and 95 per cent confidence interval, n = 9) from this study, which indicate that the contralateral bias (referred to on vertical axis as the 'Laterality Index') of delay-period activity was significantly different from 0 in Brodmann Areas (BA) 18 and 19 of the occipital cortex, and in IPS and SPL, but not in any of the frontal cortical ROIs. This contralateral bias is an operationalization of an attention-based rehearsal effect. For complete details, see Postle, Awh, Jonides *et al.* (2004). See also color plate 9.

This would follow from evidence for close linkages between spatial attention and motor control (e.g., Andersen *et al.* 2004; Fuster 1995; Goldberg, Bisley, Powell *et al.* 2002; Goodale and Westwood 2004; Hamker 2005; Hoffman and Subramaniam 1995; Moore and Fallah 2004), and may be reflected in the trend of decreasing contralateral bias in delay-period activity (an index of attention-based rehearsal) that is seen as one proceeds rostrally from peristriate, through parietal, premotor, and finally prefrontal cortex (Figure 19.1). Theeuwes and colleagues (2005) have also noted the 'evidence for a strong overlap between visual working memory, spatial attention, and the oculomotor system', and use this to articulate an emergent-property view, suggesting that it is possible 'that working memory is "nothing more" than the preparation to perform an action, whether it be oculomotor, manual, verbal, or otherwise' (pp. 198–199).

Object identity

The literature on the neural bases of object working memory of the monkey point to an important role for advanced stations of the ventral (or 'what') visual object processing stream. As is the case with spatial delayed response, sustained delay-period activity is observed in several brain regions during object delay tasks, including in inferotemporal (IT) cortex (Miller, Erickson and Desimone 1996), anterior IT cortex (Nakamura and Kubota 1995), and entorhinal cortex (Suzuki, Miller and Desimone 1997) – all in the temporal lobe – and in PFC (e.g., Miller, Erickson and Desimone 1996; Rao, Rainer and Miller 1997; Wilson, O'Scalaidhe and Goldman-Rakic 1993). Many of these temporal lobe regions, as well as PFC, demonstrate sustained object-specific delay-period activity that is not disrupted by intervening distracting stimuli. The necessity, for successful STR of object identity information, of the delay-period activity in two of these regions has been investigated by Petrides (2000). This study demonstrated a double-dissociation of working memory functions attributable to PFC vs anterior IT cortex: lesions of PFC did not impair memory for the selection of one among two object stimuli across long (90 and 120 s) delay periods, but did disrupt memory for the selection of one from among a set of three, four, or five items across shorter (10 s) delays; whereas lesions of anterior IT cortex had the converse effect. These results are logically inconsistent with the idea that PFC is a necessary neural substrate for the STR of object information. Rather, they support an alternative view that the STR of information depends on anterior IT context (and, perhaps, entorhinal cortex), whereas control functions, such as the monitoring of multiple mnemonic representations and/or the selection from among them, are supported by PFC.

In the human, fMRI studies of n-back (Nystrom *et al.* 2000; Postle, Stern, Rosen *et al.* 2000) and delayed-recognition (Postle and D'Esposito 1999) working memory for location versus identity of abstract geometric shapes have each found shape-specific memory-related activity in ventral temporal and occipital cortex, but not in PFC (Figure 19.2).[1] A subsequent fMRI study employed a multistep ABBA-like design intended to filter out delay-period activity that may be correlated with, but not necessary for, the STR of face identity. The task featured three 7 s delay periods that were interposed between the presentation of the first and second, second and third, and third and fourth stimuli. The logic was that the multiple distracting events in this task might serve to filter out activity from the first delay period that wasn't involved directly in storage, because only voxels whose activity was necessary for retaining the memory trace to the end of the trial would be expected to maintain their activity across distracting stimuli. The hierarchical analysis procedure proceeded in three steps: First, Delay 1-sensitive voxels (presumed to represent the superset of the neural correlate of mnemonic representation of the target face) were identified; second, the Delay 1 voxels that remained active during Delay 2 were identified; and third, the voxels from Step 2 that retained their activity during Delay 3 were identified. As expected, the results from each subject revealed Delay 1-specific activity in many brain areas, including PFC, posterior fusiform gyrus of the temporal lobe and posterior parietal cortex. In each subject, however, only a subset of these voxels retained the Delay 1 signal during Delay 2, and posterior fusiform gyrus was the only region in which voxels retained the signal during Delay 3 in each subject (Figure 19.3, Postle, Druzgal and D'Esposito 2003). Other studies of working memory for faces are also consistent with an important role for posterior fusiform gyrus in the STR of face information (Druzgal and D'Esposito 2003; Ranganath, Cohen, Dam *et al.* 2004; Ranganath, DeGutis and D'Esposito 2004), and of analogous, nonfrontal, visual areas for other classes of visual stimuli (Ranganath, DeGutis and D'Esposito 2004; Todd and Marois 2004, 2005; Vogel and Machizawa 2004). Thus, working memory for the identity of objects is associated with sustained activity in the very brain systems that are responsible for the visual perception of these stimuli.

Verbal material

Within the domain of overtly language-based material, neuroimaging studies designed to identify the neural loci of working memory storage have, for the most part, pinpointed left posterior perisylvian areas (e.g., Awh *et al.* 1996; Hickock, Buchsbaum, Humphreys *et al.* 2003; Paulesu, Frith and Frackowiak 1993; Postle, Berger and D'Esposito 1999; Rypma and D'Esposito 1999) – areas

---

[1] In contrast, other groups have presented results consistent with segregation-by-domain of PFC delay-period activity (e.g., Gruber and von Cramon 2003; Manoach *et al.* 2004; Rama *et al.* 2004; Rama, Sala, Gillen *et al.* 2001; Sala, Rama and Courtney 2003). Methodological factors that may underlie these divergent sets of results are considered in (Postle 2006).

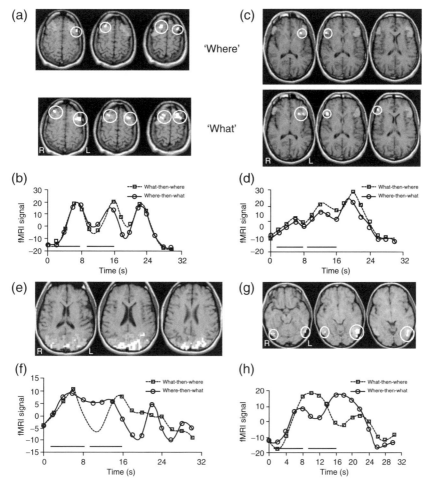

Figure19.2 Delay-period activity maps and time series plots from an fMRI study of a two-step delayed-recognition of location and shape task ('what'-then-'where' and 'where'-then- 'what' trials were randomized throughout each scanning session). (a) illustrates location ('where') and shape ('what') delay-period activity (circled) in the same slices through dorsolateral PFC of a representative subject. The dorsolateral PFC ROI is rendered in translucent white overlays. This figure illustrates the marked degree of overlap in dorsolateral PFC delay-period activity in the two conditions. (b) illustrates trial-averaged time series extracted from the voxels illustrated in (a). Values are plotted in arbitrary units of fMRI signal intensity; gray bars along the horizontal axis indicate the timing of the two delay periods during the trial. Note the similarity of fMRI signal intensity changes in spatial and object delay periods. (c) illustrates 'where' and 'what' delay-period activity in the same slices through ventrolateral PFC in a different representative subject. All display conventions for this and subsequent activation maps are the same as in (a). (d) illustrates trial-averaged time series extracted from the voxels illustrated in (c), with all display conventions for this and subsequent time series plots the same as in (b). (e) illustrates delay-period activity collapsed across 'where' and 'what' conditions from superior parietal lobule of a representative subject, and (f) illustrates the trial-averaged time series plot from these voxels. Note that, in contrast to (b) and (d), the delay-period activity is greater for 'where' than for 'what' in both trial types. (g) illustrates delay-period activity collapsed across 'where' and 'what' conditions from inferior temporal cortex of a representative subject, and (h) illustrates the trial-averaged time series plot from these voxels, which is greater for 'what' than for 'where' delay periods in both trial types. (For complete details, see (Postle and D'Esposito, 1999).)

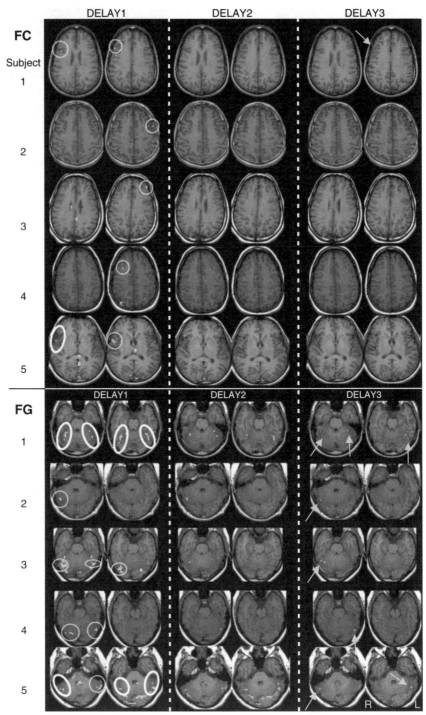

Figure 19.3 fMRI results from a multi-step delayed face-recognition task (behavioral task described in the text, and in Postle, Druzgal, and D'Esposito, 2003). The Delay 1 column illustrates the statistical maps identifying voxels in frontal cortex (FC) and fusiform gyrus (FG) with Delay 1-specific activity (critical voxels are circled). Delay 1 activity in FC was located in: right hemisphere middle

associated with speech perception and the phonological lexicon – and not PFC. Considerable additional evidence that is consistent with these observations is presented by Ruchkin *et al.* (2003), and several supporting and opposing commentaries also follow this paper. Note that many studies have implicated left inferior PFC and premotor cortex in the *rehearsal*, as opposed to the storage, of information represented in an articulatory code, and that these brain areas are also implicated in speech production. Another issue that is relevant to this question, that of the relative importance of working memory load effects in PFC vs nonPFC regions, is reviewed in Postle (2006).

Concerns about the 'activated LTM' account of the STR of information for working memory, and possible resolution

The preceding sections of this chapter have summarized evidence that the STR of information in working memory is accomplished via sustained activity in anatomical networks whose principle function is not mnemonic. Variants of this idea, particularly that the STR of information in working memory is accomplished via the temporary activation of LTM representations (e.g., Anderson 1983; Cowan 1995; Oberauer 2002; Ruchkin, Grafman, Cameron *et al.* 2003) has met with considerable resistance from many quarters (see, for example, the commentary following Ruchkin, Grafman, Cameron and Berndt 2003). Some of the concerns are in the following vein: *If working memory is accomplished via the temporary activation of long-term memory representations, how is the ordinal position of items in working memory retained? How can one account for the flexible transformation of information in working memory? and Working memory often represents the 'here and now' of a situation, and thus contains detail specific to the present moment that cannot be derived from the mere activation of representations in semantic or episodic memory.* What follows is a consideration of how an emergent-processes view of working memory can addresses these concerns. To do so, however, requires first introducing a second principle of the emergent processes account, that of multiple encoding.

Multiple encoding, the idea that mnemonic representations can include a multiplicity of features, is a venerable idea in memory research (e.g., Estes 1955; Melton and Martin 1972). For example, Wickens (1972, 1973) demonstrated that words can be encoded, in parallel, according to their semantic attributes, to the physical characteristics of their presentation at the time of encoding, and to many 'other' attributes (such as language, frequency, representing symbol, and imageability). This idea has also been fundamental to the memory systems models of working memory, as seen, for example, in the recoding of visually presented alphabetic or numeric characters into a phonological code (Baddeley 1986). More recently, several studies have extended the principle of multiple

---

frontal gyrus (MFG, Brodmann's area [BA] 9/46) and inferior frontal gyrus (IFG, BA 44) in subject 1; left MFG (BA 8) in subject 2; left MFG (BA 9/46) in subject 3; right superior frontal sulcus (BA 8) in subject 4; and IFG (BA 44) and premotor cortex (BA 6) in subject 5. FG Delay 1 activity was located bilaterally in subjects 1, 3, 4 and 5, and in right hemisphere in subject 2. The Delay 2 column illustrates the statistical maps identifying voxels in FC and FG with Delay 2-specific activity within the search space comprising the voxels that had been identified in the Delay 1 column (translucent blue). The Delay 3 column illustrates the statistical maps identifying voxels in FC and FG with Delay 3-specific activity within the search space comprising the voxels that had been identified in the Delay 2 column (translucent blue). This Delay 3 activity can be interpreted as a candidate neural correlate of the STR of face information. Such activity, identified with arrows, was seen in FC only in subject 1 (right MFG [BA 9/46]), and in FG bilaterally in subjects 1 and 5, in right hemisphere in subjects 2 and 3, and in left hemisphere in subject 4. See also color plate 10

encoding to other domains of information. One example is that the working-memory representation of visually presented object stimuli may encode not only the visual features of the object (e.g., size, color, texture, shape), but also verbal information that is spontaneously associated with the visual stimulus by the subject (Postle, D'Esposito and Corkin 2005; Postle, Idzikowski, Della Salla *et al.* 2006; Simons 1996). In addition to recoding, working memory representations can also incorporate incidental encoding-related context. This is seen, for example, when running span (or 'updating') performance suffers when the grouping of stimuli at presentation is violated by the requirement to 'drop' some of a group's items from the memory set but to keep others. This effect persists despite explicit instructions to subjects to ignore grouping information, despite intensive training and across different rates of stimulus presentation (Postle 2003). Other work has shown that the STR of letters is also sensitive to study-test manipulations of the color in which items are presented (despite instructions to ignore color), and to study-test changes in environmental context (Postle 2003; unpublished observations).

Now, back to the list of concerns laid out at the beginning of this section. The first had to do with *maintenance of ordinal position* of items represented in working memory. This is not a problem for the emergent-processes framework, because maintenance of ordinal position is a function for which the speech production system is well-suited (e.g., Bock and Levelt 1994). Thus, if the information in working memory is being represented, in part, in an articulatory code, (covertly) cycling this information through the speech production apparatus (e.g., Page and Norris 1998) would be a way to accomplish memory for order without resorting to a special-purpose memory system. (In such a case, one could invoke the operation of an 'articulatory loop', but to do so would seem to needlessly relabel a system that already exists.) The principle of multiple encoding permits the verbal recoding explanation to extend to working memory for all types of information, with the exception of egocentrically encoded location. Working memory for location is invariably insensitive to concurrent verbal interference (Logie 1995; Postle, Idzikowski, Della Salla *et al.* 2006). Consistent with this reasoning is the fact that memory for order is known to be superior when items can be represented with a verbal code (e.g., Glenberg and Fernandez 1988; O'Connor and Hermelin 1972, 1973). An analogous explanation can be invoked for ordinal memory for egocentrically encoded locations (as is required, e.g., by the Corsi blocks task) if one allows for contributions from the oculo-and/or skeletomotor system, because ordering and sequencing are also fundamental to the control of these systems.

What about the *flexible transformation of information* held in working memory? We know from the problem-solving literature that the ability to rerepresent information in a different format, or to consider it from a different perspective, can be important for solving problems. Similarly, the ability to represent an item (or a piece of information) in multiple codes, despite the unimodal channel by which it may have been perceived, should facilitate one's ability to manipulate or transform the representation of this information.

Finally, what of the *representation of the subjective present*? The multiple encoding principle holds that, for example, when one is asked to remember the seven digits of a telephone number, there is more to this process than the retrieval into conscious awareness of the seven lexical representations that were a part of one's knowledge base prior to being given the number to remember. Also represented in working memory can be, for example, information about who spoke the telephone number, about the timber, volume, and tone of the talker's voice, about one's affective classification of the talker, about whose telephone number it is, about other telephone numbers that are similar, about the ambient illumination in the room in which the number was spoken, and so on. This analysis makes clear that working memory can be construed as a special case of conscious awareness – conscious awareness of information that is not currently accessible in the environment.

Shifting theoretical perspectives on nondeclarative memory: an analogy for working memory

The shift toward an emergent-properties view of working memory function has parallels in the recent evolution of our understanding of nondeclarative, or implicit, memory phenomena. Modern research in this area began with the characterization of the amnesic syndrome, and the fact that dense anterograde amnesia spared memory for many types of information, provided that this memory was probed in the right way. This included mirror-reversed visuomotor transformations (Milner 1962), routes through a tactually guided maze (Corkin 1965), line drawings (Milner, Corkin and Teuber 1968), and words (Warrington and Weiskrantz 1968). These and subsequent observations led to a taxonomic approach of cataloguing the many nondeclarative memory 'systems' that showed sparing despite anterograde amnesia, among these, abilities organized as *skills, priming, dispositions* and *nonassociative* (Squire 1987, 1992); *structural-perceptual* and *lexical-semantic* (aka '*conceptual*') memory subsystems (Gabrieli *et al.* 1994; Keane, Gabrieli, Fennema *et al.* 1991); and *visual word form, structural description*, and *auditory word form perceptual representation systems* (Schacter 1990, 1994). This enterprise was particularly useful in delineating the boundaries of the kinds of memory performance that *are* dependent on the medial-temporal diencephalic anatomical system that supports declarative memory. As this work progressed, however, it also became apparent that an ever-subdividing taxonomy of nondeclarative memory systems and subsystems, seemingly growing with each new task and each new patient group tested, was becoming an increasingly unwieldy way to understand these empirical phenomena (e.g., Roediger 1990). Paralleling these theoretical concerns were developments in our understanding of the neurophysiological consequences of repetition. Most general was the fact that plasticity is a property of virtually all elements of the nervous system. More specifically, such plasticity could take the form of a signal increase or decrease, or in the expansion or contraction of a cortical representation, depending on the context in which repetition occurred.[2] Additionally, such plastic changes were invariably associated with changes (typically, improvements) in performance. Therefore, alternative accounts of nondeclarative memory began to emerge that emphasized the repetition-induced biasing of stimulus processing and/or task performance (e.g., Butler and Berry 2001; Postle and Corkin 1998, 1999). From this alternative perspective, nondeclarative memory didn't reveal memory systems. Instead, it simply resulted from plasticity in the networks engaged by the task. In the past few years, invocation of nondeclarative memory *systems* are increasingly infrequent, and have largely been replaced by studies that use repetition-related changes in physiological signals as probes with which to evaluate cognitive processes (e.g., Boynton 2004; Henson, Shallice, Gorno-Tempini *et al.* 2002; Stoeckel, Pollok, Schnitzler *et al.* 2004; Winston, Henson, Fine-Goulden *et al.* 2004; Yi and Chun 2005). By analogy to this evolution in viewpoints on nondecarlative memory, a similar change is now taking place with working memory.

The systems approach to working memory has, without question, been a remarkably fruitful one from which to launch the study of this cognitive phenomenon. This approach is becoming increasingly difficult to sustain, however, as our understanding of the cognitive and neural bases of working memory grows ever larger and more detailed. Particularly salient in this regard has

---

[2] Thus, repeated presentation of an item within a trial of a multi-step delayed-recognition task could produce 'repetition suppression' or 'repetition enhancement' in stimulus selective neurons of inferotemporal cortex, depending on whether the repeated item was a foil or target stimulus, respectively (Miller, Li and Desimone 1991); stem completion to previously studied words was associated with decreases in signal in inferior occipitotemporal cortex (Buckner *et al.* 1995); extensive repetition of a finger-to-thumb tapping pattern led to increases in the cortical representation of the task in the motor cortex (Karni *et al.* 1995).

been the building evidence that the STR of information is supported by sustained activity in regions whose primary function is not working memory.

Acknowledgment

The author receives support from NIH grant MH064498.

References

Andersen, RA, Meeker, D, Pesaran, B, Breznen, B, Buneo, C and Scherberger, H (2004). Sensorimotor transformations in the posterior parietal cortex. In MS Gazzaniga (ed), *The Cognitive Neurosciences*, 3rd edn (pp. 463–474). Cambridge, MA: MIT Press.

Anderson, JR (1983). *The Architecture of Cognition*. Cambridge, MA: Harvard University Press.

Anourova, I, Rama, P, Alho, K, Koivusalo, S, Kahnari, J and Carlson, S (1999). Selective interference reveals dissociation between auditory memory for location and pitch. *NeuroReport*, *10*, 3543–3547.

Awh, E, Anllo-Vento, L and Hillyard, SA (2000). The role of spatial selective attention in working memory for locations: evidence from event-related potentials. *Journal of Cognitive Neuroscience*, *12*, 840–847.

Awh, E and Jonides, J (2001). Overlapping mechanisms of attention and spatial working memory. *Trends in Cognitive Sciences*, *5*, 119–126.

Awh, E, Jonides, J, Smith, EE, Buxton, RB, Frank, LR, Love, T *et al.* (1999). Rehearsal in spatial working memory: evidence from neuroimaging. *Psychological Science*, *10*, 433–437.

Awh, E, Jonides, J, Smith, EE, Schumacher, EH, Koeppe, RA and Katz, S (1996). Dissociation of storage and rehearsal in verbal working memory: evidence from positron emission tomography. *Psychological Science*, *7*, 25–31.

Awh, E, Vogel, EK and Oh, S-H (2005). Interactions between attention and working memory. *Neuroscience*, *this special issue*.

Baddeley, AD (1986). *Working Memory*. London: Oxford University Press.

Baddeley, AD (2000). The episodic buffer: a new component of working memory? *Trends in Cognitive Sciences*, *4*, 417–423.

Baddeley, AD and Hitch, GJ (1974). Working Memory. In GH Bower (ed), *The Psychology of Learning and Motivation*, Vol. 8 (pp. 47–89). New York: Academic Press.

Baddeley, AD and Lieberman, K (1980). Spatial working memory. In RS Nickerson (ed), *Attention and Performance VIII* (pp. 521–539). Hillsdale, NJ: Erlbaum.

Baddeley, AD and Logie, RH (1999). Working memory: the multiple-component model. In A Miyake and P Shah (eds), *Models of Working Memory* (pp. 28–61). Cambridge: Cambridge University Press.

Balan, PF and Ferrera, VP (2003a). Effects of gaze shifts on maintenance of spatial memory in macaque frontal eye field. *The Journal of Neuroscience*, *23*, 5446–5454.

Balan, PF and Ferrera, VP (2003b). Effects of spontaneous eye movements on spatial memory in macaque periarcuate cortex. *The Journal of Neuroscience*, *23*, 11392–11401.

Bisley, J and Pasternak, T (2000). The multiple roles of visual cortical areas MT/MST in remembering the direction of visual motion. *Cerebral Cortex*, *10*, 1053–1065.

Bisley, J, Zaksas, D and Pasternak, T (2001). Microstimulation of cortical area MT affects performance on a visual working memory task. *Journal of Neurophysiology*, *85*, 187–196.

Bock, K and Levelt, W (1994). Language production: grammatical encoding. In M Gernsbacher (ed), *Handbook of Psycholinguistics* (pp. 945–985): Academic Press.

Boynton, GM (2004). Adaptation and attentional selection.[comment]. *Nature Neuroscience*, *7*, 8–10.

Buckner, RL, Petersen, SE, Ojemann, JG, Miezen, FM, Squire, LR and Raichle, ME (1995). Functional anatomical studies of explicit and implicit memory retrieval tasks. *Journal of Neuroscience*, *15*, 12–29.

Butler, LT and Berry, DC (2001). Implicit memory: intention and awareness revisited. *Trends in Cognitive Sciences*, *5*, 192–197.

Cheffi, S, Allport, DA and Woodin, M (1999). Hand-centered coding of target location in visuo-spatial working memory. *Neuropsychologia*, *37*, 495–502.

Chelazzi, L and Corbetta, M (2000). Cortical mechanisms of visuospatial attention in the human brain. In MS Gazzaniga (ed), *The New Cognitive Neurosciences* (pp. 667–686). Cambridge: MIT Press.

Clement, S, Demany, L and Semal, C (1999). Memory for pitch versus memory for loudness. *Journal of the Acoustical Society of America*, *106*, 2805–2811.

Constantinides, C and Steinmetz, MA (1996). Neuronal activity in posterior parietal area 7a during the delay periods of a spatial memory task. *Journal of Neurophysiology*, *76*, 1352.

Corbetta, M, Akbudak, E, Conturo, TE, Snyder, AZ, Ollinger, JM, Drury, HA *et al.* (1998). A common network of functional areas for attention and eye movements. *Neuron*, *21*(4), 761–773.

Corbetta, M, Kincade, JM and Shulman, GL (2002). Neural systems for visual orienting and their relationships to spatial working memory. *Journal of Cognitive Neuroscience*, *14*, 508–523.

Corkin, S (1965). Tactually-guided maze learning in man: Effects of unilateral cortical excisions and bilateral hippocampal lesions. *Neuropsychologia*, *3*, 339–351.

Courtney, SM (2004). Attention and cognitive control as emergent properties of information representation in working memory. *Cognitive, Affective and Behavioral Neuroscience*, *4*, 501–516.

Courtney, SM, Ungerleider, LG, Keil, K and Haxby, JV (1997). Transient and sustained activity in a distributed neural system for human working memory. *Nature*, *386*, 608–611.

Cowan, N (1995). *Attention and Memory: An Integrated Framework*. New York: Oxford University Press.

Curtis, CE and D'Esposito, M (2003). Persistent activity in the prefrontal cortex during working memory. *Trends in Cognitive Sciences*, *7*, 415–423.

Curtis, CE, Rao, VY and D'Esposito, M (2004). Maintenance of spatial and motor codes during oculomotor delayed response tasks. *The Journal of Neuroscience*, *24*, 3944–3952.

Deutsch, D (1972). Mapping of interactions in the pitch memory store. *Science*, *175*, 1020–1022.

Druzgal, TJ and D'Esposito, M (2003). Dissecting contributions of prefrontal cortex and fusiform face area to face working memory. *Journal of Cognitive Neuroscience*, *15*, 771–784.

Estes, WK (1955). Statistical theory of spontaneous recovery and regression. *Psychological Review*, *62*, 145–154.

Farmer, EW, Berman, JVF and Fletcher, YL (1986). Evidence for a visuo-spatial scratch-pad in working memory. *Quarterly Journal of Experimental Psychology*, *38A*, 675–688.

Fukushima, T, Hasegawa, I and Miyashita, Y (2004). Prefrontal neuronal activity encodes spatial target representations sequentially updated after nonspatial target-shift cues. *Journal of Neurophysiology*, *91*, 1367–1380.

Funahashi, S, Bruce, CJ and Goldman-Rakic, PS (1989). Mnemonic coding of visual space in the monkey's dorsolateral prefrontal cortex. *Journal of Neurophysiology*, *61*, 331–349.

Funahashi, S, Chafee, MV and Goldman-Rakic, PS (1993). Prefrontal neuronal activity in rhesus monkeys performing a delayed anti-saccade task. *Nature*, *365*, 753–756.

Fuster, JM (1973). Unit activity in prefrontal cortex during delayed-response performance: neuronal correlates of transient memory. *Journal of Neurophysiology*, *36*, 61–78.

Fuster, JM (1995). *Memory in the Cerebral Cortex*. Cambridge, MA: MIT Press.

Fuster, JM (2003). More than working memory rides on long-term memory. *Behavioral and Brain Sciences*, *26*, 737.

Fuster, JM and Alexander, GE (1971). Neuron activity related to short-term memory. *Science*, *173*, 652–654.

Gabrieli, JDE, Keane, MM, Stanger, BZ, Kjelgaard, MM, Corkin, S and Growdon, JH (1994). Dissociations among structural-perceptual, lexical-semantic and event-fact memory systems in amnesia, Alzheimer's disease, and normal subjects. *Cortex*, *30*, 75–103.

Glenberg, AM and Fernandez, A (1988). Evidence for auditory temporal distinctiveness: modality effects in order and frequency judgments. *Journal of Experimental Psychology: Learning, Memory, and Cognition*, *14*, 728–739.

Gnadt, JW and Andersen, RA (1988). Memory related motor planning activity in posterior parietal cortex of macaque. *Experimental Brain Research*, *70*, 216–220.

Gnadt, JW, Bracewell, RM and Andersen, RA (1991). Sensorimotor transformation during eye movements to remembered visual targets. *Vision Research, 4*, 693–715.

Goldberg, ME, Bisley, J, Powell, KD, Gottlieb, J and Kusunoki, M (2002). The role of the lateral intraparietal area of the monkey in the generation of saccades and visuospatial attention. *Annals of the New York Academy of Sciences, 956*, 205–215.

Goldman-Rakic, PS (1990). Cellular and circuit basis of working memory in prefrontal cortex of nonhuman primates. In HBM Uylings, CGV Eden, JPC DeBruin, MA Corner and MGP Feenstra (eds), *Progress in Brain Research*, Vol. 85 (pp. 325–336). Amsterdam: Elsevier Science Publishers.

Goodale, MA and Westwood, DA (2004). An evolving view of duplex vision: separate but interacting cortical pathways for perception and action. *Current Opinion in Neurobiology, 14*, 203–211.

Gruber, O and von Cramon, DY (2003). The functional neuroanatomy of human working memory revisited: Evidence from 3-T fMRI studies using classical domain-specific interference tasks. *NeuroImage, 19*, 797–809.

Hale, S, Myerson, J, Rhee, SH, Weiss, CS and Abrams, RA (1996). Selective interference with the maintenance of location information in working memory. *Neuropsychology, 10*, 228–240.

Hamker, FH (2005). The reentry hypothesis: The putative interaction of the frontal eye field, ventrolateral prefrontal cortex, and areas V4, IT for attention and eye movement. *Cerebral Cortex, 15*, 431–447.

Henson, RNA, Shallice, T, Gorno-Tempini, ML and Dolan, RJ (2002). Face repetition effects in implicit and explicit memory tests as measured by fMRI. *Cerebral Cortex, 12*, 178–186.

Hickock, G, Buchsbaum, B, Humphreys, C and Muftuler, T (2003). Auditory-motor interaction revealed by fMRI: speech, music, and working memory in area Spt. *Journal of Cognitive Neuroscience, 15*, 673–682.

Hoffman, JE and Subramaniam, B (1995). The role of visual attention in saccadic eye movements. *Perception and Psychophysics, 57*, 787–795.

Jha, A (2002). Tracking the time-course of attentional involvement in spatial working memory: an event-related potential investigation. *Cognitive Brain Research, 15*, 61–69.

Jonides, J, Lacey, SC and Nee, DE (2005). Processes of working memory in mind and brain. *Current Directions in Psychological Science, 14*, 2–5.

Kahana, MJ and Sekuler, R (2002). Recognizing spatial patterns: a noisy exemplar approach. *Vision Research, 42*, 2177–2192.

Karni, A, Meyer, G, Jezzard, P, Adams, MM, Turner, R and Ungerleider, LG (1995). Functional MRI evidence for adult motor cortex plasticity during motor skill learning. *Nature, 377*, 155–158.

Keane, MM, Gabrieli, JDE, Fennema, AC, Growdon, JH and Corkin, S (1991). Evidence for a dissociation between perceptual and conceptual priming in Alzheimer's disease. *Behavioral Neuroscience, 105*, 326–342.

LaBar, KS, Gitelman, DR, Parrish, TB and Mesulam, M (1999). Neuroanatomic overlap of working memory and spatial attention networks: a functional MRI comparison within subjects. *NeuroImage, 10*, 695–704.

Lawrence, BM, Myerson, J, Oonk, HM and Abrams, RA (2001). The effects of eye and limb movements on working memory. *Memory, 9*, 433–444.

Lebedev, MA, Messinger, A, Kralik, JD and Wise, SP (2004). Representation of attended versus remembered locations in prefrontal cortex. *PloS Biology, 2*, 1919–1935.

Logie, RH (1995). *Visuo-Spatial Working Memory*. Hove: Erlbaum.

Logie, RH and Marchetti, C (1991). Visuo-spatial working memory: visual, spatial or central executive? In RH Logie and M Denis (eds), *Mental Images in Human Cognition* (pp. 105–115). Amsterdam: Elsevier.

Magnussen, S (2000). Low-level memory processes in the brain. *Trends in Neurosciences, 23*, 247–251.

Magnussen, S and Greenlee, MW (1999). The psychophysics of perceptual memory. *Psychological Research, 62*, 81–92.

Magnussen, S, Greenlee, MW, Asplund, R and Dyrnes, S (1991). Stimulus specific mechanisms of visual short-term memory. *Vision Research, 31*, 1213–1219.

Manoach, DS, White, NS, Lindgren, KA, Heckers, S, Coleman, MJ, Dubal, S *et al.* (2004). Hemispheric specialization of the lateral prefrontal cortex for strategic processing during spatial and shape working memory. *NeuroImage, 21*, 894–903.

Melton, AW and Martin, E (eds) (1972). *Coding Processes in Human Memory*. Washington, DC: V.H. Winston and Sons.

Miller, EK, Erickson, CA and Desimone, R (1996). Neural mechanisms of visual working memory in prefrontal cortex of the Macaque. *Journal of Neuroscience, 16*, 5154–5167.

Miller, EK, Li, L and Desimone, R (1991). A neural mechanism for working and recognition memory in inferior temporal cortex. *Science, 254*, 1377–1379.

Milner, B (1962). Les troubles de la memoire accompagnant des lesions hippocampiques bilaterales. In P Passouant (ed), *Physiologie de l'Hippocampe* (pp. 257–272). Paris: Centre National de la Recherche Scientific.

Milner, B, Corkin, S and Teuber, H-L (1968). Further analysis of the hippocampal amnesic syndrome: 14 year follow-up study of H.M. *Neuropsychologia, 6*, 215–234.

Moore, T and Fallah, M (2004). Microstimulation of the frontal eye field and its effects on covert attention. *Journal of Neurophysiology, 91*, 152–162.

Nakamura, K and Kubota, K (1995). Mnemonic firing of neurons in the monkey temporal pole during a visual recognition memory task. *Journal of Neurophysiology, 74*, 162–178.

Nystrom, LE, Braver, TS, Sabb, FW, Delgado, MR, Noll, DC and Cohen, JD (2000). Working memory for letters, shapes and locations: fMRI evidence against stimulus-based regional organization of human prefrontal cortex. *NeuroImage, 11*, 424–446.

O'Connor, N and Hermelin, B (1972). Seeing and hearing in space and time. *Perception and Psychophysics, 11*, 46–48.

O'Connor, N and Hermelin, BM (1973). The spatial or temporal organization of short-term memory. *Quarterly Journal of Experimental Psychology, 25*, 335–343.

Oberauer, K (2002). Access to information in working memory: exploring the focus of attention. *Journal of Experimental Psychology: Learning, Memory, and Cognition, 28*, 411–421.

Page, MPA and Norris, D (1998). The primacy model: A new model of immediate serial recall. *Psychological Review, 105*, 761–781.

Passingham, D and Sakai, K (2004). The prefrontal cortex and working memory: physiology and brain imaging. *Current Opinion in Neurobiology, 14*, 163–168.

Pasternak, T and Greenlee, MW (2005). Working memory in primate sensory systems. *Nature Reviews Neuroscience, 6*, 96–106.

Paulesu, E, Frith, CD and Frackowiak, RSJ (1993). The neural correlates of the verbal component of working memory. *Nature, 362*, 342–345.

Pearson, DG and Sahraie, A (2003). Oculomotor control and the maintenance of spatially and temporally distributed events in visuo-spatial working memory. *Quarterly Journal of Experimental Psychology, 56A*, 1089–1111.

Petrides, M (2000). Dissociable roles of mid-dorsolateral prefrontal and anterior inferotemporal cortex in visual working memory. *Journal of Neuroscience, 20*, 7496–7503.

Postle, BR (2003). Context in verbal short-term memory. *Memory and Cognition, 31*, 1198–1207.

Postle, BR (2006). Working memory as an emergent property of the mind and brain. *Neuroscience, 139*, 23–38.

Postle, BR, Awh, E, Jonides, J, Smith, EE and D'Esposito, M (2004). The where and how of attention-based rehearsal in spatial working memory. *Cognitive Brain Research, 20*, 194–205.

Postle, BR, Berger, JS and D'Esposito, M (1999). Functional neuroanatomical double dissociation of mnemonic and executive control processes contributing to working memory performance. *Proceedings of the National Academy of Sciences (USA), 96*, 12959–12964.

Postle, BR and Corkin, S (1998). Impaired word-stem completion priming but intact perceptual identification priming with novel words: evidence from the amnesic patient H.M. *Neuropsychologia, 36*, 421–440.

Postle, BR and Corkin, S (1999). Manipulation of familiarity reveals a necessary lexical component of the word-stem completion priming effect. *Memory and Cognition, 27*, 12–25.

Postle, BR and D'Esposito, M (1999). 'What' – then – 'where' in visual working memory: an event-related fMRI study. *Journal of Cognitive Neuroscience, 11*, 585–597.

Postle, BR and D'Esposito, M (2003). Spatial working memory activity of the caudate nucleus is sensitive to frame of reference. *Cognitive, Affective, and Behavioral Neuroscience, 3*, 133–144.

Postle, BR, D'Esposito, M and Corkin, S (2005). Effects of verbal and nonverbal interference on spatial and object visual working memory. *Memory and Cognition.*

Postle, BR, Druzgal, TJ and D'Esposito, M (2003). Seeking the neural substrates of working memory storage. *Cortex, 39*, 927–946.

Postle, BR, Idzikowski, C, Della Salla, S, Logie, RH and Baddeley, AD (2006). The selective disruption of spatial working memory by eye movements. *Quarterly Journal of Experimental Psychology, 59*, 100–120.

Postle, BR, Stern, CE, Rosen, BR and Corkin, S (2000). An fMRI investigation of cortical contributions to spatial and nonspatial visual working memory. *NeuroImage, 11*, 409–423.

Quinn, JG and Ralston, GE (1986). Movement and attention in visual working memory. *Quarterly Journal of Experimental Psychology, 38A*, 689–703.

Quintana, J and Fuster, JM (1992). Mnemonic and predictive functions of cortical neurons in a memory task. *NeuroReport, 3*, 721–724.

Rama, P, Poremba, A, Sala, JB, Yee, L, Malloy, M, Mishkin, M *et al.* (2004). Dissociable functional cortical topographies for working memory maintenance of voice identity and location. *Cerebral Cortex, 14*, 768–780.

Rama, P, Sala, JB, Gillen, JS, Pek, JJ and Courtney, SM (2001). Dissociation of the neural systems for working memory maintenance of verbal and nonverbal visual information. *Cognitive, Affective, and Behavioral Neuroscience, 1*, 161–171.

Ranganath, C, Cohen, MX, Dam, C and D'Esposito, M (2004). Inferior temporal, prefrontal, and hippocampal contributions to visual working memory maintenance and associative memory recall. *The Journal of Neuroscience, 24*, 3917–3925.

Ranganath, C, DeGutis, J and D'Esposito, M (2004). Category-specific modulation of inferior temporal activity during working memory encoding and maintenance. *Cognitive Brain Research, 20*, 37–45.

Rao, SC, Rainer, G and Miller, EK (1997). Integration of what and where in the primate prefrontal cortex. *Science, 276*, 821–824.

Roediger, HL III (1990). Implicit memory. *American Psychologist, 45*, 1043–1056.

Romo, R and Salinas, E (2003). Flutter discrimination: neural codes, perception, memory and decision making. *Nature Reviews Neuroscience, 4*, 203–218.

Rose, J and Colombo, M (2005). Neural correlates of executive control in the avian brain. *PLoS Biology, 3*, 1139–1146.

Ruchkin, DS, Grafman, J, Cameron, K and Berndt, RS (2003). Working memory retention systems: a state of activated long-term memory. *Behavioral and Brain Sciences, 26*, 709–777.

Rypma, B and D'Esposito, M (1999). The roles of prefrontal brain regions in components of working memory: effects of memory load and individual differences. *Proceedings of the National Academy of Sciences (USA), 96*, 6558–6563.

Sala, JB, Rama, P and Courtney, SM (2003). Functional topography of a distributed neural system for spatial and nonspatial information maintenance in working memory. *Neuropsychologia, 41*, 341–356.

Salway, AFS and Logie, RH (1995). Visuospatial working memory, movement control and executive demands. *British Journal of Psychology, 86*, 253–269.

Schacter, DL (1990). Perceptual representation systems and implicit memory: Toward a resolution of the multiple memory systems debate. In A Diamond (ed), *Development and Neural Bases of Higher Cognitive Function* (pp. 543–571). New York: New York Academy of Sciences.

Schacter, DL (1994). Priming and multiple memory systems: perceptual mechanisms of implicit memory. In DL Schacter and E Tulving (eds), *Memory Systems 1994* (pp. 233–268). Cambridge, MA: MIT Press.

Simons, DJ (1996). In sight, out of mind: when object representations fail. *Psychological Science, 7*, 301–305.

Slotnick, SD (2005). Visual memory and visual perception recruit common neural substrates. *Behavioral and Cognitive Neuroscience Reviews, 3*, 207–221.

Smith, EE and Jonides, J (1999). Storage and executive processes of the frontal lobes. *Science*, *283*, 1657–1661.

Smyth, MM, Pearson, NA and Pendleton, LR (1988). Movement and working memory: patterns and positions in space. *Quarterly Journal of Experimental Psychology*, *40A*, 497–514.

Squire, LR (1987). *Memory and Brain*. New York: Oxford University Press.

Squire, LR (1992). Declarative and nondeclarative memory: multiple brain systems supporting learning and memory. *Journal of Cognitive Neuroscience*, *4*, 232–243.

Stoeckel, MC, Pollok, B, Schnitzler, A, Witte, OW and Seitz, RJ (2004). Use-dependent cortical plasticity in thalidomide-induced upper extremity dysplasia: evidence from somaesthesia and neuroimaging. *Experimental Brain Research*, *156*, 333–341.

Suzuki, WA, Miller, EK and Desimone, R (1997). Object and place memory in the macaque entorhinal cortex. *Journal of Neurophysiology*, *78*, 1062–1081.

Takeda, K and Funahashi, S (2002). Prefrontal task-related activity representing visual cue location or saccade direction in spatial working memory tasks. *Journal of Neurophysiology*, *87*, 567–588.

Takeda, K and Funahashi, S (2004). Population vector analysis of primate prefrontal activity during spatial working memory. *Cerebral Cortex*, *14*, 1328–1339.

Theeuwes, J, Olivers, CNL and Chizk, CL (2005). Remembering a location makes the eyes curve away. *Psychological Science*, *16*, 196–199.

Todd, JJ and Marois, R (2004). Capacity limit of visual short-term memory in human posterior parietal cortex. *Nature*, *428*, 751–754.

Todd, JJ and Marois, R (2005). Posterior parietal cortex activity predicts individual differences in visual short-term memory capacity. *Cognitive, Affective, and Behavioral Neuroscience*, *5*, 144–155.

Vogel, EK and Machizawa, MG (2004). Neural activity predicts individual differences in visual working memory capacity. *Nature*, *428*, 748–751.

Warrington, EK and Weiskrantz, L (1968). A new method of testing long-term retention with special reference to amnesic patients. *Nature*, *217*, 972–974.

Wickens, DD (1972). Characteristics of word encoding. In AW Melton and E Martin (eds), *Coding Processes in Human Memory* (pp. 191–215). Washington, DC: VH Winston and Sons.

Wickens, DD (1973). Some characteristics of word encoding. *Memory and Cognition*, *1*, 485–490.

Wilson, FAW, O'Scalaidhe, SP and Goldman-Rakic, PS (1993). Dissociation of object and spatial processing domains in primate prefrontal cortex. *Science*, *260*, 1955–1958.

Winston, JS, Henson, RN, Fine-Goulden, MR and Dolan, RJ (2004). fMRI-adaptation reveals dissociable neural representations of identity and expression in face perception. *Journal of Neurophysiology*, *92*, 1830–1839.

Yantis, S, Schwarzbach, J, Serences, JT, Carlson, RL, Steinmetz, MA, Pekar, JJ *et al.* (2002). Transient neural activity in human parietal cortex during spatial attention shifts. *Nature Neuroscience*.

Yi, D-J and Chun, MM (2005). Attentional modulation of learning-related repetition attenuation effects in human parahippocampal cortex. *The Journal of Neuroscience*, *25*.

Zarahn, E, Aguirre, GK and D'Esposito, M (1997). A trial-based experimental design for fMRI. *NeuroImage*, *6*, 122–138.

Zhou, YD and Fuster, JM (1996). Mnemonic neuronal activity in somatosensory cortex. *Proceedings of the National Academy of Sciences (USA)*, *93*, 10533–10537.

20

Activation, binding, and selective access
An embedded three-component framework for working memory

Klaus Oberauer

Suppose you want to add two three-digit numbers without paper and pencil. The task requires holding the digits that form the two numbers, and those building the result, available for cognitive processing. This cognitive function is typically attributed to working memory (Miyake and Shah 1999; Baddeley 1986; Cowan 1995), a system devoted to keeping selected representations available for goal-directed cognitive processes. More is involved, however, in accomplishing the addition than just remembering which digits the numbers were composed of. The digits must be linked to their roles in the equation to make sure that the ones of a number are not confused with the tens, and the result is not confused with one of the addends. Working memory can do this by establishing temporary *bindings* between individual digits and their places in a context representation, for instance by using a representation of two-dimensional space in which the digits are arranged as they would be when solving the problem on paper (Oberauer, Süß, Wilhelm, and Sander, 2007). Furthermore, working memory must select at any moment the subset of digits that are actually involved in the upcoming operation. For instance, the first step of the addition problem is adding the ones of the two numbers, so only these two digits must be selected for cognitive action, while the other four must be maintained but must not intrude into the current addition operation. This requirement points to the need for a focus of attention in working memory that provides *selective access* to the representations currently needed as input for an operation.

I have developed a framework for the architecture of working memory that highlights the three cognitive functions introduced above: short-term maintenance, temporary binding, and selective access (Oberauer 2002; Oberauer *et al.* 2007). The framework builds on the theory of Cowan (1995, 1999) and Halford (Halford, Wilson, and Phillips 1998), and on the work of Garavan (1998) and McElree (2001). I assume that the working memory system consists of three embedded components, the *activated part of long-term memory* (LTM), the *region of direct access* and the *focus of attention* (see Figure 20.1). The three components should not be thought of as separate subsystems, but as functionally distinct states of representations as they become selected for processing through three levels.

The first level of selection is activating a representation in LTM above baseline, either through perceptual input or through spread of activation from other representations. The set of representations activated above baseline forms the most comprehensive component of working memory, the activated part of LTM. Since activation is graded, this set has fuzzy boundaries – many representations are activated only slightly above baseline, and it is not possible to draw a sharp line between representations that are 'in' this component of working memory and representations that are 'outside'. The main consequence of activating a representation is that it is easier to retrieve (Anderson and Lebiere 1998).

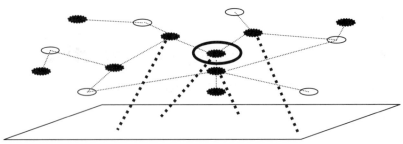

Figure 20.1 Graphical representation of the three-layer model. The small circles represent representational elements in long-term memory, linked by associations (continuous lines); the activated part of long-term memory is designated by the filled circles. A subset of the activated elements is bound to a cognitive coordinate system, sketched as a rectangular frame; the bindings are represented by broken lines. This subset of elements constitutes the direct-access region. One of the items in the direct-access region is held in the focus of attention, denoted by the thick oval. From Oberauer (2006). Is the focus of attention in working memory expanded through practice? *Journal of Experimental Psychology: Learning, Memory and Cognition, 32*, 197–214. © 2006 American Psychological Association, reprinted with permission.

Retrieving a representation means taking it into the second component of working memory, the *region of direct access*. It constitutes the second level of selection. The direct-access region consists of a small number of the activated representations which are temporarily bound to positions in a cognitive coordinate system. A cognitive coordinate system is a context representation to which content representations can be bound. The context can be a representation of space or time, such that content elements (e.g., words, letters, objects, events, faces) can be bound to positions in the represented space, or to positions on a time axis (e.g., Burgess and Hitch 1999). A coordinate system can also be a hierarchical schema that specifies roles to be filled by content elements, for instance syntactical schemas with roles for words and phrases. Elements in the region of direct access can be accessed directly through their bindings to positions or roles in a coordinate system. For instance, the cognitive system can access the ones in a multi-digit computation by focusing on the right-most positions in mental space.

Accessing an element means bringing it into the focus of attention. This constitutes the third level of selection. The focus of attention holds the representations needed as input for the upcoming cognitive operation. It is necessary to ensure selectivity of processing in tasks that require holding several similar elements in the direct-access region, and using only a subset of them for each computational step, as in the example of multi-digit computation. The focus accesses elements in the direct-access region through their positions in the cognitive coordinate system. The contents of the direct-access region therefore form the set of candidates for selection by the focus. If representations in activated LTM need to be focused on, they must first be retrieved into the direct-access region.

Working memory is a capacity-limited system: the amount of information we can hold in it at any time is limited. In my framework there are several reasons for this limitation. One is retrieval competition between activated representations in LTM, as known from classical interference theory. There is no limit to the amount of activation to be distributed among representations in LTM – in this regard my framework differs from models such as CAPS (Just and Carpenter 1992) and ACT-R (Anderson, Reder and Lebiere 1996) – but activating too many representations can be as detrimental to efficiently retrieving the relevant information as activating too few of them, because activated representations compete for retrieval. Inhibiting representations in LTM can therefore be advantageous (Anderson and Spellman 1995), and one source of individual differences in tasks with high working memory involvement could be the efficiency of inhibiting irrelevant information in LTM (Hasher, Zacks and May 1999; De Beni, Palladino, Pazzaglia *et al.* 1998). The ability to selectively inhibit activated but irrelevant representations in LTM is most relevant to tasks that require retrieval from LTM, such as across-sentence integration in reading.

A second factor relevant for the capacity of working memory is a limit to the number of independent bindings that can be held in the direct-access region. It limits the complexity of structural representations that can be set up in working memory and therefore is most relevant to reasoning tasks that require complex representations (Oberauer *et al.* 2007). A third limiting factor arises from the competition between elements in the direct-access region for entering the focus of attention. With more candidates in the direct-access region, selective access is slowed down. This limitation is most relevant to tasks that require quick and flexible access to individual elements in working memory for cognitive processing, such as speeded short-term retrieval tasks.

In this chapter I will summarize evidence from four sets of studies to support the framework. The first set demonstrates the usefulness of the distinction between activated LTM and the direct-access region. The second set provides evidence for all three components simultaneously. The third set of experiments shows that people can flexibly move information into and out of the direct-access region depending on whether they need to access that information. Finally, the fourth set of studies serves to link the focus of attention in working memory to the concept of a processing bottleneck (Pashler 1994).

Activation and binding in short-term recognition

Activation of a representation in LTM and binding of a representation to a context in the direct-access region play different roles in short-term recognition tasks. These roles can be mapped to the two processes assumed in dual-process theories of recognition (Atkinson, Herrmann and Wescourt 1974; Yonelinas 2002). One process, assumed to be fast and automatic, is the assessment of the familiarity of a probe (i.e., a stimulus to be judged as old or new). The other process, assumed to be slower and controlled, consists of recollecting information about previous encounters with the probe. I assume that familiarity assessment is based on a measurement of how quickly and fluently the probe is processed. In short-term recognition tasks, where only a few seconds separate encoding and probing of a stimulus, processing fluency is largely determined by the current level of activation of a representation of the probe in LTM. In recognition over longer time intervals familiarity is most likely driven by the strength of associations between features of the probe, so-called intra-item associations (Mandler 1980). Recollection involves retrieving that the probe has been encountered before in the relevant context – for instance, retrieving that a word has been on the last list studied (as opposed to a previous list, or in a book read before the experiment). Recollection therefore rests on retrieving a link between the content of the probe stimulus and the context of its previous encounter (if there was one), or on retrieving that there was no such element in the relevant context (if there was none). In short-term recognition tasks, I assume that this information is mostly provided by the temporary bindings between content elements and context representations in the direct-access region.

Familiarity and recollection can be separated by conflict recognition tasks (e.g., Jennings and Jacoby 1997). These are paradigms in which, for a subset of probes, familiarity and recollection support conflicting recognition decisions. An example is the modified Sternberg task (Oberauer 2001), illustrated in Figure 20.2. Participants try to remember two short lists of words, after which they receive a cue telling them which of the two lists is relevant for the upcoming recognition decision.

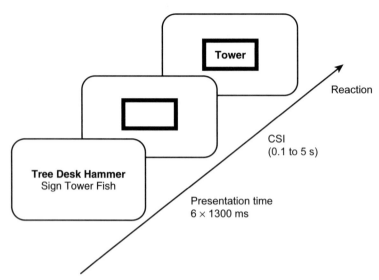

Figure 20.2 Sequence of events in a trial of the modified Sternberg task (Oberauer 2001). Two lists of words are presented simultaneously as two lines, one in blue and one in red (illustrated here through different fonts). This is followed by a frame colored red or blue, indicating which list is relevant for this trial. After a variable cue-stimulus interval (CSI), the probe appears, and reaction time is measured until the participant decides through a key-press whether the probe was in the relevant list. The example shows an intrusion trial.

After a variable cue-stimulus interval (CSI), a probe appears and participants decide whether it had been in the relevant list. Probes that had been in the irrelevant list (but not in the relevant list) are assessed as highly familiar because, up to the time where the cue is displayed, their representations are activated in LTM just as much as those of the relevant list. Recollection, however, can provide information about which list the probe was in, which eventually leads to correct rejection of these so-called *intrusion probes*. This requires that at least the relevant list is held in the region of direct access.

In an experiment involving young and old adults I investigated the time course of removing the irrelevant list from working memory (Oberauer 2001). The CSI was varied in six steps from 100 ms to 5 s. With increasing CSI, participants have more time to remove the irrelevant list from the direct-access region, thereby taking this load off the limited capacity to maintain bindings, and reducing the competition for access to elements in the relevant list. In addition, the activation of irrelevant-list items in LTM can decline over the CSI, either through passive decay or active inhibition. It turned out that both young and old adults were very efficient in removing the irrelevant list from the direct-access region. After about 1 s after the cue, there was no effect of list-length of the irrelevant list on reaction times to the probe. This indicates that elements from the irrelevant list no longer burdened the limited capacity of the direct-access region. There was no significant age difference in the speed of reducing the list-length effect of the irrelevant list to zero in that study, but later investigations with the same paradigm suggested that old adults might be somewhat less effective in this regard (Oberauer 2005b). Reducing the activation of irrelevant-list representations in LTM, in contrast, was much slower. Even after 5 s, participants had considerably more difficulties with rejecting intrusion probes than with rejecting new probes that were not part of any list, demonstrating a persistent conflict between familiarity and recollection. Moreover, these difficulties were disproportionally increased in old compared to young adults. These results are displayed in Figure 20.3.

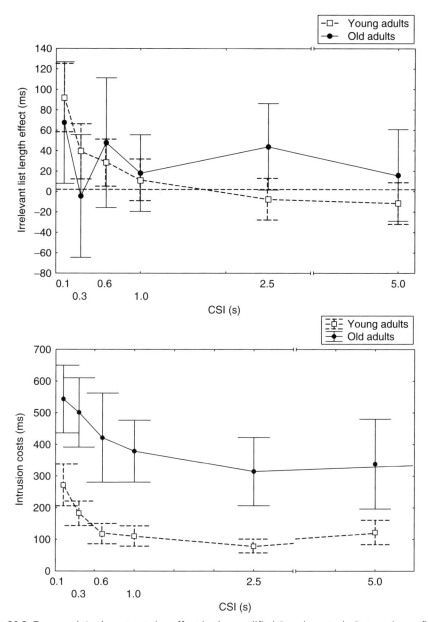

Figure 20.3 Top panel: Irrelevant-set size effect in the modified Sternberg task. Data points reflect differences between RTs on trials with irrelevant-set size 3 and trials with irrelevant-set size 1. Bottom panel: Intrusion costs in the modified Sternberg task. Data points represent differences between RTs on intrusion trials and RTs on negative trials (Oberauer 2001). Error bars reflect two standard errors (i.e., approximately 95 per cent confidence intervals).

Age differences in the difficulty of rejecting intrusion probes could arise from two sources. Old adults could have more difficulties with inhibiting irrelevant representations in LTM (Hasher *et al.* 1999). Alternatively, old adults could have problems with maintaining robust content–context bindings in the direct-access region. This deficit would compromise their recollection, leaving the misleading familiarity of intrusion probes more time to build up and influence recognition decisions.

A recent follow-up study aimed at distinguishing these possibilities (Oberauer, 2005b). I tested young and old adults with three conflict recognition tasks, the modified Sternberg task, an n-back task (Kirchner 1958), and a local recognition task. The n-back task required participants to compare each word in a 20-word sequence to the word n steps back, with n varying between one and three. The local recognition task required them to remember a list of items, each item being displayed in a separate frame. Probes were displayed in the frames and had to be compared to the list items in these frames (see Figure 20.4). In both tasks, intrusion probes were included. In the n-back task, intrusion probes were words that matched a previous word less than n steps back. These words can be assumed to be highly activated and therefore highly familiar, but they must be rejected on the basis of recollecting their ordinal position on a temporal context vector (e.g., remembering that the present word had occurred one step before instead of two). In the local recognition task, intrusion probes were probes that had been in the memory list but in a different frame. Again, these probes match a highly activated representation but must be rejected through recollection, based on the bindings between list items and their frames (i.e., their positions in a spatial coordinate system).

An important feature of the n-back task and the local recognition task that sets them apart from the modified Sternberg task is that the representations generating the familiarity signal on intrusion probes must not be inhibited, because they are not permanently irrelevant. Words less than n steps back become relevant once they are n steps back. Words that had been presented in a different frame from the one currently probed in the local recognition task will become relevant when that

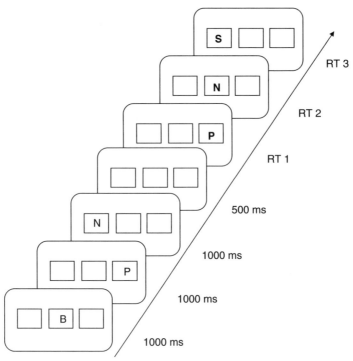

Figure 20.4 Sequence of events in a trial of the local recognition task with set size 3. Three letters are presented sequentially, each in one frame, for 1000 ms each. After a 500 ms blank, three probes appear in red (represented by bold letters). In the example, the first probe is a positive probe, the second an intrusion probe, and the third is a negative probe.

frame is probed later. If old adults are at a disadvantage in the modified Sternberg task because of an inhibition deficit, they should not be particularly impaired relative to young adults on these other conflict recognition task, because young adults could not benefit on these tasks from their more efficient inhibition mechanisms. If old adults' problems with the modified Sternberg task arise from deficits in recollection, in contrast, they should show the same problems with the other two conflict recognition tasks, too. The latter was the case: in all three conflict recognition tasks, old adults' reaction times on intrusion probes were disproportionally slowed compared to young adults'. The impairment of old adults' performance on conflict recognition tasks therefore seems to arise from a reduced capacity of the direct-access region to maintain robust content–context bindings, not from a deficit in actively reducing the activation of irrelevant representations in LTM.

I further investigated individual differences in familiarity assessment and recollection in the young group (Oberauer, 2005b). A structural-equation model analysis showed that performance in conflict recognition tasks can be decomposed into two sources of variance, one reflecting familiarity and the other reflecting recollection. The recollection factor but not the familiarity factor was correlated with a latent factor representing working memory capacity, as assessed by four established measures of that construct. This finding supports the hypothesis that working memory capacity, as reflected in performance on tasks such as reading span (Daneman and Carpenter 1980), is essentially the capacity to hold bindings in the region of direct access (Oberauer *et al.* 2007).

Observing all three components in action

My main empirical reason for distinguishing between the direct-access region and the activated part of LTM arises from findings concerning list-length effects on reaction times. An increase of reaction times with the length of the list to be held in working memory is a common finding, the most famous example being the linear slope of RTs over list length in the Sternberg (1969) task that I exploited in the first study reviewed here. List length, however, does not always affect RTs. Results from several studies support the generalization that RTs increase with list length if and only if the RT task requires access to information from the list in working memory (Kessler and Meiran 2006; Oberauer, Demmrich, Mayr *et al.* 2001; Oberauer 2002, 2005a). This can be illustrated by an experiment using an arithmetic task (Oberauer 2002, Experiment 2). In each trial participants had to remember two short lists of digits; each list could consist of one or of three digits. Each digit was presented in a separate frame. Following encoding, a cue indicated which of the two lists would be the 'active' list. After a variable CSI, a series of arithmetic operations had to be completed, using digits from the active list as input. Stimuli for these processing tasks were operation instructions such as '+ 2' or '– 6' displayed in individual frames of the active list. Participants had to retrieve the digit that had been presented in the appropriate frame, apply the operation to it, and type the result as quickly as possible. During the whole series of eight arithmetic operations they had to remember not only the digits in the active list but also the digits in the other, passive list, because at the end of the trial they had to recall the digits of both lists (see Figure 20.5). Participants were able to recall both lists reasonably well, so both lists must be assumed to be held in working memory (on successful trials). The important finding was that the length of the active list always had an effect on the latency of individual arithmetic operations. The length of the passive list, however, only affected the first operation in the series, and only on short CSIs. In other words, after about three seconds following the cue, there was no list-length effect of the passive list on arithmetic processing times (see Figure 20.6).

The three-component framework offers a straightforward explanation for this observation: because the processing task requires access to memory elements on the active list, that the list

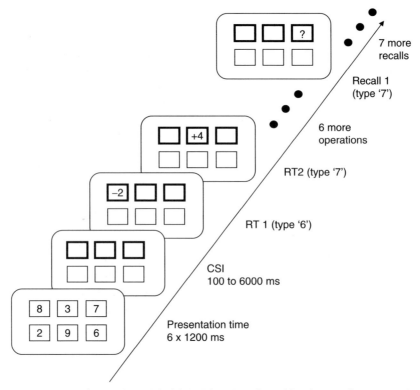

Figure 20.5 Sequence of events in a trial of the arithmetic task used in Oberauer (2002, Experiment 2). After initial encoding of two lists – here both with set size 3 – a cue indicated which list would be the active one (red frames, here marked by thick lines). Eight arithmetic operations were performed on digits of the active list. The second operation in the example represents an object switch. At the end, the digits in each frame are probed for recall.

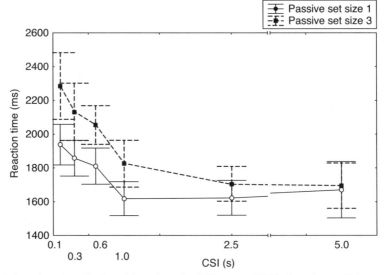

Figure 20.6 Reaction times in the arithmetic task of Oberauer (2002, Experiment 2) by set size of the passive set, for the first operation in the sequence. Error bars represent 95 per cent confidence intervals for within-subject comparisons (Bakeman and McArthur 1996).

must be held in the direct-access region. A longer list in the direct-access region places a larger burden on the limited capacity for maintaining bindings, so that the bindings are less robust for each element, and this slows down access to each element. In addition, with longer lists more elements compete for access into the focus of attention, and this competition slows down processing. The passive list, however, does not have to be accessed throughout the series of eight arithmetic tasks, so participants can remove it from the direct-access region and maintain it in activated LTM. At final recall, they can retrieve it from LTM back into the direct-access region. One consequence of this explanation is that recall should take longer for elements from the passive list than for elements from the active list. This prediction was confirmed.

The distinct behavior of active and passive lists can be explained by a framework that distinguishes only two components in working memory, such as that proposed by Cowan (1995, 1999). In his conceptualization, working memory consists of the activated part of LTM and a more central component called the focus of attention. This component, however, is more akin to the direct-access region in my framework, in that it has a capacity limit of up to four elements. Using this model, one could argue that the passive list is held in activated LTM and the active list is held in the four-item focus. This account, however, is not sufficient to explain a further finding of my experiment. In trials where the active list contained three digits, over the series of eight arithmetic operations some operations required access to the same digit as the previous operation, whereas others required switching to a new digit in the active list. Reaction times were several hundred ms longer following a switch than following repeated access to the same digit. This effect, which I call *object-switch cost*, was first described by Garavan (1998), who interpreted it as evidence for a focus of attention that selects one element in working memory. When an operation requires access to another element than the previous operation, the focus needs to select a new element, and this takes time. The observation of object-switch costs within the active list is strong evidence for a further, more narrow focus of attention operating within the component that Cowan describes as the four-item focus (i.e., the direct-access region in my framework).

An assumption in the three-component framework is that the focus of attention serves to select one element for processing among the elements currently held in the direct-access region. This implies that the difficulty of selecting a new element should depend on the content of the direct-access region (e.g., the number of elements, their discriminability and the robustness of their bindings to context representations), but not on the content of the activated part of LTM. Consistent with this, object-switch costs increased with the number of elements in active lists (Oberauer 2002, 2003; Oberauer, Wendland and Kliegl 2003), but not with the number of elements in passive lists (Oberauer 2002).

Moving out and moving in again: flexible access to working memory contents

The experiments with the modified Sternberg task have shown that people can remove an irrelevant list from the direct-access region within one second. The experiments with the arithmetic task have shown that within two to three seconds, people can also remove a passive list from the direct-access region. One difference between these two experiments is that a passive list is not permanently irrelevant – it has to be recalled at the end of the trial. This implies that the passive list must be encoded into LTM in a way that permits recall, not just an assessment of familiarity based on activation. Recall of elements from the passive list in the experiments reported in Oberauer (2002) was probed by question marks in the frames of the passive list. This means that participants must have encoded in LTM not only which digits were in the passive list but also which digit was in which frame. Possibly they have built associations in LTM between digits and their spatial positions on the screen (an alternative account requiring no association learning is that they encoded the serial order of three-digit passive lists by setting up a gradient of activation, cf. Page and Norris [1998]). These results suggest that the activated part of LTM can be used as a back-up maintenance mechanism for holding short lists of elements and their serial order over several seconds for later recall.

I carried out two experiments to investigate the flexibility with which working memory can remove information that is temporarily irrelevant for processing from the direct-access region, maintain it in activated LTM, and retrieve it back into the direct-access region later when it needs to be processed (Oberauer 2005a). One experiment used the modified Sternberg paradigm, the other the arithmetic paradigm described above. Both paradigms were modified in the following way: after encoding two lists of items (words in the case of the modified Sternberg task, digits in the case of the arithmetic task), participants performed two consecutive speeded processing operations (a recognition decision in the modified Sternberg task, an arithmetic computation in the arithmetic task). Each operation was preceded by a cue indicating which list would be relevant for the operation. In half of the trials, the second cue referred to the same list as the first cue, and in the other half the second cue required a switch to the other list. A CSI of 100 ms or 2 s followed each cue. The CSIs preceding the two operations were varied independently, yielding four combinations of CSI 1 and CSI 2. In addition, the list lengths of the two lists were varied independently, as in the previous experiments, to allow separate assessments of list-length effects for the currently relevant and the currently irrelevant list.

If the working memory system can flexibly remove a temporarily irrelevant list from the direct-access region and retrieve it back when needed, we should expect to see the following pattern: at short CSIs, there should be list-length effects for both lists at both the first and the second operation. At long CSIs, the list length effects of the currently irrelevant lists should have disappeared, while those of the currently relevant list persist. This should be the case regardless of whether or not the second cue enforced a switch to the other list. This pattern is exactly what was found in both tasks when young adults were tested. Old adults showed the same pattern with the arithmetic task, but were not entirely successful in removing the currently irrelevant list from the direct-access region in the modified Sternberg task (illustrative data from the arithmetic task are shown in Figure 20.7).

A second interesting finding from that study concerns the time for switching between lists. When the second cue demanded a switch to the previously irrelevant list, responses to the second operation took longer than when the same list was used again. The costs for switching between lists increased with the length of the list that became irrelevant for the second operation but was independent of the length of the list that became relevant. In other words, list-switch costs were a function of the length of the list to be removed from the direct-access region, but were not affected by the length of the list that had to be retrieved back from activated LTM. The latter matches previous findings with variants of the Sternberg task: the time for retrieving a list from LTM does not depend on the length of that list (Conway and Engle 1994; Wickens, Moody and Dow 1981). The finding that list-switch costs are independent of the length of the list switched to therefore supports the view that this list is retrieved from LTM. It suggests that the list is represented in activated LTM as a unitary chunk. The finding that list-switch costs increase with the length of the list switched away from, on the other hand, seems to suggest that active suppression is involved in removing a list from the direct-access region, with longer lists requiring more work to get rid of. This is not a necessary conclusion, however. An alternative is that bindings in the direct-access region decay quickly when they are no longer actively maintained, so that items no longer relevant can drop out passively. If we assume that items on a list don't drop out at the same rate, then the time until the last item from a three-item list has dropped out is, on average, longer than the time it takes

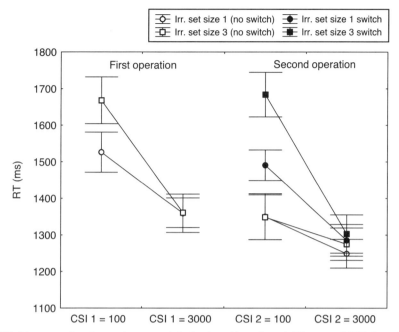

Figure 20.7 Mean reaction times of young adults in the arithmetic task (Oberauer 2005, Experiment 2), for first and second operation, broken down by irrelevant set size, CSI preceding the operation, and list switch condition (for second operation). Error bars represent 95 per cent confidence intervals for within-subject comparisons (Bakeman and McArthur 1996).

the item from a one-item list to drop out. Reaction times on the second operation following a list switch would then suffer from competition from irrelevant items longer when the previously relevant list was a long one than when it was a short one. This could explain the increase of list-switch costs with the length of the previously relevant list.

In any case, these two experiments demonstrate that the working memory system is surprisingly flexible in moving information in and out of the capacity-limited region of direct access. It seems to take something between one and three seconds to encode a short list into activated LTM so that it does no longer interfere with ongoing processes, and still can be retrieved later when it is needed as input for further processes. There seems to be little, if any, impairment of this flexibility in older age.

The focus of attention as entry gate to the processing bottleneck

Whereas research on working memory has largely been concerned with capacity limits on short-term maintenance and on executive control, research on attention and action has been interested more in constraints on basic cognitive processes. Strong evidence from the latter tradition points to the existence of a bottleneck for central cognitive processes that permits only one such process to occur at a time. The scope of the class of central processes that fall under this restriction is not fully determined yet, but it seems that at least response selection, that is the selection of a response contingent on a stimulus category (Pashler 1994), and retrieval from LTM (Rickard and Bajic 2004) belong to it. If such a strong constraint applies to processes taking perceptual stimuli as input, it is likely that the same constraint also applies to processes taking information from working memory as input. But how is the processing bottleneck related to the capacity limit (or limits) of working memory?

One possibility is that capacity limits on storage and on processing are basically the same. This view is inherent in many resource models, because a common assumption is that resources are shared between storage and processing (Just and Carpenter 1992). The concept of sharable resources does not fit well with the idea of a structural bottleneck built into the cognitive architecture, because resources can also be split between two processes running in parallel, which would not be possible in a strict bottleneck. It has been shown, however, that one formalization of resource models contains the bottleneck model as a special case (Navon and Miller 2002; Tombu and Jolicoeur 2003), implying that all data supporting the bottleneck model are also compatible with this variant of a resource model. The central idea in this model is that there is a constant pool of resources for processing, and if the pool is shared between two parallel processes, then the speed of each process is multiplied by the proportion of resources it receives. With this formalization, the total time for completing two operations demanded at the same time is always the same. They can either run sequentially with maximum speed, with full resources allocated first to one, then the other. Alternatively, they can both receive 50 per cent of the resources throughout, so that they run in parallel with half speed (and of course uneven allocation schemes are possible as well). The first scheme, with full allocation of resources first to one then the other operation, mimics the bottleneck model.

The resource-sharing model for parallel processing is interesting because its combination with resource models of working memory is straightforward. Assume a task requires holding n elements in working memory, and a demand for two central operations arises at the same time. An example for this would be if you just looked up a telephone number, and while you hold the number in memory, the door bell rings and a pot of milk boils over. You have a limited pool of resources to devote to maintaining the telephone number, deciding about pressing a button to open the door and deciding what to do about the milk. A resource model predicts that all three tasks compete with each other. That is, compared to a situation with only one processing demand, the simultaneous demand for two decisions will make at least one of them take longer. Moreover, compared to a situation with a lower memory load, or none at all, both decisions will be slowed down. Conversely, having to engage in two decisions will most likely draw more resources than having to do only one, so the simultaneous processing demand can be expected to impair memory for the telephone number, compared to a situation with only a single processing demand.

An alternative model is one in which processing capacity and storage capacity are completely independent. We could imagine that there is a storage system – or several of them as in the model of Baddeley (2000) – with limited capacity for short-term maintenance, and a processing bottleneck that performs one operation at a time. For the multitask scenario sketched above, this model predicts that the two processing demands conflict with each other – only one decision can be made at a time, so the other one has to wait until the first is completed (and we can only hope that the boiling milk is noticed a split second before the ringing door bell, because otherwise the bell would capture the bottleneck and the milk would have to wait). Maintenance of the telephone number, however, would be unaffected by the processing demand, and would have no effect on processing efficiency either.

The three-component framework advanced here takes a middle ground between these two simple conceptualizations. As should not be surprising by now, the framework distinguishes between situations where the processing demands require access to the contents to be maintained concurrently and situations where the processing tasks are independent of the storage tasks. The scenario discussed above falls in the latter category – we do not need the telephone number to decide about the milk or the door bell. If the processing tasks require input from the contents of working memory, then storage demands and processing demands are expected to interact. If the processing tasks can be done without input from the contents concurrently held in working memory, then storage demands and processing demands are largely independent. I'll explain this below.

In the three-component framework, the focus of attention has the function of selecting an object for processing, and this object is then submitted to the currently established task set. A task-set is a representation mapping categories of inputs (i.e., perceived stimuli or contents of working memory) to corresponding responses. For instance, a task-set could prescribe to react with a left button press to even numbers and with a right button press to odd numbers. Another task-set would, for example, prescribe adding two to numbers accompanied by a high tone and subtracting one to numbers accompanied by a low tone. The task-set is a representation outside the three components of working memory, so that it does not interfere with working memory contents or compete for capacity with them. It is tempting to assign task-sets to a fourth component, which might be called the executive system. At present, however, I have little to say about how this component works and how it interacts with the other three components, so this potential extension of the framework remains a construction site for now.

I assume that in most circumstances, only one task-set is established at a time (Mayr and Kliegl 2000). This constraint, together with the selection of only one object by the focus of attention, generates a functional bottleneck, such that only one object is processed according to one task-set at any time. A functional bottleneck differs from a structural bottleneck in that the former is set up by the cognitive system to optimize functionality, whereas the latter is a feature of the cognitive architecture. Permitting only one task-set to be established, and only one object to be selected, has the advantage of avoiding cross-talk between objects and between task-sets. Cross-talk means that different objects processed by the same task-set, or one object processed by different task-sets, can lead to conflicting responses and thereby impair efficient processing (Logan and Gordon 2001). I assume that the functional bottleneck arises from a default setting of the cognitive system to select a single task-set and a single object for processing to minimize cross-talk. In a task environment in which the chance of cross-talk is consistently minimal, the cognitive system can learn to relax its constraints, so that more than one task-set can be established concurrently, and more than one object can be processed at the same time (Oberauer and Kliegl 2004).

A functional bottleneck means that two processing demands arising at about the same time have to be met sequentially, resulting in dual-process costs manifest in the speed of finishing the second process (i.e., the one that has to wait) relative to a single-task condition. What if we add a demand on the maintenance function of working memory to the two processing tasks? When the two processing tasks require no access to the material to be maintained in working memory, then this material can be quickly removed from the direct-access region and encoded in the activated part of LTM. Once this is completed, the to-be-remembered information should not affect the efficiency of concurrent processes, regardless of whether there are one or two processing tasks to complete.

The situation is different when the processing tasks require access to the working-memory content. In this case, the memory contents must be held in the direct-access region. For each processing operation the focus of attention selects the element to be processed from among those elements in the direct-access region that are potential objects of the task set defining that operation. For example, imagine that three digits are held in the direct-access region, together with the spatial positions of two dots in a matrix. Two processing tasks are to be completed, one consisting of adding three to the first digit, and the other consisting of shifting the first dot to a neighboring matrix position. Assume that the dot shifting task set is selected first, so that the shifting operation is scheduled to pass first through the functional bottleneck. The focus of attention has to select the right dot for processing, and two dots compete for this selection. The three digits don't take part in this competition because they cannot be processed by the current task set. The time to finish the dot-shifting task therefore should depend on the number of dots but not the number of digits. Likewise, the second operation, adding three to one of the digits, should depend on the number of digits competing for entry into the focus of attention, but not the number of dots held concurrently in the direct-access region. For an illustration of this situation see Figure 20.8.

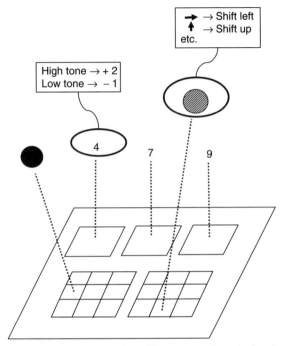

Figure 20.8 Illustration of the configuration of working memory in a dual-task experiment of Oberauer and Göthe (2006, Experiment 2). In a condition with large set sizes, participants had to remember three digits, each bound to a separate frame, and two positions of dots within matrices. The frames and matrices are representations in the cognitive coordinate system; bindings of content elements to them are depicted by the broken lines. In the simultaneous processing condition, two task demands arise at the same time, one demanding an arithmetic computation on one of the digits and the other demanding a spatial shift of one of the dots. The target digit and the target dot must be taken into the focus of attention, which is depicted by a thick-lined oval. It is linked to the currently established task set, represented by a rectangle containing the stimulus–response mappings. The default setting of the cognitive system is that a single focus selects one object at a time, and a single task set is established at any time. The two foci and the two task sets in the figure therefore would not be in place simultaneously. They can operate simultaneously, however, after extensive practice (Oberauer & Kliegl, 2004).

The example discussed above is one condition in a couple of experiments reported by Oberauer and Göthe (2006). In these experiments participants had to remember two lists, one consisting of digits displayed in frames (as in the arithmetic task described above), the other consisting of dot positions in 3 × 3 matrices. Each dot was placed in a cell of its own matrix. The digit lists could be one or three digits long, and the dot lists could consist of one or two dot positions, with the corresponding number of matrices on the screen (see Figure 20.8). Following initial encoding of the two lists, participants completed a series of operations by which they updated their working memory contents. Operations on the digits were adding two (indicated by a high tone) or subtracting one (indicated by a low tone). The digit to which the operation was to be applied was indicated by highlighting the corresponding frame in red. Operations on the dot positions were spatial shifts to adjacent matrix cells. They were indicated by arrows presented in the middle of the corresponding matrix.

There were two processing conditions. In the sequential condition, participants first completed a series of numerical operations, followed by a series of spatial operations, or the other way round. After each operation, they pressed the space bar, which immediately elicited the stimulus for the next operation. In the simultaneous condition, two operation instructions – one tone and one arrow – were presented at the same time. Participants had to complete both updating operations and then press the space bar once, upon which the next pair of operations was demanded. The time between consecutive hits on the space bar now represented the time to complete two operations, either sequentially or in parallel. By comparing the times for completing individual operations in the sequential condition to the time of completing two operations in the simultaneous condition we could determine whether participants were able to perform the two operations in parallel. It was obvious that they were not: in both experiments the time for completing both operations in the simultaneous condition was much longer than the time that would be expected if the two operations had been run in parallel with the same speed as in the sequential condition (for details of the rationale of this comparison see Oberauer and Kliegl [2004] or Oberauer and Göthe 2006). In other words, there were substantial dual-process costs, as would be expected from a bottleneck model as well as a resource-sharing model.

Of central interest in the present context is the interaction between storage and processing demands, as reflected in the effects of list length on reaction times of individual updating operations, and on the dual-process costs. This is where a critical difference between the two experiments comes into play. In Experiment 1, a single digit and a single dot position was updated throughout a trial, and when list length exceeded one, the other two digits or the other dot position (or both) were only to be maintained passively. Under these conditions, only one digit and one dot position had to be kept in the direct-access region throughout the updating sequence of a trial. The additional memory elements constituted a passive memory load analogous to the passive list in the paradigm of Oberauer (2002), and therefore could be outsourced into the activated part of LTM. This means that for the largest part of the updating sequence (i.e., after removal of the passive memory elements is completed) the load on the direct-access region was the same in all conditions regardless of the length of the two lists. Therefore, we would not expect list length to affect updating latencies – and in fact they didn't (with one exception: larger spatial lists resulted in slightly longer spatial updating RTs, but this was complemented by slightly shorter numerical updating RTs). Also, we would not expect list length to affect the size of the dual-process costs, and this expectation was also met by the data.

In Experiment 2, in contrast, updating operations were applied to all list elements; when lists were larger than one element, consecutive operations applied to different elements of the list in a random sequence. This means that participants had to hold the complete lists in the direct-access region (as illustrated in Figure 20.8). As a consequence, the number of digits to be maintained should affect the time it takes to select and process the correct digit, and likewise the number of spatial positions should affect the time for updating one of them. In fact, numerical operation latencies increased with digit list length, and spatial updating latencies increased with spatial list length. There was no cross-over effect of list length, however: The length of the digit list did not affect the spatial updating latencies, and the length of the spatial list had no effect on the digit updating times. This finding is the motivation for my assumption that list-length effects on processing latencies arise from the competition of eligible candidates for processing: only digits compete for numerical updating, and only spatial positions compete for spatial shift operations. A further expectation from the three-layer framework was that in this experiment list length should also affect dual-process costs, simply because the amount of dual-process costs reflects the time the second process must wait for the first, and the time for the first process is affected by list length (only one of the two list lengths would affect dual-process costs for each pair of updating operations, depending on which operation is done first, but there is no way to know this from the data).

An alternative explanation for the domain-specific effect of list length on latencies of individual updating operations is that there are separate storage modules for numerical and for spatial information (Baddeley 2001). Access to the numerical store would then only be affected by load on the numerical store, and access to the spatial store would depend only on load on the spatial store. The idea of separate storage systems, however, is refuted by a further finding: accuracy of recall of the final memory contents showed cross-domain effects of list lengths, that is, recall of digits was worse when the spatial list was longer, and recall of spatial positions was worse in trials with longer digit lists. This strongly suggests that representations of the two lists, maintained in the direct-access region together, mutually degrade each other. I believe that this degradation arises from interference between the bindings that link each digit to its frame, and each dot to its position in one of the matrices. In Experiment 1, where the two lists did not have to be held completely in the direct-access region, list length in one domain did not affect list length in the other domain. This is compatible with the assumption that retrieval from activated LTM is affected by similarity-based interference within domains, but not by interference between bindings across domains.

The interference between bindings across content domains in Experiment 2 could have arisen because the contents of both domains had to be bound to spatial positions (i.e., digits to the positions of the frames on the screen, and dots to the positions in their matrices). It could be the case that bindings in the direct-access region interfere less with each other when not only the contents but also the contexts they are bound to are very distinctive, for instance, when dots are bound to spatial positions and digits are bound to colors.

It should be noted that the two experiments in Oberauer and Göthe (2006) were identical in all respects except that the updating operations in Experiment 2 were applied to all list elements, as opposed to only one list element in Experiment 1. Most models of working memory would not predict a difference in the pattern of results between these experiments, because they make no difference between maintaining contents that have to be accessed and maintaining contents that don't. The striking difference in the pattern of list-length effects between the two experiments is compelling evidence that this distinction is important. Only the three-component framework makes this distinction explicitly. Other models, of course, could be augmented by an analogous distinction, and for some of them this additional assumption would not seem to be forced upon them. For instance, Baddeley (2001) assumes two modality-specific storage systems (the articulatory loop and the visuospatial sketch pad) together with one modality-independent system (the episodic buffer). It could be argued that information that doesn't have to be accessed can be held in the domain-specific slave systems, whereas information that needs to be accessed continuously must be held in the episodic buffer. In Experiment 1, only one digit and one spatial position would be held in the episodic buffer, placing a constant (low) demand on its capacity, whereas in Experiment 2 the complete lists would have to be in the episodic buffer, so that the load on its capacity varies with list lengths. There is nothing in Baddeley's model, however, that would independently motivate this assumption. Moreover, this account would not explain why in our Experiment 2 list-length effects on latencies were domain-specific whereas list-length effects on accuracies were not.

To summarize, the three-layer framework, extended by the concept of a functional processing bottleneck, can explain the complex pattern of dual-task effects in the experiments of Oberauer and Göthe (2006) – dual-process costs when attempting two processing tasks at once, dual-storage costs when combining a numerical and a spatial short-term memory task, and the mutual effects of concurrent storage and processing. This framework, therefore, provides a promising blueprint for developing an integrated model of capacity limits in working memory and attention.

References

Anderson, JR and Lebiere, C (1998). *The Atomic Components of Thought*. Mahwah, NJ: Erlbaum.

Anderson, JR, Reder, LM and Lebiere, C (1996). Working memory: Activation limits on retrieval. *Cognitive Psychology*, *30*, 221–256.

Anderson, MC and Spellman, BA (1995). On the status of inhibitory mechanisms in cognition: Memory retrieval as a model case. *Psychological Review*, *102*, 68–100.

Atkinson, RC, Herrmann, DJ and Wescourt, KT (1974). Search processes in recognition memory. In RL Solso (ed), *Theories in Cognitive Psychology: The Loyola symposium* (pp. 101–146). Potomac: Erlbaum.

Baddeley, AD (1986). *Working Memory*. Oxford: Clarendon Press.

Baddeley, AD (2000). The episodic buffer: a new component of working memory? *Trends in Cognitive Science*, *4*, 417–423.

Baddeley, AD (2001). Is working memory still working? *American Psychologist*, *56*, 851–864.

Bakeman, R and McArthur, D (1996). Picturing repeated measures: Comments on Loftus, Morrison, and others. *Behavioral Research Methods, Instruments, and Computers*, *28*, 584–589.

Burgess, N and Hitch, GJ (1999). Memory for serial order: A network model of the phonological loop and its timing. *Psychological Review*, *106*, 551–581.

Conway, ARA and Engle, RW (1994). Working memory and retrieval: A resource-dependent inhibition model. *Journal of Experimental Psychology: General*, *123*, 354–373.

Cowan, N (1995). *Attention and Memory: An integrated framework*. New York: Oxford University Press.

Cowan, N (1999). An embedded-process model of working memory. In A Miyake and P Shah (eds), *Models of Working Memory. Mechanisms of active maintenance and executive control* (pp. 62–101). Cambridge: Cambridge University Press.

Daneman, M and Carpenter, PA (1980). Individual differences in working memory and reading. *Journal of Verbal Learning and Verbal Behavior*, *19*, 450–466.

De Beni, R, Palladino, P, Pazzaglia, P and Cornoldi, C (1998). Increases in intrusion errors and working memory deficit of poor comprehenders. *Quarterly Journal of Experimental Psychology*, *51A*, 305–320.

Garavan, H (1998). Serial attention within working memory. *Memory and Cognition*, *26*, 263–276.

Halford, GS, Wilson, WH and Phillips, S (1998). Processing capacity defined by relational complexity: Implications for comparative, developmental, and cognitive psychology. *Behavioral and Brain Sciences*, *21*, 803–864.

Hasher, L, Zacks, RT and May, CP (1999). Inhibitory control, circadian arousal, and age. In D Gopher and A Koriat (eds), *Attention and Performance* (pp. 653–675). Cambridge, MA: MIT Press.

Jennings, JM and Jacoby, LL (1997). An opposition procedure for detecting age-related deficits in recollection: Telling effects of repetition. *Psychology and Aging*, *12*, 352–361.

Just, MA and Carpenter, PA (1992). A capacity theory of comprehension: Individual differences in working memory. *Psychological Review*, *99*, 122–149.

Kessler, Y and Meiran, N (2006). All updateable objects in working memory are updated whenever any of them are modified: Evidence from the memory updating paradigm. *Journal of Experimental Psychology: Learning, Memory and Cognition*, *32*, 570–585

Kirchner, WK (1958). Age differences in short-term retention of rapidly changing information. *Journal of Experimental Psychology*, *55*, 352–358.

Logan, GD and Gordon, RD (2001). Executive control of visual attention in dual-task situations. *Psychological Review*, *108*, 393–434.

Mandler, G (1980). Recognizing: The judgment of previous occurrence. *Psychological Review*, *87*, 252–271.

Mayr, U and Kliegl, R (2000). Task-set switching and long-term memory retrieval. *Journal of Experimental Psychology: Learning, Memory, and Cognition*, *26*, 1124–1140.

McElree, B (2001). Working memory and the focus of attention. *Journal of Experimental Psychology: Learning, Memory, and Cognition*, *27*, 817–835.

Miyake, A and Shah, P (1999). *Models of Working Memory. Mechanisms of active maintenance and executive control.* Cambridge: Cambridge University Press.

Navon, D and Miller, J (2002). Queuing or sharing? A critical evaluation of the single-bottleneck notion. *Cognitive Psychology, 44,* 193–251.

Oberauer, K (2001). Removing irrelevant information from working memory. A cognitive aging study with the modified Sternberg task. *Journal of Experimental Psychology: Learning, Memory, and Cognition, 27,* 948–957.

Oberauer, K (2002). Access to information in working memory: Exploring the focus of attention. *Journal of Experimental Psychology: Learning, Memory, and Cognition, 28,* 411–421.

Oberauer, K (2003). Selective attention to elements in working memory. *Experimental Psychology, 50,* 257–269.

Oberauer, K (2005a). Binding and inhibition in working memory – individual and age differences in short-term recognition. *Journal of Experimental Psychology: General, 134,* 368–387.

Oberauer, K (2005b). Control of the contents of working memory – a comparison of two paradigms and two age groups. *Journal of Experimental Psychology: Learning, Memory, and Cognition, 31,* 714–728.

Oberauer, K, Demmrich, A, Mayr, U and Kliegl, R (2001). Dissociating retention and access in working memory: An age-comparative study of mental arithmetic. *Memory and Cognition, 29,* 18–33.

Oberauer, K and Göthe, K (2006). Dual-task effects in working memory: Interference between two processing tasks, between two memory demands, and between storage and processing. *European Journal of Cognitive Psychology, 18,* 493–519.

Oberauer, K and Kliegl, R (2004). Simultaneous execution of two cognitive operations – Evidence from a continuous updating paradigm. *Journal of Experimental Psychology: Human Perception and Performance, 30,* 689–707.

Oberauer, K, Süß, H-M, Wilhelm, O and Sander, N (2007). Individual differences in working memory capacity and reasoning ability. In ARA Conway, C Jarrold, MJ Kane, A Miyake and JN Towse (eds), *Variation in working memory* (pp. 49–75). New York: Oxford University Press.

Oberauer, K, Wendland, M and Kliegl, R (2003). Age differences in working memory: The roles of storage and selective access. *Memory and Cognition, 31,* 563–569.

Page, MPA and Norris, D (1998). The primacy model: A new model of immediate serial recall. *Psychological Review, 105,* 761–781.

Pashler, H (1994). Dual-task interference in simple tasks: Data and theory. *Psychological Bulletin, 116,* 220–244.

Rickard, TC and Bajic, D (2004). Memory retrieval given two independent cues: cue selection or parallel access? *Cognitive Psychology, 48,* 243–294.

Sternberg, S (1969). Memory scanning: Mental processes revealed by reaction-time experiments. *American Scientist, 57,* 421–457.

Tombu, M and Jolicoeur, P (2003). A central capacity sharing model of dual-task performance. *Journal of Experimental Psychology: Human Perception and Performance, 29,* 3–18.

Wickens, DD, Moody, MJ and Dow, R (1981). The nature and timing of the retrieval process and of interference effects. *Journal of Experimental Psychology: General, 110,* 1–20.

Yonelinas, AP (2002). The nature of recollection and familiarity: A review of 30 years of research. *Journal of Memory and Language, 46,* 441–517.

21

A hierarchical biased-competition model of domain-dependent working memory maintenance and executive control

Susan M. Courtney, Jennifer K. Roth and
Joseph B. Sala

Introduction: defining working memory

Cognitive psychologists and neurophysiologists seem to have slightly different definitions of working memory, with the former tending to emphasize the 'working' (executive control and manipulation of information) aspect of the term and the latter tending to emphasize the 'memory' aspect. In this chapter we define 'working memory' (WM) as the ability to maintain a limited amount of task-relevant information in an active representation so that it is able to influence current and upcoming behavior and cognition. There are a couple of key elements to this definition which must be emphasized in order to understand the role of WM in cognition and behavior and the neural mechanisms that underlie this ability.

First, WM is *capacity limited*. This limitation creates the need to maintain only the information that is most important for the current task. Effective capacity can be increased if one can select or create the most efficient and effective representation that will best achieve the current goals according to the current rules. Therefore the same information may be represented neurally in different ways in order to maximize the efficiency of this limited capacity. While WM has traditionally been studied regarding the maintenance of stimulus-specific information such as locations, objects, or words, the selection and continued maintenance of this information must be guided by a maintained representation of the current rules and goals. In this chapter we will explore the possibility that the same neural mechanisms that support WM for stimulus-specific information may also be involved in the selection and maintenance of more abstract information, such as current rules and goals. The maintenance of such abstract information and its influence on the selective maintenance of more stimulus-specific information may form the basis of executive control – the ability to optimally select, manipulate and use the stimulus-specific information to be maintained.

The second key element in the definition of WM is that the representation is active and therefore *flexible and transient*. Without active maintenance, information in the WM buffer is overwritten by other competing information such as current sensory input, information retrieved from long-term memory, or other spontaneous thoughts. Much theorizing and experimentation has been directed at ascertaining whether information decays from the buffer directly due to the passage of time or whether it is necessarily replaced by interfering information (e.g., Dosher 1999). Because this interference can come from internal as well as external sources, however, including random neurophysiological fluctuations, it is difficult to separate the effects of time per se from the interference that inevitably accumulates with time.

In order to selectively maintain only the most currently relevant information, one must have both a mechanism for protecting the information that is currently in WM from interference and a mechanism for allowing information to enter and overwrite the current contents of WM when the new information becomes more important to the task than the old information. This dynamic flexibility at a millisecond timescale necessarily implies that WM be instantiated through neural activity rather than the structural changes that accompany long-term memory encoding and storage.

In the brain, the signature of WM has been considered to be the sustained neural activity over delays after the stimulus is no longer present. Sustained activity has been observed during single cell neurophysiological recordings in nonhuman primates (see reviews in Goldman-Rakic 1995; Fuster 2001) and using neuroimaging techniques in humans such as EEG (e.g., Ruchkin et al. 1992; Mecklinger and Pfeifer 1996; McEvoy et al. 1998) and fMRI (e.g., Courtney et al. 1997; Cohen et al. 1997; Zarahn et al. 1999). Working memory performance depends on this sustained activity, particularly in prefrontal cortex (PFC) (e.g., Kubota and Niki 1971; Miller et al.1996; Pessoa et al. 2002). What precisely this sustained activity represents and what its role is during performance of WM tasks, however, has been the subject of much debate (e.g., see reviews Levy and Goldman-Rakic 2000; Miller 2000; Duncan 2001; Fuster 2001; Curtis and D'Esposito 2003; Passingham and Sakai 2004; Courtney 2004). Accumulating evidence suggests that the information represented and the role of sustained neural activity in task performance may be different for different brain regions and that these representations and roles may change dynamically according to task demands.

Sustained representations of the current task demands are thought to form the basis of the biasing signal in the biased competition model for attentional selection of perceptual information (Desimone and Duncan 1995, Desimone 1998). In this model, representations of current perceptual information compete for further processing through mutually inhibitory interactions. The biasing signals enhance the strength of one of the representations, resulting in the inhibition of other possible representations. The needs of WM are very similar to those of perceptual processing. Both systems require the selection of relevant information and the suppression of irrelevant information. Both systems also require the ability either to sustain the current state or to shift states when the task demands change. Current interpretations of the biased competition model for attentional selection presume that the biasing signal, representing such information as task demands and search target templates, is maintained via PFC and that this information (in combination with perceptual salience) creates attentional priority maps in parietal cortex and the frontal eye fields, which in turn increase or decrease the strength of the representations of different locations or objects in the perceptual input (e.g., Bichot and Schall 1999; Bisley and Goldberg 2003; Serences et al. 2005). We propose that similar mechanisms may be operating in WM, influencing the relative strength of different representations of information within WM. (See also Deco and Rolls 2003; Almeida et al. 2004).

Selective maintenance of task-relevant information

Domain-dependent PFC organization: stimulus-specific information versus 'executive' information

Ever since Baddeley and Hitch (1974) proposed their Multiple Component Model with two domain-dependent 'slave systems' (i.e., the phonological loop and the visuospatial sketch pad) and a domain-independent 'central executive', most theories of WM have posited both distinct and common neural resources required for performance of WM tasks involving the maintenance of different types of information (Miyake and Shah 1999). Two tasks that both depend on the phonological loop, for example, will interfere with each other more than will two tasks that depend on different slave systems. However, even tasks that depend on separate slave systems are not entirely independent and are thus assumed to both require some common executive resources (Logie 1995).

Models of WM that include distinct systems for maintenance of verbal, spatial, and nonspatial visual information as well as a domain-independent resource necessary for all such tasks have been supported by recent neuroimaging studies. While common neural systems seem to be recruited by all of these types of WM tasks relative to nonmnemonic control tasks, double dissociations regarding the degree of activation in different cortical areas for maintenance of different types of information have also consistently been found (see Courtney 2004 for review).

While it has long been known that sensory processing areas are information domain-dependent (for review see Ungerleider and Haxby 1994), only recently has sufficient evidence accumulated to support the idea that the prefrontal cortex is also organized according to the type of information being processed or maintained. FMRI studies in humans clearly demonstrate that both dorsal and ventral frontal cortex show activation during both object and spatial WM tasks relative to nonmnemonic control tasks (Baker *et al.* 1996; Owen *et al.* 1996; D'Esposito *et al.* 1998; Nystrom *et al.* 2000; Postle *et al.* 2000a, 2000b; Stern *et al.* 2000; Postle and D'Esposito 1999). Many of these studies failed to observe any dorsal–ventral organization within the PFC related to maintenance of object versus spatial information (Petrides 1995a, b, 1996; D'Esposito *et al.* 1998; Nystrom *et al.* 2000; Stern *et al.* 2000; Postle and D'Esposito 1999). More recent studies that have found such an organization, however, suggest that the lack of dissociation was likely due to either insufficient statistical power or recoding strategies (for review see Courtney 2004). Studies that do find a spatial/nonspatial functional topography demonstrate that a region near the posterior end of the superior frontal sulcus at the junction with the precentral sulcus is activated more during spatial WM maintenance than during verbal or object WM. Similarly, posterior ventrolateral PFC (BA 44/45) is activated more during verbal and object WM than during spatial WM (Courtney *et al.* 1996, 1998; Munk *et al.* 2002; Sala *et al.* 2003; Gruber and von Cramon 2003; Sakai and Passingham 2003). This spatial/nonspatial dissociation is not limited to the visual modality (Rämä *et al.* 2004; Arnott *et al.* 2005). Verbal WM is usually left lateralized, while both visual object WM and spatial WM tend to be right lateralized, although these latter findings are less consistent (D'Esposito *et al.* 1999; Smith and Jonides 1999; Rämä *et al.* 2001; Sala and Courtney 2007), perhaps due to participants' tendencies to attempt to use verbal recoding strategies during such tasks. The functional significance of these fMRI activation differences, the nature of the representation of information in WM and the overall nature of the functional organization of prefrontal cortex, however, have remained unclear.

Studies of the effects of various prefrontal lesions in both human and nonhuman primates have also generally supported a distinction between spatial, object, and verbal WM systems, although there are some caveats to consider (for review see Curtis and D'Esposito 2004). In nonhuman primates, lesions limited to the principal sulcus and the nearby cortex dorsal to the sulcus cause deficits specifically in tasks that depend on the maintenance of spatial information across a memory delay (Mishkin *et al.* 1969; Goldman and Rosvold 1970; Goldman *et al.* 1971; Petrides 1995b). These lesions do not cause deficits on tasks that require maintenance of nonspatial information or on spatial tasks that do not involve a memory delay.

By contrast, lesions of ventrolateral PFC do frequently cause impairments in delayed object-alternation and delayed object match-to-sample recognition tasks (Mishkin and Manning 1978; Iverson and Mishkin 1970; Passingham 1975). However, deficits were also observed on similar spatial WM tasks and were present for both spatial and nonspatial tasks, even without a memory delay requirement (Iverson and Mishkin 1970; Passingham 1975). In humans, there is very little data with the lesion location specificity required to address this question. Some data do suggest that disruptions in the function of cortex within the posterior portion of the superior frontal sulcus in humans, either from stroke (Carlesimo *et al.* 2001) or from transcranial magnetic stimulation (Mottaghy *et al.* 2002) selectively disrupt spatial WM, while disruptions of ventral PFC appear to selectively impair nonspatial WM (Bechara *et al.* 1998; Mottaghy *et al.* 2002). However, both human and nonhuman primates with ventrolateral PFC lesions often have profound difficulties with inhibition of prepotent responses and rule learning that interferes with performance on a wide variety of tasks, both spatial and nonspatial (e.g., Iverson and Mishkin 1970; Stuss and Benson 1986; Shallice and Burgess 1991).

The lack of a symmetrical double-dissociation between the effects of posterior dorsal versus ventral PFC lesions may be the result of two interrelated factors. First, it may be that the brain evolved separate systems governing WM for spatial versus nonspatial WM because the two types of information are fundamentally different and thus require different neural mechanisms. The representations of spatial locations and spatial relationships are intimately tied to the sensori-motor systems. Many cells in parietal cortex, for example, receive both visual and somatosensory input and are important both for spatial perception and for reaching movements toward visual targets (Colby and Goldberg 1999). For nonspatial (object and verbal) WM, on the other hand, there is an unlimited number of possible stimuli which have a more indirect relationship to behavioral response through which we measure performance and impairment. Perhaps the neural mechanisms for representing this infinite variety of nonspatial information is necessarily more tied to the neural mechanisms that represent and implement task rules. Alternatively (or consequently) these functions may be implemented in separate cortical regions that are anatomically close together within the ventrolateral PFC and no lesion study has yet been able to distinguish them. This latter possibility is supported by the results of a study of individuals with damage in the ventral PFC by Thompson-Schill and colleagues (2002). As a group, the patients showed deficits in verbal WM relative to age-matched controls. However, one patient, RC, whose lesion extended slightly more anteriorly than any of the other patients, was the only one to have an abnormally greater difficulty with suppressing interference from memory sets presented in previous trials. Thus the ability to select currently relevant information in WM may be functionally and neurally dissociable from those regions that subsequently maintain and use that information.

Neuroimaging studies also support the idea that there are separable regions for maintenance of spatial and nonspatial information and for executive functions that do not depend on the type of stimulus-specific information. Note that these other areas may also be considered 'domain-dependent' if one considers such abstract information as task rules and goals as being another type of information domain. Of particular interest in the literature has been a mid-dorsolateral prefrontal region, likely corresponding to BA 46/9. In nonhuman primates it has been shown that many neurons in this region demonstrate sustained activity during WM delays that is selective for the task rule (White and Wise 1999; Wallis *et al.* 2001), or stimulus category (Freedman *et al.* 2003), rather than particular perceptual attributes of the sample or anticipated test stimuli. Neuroimaging studies suggest a similar interpretation. Although it is difficult to judge whether identical or merely nearby functional areas have been activated in different studies, this general region tends to be activated more when the task requires maintenance in the presence of distracting perceptual inputs (Sakai *et al.* 2002), explicit manipulation of the maintained information (D'Esposito *et al.* 1999), presumed recoding of the maintained information under conditions of high WM load (Rypma *et al.* 2002; Bor *et al.* 2003), and a large variety of other 'executive control' functions (e.g., Derrfuss *et al.* 2004). This region has also been activated in very simple executive-type tasks involving the 'refreshing' of recently presented information (Raye *et al.* 2002).

The magnitude of activation in this broadly defined region does not consistently distinguish between spatial and nonspatial tasks. Functional connectivity analyses suggest, however, that activity in this region may differentially influence the interactions among regions that are selectively involved in maintaining spatial versus nonspatial stimulus-specific information, depending on the task demands (Sakai and Passingham 2003).

In summary, there is evidence for a domain-dependent neuroanatomical functional organization within the PFC that supports models of WM that include both dissociable systems for the maintenance of spatial and nonspatial information and common resources for executive control of this information. The systems for spatial and nonspatial WM are not isolated modules, however. These two systems may have different relationships with other systems for motor behavior, rule representation and executive control. Thus the effects of lesions in these two systems may not be symmetrical. In addition, as explained in the next section, these two systems appear to change their interactions with other systems and with each other in a task-dependent manner in order to create integrated representations of spatial and nonspatial information, such as an object in its location.

Binding of objects and their locations in working memory

Despite the large literature from both human and nonhuman primate studies suggesting distinct neural systems for spatial and nonspatial information, outlined briefly above, there is an equally large literature suggesting that spatial and nonspatial information are integrated within the PFC. Single PFC neurons can integrate color and location information according to a pre-learned 'rule' (White and Wise 1999) or over the delays of delayed response tasks (Quintana *et al.* 1988; Yajeya *et al.* 1988). PFC neurons also appear to make cross-modal associations (Fuster *et al.* 2000). Prefrontal cooling implicates the prefrontal cortex specifically in the cross-temporal integration of spatial and nonspatial information (Quintana and Fuster 1993). The most telling piece of information, however, was the demonstration that cells in both dorsal and ventral frontal cortex can show selective responses to either objects, locations, or both, dynamically changing their selectivity to reflect the current task demands (Rao *et al.* 1997; Rainer *et al.* 1998).

Another critical piece of evidence in the puzzle over the nature of the representation of object and location information in WM came from a pair of fMRI experiments that, similar to the nonhuman primate experiments, tested for changes in activation during object, location, and object-in-location WM tasks. Sala and Courtney (2007) tested the ideas of a task-dependent information representation and a dynamic functional organization of the PFC in two experiments in which fMRI activation was measured while participants held in WM either fractal-like patterns, the locations of those patterns, or both the patterns and their locations. In both of those experiments, there was a dorsal/ventral, spatial/nonspatial functional topography such that the posterior part of the SFS had significantly greater activation for the location task and posterior inferior frontal cortex had greater activation for the pattern identity task. Significant activity relative to a fixation baseline or a sensorimotor control task was found in each PFC region during maintenance of both its preferred and nonpreferred information type, a result sometimes thought to be at odds with a domain-dependent functional organization. However, this activity during maintenance of that region's nonpreferred information could represent incidental encoding of the irrelevant information. Alternatively, this overlap of activation patterns could be interpreted as indicating the existence of intermixed spatially and nonspatially selective cell populations with a greater percentage of primarily spatially tuned neurons dorsally and a greater percentage of primarily object-tuned neurons ventrally, as has previously been proposed (e.g., Haxby *et al.* 2000; Duncan 2001).

This relative distributions account, however, is at odds with the results of the Sala and Courtney (2007) experiments for the task involving WM maintenance of both the patterns and their locations. That task condition resulted in an activation level, in nearly every region activated by any of the tasks, that was greater than that for each region's nonpreferred (spatial or nonspatial) information type, but less than that for each region's preferred information type. If dorsal and ventral PFC areas contained a mixture of 'what cells' and 'where cells', then activity during object-in-location delays would be greater than the activity during maintenance of either information alone, because both cell populations would now be active instead of only one or the other. Therefore, while the results of studies showing regional preferences for spatial versus nonspatial information are at odds with a stable domain-general organization, a stable domain-dependent, or even a domain-dependent organization with differential, rather than absolute, distributions of distinct cell types, has no way to account for a decrease in activity during 'bound' object-in-location WM maintenance.

The result that object-in-location WM activity was significantly less than the preferred information type suggests a more selective, integrated representation of the information during this task, perhaps with a smaller number of cells active than during the region's preferred task, but with

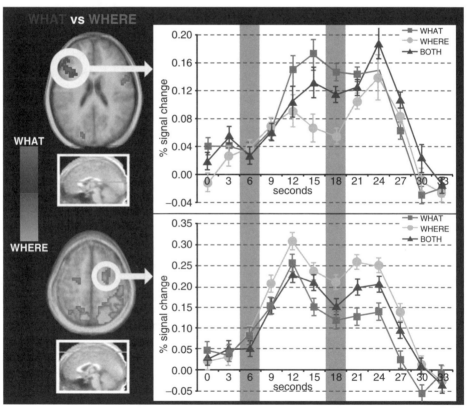

Figure 21.1 FMRI activation patterns during working memory for fractal-like patterns ('WHAT'), the locations of those patterns ('WHERE'), or both the patterns and their locations ('BOTH'). There is a dorsal/ventral spatial/nonspatial topography for the what-only and where-only tasks, but the activation for the BOTH task is in between the levels of activation for the preferred and non-preferred information types, consistent with a more selective representation for an object-in-its-location, involving fewer cells than are active during maintenance of the preferred information, but with those cells more highly active than during maintenance of the non-preferred information. Reprinted with permission from Sala and Courtney (2007). See also color plate 11.

those cells more active than during the region's nonpreferred task. What is the neural mechanism that could simultaneously account for these fMRI results and the dynamic selectivity observed in the Rao *et al.* (1997) and Rainer *et al.* (1998) studies?

Biased competition model for the selective maintenance of task-relevant information

A neural mechanism has recently been proposed that applies the principles of biased competition mechanisms for attentional selection to the problem of dynamically and selectively maintaining task-relevant information in WM (Sala and Courtney 2007). This model provides a single simple mechanism to explain both neuroimaging and single-cell physiology data regarding WM maintenance of objects, locations and the conjunction of an object and its location.

The model supposes domain-dependent inputs from parietal and inferior temporal cortices to dorsal and ventral PFC regions, respectively. Each of these PFC regions is proposed to then receive *task-dependent* input from the other. These excitatory inputs, combined with competitive interactions within each region, would result in the dual selectivity observed in the Rao *et al.* (1997) and Rainer *et al.* (1998) studies. In this model, when only spatial locations are task-relevant, the excitatory input is mainly from dorsal PFC to ventral PFC. In this case, all dorsal PFC cells which respond well to the to-be-remembered location are active, independent of their preferred object, because that object selectivity arises only when input is received from ventral PFC. When only object identities are task relevant, the excitatory input is mainly from ventral PFC to dorsal PFC. In this case, all ventral PFC cells which respond well to the to be remembered object are active, independent of their preferred location, because that location selectivity arises only when input is received from dorsal PFC. When the integrated representation of an object and its location is task relevant, then the excitatory inputs go in both directions and dual object and location selectivity is observed in both dorsal and ventral PFC. Cells would respond best *only* if the task trial required both the cell's preferred location and its preferred object to be remembered. This type of system would result in a greater number of cells in dorsal (or ventral) PFC being highly active during a task that only requires memory for locations (objects, respectively) than when both an object and its location must be remembered. The fMRI activation, which depends on the average activity of all the cells in a region, would be expected to show the intermediate response for the object-in-location task that was observed by Sala and Courtney (2007).

An important feature of this model is that the strength and direction of the interactions between dorsal and ventral PFC are task dependent. A prediction of the model is that if the task requires that objects and locations be remembered independent of their relationship with one another (i.e., which object was in which location), then both dorsal and ventral PFC regions would be expected to be more active than during an task that required an integrated representation to be remembered. In addition, functional connectivity measures between dorsal and ventral PFC would be expected to be lower when objects and locations must be maintained independently than when an integrated representation is necessary.

The question remains how the strength and direction of these interactions are determined. A promising candidate is the other regions of the PFC whose activation levels do not appear to depend on the type of stimulus-specific information being maintained. As mentioned earlier, the level of activity in these regions appears to depend on the amount and complexity of the context and the rules governing task performance (e.g., Sakai *et al.* 2002, D'Esposito *et al.* 1999; Rypma *et al.* 2002; Bor *et al.* 2003; Derrfuss *et al.* 2004). Even in simple tasks, however, these regions could provide biasing signals that control the type of information to be maintained or allowed access to WM (as in Raye *et al.* 2002). Thus, biased-competition-like interactions among PFC regions could create new representations by combining information from multiple sources according to the constraints of the current task rules. In the absence of these biasing signals and interactions both the information in WM and the resulting behavior would default to the most prepotent state, which would have been established through experience and previous behavior (see also Miller and Cohen 2001).

Interference-resistant maintenance versus updating

Another realm of WM where biased-competition-like mechanisms may be at work is in the updating of information in WM. Successful WM maintenance requires that interfering information that is not task-relevant be prevented from overwriting the current contents of the WM buffer. Indeed, many accounts of the role of PFC in WM maintenance emphasize the protection from interference aspect, rather than the storage of the information itself (e.g., Engle *et al.* 1999; Sakai *et al.* 2002). Some have suggested that WM storage capacity is fundamentally a function of attentional control over interfering information (Kane and Engle 2002). Simultaneously, however, the system must also allow the currently maintained information to be overwritten with updated information quickly whenever the new information becomes more important to the current task than the previously maintained information. This concept of relative priority is again reminiscent of biased competition for attentional selection, and data from recent neuroimaging studies support the idea that a similar mechanism is at work.

Roth and her colleagues (Roth, Serences and Courtney 2006) used fMRI to investigate the relationship between interference-resistant WM maintenance and updating the contents of WM with a new sample stimulus. They used a modified delayed-recognition task in which participants viewed a continuous stream of either faces or houses. The first object in each task block was the first sample to be maintained in WM. With the presentation of each subsequent stimulus, participants indicated with a button press whether the current stimulus matched the sample stimulus. Randomly, every 4–10 seconds, participants saw one of two well-memorized cue faces or houses. One of these cues instructed the participants that the old sample was now irrelevant and that they were to maintain in WM the next face or house that they saw and to make future match/nonmatch decisions in reference to this new sample stimulus. The other cue served as a control event. That cue instructed participants to continue to maintain the current sample stimulus. For both cue events, participants pressed a button to indicate that they recognized the cue stimulus. There were also control task blocks in which participants viewed the same stream of faces or houses, but did not need to maintain any one of them in WM. Instead, participants made a perceptual categorization decision (male/female for faces, garage/no garage for houses) for each stimulus as it was presented. Thus, the experimental design included both sustained activation components for memory blocks versus control blocks, related to WM maintenance, and transient activation components related to the update events. Contrasting the update events to the control cued maintenance events enabled identification of activity related to replacing the current contents of WM with a current perceptual stimulus.

Independent of the type of object to be remembered (face or house), transient, update-related activations were observed primarily in middle and superior frontal regions and parietal cortex. These regions partially overlapped with those regions showing sustained, maintenance-related activity. Notably, the middle frontal region activated by both maintenance and updating appears to be the same region as has been previously implicated in WM maintenance under conditions of interference (Sakai *et al.* 2002). A similar region of activation has been observed in other studies in which the task required actively maintained abstract information, such as rules, to influence cognition or behavior (Bunge *et al.* 2003; Derrfuss *et al.* 2004; see Figure 21.2.). In the Roth *et al.* study, participants needed to continue to maintain the sample stimulus while making match/nonmatch

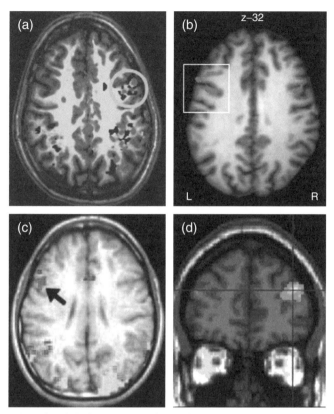

Figure 21.2 Activation of middle frontal cortex (possibly Brodmann's Area 46) in several studies involving the prioritization of one type of information over another: (a) Updating (in green), WM maintenance (blue), and their overlap (yellow) (reprinted with permission from Roth *et al.* 2006), (b) Common activation for task-switching, Stroop task, and n-back working memory task (reprinted with permission from Derrfuss *et al.* 2004), (c) Refreshing of just-seen information (reprinted with permission from Johnson *et al.* 2003), (d) Interference-resistant WM maintenance (reprinted with permission from Sakai *et al.* 2002). See also color plate 12.

and cue/not-cue decisions on highly similar stimuli. Thus, they had to attend to the current perceptual input for the purposes of immediate processing, but also keep that perceptual information from overwriting the contents of WM until an update cue was seen. The overlapping activations for interference-resistant maintenance and updating suggests that the same control mechanism may be involved for both purposes. The particular pattern of activity in this region and its interactions with other brain areas (including subcortical areas) may determine whether the current contents of WM will be maintained or overwritten by new information (see also Rougier *et al.* 2005).

Transient changes in activation have also been observed in a highly similar middle frontal region when research participants refreshed the mental representation of a recently seen (but not actively maintained) stimulus (Raye *et al.* 2002; Johnson *et al.* 2003; see Figure 21.2.). Both this refreshing task and the update events in the Roth *et al.* study involve a change in the relative priority of current versus previously seen information. The other regions that showed both sustained, maintenance-related activity and transient, update-related activity in the Roth *et al.* study were in parietal and superior frontal cortex in regions highly similar to those that have been shown to have both sustained and transient activity related to maintaining and shifting attention, respectively (Yantis *et al.* 2002; Serences *et al.* 2004).

The existence of both sustained, maintenance-related activity and transient, update-related activity in brain regions that have previously been implicated in protecting information in WM from interference and regions that have previously been implicated in controlling attentional selection among current perceptual stimuli, suggests that a common mechanism may be involved in all of these functions. We propose that the common requirement in all of these functions is the setting of relative priorities according to current task context and rules. Biased competition could be at work not only in selecting whether object identity or location or both would be attended in the perceptual input, but also which type of information would continue to be maintained during a WM delay. In addition, actively maintained information about task context and rules could also set the relative priorities for information already being maintained in WM versus current perceptual input. Changes in these relative priorities could result from either explicit instruction cues, as in the Roth *et al.* (2006) study or from unexpected reward feedback (see Rougier *et al.* 2005). Such resolution among competing sources and representations of information is necessary because of the limited storage capacity of WM.

Summary and future directions

Taken together, the studies reviewed in this chapter suggest a role for abstract contextual or rule information maintained via the mid-dorsolateral PFC to bias competitive interactions within and among other brain regions (including other regions within the PFC) in the service of selecting, creating, maintaining, and updating the optimal representation of the most important information for the current task. This select, more stimulus-specific information then in turn could serve as the biasing signal for selection of particular actions (Cisek and Kalaska 2005; for reviews see Fuster 2001, Bunge 2004), selection of competing conceptual representations in long-term memory (Kan and Thompson-Schill 2004), or for attentional selection, as in the original biased competition model (Desimone and Duncan 1995, Desimone 1998). This framework implies a hierarchical structure with domain-dependent information maintenance and selection via biased competition occurring at every level. The proposed model is shown in Figure 21.3.

In the model there are mutually inhibitory connections within each level of the hierarchy and excitatory inputs across levels. Which representation will 'win' that competition at each level depends on how the balance of competition is biased both by the saliency of feedforward perceptual information and by feedback signals from higher levels. The model allows for multiple representations to be active simultaneously, but it is their *relative* levels of activity that will ultimately determine their influence on other brain regions and, thus, on behavior (see also Bisley and Goldberg 2003).

The most powerful aspect of the model is that it enables many aspects of perception, action and cognition to be explained by a common mechanism: relative levels of sustained activity in one brain area biasing the interactions within mutually inhibitory neural networks in another brain area. While such mechanisms have been proposed before, the unusual aspect of the current proposal is that these interactions could occur *within* the PFC as well as between the PFC and perceptual or motor regions. Such a unifying framework could simplify discussions of WM, cognitive control and other executive processes. If the model holds true, the difference between the brain regions responsible for various types of executive processes or between the phonological loop and the visuospatial sketch pad would be defined primarily on the type of information represented (as determined by the inputs to that region) and the type of influence that the information

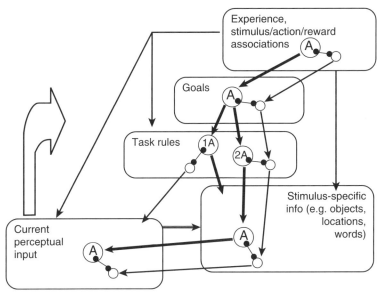

Figure 21.3 Hierarchical biased-competition (HBC) model for working memory maintenance and cognitive control. 'A' represents the current task schema with all of its associated goals, rules, and sensory information, each of which is proposed to be represented by activity in a different level of the hierarchy. Note that there are two parts to the rule representation (1A and 2A). The greater activation of 1A relative to other possible rules determines whether the current contents of working memory or the current perceptual input is more important for future maintenance in WM. The greater activation of 2A relative to other possible rules determines which objects, locations, or other stimulus-specific information will be maintained.

in that region has on the rest of the system (as determined by the output targets of that region). The model is testable at many levels, from cellular physiology and anatomy to neuroimaging and behavioral analysis. The field of WM has made great progress from identifying dissociations among different aspects of behavior and the associated neural systems. Perhaps it is now time to identify the common underlying mechanistic principles.

References

Almeida, R, Deco, G and Stetter, M (2004). Modular biased-competition and cooperation: A candidate mechanism for selective working memory. *Eur J Neurosci*, *20*, 2789–2803.

Arnott, SR, Grady, CL, Hevenor, SJ, Graham, S and Alain, C (2005). The functional organization of auditory working memory as revealed by fMRI. *Journal of Cognitive Neuroscience*, *17*(5), 819–831.

Baddeley, A and Hitch, GJ (1974). Working memory. In GA Bower (ed), *Recent Advances in Learning and Memory* (pp. 17–90). New York: Academic Press.

Baker, SC, Frith, CD, Frackowiak, RS and Dolan, RJ (1996). Active representation of shape and spatial location in man. *Cereb Cortex*, *6*, 612–619.

Bechara, A, Damasio, H, Tranel, D and Anderson, SW (1998). Dissociation of working memory from decision making within the human prefrontal cortex. *J Neurosci*, *18*, 428–437.

Bichot, NP and Schall, JD (1999). Effects of similarity and history on neural mechanisms of visual selection. *Nat Neurosci*, *2*(6), 549–554.

Bisley JW and Goldberg, ME (2003). Neuronal activity in the lateral intraparietal area and spatial attention. *Science*, *299*, 81–86.

Bor, D, Duncan, J, Wiseman, RJ and Owen, AM (2003). Encoding strategies dissociate prefrontal activity from working memory demand. *Neuron, 37*(2), 361–367.

Bunge, SA (2004). How we use rules to select actions: a review of evidence from cognitive neuroscience. *Cognitive, Affective, and Behavioral Neuroscience, 4*(4), 564–579.

Bunge, SA, Kahn, I, Wallis, JD, Miller, EK and Wagner, AD (2003). Neural circuits subserving the retrieval and maintenance of abstract rules. *J Neurophysiol, 90*(5), 3419–3428.

Carlesimo, GA, Perri, R, Turriziani, P, Tomaiuolo, F and Caltagirone, C (2001). Remembering what but not where: Independence of spatial and visual working memory in the human brain. *Cortex, 37*, 519–534.

Cisek, P and Kalaska, JF (2005). Neural correlates of reaching decisions in dorsal premotor cortex: Specification of multiple direction choices and final selection of action. *Neuron, 45*(5), 801–814.

Cohen, JD, Perlstein, WM, Braver, TS, Nystrom, LE, Noll, DC, Jonides, J and Smith, EE (1997). Temporal dynamics of brain activation during a working memory task. *Nature, 386*(6625), 604–608.

Colby, CL and Goldberg, ME (1999). Space and attention in parietal cortex. *Annu Rev Neurosci, 22*, 319–349.

Courtney, SM (2004). Attention and cognitive control as emergent properties of information representation in working memory. *Cognitive, Affective, and Behavioral Neuroscience, 4*(4), 501–516.

Courtney, SM, Petit, L, Maisog, JM, Ungerleider, LG and Haxby, JV (1998). An area specialized for spatial working memory in human frontal cortex. *Science, 279*, 1347–1351.

Courtney, SM, Ungerleider, LG, Keil, K and Haxby, JV (1997). Transient and sustained activity in a distributed neural system for human working memory task. *Nature, 386*(6625), 608–611.

Courtney, SM, Ungerleider, LG, Keil, K and Haxby, JV (1996). Object and spatial visual working memory activate separate neural systems in human cortex. *Cereb Cortex, 6*, 39–49.

Curtis, CE and D'Esposito, M (2003). Persistent activity in the prefrontal cortex during working memory. *Trends in Cognitive Science, 7*(9), 415–423.

Curtis, CE and D'Esposito, M (2004). The effects of prefrontal lesions on working memory performance and theory. *Cognitive, Affective, and Behavioral Neuroscience, 4*(4), 528–539.

D'Esposito, M, Aguirre, GK, Zarahn, E, Ballard, D, Shin, RK and Lease, J (1998). Functional MRI studies of spatial and nonspatial working memory. *Brain Res Cogn Brain Res, 7*, 1–13.

D'Esposito, M, Postle, BR, Ballard D and Lease, J (1999). Maintenance versus manipulation of information held in working memory: An event-related fmri study. *Brain Cogn, 41*, 66–86.

Deco, G and Rolls, ET (2003). Attention and working memory: A dynamical model of neuronal activity in the prefrontal cortex. *Eur J Neurosci, 18*, 2374–2390.

Derrfuss, J, Brass, M and von Cramon DY (2004). Cognitive control in the posterior frontolateral cortex: evidence from common activations in task coordination, interference control, and working memory. *Neuroimage, 23*(2), 604–612.

Desimone, R (1998). Visual attention mediated by biased competition in extrastriate visual cortex. *Philos Trans R Soc Lond B Biol Sci, 353*, 1245–1255.

Desimone, R and Duncan, J (1995). Neural mechanisms of selective visual attention. *Annu Rev Neurosci, 18*, 193–222.

Dosher, BA (1999). Item interference and time delays in working memory: immediate serial recall. *International Journal Of Psychology, 34*(5/6), 276–284.

Duncan, J (2001). An adaptive coding model of neural function in prefrontal cortex. *Nat Rev Neurosci, 2*, 820–829.

Engle, RW, Kane, MJ and Tuholski, SW (1999). Individual differences in working memory capacity and what they tell us about controlled attention, general fluid intelligence, and functions of the prefrontal cortex. In A Miyake and P Shah (eds), *Models of Working Memory: Mechanisms of active maintenance and executive control* (pp. 102–134). Cambridge: Cambridge University Press.

Freedman, DJ, Riesenhuber, M, Poggio, T and Miller, EK (2003). A comparison of primate prefrontal and inferior temporal cortices during visual categorization. *Journal of Neuroscience, 23*(12), 5235–5246.

Fuster, JM (2001). The prefrontal cortex—an update: Time is of the essence. *Neuron, 30*, 319–333.

Fuster, JM, Bodner, M and Kroger, JK. (2000). Cross-modal and cross-temporal association in neurons of frontal cortex. *Nature, 405,* 347–351.

Goldman, PS, Rosvold, HE, Vest, B and Galkin, TW (1971). Analysis of the delayed-alternation deficit produced by dorsolateral prefrontal lesions in the rhesus monkey. *J Comp Physiol Psychol, 77*(2), 212–220.

Goldman, PS and Rosvold, HE (1970). Localization of function within the dorsolateral prefrontal cortex of the rhesus monkey. *Exp Neurol, 27*(2), 291–304.

Goldman-Rakic, PS (1995). Cellular basis of working memory. *Neuron, 14,* 477–485.

Gruber, O and von Cramon, Y (2003). The functional neuroanatomy of human working memory revisited. Evidence from 3-T fMRI studies using classical domain-specific interference tasks. *Neuroimage, 19*(3), 797–809.

Haxby, JV, Petit, L, Ungerleider, LG and Courtney, SM (2000). Distinguishing the functional roles of multiple regions in distributed neural systems for visual working memory. *Neuroimage, 11,* 145–156.

Iverson, SD and Mishkin, M (1970). Perseverative interference in monkeys following selective lesions of the inferior prefrontal convexity. *Exp Brain Res, 11,* 376–386.

Johnson, MK, Raye, CL, Mitchell, KJ, Greene, EJ and Anderson, AW (2003). fMRI evidence for an organization of prefrontal cortex by both type of process and type of information. *Cereb Cortex, 13,* 265–273.

Kan, IP and Thompson-Schill, SL (2004). Selection from perceptual and conceptual representations. *Cogn Affect Behav Neurosci, 4*(4), 466–482.

Kane, MJ and Engle, RW (2002). The role of prefrontal cortex in working-memory capacity, executive attention, and general fluid intelligence: an individual-differences perspective. *Psychonomic Bull Rev, 9*(4), 637–671.

Kubota, K and Niki, H (1971). Prefrontal cortical unit activity and delayed alternation performance in monkeys. *Journal of Neurophysiology, 34,* 337–347.

Levy, R and Goldman-Rakic, PS (2000). Segregation of working memory functions within the dorsolateral prefrontal cortex. *Exp Brain Res, 133,* 23–32.

Logie, R (1995). *Visuo-spatial Working Memory.* Hove: Lawrence Erlbaum Associates, Inc.

McEvoy, LK, Smith, ME and Gevins, A (1998). Dynamic cortical networks of verbal and spatial working memory: Effects of memory load and task practice. *Cerebral Cortex, 8*(7), 563–574.

Mecklinger, A and Pfeifer, E (1996). Event-related potentials reveal topographical and temporally distinct neuronal activation patterns for spatial and object working memory. *Cognitive Brain Research, 4,* 211–224.

Miller, EK (2000). The prefrontal cortex and cognitive control. *Nat Rev Neurosci, 1,* 59–65.

Miller, EK and Cohen, JD (2001). An integrative theory of prefrontal cortex function. *Annu Rev Neurosci, 24,* 167–202.

Miller, EK, Erickson, CA and Desimone, R (1996). Neural mechanisms of visual working memory in prefrontal cortex of the macaque. *Journal of Neuroscience, 16,* 5154–5167.

Mishkin, M and Manning, FJ (1978). Non-spatial memory after selective prefrontal lesions in monkeys. *Brain Research, 143*(2), 313–323.

Mishkin, M, Vest, B, Waxler, M and Rosvold, HE (1969). A re-examination of the effects of frontal lesions on object alternation. *Neuropsychologia, 7,* 357–364.

Miyake, A and Shah, P (1999). *Models of Working Memory: Mechanisms of active maintenance and executive control.* Cambridge: Cambridge University Press,.

Mottaghy, FM, Gangitano, M, Sparing, R, Krause, BJ and Pascual-Leone, A. (2002). Segregation of areas related to visual working memory in the prefrontal cortex revealed by rtms. *Cereb Cortex, 12,* 369–375.

Munk, M, Linden, D, Muckli, L, Lanfermann, H, Zanella, F, Singer, W and Goebel, R (2002). Distributed cortical systems in visual short-term memory revealed by event-related functional magnetic resonance imaging. *Cerebral Cortex, 12,* 866–887.

Nystrom, LE, Braver, TS, Sabb, FW, Delgado, MR, Noll, DC and Cohen, JD (2000). Working memory for letters, shapes, and locations: Fmri evidence against stimulus-based regional organization in human prefrontal cortex. *Neuroimage, 11,* 424–446.

Owen, AM, Evans, AC and Petrides, M (1996). Evidence for a two-stage model of spatial working memory processing within the lateral frontal cortex: A positron emission tomography study. *Cereb Cortex*, 6, 31–38.

Passingham, R (1975). Delayed matching after selective prefrontal lesions in monkeys (*Macaca mulatta*). *Brain Research*, 92, 89–102.

Passingham, D and Sakai, K (2004). The prefrontal cortex and working memory: physiology and brain imaging. *Curr Opin Neurobiol*, 14(2), 163–168.

Pessoa, L, Gutierrez, E, Bandettini, P and Ungerleider, L (2002). Neural correlates of visual working memory: Fmri amplitude predicts task performance. *Neuron*, 35, 975–987.

Petrides, M (1995a). Functional organization of the human frontal cortex for mnemonic processing. Evidence from neuroimaging studies. *Ann N Y Acad Sci*, 769, 85–96.

Petrides, M (1995b). Impairments on nonspatial self-ordered and externally ordered working memory tasks after lesions of the mid-dorsal part of the lateral frontal cortex in the monkey. *J Neurosci*, 15, 359–375.

Petrides, M (1996). Specialized systems for the processing of mnemonic information within the primate frontal cortex. *Philos Trans R Soc Lond B Biol Sci*, 351, 1455–1461.

Postle, BR and D'Esposito, M (1999). 'What'-then-where' in visual working memory: An event-related fmri study. *J Cogn Neurosci*, 11, 585–597.

Postle, BR, Stern, CE, Rosen, BR and Corkin, S (2000a). An fMRI investigation of cortical contributions to spatial and nonspatial visual working memory. *NeuroImage*, 11, 409–423.

Postle, BR, Zarahn, E and D'Esposito, M (2000b). Using event-related fmri to assess delay-period activity during performance of spatial and nonspatial working memory tasks. *Brain Res Brain Res Protoc*, 5, 57–66.

Quintana, J and Fuster, JM (1993). Spatial and temporal factors in the role of prefrontal and parietal cortex in visuomotor integration. *Cereb Cortex*, 3, 122–132.

Quintana, J, Yajeya, J and Fuster, JM (1988). Prefrontal representation of stimulus attributes during delay tasks. I. Unit activity in cross-temporal integration of sensory and sensory-motor information. *Brain Res*, 474, 211–221.

Rainer, G, Asaad, WF and Miller, EK (1998). Memory fields of neurons in the primate prefrontal cortex. *Proc Natl Acad Sci USA*, 95, 15008–15013.

Rämä, P, Poremba, A, Yee, L, Malloy, M, Mishkin, M and Courtney, SM (2004). Dissociable functional cortical topographies for working memory maintenance of voice identity and location. *Cerebral Cortex*, 14, 768–780.

Rämä, P, Sala, JB, Gillen, JS, Pekar, JJ and Courtney, SM (2001). Dissociation of the neural systems for working memory maintenance of verbal and nonspatial visual information. *Cognitive, Affective, and Behavioral Neuroscience*, 1, 161–171.

Rao, SC, Rainer, G and Miller, EK (1997). Integration of what and where in the primate prefrontal cortex. *Science*, 276, 821–824.

Raye, CL, Johnson, MK, Mitchell, KJ, Reeder, JA and Greene, EJ (2002). Neuroimaging a single thought: dorsolateral PFC activity associated with refreshing just-activated information. *NeuroImage*, 15, 447–453.

Roth, JK, Serences, JT and Courtney, SM (2006). Neural system for controlling the contents of object working memory in humans. *Cerebral Cortex*, 16(11), 1595–1603.

Rougier, NP, Noelle, DC, Braver, TS, Cohen, JD and O'Reilly, RC (2005). Prefrontal cortex and flexible cognitive control: Rules without symbols. *Proceedings of the National Academy of Sciences*, 102(207), 7338–7343.

Ruchkin, DS, Johnson, R Jr, Grafman, J, Canoune, H and Ritter, W (1992). Distinctions and similarities among working memory processes: an event-related potential study. *Brain Res Cogn Brain Res*, 1(1), 53–66.

Rypma, B, Berger, JS and D'Esposito, M. (2002). The influence of working-memory demand and subject performance on prefrontal cortical activity. *J Cogn Neurosci*, 14(5), 721–731.

Sakai, K and Passingham, RE. (2003). Prefrontal interactions reflect future task operations. *Nat Neurosci*, 6, 75–81.

Sakai, K, Rowe, JB and Passingham, RE (2002). Active maintenance in prefrontal area 46 creates distractor-resistant memory *Nature Neuroscience*, 5(5), 479–484.

Sala, JB and Courtney, SM (2007). Binding of what and where during working memory maintenance. *Cortex*, 43, 5–21.

Sala, JB, Rama, P, and Courtney, SM (2003). Functional topography of a distributed neural system for spatial and nonspatial information maintenance in working memory. *Neuropsychologia*, 41, 341–356.

Serences, JT, Schwarzbach, J, Courtney, SM and Yantis, S (2004). Control of object-based visual attention in human cortex. *Cerebral Cortex*, 14, 1346–1357.

Serences, JT, Shomstein, S, Leber, AB, Golay, X, Egeth, HE and Yantis S. (2005). Coordination of voluntary and stimulus-driven attentional control in human cortex. *Psychol Sci*, 16(2), 114–122.

Shallice, T and Burgess, PW (1991). Deficits in strategy application following frontal lobe damage in man. *Brain*, 114, 727–41.

Smith, EE and Jonides, J (1999). Storage and executive processes in the frontal lobes. *Science*, 283, 1657–1661.

Stern, CE, Owen, AM, Tracey, I, Look, RB, Rosen, BR and Petrides, M (2000). Activity in ventrolateral and mid-dorsolateral prefrontal cortex during nonspatial visual working memory processing: Evidence from functional magnetic resonance imaging. *NeuroImage*, 11, 392–399.

Stuss, DT and Benson, DF (1986). *The Frontal Lobes*. New York: Raven Press.

Thompson-Schill, SL, Jonides, J, Marshuetz, C, Smith, EE, D'Esposito, M, Kan, IP, Knight, RT, Swick D (2002). Effects of frontal lobe damage on interference effects in working memory. *Cogn Affect Behav Neurosci*, 2(2), 109–120.

Ungerleider, LG and Haxby, JV (1994). 'What' and 'where' in the human brain. *Curr Opin Neurobiol*, 4(2), 157–165.

Wallis, JD, Anderson, KC and Miller, EK (2001). Single neurons in the prefrontal cortex encode abstract rules. *Nature*, 411, 953–956.

White, IM and Wise, SP (1999). Rule-dependent neuronal activity in the prefrontal cortex. *Exp Brain Res*, 126, 315–335.

Yajeya, J, Quintana, J and Fuster, JM (1988). Prefrontal representation of stimulus attributes during delay tasks: The role of behavioral significance. *Brain Res*, 474, 222–230.

Yantis, S, Schwarzbach, J, Serences, JT, Carlson, RL, Steinmetz, MA, Pekar, JJ and Courtney, SM (2002). Transient neural activity in human parietal cortex during spatial attention shifts. *Nature Neuroscience*, 5, 995–1002.

Zarahn, E, Aguirre, GK, D'Esposito, M. (1999). Temporal isolation of the neural correlates of spatial mnemonic processing with fMRI. *Brain Res Cogn Brain Res*, 7(3), 255–268.

Index